Database System Implementation

Hector Garcia-Molina

Jeffrey D. Ullman

Jennifer Widom

Department of Computer Science
Stanford University

An Alan R. Apt Book

OUT-OF-PRINT PURCHASE

Prentice Hall
Upper Saddle River, New Jersey 07458

Library of Congress Cataloging-in-Publication Data

Garcia-Molina, Hector.
      Databse System Implementation
  Hector Garcia-Molina, Jeffrey D. Ullman, Jennifer Widom
          p. cm.
  Includes bibliographical references and index.
  ISBN: 0-13-040264-8
  1. Database management. I. Ullman, Jeffrey D. II. Widom, Jennifer
III. Title.
QA76.9.D3G365   2000
005.74--dc21   99-31049
                                                           CIP

Publisher: **ALAN APT**
Editor-in-chief: **MARCIA HORTON**
Project manager: **ANA ARIAS TERRY**
Production editor: **IRWIN ZUCKER**
Managing editor: **EILEEN CLARK**
Manufacturing buyer: **PAT BROWN**
Assistant vice president of production and manufacturing: **DAVID W. RICCARDI**
Cover director: **HEATHER SCOTT**
Cover designer: **TAMARA NEWNAM-CAVALLO**
Editorial assistant: **TONI HOLM**

The author and publisher of this book have used their best efforts in preparing this book. These efforts include the development, research, and testing of the theories and programs to determine their effectiveness. The author and publisher make no warranty of any kind, expressed or implied, with regard to these programs or the documentation contained in this book. The author and publisher shall not be liable in any event for incidental or consequential damages in connection with, or arising out of, the furnishing, performance, or use of these programs.

Printed in the United States of America

10 9 8 7 6 5 4 3 2 1

ISBN   0-13-040264-8

Prentice-Hall International (UK) Limited, London
Prentice-Hall of Australia Pty. Limited, Sydney
Prentice-Hall Canada Inc., Toronto
Prentice-Hall Hispanoamericana, S.A., Mexico
Prentice-Hall of India Private Limited, New Delhi
Prentice-Hall of Japan, Inc., Tokyo
Prentice-Hall (Singapore) Pte. Ltd., Singapore
Editora Prentice-Hall do Brasil, Ltda., Rio de Janeiro

Preface

This book was designed for CS245, the second course in the database sequence at Stanford. Here, the first database course, CS145, covers database design and programming, for which the book *A First Course in Database Systems* by Jeff Ullman and Jennifer Widom, Prentice-Hall, 1997, was written. The CS245 course then covers implementation of a DBMS, notably storage structures, query processing, and transaction management.

Use of the Book

We're on a quarter system at Stanford, so the principal course using this book — CS245 — is only ten weeks long. In the Winter of 1999, Hector Garcia-Molina used a "beta" version of this book, and covered the following parts: Sections 2.1–2.4, all of Chapters 3 and 4, Sections 5.1 and 5.2, Sections 6.1–6.7, Sections 7.1–7.4, all of Chapter 8, Chapter 9 except for Section 9.8, Sections 10.1–10.3, Section 11.1, and Section 11.5.

The balance of Chapters 6 and 7 (query optimization) is covered in an advanced course, CS346, where students implement their own DBMS. Other portions of the book that are not covered in CS245 may appear in another advanced course, CS347, which talks about distributed databases and advanced transaction processing.

Schools that are on the semester system have the opportunity to combine the use of this book with its predecessor: *A First Course in Database Systems*. We recommend using that book in the first semester, coupled with a database-application programming project. The second semester could cover most or all of the content of this book. An advantage to splitting the study of databases into two courses is that students not planning to specialize in DBMS construction can take only the first course and be able to use databases in whatever branch of Computer Science they enter.

Prerequisites

The course on which the book is based is rarely taken before the senior year, so we expect the reader to have a fairly broad background in the traditional areas of Computer Science. We assume that the reader has learned something about database programming, especially SQL. It is helpful to know about relational algebra and to have some familiarity with basic data structures. Likewise, some knowledge of file systems and operating systems is useful.

Exercises

The book contains extensive exercises, with some for almost every section. We indicate harder exercises or parts of exercises with an exclamation point. The hardest exercises have a double exclamation point.

Some of the exercises or parts are marked with a star. For these exercises, we shall endeavor to maintain solutions accessible through the book's Web page. These solutions are publicly available and should be used for self-testing. Note that in a few cases, one exercise B asks for modification or adaptation of your solution to another exercise A. If certain parts of A have Web-published solutions, then you should expect the corresponding parts of B to have solutions as well.

Support on the World-Wide Web

The book's home page is

    http://www-db.stanford.edu/~ullman/dbsi.html

Here you will find solutions to starred exercises, errata as we learn of them, and backup materials. We hope to make available the notes for each offering of CS245 and relevant portions of other database courses, as we teach them, including homeworks, exams, and solutions.

Acknowledgements

Thanks go to Brad Adelberg, Karen Butler, Ed Chang, Surajit Chaudhuri, Rada Chirkova, Tom Dienstbier, Xavier Faz, Tracy Fujieda, Luis Gravano, Ben Holzman, Fabien Modoux, Peter Mork, Ken Ross, Mema Roussopolous, and Jonathan Ullman for assistance gathering material and/or discovering errors in earlier drafts of this work. Remaining errors are ours, of course.

H. G.-M.
J. D. U.
J. W.
Stanford, CA

Table of Contents

About the Authors

Hector Garcia-Molina is the Leonard Bosack and Sandra Lerner Professor in the Computer Science and Electrical Engineering Departments at Stanford University. He has published extensively in the fields of database systems, distributed systems, and digital libraries. His research interests also include distributed computing systems, database systems, and digital libraries.

Jeffrey D. Ullman is the Stanford W. Ascherman Professor of Computer Science at Stanford University. He is the author or co-author of 15 books and 170 technical publications, including *A First Course in Database Systems* (Prentice Hall 1997) and *Elements of ML Programming* (Prentice Hall 1998). His research interests include database theory, database integration, data mining, and education using the information infrastructure. He has received numerous awards such as the Guggenheim Fellowship and election to the National Academy of Engineering. He also received the 1996 Sigmod Contribution Award and the 1998 Karl V. Karstrom Outstanding Educator Award.

Jennifer Widom is an Associate Professor in the Computer Science and Electrical Engineering Departments at Stanford University. She has served on numerous editorial boards and program committees, she has published widely in computer science conferences and journals, and is co-author of *A First Course in Database Systems* (Prentice Hall 1997). Her research interests include database systems for semistructured data and XML, data warehousing, and active database systems.

Chapter 1

Introduction to DBMS Implementation

Databases today are essential to every business. They are used to maintain internal records, to present data to customers and clients on the World-Wide-Web, and to support many other commercial processes. Databases are likewise found at the core of many scientific investigations. They represent the data gathered by astronomers, by investigators of the human genome, and by biochemists exploring the medicinal properties of proteins, along with many other scientists.

The power of databases comes from a body of knowledge and technology that has developed over several decades and is embodied in specialized software called a *database management system*, or *DBMS*, or more colloquially a "database system." A DBMS is a powerful tool for creating and managing large amounts of data efficiently and allowing it to persist over long periods of time, safely. These systems are among the most complex types of software available. The capabilities that a DBMS provides the user are:

1. *Persistent storage.* Like a file system, a DBMS supports the storage of very large amounts of data that exists independently of any processes that are using the data. However, the DBMS goes far beyond the file system in providing flexibility, such as data structures that support efficient access to very large amounts of data.

2. *Programming interface.* A DBMS allows the user to access and modify data through a powerful query language. Again, the advantage of a DBMS over a file system is the flexibility to manipulate stored data in much more complex ways than the reading and writing of files.

3. *Transaction management.* A DBMS supports concurrent access to data, i.e., simultaneous access by many distinct processes (called "transactions") at once. To avoid some of the undersirable consequences of si-

---

Core Terminology Review

This book is designed for someone who has studied database systems from the point of view of the user (e.g., SQL programming) at the level of Ullman and Widom's *A First Course in Database Systems*, Prentice-Hall, 1997. The following terms should thus be familiar:

- *Data*: any information worth preserving, most likely in electronic form.

- *Database*: a collection of data, organized for access and modification, preserved over a long period.

- *Query*: an operation that extracts specified data from the database.

- *Relation*: an organization of data into a two-dimensional table, where rows (tuples) represent basic entities or facts of some sort, and columns (attributes) represent properties of those entities.

- *Schema*: a description of the structure of the data in a database, often called "metadata."

---

multaneous access, the DBMS supports *isolation*, the appearance that transactions execute one-at-a-time, and *atomicity*, the requirement that transactions execute either completely or not at all. A DBMS also supports *resiliency*, the ability to recover from failures or errors of many types.

1.1 Introducing: The Megatron 2000 Database System

If you have used a DBMS, perhaps one supporting the common SQL query language, you might imagine that implementing such a system is not hard. You might have in mind an implementation such as the recent (fictitious) offering from Megatron Systems Inc.: the Megatron 2000 Database Management System. This system, which is available under UNIX and other operating systems, and which uses the relational approach, supports the SQL query language.

1.1.1 Megatron 2000 Implementation Details

To begin, Megatron 2000 uses the file system to store its relations. For example, the relation `Students(name, id, dept)` would be stored in the file

/usr/db/Students. The file Students has one line for each tuple. Values of components of a tuple are stored as character strings, separated by the special marker character #. For instance, the file /usr/db/Students might look like:

```
Smith#123#CS
Johnson#522#EE
    . . .
```

The database schema is stored in a special file named /usr/db/schema. For each relation, the file schema has a line beginning with that relation name, in which attribute names alternate with types. The character # separates elements of these lines. For example, the schema file might contain lines such as

```
Students#name#STR#id#INT#dept#STR
Depts#name#STR#office#STR
    . . .
```

Here the relation Students(name, id, dept) is described; the type of attributes name and dept are strings while id is an integer. Another relation with schema Depts(name, office) is shown as well.

Example 1.1: Here is an example of a session using the Megatron 2000 DBMS. We are running on a machine called dbhost, and we invoke the DBMS by the UNIX-level command megatron2000.

```
dbhost> megatron2000
```

produces the response

```
WELCOME TO MEGATRON 2000!
```

We are now talking to the Megatron 2000 user interface, to which we can type SQL queries[1] in response to the Megatron prompt (&). A # ends a query. For instance,

```
& SELECT *
  FROM Students #
```

produces as an answer the table

name	id	dept
Smith	123	CS
Johnson	522	EE

Megatron 2000 also allows us to execute a query and store the result in a new file, if we end the query with a vertical bar and the name of the file. For instance,

---

[1]There is a brief review of SQL in Section 1.4.2.

```
& SELECT *
  FROM Students
  WHERE id >= 500 | HighId #
```

creates a new file **/usr/db/HighId** in which only the line

```
Johnson#522#EE
```

appears.   □

1.1.2   How Megatron 2000 Executes Queries

Let us consider a common form of SQL query:

```
SELECT * FROM R WHERE <Condition>
```

Megatron 2000 will do the following:

1. Read the file **schema** to determine the attributes of relation R and their types.

2. Check that the <Condition> is semantically valid for R.

3. Display each of the attribute names as the header of a column, and draw a line.

4. Read the file named R, and for each line:

   (a) Check the condition, and

   (b) Display the line as a tuple, if the condition is true.

To execute

```
SELECT * FROM R WHERE <condition> | T
```

Megatron 2000 does the following:

1. Process query as before, but omit step (2), which generates column headers and a line separating the headers from the tuples.

2. Write the result to a new file **/usr/db/T**.

3. Add to the file **/usr/db/schema** an entry for T that looks just like the entry for R, except that relation name T replaces R. That is, the schema for T is the same as the schema for R.

Example 1.2: Now, let us consider a more complicated query, one involving a join of our two example relations **Students** and **Depts**:

```
SELECT office
FROM Students, Depts
WHERE Students.name = 'Smith' AND
      Students.dept = Depts.name #
```

This query requires that Megatron 2000 "join" relations `Students` and `Depts`. That is, the system must consider in turn each pair of tuples, one from each relation, and determine whether:

a) The tuples represent the same department, and

b) The name of the student is Smith.

The algorithm can be described informally as:

```
for(each tuple s in Students)
    for(each tuple d in Depts)
        if(s and d satisfy the WHERE-condition)
            display the office value from Depts;
```

□

1.1.3   What's Wrong With Megatron 2000?

It may come as no surprise that a DBMS is not implemented like our imaginary Megatron 2000. There are a number of ways that the implementation described here is inadequate for applications involving significant amounts of data or multiple users of data. A partial list of problems follows:

- The tuple layout on disk is inadequate, with no flexibility when the database is modified. For instance, if we change `EE` to `ECON` in one `Students` tuple, the entire file has to be rewritten, as every subsequent character is moved two positions down the file.

- Search is very expensive. We always have to read an entire relation, even if the query gives us a value or values that enable us to focus on one tuple, as in the query of Example 1.2. There, we had to look at the entire `Student` relation, even though the only one we wanted was that for student Smith.

- Query-processing is by "brute force," and much cleverer ways of performing operations like joins are available. For instance, we shall see that in a query like that of Example 1.2, it is not necessary to look at all pairs of tuples, one from each relation, even if the name of one student (Smith) were not specified in the query.

- There is no way for useful data to be buffered in main memory; all data comes off the disk, all the time.

- There is no concurrency control. Several users can modify a file at the same time with unpredictable results.

- There is no reliability; we can lose data in a crash or leave operations half done.

- There is little security. Presumably the underlying operating system controls access in some coarse manner, e.g., different users are either permitted or forbidden to access the file holding a given relation, but one cannot be given access, say, to certain attributes of a relation and not others.

It is the purpose of this book to introduce the reader to better ways of building a database management system. We hope you will enjoy the study.

1.2 Overview of a Database Management System

In Fig. 1.1 we see an outline of a complete DBMS. Single boxes represent system components, while double boxes represent in-memory data structures. The solid lines indicate control and data flow, while dashed lines indicate data flow only. Since the diagram is complicated, we shall consider the details in several stages. First, at the top, we suggest that there are two distinct sources of commands to the DBMS:

1. Conventional users and application programs that ask for data or modify data.

2. A *database administrator*: a person or persons responsible for the structure or *schema* of the database.

1.2.1 Data-Definition Language Commands

The second kind of command is the simpler to process, and we show its trail beginning at the upper right side of Fig. 1.1. For example, the database administrator, or *DBA*, for a university registrar's database might decide that there should be a table or relation with columns for a student, a course the student has taken, and a grade for that student in that course. The DBA might also decide that the only allowable grades are A, B, C, D, and F. This structure and constraint information is all part of the schema of the database. It is shown in Fig. 1.1 as entered by the DBA, who needs special authority to execute schema-altering commands, since these can have profound effects on the database. These schema-altering *DDL commands* ("DDL" stands for "data-definition language") are parsed by a DDL processor and passed to the execution engine, which then goes through the index/file/record manager to alter the *metadata*, that is, the schema information for the database.

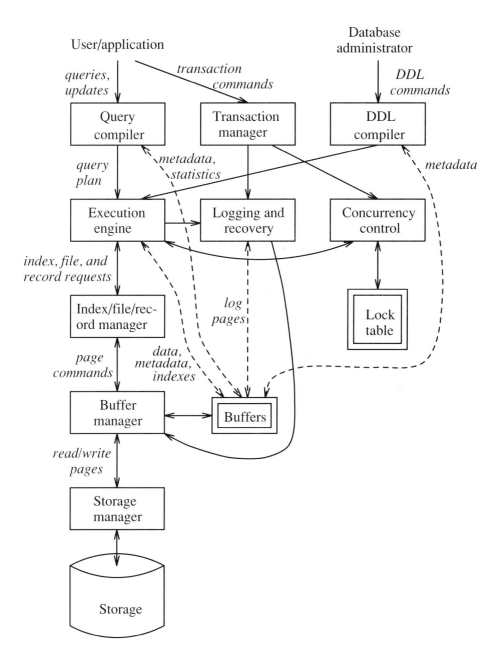

Figure 1.1: Database management system components

1.2.2 Overview of Query Processing

The great majority of interactions with the DBMS follow the path on the left side of Fig. 1.1. A user or an application program initiates some action that does not affect the schema of the database, but may affect the content of the database (if the action is a modification command) or will extract data from the database (if the action is a query). There are two paths along which user actions affect the database:

1. *Answering the query.* The query is parsed and optimized by a *query compiler.* The resulting *query plan*, or sequence of actions to be taken to answer the query, is passed to the *execution engine.* The execution engine issues a sequence of requests for small pieces of data, typically records or tuples of a relation, to a resource manager that knows about *data files* (holding relations), the format and size of records in those files, and *index files*, which help find elements of data files quickly. The requests for data are translated into pages and these requests are passed to the *buffer manager.* We shall discuss the role of the buffer manager in Section 1.2.3, but briefly, its task is to bring appropriate portions of the data from secondary storage (disk, normally) where it is kept permanently, to main-memory buffers. Normally, the page or "disk block" is the unit of transfer between buffers and disk. The buffer manager communicates with a storage manager to get data from disk. The storage manager might involve operating-system commands, but more typically, the DBMS issues commands directly to the disk controller.

2. *Transaction processing.* Queries and other actions are grouped into *transactions*, which are units that must be executed atomically and in isolation, as discussed in the introduction to this chapter; often each query or modification action is a transaction by itself. In addition, the execution of transactions must be *durable*, meaning that the effect of any completed transaction must be preserved even if the system fails in some way right after completion of the transaction. We divide the transaction processor into two major parts:

   (a) A *concurrency-control manager*, (or *scheduler*), responsible for assuring atomicity and isolation of transactions, and

   (b) A *logging and recovery manager* responsible for the durability of transactions.

We shall consider these components further in Section 1.2.4.

1.2.3 Main-Memory Buffers and the Buffer Manager

The data of a database normally resides in secondary storage; in today's computer systems "secondary storage" generally means magnetic disk. However, to perform any useful operation on data, that data must be in main memory.

Thus, a DBMS component called the *buffer manager* is responsible for partitioning the available main memory into *buffers*, which are page-sized regions into which disk blocks can be transferred. Thus, all DBMS components that need information from the disk will interact with the buffers and the buffer manager, either directly or through the execution engine. The kinds of information that various components may need include:

1. *Data*: the contents of the database itself.

2. *Metadata*: the database schema that describes the structure of, and constraints on, the database.

3. *Statistics*: information gathered and stored by the DBMS about data properties such as the sizes of, and values in, various relations or other components of the database.

4. *Indexes*: data structures that support efficient access to the data.

A more complete discussion of the buffer manager and its role appears in Section 6.8.

1.2.4 Transaction Processing

As we mentioned, it is normal to group one or more database operations into a *transaction*, which is a unit of work that must be executed atomically and in apparent isolation from other transactions. In addition, a DBMS offers the guarantee of durability: that the work of a completed transaction will never be lost. The *transaction manager* therefore accepts *transaction commands* from an application, which tell the transaction manager when transactions begin and end, as well as information about the expectations of the application (some may not wish to require atomicity, for example). The transaction processor performs the following tasks:

1. *Logging*: In order to assure durability, every change in the database is logged separately on disk. The *log manager* follows one of several policies designed to assure that no matter when a system failure or "crash" occurs, a *recovery manager* will be able to examine the log of changes and restore the database to some consistent state. The log manager initially writes the log in buffers and negotiates with the buffer manager to make sure that buffers are written to disk (where data can survive a crash) at appropriate times.

2. *Concurrency control*: Transactions must appear to execute in isolation. But in most systems, there will in truth be many transactions executing at once. Thus, the scheduler (concurrency-control manager) must assure that the individual actions of multiple transactions are executed in such an order that the net effect is the same as if the transactions had in

---

The ACID Properties of Transactions

Properly implemented transactions are commonly said to meet the "ACID test," where:

- "A" stands for "atomicity," the all-or-nothing execution of transactions.

- "I" stands for "isolation," the fact that each transaction must appear to be executed as if no other transaction is executing at the same time.

- "D" stands for "durability," the condition that the effect on the database of a transaction must never be lost, once the transaction has completed.

The remaining letter, "C," stands for "consistency." That is, all databases have consistency constraints, or expectations about relationships among data elements (e.g., a certain attribute is a key, students may not take more than 8 courses at a time, and so on). Transactions are expected to preserve the consistency of the database. We discuss this matter in more detail in Section 9.1.

---

fact executed in their entirety, one-at-a-time. A typical scheduler does its work by maintaining *locks* on certain pieces of the database. These locks prevent two transactions from accessing the same piece of data in ways that interact badly. Locks are generally stored in a main-memory *lock table*, as suggested by Fig. 1.1. The scheduler affects the execution of queries and other database operations by forbidding the execution engine from accessing locked parts of the database.

3. *Deadlock resolution*: As transactions compete for resources through the locks that the scheduler grants, they can get into a situation where none can proceed because each needs something another transaction has. The transaction manager has the responsibility to intervene and cancel ("abort") one or more transactions to let the others proceed.

1.2.5   The Query Processor

The portion of the DBMS that most affects the performance that the user sees is the *query processor*. In Fig. 1.1 the query processor is represented by two components:

1. The *query compiler*, which translates the query into an internal form called a *query plan*. The latter is a sequence of operations to be performed on

the data. Often the operations in a query plan are implementations of "relational algebra" operations, which are discussed in Section 6.1 and with which you may be familiar already. The query compiler consists of three major units:

(a) A *query parser*, which builds a tree structure from the textual form of the query.

(b) A *query preprocessor*, which performs semantic checks on the query (e.g., making sure all relations mentioned by the query actually exist), and performing some tree transformations to turn the parse tree into a tree of algebraic operators representing the initial query plan.

(c) A *query optimizer*, which transforms the initial query plan into the best available sequence of operations on the actual data.

The query compiler uses metadata and statistics about the data to decide which sequence of operations is likely to be the fastest. For example, the existence of an index can make one plan much faster than another.

2. The *execution engine*, which has the responsibility for executing each of the steps in the chosen query plan. The execution engine interacts with most of the other components of the DBMS, either directly or through the buffers. It must get the data from the database into buffers in order to manipulate that data. It needs to interact with the scheduler to avoid accessing data that is locked, and with the log manager to make sure that all database changes are properly logged.

1.3 Outline of This Book

The subject of database system implementation can be divided roughly into three parts:

1. *Storage management*: how secondary storage is used effectively to hold data and allow it to be accessed quickly.

2. *Query processing*: how queries expressed in a very high-level language such as SQL can be executed efficiently.

3. *Transaction management*: how to support transactions with the ACID properties discussed in Section 1.2.4.

Each of these topics is covered by several chapters of the book.

1.3.1 Prerequisites

Although this book assumes you have no prior knowledge of DBMS implementation, it is intended as the text for a "second course" in a sequence of courses covering databases, or as part of a comprehensive, one-semester course. In particular, it is a follow-on to the text *A First Course in Database Systems* by Jeff Ullman and Jennifer Widom. The latter book covers:

1. *Database design*: the informal, high-level, specification of the schema of a database, using notations such as the entity/relationship model or ODL (Object Description Language), and the implementation of designs in the data-definition portion of SQL.

2. *Database programming*: writing queries and database modification commands using appropriate languages, especially SQL.

The impact of database-design technology on DBMS implementation is small, but you should have familiarity with the relational model and how data is represented by relations, since much of what we say in this book addresses how one stores relations, optimizes queries about relations, and how one controls access to relations by methods such as locking. Further, in order to appreciate the technology behind query processing, you should be familiar with SQL programming. A brief review of these topics is in Section 1.4.

Additionally, we assume you are familiar with *files* (named storage areas in which data can be kept). We expect that you are familiar with the architecture of a conventional file system, i.e., the part of an operating system that manages its files. The way a DBMS manages files is rather different, and we cover the basics of this important topic.

1.3.2   Storage-Management Overview

This book begins with chapters on storage management. Chapter 2 introduces the memory hierarchy. However, since secondary storage, especially disk, is so central to the way a DBMS manages data, we examine in the greatest detail the way data is stored and accessed on disk. The "block model" for disk-based data is introduced; it influences the way almost everything is done in a database system.

Chapter 3 relates the storage of data elements — relations, tuples, attribute-values, and their equivalents in other data models — to the requirements of the block model of data. Then we look at the important data structures that are used for the construction of indexes. Recall that an index is a data structure that supports efficient access to data. Chapter 4 covers the important one-dimensional index structures — indexed-sequential files, B-trees, and hash tables. These indexes are commonly used in a DBMS to support queries in which a value for an attribute is given and the tuples with that value are desired. Chapter 5 discusses multidimensional indexes, which are data structures for specialized applications such as geographic databases, where queries typically ask for the contents of some region. These index structures can also support complex SQL queries that limit the values of two or more attributes, and some of these structures are beginning to appear in commercial DBMS's.

1.3.3 Query-Processing Overview

Chapter 6 introduces the relational algebra as a way to describe the execution of queries. This chapter then covers the basics of query execution, including a number of algorithms for efficient implementation of key operations such as joins of relations.

In Chapter 7 we consider the architecture of the query compiler and optimizer. We begin with the parsing of queries and their semantic checking. Next, we consider the conversion of queries from SQL to relational algebra and the selection of a *logical query plan*, that is, an algebraic expression that represents the particular operations to be performed on data and the necessary constraints regarding order of operations. Finally, we explore the selection of a *physical query plan*, in which the particular order of operations and the algorithm used to implement each operation have been specified.

1.3.4 Transaction-Processing Overview

In Chapter 8 we see how a DBMS supports durability of transactions. The central idea is that a log of all changes to the database is made. Since anything that is in main-memory but not on disk can be lost in a crash (say, if the power supply is interrupted), we have to be careful to move from buffer to disk, in the proper order, both the database changes themselves and the log of what changes were made. There are several log strategies available, but each limits our freedom of action in some ways.

Then, we take up the matter of concurrency control — assuring atomicity and isolation — in Chapter 9. We view transactions as sequences of operations that read or write database elements. The major topic of the chapter is how to manage locks on database elements: the different types of locks that may be used, and the ways that transactions may be allowed to acquire locks and release their locks on elements. Also studied are a number of ways to assure atomicity and isolation without using locks.

Chapter 10 concludes our study of transaction processing. We consider the interaction between the requirements of logging, as discussed in Chapter 8, and the requirements of concurrency that were discussed in Chapter 9. Handling of deadlocks, another important function of the transaction manager, is covered here as well. The extension of concurrency control to a distributed environment is also considered in Chapter 10. Finally, we introduce the possibility that transactions are "long," taking hours or days rather than milliseconds. A long transaction cannot lock data without causing chaos among other potential users of that data, which forces us to rethink concurrency control for applications that involve long transactions.

1.3.5 Information Integration Overview

Much of the recent evolution of database systems has been toward capabilities that allow different *data sources*, which may be databases and/or information resources that are not managed by a DBMS, to work together in a larger whole. Thus, Chapter 11 is devoted to a study of important aspects of this new technology, called *information integration*. We discuss the principal modes of integration, including translated and integrated copies of sources called a *data warehouse*, and virtual "views" of a collection of sources, called a *mediator*.

1.4 Review of Database Models and Languages

In this section, we shall give the reader a brief review of SQL and the relational model. We also review the notion of objects as in an object-oriented database. The examples are taken from Ullman and Widom's, *A First Course in Database Systems*.

1.4.1 Relational Model Review

A *relation* is a set of *tuples*, which in turn are lists of values. All tuples of a relation have the same number of components, and corresponding components from different tuples are of the same type. We display a relation by listing each of its tuples as a row. Column headers called *attributes* represent the meaning of each component of the tuples. The relation name and its attribute names and types are the *schema* for the relation.

Example 1.3: The relation Movie, which we use frequently in examples, might consist of the following:

title	*year*	*length*
Star Wars	1977	124
Mighty Ducks	1991	104
Wayne's World	1992	95

The schema for the relation is

```
Movie(title, year, length)
```

The attributes are `title`, `year`, and `length`, which we may suppose are of types string, integer, and integer, respectively. Each of the three rows below the line is a tuple. For instance, the first tuple says that "Star Wars" was made in 1977 and is 124 minutes long.   □

A *database schema* is a collection of relation schemas. In our running example of movies, we shall often use relations

```
Movie(title, year, length, studioName)
MovieStar(name, address, gender, birthdate)
StarsIn(title, year, starName)
Studio(name, address)
```

The first is like the `Movie` relation from Example 1.3, although it adds the name of the producing studio when we need some additional connections in examples. The second gives information about movie stars, and the third connects movies to their stars. The fourth gives some information about movie studios. The intent of the various attributes should be clear from their names.

1.4.2   SQL Review

The database language SQL has a large number of capabilities, including statements that query and modify the database. Database modification is through three commands, called `INSERT`, `DELETE`, and `UPDATE`, whose syntaxes we shall not review here. Queries are generally expressed with a "select-from-where" statement, which actually has the general form shown in Fig. 1.2. Only the first two lines (*clauses*), the ones introduced by the keywords `SELECT` and `FROM`, are required.

```
SELECT <attribute list>
FROM <relation list>
WHERE <condition>
GROUP BY <attribute list>
HAVING <condition>
ORDER BY <attribute list>
```

Figure 1.2: General form of an SQL query

Although better ways exist, the result of such a query can be computed by:

1. Taking all possible combinations of tuples from the relations in the `FROM` clause,

2. Throwing away any that do not meet the condition of the `WHERE` clause,

3. Grouping the remaining tuples according to their values in the attributes mentioned in the `GROUP BY` clause (if any),

4. Testing each group according to the condition in the `HAVING` clause (if any), and rejecting all groups that do not meet this condition,

5. Computing tuples from specified attributes and aggregations of attributes (e.g., sum within a group) as specified by the `SELECT` clause, and finally

6. Ordering the resulting tuples according to values in the list of attributes in the `ORDER BY` clause.

Example 1.4 : Figure 1.3 is a simple SQL query with only the first three clauses. It asks for the names of stars that starred in movies made by Paramount

Studios, and the titles of the movies that they starred in. Note that `title` and `year` together are the key for `Movie`, since there could be two movies of the same title (but not in the same year, we hope).   □

```
SELECT starName, Movie.title
FROM Movie, StarsIn
WHERE Movie.title = StarsIn.title AND
      Movie.year = StarsIn.year AND
      studioName = 'Paramount';
```

Figure 1.3: Finding the Paramount stars

Example 1.5: Figure 1.4 is a more complicated query. It asks us first to find the stars who starred in at least three movies. That part of the query is accomplished by grouping the `StarsIn` tuples by the name of the star (the `GROUP BY` clause) and then filtering out the groups that have two or fewer tuples (the `HAVING` clause).

```
SELECT starName, MIN(year) AS minYear
FROM StarsIn
GROUP BY starName
HAVING COUNT(*) >= 3
ORDER BY minYear;
```

Figure 1.4: Finding earliest years of stars appearing in at least three movies

Next, from each of the surviving groups, the `SELECT` clause tells us to produce the name of the star and the earliest year that star appeared in a movie. The second component of the select-list, which is `MIN(year)`, is given the attribute name `minYear`. Last, the `ORDER BY` clause says that the output tuples are to be listed in increasing order of the value of `minYear`; that is, the stars appear in the order of their first movie.   □

Subqueries

One of the powerful features that SQL provides is the ability to use *subqueries* within a `WHERE`, `FROM`, or `HAVING` clause. A subquery is a complete select-from-where statement whose value is tested in one of these clauses.

Example 1.6: In Fig. 1.5 is an SQL query with a subquery. The overall query finds the title and year of the movies made not in Hollywood. The subquery

```
SELECT title, year
FROM Movie
WHERE studioName IN (
    SELECT name
    FROM Studio
    WHERE address NOT LIKE '%Hollywood%'
);
```

Figure 1.5: Finding the movies not made in Hollywood

```
SELECT name
FROM Studio
WHERE address NOT LIKE '%Hollywood%'
```

produces a one-column relation consisting of the names of all the studios that do not have "Hollywood" somewhere in their address. This subquery is then used in the WHERE clause of the outer query to identify those movies whose studio appears in this set of studio names. □

Views

Another important capability of SQL is the definition of *views*, which are descriptions of relations that are not stored, but constructed as needed from stored relations.

Example 1.7: Figure 1.6 shows the definition of a view; it is the title and year of movies made by Paramount studios. The definition of view ParamountMovie is stored as part of the schema of the database, but its tuples are not computed at this time. If we use ParamountMovie as a relation in a query, then its tuples, or the necessary subset of its tuples if the query does not need the whole relation, will be constructed logically by folding the view definition into the query. Thus, these tuples are never actually stored in the database. □

```
CREATE VIEW ParamountMovie AS
    SELECT title, year
    FROM Movie
    WHERE studioName = 'Paramount';
```

Figure 1.6: View for only the movies made by Paramount

1.4.3 Relational and Object-Oriented Data

Most of what is discussed in this book assumes that the database is relational: data is modeled by tables, data items are tuples or rows of the table, and tuples have a fixed number of components, each of a fixed type determined by the relation's schema. This view of data was suggested in Example 1.3. At a different level, we can think of a tuple as a "struct" (the C term) or record, with one field for the value of each attribute.

There is another model of data that is used in some database systems: data as objects. In this model, the elementary data item is an *object*. Objects are grouped into *classes*, and each class has a schema that is a list of of *properties*:

1. Some of those properties are attributes, which can be represented like attributes of a relational tuple.

2. Other properties are *relationships*, which connect an object to one or more other objects. We can think, at an implementation level, of a relationship as a list of pointers to these objects.

3. Still other properties are *methods*, that is, functions that can be applied to objects of the class.

While the code for methods will typically be stored outside of the objects, the rest of the object-oriented formulation of data fits well into our general framework. That is, we shall generally think of "files" as the largest units of data. Files are simply named collections of data, and files are generally composed of smaller units, for which the following terminology is used:

a) In the earliest databases, files were composed of *records*, which were composed of *fields*. A record is analogous to a "struct" in C and its descendant programming languages such as C++ or Java.

b) In relational databases, files are *relations*; they are composed of *tuples*, which are composed of *attributes*.

c) In object-oriented databases, files are the *extents* of *classes*, that is, the set of currently existing objects of one class. Extents are composed of *objects*, and the objects have *fields* or "instance variables," whose values represent either attributes of the object or the set of related objects according to some relationship.

It is useful to draw the following analogies:

1. A file, relation, and extent are similar concepts; they are each values consisting of some smaller elements that have a common schema (records, tuples, or objects).

2. The schema of a file or relation and the definition of a class are similar concepts; each describes the elements of a file, relation, or an extent (of the class).

3. Records, tuples, and objects are similar concepts. Each is often implemented as if they were "structs" in C.

1.5 Summary of Chapter 1

✦ *Database Management Systems*: These systems are characterized by their ability to support efficient access to large amounts of data, which persists over time. They are also characterized by their support for powerful query languages and for durable transactions that can execute concurrently in a manner that appears atomic and independent of other transactions.

✦ *Comparison With File Systems*: Converntional file systems are inadequate as database systems, because they fail to support efficient search, efficient modifications to small pieces of data, complex queries, controlled buffering of useful data in main memory, or atomic and independent execution of transactions.

✦ *Components of a DBMS*: The major components of a database management system are the storage manager, the query processor, and the transaction manager.

✦ *The Storage Manager*: This component is responsible for storing data, metadata (information about the schema or structure of the data), indexes (data structures to speed the access to data), and logs (records of changes to the database). This material is kept on disk. An important storage-management component is the buffer manager, which keeps portions of the disk contents in main memory.

✦ *The Query Processor*: This component parses queries, optimizes them by selecting a query plan, and executes the plan on the stored data.

✦ *The Transaction Manager*: This component is responsible for logging database changes to support recovery after a system crashes. It also supports concurrent execution of transactions in a way that assures atomicity (a transaction is performed either completely or not at all), and isolation (transactions are executed as if there were no other concurrently executing transactions).

✦ *SQL*: This query language, based on the relational model, is an important standard. Both the language and the relational model are central to large portions of this book.

✦ *Data Concepts*: File systems, conventional programming languages like C, the relational model, and object-oriented data models share many common notions, often with different terminology. There are analogies among structs, tuples, and objects, and among files, relations, and classes.

1.6 References for Chapter 1

Today, on-line searchable bibliographies cover essentially all recent papers concerning database systems. Thus, in this book, we shall not try to be exhaustive in our citations, but rather shall mention only the papers of historical importance and major secondary sources or useful surveys. One searchable index of database research papers has been constructed by Michael Ley [6]. Alf-Christian Achilles maintains a searchable directory of many indexes relevant to the database field [1].

The background assumed for this text is obtainable from [8]. The SQL2 and SQL3 standards are obtainable on-line by anonymous FTP from [5]. We suggest [4] for those wanting an SQL2 manual.

While many prototype implementations of database systems contributed to the technology of the field, two of the most widely known are the System R project at IBM Almaden Research Center [2] and the INGRES project at Berkeley [7]. Each was an early relational system and helped establish this type of system as the dominant database technology.

The 1998 "Asilomar report" [3] is the most recent in a series of reports on database-system research and directions. It also has references to earlier reports of this type.

1. `http://www.ira.uka.de/bibliography/Database` .

2. M. M. Astrahan et al., "System R: a relational approach to database management," *ACM Trans. on Database Systems* **1**:2 (1976), pp. 97–137.

3. P. A. Bernstein et al., "The Asilomar report on database research," `http://s2k-ftp.cs.berkeley.edu:8000/postgres/papers/Asilomar_Final.htm` .

4. Date, C. J. and H. Darwen, *A Guide to the SQL Standard*, Fourth Edition, Addison-Wesley, Reading, MA, 1997.

5. `ftp://jerry.ece.umassd.edu/isowg3` .

6. `http://www.informatik.uni-trier.de/~ley/db/index.html` . A mirror site is found at `http://www.acm.org/sigmod/dblp/db/index.html` .

7. M. Stonebraker, E. Wong, P. Kreps, and G. Held, "The design and implementation of INGRES," *ACM Trans. on Database Systems* **1**:3 (1976), pp. 189–222.

8. J. D. Ullman and J. Widom, *A First Course in Database Systems*, Prentice-Hall, Englewood Cliffs NJ, 1997.

Chapter 2

Data Storage

One of the important ways that database systems are distinguished from other systems is the ability of a DBMS to deal with very large amounts of data efficiently. In this chapter and the next we shall learn the basic techniques for managing data within the computer. The study can be divided into two parts:

1. How does a computer system store and manage very large volumes of data?

2. What representations and data structures best support efficient manipulations of this data?

We cover the first issue in this chapter, while the second is the topic of Chapters 3 through 5.

This chapter begins with the technology used for physically storing massive amounts of data. We shall study the devices used to store information, especially rotating disks. We introduce the "memory hierarchy," and see how the efficiency of algorithms involving very large amounts of data depends on the pattern of data movement between main memory and secondary storage (typically disks) or even "tertiary storage" (robotic devices for storing and accessing large numbers of optical disks or tape cartridges). A particular algorithm — two-phase, multiway merge sort — is used as an important example of an algorithm that uses the memory hierarchy effectively.

We also consider, in Section 2.4, a number of techniques for lowering the time it takes to read or write data from disk. The last two sections discuss methods for improving the reliability of disks. Problems addressed include intermittent read- or write-errors, and "disk crashes," where data becomes permanently unreadable.

2.1   The Memory Hierarchy

A typical computer system has several different components in which data may
be stored. These components have data capacities ranging over at least seven
orders of magnitude and also have access speeds ranging over seven or more
orders of magnitude. The cost per byte of these components also varies, but
more slowly, with perhaps three orders of magnitude between the cheapest and
most expensive forms of storage. Not surprisingly, the devices with smallest
capacity also offer the fastest access speed and have the highest cost per byte.
A schematic of the memory hierarchy is shown in Fig. 2.1.

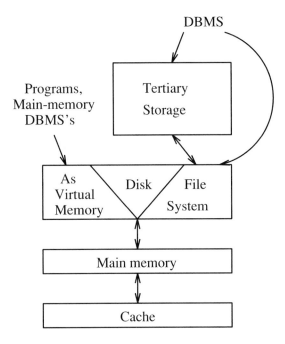

Figure 2.1: The memory hierarchy

2.1.1   Cache

At the lowest level of the hierarchy is a *cache*. The cache is an integrated cir-
cuit ("chip"), or part of the processor's chip, that is capable of holding data
or machine instructions. The data (including instructions) in the cache are a
copy of certain locations of main memory, the next higher level of the memory
hierarchy. Sometimes, the values in the cache are changed, but the corresponding change to the main memory is delayed. Nevertheless, each value in the
cache at any one time corresponds to one place in main memory. The unit of
transfer between cache and main memory is typically a small number of bytes.

We may therefore think of the cache as holding individual machine instructions, integers, floating-point numbers or short character strings.

Often, a machine's cache is divided into two levels. *On-board cache* is found on the same chip as the microprocessor itself, and additional *level-2 cache* is found on another chip.

When the machine executes instructions, it looks for both the instructions and the data used by those instructions in the cache. If it doesn't find them there, it goes to main-memory and copies the instructions or data into the cache. Since the cache can hold only a limited amount of data, it is usually necessary to move something out of the cache in order to accommodate the new data. If what is moved out of cache has not changed since it was copied to cache, then nothing more needs to be done. However, if the data being expelled from the cache has been modified, then the new value must be copied into its proper location in main memory.

When data in the cache is modified, a simple computer with a single processor has no need to update the corresponding location in main memory. However, in a multiprocessor system that allows several processors to access the same main memory and keep their own private caches, it is often necessary for cache updates to *write through*, that is, to change the corresponding place in main memory immediately.

Typical caches at the end of the millenium have capacities up to a megabyte. Data can be read or written between the cache and processor at the speed of the processor instructions, commonly 10 nanoseconds (10^{-8} seconds) or less. On the other hand, moving an instruction or data item between cache and main memory takes much longer, perhaps 100 nanoseconds (10^{-7} seconds).

2.1.2 Main Memory

In the center of the action is the computer's *main memory*. We may think of everything that happens in the computer — instruction executions and data manipulations — as working on information that is resident in main memory (although in practice, it is normal for what is used to migrate to the cache, as we discussed in Section 2.1.1).

In 1999, typical machines are configured with around 100 megabytes (10^8 bytes) of main memory. However, machines with much larger main memories, 10 gigabytes or more (10^{10} bytes) can be found.

Main memories are *random access*, meaning that one can obtain any byte in the same time.[1] Typical times to access data from main memories are in the 10–100 nanosecond range (10^{-8} to 10^{-7} seconds).

---

[1] Although some modern parallel computers have a main memory shared by many processors in a way that makes the access time of certain parts of memory different, by perhaps a factor of 3, for different processors.

Computer Quantities are Powers of 2

It is conventional to talk of sizes or capacities of computer components as if they were powers of 10: megabytes, gigabytes, and so on. In reality, since it is most efficient to design components such as memory chips to hold a number of bits that is a power of 2, all these numbers are really shorthands for nearby powers of 2. Since $2^{10} = 1024$ is very close to a thousand, we often maintain the fiction that $2^{10} = 1000$, and talk about 2^{10} with the prefix "kilo," 2^{20} as "mega," 2^{30} as "giga," 2^{40} as "tera," and 2^{50} as "peta," even though these prefixes in scientific parlance refer to 10^3, 10^6, 10^9, and 10^{12}, respectively. The discrepancy grows as we talk of larger numbers. A "gigabyte" is really 1.074×10^9 bytes.

We use the standard abbreviations for these numbers: K, M, G, T, and P for kilo, mega, giga, tera, and peta, respectively. Thus, 16G bytes is sixteen gigabytes, or strictly speaking 2^{34} bytes. Since we sometimes want to talk about numbers that are the conventional powers of 10, we shall reserve for these the traditional numbers, without the prefixes "kilo," "mega," and so on. For example, "one million bytes" is 1,000,000 bytes, while "one megabyte" is 1,048,576 bytes.

2.1.3 Virtual Memory

When we write programs, the data we use — variables of the program, files read, and so on — occupies a *virtual memory address space*. Instructions of the program likewise occupy an address space of their own. Many machines use a 32-bit address space; that is, there are 2^{32}, or about 4 billion, different addresses. Since each byte needs its own address, we can think of a typical virtual memory as 4 gigabytes.

Since a virtual memory space is much bigger than the usual main memory, most of the content of a fully occupied virtual memory is actually stored on the disk. We discuss the typical operation of a disk in Section 2.2, but for the moment we only need to be aware that the disk is divided logically into *blocks*. The block size on common disks is in the range 4K to 56K bytes, i.e., 4 to 56 kilobytes. Virtual memory is moved between disk and main memory in entire blocks, which are usually called *pages* in main memory. The machine hardware and the operating system allow pages of virtual memory to be brought into any part of the main memory and to have each byte of that block referred to properly by its virtual memory address. We shall not discuss the mechanisms for doing so in this book.

The path in Fig. 2.1 involving virtual memory represents the treatment of conventional programs and applications. It does not represent the typical way data in a database is managed. However, there is increasing interest in *main-memory database systems*, which do indeed manage their data through

---

Moore's Law

Gordon Moore observed many years ago that integrated circuits were improving in many ways, following an exponential curve that doubles about every 18 months. Some of these parameters that follow "Moore's law" are:

1. The speed of processors, i.e., the number of instructions executed per second and the ratio of the speed to cost of a processor.

2. The cost of main memory per bit and the number of bits that can be put on one chip.

3. The cost of disk per bit and the number of bytes that a disk can hold.

On the other hand, there are some other important parameters that do not follow Moore's law; they grow slowly if at all. Among these slowly growing parameters are the speed of accessing data in main memory, or the speed at which disks rotate. Because they grow slowly, "latency" becomes progressively larger. That is, the time to move data between levels of the memory hierarchy appears to take progressively longer compared with the time to compute. Thus, in future years, we expect that main memory will appear much further away from the processor than cache, and data on disk will appear even further away from the processor. Indeed, these effects of apparent "distance" are already quite severe in 1999.

---

virtual memory, relying on the operating system to bring needed data into main memory through the paging mechanism. Main-memory database systems, like most applications, are most useful when the data is small enough to remain in main memory without being swapped out by the operating system. If a machine has a 32-bit address space, then main-memory database systems are appropriate for applications that need to keep no more than 4 gigabytes of data in memory at once (or less if the machine's actual main memory is smaller than 2^{32} bytes). That amount of space is sufficient for many applications, but not for large, ambitious applications of DBMS's.

Thus, large-scale database systems will manage their data directly on the disk. These systems are limited in size only by the amount of data that can be stored on all the disks and other storage devices available to the computer system. We shall introduce this mode of operation next.

2.1.4 Secondary Storage

Essentially every computer has some sort of *secondary storage*, which is a form of storage that is both significantly slower and significantly more capacious than

main memory, yet is essentially random-access, with relatively small differences
among the times required to access different data items (these differences are
discussed in Section 2.2). Modern computer systems use some form of disk as
secondary memory. Usually this disk is magnetic, although sometimes optical
or magneto-optical disks are used. The latter types are cheaper, but may not
support writing of data on the disk easily or at all; thus they tend to be used
only for archival data that doesn't change.

We observe from Fig. 2.1 that the disk is considered the support for both
virtual memory and a file system. That is, while some disk blocks will be used
to hold pages of an application program's virtual memory, other disk blocks are
used to hold (parts of) files. Files are moved between disk and main memory
in blocks, under the control of the operating system or the database system.
Moving a block from disk to main memory is a *disk read*; moving the block
from main memory to the disk is a *disk write*. We shall refer to either as a
disk I/O. Certain parts of main memory are used to *buffer* files, that is, to hold
block-sized pieces of these files.

For example, when you open a file for reading, the operating system might
reserve a 4K block of main memory as a buffer for this file, assuming disk blocks
are 4K bytes. Initially, the first block of the file is copied into the buffer. When
the application program has consumed those 4K bytes of the file, the next block
of the file is brought into the buffer, replacing the old contents. This process,
illustrated in Fig. 2.2, continues until either the entire file is read or the file is
closed.

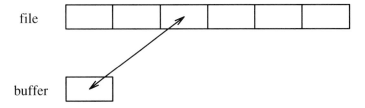

Figure 2.2: A file and its main-memory buffer

A database management system will manage disk blocks itself, rather than
relying on the operating system's file manager to move blocks between main
and secondary memory. However, the issues in management are essentially the
same whether we are looking at a file system or a DBMS. It takes roughly 10–30
milliseconds (.01 to .03 seconds) to read or write a block on disk. In that time,
a typical machine can execute perhaps one million instructions. As a result, it
is common for the time to read or write a disk block to dominate the time it
takes to do whatever must be done with the contents of the block. Therefore it
is vital that, whenever possible, a disk block containing data we need to access
should already be in a main-memory buffer. Then, we do not have to pay the
cost of a disk I/O. We shall return to this problem in Sections 2.3 and 2.4,
where we see some examples of how to deal with the high cost of moving data

between levels in the memory hierarchy.

In 1999, single disk units have capacities in the range from 1 to over 10 gigabytes. Moreover, machines can use several disk units, so secondary-storage capacity of 100 gigabytes for a single machine is realistic. Thus, secondary memory is on the order of 10^5 times slower but at least 100 times more capacious than typical main memory. Secondary memory is also significantly cheaper than main memory. In 1999, prices for magnetic disk units range from 5 to 10 cents per megabyte, while the cost of main memory is 1 to 2 dollars per megabyte.

2.1.5 Tertiary Storage

As capacious as a collection of disk units can be, there are databases much larger than what can be stored on the disk(s) of a single machine, or even of a substantial collection of machines. For example, chains of retail stores retain terabytes of data about their sales. Data gathered from satellite images often measures in the terabytes, and satellites will soon return petabytes (10^{15} bytes) of information per year.

To serve such needs, *tertiary storage* devices have been developed to hold data volumes measured in terabytes. Tertiary storage is characterized by significantly higher read/write times than secondary storage, but also by much larger capacities and smaller cost per byte than is available from magnetic disks. While main memory offers uniform access time for any datum, and disk offers an access time that does not differ by more than a small factor for accessing any datum, tertiary storage devices generally offer access times that vary widely, depending on how close to a read/write point the datum is. Here are the principal kinds of tertiary storage devices:

1. *Ad-hoc Tape Storage.* The simplest — and in past years the only — approach to tertiary storage is to put data on tape reels or cassettes and to store the cassettes in racks. When some information from the tertiary store is wanted, a human operator locates and mounts the tape on a tape reader. The information is located by winding the tape to the correct position, and the information is copied from tape to secondary storage or to main memory. To write into tertiary storage, the correct tape and point on the tape is located, and the copy proceeds from disk to tape.

2. *Optical-Disk Juke Boxes.* A "juke box" consists of racks of CD-ROM's (CD = "compact disk"; ROM = "read-only memory." These are optical disks of the type used commonly to distribute software). Bits on an optical disk are represented by small areas of black or white, so bits can be read by shining a laser on the spot and seeing whether the light is reflected. A robotic arm that is part of the jukebox can quickly extract any one CD-ROM and move it to a CD reader. The CD can then have its contents, or part thereof, read into secondary memory. It is not normally possible to write onto CD's without using special equipment. Low-cost CD writers

are available, and it is likely that read/write tertiary storage based on optical disks will soon be economical.

3. *Tape Silos* A "silo" is a room-sized device that holds racks of tapes. The tapes are accessed by robotic arms that can bring them to one of several tape readers. The silo is thus an automated version of the earlier ad-hoc storage of tapes. Since it uses computer control of inventory and automates the tape-retrieval process, it is at least an order of magnitude faster than human-powered systems.

The capacity of a tape cassette in 1999 is as high as 50 gigabytes. Tape silos can therefore hold many terabytes. CD's have a standard of about 2/3 of a gigabyte, with a next-generation standard of about 2.5 gigabytes becoming prevalent. CD-ROM jukeboxes in the multiterabyte range are also available.

The time taken to access data from a tertiary storage device ranges from a few seconds to a few minutes. A robotic arm in a jukebox or silo can find the desired CD-ROM or cassette in several seconds, while human operators probably require minutes to locate and retrieve tapes. Once loaded in the reader, any part of the CD can be accessed in a fraction of a second, while it can take many additional seconds to move the correct portion of a tape under the read-head of the tape reader.

In summary, tertiary storage access can be about 1000 times slower than secondary-memory access (milliseconds versus seconds). However, single tertiary-storage units can be 1000 times more capacious than secondary storage devices (gigabytes versus terabytes). Figure 2.3 shows, on a log-log scale, the relationship between access times and capacities for the four levels of memory hierarchy that we have studied. We include "zip" and "floppy" disks ("diskettes"), which are common storage devices, although not typical of secondary storage used for database systems. The horizontal axis measures seconds in exponents of 10; e.g., -3 means 10^{-3} seconds, or one millisecond. The vertical axis measures bytes, also in exponents of 10; e.g., 8 means 100 megabytes.

2.1.6 Volatile and Nonvolatile Storage

An additional distinction among storage devices is whether they are *volatile* or *nonvolatile*. A volatile device "forgets" what is stored in it when the power goes off. A nonvolatile device, on the other hand, is expected to keep its contents intact even for long periods when the device is turned off or there is a power failure. The question of volatility is important, because one of the characteristic capabilities of a DBMS is the ability to retain its data even in the presence of power failures.

Magnetic materials will hold their magnetism in the absence of power, so devices such as magnetic disks and tapes are nonvolatile. Likewise, optical devices such as CD's hold the black or white dots with which they are imprinted, even in the absence of power. Indeed, for many of these devices it is impossible

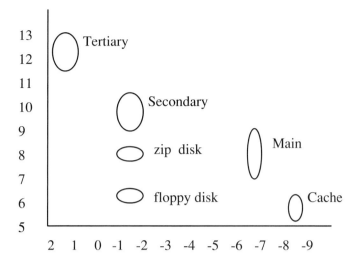

Figure 2.3: Access time versus capacity for various levels of the memory hierarchy

to change what is written on their surface by any means. Thus, essentially all secondary and tertiary storage devices are nonvolatile.

On the other hand, main memory is generally volatile. It happens that a memory chip can be designed with simpler circuits if the value of the bit is allowed to degrade over the course of a minute or so; the simplicity lowers the cost per bit of the chip. What actually happens is that the electric charge that represents a bit drains slowly out of the region devoted to that bit. As a result, a so-called *dynamic random-access memory*, or DRAM, chip needs to have its entire contents read and rewritten periodically. If the power is off, then this refresh does not occur, and the chip will quickly lose what is stored.

A database system that runs on a machine with volatile main memory must back up every change on disk before the change can be considered part of the database, or else we risk losing information in a power failure. As a consequence, query and database modifications must involve a large number of disk writes, some of which could be avoided if we didn't have the obligation to preserve all information at all times. An alternative is to use a form of main memory that is not volatile. New types of memory chips, called *flash memory*, are nonvolatile and are becoming economical. An alternative is to build a so-called *RAM disk* from conventional memory chips by providing a battery backup to the main power supply.

2.1.7 Exercises for Section 2.1

Exercise 2.1.1: Suppose that in 1999 the typical computer has a processor that runs at 500 megahertz, has a disk of 10 gigabytes, and a main memory of 100 megabytes. Assume that Moore's law (these factors double every 18 months) continues to hold into the indefinite future.

* a) When will terabyte disks be common?

   b) When will gigabyte main memories be common?

   c) When will terahertz processors be common?

   d) What will be a typical configuration (processor, disk, memory) in the year 2008?

! **Exercise 2.1.2 :** Commander Data, the android from the 24th century on *Star Trek: The Next Generation* (but you knew that, didn't you?) once proudly announced that his processor runs at "12 teraops." While an operation and a cycle may not be the same, let us suppose they are, and that Moore's law continues to hold for the next 300 years. If so, what would Data's true processor speed be?

2.2 Disks

The use of secondary storage is one of the important characteristics of database management systems, and secondary storage is almost exclusively based on magnetic disks. Thus, to motivate many of the ideas used in DBMS implementation, we must examine the operation of disks in detail.

2.2.1 Mechanics of Disks

The two principal moving pieces of a disk drive are shown in Fig. 2.4; they are a *disk assembly* and a *head assembly*. The disk assembly consists of one or more circular *platters* that rotate around a central spindle. The upper and lower surfaces of the platters are covered with a thin layer of magnetic material, on which bits are stored. A 0 is represented by orienting the magnetism of a small area in one direction and a 1 by orienting the magnetism in the opposite direction. A common diameter for disk platters is 3.5 inches, although disks with diameters from an inch to several feet have been built.

The locations where bits are stored are organized into *tracks*, which are concentric circles on a single platter. Tracks occupy most of a surface, except for the region closest to the spindle, as can be seen in the top view of Fig. 2.5. A track consists of many points, each of which represents a single bit by the direction of its magnetism.

Tracks are organized into *sectors*, which are segments of the circle separated by *gaps* that are not magnetized in either direction.[2] The sector is an indivisible

---

[2] We show each track with the same number of sectors in Fig. 2.5. However, as we shall discuss in Example 2.1, the number of sectors per track may vary, with the outer tracks having more sectors than inner tracks.

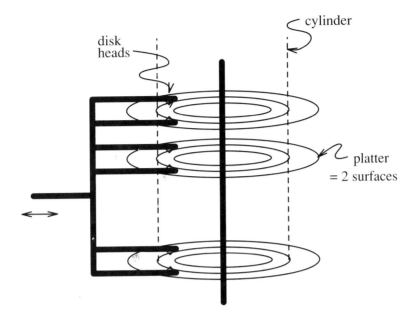

Figure 2.4: A typical disk

unit, as far as reading and writing the disk is concerned. It is also indivisible as far as errors are concerned. Should a portion of the magnetic layer be corrupted in some way, so that it cannot store information, then the entire sector containing this portion cannot be used. Gaps often represent about 10% of the total track and are used to help identify the beginnings of sectors. The blocks, which, as we mentioned in Section 2.1.3, are logical units of data that are transferred between disk and main memory, consist of one or more sectors.

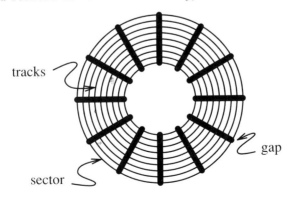

Figure 2.5: Top view of a disk surface

The second movable piece shown in Fig. 2.4, the head assembly, holds the *disk heads*. There is one head for each surface, riding extremely close to the

---

Sectors Versus Blocks

Remember that a "sector" is a physical unit of the disk, while a "block" is a logical unit, a creation of whatever software system — operating system or DBMS, for example — is using the disk. As we mentioned, it is typical today for blocks to be at least as large as sectors and to consist of one or more sectors. However, there is no reason why a block cannot be a fraction of a sector, with several blocks packed into one sector. In fact, some older systems did use this strategy.

---

surface, but never touching it (or else a "head crash" occurs and the disk is destroyed, along with everything stored thereon). A head reads the magnetism passing under it, and can also alter the magnetism to write information on the disk. The heads are each attached to an arm, and the arms for all the surfaces move in and out together, being part of the rigid head assembly.

2.2.2 The Disk Controller

One or more disk drives are controlled by a *disk controller*, which is a small processor capable of:

1. Controlling the mechanical actuator that moves the head assembly, to position the heads at a particular radius. At this radius, one track from each surface will be under the head for that surface and will therefore be readable and writable. The tracks that are under the heads at the same time are said to form a *cylinder*.

2. Selecting a surface from which to read or write, and selecting a sector from the track on that surface that is under the head. The controller is also responsible for knowing when the rotating spindle has reached the point where the desired sector is beginning to move under the head.

3. Transferring the bits read from the desired sector to the computer's main memory or transferring the bits to be written from main memory to the intended sector.

Figure 2.6 shows a simple, single-processor computer. The processor communicates via a data bus with the main memory and the disk controller. A disk controller can control several disks; we show three disks in this computer.

2.2.3 Disk Storage Characteristics

Disk technology is in flux, as the space needed to store a bit shrinks rapidly. In 1999, some of the typical measures associated with disks are:

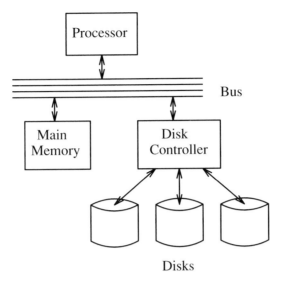

Figure 2.6: Schematic of a simple computer system

- *Rotation Speed of the Disk Assembly.* 5400 RPM, i.e., one rotation every 11 milliseconds, is common, although higher and lower speeds are found.

- *Number of Platters per Unit.* A typical disk drive has about five platters and therefore ten surfaces. However, the common diskette ("floppy" disk) and "zip" disk have a single platter with two surfaces, and disk drives with up to 30 surfaces are found. "Single-sided floppies," with a single surface on one platter, are old-fashioned but may still be found.

- *Number of Tracks per Surface.* A surface may have as many as 10,000 tracks, although diskettes have a much smaller number; see Example 2.2.

- *Number of Bytes per Track.* Common disk drives have 10^5 or more bytes per track, although diskettes' tracks hold less. As mentioned, tracks are divided into sectors. Figure 2.5 shows 12 sectors per track, but in fact as many as 500 sectors per track are found in modern disks. Sectors, in turn, hold perhaps 512 to 4096 bytes each.

Example 2.1 : The *Megatron 747* disk has the following characteristics, which are typical of a medium-size, vintage-1999 disk drive.

- There are four platters providing eight surfaces.

- There are 2^{13}, or 8192 tracks per surface.

- There are (on average) $2^8 = 256$ sectors per track.

- There are $2^9 = 512$ bytes per sector.

The capacity of the disk is the product of 8 surfaces, times 8192 tracks, times 256 sectors, times 512 bytes, or 2^{33} bytes. The Megatron 747 is thus an 8 gigabyte disk. A single track holds 256×512 bytes, or 128K bytes. If blocks are 2^{12}, or 4096 bytes, then one block uses 8 sectors, and there are $256/8 = 32$ blocks on a track.

The Megatron 747 has surfaces of 3.5-inch diameter. The tracks occupy the outer inch of the surfaces, and the inner 0.75 inch is unoccupied. The density of bits in the radial direction is thus 8192 per inch, because that is the number of tracks.

The density of bits around the tracks is far greater. Let us suppose at first that each track has the average number of sectors, 256. Suppose that the gaps occupy 10% of the tracks, so the 128K bytes per track (or 1M bits) occupy 90% of the track. The length of the outermost track is 3.5π or about 11 inches. Ninety percent of this distance, or about 9.9 inches, holds a megabit. Hence the density of bits in the occupied portion of the track is about 100,000 bits per inch.

On the other hand, the innermost track has a diameter of only 1.5 inches and would store the same one megabit in $0.9 \times 1.5 \times \pi$ or about 4.2 inches. The bit density of the inner tracks is thus around a 250,000 bits per inch.

Since the densities of inner and outer tracks would vary too much if the number of sectors and bits were kept uniform, the Megatron 747, like other modern disk drives, stores more sectors on the outer tracks than on inner tracks. For example, we could store 256 sectors per track on the middle third, but only 192 sectors on the inner third and 320 sectors on the outer third of the tracks. If we did, then the density would range from 114,000 bits to 182,000 bits per inch, at the outermost and innermost tracks, respectively. □

Example 2.2: At the small end of the range of disks is the standard 3.5-inch diskette. It has two surfaces with 40 tracks each, for a total of 80 tracks. The capacity of this disk, formatted in either the MAC or PC formats, is about 1.5 megabytes of data, or 150,000 bits (18,750 bytes) per track. About one quarter of the available space is taken up by gaps and other disk overhead in either format. □

2.2.4 Disk Access Characteristics

Our study of database management systems requires us to understand not only the way data is stored on disks but the way it is manipulated. Since all computation takes place in main memory or cache, the only issue as far as the disk is concerned is how to move blocks of data between disk and main memory. As we mentioned in Section 2.2.2, blocks (or the consecutive sectors that comprise the blocks) are read or written when:

a) The heads are positioned at the cylinder containing the track on which the block is located, and

b) The sectors containing the block move under the disk head as the entire disk assembly rotates.

The time taken between the moment at which the command to read a block is issued and the time that the contents of the block appear in main memory is called the *latency* of the disk. It can be broken into the following components:

1. The time taken by the processor and disk controller to process the request, usually a fraction of a millisecond, which we shall neglect. We shall also neglect time due to contention for the disk controller (some other process might be reading or writing the disk at the same time) and other delays due to contention, such as for the bus.

2. The time to position the head assembly at the proper cylinder. This time, called *seek time*, can be 0 if the heads happen already to be at the proper cylinder. If not, then the heads require some minimum time to start moving and stop again, plus additional time that is roughly proportional to the distance traveled. Typical minimum times, the time to start, move by one track, and stop, are a few milliseconds, while maximum times to travel across all tracks are in the 10 to 40 millisecond range. Figure 2.7 suggests how seek time varies with distance. It shows seek time beginning at some value x for a distance of one cylinder and suggests that the maximum seek time is in the range $3x$ to $20x$. The average seek time is often used as a way to characterize the speed of the disk. We discuss how to calculate this average in Example 2.3.

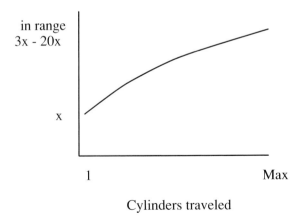

Figure 2.7: Seek time varies with distance traveled

3. The time for the disk to rotate so the first of the sectors containing the block reaches the head. This delay is called *rotational latency*. A typical disk rotates completely about once every 10 milliseconds. On the average, the desired sector will be about half way around the circle when the

heads arrive at its cylinder, so the average rotational latency is around 5 milliseconds. Figure 2.8 illustrates the problem of rotational latency.

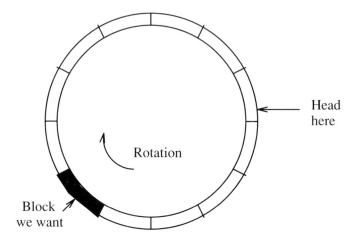

Figure 2.8: The cause of rotational latency

4. The *transfer time*, during which the sectors of the block, and any gaps between them, rotate past the head. Since a typical disk has about 100,000 bytes per track and rotates once in approximately 10 milliseconds, we can read from disk at about 10 megabytes per second. The transfer time for a 4096 byte block is less than half a millisecond.

Example 2.3 : Let us examine the time it takes to read a 4096-byte block from the Megatron 747 disk. First, we need to know some timing properties of the disk:

- The disk rotates at 3840 rpm; i.e., it makes one rotation in 1/64th of a second.

- To move the head assembly between cylinders takes one millisecond to start and stop, plus one additional millisecond for every 500 cylinders traveled. Thus, the heads move one track in 1.002 milliseconds and move from the innermost to the outermost track, a distance of 8191 tracks, in about 17.4 milliseconds.

Let us calculate the minimum, maximum, and average times to read that 4096-byte block. The minimum time, since we are neglecting overhead and contention due to use of the controller, is just the transfer time. That is, the block might be on a track over which the head is positioned already, and the first sector of the block might be about to pass under the head.

Since there are 512 bytes per sector on the Megatron 747 (see Example 2.1 for the physical specifications of the disk), the block occupies eight sectors. The

---

Trends in Disk-Controller Architecture

As the cost of digital hardware drops precipitously, disk controllers are beginning to look more like computers of their own, with general-purpose processors and substantial random-access memory. Among the many things that might be done with such additional hardware, disk controllers are beginning to read and store in their local memory entire tracks of a disk, even if only one block from that track is requested. This capability greatly reduces the average access time for blocks, as long as we need all or most of the blocks on a single track. Section 2.4.1 discusses some of the applications of full-track or full-cylinder reads and writes.

---

heads must therefore pass over eight sectors and the seven gaps between them. Recall that the gaps represent 10% of the circle and sectors the remaining 90%. There are 256 gaps and 256 sectors around the circle. Since the gaps together cover 36 degrees of arc and sectors the remaining 324 degrees, the total degrees of arc covered by seven gaps and 8 sectors is:

$$36 \times \frac{7}{256} + 324 \times \frac{8}{256} = 11.109$$

degrees. The transfer time is thus $(11.109/360)/64$ seconds; that is, we divide by 360 to get the fraction of a rotation needed, and then divide by 64 because the Megatron 747 rotates 64 times a second. This transfer time, and thus the minimum latency, is about 0.5 milliseconds.

Now, let us look at the maximum possible time to read the block. In the worst case, the heads are positioned at the innermost cylinder, and the block we want to read is on the outermost cylinder (or vice versa). Thus, the first thing the controller must do is move the heads. As we observed above, the time it takes to move the Megatron 747 heads across all cylinders is about 17.4 milliseconds. This quantity is the seek time for the read.

The worst thing that can happen when the heads arrive at the correct cylinder is that the beginning of the desired block has just passed under the head. Assuming we must read the block starting at the beginning, we have to wait essentially a full rotation, or 15.6 milliseconds (i.e., 1/64th of a second), for the beginning of the block to reach the head again. Once that happens, we have only to wait an amount equal to the transfer time, 0.5 milliseconds, to read the entire block. Thus, the worst-case latency is $17.4 + 15.6 + 0.5 = 33.5$ milliseconds.

Last let us compute the average time to read a block. Two of the components of the latency are easy to compute: the transfer time is always 0.5 milliseconds, and the average rotational latency is the time to rotate the disk half way around, or 7.8 milliseconds. We might suppose that the average seek time is just the time to move across half the tracks. However, that is not quite right, since typically, the heads are initially somewhere near the middle and therefore will have to move less than half the distance, on average, to the desired cylinder.

A more detailed estimate of the average number of tracks the head must move is obtained as follows. Assume the heads are initially at any of the 8192 cylinders with equal probability. If at cylinder 1 or cylinder 8192, then the average number of tracks to move is $(1 + 2 + \cdots + 8191)/8192$, or about 4096 tracks. If at cylinder 4096, in the middle, then the head is about equally likely to move in as out, and either way, it will move on average about a quarter of the tracks, or 2048 tracks. A bit of calculation shows that as the initial head position varies from cylinder 1 to cylinder 4096, the average distance the head needs to move decreases quadratically from 4096 to 2048. Likewise, as the initial position varies from 4096 up to 8192, the average distance to travel increases quadratically back up to 4096, as suggested in Fig. 2.9.

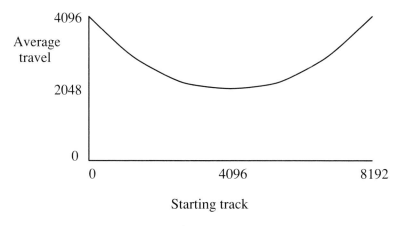

Figure 2.9: Average travel distance as a function of initial head position

If we integrate the quantity in Fig. 2.9 over all initial positions, we find that the average distance traveled is one third of the way across the disk, or 2730 cylinders. That is, the average seek time will be one millisecond, plus the time to travel 2730 cylinders, or $1 + 2730/500 = 6.5$ milliseconds.[3] Our estimate of the average latency is thus $6.5 + 7.8 + 0.5 = 14.8$ milliseconds; the three terms represent average seek time, average rotational latency, and transfer time, respectively. □

2.2.5 Writing Blocks

The process of writing a block is, in its simplest form, quite analogous to reading a block. The disk heads are positioned at the proper cylinder, we wait for the

---

[3]Note that this calculation ignores the possibility that we do not have to move the head at all, but that case occurs only once in 8192 times assuming random block requests. On the other hand, random block requests is not necessarily a good assumption, as we shall see in Section 2.4.

proper sector(s) to rotate under the head, but, instead of reading the data under the head we use the head to write new data. The minimum, maximum and average times to write would thus be exactly the same as for reading.

A complication occurs if we want to verify that the block was written correctly. If so, then we have to wait for an additional rotation and read each sector back to check that what was intended to be written is actually stored there. A simple way to verify correct writing by using checksums is discussed in Section 2.5.2.

2.2.6 Modifying Blocks

It is not possible to modify a block on disk directly. Rather, even if we wish to modify only a few bytes (e.g., a component of one of several tuples stored on the block), we must do the following:

1. Read the block into main memory.

2. Make whatever changes to the block are desired in the main-memory copy of the block.

3. Write the new contents of the block back onto the disk.

4. If appropriate, verify that the write was done correctly.

The total time for this block modification is thus the sum of time it takes to read, the time to perform the update in main memory (which is usually negligible compared to the time to read or write to disk), the time to write, and, if verification is performed, another rotation time of the disk.[4]

2.2.7 Exercises for Section 2.2

Exercise 2.2.1: The *Megatron 777* disk has the following characteristics:

1. There are ten surfaces, with 10,000 tracks each.

2. Tracks hold an average of 1000 sectors of 512 bytes each.

3. 20% of each track is used for gaps.

4. The disk rotates at 10,000 rpm.

5. The time it takes the head to move n tracks is $1 + 0.001n$ milliseconds.

---

[4]We might wonder whether the time to write the block we just read is the same as the time to perform a "random" write of a block. If the heads stay where they are, then we know we have to wait a full rotation to write, but the seek time is zero. However, since the disk controller does not know when the application will finish writing the new value of the block, the heads may well have moved to another track to perform some other disk I/O before the request to write the new value of the block is made.

Answer the following questions about the Megatron 777.

* a) What is the capacity of the disk?

  b) If all tracks hold the same number of sectors, what is the density of bits in the sectors of a track?

* c) What is the maximum seek time?

* d) What is the maximum rotational latency?

  e) If a block is 16,384 bytes (i.e., 32 sectors), what is the transfer time of a block?

  ! f) What is the average seek time?

  g) What is the average rotational latency?

! **Exercise 2.2.2:** Suppose the Megatron 747 disk head is at track 1024, i.e., 1/8 of the way across the tracks. Suppose that the next request is for a block on a random track. Calculate the average time to read this block.

*!! **Exercise 2.2.3:** At the end of Example 2.3 we computed the average distance that the head travels moving from one randomly chosen track to another randomly chosen track, and found that this distance is 1/3 of the tracks. Suppose, however, that the number of sectors per track were inversely proportional to the length (or radius) of the track, so the bit density is the same for all tracks. Suppose also that we need to move the head from a random *sector* to another random sector. Since the sectors tend to congregate at the outside of the disk, we might expect that the average head move would be less than 1/3 of the way across the tracks. Assuming, as in the Megatron 747, that tracks occupy radii from 0.75 inches to 1.75 inches, calculate the average number of tracks the head travels when moving between two random sectors.

!! **Exercise 2.2.4:** At the end of Example 2.1 we suggested that the maximum density of tracks could be reduced if we divided the tracks into three regions, with different numbers of sectors in each region. If the divisions between the three regions could be placed at any radius, and the number of sectors in each region could vary, subject only to the constraint that the total number of bytes on the 8192 tracks of one surface be 1 gigabyte, what choice for the five parameters (radii of the two divisions between regions and the numbers of sectors per track in each of the three regions) minimizes the maximum density of any track?

2.3   Using Secondary Storage Effectively

In most studies of algorithms, one assumes that the data is in main memory, and access to any item of data takes as much time as any other. This model of computation is often called the "RAM model" or random-access model of computation. However, when implementing a DBMS, one must assume that the data does *not* fit into main memory. One must therefore take into account the use of secondary, and perhaps even tertiary storage in designing efficient algorithms. The best algorithms for processing very large amounts of data thus often differ from the best main-memory algorithms for the same problem.

In this section, we shall consider primarily the interaction between main and secondary memory. In particular, there is a great advantage in designing algorithms that limit the number of disk accesses, even if the actions taken by the algorithm on data in main memory are not what we might consider the best use of the main memory. A similar principle applies at each level of the memory hierarchy. Even a main-memory algorithm can sometimes be improved if we remember the size of the cache and design our algorithm so that data moved to cache tends to be used many times. Likewise, an algorithm using tertiary storage needs to take into account the volume of data moved between tertiary and secondary memory, and it is wise to minimize this quantity even at the expense of more work at the lower levels of the hierarchy.

2.3.1 The I/O Model of Computation

Let us imagine a simple computer running a DBMS and trying to serve a number of users who are accessing the database in various ways: queries and database modifications. For the moment, assume our computer has one processor, one disk controller, and one disk. The database itself is much too large to fit in main memory. Key parts of the database may be buffered in main memory, but generally, each piece of the database that one of the users accesses will have to be retrieved initially from disk.

We shall assume that the disk is a Megatron 747, with 4K-byte blocks and the timing characteristics determined in Example 2.3. In particular, the average time to read or write a block is about 15 milliseconds. Since there are many users, and each user issues disk-I/O requests frequently, the disk controller will often have a queue of requests, which we initially assume it satisfies on a first-come-first-served basis. A consequence of this strategy is that each request for a given user will appear random (i.e., the disk head will be in a random position before the request), even if this user is reading blocks belonging to a single relation, and that relation is stored on a single cylinder of the disk. Later in this section we shall discuss how to improve the performance of the system in various ways. However, the following rule, which defines the *I/O model of computation*, continues to hold:

> **Dominance of I/O cost**: If a block needs to be moved between disk and main memory, then the time taken to perform the read or write is much larger than the time likely to be used manipulating that data in main memory. Thus, the number of block accesses (reads and writes) is a good approximation to the time needed by the algorithm and should be minimized.

Example 2.4: Suppose our database has a relation R and a query asks for the tuple of R that has a certain key value k. As we shall see, it is quite desirable that an index on R be created and used to identify the disk block on which the tuple with key value k appears. However it is generally unimportant whether the index tells us where on the block this tuple appears.

The reason is that it will take on the order of 15 milliseconds to read this 4K-byte block. In 15 milliseconds, a modern microprocessor can execute millions of instructions. However, searching for the key value k once the block is in main memory will only take thousands of instructions, even if the dumbest possible linear search is used. The additional time to perform the search in main memory will therefore be less than 1% of the block access time and can be neglected safely. □

2.3.2   Sorting Data in Secondary Storage

As an extended example of how algorithms need to change under the I/O model of computation cost, let us consider sorting when the data is much larger than main memory. To begin, we shall introduce a particular sorting problem and give some details of the machine on which the sorting occurs.

Example 2.5: Let us assume that we have a large relation R consisting of 10,000,000 tuples. Each tuple is represented by a record with several fields, one of which is the *sort key* field, or just "key field" if there is no confusion with other kinds of keys. The goal of a sorting algorithm is to order the records by increasing value of their sort keys.

A sort key may or may not be a "key" in the usual SQL sense of a *primary key*, where records are guaranteed to have unique values in their primary key. If duplicate values of the sort key are permitted, then any order of records with equal sort keys is acceptable. For simplicity, we shall assume sort keys are unique. Also for simplicity, we assume records are of fixed length, namely 100 bytes per record. Thus, the entire relation occupies a gigabyte.

The machine on which the sorting occurs has one Megatron 747 disk and 50 megabytes of main memory available for buffering blocks of the relation. The actual main memory is 64M bytes, but the rest of main-memory is used by the system.

We assume disk blocks are 4096 bytes. We may thus pack 40 100-byte tuples or records to the block, with 96 bytes left over that may be used for certain bookkeeping functions or left unused. The relation thus occupies 250,000 blocks. The number of blocks that can fit in 50M bytes of memory (which, recall, is really 50×2^{20} bytes), is $50 \times 2^{20}/2^{12}$, or 12,800 blocks. □

If the data fits in main memory, there are a number of well-known algorithms that work well;[5] variants of "Quicksort" are generally considered the

---

[5]See D. E. Knuth, *The Art of Computer Programming, Vol. 3: Sorting and Searching, 2nd Edition*, Addison-Wesley, Reading MA, 1998.

fastest. Moreover, we would use a strategy where we sort only the key fields with attached pointers to the full records. Only when the keys and their pointers were in sorted order, would we use the pointers to bring every record to its proper position.

Unfortunately, these ideas do not work very well when secondary memory is needed to hold the data. The preferred approaches to sorting, when the data is mostly in secondary memory, involve moving each block between main and secondary memory only a small number of times, in a regular pattern. Often, these algorithms operate in a small number of *passes*; in one pass every record is read into main memory once and written out to disk once. In the next section, we shall consider one such algorithm.

2.3.3 Merge-Sort

The reader may be familiar with a sorting algorithm called Merge-Sort that works by merging sorted lists into larger sorted lists. To *merge* sorted lists, we repeatedly compare the smallest remaining keys of each list, move the record with the smaller key to the output, and repeat, until one list is exhausted. At that time, the output, in the order selected, followed by what remains of the nonexhausted list is the complete set of records, in sorted order.

Example 2.6 : Suppose we have two sorted lists of four records each. To make matters simpler, we shall represent records by their keys and no other data, and we assume keys are integers. One of the sorted lists is $(1, 3, 4, 9)$ and the other is $(2, 5, 7, 8)$. In Fig. 2.10 we see the stages of the merge process.

Step	List 1	List 2	Output
start	$1, 3, 4, 9$	$2, 5, 7, 8$	none
1)	$3, 4, 9$	$2, 5, 7, 8$	1
2)	$3, 4, 9$	$5, 7, 8$	$1, 2$
3)	$4, 9$	$5, 7, 8$	$1, 2, 3$
4)	9	$5, 7, 8$	$1, 2, 3, 4$
5)	9	$7, 8$	$1, 2, 3, 4, 5$
6)	9	8	$1, 2, 3, 4, 5, 7$
7)	9	none	$1, 2, 3, 4, 5, 7, 8$
8)	none	none	$1, 2, 3, 4, 5, 7, 8, 9$

Figure 2.10: Merging two sorted lists to make one sorted list

At the first step, the head elements of the two lists, 1 and 2, are compared. Since $1 < 2$, the 1 is removed from the first list and becomes the first element of the output. At step (2), the heads of the remaining lists, now 3 and 2, are compared; 2 wins and is moved to the output. The merge continues until step (7), when the second list is exhausted. At that point, the remainder of the first list, which happens to be only one element, is appended to the output and the merge is done. Note that the output is in sorted order, as must be the case, because at each step we chose the smallest of the remaining elements.   □

The time to merge in main memory is linear in the sum of the lengths of the lists. The reason is that, because the given lists are sorted, only the heads of the two lists are ever candidates for being the smallest unselected element, and we can compare them in a constant amount of time. The classic merge-sort algorithm sorts recursively, using $\log_2 n$ phases if there are n elements to be sorted. It can be described as follows:

BASIS: If there is a list of one element to be sorted, do nothing, because the list is already sorted.

INDUCTION: If there is a list of more than one element to be sorted, then divide the list arbitrarily into two lists that are either of the same length, or as close as possible if the original list is of odd length. Recursively sort the two sublists. Then merge the resulting sorted lists into one sorted list.

The analysis of this algorithm is well known and not too important here. Briefly $T(n)$, the time to sort n elements, is some constant times n (to split the list and merge the resulting sorted lists) plus the time to sort two lists of size $n/2$. That is, $T(n) = 2T(n/2) + an$ for some constant a. The solution to this recurrence equation is $T(n) = O(n \log n)$, that is, proportional to $n \log n$.

2.3.4   Two-Phase, Multiway Merge-Sort

We shall use a variant of Merge-Sort, called *Two-Phase, Multiway Merge-Sort*, to sort the relation of Example 2.5 on the machine described in that example. It is the preferred sorting algorithm in many database applications. Briefly, this algorithm consists of:

- *Phase 1*: Sort main-memory-sized pieces of the data, so every record is part of a sorted list that just fits in the available main memory. There may thus be any number of these *sorted sublists*, which we merge in the next phase.

- *Phase 2*: Merge all the sorted sublists into a single sorted list.

Our first observation is that with data on secondary storage, we do not want to start with a basis to the recursion that is one record or a few records. The reason is that Merge-Sort is not as fast as some other algorithms when the records to be sorted fit in main memory. Thus, we shall begin the recursion by taking an entire main memory full of records, and sorting them using an appropriate main-memory sorting algorithm such as Quicksort. We repeat this process for as many times as necessary:

1. Fill all available main memory with blocks from the original relation to be sorted.

2. Sort the records that are in main memory.

3. Write the sorted records from main memory onto new blocks of secondary memory, forming one sorted sublist.

At the end of this *first phase*, all the records of the original relation will have been read once into main memory, and become part of a main-memory-size sorted sublist that has been written onto disk.

Example 2.7: Consider the relation described in Example 2.5. We determined that 12,800 of the 250,000 blocks will fill main memory. We thus fill memory 20 times, sort the records in main memory, and write the sorted sublists out to disk. The last of the 20 sublists is shorter than the rest; it occupies only 6,800 blocks, while the other 19 sublists occupy 12,800 blocks.

How long does this phase take? We read each of the 250,000 blocks once, and we write 250,000 new blocks. Thus, there are half a million disk I/O's. We have assumed, for the moment, that blocks are stored at random on the disk, an assumption that, as we shall see in Section 2.4, can be improved upon greatly. However, on our randomness assumption, each block read or write takes about 15 milliseconds. Thus, the I/O time for the first phase is 7500 seconds, or 125 minutes. It is not hard to reason that at a processor speed of tens of millions of instructions per second, the 10,000,000 records can be formed into 20 sorted sublists in far less than the I/O time. We thus estimate the total time for phase one as 125 minutes. □

Now, let us consider how we complete the sort by merging the sorted sublists. We could merge them in pairs, as in the classical Merge-Sort, but that would involve reading all data in and out of memory $2 \log_2 n$ times if there were n sorted sublists. For instance, the 20 sorted sublists of Example 2.7 would be read in and out of secondary storage once to merge into 10 lists; another complete reading and writing would reduce them to 5 sorted lists, a read/write of 4 of the five lists would reduce them to 3, and so on.

A better approach is to read the first block of each sorted sublist into a main-memory buffer. For some huge relations, there would be too many sorted sublists from phase one to read even one block per list into main memory, a problem we shall deal with in Section 2.3.5. But for data such as that of Example 2.5, there are relatively few lists, 20 in that example, and a block from each list fits easily in main memory.

We also use a buffer for an output block that will contain as many of the first elements in the complete sorted list as it can hold. Initially, the output block is empty. The arrangement of buffers is suggested by Fig. 2.11. We merge the sorted sublists into one sorted list with all the records as follows.

1. Find the smallest key among the first remaining elements of all the lists. Since this comparison is done in main memory, a linear search is sufficient, taking a number of machine instructions proportional to the number of sublists. However, if we wish, there is a method based on "priority

Input buffers, one for each sorted list

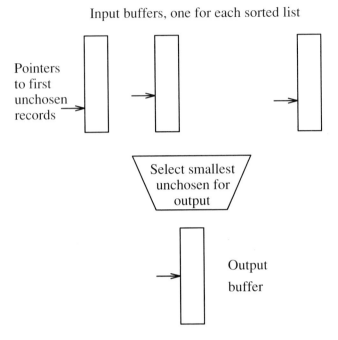

Figure 2.11: Main-memory organization for multiway merging

queues"[6] that takes time proportional to the logarithm of the number of sublists to find the smallest element.

2. Move the smallest element to the first available position of the output block.

3. If the output block is full, write it to disk and reinitialize the same buffer in main memory to hold the next output block.

4. If the block from which the smallest element was just taken is now exhausted of records, read the next block from the same sorted sublist into the same buffer that was used for the block just exhausted. If no blocks remain, then leave its buffer empty and do not consider elements from that list in any further competition for smallest remaining elements.

In the second phase, unlike the first phase, the blocks are read in an unpredictable order, since we cannot tell when an input block will become exhausted. However, notice that every block holding records from one of the sorted lists is read from disk exactly once. Thus, the total number of block reads is 250,000 in the second phase, just as for the first. Likewise, each record is placed once in

---

[6]See Aho, A. V. and J. D. Ullman *Foundations of Computer Science*, Computer Science Press, 1992.

How Big Should Blocks Be?

We have assumed a 4K byte block in our analysis of algorithms using the Megatron 747 disk. However, there are arguments that a larger block size would be advantageous. Recall from Example 2.3 that it takes about half a millisecond for transfer time of a 4K block and 14 milliseconds for average seek time and rotational latency. If we doubled the size of blocks, we would halve the number of disk I/O's for an algorithm like the Multiway Merge-Sort described here. On the other hand, the only change in the time to access a block would be that the transfer time increases to 1 millisecond. We would thus approximately halve the time the sort takes.

If we doubled the block size again, to 16K, the transfer time would rise only to 2 milliseconds, and for a block size of 64K it would be 8 milliseconds. At that point, the average block access time would be 22 milliseconds, but we would need only 62,500 block accesses for a speedup in sorting by a factor of 10.

There are reasons to keep the block size fairly small. First, we cannot effectively use blocks that cover several tracks. Second, small relations would occupy only a fraction of a block, and thus there could be much wasted space on the disk. There are also certain data structures for secondary storage organization that prefer to divide data among many blocks and therefore work less well when the block size is too large. In fact, we shall see in Section 2.3.5 that the larger the blocks are, the fewer the number of records we can sort by the two-phase, multiway method described here. Nevertheless, as machines get faster and disks more capacious, there is a tendency for block sizes to grow.

---

an output block, and each of these blocks is written to disk. Thus, the number of block writes in the second phase is also 250,000. As the amount of second-phase computation in main memory can again be neglected compared to the I/O cost, we conclude that the second phase takes another 125 minutes, or 250 minutes for the entire sort.

2.3.5 Extension of Multiway Merging to Larger Relations

The Two-Phase, Multiway Merge-Sort described above can be used to sort some very large sets of records. To see how large, let us suppose that:

1. The block size is B bytes.

2. The main memory available for buffering blocks is M bytes.

3. Records take R bytes.

The number of buffers available in main memory is thus M/B. On the second phase, all but one of these buffers may be devoted to one of the sorted sublists; the remaining buffer is for the output block. Thus, the number of sorted sublists that may be created in phase one is $(M/B) - 1$. This quantity is also the number of times we may fill main memory with records to be sorted. Each time we fill main memory, we sort M/R records. Thus, the total number of records we can sort is $(M/R)\big((M/B)-1\big)$, or approximately M^2/RB records.

Example 2.8: If we use the parameters outlined in Example 2.5, then $M = 50,000,000$, $B = 4096$, and $R = 100$. We can thus sort up to $M^2/RB = 6.1$ billion records, occupying six tenths of a terabyte.

Note that relations this size will not fit on a Megatron 747 disk, or on any reasonably small number of them. We would probably need to use a tertiary storage device to store the records, and we would have to move records from tertiary storage to a disk or disks, using a strategy like Multiway Merge-Sort, but with tertiary storage and secondary storage playing the roles we have ascribed to secondary storage and main memory, respectively.   □

If we need to sort more records, we can add a third pass. Use the Two-Phase, Multiway Merge-Sort to sort groups of M^2/RB records, turning them into sorted sublists. Then, in a third phase, we would merge up to $(M/B) - 1$ of these lists in a final multiway merge.

The third phase lets us sort approximately M^3/RB^2 records occupying M^3/B^2 blocks. For the parameters of Example 2.5, this amount is about 75 trillion records occupying 7500 petabytes. Such an amount is unheard of today. Since even the 0.61 terabyte limit for the Two-Phase, Multiway Merge-Sort is unlikely to be carried out in secondary storage, we suggest that the two-phase version of Multiway Merge-Sort is likely to be enough for all practical purposes.

2.3.6   Exercises for Section 2.3

Exercise 2.3.1: Using Two-Phase, Multiway Merge-Sort, how long would it take to sort the relation of Example 2.5 if the Megatron 747 disk were replaced by the Megatron 777 disk described in Exercise 2.2.1, and all other characteristics of the machine and data remained the same?

Exercise 2.3.2: Suppose we use Two-Phase, Multiway Merge-Sort on the machine and relation R of Example 2.5, with certain modifications. Tell how many disk I/O's are needed for the sort if the relation R and/or machine characteristics are changed as follows:

* a) The number of tuples in R is doubled (and everything else remains the same).

  b) The length of tuples is doubled to 200 bytes (and everything else remains as in Example 2.5).

* c) The size of blocks is doubled, to 8192 bytes (again, as throughout this exercise, all other parameters are unchanged).

d) The size of available main memory is doubled to 100 megabytes.

! **Exercise 2.3.3:** Suppose the relation R of Example 2.5 grows to have as many tuples as can be sorted using Two-Phase, Multiway Merge-Sort on the machine described in that example. Also assume that the disk grows to accomodate R, but all other characteristics of the disk, machine, and relation R remain the same. How long would it take to sort R?

* **Exercise 2.3.4:** Let us again consider the relation R of Example 2.5, but assume that it is stored sorted by the sort key (which is in fact a "key" in the usual sense, and uniquely identifies records). Also, assume that R is stored in a sequence of blocks whose locations are known, so that for any i it is possible to locate and retrieve the ith block of R using one disk I/O. Given a key value K, we can find the tuple with that key value by using a standard binary search technique. What is the maximum number of disk I/O's needed to find the tuple with key K?

!! **Exercise 2.3.5:** Suppose we have the same situation as in Exercise 2.3.4, but we are given 10 key values to find. What is the maximum number of disk I/O's needed to find all 10 tuples?

* **Exercise 2.3.6:** Suppose we have a relation whose n tuples each require R bytes, and we have a machine whose main memory M and disk-block size B are just sufficient to sort the n tuples using Two-Phase, Multiway Merge-Sort. How would the maximum n change if we made one of the following alterations to the parameters?

a) Double B.

b) Double R.

c) Double M.

! **Exercise 2.3.7:** Repeat Exercise 2.3.6 if it is just possible to perform the sort using Three-Phase, Multiway Merge-Sort.

*! **Exercise 2.3.8:** As a function of parameters R, M, and B (as in Exercise 2.3.6) and the integer k, how many records can be sorted using a k-phase, Multiway Merge-Sort?

2.4 Improving the Access Time of Secondary Storage

The analysis of Section 2.3.4 assumed that data was stored on a single disk and that blocks were chosen randomly from the possible locations on the disk. That assumption may be appropriate for a system that is executing a large number of small queries simultaneously. But if all the system is doing is sorting a large relation, then we can save a significant amount of time by being judicious about where we put the blocks involved in the sort, thereby taking advantage of the way disks work. In fact, even if the load on the system is from a large number of unrelated queries accessing "random" blocks on disk, we can do a number of things to make the queries run faster and/or allow the system to process more queries in the same time ("increase the *throughput*"). Among the strategies we shall consider in this section are:

- Place blocks that are accessed together on the same cylinder so we can often avoid seek time, and possibly rotational latency as well.

- Divide the data among several smaller disks rather than one large one. Having more head assemblies that can go after blocks independently can increase the number of block accesses per unit time.

- "Mirror" a disk: making two or more copies of the data on single disk. In addition to saving the data in case one of the disks fails, this strategy, like dividing the data among several disks, lets us access several blocks at once.

- Use a disk-scheduling algorithm, either in the operating system, in the DBMS, or in the disk controller, to select the order in which several requested blocks will be read or written.

- Prefetch blocks to main memory in anticipation of their later use.

In our discussion, we shall emphasize the improvements possible when the system is dedicated, at least momentarily, to doing a particular task such as the sorting operation we introduced in Section 2.5. However, there are at least two other viewpoints with which to measure the performance of systems and their use of secondary storage:

1. What happens when there are a large number of processes being supported simultaneously by the system? An example is an airline reservation system that accepts queries about flights and new bookings from many agents at the same time.

2. What do we do if we have a fixed budget for a computer system, or we must execute a mix of queries on a system that is already in place and not easily changed?

We address these questions in Section 2.4.6 after exploring the options.

2.4.1 Organizing Data by Cylinders

Since seek time represents about half the average time to access a block, there are a number of applications where it makes sense to store data that is likely to be accessed together, such as relations, on a single cylinder. If there is not enough room, then several adjacent cylinders can be used.

In fact, if we choose to read all the blocks on a single track or on a cylinder consecutively, then we can neglect all but the first seek time (to move to the cylinder) and the first rotational latency (to wait until the first of the blocks moves under the head). In that case, we can approach the theoretical transfer rate for moving data on or off the disk.

Example 2.9: Let us review the performance of the Two-Phase, Multiway Merge-Sort described in Section 2.3.4. Recall from Example 2.3 that we determined the average block transfer time, seek time, and rotational latency to be 0.5 milliseconds, 6.5 milliseconds, and 7.8 milliseconds, respectively, for the Megatron 747 disk. We also found that the sorting of 10,000,000 records occupying a gigabyte took about 250 minutes. This time was divided into four large operations, two for reading and two for writing. One read- and one write-operation was associated with each of the two phases of the algorithm.

Let us consider whether the organization of data by cylinders can improve the time of these operations. The first operation was the reading of the original records into main memory. Recall from Example 2.7 that we loaded main memory 20 times, with 12,800 blocks each time.

The original data may be stored on consecutive cylinders. Each of the 8,192 cylinders of the Megatron 747 stores about a megabyte; technically this figure is an average, because inner tracks store less and outer tracks more, but we shall for simplicity assume all tracks and cylinders are average. We must thus store the initial data on 1000 cylinders, and we read 50 cylinders to fill main memory. Therefore we can read one cylinder with a single seek time. We do not even have to wait for any particular block of the cylinder to pass under the head, because the order of records read is not important at this phase. We must move the heads 49 times to adjacent cylinders, but recall that a move of one track takes only one millisecond according to the parameters of Example 2.3. The total time to fill main memory is thus:

1. 6.5 milliseconds for one average seek.

2. 49 milliseconds for 49 one-cylinder seeks.

3. 6.4 seconds for the transfer of 12,800 blocks.

All but the last quantity can be neglected. Since we fill memory 20 times, the total reading time for phase 1 is about 2.15 minutes. This number should be compatred with the hour that the reading part of phase 1 took in Example 2.7 when we assumed blocks were distributed randomly on disk. The writing part of phase 1 can likewise use adjacent cylinders to store the 20 sorted sublists of records. They can be written out onto another 1000 cylinders, using the same head motions as for reading: one random seek and 49 one-cylinder seeks for each of the 20 lists. Thus, the writing time for phase 1 is also about 2.15 minutes, or 4.3 minutes for all of phase 1, compared with 125 minutes when randomly distributed blocks were used.

On the other hand, storage by cylinders does not help with the second phase of the sort. Recall that in the second phase, blocks are read from the fronts of the 20 sorted sublists in an order that is determined by the data and by which list next exhausts its current block. Likewise, output blocks, containing the complete sorted list, are written one at a time, interspersed with block reads. Thus, the second phase will still take about 125 minutes. We have consequently cut the sorting time almost in half, but cannot do better by judicious use of cylinders alone.   □

2.4.2 Using Multiple Disks

We can often improve the speed of our system if we replace one disk, with many heads locked together, by several disks with their independent heads. The arrangement was suggested in Fig. 2.6, where we showed three disks connected to a single controller. As long as the disk controller, bus, and main memory can handle the data transferred at a higher rate, the effect will be approximately as if all times associated with reading and writing the disk were divided by the number of disks. An example should illustrate the difference.

Example 2.10 : The Megatron 737 disk has all the characteristics of the Megatron 747 outlined in Examples 2.1 and 2.3, but it has only one platter and two surfaces. Thus, each Megatron 737 holds 2 gigabytes. Suppose that we replace our one Megatron 747 by four Megatron 737's. Let us consider how the Two-Phase, Multiway Merge-Sort can be conducted.

First, we can divide the given records among the four disks; the data will occupy 1000 adjacent cylinders on each disk. When we want to load main memory from disk during phase 1, we shall fill 1/4 of main memory from each of the four disks. We still get the benefit observed in Example 2.9 that the seek time and rotational latency go essentially to zero. However, we can read enough blocks to fill 1/4 of main memory, which is 3,200 blocks, from a disk in about 1,600 milliseconds, or 1.6 seconds. As long as the system can handle data at this rate coming from four disks, we can fill the 50 megabytes of main memory in 1.6 seconds, compared with 6.4 seconds when we used one disk.

Similarly, when we write out main memory during phase 1, we can distribute each sorted sublist onto the four disks, occupying about 50 adjacent cylinders on each disk. Thus, there is a factor-of-4 speedup for the writing part of phase 1 too, and the entire phase 1 takes about a minute, compared with 4 minutes using only the cylinder-based improvement of Section 2.4.1 and 125 minutes for the original, random approach.

Now, let us consider the second phase of the Two-Phase, Multiway Merge-Sort. We must still read blocks from the fronts of the various lists in a seemingly random, data-dependent way. If the core algorithm of phase 2 — the selection of smallest remaining elements from the 20 sublists — requires that all 20 lists be represented by blocks completely loaded into main memory, then we cannot use the four disks to advantage. Every time a block is exhausted, we must wait until a new block is read from the same list to replace it. Thus, only one disk at a time gets used.

However, if we write our code more carefully, we can resume comparisons among the 20 smallest elements as soon as the first element of the new block appears in main memory.[7] If so, then several lists might be having their blocks loaded into main memory at the same time. As long as they are on separate disks, then we can perform several block reads at the same time, and we have the potential of a factor-of-4 increase in the speed of the reading part of phase 2. We are also limited by the random order in which blocks must be read; if the next two blocks we need happen to be on the same disk, then one has to wait for the other, and all main-memory processing stops until at least the beginning of the second arrives in main memory.

The writing part of phase 2 is easier to speed up. We can use four output buffers, and fill each in turn. Each buffer, when full, is written to one particular disk, filling cylinders in order. We can thus fill one of the buffers while the other three are written out.

Nevertheless, we cannot possibly write out the complete sorted list faster than we can read the data from the 20 intermediate lists. As we saw above, it is not possible to keep all four disks doing useful work all the time, and our speedup for phase 2 is probably in the 2-3 times range. However, even a factor of 2 saves us an hour. By using cylinders to organize data and four disks to hold data, we can reduce the time for our sorting example from 125 minutes for each of the two phases to 1 minute for the first phase and an hour for the second.   □

2.4.3   Mirroring Disks

There are situations where it makes sense to have two or more disks hold identical copies of data. The disks are said to be *mirrors* of each other. One important motivation is that the data will survive a head crash by either disk, since it is still readable on a mirror of the disk that crashed. Systems designed to enhance reliability often use pairs of disks as mirrors of each other.

However, mirror disks can also speed up access to data. Recall our discussion of phase 2 of multiway merge-sorting Example 2.10, where we observed that if we were very careful about timing, we could arrange to load up to four blocks from four different sorted lists whose previous blocks were exhausted. However, we could not choose which four lists would get new blocks. Thus, we could be

---

[7]We should emphasize that this approach requires extremely delicate implementation and should only be attempted if there is an important benefit to doing so. There is a significant risk that, if we are not careful, there will be an attempt to read a record before it actually arrives in main memory.

unlucky and find that the first two lists were on the same disk, or two of the first three lists were on the same disk.

If we are willing to waste disk space by making four copies of a single large disk, then we can guarantee that the system can always be retrieving four blocks at once. That is, no matter which four blocks we need, we can assign each one to any one of the four disks and have the block read off of that disk.

In general, if we make n copies of a disk, we can read any n blocks in parallel. If we have fewer than n blocks to read at once, then we can often obtain a speed increase by judiciously choosing which disk to read from. That is, we can pick the available disk whose head is closest to the cylinder from which we desire to read.

Using mirror disks does not speed up writing, but neither does it slow writing down, when compared with using a single disk. That is, whenever we need to write a block, we write it on all disks that have a copy. Since the writing can take place in parallel, the elapsed time is about the same as for writing to a single disk. There is a slight opportunity for differences among the writing times for the various mirror disks, because we cannot rely on them rotating in exact synchronism. Thus, one disk's head might just miss a block, while another disk's head might be about to pass over the position for the same block. However, these differences in rotational latency average out, and if we are using the cylinder-based strategy of Section 2.4.1, then the rotational latency can be neglected anyway.

2.4.4   Disk Scheduling and the Elevator Algorithm

Another effective way to speed up disk accesses in some situations is to have the disk controller choose which of several requests to execute first. This opportunity is not useful when the system needs to read or write disk blocks in a certain sequence, such as is the case in parts of our running merge-sort example. However, when the system is supporting many small processes that each access a few blocks, one can often increase the throughput by choosing which process' request to honor first.

A simple and effective way to schedule large numbers of block requests is known as the *elevator algorithm*. We think of the disk head as making sweeps across the disk, from innermost to outermost cylinder and then back again, just as an elevator makes vertical sweeps from the bottom to top of a building and back again. As heads pass a cylinder, they stop if there are one or more requests for blocks on that cylinder. All these blocks are read or written, as requested. The heads then proceed in the same direction they were traveling until the next cylinder with blocks to access is encountered. When the heads reach a position where there are no requests ahead of them in their direction of travel, they reverse direction.

Example 2.11 : Suppose we are scheduling a Megatron 747 disk, which we recall has average seek, rotational latency, and transfer times of 6.5, 7.8, and

0.5. In this example, all times are in milliseconds. Suppose that at some time there are existing requests for block accesses at cylinders 1000, 3000, and 7000. The heads are located at cylinder 1000. In addition, there are three more requests for block accesses that come in at later times, as summarized in Fig. 2.12. For instance, the request for a block from cylinder 2000 is made at time 20 milliseconds.

We shall assume that each block access incurs time 0.5 for transfer and 7.8 for average rotational latency, i.e., we need 8.3 milliseconds plus whatever the seek time is for each block access. The seek time can be calculated by the rule for the Megatron 747 given in Example 2.3: 1 plus the number of tracks divided by 500. Let us see what happens if we schedule by the elevator algorithm. The first request at cylinder 1000 requires no seek, since the heads are already there. Thus, at time 8.3 the first access will be complete. The request for cylinder 2000 has not arrived at this point, so we move the heads to cylinder 3000, the next requested "stop" on our sweep to the highest-numbered tracks. The seek from cylinder 1000 to 3000 takes 5 milliseconds, so we arrive at time 13.3 and complete the access in another 8.3. Thus, the second access is complete at time 21.6. By this time, the request for cylinder 2000 has arrived, but we passed that cylinder at time 11.3 and will not come back to it until the next pass.

We thus move next to cylinder 7000, taking time 9 to seek and 8.3 for rotation and transfer. The third access is thus complete at time 38.9. Now, the request for cylinder 8000 has arrived, so we continue outward. We require 3 milliseconds for seek time, so this access is complete at time $38.9+3+8.3 = 50.2$. At this time, the request for cylinder 5000 has been made, so it and the request at cylinder 2000 remain. We thus sweep inward, honoring these two requests. Figure 2.13 summarizes the times at which requests are honored.

Let us compare the performance of the elevator algorithm with a more naive approach such as first-come-first-served. The first three requests are satisfied in exactly the same manner, assuming that the order of the first three requests was 1000, 3000, 7000. However, at that point, we go to cylinder 2000, because that was the fourth request to arrive. The seek time is 11.0 for this request, since we travel from cylinder 7000 to 2000, more than half way across the disk. The fifth request, at cylinder 8000, requires a seek time of 13, and the last, at 5000, uses seek time 7. Figure 2.14 summarizes the activity caused by first-come-first-serve scheduling. The difference between the two algorithms — 14 milliseconds — may appear not significant, but recall that the number of requests in this simple example is small and the algorithms were assumed not to deviate until the fourth of the six requests. □

If the average number of requests waiting for the disk increases, the elevator algorithm further improves the throughput. For instance, should the pool of waiting requests equal the number of cylinders, then each seek will cover but a few cylinders, and the average seek time will approximate the minimum. If the pool of requests grows beyond the number of cylinders, then there will typically be more than one request at each cylinder. The disk controller can then order

Cylinder of Request	First time available
1000	0
3000	0
7000	0
2000	20
8000	30
5000	40

Figure 2.12: Arrival times for six block-access requests

Cylinder of Request	Time completed
1000	8.3
3000	21.6
7000	38.9
8000	50.2
5000	65.5
2000	80.8

Figure 2.13: Finishing times for block accesses using the elevator algorithm

Cylinder of Request	Time completed
1000	8.3
3000	21.6
7000	38.9
2000	58.2
8000	79.5
5000	94.8

Figure 2.14: Finishing times for block accesses using the first-come-first-served algorithm

---

Effective Latency of the Elevator Algorithm

Although we saw in Example 2.11 how the average time taken per disk access can be reduced, the benefit is not uniform among requests. For example, the request from cylinder 2000 is satisfied at time 58.2 using first-come-first-served, but time 80.8 using the elevator algorithm, as we find by examining Figs. 2.13 and 2.14. Since the request was issued at time 20, the apparent latency of the disk as far as the requesting process is concerned went from 38.2 to 60.8 milliseconds.

If there were many more disk-access requests waiting, then each sweep of the heads during the elevator algorithm would take a very long time. A process whose request just missed the "elevator" would see an apparent latency that was very high indeed. The compensation is that without using the elevator algorithm or another good scheduling approach, throughput would decrease, and the disk could not satisfy requests at the rate they were generated. The system would eventually experience arbitrarily long delays, or fewer processes per second could be served.

---

the requests around the cylinder, reducing the average rotational latency as well as the average seek time. However, should request pools grow that big, the time taken to serve any request becomes extremely large. An example should illustrate the situation.

Example 2.12: Suppose again we are operating a Megatron 747 disk, with its 8192 cylinders. Imagine that there are 1000 disk access requests waiting. For simplicity, assume that these are all for blocks on different cylinders, spaced 8 apart. If we start at one end of the disk and sweep across, each of the 1000 requests has just a fraction more than 1 millisecond for seek time, 7.8 milliseconds for rotational latency, and 0.5 milliseconds for transfer. We can thus satisfy one request every 9.3 milliseconds, about 60% of the 14.4 millisecond average time for random block accesses. However, the entire 1000 accesses take 9.3 seconds, so the average delay in satisfying a request is half that, or 4.65 seconds, a quite noticeable delay.

Now, suppose the pool of requests is as large as 16,384, which we shall assume for simplicity is exactly two accesses per cylinder. In this case, each seek time is one millisecond, and of course the transfer time is half a millisecond. Since there are two blocks accessed on each cylinder, on average the further of the two blocks will be 2/3 of the way around the disk when the heads arrive at that track. The proof of this estimate is tricky; we explain it in the box entitled "Waiting for the Last of Two Blocks."

Thus the average latency for these two blocks will be half of 2/3 of the time for a single revolution, or $2 \times \frac{2}{3} \times 15.6 = 5.2$ milliseconds. We have thus reduced the average time to access a block to $1 + 0.5 + 5.2 = 6.7$ milliseconds, or less

---

Waiting for the Last of Two Blocks

Suppose there are two blocks at random positions around a cylinder. Let x_1 and x_2 be the positions, in fractions of the full circle, so these are numbers between 0 and 1. The probability that both x_1 and x_2 are less than some number y between 0 and 1 is y^2. Thus, the probability density for y is the derivative of y^2, or $2y$. That is, the probability that y has a given value increases linearly, as y grows from 0 to 1. The average of y is the integral of y times the probability density of y, that is $\int_0^1 2y^2$ or $2/3$.

---

than half the average time with first-come-first-served scheduling. On the other hand, the 16,384 accesses take a total of 110 seconds, so the average delay in satisfying a request is 55 seconds.   □

2.4.5   Prefetching and Large-Scale Buffering

Our final suggestion for speeding up some secondary-memory algorithms is called *prefetching* or sometimes *double buffering*. In some applications we can predict the order in which blocks will be requested from disk. If so, then we can load them into main memory buffers before they are needed. One advantage to doing so is that we are thus better able to schedule the disk, such as by using the elevator algorithm, to reduce the average time needed to access a block. We could gain the speedup in block access suggested by Example 2.12 without the long delay in satisfying requests that we also saw in that example.

Example 2.13 : For an example of the use of double buffering, let us again focus on the second phase of the Two-Phase, Multiway Merge-Sort outlined in Section 2.3.4. Recall that we merged 20 sorted sublists by bringing into main memory one block from each list. If we had so many sorted sublists to merge that one block from each would fill main memory, then we could not do any better. But in our example, there is plenty of main memory left over. For example, we could devote two block buffers to each list and fill one buffer while records were being selected from the other during the merge. When a buffer was exhausted, we would switch to the other buffer for the same list, with no delay.   □

However, the scheme of Example 2.13 would still take as much time as is required to read all the blocks of the sorted sublists, which is 250,000 blocks. We could combine prefetching with the cylinder-based strategy of Section 2.4.1 if we:

1. Store the sorted sublists on whole, consecutive cylinders, with the blocks on each track being consecutive blocks of the sorted sublist.

2. Read whole tracks or whole cylinders whenever we need some more records from a given list.

Example 2.14: To appreciate the benefit of track-sized or cylinder-sized reads, again let us consider the second phase of the Two-Phase, Multiway Merge-Sort We have room in main memory for two track-sized buffers for each of the 20 lists. Recall a track of the Megatron 747 holds 128K bytes, so the total space requirement is about 5 megabytes of main memory. We can read a track starting at any sector, so the time to read a track is essentially the average seek time plus the time for the disk to rotate once, or $6.5 + 15.6 = 22.1$ milliseconds. Since we must read all the blocks on 1000 cylinders, or 8000 tracks, to read the 20 sorted sublists, the total time for reading of all data is about 2.95 minutes.

We can do even better if we use two cylinder-sized buffers per sorted sublist, and fill one while the other is being used. Since there are eight tracks on a cylinder of the Megatron 747, we use 40 buffers of a megabyte each. With 50 megabytes available for the sort, we have enough room in main memory to do so. Using cylinder-sized buffers, we need only do a seek once per cylinder. The time to seek and read all eight tracks of a cylinder is thus $6.5 + 8 \times 15.6 = 131.3$ milliseconds. The time to read all 1000 cylinders is 1000 times as long, or about 2.19 minutes. □

The ideas just discussed for reading have their analogs for writing. In the spirit of prefetching, we can delay the writing of buffered blocks, as long as we don't need to reuse the buffer immediately. This strategy allows us to avoid delays while we wait for a block to be written out.

However, much more powerful is the strategy of using large output buffers — track-sized or cylinder-sized. If our application permits us to write in such large chunks, then we can essentially eliminate seek time and rotational latency, and write to disk at the maximum transfer rate of the disk. For instance, if we modified the writing part of the second phase of our sorting algorithm so there were two output buffers of a megabyte each, then we could fill one buffer with sorted records, and write it to a cylinder at the same time we filled the other output buffer with the next sorted records. Then, the writing time would be 2.15 minutes, like the reading time in Example 2.14, and the entire phase 2 would take 4.3 minutes, just like the improved phase 1 of Example 2.9. In essence, a combination of the tricks of cylinderization and cylinder-sized buffering and prefetching has given us a sort in 8.6 minutes that takes over 4 hours by a naive disk-management strategy.

2.4.6 Summary of Strategies and Tradeoffs

We have seen five different "tricks" that can sometimes improve the performance of a disk system. They are:

1. Organizing data by cylinders.

2. Using several disks in place of one.

3. Mirroring disks.

4. Scheduling requests by the elevator algorithm.

5. Prefetching data in track- or cylinder-sized chunks.

We also considered their effect on two situations, which represent the extremes of disk-access requirements:

a) A very regular situation, exemplified by phase 1 of the Two-Phase, Multi-way Merge-Sort, where blocks can be read and written in a sequence that can be predicted in advance, and there is only one process using the disk.

b) A collection of short processes, such as airline reservations or bank-account changes, that execute in parallel, share the same disk(s), and cannot be predicted in advance. Phase 2 of Two-Phase, Multiway Merge-Sort has some of these characteristics.

Below we summarize the advantages and disadvantages of each of these methods for these applications and those in between.

Cylinder-Based Organization

- Advantage: Excellent for type (a) applications, where accesses can be predicted in advance, and only one process is using the disk.

- Disadvantage: No help for type (b) applications, where accesses are unpredictable.

Multiple Disks

- Advantage: Increases the rate at which read/write requests can be satisfied, for both types of applications.

- Problem: Read or write requests for the same disk cannot be satisfied at the same time, so speedup factor may be less than the factor by which the number of disks increases.

- Disadvantage: The cost of several small disks exceeds the cost of a single disk with the same total capacity.

Mirroring

- Advantage: Increases the rate at which read/write requests can be satisfied, for both types of applications; does not have the problem of colliding accesses mentioned for multiple disks.

- Advantage: Improves fault tolerance for all applications.

- Disadvantage: We must pay for two or more disks but get the storage capacity of only one.

Cylinder of Request	First time available
1000	0
6000	1
500	10
5000	20

Figure 2.15: Arrival times for six block-access requests

Elevator Algorithm

- Advantage: Reduces the average time to read/write blocks when the accesses to blocks are unpredictable.

- Problem: The algorithm is most effective in situations where there are many waiting disk-access requests and therefore the average delay for the requesting processes is high.

Prefetching/Double Buffering

- Advantage: Speeds up access when the needed blocks are known but the timing of requests is data-dependent, as in phase 2 of the multiway merge-sort.

- Disadvantage: Requires extra main-memory buffers. No help when accesses are random.

2.4.7 Exercises for Section 2.4

Exercise 2.4.1: Suppose we are scheduling I/O requests for a Megatron 747 disk, and the requests in Fig. 2.15 are made, with the head initially at track 4000. At what time is each request seviced fully if:

a) We use the elevator algorithm (it is permissible to start moving in either direction at first).

b) We use first-come, first-served scheduling.

*! **Exercise 2.4.2:** Suppose we use two Megatron 747 disks as mirrors of one another. However, instead of allowing reads of any block from either disk, we keep the head of the first disk in the inner half of the cylinders, and the head of the second disk in the outer half of the cylinders. Assuming read requests are on random tracks, and we never have to write:

a) What is the average rate at which this system can read blocks?

b) How does this rate compare with the average rate for mirrored Megatron 747 disks with no restriction?

c) What disadvantages do you forsee for this system?

! **Exercise 2.4.3:** Let us explore the relationship between the arrival rate of requests, the throughput of the elevator algorithm, and the average delay of requests. To simplify the problem, we shall make the following assumptions:

1. A pass of the elevator algorithm always proceeds from the innermost to outermost track, or vice-versa, even if there are no requests at the extreme cylinders.

2. When a pass starts, only those requests that are already pending will be honored, not requests that come in while the pass is in progress, even if the head passes their cylinder.[8]

3. There will never be two requests for blocks on the same cylinder waiting on one pass.

Let A be the interarrival rate, that is the time between requests for block accesses. Assume that the system is in steady state, that is, it has been accepting and answering requests for a long time. For a Megatron 747 disk, compute as a function of A:

* a) The average time taken to perform one pass.

b) The number of requests serviced on one pass.

c) The average time a request waits for service.

*!! **Exercise 2.4.4:** In Example 2.10, we saw how dividing the data to be sorted among four disks could allow more than one block to be read at a time. On the assumption that the merging phase generates read requests for blocks that are on random disks, and that all read requests are honored unless they are for a disk that is currently serving another request, what is the average number of disks that are serving requests at any time? Note: there are a two observations that simplify the problem:

1. Once a request to read a block is unable to proceed, then the merging must stop and generate no more requests, because there is no data from the exhausted sublist that generated the unsatisfied read request.

---

[8]The purpose of this assumption is to avoid having to deal with the fact that a typical pass of the elevator algorithm goes fast as first, as there will be few waiting requests where the head has recently been, and speeds up as it moves into an area of the disk where it has not recently been. The analysis of the way request density varies during a pass is an interesting exercise in its own right.

2. As soon as merging is able to proceed, it will generate a read request, since main-memory merging takes essentially no time compared with the time to satisfy a read request.

! **Exercise 2.4.5:** If we are to read k randomly chosen blocks from one cylinder, on the average how far around the cylinder must we go before we pass all of the blocks?

2.5 Disk Failures

In this and the next section we shall consider the ways in which disks can fail and what can be done to mitigate these failures.

1. The most common form of failure is an *intermittent failure*, where an attempt to read or write a sector is unsuccessful, but with repeated tries we are able to read or write successfully.

2. A more serious form of failure is one in which a bit or bits are permanently corrupted, and it becomes impossible to read a sector correctly no matter how many times we try. This form of error is called *media decay*.

3. A related type of error is a *write failure*, where we attempt to write a sector, but we can neither write successfully nor can we retrieve the previously written sector. A possible cause is that there was a power outage during the writing of the sector.

4. The most serious form of disk failure is a *disk crash*, where the entire disk becomes unreadable, suddenly and permanently.

In this section we consider a simple model of disk failures. We cover parity checks as a way to detect intermittent failures. We also discuss "stable storage," a technique for organizing a disk so that media decays or failed writes do not result in permanent loss. In Section 2.6 we examine techniques collectively known as "RAID" for coping with disk crashes.

2.5.1 Intermittent Failures

Disk sectors are ordinarily stored with some redundant bits, which we discuss in Section 2.5.2. The purpose of these bits is to enable us to tell whether what we are reading from the sector is correct or not; they similarly allow us to tell whether a sector we wrote has been written correctly.

A useful model of disk reads is that the reading function returns a pair (w, s), where w is the data in the sector that is read, and s is a *status* bit that tells whether or not the read was successful; i.e., whether or not we can rely on w being the true contents of the sector. In an intermittent failure, we may get a status "bad" several times, but if the read function is repeated enough times

(100 times is a typical limit), then eventually a status "good" will be returned, and we rely on the data returned with this status to be the correct contents of the disk sector. As we shall see in Section 2.5.2, there is a chance that we are being fooled; the status is "good" but the data returned is wrong. However, we can make the probability of this event as low as we like, if we add more redundancy to the sectors.

Writing of sectors can also profit by observing the status of what we write. As we mentioned in Section 2.2.5, we may try to read each sector after we write it and determine whether the write was successful. A straightforward way to perform the check is to read the sector and compare it with the sector we intended to write. However, instead of performing the complete comparison at the disk controller, it is simpler to attempt to read the sector and see if its status is "good." If so, we assume the write was correct, and if the status is "bad" then the write was apparently unsuccessful and must be repeated. Notice that, as with reading, we can be fooled if the status is "good" but the write was actually unsuccessful. Also as with reading, we can make the probability of such an event as small as we like.

2.5.2   Checksums

How a reading operation can determine the good/bad status of a sector may appear mysterious at first. Yet the technique used in modern disk drives is quite simple: each sector has some additional bits, called the *checksum*, that are set depending on the values of the data bits stored in that sector. If, on reading, we find that the checksum is not proper for the data bits, then we return status "bad"; otherwise we return "good." While there is a small probability that the data bits may be misread, but the incorrect bits happen to have the same checksum as the correct bits (and therefore incorrect bits will be given the status "good"), by using a sufficiently large number of checksum bits, we can reduce this probability to whatever small level we wish.

A simple form of checksum is based on the *parity* of all the bits in the sector. If there is an odd number of 1's among a collection of bits, we say the bits have *odd* parity, or that their parity bit is 1. Similarly, if there is an even number of 1's among the bits, then we say the bits have *even* parity, or that their parity bit is 0. As a result:

- The number of 1's among a collection of bits and their parity bit is always even.

When we write a sector, the disk controller can compute the parity bit and append it to the sequence of bits written in the sector. Thus, every sector will have even parity.

Example 2.15 : If the sequence of bits in a sector were 01101000, then there is an odd number of 1's, so the parity bit is 1. If we follow this sequence by its parity bit we have 011010001. If the given sequence of bits were 11101110, we have an even number of 1's, and the parity bit is 0. The sequence followed by its parity bit is 111011100. Note that each of the nine-bit sequences constructed by adding a parity bit has even parity. □

Any one-bit error in reading or writing the bits and their parity bit results in a sequence of bits that has *odd parity*; i.e., the number of 1's is odd. It is easy for the disk controller to count the number of 1's and to determine the presence of an error if a sector has odd parity.

Of course, more than one bit of the sector may be corrupted. If so, the probability is 50% that the number of 1-bits will be even, and the error will not be detected. We can increase our chances of detecting even large numbers of errors if we keep several parity bits. For example, we could keep eight parity bits, one for the first bit of every byte, one for the second bit of every byte, and so on, up to the eighth and last bit of every byte. Then, on a massive error, the probability is 50% that any one parity bit will detect an error, and the chance that none of the eight do so is only one in 2^8, or $1/256$. In general, if we use n independent bits as a checksum, then the chance of missing an error is only $1/2^n$. For instance, if we devote 4 bytes to a checksum, then there is only one chance in about four billion that the error will go undetected.

2.5.3 Stable Storage

While checksums will almost certainly detect the existence of a media failure or a failure to read or write correctly, it does not help us correct the error. Moreover, when writing we could find ourselves in a position where we overwrite the previous contents of a sector and yet cannot read the new contents. That situation could be serious in a situation where, say, we were adding a small increment to an account balance and have now lost both the original balance and the new balance. If we could be assured that the contents of the sector contained either the new or old balance, then we would only have to determine whether the write was successful or not.

To deal with the problems above, we can implement a policy known as *stable storage* on a disk or on several disks. The general idea is that sectors are paired, and each pair represents one sector-contents X. We shall refer to the pair of sectors representing X as the "left" and "right" copies, X_L and X_R. We continue to assume that the copies are written with a sufficient number of parity-check bits so that we can rule out the possibility that a bad sector looks good when the parity checks are considered. Thus, we shall assume that if the read function returns (w, good) for either X_L or X_R, then w is the true value of X. The stable-storage writing policy is:

1. Write the value of X into X_L. Check that the value has status "good"; i.e., the parity-check bits are correct in the written copy. If not, repeat the write. If after a set number of write attempts, we have not successfully written X into X_L, assume that there is a media failure in this sector. A fix-up such as substituting a spare sector for X_L must be adopted.

2. Repeat (1) for X_R.

The stable-storage reading policy is:

1. To obtain the value of X, read X_L. If status "bad" is returned, repeat the read a set number of times. If a value with status "good" is eventually returned, take that value as X.

2. If we cannot read X_L, repeat (1) with X_R.

2.5.4 Error-Handling Capabilities of Stable Storage

The policies described in Section 2.5.3 are capable of compensating for several different kinds of errors. We shall outline them here.

1. *Media failures.* If, after storing X in sectors X_L and X_R, one of them undergoes a media failure and becomes permanently unreadable, we can always read X from the other. If X_R has failed but X_L has not, then the read policy will correctly read X_L and not even look at X_R; we shall discover that X_R is failed when we next try to write a new value for X. If only X_L has failed, then we shall not be able to get a "good" status for X in any of our attempts to read X_L (recall that we assume a bad sector will always return status "bad," even though in reality there is a tiny chance that "good" will be returned because all the parity-check bits happen to match). Thus, we proceed to step (2) of the read algorithm and correctly read X from X_R. Note that if both X_L and X_R have failed, then we cannot read X, but the probability of both failing is extremely small.

2. *Write failure.* Suppose that as we write X, there is a system failure — e.g., a power outage. It is possible that X will be lost in main memory, and also the copy of X being written at the time will be garbled. For example, half the sector may be written with part of the new value of X, while the other half remains as it was. When the system becomes available and we examine X_L and X_R, we are sure to be able to determine either the old or new value of X. The possible cases are:

   (a) The failure occurred as we were writing X_L. Then we shall find that the status of X_L is "bad." However, since we never got to write X_R, its status will be "good" (unless there is a coincident media failure at X_R, which we rule out as extremely unlikely). Thus, we can obtain the old value of X. We may also copy X_R into X_L to repair the damage to X_L.

   (b) The failure occurred after we wrote X_L. Then we expect that X_L will have status "good," and we may read the new value of X from X_L. Note that X_R may have status bad, and we should copy X_L into X_R if so.

2.5.5 Exercises for Section 2.5

Exercise 2.5.1: Compute the parity bit for the following bit sequences:

* a) 00111011.

  b) 00000000.

  c) 10101101.

Exercise 2.5.2: We can have two parity bits associated with a string if we follow the string by one bit that is a parity bit for the odd positions and a second that is the parity bit for the even positions. For each of the strings in Exercise 2.5.1, find the two bits that serve in this way.

2.6 Recovery from Disk Crashes

In this section, we shall consider the most serious mode of failure for disks — the "head crash," where data is permanently destroyed. In this event, if data is not backed up on another medium, such as a tape backup system, or on a mirror disk as we discussed in Section 2.4.3, then there is nothing we can do to recover the data. This situation represents a disaster for major DBMS applications, such as banking and other financial applications, airline or other reservation-booking databases, inventory-management systems, and many others.

There are a number of schemes that have been developed to reduce the risk of data loss by disk crashes. They generally involve redundancy, extending the idea of parity checks, as discussed in Section 2.5.2, or duplicated sectors, as in Section 2.5.3. The common term for this class of strategies is RAID, or *Redundant Arrays of Independent Disks*.[9] Here, we shall discuss primarily three schemes, called RAID levels 4, 5, and 6. These RAID schemes also handle failures in the modes discussed in Section 2.5: media failures and corruption of data in a single sector due to a temporary system failure.

2.6.1 The Failure Model for Disks

To begin our discussion of disk crashes, we need to consider first the statistics of such failures. The simplest way to describe failure behavior is through a measurement known as *mean time to failure*. This number is the length of time by which 50% of a population of disks will have failed catastrophically, i.e., had a head crash so they are no longer readable. For modern disks, the mean time to failure is about 10 years.

The simplest way to use this number is to assume that failures occur linearly. That is, if 50% have failed by 10 years, then 5% will fail in the first year, 5% in the second, and so on, for 20 years. More realistically, the survival

---

[9]Previously, the acronym RAID was translated as "Redundant Array of Inexpensive Disks," and this meaning may still appear in literature.

percentage of disks looks more like Fig. 2.16. As for most types of electronic equipment, many disk failures occur early in the life cycle, due to tiny defects in the manufacture of that disk. Hopefully, most of these are caught before the disk leaves the factory, but some do not show up for months. A disk that does not suffer an early failure will probably serve for many years. Later in the life cycle, factors such as "wear-and-tear" and the accumulated effects of tiny dust particles increase the chances of a crash.

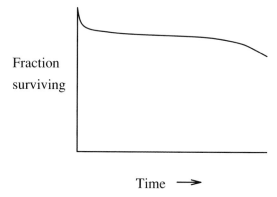

Figure 2.16: A survival rate curve for disks

However, the mean time to a disk crash does not have to be the same as the mean time to data loss. The reason is that there are a number of schemes available for assuring that if one disk fails, there are others to help recover the data of the failed disk. In the balance of this section, we shall study the most common schemes.

Each of these schemes starts with one or more disks that hold the data (we'll call these the *data disks*) and adding one or more disks that hold information that is completely determined by the contents of the data disks. The latter are called *redundant disks*. When there is a disk crash of either a data disk or a redundant disk, the other disks can be used to restore the failed disk, and there is no permanent information loss.

2.6.2   Mirroring as a Redundancy Technique

The simplest scheme is to mirror each disk, as discussed in Section 2.4.3. We shall call one of the disks the *data disk*, while the other is the *redundant disk*; which is which doesn't matter in this scheme. Mirroring, as a protection against data loss, is often referred to as *RAID level 1*. It gives a mean time to memory loss that is much greater than the mean time to disk failure, as the following example illustrates. Essentially, with mirroring and the other redundancy schemes we discuss, the only way data can be lost is if there is a second disk crash while the first crash is being repaired.

Example 2.16: Suppose each disk has a 10 year mean time to failure. We shall use the linear model of failures described in Section 2.6.1, which means that the chance a disk will fail is 5% per year. If disks are mirrored, then when a disk fails, we have only to replace it with a good disk and copy the mirror disk to the new one. At the end, we have two disks that are mirrors of each other, and the system is restored to its former state.

The only thing that could go wrong is that during the copying the mirror disk fails. Now, both copies of at least part of the data have been lost, and there is no way to recover.

But how often will this sequence of events occur? Suppose that the process of replacing the failed disk takes 3 hours, which is 1/8 of a day, or 1/2920 of a year. Since we assume a failure rate of 5% per year, the probability that the mirror disk will fail during copying is $(1/20) \times (1/2920)$, or one in 58,400. If one disk fails every 10 years, then one of the two disks will fail once in 5 years on the average. One in every 58,400 of these failures results in data loss. Put another way, the mean time to a failure involving data loss is $5 \times 58,400 = 292,000$ years. □

2.6.3 Parity Blocks

While mirroring disks is an effective way to reduce the probability of a disk crash involving data loss, it uses as many redundant disks as there are data disks. Another approach, often called *RAID level 4*, uses only one redundant disk no matter how many data disks there are. We assume the disks are identical, so we can number the blocks on each disk from 1 to some number n. Of course, all the blocks on all the disks have the same number of bits; for instance, the 4096-byte blocks in our Megatron 747 running example have $8 \times 4096 = 32,768$ bits. In the redundant disk, the ith block consists of parity checks for the ith blocks of all the data disks. That is, the jth bits of all the ith blocks, including both the data disks and the redundant disk, must have an even number of 1's among them, and we always choose the bit of the redundant disk to make this condition true.

We saw in Example 2.15 how to force the condition to be true. In the redundant disk, we choose bit j to be 1 if an odd number of the data disks have 1 in that bit, and we choose bit j of the redundant disk to be 0 if there are an even number of 1's in that bit among the data disks. The term for this calculation is the *modulo-2 sum*. That is, the modulo-2 sum of bits is 0 if there are an even number of 1's among those bits, and 1 if there are an odd number of 1's.

Example 2.17: Suppose for sake of an extremely simple example that blocks consist of only one byte — eight bits. Let there be three data disks, called 1, 2, and 3, and one redundant disk, called disk 4. Focus on, say, the first block of all these disks. If the data disks have in their first blocks the following bit sequences:

                              disk 1: 11110000
                              disk 2: 10101010
                              disk 3: 00111000

then the redundant disk will have in block 1 the parity check bits:

                              disk 4: 01100010

Notice how in each position, an even number of the four 8-bit sequences have
1's. There are two 1's in positions 1, 2, 4, 5, and 7, four 1's in position 3, and
zero 1's in positions 6 and 8.   □

Reading

Reading blocks from a data disk is no different from reading blocks from any
disk. There is generally no reason to read from the redundant disk, but we could.
In some circumstances, we can actually get the effect of two simultaneous reads
from one of the data disks; the following example shows how, although the
conditions under which it could be used are expected to be rare.

Example 2.18: Suppose we are reading a block of the first data disk, and
another request comes in to read a different block, say block 1, of the same
data disk. Ordinarily, we would have to wait for the first request to finish.
However, if none of the other disks are busy, we could read block 1 from each
of them, and compute block 1 of the first disk by taking the modulo-2 sum.

   Specifically, if the disks and their first blocks were as in Example 2.17, then
we could read the second and third data disks and the redundant disk, to get
the following blocks:

                              disk 2: 10101010
                              disk 3: 00111000
                              disk 4: 01100010

If we take the modulo-2 sum of the bits in each column, we get

                              disk 1: 11110000

which is the same as block 1 of the first disk.   □

Writing

When we write a new block of a data disk, we need not only to change that
block, but we need to change the corresponding block of the redundant disk
so it continues to hold the parity checks for the corresponding blocks of all the
data disks. A naive approach would read the corresponding blocks of the n data
disks, take their modulo-2 sum, and rewrite the block of the redundant disk.
That approach requires $n - 1$ reads of the data blocks not being rewritten,

---

The Algebra of Modulo-2 Sums

It may be helpful for understanding some of the tricks used with parity checks to know the algebraic rules involving the modulo-2 sum operation on bit vectors. We shall denote this operation $\oplus$. For instance, $1100 \oplus 1010 = 0110$. Here are some useful rules about $\oplus$:

- The *commutative law*: $x \oplus y = y \oplus x$.

- The *associative law*: $x \oplus (y \oplus z) = (x \oplus y) \oplus z$.

- The all-0 vector of the appropriate length, which we denote $\bar{0}$, is the *identity* for $\oplus$; that is, $x \oplus \bar{0} = \bar{0} \oplus x = x$.

- $\oplus$ is its own inverse: $x \oplus x = \bar{0}$. As a useful consequence, if $x \oplus y = z$, then we can "add" x to both sides and get $y = x \oplus z$.

---

a write of the data block that is rewritten, and a write of the block of the redundant disk. The total is thus $n + 1$ disk I/O's.

A better approach is to look only at the old and new versions of the data block i being rewritten. If we take their modulo-2 sum, we know in which positions there is a change in the number of 1's among the blocks numbered i on all the disks. Since these changes are always by one, any even number of 1's changes to an odd number. If we change the same positions of the redundant block, then the number of 1's in each position becomes even again. We can perform these calculations using four disk I/O's:

1. Read the old value of the data block being changed.

2. Read the corresponding block of the redundant disk.

3. Write the new data block.

4. Recalculate and write the block of the redundant disk.

Example 2.19: Suppose the three first blocks of the data disks are as in Example 2.17:

$$\text{disk 1: } 11110000$$
$$\text{disk 2: } 10101010$$
$$\text{disk 3: } 00111000$$

Suppose also that the block on the second disk changes from 10101010 to 11001100. We take the modulo-2 sum of the old and new values of the block on disk 2, to get 01100110. That tells us we must change positions 2, 3, 6, and 7 of the first block of the redundant disk. We read that block: 01100010. We replace this block by a new block that we get by changing the appropriate positions; in effect we replace the redundant block by the modulo-2 sum of itself and 01100110, to get 00000100. Another way to express the new redundant block is that it is the modulo-2 sum of the old and new versions of the block being rewritten and the old value of the redundant block. In our example, the first blocks of the four disks — three data disks and one redundant — have become

disk 1: 11110000
disk 2: 11001100
disk 3: 00111000
disk 4: 00000100

after the write to the block on the second disk and the necessary recomputation of the redundant block. Notice that in the blocks above, each column continues to have an even number of 1's.

Incidentally, notice that this write of a data block, like all writes of data blocks using the scheme described above, takes four disk I/O's. The naive scheme — read all but the rewritten block and recompute the redundant block directly — would also require four disk I/O's in this example: two to read data from the first and third data disks, and two to write the second data disk and the redundant disk. However, if we had more than three data disks, the number of I/O's for the naive scheme rises linearly with the number of data disks, while the cost of the scheme advocated here continues to require only four.   □

Failure Recovery

Now, let us consider what we would do if one of the disks crashed. If it is the redundant disk, we swap in a new disk, and recompute the redundant blocks. If the failed disk is one of the data disks, then we need to swap in a good disk and recompute its data from the other disks. The rule for recomputing any missing data is actually simple, and doesn't depend on which disk, data or redundant, is failed. Since we know that the number of 1's among corresponding bits of all disks is even, it follows that:

- The bit in any position is the modulo-2 sum of all the bits in the corresponding positions of all the other disks.

If one doubts the above rule, one has only to consider the two cases. If the bit in question is 1, then the number of corresponding bits that are 1 must be odd, so their modulo-2 sum is 1. If the bit in question is 0, then there are an even number of 1's among the corresponding bits, and their modulo-2 sum is 0.

Example 2.20 : Suppose that disk 2 fails. We need to recompute each block of the replacement disk. Following Example 2.17, let us see how to recompute the first block of the second disk. We are given the corresponding blocks of the first and third data disks and the redundant disk, so the situation looks like:

$$
\begin{array}{l}
\text{disk 1: 11110000} \\
\text{disk 2: ????????} \\
\text{disk 3: 00111000} \\
\text{disk 4: 01100010}
\end{array}
$$

If we take the modulo-2 sum of each column, we deduce that the missing block is 10101010, as was initially the case in Example 2.17. □

2.6.4 An Improvement: RAID 5

The RAID level 4 strategy described in Section 2.6.3 effectively preserves data unless there are two, almost-simultaneous disk crashes. However, it suffers from a bottleneck defect that we can see when we re-examine the process of writing a new data block. Whatever scheme we use for updating the disks, we need to read and write the redundant disk's block. If there are n data disks, then the number of disk writes to the redundant disk will be n times the average number of writes to any one data disk.

However, as we observed in Example 2.20, the rule for recovery is the same as for the data disks and redundant disks: take the modulo-2 sum of corresponding bits of the other disks. Thus, we do not have to treat one disk as the redundant disk and the others as data disks. Rather, we could treat each disk as the redundant disk for some of the blocks. This improvement is often called *RAID level 5*.

For instance, if there are $n + 1$ disks numbered 0 through n, we could treat the ith cylinder of disk j as redundant if j is the remainder when i is divided by $n + 1$.

Example 2.21: If, as in our running example, $n = 3$ so there are 4 disks, the first disk, numbered 0, would be redundant for its cylinders numbered 4, 8, 12, and so on, because these are the numbers that leave remainder 0 when divided by 4. The disk numbered 1 would be redundant for blocks numbered 1, 5, 9, and so on; disk 2 is redundant for blocks 2, 6, 10,..., and disk 3 is redundant for 3, 7, 11,.... .

As a result, the reading and writing load for each disk is the same. If all blocks are equally likely to be written, then for one write, each disk has a 1/4 chance that the block is on that disk. If not, then it has a 1/3 chance that it will be the redundant disk for that block. Thus, each of the four disks is involved in $\frac{1}{4} + \frac{3}{4} \times \frac{1}{3} = \frac{1}{2}$ of the writes. □

2.6.5 Coping With Multiple Disk Crashes

There is a theory of error-correcting codes that allows us to deal with any number of disk crashes — data or redundant — if we use enough redundant disks. This strategy leads to the highest RAID "level," *RAID level 6*. We shall give only a simple example here, where two simultaneous crashes are correctable, and the strategy is based on the simplest error-correcting code, known as a *Hamming code*.

In our description we focus on a system with seven disks, numbered 1 through 7. The first four are data disks, and disks 5 through 7 are redundant. The relationship between data and redundant disks is summarized by the 3×7 matrix of 0's and 1's in Fig. 2.17. Notice that:

a) Every possible column of three 0's and 1's, except for the all-0 column, appears in the matrix of Fig. 2.17.

b) The columns for the redundant disks have a single 1.

c) The columns for the data disks each have at least two 1's.

	Data				Redundant		
Disk number	1	2	3	4	5	6	7
	1	1	1	0	1	0	0
	1	1	0	1	0	1	0
	1	0	1	1	0	0	1

Figure 2.17: Redundancy pattern for a system that can recover from two simultaneous disk crashes

The meaning of each of the three rows of 0's and 1's is that if we look at the corresponding bits from all seven disks, and restrict our attention to those disks that have 1 in that row, then the modulo-2 sum of these bits must be 0. Put another way, the disks with 1 in a given row are treated as if they were the entire set of disks in a RAID level 4 scheme. Thus, we can compute the bits of one of the redundant disks by finding the row in which that disk has 1, and taking the modulo-2 sum of the corresponding bits of the other disks that have 1 in the same row.

For the matrix of Fig. 2.17, this rule implies:

1. The bits of disk 5 are the modulo-2 sum of the corresponding bits of disks 1, 2, and 3.

2. The bits of disk 6 are the modulo-2 sum of the corresponding bits of disks 1, 2, and 4.

3. The bits of disk 7 are the modulo-2 sum of the corresponding bits of disks 1, 3, and 4.

We shall see shortly that the particular choice of bits in this matrix gives us a simple rule by which we can recover from two simultaneous disk crashes.

Reading

We may read data from any data disk normally. The redundant disks can be ignored.

Writing

The idea is similar to the writing strategy outlined in Section 2.6.4, but now several redundant disks may be involved. To write a block of some data disk, we compute the modulo-2 sum of the new and old versions of that block. These bits are then added, in a modulo-2 sum, to the corresponding blocks of all those redundant disks that have 1 in a row in which the written disk also has 1.

Example 2.22: Let us again assume that blocks are only eight bits long, and focus on the first blocks of the seven disks involved in our RAID level 6 example. First, suppose the data and redundant first blocks are as given in Fig. 2.22. Notice that the block for disk 5 is the modulo-2 sum of the blocks for the first three disks, the sixth row is the modulo-2 sum of rows 1, 2, and 4, and the last row is the modulo-2 sum of rows 1, 3, and 4.

Disk	Contents
1)	11110000
2)	10101010
3)	00111000
4)	01000001
5)	01100010
6)	00011011
7)	10001001

Figure 2.18: First blocks of all disks

Suppose we rewrite the first block of disk 2 to be 00001111. If we sum this sequence of bits modulo-2 with the sequence 10101010 that is the old value of this block, we get 10100101. If we look at the column for disk 2 in Fig. 2.17, we find that this disk has 1's in the first two rows, but not the third. Since redundant disks 5 and 6 have 1 in rows 1 and 2, respectively, we must perform the sum modulo-2 operation on the current contents of their first blocks and the sequence 10100101 just calculated. That is, we flip the values of positions 1, 3, 6, and 8 of these two blocks. The resulting contents of the first blocks of all disks is shown in Fig. 2.19. Notice that the new contents continue to satisfy the constraints implied by Fig. 2.17: the modulo-2 sum of corresponding blocks that have 1 in a particular row of the matrix of Fig. 2.17 is still all 0's. □

Disk	Contents
1)	11110000
2)	00001111
3)	00111000
4)	01000001
5)	11000111
6)	10111110
7)	10001001

Figure 2.19: First blocks of all disks after rewriting disk 2 and changing the redundant disks

Failure Recovery

Now, let us see how the redundancy scheme outlined above can be used to correct up to two simultaneous disk crashes. Let the failed disks be a and b. Since all columns of the matrix of Fig. 2.17 are different, we must be able to find some row r in which the columns for a and b are different. Suppose that a has 0 in row r, while b has 1 there.

Then we can compute the correct b by taking the modulo-2 sum of corresponding bits from all the disks other than b that have 1 in row r. Note that a is not among these, so none of them have failed. Having done so, we must recompute a, with all other disks available. Since every column of the matrix of Fig. 2.17 has a 1 in some row, we can use this row to recompute disk a by taking the modulo-2 sum of bits of those other disks with a 1 in this row.

Example 2.23 : Suppose that disks 2 and 5 fail at about the same time. Consulting the matrix of Fig. 2.17, we find that the columns for these two disks differ in row 2, where disk 2 has 1 but disk 5 has 0. We may thus reconstruct disk 2 by taking the modulo-2 sum of corresponding bits of disks 1, 4, and 6, the other three disks with 1 in row 2. Notice that none of these three disks has failed. For instance, following from the situation regarding the first blocks in Fig. 2.19, we would initially have the data of Fig. 2.20 available after disks 2 and 5 failed.

If we take the modulo-2 sum of the contents of the blocks of disks 1, 4, and 6, we find that the block for disk 2 is 00001111. This block is correct as can be verified from Fig. 2.19. The situation is now as in Fig. 2.21.

Now, we see that disk 5's column in Fig. 2.17 has a 1 in the first row. We can therefore recompute disk 5 by taking the modulo-2 sum of corresponding bits from disks 1, 2, and 3, the other three disks that have 1 in the first row. For block 1, this sum is 11000111. Again, the correctness of this calculation can be confirmed by Fig. 2.19. □

Additional Observations About RAID Level 6

1. We can combine the ideas of RAID levels 5 and 6, by varying the redundant disks according to the block or cylinder number. Doing so will avoid bottlenecks when writing; the scheme described in Section 2.6.5 will cause bottlenecks at the redundant disks.

2. The scheme described in Section 2.6.5 is not restricted to four data disks. The number of disks can be one less than any power of 2, say $2^k - 1$. Of these disks, k are redundant, and the remaining $2^k - k - 1$ are data disks, so the redundancy grows roughly as the logarithm of the number of data disks. For any k, we can construct the matrix corresponding to Fig. 2.17 by writing all possible columns of k 0's and 1's, except the all-0's column. The columns with a single 1 correspond to the redundant disks, and the columns with more than one 1 are the data disks.

Disk	Contents
1)	11110000
2)	????????
3)	00111000
4)	01000001
5)	????????
6)	10111110
7)	10001001

Figure 2.20: Situation after disks 2 and 5 fail

2.6.6 Exercises for Section 2.6

Exercise 2.6.1: Suppose we use mirrored disks as in Example 2.16, the failure rate is 4% per year, and it takes 8 hours to replace a disk. What is the mean time to a disk failure involving loss of data?

*! Exercise 2.6.2: Suppose disks have a failure rate of fraction F per year and it takes H hours to replace a disk.

    a) If we use mirrored disks, what is the mean time to data loss, as a function of F and H?

    b) If we use a RAID level 4 or 5 scheme, with N disks, what is the mean time to data loss?

Disk	Contents
1)	11110000
2)	00001111
3)	00111000
4)	01000001
5)	????????
6)	10111110
7)	10001001

Figure 2.21: After recovering disk 2

!! Exercise 2.6.3: Suppose we use three disks as a mirrored group; i.e., all three hold identical data. If the failure rate for one disk is F per year and it takes H hours to restore a disk, what is the mean time to data loss?

Exercise 2.6.4: Suppose we are using a RAID level 4 scheme with four data disks and one redundant disk. As in Example 2.17 assume blocks are a single byte. Give the block of the redundant disk if the corresponding blocks of the data disks are:

* a) 01010110, 11000000, 00111011, and 11111011.

  b) 11110000, 11111000, 00111111, and 00000001.

Exercise 2.6.5: Using the same RAID level 4 scheme as in Exercise 2.6.4, suppose that data disk 1 has failed. Recover the block of that disk under the following circumstances:

* a) The contents of disks 2 through 4 are 01010110, 11000000, and 00111011, while the redundant disk holds 11111011.

  b) The contents of disks 2 through 4 are 11110000, 11111000, and 00111111, while the redundant disk holds 00000001.

Exercise 2.6.6: Suppose the block on the first disk in Exercise 2.6.4 is changed to 10101010. What changes to the corresponding blocks on the other disks must be made?

Exercise 2.6.7: Suppose we have the RAID level 6 scheme of Example 2.22, and the blocks of the four data disks are 00111100, 11000111, 01010101, and 10000100, respectively.

  a) What are the corresponding blocks of the redundant disks?

  b) If the third disk's block is rewritten to be 10000000, what steps must be taken to change other disks?

Error-Correcting Codes and RAID Level 6

There is a broad theory that guides our selection of a suitable matrix, like that of Fig. 2.17, to determine the content of redundant disks. A *code* of length n is a set of bit-vectors (called *code words*) of length n. The *Hamming distance* between two code words is the number of positions in which they differ, and the *minimum distance* of a code is the smallest Hamming distance of any two different code words.

If C is any code of length n, we can require that the corresponding bits on n disks have one of the sequences that are members of the code. As a very simple example, if we are using a disk and its mirror, then $n = 2$, and we can use the code $C = \{00, 11\}$. That is, the corresponding bits of the two disks must be the same. For another example, the matrix of Fig. 2.17 defines the code consisting of the 16 bit-vectors of length 7 that have arbitrary values for the first four bits and have the remaining three bits determined by the rules for the three redundant disks.

If the minimum distance of a code is d, then disks whose corresponding bits are required to be a vector in the code will be able to tolerate $d - 1$ simultaneous disk crashes. The reason is that, should we obscure $d - 1$ positions of a code word, and there were two different ways these positions could be filled in to make a code word, then the two code words would have to differ in at most the $d - 1$ positions. Thus, the code could not have minimum distance d. As an example, the matrix of Fig. 2.17 actually defines the well-known *Hamming code*, which has minimum distance 3. Thus, it can handle two disk crashes.

Exercise 2.6.8: Describe the steps taken to recover from the following failures using the RAID level 6 scheme with seven disks:

* a) Disks 1 and 7.

  b) Disks 1 and 4.

  c) Disks 3 and 6.

Exercise 2.6.9: Find a RAID level 6 scheme using 15 disks, four of which are redundant. *Hint*: Generalize the 7-disk Hamming matrix.

Exercise 2.6.10: List the 16 code words for the Hamming code of length 7. That is, what are the 16 lists of bits that could be corresponding bits on the seven disks of the RAID level 6 scheme based on the matrix of Fig. 2.17?

Exercise 2.6.11: Suppose we have four disks, of which disks 1 and 2 are data disks, and disks 3 and 4 are redundant. Disk 3 is a mirror of disk 1. Disk 4 holds the parity check bits for the corresponding bits of disks 2 and 3.

a) Express this situation by giving a parity check matrix analogous to Fig. 2.17.

!! b) It is possible to recover from *some* but not all situations where two disks fail at the same time. Determine for which pairs it is possible to recover and for which pairs it is not.

*! **Exercise 2.6.12:** Suppose we have eight data disks numbered 1 through 8, and three redundant disks: 9, 10, and 11. Disk 9 is a parity check on disks 1 through 4, and disk 10 is a parity check on disks 5 through 8. If all pairs of disks are equally likely to fail simultaneously, and we want to maximize the probability that we can recover from the simultaneous failure of two disks, then on which disks should disk 11 be a parity check?

!! **Exercise 2.6.13:** Find a RAID level 6 scheme with ten disks, such that it is possible to recover from the failure of any three disks simultaneously. You should use as many data disks as you can.

2.7   Summary of Chapter 2

✦ *Memory Hierarchy*: A computer system uses storage components ranging over many orders of magnitude in speed, capacity, and cost per bit. From the smallest/most expensive to largest/cheapest, they are: cache, main memory, secondary memory (disk), and tertiary memory.

✦ *Tertiary Storage*: The principal devices for tertiary storage are tape cassettes, tape silos (mechanical devices for managing tape cassettes), and "juke boxes" (mechanical devices for managing CD-ROM disks). These storage devices have capacities of many terabytes, but are the slowest available storage devices.

✦ *Disks/Secondary Storage*: Secondary storage devices are principally magnetic disks with multigigabyte capacities. Disk units have several circular platters of magnetic material, with concentric tracks to store bits. Platters rotate around a central spindle. The tracks at a given radius from the center of a platter form a cylinder.

✦ *Blocks and Sectors*: Tracks are divided into sectors, which are separated by unmagnetized gaps. Sectors are the unit of reading and writing from the disk. Blocks are logical units of storage used by an application such as a DBMS. Blocks typically consist of several sectors.

✦ *Disk Controller*: The disk controller is a processor that controls one or more disk units. It is responsible for moving the disk heads to the proper cylinder to read or write a requested track. It also may schedule competing requests for disk access and buffers the blocks to be read or written.

✦ *Disk Access Time*: The latency of a disk is the time between a request to read or write a block, and the time the access is completed. Latency is caused principally by three factors: the seek time to move the heads to the proper cylinder, the rotational latency during which the desired block rotates under the head, and the transfer time, while the block moves under the head and is read or written.

✦ *Moore's Law*: A consistent trend sees parameters such as processor speed and capacities of disk and main memory doubling every 18 months. However, disk access times shrink little if at all in a similar period. An important consequence is that the (relative) cost of accessing disk appears to grow as the years progress.

✦ *Algorithms Using Secondary Storage*: When the data is so large it does not fit in main memory, the algorithms used to manipulate the data must take into account the fact that reading and writing disk blocks between disk and memory often takes much longer than it does to process the data once it is in main memory. The evaluation of algorithms for data in secondary storage thus focuses on the number of disk I/O's required.

✦ *Two-Phase, Multiway Merge-Sort*: This algorithm for sorting is capable of sorting enormous amounts of data on disk using only two disk reads and two disk writes of each datum. It is the sorting method of choice in most database applications.

✦ *Speeding Up Disk Access*: There are several techniques for accessing disk blocks faster for some applications. They include dividing the data among several disks (to allow parallel access), mirroring disks (maintaining several copies of the data, also to allow parallel access), organizing data that will be accessed together by tracks or cylinders, and prefetching or double buffering by reading or writing entire tracks or cylinders together.

✦ *Elevator Algorithm*: We can also speed accesses by queueing access requests and handling them in an order that allows the heads to make one sweep across the disk. The heads stop to handle a request each time it reaches a cylinder containing one or more blocks with pending access requests.

✦ *Disk Failure Modes*: To avoid loss of data, systems must be able to handle errors. The principal types of disk failure are intermittent (a read or write error that will not reoccur if repeated), permanent (data on the disk is corrupted and cannot be properly read), and the disk crash, where the entire disk becomes unreadable.

✦ *Checksums*: By adding a parity check (extra bit to make the number of 1's in a bit string even), intermittent failures and permanent failures can be detected, although not corrected.

✦ *Stable Storage*: By making two copies of all data and being careful about the order in which those copies are written, a single disk can be used to protect against almost all permanent failures of a single sector.

✦ *RAID*: There are several schemes for using an extra disk or disks to enable data to survive a disk crash. RAID level 1 is mirroring of disks; level 4 adds a disk whose contents are a parity check on corresponding bits of all other disks, level 5 varies the disk holding the parity bit to avoid making the parity disk a writing bottleneck. Level 6 involves the use of error-correcting codes and may allow survival after several simultaneous disk crashes.

2.8   References for Chapter 2

The RAID idea can be traced back to [6] on disk striping. The name and error-correcting capability is from [5].

The model of disk failures in Section 2.5 appears in unpublished work of Lampson and Sturgis [4].

There are several useful surveys of material relevant to this chapter. [2] discusses trends in disk storage and similar systems. A study of RAID systems is in [1]. [7] surveys algorithms suitable for the secondary storage model (block model) of computation.

[3] is an important study of how one optimizes a system involving processor, memory, and disk, to perform specific tasks.

1. P. M. Chen et al., "RAID: high-performance, reliable secondary storage," *Computing Surveys* **26**:2 (1994), pp. 145–186.

2. G. A. Gibson et al., "Strategic directions in storage I/O issues in large-scale computing," *Computing Surveys* **28**:4 (1996), pp. 779–793.

3. J. N. Gray and F. Putzolo, "The five minute rule for trading memory for disk accesses and the 10 byte rule for trading memory for CPU time," *Proc. ACM SIGMOD Intl. Conf. on Management of Data* (1987), pp. 395–398.

4. B. Lampson and H. Sturgis, "Crash recovery in a distributed data storage system," Technical report, Xerox Palo Alto Research Center, 1976.

5. D. A. Patterson, G. A. Gibson, and R. H. Katz, "A case for redundant arrays of inexpensive disks," *Proc. ACM SIGMOD Intl. Conf. on Management of Data*, pp. 109–116, 1988.

6. K. Salem and H. Garcia-Molina, "Disk striping," *Proc. Second Intl. Conf. on Data Engineering*, pp. 336–342, 1986.

7. J. S. Vitter, "External memory algorithms," *Proc. Seventeenth Annual ACM Symposium on Principles of Database Systems*, pp. 119–128, 1998.

Chapter 3

Representing Data Elements

This chapter relates the block model of secondary storage that we covered in Section 2.3 to the requirements of database management systems. We begin by looking at the way that relations or sets of objects are represented in secondary storage.

- Attributes need to be represented by fixed- or variable-length sequences of bytes, called "fields."

- Fields, in turn, are put together in fixed- or variable-length collections called "records," which correspond to tuples or objects.

- Records need to be stored in physical blocks. Various data structures are useful, especially if blocks of records need to be reorganized when the database is modified.

- A collection of records that forms a relation or the extent of a class is stored as a collection of blocks, called a *file*.[1] To support efficient querying and modification of these collections, we put one of a number of "index" structures on the file; these structures are the subject of Chapters 4 and 5.

3.1 Data Elements and Fields

We shall begin by looking at the representation of the most basic data elements: the values of attributes found in relational or object-oriented database systems. These are represented by "fields." Subsequently, we shall see how fields are put

---

[1]The database notion of a "file" is somewhat more general that the "file" in an operating system. While a database file could be an unstructured stream of bytes, it is more common for the file to consist of a collection of blocks organized in some useful way, with indexes or other specialized access methods. We discuss these organizations in Chapter 4.

together to form the larger elements of a storage system: records, blocks, and files.

3.1.1 Representing Relational Database Elements

Suppose we have declared a relation in an SQL system, by a CREATE TABLE statement such as that of Fig. 3.1. The DBMS has the job of representing and storing the relation described by this declaration. Since a relation is a set of tuples, and tuples are similar to records or "structs" (the C or C++ term), we may imagine that each tuple will be stored on disk as a record. The record will occupy (part of) some disk block, and within the record there will be one field for every attribute of the relation.

```
CREATE TABLE MovieStar(
    name CHAR(30) PRIMARY KEY,
    address VARCHAR(255),
    gender CHAR(1),
    birthdate DATE
);
```

Figure 3.1: An SQL table declaration

While the general idea appears simple, the "devil is in the details," and we shall have to discuss a number of issues:

1. How do we represent SQL datatypes as fields?

2. How do we represent tuples as records?

3. How do we represent collections of records or tuples in blocks of memory?

4. How do we represent and store relations as collections of blocks?

5. How do we cope with record sizes that may be different for different tuples or that do not divide the block size evenly, or both?

6. What happens if the size of a record changes because some field is updated? How do we find space within its block, especially when the record grows?

The first item is the subject of this section. The next two items are covered in Section 3.2. We shall discuss the last two in Sections 3.4 and 3.5, respectively. The fourth question — representing relations so their tuples can be accessed efficiently — will be studied in Chapter 4.

Further, we need to consider how to represent certain kinds of data that are found in modern object-relational or object-oriented systems, such as object identifiers (or other pointers to records) and "blobs" (binary, large objects, such as a 2-gigabyte MPEG video). These matters are addressed in Sections 3.3 and 3.4.

3.1.2 Representing Objects

Today, many database systems support "objects." These systems include pure object-oriented DBMS's, where an object-oriented language like C++, extended with an object-oriented query language such as OQL,[2] is used as the query and host language. They also include object-relational extensions of the classical relational systems; these systems support objects as values of attributes in a relation.

To a first approximation, an object is a tuple, and its fields or "instance variables" are attributes. However, there are two important differences:

1. Objects can have *methods* or special-purpose functions associated with them. The code for these functions is part of the schema for a class of objects.

2. Objects may have an *object identifier* (OID), which is an address in some global address space that refers uniquely to that object. Moreover, objects can have relationships to other objects, and these relationships are represented by pointers or lists of pointers. Relational data does not have addresses as values, although we shall see that "behind the scenes" the implementation of relations requires the manipulation of addresses or pointers in many ways. The matter of representing addresses is complex, both for large relations and for classes with large extents. We discuss the matter in Section 3.3.

Example 3.1 : We see in Fig. 3.2 an ODL definition of a class Star. It represents movie stars, although the information is somewhat different from that in the relation MovieStar of Fig. 3.1. In particular, we do not represent gender or birthdate of stars, but we have a relationship between stars and the movies they starred in. This relationship is represented by starredIn from stars to their movies, and its inverse, stars, from a movie to its stars. We do not show the definition of the class Movie, which is involved in this relationship.

A Star object can be represented by a record. This record will have fields for attributes name and address. Since the latter is a structure, we might prefer to use two fields, named street and city in place of a field named address. More problematic is the representation of the relationship starredIn. This relationship is a set of references to Movie objects. We need a way to represent the locations of these Movie objects, which normally means we must specify

---

[2]OQL is the standard object-oriented query language described in R. G. G. Cattell (ed.) *The Object Database Standard ODMG*, third edition, Morgan-Kaufmann, San Francisco, 1998. Its companion language, ODL, is used to describe database schemas in object-oriented terms.

```
interface Star {
    attribute string name;
    attribute Struct Addr {
        string street, string city} address;
    relationship Set<Movie> starredIn
                    inverse Movie::stars;
};
```

Figure 3.2: The ODL definition of a movie star class

the place on the disk of some machine where they are stored. Techniques for representing such addresses are discussed in Section 3.3. We also need the ability to represent arbitrarily long lists of movies for a given star; this problem of "variable-length records" is the subject of Section 3.4. □

3.1.3 Representing Data Elements

Let us begin by considering how the principal SQL datatypes are represented as fields of a record. Ultimately, all data is represented as a sequence of bytes. For example, an attribute of type INTEGER is normally represented by two or four bytes, and an attribute of type FLOAT is normally represented by four or eight bytes. The integers and real numbers are represented by bit strings that are specially interpreted by the machine's hardware so the usual arithmetic operations can be performed on them.

Fixed-Length Character Strings

The simplest kind of character strings to represent are those described by the SQL type CHAR(n). These are fixed-length character strings of length n. The field for an attribute with this type is an array of n bytes. Should the value for this attribute be a string of length shorter than n, then the array is filled out with a special *pad* character, whose 8-bit code is not one of the legal characters for SQL strings.

Example 3.2 : If an attribute A were declared to have type CHAR(5), then the field corresponding to A in all tuples is an array of five characters. If in one tuple the component for attribute A were 'cat', then the value of the array would be:

$$c \ a \ t \ \bot \ \bot$$

Here, $\bot$ is the "pad" character, which occupies the fourth and fifth bytes of the array. Note that the quote marks, which are needed to indicate a character string in SQL programs, are not stored with the value of the string. □

A Note on Terminology

Depending on whether you have experience with file systems, conventional programming languages like C, with relational database languages (SQL in particular), or object-oriented languages (e.g., Smalltalk, C++, or the object-oriented database language OQL), you may know different terms for essentially the same concepts. The following table summarizes the correspondence, although there are some differences, e.g., a class can have methods; a relation cannot.

	Data Element	Record	Collection
Files	field	record	file
C	field	struct	array, file
SQL	attribute	tuple	relation
OQL	attribute, relationship	object	extent (of a class)

We shall tend to use file-system terms — fields and records — unless we are referring to specific uses of these concepts in database applications. In the latter case we shall use relational and/or object-oriented terms.

Variable-Length Character Strings

Sometimes the values in a column of a relation are character strings whose length may vary widely. The SQL type VARCHAR(n) is often used as the type of such a column. However, there is an intended implementation of attributes declared this way, in which $n + 1$ bytes are dedicated to the value of the string regardless of how long it is. Thus, the SQL VARCHAR type actually represents fields of fixed length, although its value has a length that varies. We shall examine character strings whose representation's length varies in Section 3.4. There are two common representations for VARCHAR strings:

1. *Length plus content.* We allocate an array of $n + 1$ bytes. The first byte holds, as an 8-bit integer, the number of bytes in the string. The string cannot exceed n characters, and n itself cannot exceed 255, or we shall not be able to represent the length in a single byte.[3] The second and subsequent bytes hold the characters of the string. Any bytes of the array that are not used, because the string is shorter than the maximum possible, are ignored. These bytes cannot possibly be construed as part of the value, because the first byte tells us when the string ends.

2. *Null-terminated string.* Again allocate an array of $n+1$ bytes for the value of the string. Fill this array with the characters of the string, followed by

---

[3]Of course we could use a scheme in which two or more bytes are dedicated to the length.

a *null* character, which is not one of the legal characters that can appear in character strings. As with the first method, unused positions of the array cannot be construed as part of the value; here the null terminator warns us not to look further, and also makes the representation of VARCHAR strings compatible with that of character strings in C.

Example 3.3 : Suppose attribute A is declared VARCHAR(10). We allocate an array of 11 characters in each tuple's record for the value of A. Suppose 'cat' is the string to represent. Then in method 1, we would put 3 in the first byte to represent the length of the string, and the next three characters would be the string itself. The final seven positions are irrelevant. Thus, the value appears as:

$$3\ \texttt{c}\ \texttt{a}\ \texttt{t}$$

Note that the "3" is the 8-bit integer 3, i.e., 00000011, not the character '3'.

In the second method, we fill the first three positions with the string; the fourth is the null character (for which we use the symbol $\perp$, as we did for the "pad" character), and the remaining seven positions are irrelevant. Thus,

$$\texttt{c}\ \texttt{a}\ \texttt{t}\ \perp$$

is the representation of 'cat' as a null-terminated string.   □

Dates and Times

A date is usually represented as a fixed-length character string, following some format. Thus, a date can be represented just as we would represent any other fixed-length character string.

Example 3.4 : As an example, the SQL2 standard has dates represented by 10-character strings of the form YYYY-MM-DD. That is, the first four characters are digits representing the year, the fifth is a hyphen, the sixth and seventh are digits representing the month, with a leading 0 if necessary, the eighth character is another hyphen, and last come two digits representing the day, with a leading 0 if necessary. For instance, the character string '1948-05-14' represents May 14, 1948.   □

Times may similarly be represented as if they were character strings. For example, the SQL2 standard represents times that are integral numbers of seconds by an 8-character string of the form HH:MM:SS. That is, the first two characters are the hour, represented on a 24-hour clock, with a leading 0 if needed. Thus, 7AM is represented by the digits 07, and 7PM is represented by the digits 19. Following a colon are two digits representing the minutes, another colon, and two digits representing the seconds. Both minutes and seconds require a leading 0 if necessary to make two digits. For instance, '20:19:02' represents two seconds after 8:19 PM.

The "Year 2000" Problem

Many database systems and other application programs have a representation for dates that involves only two digits for the year, for example YYMMDD. Since these applications never have had to deal with a date other than one in the 1900's, the "19" could be understood, and a date like May 14, 1948 would be represented as '480514'.

The problem is that these applications can take advantage of the fact that if date d_1 is earlier than date d_2, then d_1 is represented by a string that is lexicographically less than the string that represents date d_2. This observation allows us to write queries like

```
SELECT name FROM MovieStar WHERE birthdate < '980601'
```

to select (from the relation MovieStar declared in Fig. 3.1) those movie stars who were born before June 1, 1998. When our database starts getting some child stars born in the third millennium, their birthdates will be lexicographically less than '980601'. For example, a star born on Aug. 31, 2001 has a birthdate value of '010831', which is lexicographically less than '980601'. The only way to avoid this problem (at least until the year 10,000) in systems that compare dates is to recode dates to use a four-digit year, as the SQL2 standard does.

Such a time is easily represented as a fixed-length character string of length 8. However, the SQL2 standard also allows a value of type TIME to include fractions of a second. We follow the 8 characters described above by a period, and as many digits as needed to describe the fraction of a second. For instance, two and a quarter seconds after 8:19 PM is represented in SQL2 by '20:19:02.25'. Since such strings are of arbitrary length, we have two choices:

1. The system can put a limit on the precision of times, and times can then be stored as if they were type VARCHAR(n), where n is the greatest length a time can have: 9 plus the number of fractional digits allowed in seconds.

2. Times can be stored as true variable-length values and dealt with as discussed in Section 3.4.

Bits

A sequence of bits — that is, data described in SQL2 by the type BIT(n) — can be packed eight to a byte. If n is not divisible by 8, then we are best off ignoring the unused bits of the last byte. For instance, the bit sequence 010111110011 might be represented by 01011111 as the first byte and 00110000 as the second; the final four 0's are not part of any field. As a special case, we can represent

---

Packing Fields Into a Single Byte

One may be tempted to take advantage of fields that have small enumerated types or that are boolean-valued, to pack several fields into a single byte. For instance, if we had three fields that were a boolean, a day of the week, and one of four colors, respectively, we could use one bit for the first, 3 bits for the second, and two bits for the third, put them all in a single byte and still have two bits left over. There is no impediment to doing so, but it makes retrieval of values from one of the fields or the writing of new values for one of the fields more complex and error-prone. Such packing of fields used to be more important when storage space was more expensive. Today, we do not advise it in common situations.

---

a boolean value, that is, a single bit, as 10000000 for true and 00000000 for false. However, it may in some contexts be easier to test a boolean if we make the distinction appear in all bits; i.e., use 11111111 for true and 00000000 for false.

Enumerated Types

Sometimes it is useful to have an attribute whose values take on a small, fixed set of values. These values are given symbolic names, and the type consisting of all those names is an *enumerated type*. Common examples of enumerated types are days of the week, e.g., {SUN, MON, TUE, WED, THU, FRI, SAT}, or a set of colors, e.g., {RED, GREEN, BLUE, YELLOW}.

We can represent the values of an enumerated type by integer codes, using only as many bytes as needed. For instance, we could represent RED by 0, GREEN by 1, BLUE by 2, and YELLOW by 3. These integers can all be represented by two bits, 00, 01, 10, and 11, respectively. It is more convenient, however, to use full bytes for representing integers chosen from a small set. For example, YELLOW is represented by the integer 3, which is 00000011 as an eight-bit byte. Any enumerated type with up to 256 values can be represented by a single byte. If the enumerated type has up to 2^{16} values, a short integer of two bytes will suffice, and so on.

3.2 Records

We shall now begin the discussion of how fields are grouped together into records. The study continues in Section 3.4, where we look at variable-length fields and records.

In general, each type of record used by a database system must have a *schema*, which is stored by the database. The schema includes the names and data types of fields in the record, and their offsets within the record. The schema is consulted when it is necessary to access components of the record.

3.2.1 Building Fixed-Length Records

Tuples are represented by records consisting of the sorts of fields discussed in Section 3.1.3. The simplest situation occurs when all the fields of the record have a fixed length. We may then concatenate the fields to form the record.

Example 3.5 : Consider the declaration of the `MovieStar` relation in Fig. 3.1. There are four fields:

1. `name`, a 30-byte string of characters.

2. `address`, of type `VARCHAR(255)`. This field will be represented by 256 bytes, using the schema discussed in Example 3.3.

3. `gender`, a single byte, which we suppose will always hold either the character 'F' or the character 'M'.

4. `birthdate`, of type `DATE`. We shall assume that the 10-byte SQL2 representation of dates is used for this field.

Thus, a record of type `MovieStar` takes $30 + 256 + 1 + 10 = 297$ bytes. It looks as suggested in Fig. 3.3. We have indicated the *offset* of each field, which is the number of bytes from the beginning of the record at which the field itself begins. Thus, field `name` begins at offset 0; `address` begins at offset 30, `gender` at 286, and `birthdate` at offset 287. $\square$

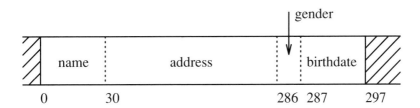

Figure 3.3: A `MovieStar` record

Some machines allow more efficient reading and writing of data that begins at a byte of main memory whose address is a multiple of 4 (or 8 if the machine has a 64-bit processor). Certain types of data, such as integers, may be absolutely required to begin at an address that is a multiple of 4, while others, such as double-precision reals, may need to begin with a multiple of 8.

While the tuples of a relation are stored on disk and not in main memory, we have to be aware of this issue. The reason is that when we read a block from disk to main memory, the first byte of the block will surely be placed at a memory address that is a multiple of 4, and in fact will be a multiple of some high power of 2, such as 2^{12} if blocks and pages have length $4096 = 2^{12}$. Requirements that certain fields be loaded into a main-memory position whose first byte address is a multiple of 4 or 8 thus translate into the requirement that those fields have an offset within their block that has the same divisor.

For simplicity, let us assume that the only requirement on data is that fields start at a main-memory byte whose address is a multiple of 4. Then it is sufficient that

a) Each record start at a byte within its block that is a multiple of 4, and

b) All fields within the record start at a byte that is offset from the beginning of the record by a multiple of 4.

Put another way, we round all field and record lengths up to the next multiple of 4.

Example 3.6 : Suppose that the tuples of the `MovieStar` relation need to be represented so each field starts at a byte that is a multiple of 4. Then the offsets of the four fields would be 0, 32, 288, and 292, and the entire record would take 304 bytes. The format is suggested by Fig. 3.4.

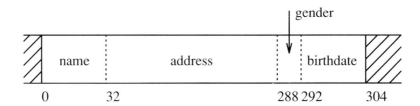

Figure 3.4: The layout of `MovieStar` tuples when fields are required to start at multiple of 4 bytes

For instance, the first field, `name`, takes 30 bytes, but we cannot start the second field until the next multiple of 4, or offset 32. Thus, `address` has offset 32 in this record format. The second field is of length 256 bytes, which means the first available byte following `address` is 288. The third field, `gender`, needs only one byte, but we cannot start the last field until a total of 4 bytes later, at 292. The fourth field, `birthdate`, being 10 bytes long, ends at byte 301, which makes the record length 302 (notice that the first byte is 0). However if all fields of all records must start at a multiple of 4, the bytes numbered 302 and 303 are useless, and effectively, the record consumes 304 bytes. We shall assign bytes 302 and 303 to the `birthdate` field, so they do not get used for any other purpose accidentally.   □

The Need for a Record Schema

We might wonder why we need to indicate the record schema in the record itself, since currently we are only considering fixed-format records. For example, fields in a "struct," as used in C or similar languages, do not have their offsets stored when the program is running; rather the offsets are compiled into the application programs that access the struct.

However, there are several reasons why the record schema must be stored and accessible to the DBMS. For one, the schema of a relation (and therefore the schema of the records that represent its tuples) can change. Queries need to use the current schema for these records, and so need to know what the schema currently is. In other situations, we may not be able to tell immediately what the record type is simply from its location in the storage system. For example, some storage organizations permit tuples of different relations to appear in the same block of storage.

3.2.2 Record Headers

There is another issue that must be raised when we design the layout of a record. Often, there is information that must be kept in the record but that is not the value of any field. For example, we may want to keep in the record:

1. The record schema, or more likely, a pointer to a place where the DBMS stores the schema for this type of record,

2. The length of the record,

3. Timestamps indicating the time the record was last modified, or last read,

among other possible pieces of information. Thus, many record layouts include a *header* of some small number of bytes to provide this additional information.

The database system maintains *schema information*, which is essentially what appears in the `CREATE TABLE` statement for that relation:

1. The attributes of the relation,

2. Their types,

3. The order in which attributes appear in the tuple,

4. Constraints on the attributes and the relation itself, such as primary key declarations, or a constraint that some integer attribute must have a value in a certain range.

We do not have to put all this information in the header of a tuple's record. It is sufficient to put there a pointer to the place where the information about the tuple's relation is stored. Then all this information can be obtained when needed.

As another example, even though the length of the tuple may be deducible from its schema, it may be convenient to have the length in the record itself. For instance, we may not wish to examine the record contents, but just find the beginning of the next record quickly. A length field lets us avoid accessing the record's schema, which may involve a disk I/O.

Example 3.7 : Let us modify the layout of Example 3.6 to include a header of 12 bytes. The first four bytes are the type. It is actually an offset in an area where the schemas for all the relations are kept. The second is the record length, a 4-byte integer, and the third is a timestamp indicating when the tuple was inserted or last updated. The timestamp is also a 4-byte integer. The resulting layout is shown in Fig. 3.5. The length of the record is now 316 bytes. □

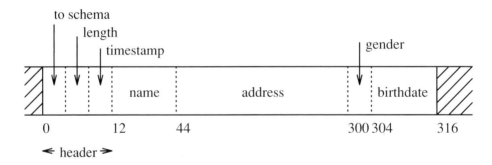

Figure 3.5: Adding some header information to records representing tuples of the MovieStar relation

3.2.3 Packing Fixed-Length Records into Blocks

Records representing tuples of a relation are stored in blocks of the disk and moved into main memory (along with their entire block) when we need to access or update them. The layout of a block that holds records is suggested in Fig. 3.6.

Figure 3.6: A typical block holding records

There is an optional *block header* that holds information such as:

1. Links to one or more other blocks that are part of a network of blocks such as those described in Chapter 4 for creating indexes to the tuples of a relation.

2. Information about the role played by this block in such a network.

3. Information about which relation the tuples of this block belong to.

4. A "directory" giving the offset of each record in the block.

5. A "block ID"; see Section 3.3.

6. Timestamp(s) indicating the time of the block's last modification and/or access.

By far the simplest case is when the block holds tuples from one relation, and the records for those tuples have a fixed format. In that case, following the header, we pack as many records as we can into the block and leave the remaining space unused.

Example 3.8 : Suppose we are storing records with the layout developed in Example 3.7. These records are 316 bytes long. Suppose also that we use 4096-byte blocks. Of these bytes, say 12 will be used for a block header, leaving 4084 bytes for data. In this space we can fit twelve records of the given 316-byte format, and 292 bytes of each block are wasted space. □

3.2.4   Exercises for Section 3.2

* **Exercise 3.2.1 :** Suppose a record has the following fields in this order: A character string of length 15, an integer of 2 bytes, an SQL2 date, and an SQL2 time (no decimal point). How many bytes does the record take if:

   a) Fields can start at any byte.

   b) Fields must start at a byte that is a multiple of 4.

   c) Fields must start at a byte that is a multiple of 8.

Exercise 3.2.2 : Repeat Exercise 3.2.1 for the list of fields: A real of 8 bytes, a character string of length 17, a single byte, and an SQL2 date.

* **Exercise 3.2.3 :** Assume fields are as in Exercise 3.2.1, but records also have a record header consisting of two 4-byte pointers and a character. Calculate the record length for the three situations regarding field alignment (a) through (c) in Exercise 3.2.1.

Exercise 3.2.4 : Repeat Exercise 3.2.2 if the records also include a header consisting of an 8-byte pointer, and ten 2-byte integers.

* **Exercise 3.2.5:** Suppose records are as in Exercise 3.2.3, and we wish to pack as many records as we can into a block of 4096 bytes, using a block header that consists of ten 4-byte integers. How many records can we fit in the block in each of the three situations regarding field alignment (a) through (c) of Exercise 3.2.1?

Exercise 3.2.6: Repeat Exercise 3.2.5 for the records of Exercise 3.2.4, assuming that blocks are 16,384 bytes long, and that block headers consist of three 4-byte integers and a directory that has a 2-byte integer for every record in the block.

3.3 Representing Block and Record Addresses

Before proceeding with the study of how records with more complex structure are represented, we must consider how addresses, pointers, or references to records and blocks can be represented, since these pointers often form part of complex records. There are other reasons for knowing about secondary-storage address representation as well. When we look at efficient structures for representing files or relations in Chapter 4, we shall see several important uses for the address of a block or the address of a record.

The address of a block when it is loaded into a buffer of main memory can be taken to be the virtual-memory address of its first byte, and the address of a record within that block is the virtual-memory address of the first byte of that record. However, in secondary storage, the block is not part of the application's virtual-memory address space. Rather, a sequence of bytes describes the location of the block within the overall system of data accessible to the DBMS: the device ID for the disk, the cylinder number, and so on. A record can be identified by giving its block and the offset of the first byte of the record within the block.

To complicate further the matter of representing addresses, a recent trend toward "object brokers" allows independent creation of objects by many cooperating systems. These objects may be represented by records that are part of an object-oriented DBMS, although we can think of them as tuples of relations without losing the principal idea. However, the capability for independent creation of objects or records puts additional stress on the mechanism that maintains addresses of these records.

In this section, we shall begin with a discussion of address spaces, especially as they pertain to the common "client-server" architecture for DBMS's. We then discuss the options for representing addresses, and finally look at "pointer swizzling," the ways in which we can convert addresses in the data server's world to the world of the client application programs.

3.3.1 Client-Server Systems

Commonly, a database consists of a *server* process that provides data from secondary storage to one or more *client* processes that are applications using the data. The server and client processes may be on one machine, or the server and the various clients can be distributed over many machines.

The client application uses a conventional "virtual" address space, typically 32 bits, or about 4 billion different addresses. The operating system or DBMS decides which parts of the address space are currently located in main memory, and hardware maps the virtual address space to physical locations in main memory. We shall not think further of this virtual-to-physical translation, and shall think of the client address space as if it were main memory itself.

The server's data lives in a *database address space*. The addresses of this space refer to blocks, and possibly to offsets within the block. There are several ways that addresses in this address space can be represented:

1. *Physical Addresses.* These are byte strings that let us determine the place within the secondary storage system where the block or record can be found. One or more bytes of the physical address are used to indicate each of:

    (a) The host to which the storage is attached (if the database is stored across more than one machine),

    (b) An identifier for the disk or other device on which the block is located,

    (c) The number of the cylinder of the disk,

    (d) The number of the track within the cylinder (if the disk has more than one surface),

    (e) The number of the block within the track.

    (f) (In some cases) the offset of the beginning of the record within the block.

2. *Logical Addresses.* Each block or record has a "logical address," which is an arbitrary string of bytes of some fixed length. A *map table*, stored on disk in a known location, relates logical to physical addresses, as suggested in Fig. 3.7.

Notice that physical addresses are long. Eight bytes is about the minimum we could use if we incorporate all the listed elements, and some systems use up to 16 bytes. For example, imagine a database of objects that is designed to last for 100 years. In the future, the database may grow to encompass one million machines, and each machine might be fast enough to create one object every nanosecond. This system would create around 2^{77} objects, which requires a minimum of ten bytes to represent addresses. Since we would probably prefer to reserve some bytes to represent the host, others to represent the storage unit,

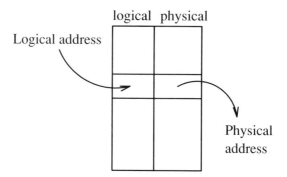

Figure 3.7: A map table translates logical to physical addresses

and so on, a rational address notation would probably use considerably more than 10 bytes for a system of this scale.

3.3.2 Logical and Structured Addresses

One might wonder what the purpose of logical addresses could be. All the information needed for a physical address is found in the map table, and following logical pointers to records requires consulting the map table and then going to the physical address. However, the level of indirection involved in the map table allows us considerable flexibility. For example, many data organizations require us to move records around, either within a block or from block to block. If we use a map table, then all pointers to the record refer to this map table, and all we have to do when we move or delete the record is to change the entry for that record in the table.

Many combinations of logical and physical addresses are possible as well, yielding *structured* address schemes. For instance, one could use a physical address for the block (but not the offset within the block), and add the key value for the record being referred to. Then, to find a record given this structured address, we use the physical part to reach the block containing that record, and we examine the records of the block to find the one with the proper key.

Of course, to survey the records of the block, we need enough information to locate them. The simplest case is when the records are of a known, fixed-length type, with the key field at a known offset. Then, we only have to find in the block header a count of how many records are in the block, and we know exactly where to find the key fields that might match the key that is part of the address. However, there are many other ways that blocks might be organized so that we could survey the records of the block; we shall cover others shortly.

A similar, and very useful, combination of physical and logical addresses is to keep in each block an *offset table* that holds the offsets of the records within the block, as suggested in Fig. 3.8. Notice that the table grows from the front end of the block, while the records are placed starting at the end of the block.

This strategy is useful when the records need not be of equal length. Then, we do not know in advance how many records the block will hold, and we do not have to allocate a fixed amount of the block header to the table initially.

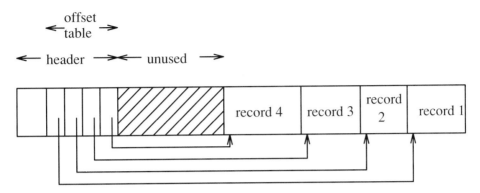

Figure 3.8: A block with a table of offsets telling us the position of each record within the block

The address of a record is now the physical address of its block plus the offset of the entry in the block's offset table for that record. This level of indirection within the block offers many of the advantages of logical addresses, without the need for a global map table.

- We can move the record around within the block, and all we have to do is change the record's entry in the offset table; pointers to the record will still be able to find it.

- We can even allow the record to move to another block, if the offset table entries are large enough to hold a "forwarding address" for the record.

- Finally, we have an option, should the record be deleted, of leaving in its offset-table entry a *tombstone*, a special value that indicates the record has been deleted. Prior to its deletion, pointers to this record may have been stored at various places in the database. After record deletion, following a pointer to this record leads to the tombstone, whereupon the pointer can either be replaced by a null pointer, or the data structure otherwise modified to reflect the deletion of the record. Had we not left the tombstone, the pointer might lead to some new record, with surprising, and erroneous, results.

3.3.3 Pointer Swizzling

Often, pointers or addresses are part of records. This situation is not common for records that represent tuples of a relation, but it is for tuples that represent objects. Also, modern object-relational database systems allow attributes of

---

Ownership of Memory Address Spaces

In this section we have presented a view of the transfer between secondary and main memory in which each client owns its own memory address space, and the database address space is shared. This model is common in object-oriented DBMS's. However, relational systems often treat the memory address space as shared; the motivation is to support recovery and concurrency as we shall discuss in Chapters 8 and 9.

A useful compromise is to have a shared memory address space on the server side, with copies of parts of that space on the clients' side. That organization supports recovery and concurrency, while also allowing processing to be distributed in "scalable" way: the more clients the more processors can be brought to bear.

---

pointer type (called references), so even relational systems need the ability to represent pointers in tuples. Finally, index structures are composed of blocks that usually have pointers within them. Thus, we need to study the management of pointers as blocks are moved between main and secondary memory; we do so in this section.

As we mentioned earlier, every block, record, object, or other referenceable data item has two forms of address:

1. Its address in the server's database address space, which is typically a sequence of eight or so bytes locating the item in the secondary storage of the system. We shall call this address the *database address*.

2. An address in virtual memory (provided that item is currently buffered in virtual memory). These addresses are typically four bytes. We shall refer to such an address as the *memory address* of the item.

When in secondary storage, we surely must use the database address of the item. However, when the item is in the main memory, we can refer to the item by either its database address or its memory address. It is more efficient to put memory addresses wherever an item has a pointer, because these pointers can be followed using single machine instructions.

In contrast, following a database address is much more time-consuming. We need a table that translates from all those database addresses that are currently in virtual memory to their current memory address. Such a *translation table* is suggested in Fig. 3.9. It may be reminiscent of the map table of Fig. 3.7 that translates between logical and physical addresses. However:

a) Logical and physical addresses are both representations for the database address. In contrast, memory addresses in the translation table are for copies of the corresponding object in memory.

b) All addressable items in the database have entries in the map table, while only those items currently in memory are mentioned in the translation table.

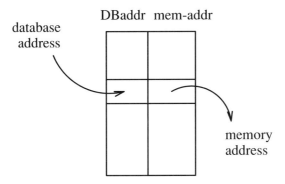

Figure 3.9: The translation table turns database addresses into their equivalents in memory

To avoid the cost of translating repeatedly from database addresses to memory addresses, several techniques have been developed that are collectively known as *pointer swizzling*. The general idea is that when we move a block from secondary to main memory, pointers within the block may be "swizzled," that is, translated from the database address space to the virtual address space. Thus, a pointer actually consists of:

1. A bit indicating whether the pointer is currently a database address or a (swizzled) memory address.

2. The database or memory pointer, as appropriate. The same space is used for whichever address form is present at the moment. Of course, not all the space may be used when the memory address is present, because it is typically shorter than the database address.

Example 3.9 : Figure 3.10 shows a simple situation in which the Block 1 has a record with pointers to a second record on the same block and to a pointer on another block. The figure also shows what might happen when Block 1 is copied to memory. The first pointer, which points within Block 1, can be swizzled so it points directly to the memory address of the target record.

However, if Block 2 is not in memory at this time, then we cannot swizzle the second pointer; it must remain unswizzled, pointing to the database address of its target. Should Block 2 be brought to memory later, it becomes theoretically possible to swizzle the second pointer of Block 1. Depending on the swizzling strategy used, there may or may not be a list of such pointers that are in memory, referring to Block 2; if so, then we have the option of swizzling the pointer at that time. □

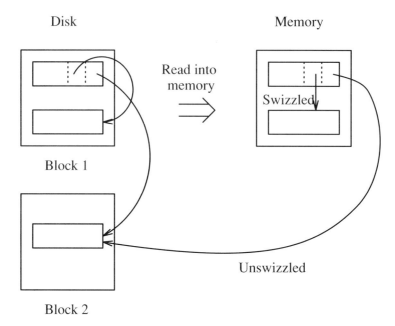

Figure 3.10: Structure of a pointer when swizzling is used

There are several strategies we can use to determine when to swizzle pointers.

Automatic Swizzling

As soon as a block is brought into memory, we locate all its pointers and addresses and enter them into the translation table if they are not already there. These pointers include both the pointers *from* records in the block to elsewhere and the addresses of the block itself and/or its records, if these are addressable items. We need some mechanism to locate the pointers within the block. For example:

1. If the block holds records with a known schema, the schema will tell us where in the records the pointers are found.

2. If the block is used for one of the index structures we shall discuss in Chapter 4, then the block will hold pointers at known locations.

3. We may keep within the block header a list of where the pointers are.

When we enter into the translation table the addresses for the block just moved into memory, and/or its records, we know where in memory the block has been buffered. We may thus create the translation-table entry for these database addresses straightforwardly. When we insert one of these database addresses A into the translation table, we may find it in the table already, because its block is currently in memory. In this case, we replace A in the block just moved to memory by the corresponding memory address, and we set the "swizzled" bit to true. On the other hand, if A is not yet in the translation table, then its block has not been copied into main memory. We therefore cannot swizzle this pointer and leave it in the block as a database pointer.

If we try to follow a pointer P from a block, and we find that pointer P is still unswizzled, i.e., in the form of a database pointer, then we need to make sure the block B containing the item that P points to is in memory (or else why are we following that pointer?). We consult the translation table to see if database address P currently has a memory equivalent. If not, we copy block B into a memory buffer. Once B is in memory, we can "swizzle" P by replacing its database form by the equivalent memory form.

Swizzling on Demand

Another approach is to leave all pointers unswizzled when the block is first brought into memory. We enter its address, and the addresses of its pointers, into the translation table, along with their memory equivalents. If and when we follow a pointer P that is inside some block of memory, we swizzle it, using the same strategy that we followed when we found an unswizzled pointer using automatic swizzling.

The difference between on-demand and automatic swizzling is that the latter tries to get all the pointers swizzled quickly and efficiently when the block is loaded into memory. The possible time saved by swizzling all of a block's pointers at one time must be weighed against the possibility that some swizzled pointers will never be followed. In that case, any time spent swizzling and unswizzling the pointer will be wasted.

An interesting option is to arrange that database pointers look like invalid memory addresses. If so, then we can allow the computer to follow any pointer as if it were in its memory form. If the pointer happens to be unswizzled, then the memory reference will cause a hardware trap. If the DBMS provides a function that is invoked by the trap, and this function "swizzles" the pointer in the manner described above, then we can follow swizzled pointers in single instructions, and only need to do something more time consuming when the pointer is unswizzled.

No Swizzling

Of course it is possible never to swizzle pointers. We still need the translation table, so the pointers may be followed in their unswizzled form. This approach does offer the advantage that records cannot be pinned in memory, as discussed in Section 3.3.5, and decisions about which form of pointer is present need not be made.

Programmer Control of Swizzling

In some applications, it may be known by the application programmer whether the pointers in a block are likely to be followed. This programmer may be able to specify explicitly that a block loaded into memory is to have its pointers swizzled, or the programmer may call for the pointers to be swizzled only as needed. For example, if a programmer knows that a block is likely to be accessed heavily, such as the root block of a B-tree (discussed in Section 4.3), then the pointers would be swizzled. However, blocks that are loaded into memory, used once, and then likely dropped from memory, would not be swizzled.

3.3.4 Returning Blocks to Disk

When a block is moved from memory back to disk, any pointers within that block must be "unswizzled"; that is, their memory addresses must be replaced by the corresponding database addresses. The translation table can be used to associate addresses of the two types in either direction, so in principle it is possible to find, given a memory address, the database address to which the memory address is assigned.

However, we do not want each unswizzling operation to require a search of the entire translation table. While we have not discussed the implementation of this table, we might imagine that the table of Fig. 3.9 has appropriate indexes. If we think of the translation table as a relation, then the problem of finding the memory address associated with a database address x can be expressed as the query:

```
SELECT memAddr
FROM TranslationTable
WHERE dbAddr = x;
```

For instance, a hash table using the database address as the key might be appropriate for an index on the **dbAddr** attribute; Chapter 4 suggests many possible data structures.

If we want to support the reverse query,

```
SELECT dbAddr
FROM TranslationTable
WHERE memAddr = y;
```

then we need to have an index on attribute **memAddr** as well. Again, Chapter 4 suggest data structures suitable for such an index. Also, Section 3.3.5 talks about linked-list structures that in some circumstances can be used to go from a memory address to all main-memory pointers to that address.

3.3.5 Pinned Records and Blocks

A block in memory is said to be *pinned* if it cannot at the moment be safely written back to disk. A bit telling whether or not a block is pinned can be located in the header of the block. There are many reasons why a block could be pinned, including requirements of a recovery system as discussed in Chapter 8. Pointer swizzling introduces an important reason why certain blocks must be pinned.

If a block B_1 has within it a swizzled pointer to some data item in block B_2, then we must be very careful about moving block B_2 back to disk and reusing its main-memory buffer. The reason is that, should we follow the pointer in B_1, it will lead us to the buffer, which no longer holds B_2; in effect, the pointer has become dangling. A block, like B_2, that is referred to by a swizzled pointer from somewhere else is therefore pinned.

When we write a block back to disk, we not only need to "unswizzle" any pointers in that block. We also need to make sure it is not pinned. If it is pinned, we must either unpin it, or let the block remain in memory, occupying space that could otherwise be used for some other block. To unpin a block that is pinned because of swizzled pointers from outside, we must "unswizzle" any pointers to it. Consequently, the translation table must record, for each database address whose data item is in memory, the places in memory where swizzled pointers to that item exist. Two possible approaches are:

1. Keep the list of references to a memory address as a linked list attached to the entry for that address in the translation table.

2. If memory addresses are significantly shorter than database addresses, we can create the linked list in the space used for the pointers themselves. That is, each space used for a database pointer is replaced by

   (a) The swizzled pointer, and

   (b) Another pointer that forms part of a linked list of all occurrences of this pointer.

   Figure 3.11 suggests how all the occurrences of a memory pointer y could be linked, starting at the entry in the translation table for database address x and its corresponding memory address y.

3.3.6 Exercises for Section 3.3

* **Exercise 3.3.1:** If we represent physical addresses for the Megatron 747 disk by allocating a separate byte or bytes to each of the cylinder, track within a cylinder, and block within a track, how many bytes do we need? Make a reasonable assumption about the maximum number of blocks on each track; recall that the Megatron 747 has a variable number of sectors/track.

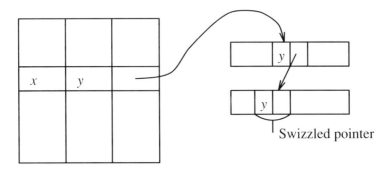

Translation table

Figure 3.11: A linked list of occurrences of a swizzled pointer

Exercise 3.3.2: Repeat Exercise 3.3.1 for the Megatron 777 disk described in Exercise 2.2.1

* **Exercise 3.3.3:** If we wish to represent record addresses as well as block addresses, we need additional bytes. Assuming we want addresses for a single Megatron 747 disk as in Exercise 3.3.1, how many bytes would we need for record addresses if we:

   * a) Included the number of the byte within a block as part of the physical address.

   b) Used structured addresses for records. Assume that the stored records have a 4-byte integer as a key.

Exercise 3.3.4: Today, IP addresses have four bytes. Suppose that block addresses for a world-wide address system consist of an IP address for the host, a device number between 1 and 1000, and a block address on an individual device (assumed to be a Megatron 747 disk). How many bytes would block addresses require?

Exercise 3.3.5: In the future, IP addresses will use 16 bytes. In addition, we may want to address not only blocks, but records, which may start at any byte of a block. However, devices will have their own IP address, so there will be no need to represent a device within a host, as we suggested was necessary in Exercise 3.3.4. How many bytes would be needed to represent addresses in these circumstances, again assuming devices were Megatron 747 disks?

! **Exercise 3.3.6:** Suppose we wish to represent the addresses of blocks on a Megatron 747 disk logically, i.e., using identifiers of k bytes for some k. We also need to store on the disk itself a map table, as in Fig. 3.7, consisting of pairs of logical and physical addresses. The blocks used for the map table itself are not part of the database, and therefore do not have their own logical addresses in the map table. Assuming that physical addresses use the minimum possible number of bytes for physical addresses (as calculated in Exercise 3.3.1), and logical addresses likewise use the minimum possible number of bytes for logical addresses, how many blocks of 4096 bytes does the map table for the disk occupy?

*! Exercise 3.3.7: Suppose that we have 4096-byte blocks in which we store records of 100 bytes. The block header consists of an offset table, as in Fig. 3.8, using 2-byte pointers to records within the block. On an average day, two records per block are inserted, and one record is deleted. A deleted record must have its pointer replaced by a "tombstone," because there may be dangling pointers to it. For specificity, assume the deletion on any day always occurs before the insertions. If the block is initially empty, after how many days will there be no room to insert any more records?

! Exercise 3.3.8: Repeat Exercise 3.3.7 on the assumption that each day there is one deletion and 1.1 insertions on the average.

Exercise 3.3.9: Repeat Exercise 3.3.7 on the assumption that instead of deleting records, they are moved to another block and must be given an 8-byte forwarding address in their offset-table entry. Assume either:

! a) All offset-table entries are given the maximum number of bytes needed in an entry.

!! b) Offset-table entries are allowed to vary in length in such a way that all entries can be found and interpreted properly.

* Exercise 3.3.10: Suppose that if we swizzle all pointers automatically, we can perform the swizzling in half the time it would take to swizzle each one separately. If the probability that a pointer in main memory will be followed at least once is p, for what values of p is it more efficient to swizzle automatically than on demand?

! Exercise 3.3.11: Generalize Exercise 3.3.10 to include the possibility that we never swizzle pointers. Suppose that the important actions take the following times, in some arbitrary time units:

   i. On-demand swizzling of a pointer: 30.

   ii. Automatic swizzling of pointers: 20 per pointer.

   iii. Following a swizzled pointer: 1.

   iv. Following an unswizzled pointer: 10.

Suppose that in-memory pointers are either not followed (probability $1 - p$) or are followed k times (probability p). For what values of k and p do no-swizzling, automatic-swizzling, and on-demand-swizzling each offer the best average performance?

3.4 Variable-Length Data and Records

Until now, we have made the simplifying assumption that every data item has a fixed length, that records have a fixed schema, and that the schema is a list of fixed-length fields. However, in practice, life is rarely so simple. We may wish to represent:

1. *Data items whose size varies.* For instance, in Fig. 3.1 we considered a MovieStar relation that had an address field of up to 255 bytes. While there might be some addresses that long, the vast majority of them will probably be 50 bytes or less. We could probably save more than half the space used for storing MovieStar tuples if we used only as much space as the actual address needed.

2. *Repeating fields.* In Example 3.1 we discussed a class of movie-star objects that contained a relationship to a set of movies in which the star appeared. The number of movies varies from star to star, so the amount of space needed to store such a star object as a record would vary, with no obvious limit.

3. *Variable-format records.* Sometimes we do not know in advance what the fields of a record will be, or how many occurrences of each field there will be. For example, some movie stars also direct movies, and we might want to add fields to their record referring to the movies they directed. Likewise, some stars produce movies or participate in other ways, and we might wish to put this information into their record as well. However, since most stars are neither producers nor directors, we would not want to reserve space for this information in every star's record.

4. *Enormous fields.* Modern DBMS's support attributes whose value is a very large data item. For instance, we might want to include a picture attribute with a movie-star record that is a GIF image of the star. A movie record might have a field that is a 2-gigabyte MPEG encoding of the movie itself, as well as more mundane fields such as the title of the movie. These fields are so large, that our intuition that records fit within blocks is contradicted.

3.4.1 Records With Variable-Length Fields

If one or more fields of a record have variable length, then the record must contain enough information to let us find any field of the record. A simple but effective scheme is to put all fixed-length fields ahead of the variable-length fields. We then place in the record header:

1. The length of the record.

2. Pointers to (i.e., offsets of) the beginnings of all the variable-length fields. However, if the variable-length fields always appear in the same order, then the first of them needs no pointer; we know it immediately follows the fixed-length fields.

Example 3.10: Suppose that we have movie-star records with name, address, gender, and birthdate. We shall assume that the gender and birthdate are fixed-length fields, taking 4 and 12 bytes, respectively. However, both name and address will be represented by character strings of whatever length is appropriate. Figure 3.12 suggests what a typical movie-star record would look like. We shall always put the name before the address. Thus, no pointer to the beginning of the name is needed; that field will always begin right after the fixed-length portion of the record. □

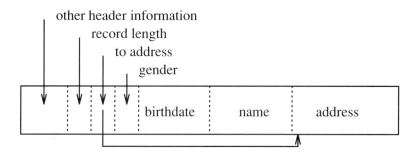

Figure 3.12: A `MovieStar` record with `name` and `address` implemented as variable-length character strings

3.4.2 Records With Repeating Fields

A similar situation occurs if a record contains a variable number of occurrences of a field F, but the field itself is of fixed length. It is sufficient to group all occurrences of field F together and put in the record header a pointer to the first. We can locate all the occurrences of the field F as follows. Let the number of bytes devoted to one instance of field F be L. We then add to the offset for the field F all integer multiples of L, starting at 0, then L, $2L$, $3L$, and so on. Eventually, we reach the offset of the field following F, whereupon we stop.

Example 3.11: Suppose that we redesign our movie-star records to hold only the name and address (which are variable-length strings) and pointers to all the movies of the star. Figure 3.13 shows how this type of record could be represented. The header contains pointers to the beginning of the address field (we assume the name field always begins right after the header) and to the first of the movie pointers. The length of the record tells us how many movie pointers there are. □

Representing Null Values

Tuples often have fields that may be NULL. The record format of Fig. 3.12 offers a convenient way to represent NULL values. If a field such as address is null, then we put a null pointer in the place where the pointer to an address goes. Then, we need no space for an address, except the place for the pointer. This arrangement can save space on average, even if address is a fixed-length field but frequently has the value NULL.

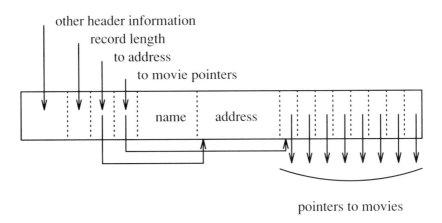

Figure 3.13: A record with a repeating group of references to movies

An alternative representation is to keep the record of fixed length, and put the variable-length portion — be it fields of variable length or fields that repeat an indefinite number of times — on a separate block. In the record itself we keep

1. Pointers to the place where each repeating field begins, and

2. Either how many repetitions there are, or where the repetitions end.

Figure 3.14 shows the layout of a record for the problem of Example 3.11, but with the variable-length fields name and address, and the repeating field starredIn (a set of movie references) kept on a separate block or blocks.

There are advantages and disadvantages to using indirection for the variable-length components of a record:

- Keeping the record itself fixed-length allows records to be searched more efficiently, minimizes the overhead in block headers, and allows records to be moved within or among blocks with minimum effort.

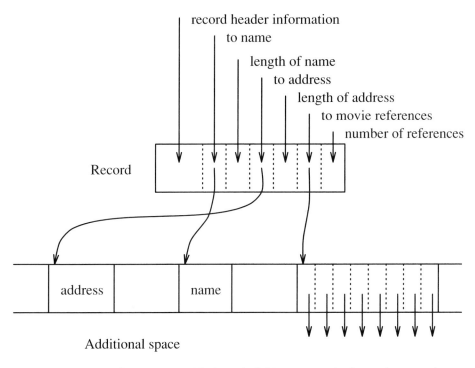

Figure 3.14: Storing variable-length fields separately from the record

- On the other hand, storing variable-length components on another block increases the number of disk I/O's needed to examine all components of a record.

A compromise strategy is to keep in the fixed-length portion of the record enough space for:

1. Some reasonable number of occurrences of the repeating fields,

2. A pointer to a place where additional occurrences could be found, and

3. A count of how many additional occurrences there are.

If there are fewer than this number, some of the space would be unused. If there are more than can fit in the fixed-length portion, then the pointer to additional space will be nonnull, and we can find the additional occurrences by following this pointer.

3.4.3 Variable-Format Records

An even more complex situation occurs when records do not have a fixed schema. That is, the fields or their order are not completely determined by the relation or class whose tuple or object the record represents. The simplest representation of variable-format records is a sequence of *tagged fields*, each of which consists of:

1. Information about the role of this field, such as:

   (a) The attribute or field name,

   (b) The type of the field, if it is not apparent from the field name and some readily available schema information, and

   (c) The length of the field, if it is not apparent from the type.

2. The value of the field.

There are at least two reasons why tagged fields would make sense.

1. *Information-integration applications.* Sometimes, a relation has been constructed from several earlier sources, and these sources have different kinds of information; see Section 11.1 for a discussion. For instance, our movie-star information may have come from several sources, one of which records birthdates and the others do not, some give addresses, others not, and so on. If there are not too many fields, we are probably best off leaving NULL those values we do not know. However, if there are many sources, with many different kinds of information, then there may be too many NULL's, and we can save significant space by tagging and listing only the nonnull fields.

2. *Records with a very flexible schema.* If many fields of a record can repeat and/or not appear at all, then even if we know the schema, tagged fields may be useful. For instance, medical records may contain information about many tests, but there are thousands of possible tests, and each patient has results for relatively few of them.

Example 3.12: Suppose some movie stars have information such as movies directed, former spouses, restaurants owned, and a number of other fixed but unusual pieces of information. In Fig. 3.15 we see the beginning of a hypothetical movie-star record using tagged fields. We suppose that single-byte codes are used for the various possible field names and types. Appropriate codes are indicated on the figure, along with lengths for the two fields shown, both of which happen to be of type string. □

3.4.4 Records That Do Not Fit in a Block

We shall now address another problem whose importance has been increasing as DBMS's are more frequently used to manage datatypes with large values: often values do not fit in one block. Typical examples are video or audio "clips."

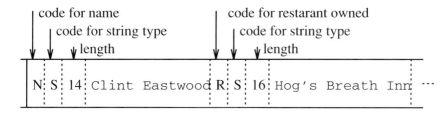

Figure 3.15: A record with tagged fields

Often, these large values have a variable length, but even if the length is fixed for all values of the type, we need to use some special techniques to represent these values. In this section we shall consider a technique called "spanned records" that can be used to manage records that are larger than blocks. The management of extremely large values (megabytes or gigabytes) is addressed in Section 3.4.5.

Spanned records also are useful in situations where records are smaller than blocks, but packing whole records into blocks wastes significant amounts of space. For instance, the waste space in Example 3.8 was only 7%, but if records are just slightly larger than half a block, the wastage can approach 50%. The reason is that then we can pack only one record per block.

For both these reasons, it is sometimes desirable to allow records to be split across two or more blocks. The portion of a record that appears in one block is called a *record fragment*. A record with two or more fragments is called *spanned*, and records that do not cross a block boundary are *unspanned*.

If records can be spanned, then every record and record fragment requires some extra header information:

1. Each record or fragment header must contain a bit telling whether or not it is a fragment.

2. If it is a fragment, then it needs bits telling whether it is the first or last fragment for its record.

3. If there is a next and/or previous fragment for the same record, then the fragment needs pointers to these other fragments.

Example 3.13: Figure 3.16 suggests how records that were about 60% of a block in size could be stored with three records for every two blocks. The header for record fragment 2a contains an indicator that it is a fragment, an indicator that it is the first fragment for its record, and a pointer to next fragment, 2b. Similarly, the header for 2b indicates it is the last fragment for its record and holds a back-pointer to the previous fragment 2a. □

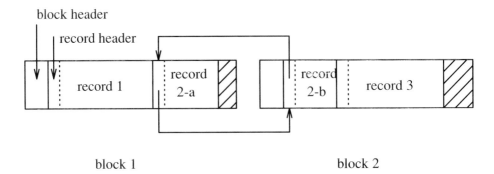

Figure 3.16: Storing spanned records across blocks

3.4.5   BLOBS

Now, let us consider the representation of truly large values for records or fields of records. The common examples include images in various formats (e.g., GIF, or JPEG), movies in formats such as MPEG, or signals of all sorts: audio, radar, and so on. Such values are often called *binary, large objects*, or BLOBS. When a field has a BLOB as value, we must rethink at least two issues.

Storage of BLOBS

A BLOB must be stored on a sequence of blocks. Often we prefer that these blocks are allocated consecutively on a cylinder or cylinders of the disk, so the BLOB may be retrieved efficiently. However, it is also possible to store the BLOB on a linked list of blocks.

Moreover, it is possible that the BLOB needs to be retrieved so quickly (e.g., a movie that must be played in real time), that storing it on one disk does not allow us to retrieve it fast enough. Then, it is necessary to *stripe* the BLOB across several disks, that is, to alternate blocks of the BLOB among these disks. Thus, several blocks of the BLOB can be retrieved simultaneously, increasing the retrieval rate by a factor approximately equal to the number of disks involved in the striping.

Retrieval of BLOBS

Our assumption that when a client wants a record, the block containing the record is passed from the database server to the client in its entirety may not hold. We may want to pass only the "small" fields of the record, and allow the client to request blocks of the BLOB one at a time, independently of the rest of the record. For instance, if the BLOB is a 2-hour movie, and the client requests to have the movie played, the movie could be shipped several blocks at a time to the client, at just the rate necessary to play the movie.

In many applications, it is also important that the client be able to request interior portions of the BLOB without having to receive the entire BLOB. Examples would be a request to see the 45th minute of a movie, or the ending of an audio clip. If the DBMS is to support such operations, then it requires a suitable index structure, e.g., an index by seconds on a movie BLOB.

3.4.6 Exercises for Section 3.4

* **Exercise 3.4.1:** A patient record consists of the following fixed-length fields: the patient's date of birth, social-security number, and patient ID, each 10 bytes long. It also has the following variable-length fields: name, address, and patient history. If pointers within a record require 4 bytes, and the record length is a 4-byte integer, how many bytes, exclusive of the space needed for the variable-length fields, are needed for the record? You may assume that no alignment of fields is required.

* **Exercise 3.4.2:** Suppose records are as in Exercise 3.4.1, and the variable-length fields name, address, and history each have a length that is uniformly distributed. For the name, the range is 10–50 bytes; for address it is 20–80 bytes, and for history it is 0–1000 bytes. What is the average length of a patient record?

Exercise 3.4.3: Suppose that the patient records of Exercise 3.4.1 are augmented by an additional repeating field that represents cholesterol tests. Each cholesterol test requires 16 bytes for a date and an integer result of the test. Show the layout of patient records if:

a) The repeating tests are kept with the record itself.

b) The tests are stored on a separate block, with pointers to them in the record.

Exercise 3.4.4: Starting with the patient records of Exercise 3.4.1, suppose we add fields for tests and their results. Each test consists of a test name, a date, and a test result. Assume that each such test requires 40 bytes. Also, suppose that for each patient and each test a result is stored with probability p.

a) Assuming pointers and integers each require 4 bytes, what is the average number of bytes devoted to test results in a patient record, assuming that all test results are kept within the record itself, as a variable-length field?

b) Repeat (a), if test results are represented by pointers within the record to test-result fields kept elsewhere.

! c) Suppose we use a hybrid scheme, where room for k test results are kept within the record, and additional test results are found by following a pointer to another block (or chain of blocks) where those results are kept. As a function of p, what value of k minimizes the amount of storage used for test results?

!! d) The amount of space used by the repeating test-result fields is not the only issue. Let us suppose that the figure of merit we wish to minimize is the number of bytes used, plus a penalty of 10,000 if we have to store some results on another block (and therefore will require a disk I/O for many of the test-result accesses we need to do. Under this assumption, what is the best value of k as a function of p?

*!! **Exercise 3.4.5:** Suppose blocks have 1000 bytes available for the storage of records, and we wish to store on them fixed-length records of length r, where $500 < r \leq 1000$. The value of r includes the record header, but a record fragment requires an additional 16 bytes for the fragment header. For what values of r can we improve space utilization by spanning records?

! **Exercise 3.4.6:** Recall from Example 2.3 that the transfer rate of the Megatron 747 disk is 1/2 millisecond per 4096-byte block. An MPEG movie uses about one gigabyte per hour of play. If we organize the blocks of an MPEG movie as best we can on a Megatron 747, can we play the movie in real time? If not, how many Megatron disks would we need? How could we organize the blocks so that the movie could be played with only a very small delay?

3.5   Record Modifications

Insertions, deletions, and update of records often create special problems. These problems are most severe when the records change their length, but they come up even when records and fields are all of fixed length.

3.5.1   Insertion

First, let us consider insertion of new records into a relation (or equivalently, into the current extent of a class). If the records of a relation are kept in no particular order, we can just find a block with some empty space, or get a new block if there is none, and put the record there. Usually, there is some mechanism for finding all the blocks holding tuples of a given relation or objects of a class, but we shall defer the question of how to keep track of these blocks until Section 4.1.

There is more of a problem when the tuples must be kept in some fixed order, such as sorted by their primary key. There is good reason to keep records sorted, since it facilitates answering certain kinds of queries, as we shall see in Section 4.1. If we need to insert a new record, we first locate the appropriate block for that record. Fortuitously, there may be space in the block to put the new record. Since records must be kept in order, we may have to slide records around in the block to make space available at the proper point.

If we need to slide records, then the block organization that we showed in Fig. 3.8, which we reproduce here as Fig. 3.17, is useful. Recall from our discussion in Section 3.3.2 that we may create an "offset table" in the header of each block, with pointers to the location of each record in the block. A pointer to a record from outside the block is a "structured address," that is, the block address and the location of the entry for the record in the offset table.

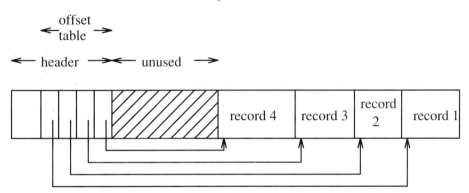

Figure 3.17: An offset table lets us slide records within a block to make room for new records

If we can find room for the inserted record in the block at hand, then we simply slide the records within the block and adjust the pointers in the offset table. The new record is inserted into the block, and a new pointer to the record is added to the offset table for the block.

However, there may be no room in the block for the new record, in which case we have to find room outside the block. There are two major approaches to solving this problem, as well as combinations of these approaches.

1. *Find space on a "nearby" block.* For example, if block B_1 has no available space for a record that needs to be inserted in sorted order into that block, then look at the following block B_2 in the sorted order of the blocks. If there is room in B_2, move the highest record(s) of B_1 to B_2, and slide the records around on both blocks. However, if there are external pointers to records, then we have to be careful to leave a *forwarding address* in the offset table of B_1 to say that a certain record has been moved to B_2 and where its entry in the offset table of B_2 is. Allowing forwarding addresses typically increases the amount of space needed for entries of the offset table.

2. *Create an overflow block.* In this scheme, each block B has in its header a place for a pointer to an *overflow* block where additional records that theoretically belong in B can be placed. The overflow block for B can point to a second overflow block, and so on. Figure 3.18 suggests the situation. We show the pointer for overflow blocks as a nub on the block, although it is in fact part of the block header.

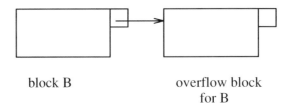

block B   overflow block
                              for B

Figure 3.18: A block and its first overflow block

3.5.2 Deletion

When we delete a record, we may be able to reclaim its space. If we use an offset table as in Fig. 3.17 and records can slide around the block, then we can compact the space in the block so there is always one unused region in the center, as suggested by that figure.

If we cannot slide records, we should maintain an available-space list in the block header. Then we shall know where, and how large, the available regions are if a new record is inserted into the block. Note that the block header normally does not need to hold the entire available space list. It is sufficient to put the list head in the block header, and use the available regions themselves to hold the links in the list, much as we did in Fig. 3.11.

When a record is deleted, we may be able to do away with an overflow block. If the record is deleted either from a block B or from any block on its overflow chain, we can consider the total amount of used space on all the blocks of that chain. If the records can fit on fewer blocks, and we can safely move records among blocks of the chain, then a reorganization of the entire chain can be performed.

However, there is one additional complication involved in deletion, which we must remember regardless of what scheme we use for reorganizing blocks. There may be pointers to the deleted record, and if so, we don't want these pointers to dangle or wind up pointing to a new record that is put in the place of the deleted record. The usual technique, which we pointed out in Section 3.3.2, is to place a *tombstone* in place of the record. This tombstone is permanent; it must exist until the entire database is reconstructed.

Where the tombstone is placed depends on the nature of record pointers. If pointers go to fixed locations from which the location of the pointer is found, then we put the tombstone in that fixed location. Here are two examples:

1. We suggested in Section 3.3.2 that if the offset-table scheme of Fig. 3.17 were used, then the tombstone could be a null pointer in the offset table, since pointers to the record were really pointers to the offset table entries.

2. If we are using a map table, as in Fig. 3.7, to translate logical record addresses to physical addresses, then the tombstone can be a null pointer in place of the physical address.

If we need to replace records by tombstones, it would be wise to have at the very beginning of the record header a bit that serves as a tombstone; i.e., it is 0 if the record is *not* deleted, while 1 means that the record has been deleted. Then, only this bit must remain where the record used to begin, and subsequent bytes can be reused for another record, as suggested by Fig. 3.19.[4] When we follow a pointer to the deleted record, the first thing we see is the "tombstone" bit telling us that the record was deleted. We then know not to look at the following bytes.

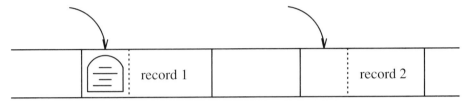

Figure 3.19: Record 1 can be replaced, but the tombstone remains; record 2 has no tombstone and can be seen by following a pointer to it

3.5.3 Update

When a fixed-length record is updated, there is no effect on the storage system, because we know it can occupy exactly the same space it did before the update. However, when a variable-length record is updated, we have all the problems associated with both insertion and deletion, except that it is never necessary to create a tombstone for the old version of the record.

If the updated record is longer than the old version, then we may need to create more space on its block. This process may involve sliding records or even the creation of an overflow block. If variable-length portions of the record are stored on another block, as in Fig. 3.14, then we may need to move elements around that block or create a new block for storing variable-length fields. Conversely, if the record shrinks because of the update, we have the same opportunities as with a deletion to recover or consolidate space, or to eliminate overflow blocks.

3.5.4 Exercises for Section 3.5

Exercise 3.5.1: Suppose we have blocks of records sorted by their sort key field and partitioned among blocks in order. Each block has a range of sort keys that is known from outside (the sparse-index structure in Section 4.1.3 is an example of this situation). There are no pointers to records from outside, so it is possible to move records between blocks if we wish. Here are some of the ways we could manage insertions and deletions.

---

[4]However, the field-alignment problem discussed in Section 3.2.1 may force us to leave four bytes or more unused.

i. Split blocks whenever there is an overflow. Adjust the range of sort keys for a block when we do.

ii. Keep the range of sort keys for a block fixed, and use overflow blocks as needed. Keep for each block and each overflow block an offset table for the records in that block alone.

iii. Same as (*ii*), but keep the offset table for the block and all its overflow blocks in the first block (or overflow blocks if the offset table needs the space). Note that if more space for the offset table is needed, we can move records from the first block to an overflow block to make room.

iv. Same as (*ii*), but keep the sort key along with a pointer in the offset tables.

v. Same as (*iii*), but keep the sort key along with a pointer in the offset table.

Answer the following questions:

* a) Compare methods (*i*) and (*ii*) for the average numbers of disk I/O's needed to retrieve the record, once the block (or first block in a chain with overflow blocks) that could have a record with a given sort key is found. Are there any disadvantages to the method with the fewer average disk I/O's?

  b) Compare methods (*ii*) and (*iii*) for their average numbers of disk I/O's per record retrival, as a function of b, the total number of blocks in the chain. Assume that the offset table takes 10% of the space, and the records take the remaining 90%.

! c) Include methods (*iv*) and (*v*) in the comparison from part (b). Assume that the sort key is 1/9 of the record. Note that we do not have to repeat the sort key in the record if it is in the offset table. Thus, in effect, the offset table uses 20% of the space and the remainders of the records use 80% of the space.

Exercise 3.5.2: Relational database systems have always preferred to use fixed-length tuples if possible. Give three reasons for this preference.

3.6   Summary of Chapter 3

◆ *Fields*: Fields are the most primitive data elements. Many, such as integers or fixed-length character strings are simply given an appropriate number of bytes in secondary storage. Variable-length character strings are encoded either with a fixed-length block and an endmarker, or stored in an area for varying strings, with a length indicated by an integer at the beginning or an endmarker at the end.

◆ *Records*: Records are composed of several fields plus a record header. The header contains information about the record, possibly including such matters as a timestamp, schema information, and a record length.

◆ *Variable-Length Records*: If records contain one or more variable-length fields or contain an unknown number of repetitions of a field, then additional structure is necessary. A directory of pointers in the record header can be used to locate variable-length fields within the record. Alternatively, we can replace the variable-length or repeating fields by (fixed-length) pointers to a place outside the record where the field value is kept.

◆ *Blocks*: Records are generally stored within blocks. A block header, with information about that block consumes some of the space in the block, with the remainder occupied by one or more records.

◆ *Spanned Records*: Generally, a record exists within one block. However, if records are longer than blocks, or we wish to make use of leftover space within blocks, then we can break records into two or more fragments, one on each block. A fragment header is then needed to link the fragments of a record.

◆ *BLOBS*: Very large values, such as images and videos, are called BLOBS (binary, large objects). These values must be stored across many blocks. Depending on the requirements for access, it may be desirable to keep the BLOB on one cylinder, to reduce the access time for the BLOB, or it may be necessary to stripe the BLOB across several disks, to allow parallel retrieval of its contents.

◆ *Offset Tables*: To support insertions and deletions of records, as well as records that change their length due to modification of varying-length fields, we can put in the block header an offset table that has pointers to each of the records in the block.

◆ *Overflow Blocks*: Also used to support insertions and growing records, a block may have a link to an overflow block or chain of blocks, wherein are kept some records that logically belong in the first block.

◆ *Database Addresses*: Data managed by a DBMS is found among several storage devices, typically disks. To locate blocks and records in this storage system, we can use physical addresses, which are a description of the device number, cylinder, track, sector(s), and possibly byte within a sector. We can also use logical addresses, which are arbitrary character strings that are translated into physical addresses by a map table.

◆ *Structured Addresses*: We may also locate records by using part of the physical address, e.g., the location of the block whereon a record is found, plus additional information such as a key for the record or a position in the offset table of a block that locates the record.

◆ *Pointer Swizzling*: When disk blocks are brought to main memory, the database addresses need to be translated to memory addresses, if pointers are to be followed. The translation is called swizzling, and can either be done automatically, when blocks are brought to memory, or on-demand, when a pointer is first followed.

◆ *Tombstones*: When a record is deleted, it may cause pointers to it to dangle. A tombstone in place of (part of) the deleted record warns the system that the record is no longer there.

◆ *Pinned Blocks*: For various reasons, including the fact that a block may contain swizzled pointers, it may be unacceptable to copy a block from memory back to its place on disk. Such a block is said to be pinned. If the pinning is due to swizzled pointers, then they must be unswizzled before returning the block to disk.

3.7   References for Chapter 3

The classic 1968 text on the subject of data structures [2] has been updated recently. [4] has information on structures relevant to this chapter and also Chapter 4.

Tombstones as a technique for dealing with deletion is from [3]. [1] covers data representation issues, such as addresses and swizzling in the context of object-oriented DBMS's.

1. R. G. G. Cattell, *Object Data Management*, Addison-Wesley, Reading MA, 1994.

2. D. E. Knuth, *The Art of Computer Programming, Vol. I, Fundamental Algorithms, Third Edition*, Addison-Wesley, Reading MA, 1997.

3. D. Lomet, "Scheme for invalidating free references," *IBM J. Research and Development* **19**:1 (1975), pp. 26–35.

4. G. Wiederhold, *File Organization for Database Design*, McGraw-Hill, New York, 1987.

Chapter 4

Index Structures

Having seen the options available for representing records, we must now consider how whole relations, or the extents of classes, are represented. It is not sufficient simply to scatter the records that represent tuples of the relation or objects of the extent among various blocks. To see why, ask how we would answer even the simplest query, such as SELECT * FROM R. We would have to examine every block in the storage system, and we would have to rely on there being:

1. Enough information in block headers to identify where in the block records begin.

2. Enough information in record headers to tell what relation the record belongs to.

A slightly better organization is to reserve some blocks, perhaps several whole cylinders, for a given relation. All blocks in those cylinders may be assumed to hold records that represent tuples of our relation. Now, at least we can find the tuples of the relation without scanning the entire data store.

However, this organization offers no help should we want to answer the next-simplest query: "find a tuple given the value of its primary key." For example, name is the primary key of the MovieStar relation from Fig. 3.1. A query like

```
SELECT *
FROM MovieStar
WHERE name = 'Jim Carrey';
```

requires us to scan all the blocks on which MovieStar tuples could be found. To facilitate queries such as this one, we often create one or more *indexes* on a relation. As suggested in Fig. 4.1, an index is any data structure that takes as input a property of records — typically the value of one or more fields — and finds the records with that property "quickly." In particular, an index lets us find a records without having to look at more than a small fraction of all

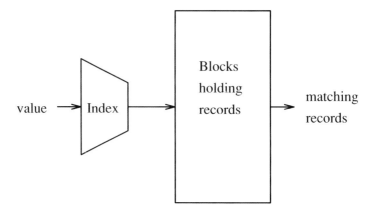

Figure 4.1: An index takes a value for some field(s) and finds records with the matching value

possible records. The field(s) on whose values the index is based is called the *search key*, or just "key" if the index is understood.

There are many different data structures that serve as indexes. In the remainder of this chapter we consider methods for designing and implementing indexes:

1. Simple indexes on sorted files.

2. Secondary indexes on unsorted files.

3. B-trees, a commonly used way to build indexes on any file.

4. Hash tables, another useful and important index structure.

4.1 Indexes on Sequential Files

We begin our study of index structures by considering what is probably the simplest structure: A sorted file, called the *data file*, is given another file, called the *index file*, consisting of key-pointer pairs. A search key K in the index file is associated with a pointer to a data-file record that has search key K. These indexes can be "dense," meaning there is an entry in the index file for every record of the data file, or "sparse," meaning that only some of the data records are represented in the index file, often one index pair per block of the data file.

4.1.1 Sequential Files

One of the simplest index types relies on the file being sorted on the attribute(s) of the index. Such a file is called a *sequential file*. This structure is especially

---

Keys and More Keys

The term "key" has several meanings, and this book uses "key" in each of these ways when the situation warrants it. You surely are familiar with the use of "key" to mean "primary key of a relation." These keys are declared in SQL and require that the relation not have two tuples that agree on the attribute or attributes of the primary key.

In Section 2.3.4 we learned about "sort keys," the attribute(s) on which a file of records is sorted. Now, we shall speak of "search keys," the attribute(s) for which we are given values and asked to search, through an index," for tuples with matching values. We try to use the appropriate adjective — "primary," "sort," or "search" — when the meaning of "key" is unclear. However, notice in sections such as 4.1.2 and 4.1.3 that there are many times when the three kinds of keys are one and the same.

---

useful when the search key is the primary key of the relation, although it can be used for other attributes. Figure 4.2 suggests a relation represented as a sequential file.

In this file, the tuples are sorted by their primary key. We imagine that keys are integers; we show only the key field, and we make the atypical assumption that there is room for only two records in one block. For instance, the first block of the file holds the records with keys 10 and 20. In this and many other examples, we use integers that are sequential multiples of 10 as keys, although there is surely no requirement that keys be multiples of 10 or that records with all multiples of 10 appear.

4.1.2 Dense Indexes

Now that we have our records sorted, we can build on them a *dense index*, which is a sequence of blocks holding only the keys of the records and pointers to the records themselves; the pointers are addresses in the sense discussed in Section 3.3. The index is called "dense" because every key from the data file is represented in the index. In comparison, "sparse" indexes, to be discussed in Section 4.1.3, normally keep only one key per data block in the index.

The index blocks of the dense index maintain these keys in the same sorted order as in the file itself. Since keys and pointers presumably take much less space than complete records, we expect to use many fewer blocks for the index than for the file itself. The index is especially advantageous when it, but not the data file, can fit in main memory. Then, by using the index, we can find any record given its search key, with only one disk I/O per lookup.

Example 4.1 : Figure 4.3 suggests a dense index on a sorted file that begins as Fig. 4.2. For convenience, we have assumed that the file continues with a

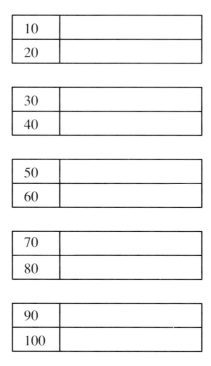

Figure 4.2: A sequential file

key every 10 integers, although in practice we would not expect to find such a regular pattern of keys. We have also assumed that index blocks can hold only four key-pointer pairs. Again, in practice we would find typically that there were many more pairs per block, perhaps hundreds.

The first index block contains pointers to the first four records, the second block has pointers to the next four, and so on. For reasons that we shall discuss in Section 4.1.6, in practice we may not want to fill all the index blocks completely.   □

The dense index supports queries that ask for records with a given search key value. Given key value K, we search the index blocks for K, and when we find it, we follow the associated pointer to the record with key K. It might appear that we need to examine every block of the index, or half the blocks of the index, on average, before we find K. However, there are several factors that make the index-based search more efficient than it seems.

1. The number of index blocks is usually small compared with the number of data blocks.

2. Since keys are sorted, we can use binary search to find K. If there are n blocks of the index, we only look at $\log_2 n$ of them.

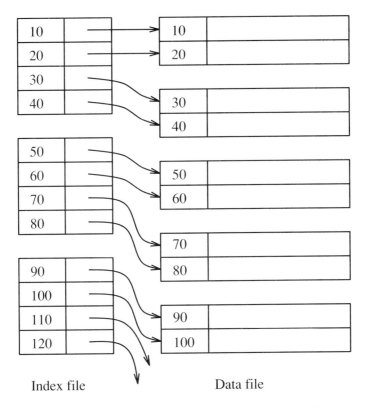

Figure 4.3: A dense index (left) on a sequential data file (right)

3. The index may be small enough to be kept permanently in main memory buffers. If so, the search for key K involves only main-memory accesses, and there are no expensive disk I/O's to be performed.

Example 4.2 : Imagine a relation of 1,000,000 tuples that fit ten to a 4096-byte block. The total space required by the data is over 400 megabytes, probably far too much to keep in main memory. However, suppose that the key field is 30 bytes, and pointers are 8 bytes. Then with a reasonable amount of block-header space we can keep 100 key-pointer pairs in a 4096-byte block.

A dense index therefore requires 10,000 blocks, or 40 megabytes. We might be able to allocate main-memory buffers for these blocks, depending on what else we needed in main memory, and how much main memory there was. Further, $\log_2(10000)$ is about 13, so we only need to access 13 or 14 blocks in a binary search for a key. And since all binary searches would start out accessing only a small subset of the blocks (the block in the middle, those at the 1/4 and 3/4 points, those at 1/8, 3/8, 5/8, and 7/8, and so on), even if we could not afford to keep the whole index in memory, we might be able to keep the most important blocks in main memory, thus retrieving the record for any key with

---

Locating Index Blocks

We have assumed that some mechanism exists for locating the index blocks, from which the individual tuples (if the index is dense) or blocks of the data file (if the index is sparse) can be found. Many ways of locating the index can be used. For example, if the index is small, we may store it in reserved locations of memory or disk. If the index is larger, we can build another layer of index on top of it as we discuss in Section 4.1.4 and keep that in fixed locations. The ultimate extension of this idea is the B-tree of Section 4.3, where we need to know the location of only a single root block.

---

significantly fewer than 14 disk I/O's.   □

4.1.3   Sparse Indexes

If a dense index is too large, we can use a similar structure, called a *sparse index*, that uses less space at the expense of somewhat more time to find a record given its key. A sparse index, as seen in Fig. 4.4, holds only one key-pointer per data block. The key is for the first record on the data block.

Example 4.3: As in Example 4.1, we assume that the data file is sorted, and keys are all the integers divisible by 10, up to some large number. We also continue to assume that four key-pointer pairs fit on an index block. Thus, the first index block has entries for the first keys on the first four blocks, which are 10, 30, 50, and 70. Continuing the assumed pattern of keys, the second index block has the first keys of the fifth through eighth blocks, which we assume are 90, 110, 130, and 150. We also show a third index block with first keys from the hypothetical ninth through twelfth data blocks.   □

Example 4.4: A sparse index can require many fewer blocks than a dense index. Using the more realistic parameters of Example 4.2, since there are 100,000 data blocks, and 100 key-pointer pairs fit on one index block, we need only 1000 index blocks if a sparse index is used. Now the index uses only four megabytes, an amount that could plausibly be allocated in main memory.

On the other hand, the dense index allows us to answer queries of the form "does there exist a record with key value K?" without having to retrieve the block containing the record. The fact that K exists in the dense index is enough to guarantee the existence of the record with key K. On the other hand, the same query, using a sparse index, requires a disk I/O to retrieve the block on which key K *might* be found.   □

To find the record with key K, given a sparse index, we search the index for the largest key less than or equal to K. Since the index file is sorted by

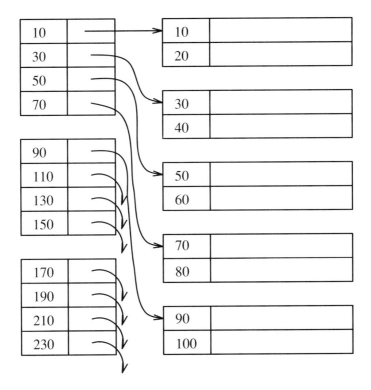

Figure 4.4: A sparse index on a sequential file

key, we may again be able to use binary search to locate this entry. We follow the associated pointer to a data block. Now, we must search this block for the record with key K. Of course the block must have enough format information that the records and their contents can be identified. Any of the techniques from Sections 3.2 and 3.4 can be used, as appropriate.

4.1.4 Multiple Levels of Index

An index can itself cover many blocks, as we saw in Examples 4.2 and 4.4. If these blocks are not in some place where we know we can find them, e.g., designated cylinders of a disk, then we may need another data structure to find them. Even if we can locate the index blocks, and we can use a binary search to find the desired index entry, we still may need to do many disk I/O's to get to the record we want.

By putting an index on the index, we can make the use of the first level of index more efficient. Figure 4.5 extends Fig. 4.4 by adding a second index level (as before, we assume the unusual pattern of keys every 10 integers). The same idea would let us place a third-level index on the second level, and so on. However, this idea has its limits, and we might consider using the B-tree structure described in Section 4.3 in preference to building many levels of index.

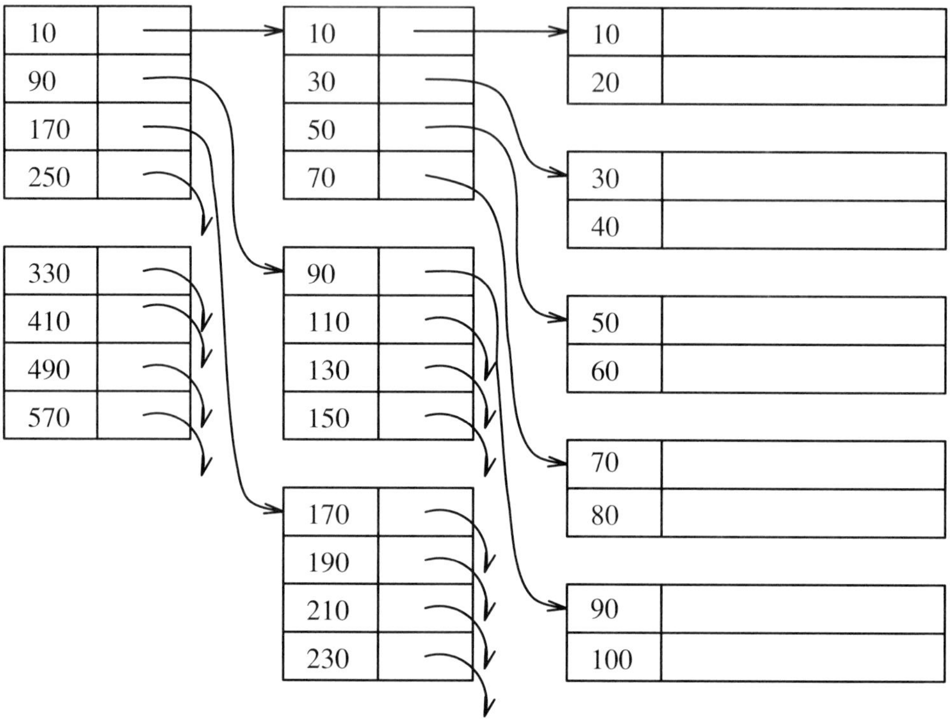

Figure 4.5: Adding a second level of sparse index

In this example, the first-level index is sparse, although we could have chosen a dense index for the first level. However, the second and higher levels must be sparse. The reason is that a dense index on an index would have exactly as many key-pointer pairs as the first-level index, and therefore would take exactly as much space as the first-level index. A second-level dense index thus introduces additional structure for no advantage.

Example 4.5 : Continuing with a study of the hypothetical relation of Example 4.4, suppose we put a second-level index on the first-level sparse index. Since the first-level index occupies 1000 blocks, and we can fit 100 key-pointer pairs in a block, we need 10 blocks for the second-level index.

It is very likely that these 10 blocks can remain buffered in memory. If so, then to find the record with a given key K, we look up in the second-level index to find the largest key less than or equal to K. The associated pointer leads to a block B of the first-level index that will surely guide us to the desired record. We read block B into memory if it is not already there; this read is the first disk I/O we need to do. We look in block B for the greatest key less than or equal to K, and that key gives us a data block that will contain the record with key K if such a record exists. That block requires a second disk I/O, and we are done, having used only two I/O's. □

4.1.5 Indexes With Duplicate Search Keys

Until this point we have supposed that the search key, upon which the index is based, was also a key of the relation, so there could be at most one record with any key value. However, indexes are often used for nonkey attributes, so it is possible that more than one record has a given key value. If we sort the records by the search key, leaving records with equal search key in any order, then we can adapt the ideas mentioned earlier to search keys that are not keys of the relation.

Perhaps the simplest extension of previous ideas is to have a dense index with one entry with key K for each record of the data file that has search key K. That is, we allow duplicate search keys in the index file. Finding all the records with a given search key K is thus simple: Look for the first K in the index file, find all the other K's, which must immediately follow, and pursue all the associated pointers to find the records with search key K.

A slightly more efficient approach is to have only one record in the dense index for each search key K. This key is associated with a pointer to the first of the records with K. To find the others, move forward in the data file to find any additional records with K; these must follow immediately in the sorted order of the data file. Figure 4.6 illustrates this idea.

Example 4.6: Suppose we want to find all the records with search key 20 in Fig. 4.6 We find the 20 entry in the index and follow its pointer to the first record with search key 20. We then search forward in the data file. Since we are at the last record of the second block of this file, we move forward to the third block.[1] We find the first record of this block has 20, but the second has 30. Thus, we need search no further; we have found the two records with search key 20. □

Figure 4.7 shows a sparse index on the same data file as Fig. 4.6. The sparse index is quite conventional; it has key-pointer pairs corresponding to the first search key on each block of the data file.

To find the records with search key K in this data structure, we find the last entry of the index, call it E_1, that has a key less than or equal to K. We then move towards the front of the index until we either come to the first entry or we come to an entry E_2 with a key strictly less than K. All the data blocks that might have a record with search key K are pointed to by the index entries from E_2 to E_1, inclusive.

---

[1] To find the next block of the data file, we could chain the blocks in a linked list; i.e., give each block a pointer to the next. We could also go back to the index and follow the next pointer of the index to the next data-file block.

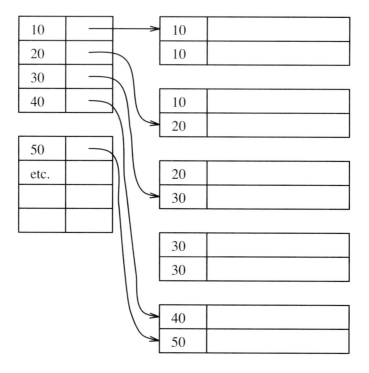

Figure 4.6: A dense index when duplicate search keys are allowed

Example 4.7: Suppose we want to look up key 20 in Fig. 4.7. The third entry in the first index block is E_1; it is the last entry with a key ≤ 20. When we search backward, we immediately find an entry with a key smaller than 20. Thus, the second entry of the first index block is E_2. The two associated pointers take us to the second and third data blocks, and it is on these two blocks that we find records with search key 20.

For another example, if $K = 10$, then E_1 is the second entry of the first index block, and E_2 doesn't exist because we never find a smaller key. Thus, we follow the pointers in all index entries up to and including the second. That takes us to the first two data blocks, where we find all of the records with search key 10. □

A slightly different scheme is shown in Fig. 4.8. There, the index entry for a data block holds the smallest search key that is *new*; i.e., it did not appear in a previous block. If there is no new search key in a block, then its index entry holds the lone search key found in that block. Under this scheme, we can find the records with search key K by looking in the index for the first entry whose key is either

a) Equal to K, or

b) Less than K, but the next key is greater than K.

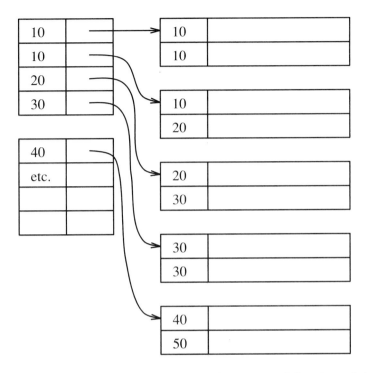

Figure 4.7: A sparse index indicating the lowest search key in each block

We follow the pointer in this entry, and if we find at least one record with search key K in that block, then we search forward through additional blocks until we find all records with search key K.

Example 4.8: Suppose that $K = 20$ in the structure of Fig. 4.8. The second index entry is indicated by the above rule, and its pointer leads us to the first block with 20. We must search forward, since the following block also has a 20.

If $K = 30$, the rule indicates the third entry. Its pointer leads us to the third data block, where the records with search key 30 begin. Finally, if $K = 25$, then part (b) of the selection rule indicates the second index entry. We are thus led to the second data block. If there were any records with search key 25, at least one would have to follow the records with 20 on that block, because we know that the first new key in the third data block is 30. Since there are no 25's, we fail in our search. □

4.1.6 Managing Indexes During Data Modifications

Until this point, we have shown data files and indexes as if they were sequences of blocks, fully packed with records of the appropriate type. Since data evolves with time, we expect that records will be inserted, deleted, and sometimes updated. As a result, an organization like a sequential file will evolve so that

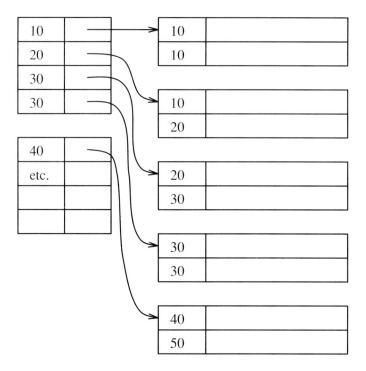

Figure 4.8: A sparse index indicating the lowest new search key in each block

what once fit in one block no longer does. We can use the techniques discussed in Section 3.5 to reorganize the data file. Recall that the three big ideas from that section are:

1. Create overflow blocks if extra space is needed, or delete overflow blocks if enough records are deleted that the space is no longer needed. Overflow blocks do not have entries in a sparse index. Rather, they should be considered as extensions of their primary block.

2. Instead of overflow blocks, we may be able to insert new blocks in the sequential order. If we do, then the new block needs an entry in a sparse index. We should remember that changing an index can create the same kinds of problems on the index file that insertions and deletions to the data file create. If we create new index blocks, then these blocks must be located somehow, e.g., with another level of index as in Section 4.1.4.

3. When there is no room to insert a tuple into a block, we can sometimes slide tuples to adjacent blocks. Conversely, if adjacent blocks grow too empty, they can be combined.

However, when changes occur to the data file, we must often change the index to adapt. The correct approach depends on whether the index is dense or sparse, and on which of the three actions discussed above is used. However, one general principle should be remembered:

- An index file is an example of a sequential file; the key-pointer pairs can be treated as records sorted by the value of the search key. Thus, the same strategies used to maintain data files in the face of modifications can be applied to its index file.

In Fig. 4.9, we summarize the actions that must be taken on a sparse or dense index when seven different actions on the data file are taken. These seven actions include creating or deleting empty overflow blocks, creating or deleting empty blocks of the sequential file, inserting, deleting, and moving records. Notice that we assume only empty blocks can be created or destroyed. In particular, if we want to delete a block that contains records, we must first delete the records or move them to another block.

Action	Dense Index	Sparse Index
Create empty overflow block	none	none
Delete empty overflow block	none	none
Create empty sequential block	none	insert
Delete empty sequential block	none	delete
Insert record	insert	update(?)
Delete record	delete	update(?)
Slide record	update	update(?)

Figure 4.9: How actions on the sequential file affect the index file

In this table, we notice the following:

- Creating or destroying an empty overflow block has no effect on either type of index. It has no effect on a dense index, because that index refers to records. It has no effect on a sparse index, because it is only the primary blocks, not the overflow blocks, that have entries in the sparse index.

- Creating or destroying blocks of the sequential file has no effect on a dense index, again because that index refers to records, not blocks. It *does* affect a sparse index, since we must insert or delete an index entry for the block created or destroyed, respectively.

- Inserting or deleting records results in the same action on a dense index, as a key-pointer pair for that record is inserted or deleted. However, there is typically no effect on a sparse index. The exception is when the record is the first of its block, in which case the corresponding key value in the sparse index must be updated. Thus, we have put a question mark after

---

Preparing for Evolution of Data

Since it is common for relations or class extents to grow with time, it is often wise to distribute extra space among blocks — both data and index blocks. If blocks are, say, 75% full to begin with, then we can run for some time before having to create overflow blocks or slide records between blocks. The advantage to having no overflow blocks, or few overflow blocks, is that the average record access then requires only one disk I/O. The more overflow blocks, the higher will be the average number of blocks we need to look at in order to find a given record.

"update" for these actions in the table of Fig. 4.9, indicating that the update is possible, but not certain.

- Similarly, sliding a record, whether within a block or between blocks, results in an update to the corresponding entry of a dense index, but only affects a sparse index if the moved record was or becomes the first of its block.

We shall illustrate the family of algorithms implied by these rules in a series of examples. These examples involve both sparse and dense indexes and both "record sliding" and overflow-block approaches.

Example 4.9: First, let us consider the deletion of a record from a sequential file with a dense index. We begin with the file and index of Fig. 4.3. Suppose that the record with key 30 is deleted. Figure 4.10 shows the result of the deletion.

First, the record 30 is deleted from the sequential file. We assume that there are possible pointers from outside the block to records in the block, so we have elected not to slide the remaining record, 40, forward in the block. Rather, we suppose that a tombstone has been left in place of the record 30.

In the index, we delete the key-pointer pair for 30. We suppose that there cannot be pointers to index records from outside, so there is no need to leave a tombstone for the pair. Therefore, we have taken the option to consolidate the index block and move following records forward.   □

Example 4.10: Now, let us consider two deletions from a file with a sparse index. We begin with the structure of Fig. 4.4 and again suppose that the record with key 30 is deleted. We also assume that there is no impediment to sliding records around in blocks — either we know there are no pointers to records from anywhere, or we are using an offset table as in Fig. 3.17 to support such sliding.

The effect of the deletion of record 30 is shown in Fig. 4.11. The record has been deleted, and the following record, 40, slides forward to consolidate the

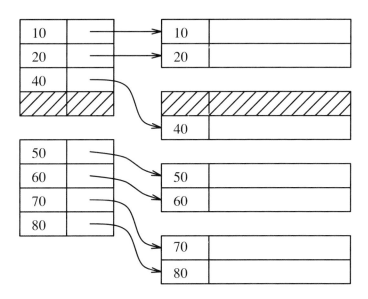

Figure 4.10: Deletion of record with search key 30 in a dense index

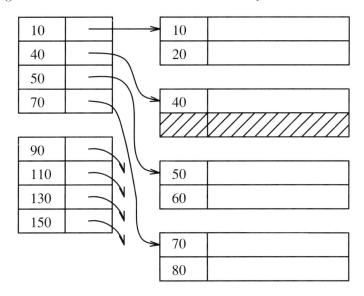

Figure 4.11: Deletion of record with search key 30 in a sparse index

block at the front. Since 40 is now the first key on the second data block, we need to update the index record for that block. We see in Fig. 4.11 that the key associated with the pointer to the second data block has been updated from 30 to 40.

Now, suppose that record 40 is also deleted. We see the effect of this action in Fig. 4.12. The second data block now has no records at all. If the sequential file is stored on arbitrary blocks (rather than, say, consecutive blocks of a cylinder), then we may link the unused block to a list of available space.

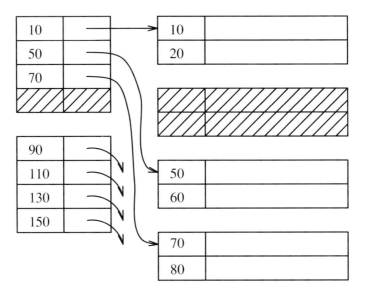

Figure 4.12: Deletion of record with search key 40 in a sparse index

We complete the deletion of record 40 by adjusting the index. Since the second data block no longer exists, we delete its entry from the index. We also show in Fig 4.12 the first index block having been consolidated by moving forward the following pairs. That step is optional.   □

Example 4.11 : Now, let us consider the effect of an insertion. Begin at Fig. 4.11, where we have just deleted record 30 from the file with a sparse index, but the record 40 remains. We now insert a record with key 15. Consulting the sparse index, we find that this record belongs in the first data block. But that block is full; it holds records 10 and 20.

One thing we can do is look for a nearby block with some extra space, and in this case we find it in the second data block. We thus slide blocks backward in the file to make room for record 15. The result is shown in Fig. 4.13. Record 20 has been moved from the first to the second data block, and 15 put in its place. To fit record 20 on the second block and keep records sorted, we slide record 40 back in the second block and put 20 ahead of it.

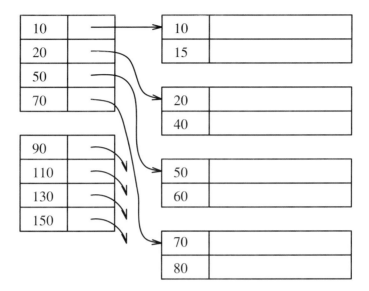

Figure 4.13: Insertion into a file with a sparse index, using immediate reorganization

Our last step is to modify the index entries of the changed blocks. We might have to change the key in the index pair for block 1, but we do not in this case, because the inserted record is not the first in its block. We do, however, change the key in the index entry for the second data block, since the first record of that block, which used to be 40, is now 20. □

Example 4.12: The problem with the strategy exhibited in Example 4.11 is that we were lucky to find an empty space in an adjacent data block. Had the record with key 30 not been deleted previously, we would have searched in vain for an empty space. In principle, we would have had to slide every record from 20 to the end of the file back until we got to the end of the file and could create an additional block.

Because of this risk, it is often wiser to allow overflow blocks to supplement the space of a primary block that has too many records. Figure 4.14 shows the effect of inserting a record with key 15 into the structure of Fig. 4.11. As in Example 4.11, the first data block has too many records. Instead of sliding records to the second block, we create an overflow block for the data block. We have shown in Fig. 4.14 a "nub" on each block, representing a place in the block header where a pointer to an overflow block may be placed. Any number of overflow blocks may be linked in a chain using these pointer spaces.

In our example, record 15 is inserted in its rightful place, after record 10. Record 20 slides to the overflow block to make room. No changes to the index are necessary, since the first record in data block 1 has not changed. Notice that no index entry is made for the overflow block, which is considered an extension

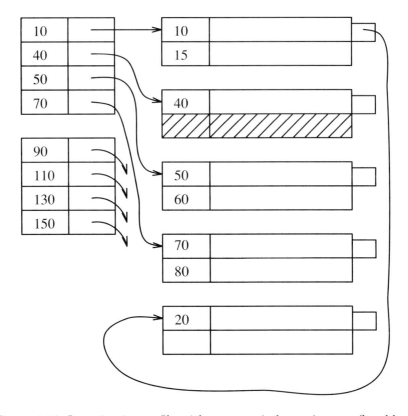

Figure 4.14: Insertion into a file with a sparse index, using overflow blocks

of data block 1, not a block of the sequential file on its own.   □

4.1.7   Exercises for Section 4.1

* **Exercise 4.1.1:** Suppose blocks hold either three records, or ten key-pointer pairs. As a function of n, the number of records, how many blocks do we need to hold a data file and:

    a) A dense index?

    b) A sparse index?

Exercise 4.1.2: Repeat Exercise 4.1.1 if blocks can hold up to 30 records or 200 key-pointer pairs, but neither data- nor index-blocks are allowed to be more than 80% full.

! **Exercise 4.1.3:** Repeat Exercise 4.1.1 if we use as many levels of index as is appropriate, until the final level of index has only one block.

*!! Exercise 4.1.4: Suppose that blocks hold three records or ten key-pointer pairs, as in Exercise 4.1.1, but duplicate search keys are possible. To be specific, 1/3 of all search keys in the database appear in one record, 1/3 appear in exactly two records, and 1/3 appear in exactly three records. Suppose we have a dense index, but there is only one key-pointer pair per search-key value, to the first of the records that has that key. If no blocks are in memory initially, compute the average number of disk I/O's needed to find all the records with a given search key K. You may assume that the location of the index block containing key K is known, although it is on disk.

! Exercise 4.1.5: Repeat Exercise 4.1.4 for:

    a) A dense index with a key-pointer pair for each record, including those with duplicated keys.

    b) A sparse index indicating the lowest key on each data block, as in Fig. 4.7.

    c) A sparse index indicating the lowest *new* key on each data block, as in Fig. 4.8.

! Exercise 4.1.6: If we have a dense index on the primary key attribute of a relation, then it is possible to have pointers to tuples (or the records that represent those tuples) go to the index entry rather than to the record itself. What are the advantages of each approach?

Exercise 4.1.7: Continue the changes to Fig. 4.13 if we next delete the records with keys 60, 70, and 80, then insert records with keys 21, 22, and so on, up to 29. Assume that extra space is obtained by:

    * a) Adding overflow blocks to either the data file or index file.

    b) Sliding records as far back as necessary, adding additional blocks to the end of the data file and/or index file if needed.

    c) Inserting new data or index blocks into the middle of these files as necessary.

*! Exercise 4.1.8: Suppose that we handle insertions into a data file of n records by creating overflow blocks as needed. Also, suppose that the data blocks are currently half full on the average. If we insert new records at random, how many records do we have to insert before the average number of data blocks (including overflow blocks if necessary) that we need to examine to find a record with a given key reaches 2? Assume that on a lookup, we search the block pointed to by the index first, and only search overflow blocks, in order, until we find the record, which is definitely in one of the blocks of the chain.

4.2   Secondary Indexes

The data structures described in Section 4.1 are called *primary indexes*, because they determine the location of the indexed records. In Section 4.1, the location was determined by the fact that the underlying file was sorted on the search key. Section 4.4 will discuss another common example of a primary index: a hash table in which the search key determines the "bucket" into which the record goes.

However, frequently we want several indexes on a relation, to facilitate a variety of queries. For instance, consider again the MovieStar relation declared in Fig. 3.1. Since we declared name to be the primary key, we expect that the DBMS will create a primary index structure to support queries that specify the name of the star. However, suppose we also want to use our database to acknowledge stars on milestone birthdays. We may then run queries like

```
SELECT name, address
FROM MovieStar
WHERE birthdate = DATE '1950-01-01';
```

We need a *secondary index* on birthdate to help with such queries. In an SQL system, we might call for such an index by an explicit command such as

```
CREATE INDEX BDIndex ON MovieStar(birthdate);
```

A secondary index serves the purpose of any index: it is a data structure that facilitates finding records given a value for one or more fields. However, the secondary index is distinguished from the primary index in that a secondary index does not determine the placement of records in the data file. Rather the secondary index tells us the current locations of records; that location may have been decided by a primary index on some other field. One interesting consequence of the distinction between primary and secondary indexes is that:

- It makes no sense to talk of a sparse, secondary index. Since the secondary index does not influence location, we could not use it to predict the location of any record whose key was not mentioned in the index file explicitly.

- Thus, secondary indexes are always dense.

4.2.1   Design of Secondary Indexes

A secondary index is a dense index, usually with duplicates. As before, this index consists of key-pointer pairs; the "key" is a search key and need not be unique. Pairs in the index file are sorted by key value, to help find the entries given a key. If we wish to place a second level of index on this structure, then that index would be sparse, for the reasons discussed in Section 4.1.4.

Example 4.13 : Figure 4.15 shows a typical secondary index. The data file is shown with two records per block, as has been our standard for illustration. The records have only their search key shown; this attribute is integer valued, and as before we have taken the values to be multiples of 10. Notice that, unlike the data file in Section 4.1.5, here the data is not sorted by the search key.

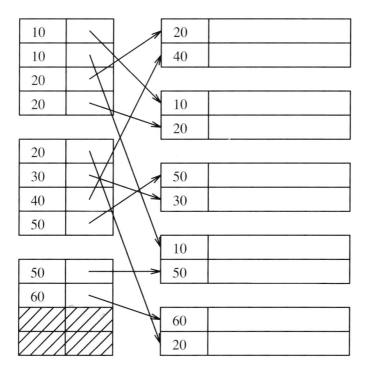

Figure 4.15: A secondary index

However, the keys in the index file *are* sorted. The result is that the pointers in one index block can go to many different data blocks, instead of one or a few consecutive blocks. For example, to retrieve all the records with search key 20, we not only have to look at two index blocks, but we are sent by their pointers to three different data blocks. Thus, using a secondary index may result in many more disk I/O's than if we get the same number of records via a primary index. However, there is no help for this problem; we cannot control the order of tuples in the data block, because they are presumably ordered according to some other attribute(s).

It would be possible to add a second level of index to Fig. 4.15. This level would be sparse, with pairs corresponding to the first key or first new key of each index block, as discussed in Section 4.1.4. □

4.2.2   Applications of Secondary Indexes

Besides supporting additional indexes on relations (or extents of classes) that
are organized as sequential files, there are some data structures where secondary
indexes are needed for even the primary key. One of these is the "heap" structure, where the records of the relation are kept in no particular order.

A second common structure needing secondary indexes is the *clustered file*.
In this structure, two or more relations are stored with their records intermixed.
An example will illustrate why this organization makes good sense in special
situations.

Example 4.14 : Suppose we have two relations, whose schemas we may describe briefly as

```
Movie(title, year, length, studioName)
Studio(name, address, president)
```

Attributes `title` and `year` together are the key for `Movie`, while `name` is the
key for `Studio`. Attribute `studioName` in `Movie` is a foreign key referencing
`name` in `Studio`. Suppose further that a common form of query is:

```
SELECT title, year
FROM Movie
WHERE studioName = 'zzz';
```

Here, *zzz* is intended to represent the name of a particular studio, e.g. `'Disney'`.

If we are convinced that the above is a typical query, then instead of ordering
`Movie` tuples by the primary key `title` and `year`, we can order the tuples by
`studioName`. We could then place on this sequential file a primary index with
duplicates, as was discussed in Section 4.1.5. The value of doing so is that
when we query for the movies by a given studio, we find all our answers on a
few blocks, perhaps one more than the minimum number on which they could
possibly fit. That minimizes disk I/O's for this query and thus makes the
answering of this query form very efficient.

However, merely sorting the `Movie` tuples by an attribute other than its
primary key will not help if we need to relate information about movies to
information about studios, such as:

```
SELECT president
FROM Movie, Studio
WHERE title = 'Star Wars' AND
      Movie.studioName = Studio.name
```

i.e., find the president of the studio that made "Star Wars," or:

```
SELECT title, year
FROM Movie, Studio
WHERE address LIKE '%Hollywood%' AND
      Movie.studioName = Studio.name
```

i.e., find all the movies that were made in Hollywood. For these queries, we need to join Movie and Studio.

If we are sure that joins on the studio name between relations Movie and Studio will be common, we can make those joins efficient by choosing a *clustered file structure*, where the Movie tuples are placed with Studio tuples in the same sequence of blocks. More specifically, we place after each Studio tuple all the Movie tuples for the movies made by that studio. The pattern is suggested in Fig. 4.16.

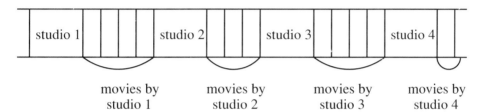

Figure 4.16: A clustered file with each studio clustered with the movies made by that studio

Now, if we want the president of the studio that made a particular movie, we have a good chance of finding the record for the studio and the movie on the same block, saving an I/O step. If we want the movies made by certain studios, we again will tend to find those movies on the same block as one of the studios, saving I/O's.

If these queries are to be efficient, however, we need to find the given movie or given studio efficiently. Thus, we need a secondary index on Movie.title to find the movie (or movies, since two or more movies with the same title can exist) with that title, wherever they may be among the blocks that hold Movie and Studio tuples. We also need an index on Studio.name to find the tuple for a given studio. □

4.2.3 Indirection in Secondary Indexes

There is some wasted space, perhaps a significant amount of wastage, in the structure suggested by Fig. 4.15. If a search-key value appears n times in the data file, then the value is written n times in the index file. It would be better if we could write the key value once for all the pointers to data records with that value.

A convenient way to avoid repeating values is to use a level of indirection, called *buckets*, between the secondary index file and the data file. As shown in Fig. 4.17, there is one pair for each search key K. The pointer of this pair goes to a position in a "bucket file," which holds the "bucket" for K. Following this position, until the next position pointed to by the index, are pointers to all the records with search-key value K.

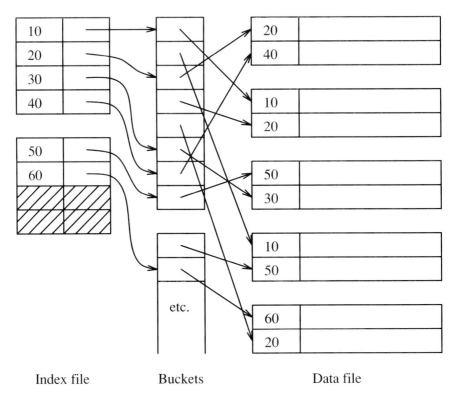

Figure 4.17: Saving space by using indirection in a secondary index

Example 4.15 : For instance, if we follow the pointer from search key 50 in the index file of Fig. 4.17 to the intermediate "bucket" file. This pointer happens to take us to the last pointer of one block of the bucket file. We search forward, to the first pointer of the next block. We stop at that point, because the next pointer of the index file, associated with search key 60, points to the second pointer of the second block of the bucket file.   □

The scheme suggested by Fig. 4.17 will save space as long as search-key values are larger than pointers. However, even when the keys and pointers are comparable in size, there is an important advantage to using indirection with secondary indexes: often, we can use the pointers in the buckets to help answer queries without ever looking at most of the records in the data file. Specifically, when there are several conditions to a query, and each condition has a secondary index to help it, we can find the bucket pointers that satisfy all the conditions by intersecting sets of pointers in memory, and retrieving only the records pointed to by the surviving pointers. We thus save the I/O cost of retrieving records that satisfy some, but not all, of the conditions.[2]

---

[2]We could also use this pointer-intersection trick if we got the pointers directly from the

Example 4.16: Consider the relation

```
Movie(title, year, length, studioName)
```

of Example 4.14. Suppose we have secondary indexes with indirect buckets on both `studioName` and `year`, and we are asked the query

```
SELECT title
FROM Movie
WHERE studioName = 'Disney' AND
      year = 1995;
```

that is, find all the Disney movies made in 1995.

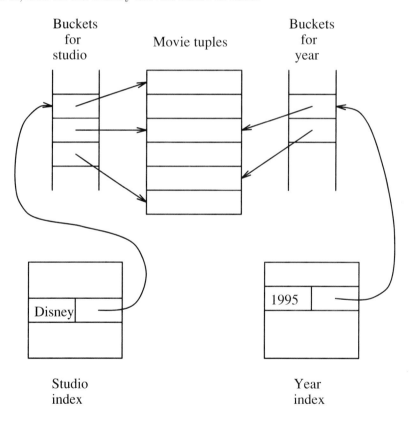

Figure 4.18: Intersecting buckets in main memory

Figure 4.18 shows how we can answer this query using the indexes. Using the index on `studioName`, we find the pointers to all records for Disney movies,

---

index, rather than from buckets. However, the use of buckets often saves disk I/O's, since the pointers use less space than key-pointer pairs.

but we do not yet bring any of those records from disk to memory. Instead, using the index on `year`, we find the pointers to all the movies of 1995. We then intersect the two sets of pointers, getting exactly the movies that were made by Disney in 1995. Now, we need to retrieve from disk all the blocks holding one or more of these movies, thus retrieving the minimum possible number of data blocks. □

4.2.4 Document Retrieval and Inverted Indexes

For many years, the information-retrieval community has dealt with the storage of documents and the efficient retrieval of documents with a given set of keywords. With the advent of the World-Wide Web and the feasibility of keeping all documents on-line, the retrieval of documents given keywords has become one of the largest database problems. While there are many kinds of queries that one can use to find relevant documents, the simplest and most common form can be seen in relational terms as follows:

- A document may be thought of as a tuple in a relation `Doc`. This relation has very many attributes, one corresponding to each possible word in a document. Each attribute is boolean — either the word is present in the document, or it is not. Thus, the relation schema may be thought of as

    `Doc(hasCat, hasDog, ... )`

    where `hasCat` is true if and only if the document has the word "cat" at least once.

- There is a secondary index on each of the attributes of `Doc`. However, we save the trouble of indexing those tuples for which the value of the attribute is `FALSE`; instead, the index only leads us to the documents for which the word is present. That is, the index has entries only for the search-key value `TRUE`.

- Instead of creating a separate index for each attribute (i.e., for each word), the indexes are combined into one, called an *inverted index*. This index uses indirect buckets for space efficiency, as was discussed in Section 4.2.3.

Example 4.17 : An inverted index is illustrated in Fig. 4.19. In place of a data file of records is a collection of documents, each of which may be stored on one or more disk blocks. The inverted index itself consists of a set of word-pointer pairs; the words are in effect the search key for the index. The inverted index is kept in a sequence of blocks, just like any of the indexes discussed so far. However, in some document-retrieval applications, the data may be more static than the typical database, so there may be no provision for overflow of blocks or changes to the index in general.

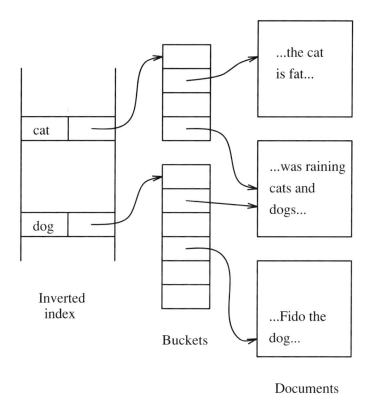

Figure 4.19: An inverted index on documents

The pointers refer to positions in a "bucket" file. For instance, we have shown in Fig. 4.19 the word "cat" with a pointer to the bucket file. Following the position of the bucket file pointed to are pointers to all the documents that contain the word "cat." We have shown some of these in the figure. Similarly, the word "dog" is shown pointing to a list of pointers to all the documents with "dog." □

Pointers in the bucket file can be:

1. Pointers to the document itself.

2. Pointers to an occurrence of the word. In this case, the pointer might be a pair consisting of the first block for the document and an integer indicating the number of the word in the document.

Once we have the idea of using "buckets" of pointers to occurrences of each word, we may also want to extend the idea to include in the bucket array some information about the occurrence. Now, the bucket file itself becomes a collection of records with important structure. Early uses of the idea distinguished

---

More About Information Retrieval

There are a number of techniques for improving the effectiveness of retrieval of documents given keywords. While a complete treatment is beyond the scope of this book, here are two useful techniques:

1. *Stemming.* We remove suffixes to find the "stem" of each word, before entering its occurrence into the index. For example, plural nouns can be treated as their singular versions. Thus, in Example 4.17, the inverted index evidently uses stemming, since the search for word "dog" got us not only documents with "dog," but also a document with the word "dogs."

2. *Stop words.* The most common words, such as "the" or "and," are called *stop words* and are often not included in the inverted index. The reason is that the several hundred most common words appear in too many documents to make them useful as a way to find documents about specific subjects. Eliminating stop words also reduces the size of the index significantly.

---

occurrences of a word in the title of a document, the abstract, and the body of text. With the growth of documents on the Web, especially documents using HTML, XML, or another markup language, we can also indicate the markings associated with words. For instance, we can distinguish words appearing in titles headers, tables, or anchors, as well as words appearing in different fonts or sizes.

Example 4.18 : Figure 4.20 illustrates a bucket file that has been used to indicate occurrences of words in HTML documents. The first column indicates the type of occurrence, i.e., its marking, if any. The second and third columns are together the pointer to the occurrence. The third column indicates the document, and the second column gives the number of the word in the document.

We can use this data structure to answer various queries about documents without having to examine the documents in detail. For instance, suppose we want to find documents about dogs that compare them with cats. Without a deep understanding of the meaning of text, we cannot answer this query precisely. However, we could get a good hint if we searched for documents that

a) Mention dogs in the title, and

b) Mention cats in some anchor — presumably a link to a document about cats.

Insertion and Deletion From Buckets

We show buckets in figures such as Fig. 4.19 as compacted arrays of appropriate size. In practice, they are records with a single field (the pointer) and are stored in blocks like any other collection of records. Thus, when we insert or delete pointers, we may use any of the techniques seen so far, such as leaving extra space in blocks for expansion of the file, overflow blocks, and possibly moving records within or among blocks. In the latter case, we must be careful to change the pointer from the inverted index to the bucket file, as we move the records it points to.

We can answer this query by intersecting pointers. That is, we follow the pointer associated with "cat" to find the occurrences of this word. We select from the bucket file the pointers to documents associated with occurrences of "cat" where the type is "anchor." We then find the bucket entries for "dog" and select from them the document pointers associated with the type "title." If we intersect these two sets of pointers, we have the documents that meet the conditions: they mention "dog" in the title and "cat" in an anchor. □

4.2.5 Exercises for Section 4.2

* Exercise 4.2.1: As insertions and deletions are made on a data file, a secondary index file needs to change as well. Suggest some ways that the secondary index can be kept up to date as the data file changes.

! Exercise 4.2.2: Suppose we have blocks that can hold three records or ten key-pointer pairs, as in Exercise 4.1.1. Let these blocks be used for a data file and a secondary index on search key K. For each K-value v present in the file, there are either 1, 2, or three records with v in field K. Exactly 1/3 of the values appear once, 1/3 appear twice, and 1/3 appear three times. Suppose further that the index blocks and data blocks are all on disk, but there is a structure that allows us to take any K-value v and get pointers to all the index blocks that have search-key value v in one or more records (perhaps there is a second level of index in main memory). Calculate the average number of disk I/O's necessary to retrieve all the records with search-key value v.

*! Exercise 4.2.3: Consider a clustered file organization like Fig. 4.16, and suppose that ten records, either studio records or movie records, will fit on one block. Also assume that the number of movies per studio is uniformly distributed between 1 and m. As a function of m, what is the averge number of disk I/O's needed to retrieve a studio and all its movies? What would the number be if movies were randomly distributed over a large number of blocks?

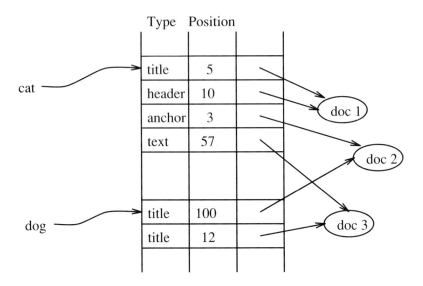

Figure 4.20: Storing more information in the inverted index

Exercise 4.2.4: Suppose that blocks can hold either three records, ten key-pointer pairs, or fifty pointers. If we use the indirect buckets scheme of Fig. 4.17:

* a) If the average search-key value appears in 10 records, how many blocks do we need to hold 3000 records and its secondary index structure? How many blocks would be needed if we did *not* use buckets?

! b) If there are no constraints on the number of records that can have a given search-key value, what are the minimum and maximum number of blocks needed?

! **Exercise 4.2.5:** On the assumptions of Exercise 4.2.4(a), what is the average number of disk I/O's to find and retrieve the ten records with a given search-key value, both with and without the bucket structure? Assume nothing is in memory to begin, but it is possible to locate index or bucket blocks without incurring additional I/O's beyond what is needed to retrieve these blocks into memory.

Exercise 4.2.6: Suppose that as in Exercise 4.2.4, a block can hold either three records, ten key-pointer pairs, or fifty pointers. Let there be secondary indexes on studioName and year of the relation Movie, as in Example 4.16. Suppose there are 51 Disney movies, and 101 movies made in 1995. Only one of these movies was a Disney movie. Compute the number of disk I/O's needed to answer the query of Example 4.16 (find the Disney movies made in 1995) if we:

* a) Use buckets for both secondary indexes, retrieve the pointers from the buckets, intersect them in main memory, and retrieve only the one record for the Disney movie of 1995.

  b) Do not use buckets, use the index on `studioName` to get the pointers to Disney movies, retrieve them, and select those that were made in 1995. Assume no two Disney movie records are on the same block.

  c) Proceed as in (b), but starting with the index on `year`. Assume no two movies of 1995 are on the same block.

Exercise 4.2.7: Suppose we have a repository of 1000 documents, and we wish to build an inverted index with 10,000 words. A block can hold ten word-pointer pairs or 50 pointers to either a document or a position within a document. The distribution of words is Zipfian (see the box on "The Zipfian Distribution" in Section 7.4.3); the number of occurrences of the ith most frequent word is $100000/\sqrt{i}$, for $i = 1, 2, \ldots, 10000$.

* a) What is the averge number of words per document?

* b) Suppose our inverted index only records for each word all the documents that have that word. What is the maximum number of blocks we could need to hold the inverted index?

  c) Suppose our inverted index holds pointers to each occurrence of each word. How many blocks do we need to hold the inverted index?

  d) Repeat (b) if the 400 most common words ("stop" words) are *not* included in the index.

  e) Repeat (c) if the 400 most common words are not included in the index.

Exercise 4.2.8: If we use an augmented inverted index, such as in Fig. 4.20, we can perform a number of other kinds of searches. Suggest how this index could be used to find:

* a) Documents in which "cat" and "dog" appeared within five positions of each other in the same type of element (e.g., title, text, or anchor).

  b) Documents in which "dog" followed "cat" separated by exactly one position.

  c) Documents in which "dog" and "cat" both appear in the title.

4.3 B-Trees

While one or two levels of index are often very helpful in speeding up queries, there is a more general structure that is commonly used in commercial systems. The general family of data structures is called a *B-tree*, and the particular variant that is most often used is known as a *B+ tree*. In essence:

- B-trees automatically maintain as many levels of index as is appropriate for the size of the file being indexed.

- B-trees manage the space on the blocks they use so that every block is between half used and completely full. No overflow blocks are ever needed for the index.

In the following discussion, we shall talk about "B-trees," but the details will all be for the B+ tree variant. Other types of B-tree are discussed in exercises.

4.3.1 The Structure of B-trees

As implied by the name, a B-tree organizes its blocks into a tree. The tree is *balanced*, meaning that all paths from the root to a leaf have the same length. Typically, there are three layers in a B-tree: the root, an intermediate layer, and leaves, but any number of layers is possible. To help visualize B-trees, you may wish to look ahead at Figs. 4.21 and 4.22, which show nodes of a B-tree, and Fig. 4.23, which shows a small, complete B-tree.

There is a parameter n associated with each B-tree index, and this parameter determines the layout of all blocks of the B-tree. Each block will have space for n search-key values and $n + 1$ pointers. In a sense, a B-tree block is similar to the index blocks introduced in Section 4.1, except that the B-tree block has an extra pointer, along with n key-pointer pairs. We pick n to be as large as will allow $n + 1$ pointers and n keys to fit in one block.

Example 4.19 : Suppose our blocks are 4096 bytes. Also let keys be integers of 4 bytes and let pointers be 8 bytes. If there is no header information kept on the blocks, then we want to find the largest integer value of n such that $4n + 8(n + 1) \leq 4096$. That value is $n = 340$. □

There are several important rules that constrain what can appear in the blocks of a B-tree.

- At the root, there are at least two used pointers.[3] All pointers point to B-tree blocks at the level below.

---

[3]Technically, there is a possibility that the entire B-tree has only one pointer because it is an index into a data file with only one record. In this case, the entire tree is a root block that is also a leaf, and this block has only one key and one pointer. We shall ignore this trivial case in the descriptions that follow.

- At a leaf, the last pointer points to the next leaf block to the right, i.e., to the block with the next higher keys. Among the other n pointers in a leaf block, at least $\lfloor \frac{n+1}{2} \rfloor$ of these pointers are used and point to data records; unused pointers may be thought of as null and do not point anywhere. The ith pointer, if it is used, points to a record with the ith key.

- At an interior node, all $n + 1$ pointers can be used to point to B-tree blocks at the next lower level. At least $\lceil \frac{n+1}{2} \rceil$ of them are actually used (but if the node is the root, then we require only that at least 2 be used, regardless of how large n is). If j pointers are used, then there will be $j - 1$ keys, say $K_1, K_2, \ldots, K_{j-1}$. The first pointer points to a part of the B-tree where some of the records with keys less than K_1 will be found. The second pointer goes to that part of the tree where all records with keys that are at least K_1, but less than K_2 will be found, and so on. Finally, the jth pointer gets us to the part of the B-tree where some of the records with keys greater than or equal to K_{j-1} are found. Note that some records with keys far below K_1 or far above K_{j-1} may not be reachable from this block at all, but will be reached via another block at the same level.

- Suppose we draw a B-tree in the conventional manner for trees, with the children of a given node placed in order from left (the "first child") to right (the "last child"). Then if we look at the nodes of the B-tree at any one level, from left to right, the keys at those nodes appear in nondecreasing order.

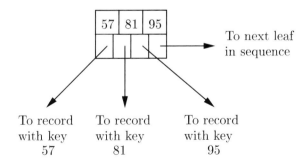

Figure 4.21: A typical leaf of a B+ tree

Example 4.20 : In this and our running examples of B-trees, we shall use $n = 3$. That is, blocks have room for three keys and four pointers, which are atypically small numbers. Keys are integers. Figure 4.21 shows a leaf that is completely used. There are three keys, 57, 81, and 95. The first three pointers go to records with these keys. The last pointer, as is always the case with leaves, points to the next leaf to the right in the order of keys; it would be null if this leaf were the last in sequence.

A leaf is not necessarily full, but in our example with $n = 3$, there must be at least two key-pointer pairs. That is, the key 95 in Fig. 4.21 might be missing, and with it the third of the pointers, the one labeled "to record with key 95."

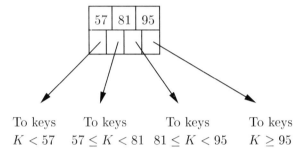

Figure 4.22: A typical interior node of a B+ tree

Figure 4.22 shows a typical interior node. There are three keys; we have picked the same keys as in our leaf example: 57, 81, and 95.[4] There are also four pointers in this node. The first points to a part of the B-tree from which we can reach only records with keys less than 57, the first of the keys. The second pointer leads to records with keys between the first and second keys of the B-tree block, the third pointer for those records between the second and third keys of the block, and the fourth pointer lets us reach records with keys equal to or above the third key of the block.

As with our example leaf, it is not necessarily the case that all slots for keys and pointers are occupied. However, with $n = 3$, at least one key and two pointers must be present in an interior node. The most extreme case of missing elements would be if the only key were 57, and only the first two pointers were used. In that case, the first pointer would be to keys less than 57, and the second pointer would be to keys greater than or equal to 57. □

Example 4.21 : Figure 4.23 shows a complete, three-level B+ tree,[5] using the nodes described in Example 4.20. We have assumed that the data file consists of records whose keys are all the primes from 2 to 47. Notice that at the leaves, each of these keys appears once, in order. All leaf blocks have two or three key-pointer pairs, plus a pointer to the next leaf in sequence. The keys are in sorted order as we look across the leaves from left to right.

The root has only two pointers, the minimum possible number, although it could have up to four. The one key at the root separates those keys reachable

---

[4]Although the keys are the same, the leaf of Fig. 4.21 and the interior node of Fig. 4.22 have no relationship. In fact, they could never appear in the same B-tree.

[5]Remember all B-trees discussed in this section are B+ trees, but we shall, in the future, omit the "+" when referring to them.

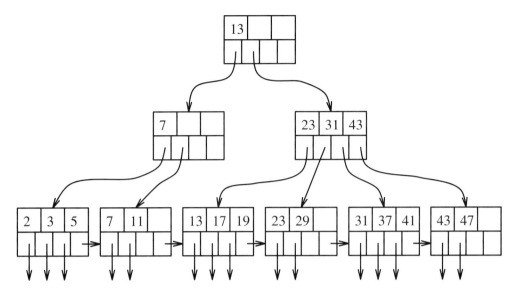

Figure 4.23: A B+ tree

via the first pointer from those reachable via the second. That is, keys up to 12 could be found in the first subtree of the root, and keys 13 and up are in the second subtree.

If we look at the first child of the root, with key 7, we again find two pointers, one to keys less than 7 and the other to keys 7 and above. Note that the second pointer in this node gets us only to keys 7 and 11, not to *all* keys ≥ 7, such as 13 (although we could reach the larger keys by following the next-block pointers in the leaves).

Finally, the second child of the root has all four pointer slots in use. The first gets us to some of the keys less than 23, namely 13, 17, and 19. The second pointer gets us to all keys K such that $23 \leq K < 31$; the third pointer lets us reach all keys K such that $31 \leq K < 43$, and the fourth pointer gets us to some of the keys ≥ 43 (in this case, to all of them). $\Box$

4.3.2   Applications of B-trees

The B-tree is a powerful tool for building indexes. The sequence of pointers to records at the leaves can play the role of any of the pointer sequences coming out of an index file that we learned about in Sections 4.1 or 4.2. Here are some examples:

1. The search key of the B-tree is the primary key for the data file, and the index is dense. That is, there is one key-pointer pair in a leaf for every record of the data file. The data file may or may not be sorted by primary key.

2. The data file is sorted by its primary key, and the B+ tree is a sparse index with one key-pointer pair at a leaf for each block of the data file.

3. The data file is sorted by an attribute that is not a key. This attribute is the search key for the B+ tree. For each value K of the search key that appears in the data file there is one key-pointer pair at a leaf. The pointer goes to the first of the records that have K as their sort-key value.

There are additional applications of B-tree variants that allow multiple occurrences of the search key[6] at the leaves. Figure 4.24 suggests what such a B-tree might look like. The extension is analogous to the indexes with duplicates that we discussed in Section 4.1.5.

If we do allow duplicate occurrences of a search key, then we need to change slightly the definition of what the keys at interior nodes mean, which we discussed in Section 4.3.1. Now, suppose there are keys $K_1, K_2, \ldots, K_n$ at an interior node. Then K_i will be the smallest new key that appears in the part of the subtree accessible from the $(i+1)$st pointer. By "new," we mean that there are no occurrences of K_i in the portion of the tree to the left of the $(i+1)$st subtree, but at least one occurrence of K_i in that subtree. Note that in some situations, there will be no such key, in which case K_i can be taken to be null. Its associated pointer is still necessary, as it points to a significant portion of the tree that happens to have only one key value within it.

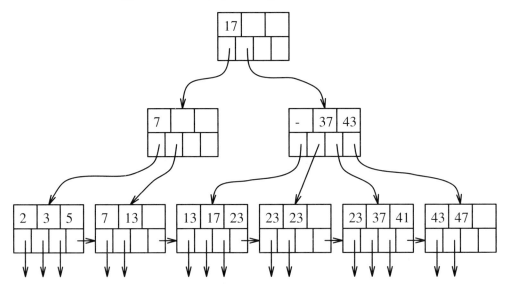

Figure 4.24: A B-tree with duplicate keys

Example 4.22: Figure 4.24 shows a B-tree similar to Fig. 4.23, but with duplicate values. In particular, key 11 has been replaced by 13, and keys 19,

---
[6]Remember that a "search key" is not necessarily a "key" in the sense of being unique.

29, and 31 have all been replaced by 23. As a result, the key at the root is 17, not 13. The reason is that, although 13 is the lowest key in the second subtree of the root, it is not a *new* key for that subtree, since it also appears in the first subtree.

We also had to make some changes to the second child of the root. The second key is changed to 37, since that is the first new key of the third child (fifth leaf from the left). Most interestingly, the first key is now null. The reason is that the second child (fourth leaf) has no new keys at all. Put another way, if we were searching for any key and reached the second child of the root, we would never want to start at its second child. If we are searching for 23 or anything lower, we want to start at its first child, where we will either find what we are looking for (if it is 17), or find the first of what we are looking for (if it is 23). Note that:

- We would not reach the second child of the root searching for 13; we would be directed at the root to its first child instead.

- If we are looking for any key between 24 and 36, we are directed to the third leaf, but when we don't find even one occurrence of what we are looking for, we know not to search further right. For example, if there were a key 24 among the leaves, it would either be on the 4th leaf, in which case the null key in the second child of the root would be 24 instead, or it would be in the 5th leaf, in which case the key 37 at the second child of the root would be 24.

□

4.3.3 Lookup in B-Trees

We now revert to our original assumption that there are no duplicate keys at the leaves. This assumption makes the discussion of B-tree operations simpler, but is not essential for these operations. Suppose we have a B-tree index and we want to find a record with search-key value K. We search for K recursively, starting at the root and ending at a leaf. The search procedure is:

BASIS: If we are at a leaf, look among the keys there. If the ith leaf is K, then the ith pointer will take us to the desired record.

INDUCTION: If we are at an interior node with keys $K_1, K_2, \ldots, K_n$, follow the rules given in Section 4.3.1 to decide which of the children of this node should next be examined. That is, there is only one child that could lead to a leaf with key K. If $K < K_1$, then it is the first child, if $K_1 \leq K < K_2$, it is the second child, and so on. Recursively apply the search procedure at this child.

Example 4.23 : Suppose we have the B-tree of Fig. 4.23, and we want to find a record with search key 40. We start at the root, where there is one key, 13. Since $13 \leq 40$, we follow the second pointer, which leads us to the second-level node with keys 23, 31, and 43.

At that node, we find $31 \leq 40 < 43$, so we follow the third pointer. We are thus led to the leaf with keys 31, 37, and 41. If there had been a record in the data file with key 40, we would have found key 40 at this leaf. Since we do not find 40, we conclude that there is no record with key 40 in the underlying data.

Note that had we been looking for a record with key 37, we would have taken exactly the same decisions, but when we got to the leaf we would find key 37. Since it is the second key in the leaf, we follow the second pointer, which will lead us to the data record with key 37. $\square$

4.3.4   Range Queries

B-trees are useful not only for queries in which a single value of the search key is sought, but for queries in which a range of values are asked for. Typically, *range queries* have a term in the WHERE-clause that compares the search key with a value or values, using one of the comparison operators other than = or <>. Examples of range queries using a search-key attribute k could look like

```
SELECT *
FROM R
WHERE R.k > 40;
```

or

```
SELECT *
FROM R
WHERE R.k >= 10 AND R.k <= 25;
```

If we want to find all keys in the range $[a, b]$ at the leaves of a B-tree, we do a lookup to find the key a. Whether or not it exists, we are led to a leaf where a could be, and we search the leaf for keys that are a or greater. Each such key we find has an associated pointer to one of the records whose key is in the desired range.

If we do not find a key higher than b, we use the pointer in the current leaf to the next leaf, and keep examining keys and following the associated pointers, until we either

1. Find a key higher than b, at which point we stop, or

2. Reach the end of the leaf, in which case we go to the next leaf and repeat the process.

The above search algorithm also works if b is infinite; i.e., there is only a lower bound and no upper bound. In that case, we search all the leaves from the one that would hold key a to the end of the chain of leaves. If a is $-\infty$ (that is, there is an upper bound on the range but no lower bound), then the search for "minus infinity" as a search key will always take us to the first child of whatever B-tree node we are at; i.e., we eventually find the first leaf. The search then proceeds as above, stopping only when we pass the key b.

Example 4.24: Suppose we have the B-tree of Fig. 4.23, and we are given the range $(10, 25)$ to search for. We look for key 10, which leads us to the second leaf. The first key is less than 10, but the second, 11, is at least 10. We follow its associated pointer to get the record with key 11.

Since there are no more keys in the second leaf, we follow the chain to the third leaf, where we find keys 13, 17, and 19. All are less than or equal to 25, so we follow their associated pointers and retrieve the records with these keys. Finally, we move to the fourth leaf, where we find key 23. But the next key of that leaf, 29, exceeds 25, so we are done with our search. Thus, we have retrieved the five records with keys 11 through 23.   □

4.3.5   Insertion Into B-Trees

We see some of the advantage of B-trees over the simpler multilevel indexes introduced in Section 4.1.4 when we consider how to insert a new key into a B-tree. The corresponding record will be inserted into the file being indexed by the B-tree, using any of the methods discussed in Section 4.1; here we consider how the B-tree changes in response. The insertion is in principle recursive:

- We try to find a place for the new key in the appropriate leaf, and we put it there if there is room.

- If there is no room in the proper leaf, we split the leaf into two and divide the keys between the two new nodes, so each is half full or just over half full.

- The splitting of nodes at one level appears to the level above as if a new key-pointer pair needs to be inserted at that higher level. We may thus recursively apply this strategy to insert at the next level: if there is room, insert it; if not, split the parent node and continue up the tree.

- As an exception, if we try to insert into the root, and there is no room, then we split the root into two nodes and create a new root at the next higher level; the new root has the two nodes resulting from the split as its children. Recall that no matter how large n (the number of slots for keys at a node) is, it is always permissible for the root to have only one key and two children.

When we split a node and insert into its parent, we need to be careful how the keys are managed. First, suppose N is a leaf whose capacity is n keys. Also suppose we are trying to insert an $(n + 1)$st key and its associated pointer. We create a new node M, which will be the sibling of N, immediately to its right. The first $\lceil \frac{n+1}{2} \rceil$ key-pointer pairs, in sorted order of the keys, remain with N, while the other key-pointer pairs move to M. Note that both nodes N and M are left with a sufficient number of key-pointer pairs — at least $\lfloor \frac{n+1}{2} \rfloor$ such pairs.

Now, suppose N is an interior node whose capacity is n keys and $n + 1$ pointers, and N has just been assigned $n+2$ pointers because of a node splitting below. We do the following:

1. Create a new node M, which will be the sibling of N, immediately to its right.

2. Leave at N the first $\lceil \frac{n+2}{2} \rceil$ pointers, in sorted order, and move to M the remaining $\lfloor \frac{n+2}{2} \rfloor$ pointers.

3. The first $\lceil \frac{n}{2} \rceil$ keys stay with N, while the last $\lfloor \frac{n}{2} \rfloor$ keys move to M. Note that there is always one key in the middle left over; it goes with neither N nor M. The leftover key K indicates the smallest key reachable via the first of M's children. Although this key doesn't appear in N or M, it is associated with M, in the sense that it represents the smallest key reachable via M. Therefore K will be used by the parent of N and M to divide searches between those two nodes.

Example 4.25 : Let us insert key 40 into the B-tree of Fig. 4.23. We find the proper leaf for the insertion by the lookup procedure of Section 4.3.3. As found in Example 4.23, the insertion goes into the fifth leaf. Since $n = 3$, but this leaf now has four key-pointer pairs — 31, 37, 40, and 41 — we need to split the leaf. Our first step is to create a new node and move the highest two keys, 40 and 41, along with their pointers, to that node. Figure 4.25 shows this split.

Notice that although we now show the nodes on four ranks, there are still only three levels to the tree, and the seven leaves occupy the last two ranks of the diagram. They are linked by their last pointers, which still form a chain from left to right.

We must now insert a pointer to the new leaf (the one with keys 40 and 41) into the node above it (the node with keys 23, 31, and 43). We must also associate with this pointer the key 40, which is the least key reachable through the new leaf. Unfortunately, the parent of the split node is already full; it has no room for another key or pointer. Thus, it too must be split.

We start with pointers to the last five leaves and the list of keys representing the least keys of the last four of these leaves. That is, we have pointers P_1, P_2, P_3, P_4, P_5 to the leaves whose least keys are 13, 23, 31, 40, and 43, and we have the key sequence 23, 31, 40, 43 to separate these pointers. The first three pointers and first two keys remain with the split interior node, while the last two pointers and last key go to the new node. The remaining key, 40, represents the least key accessible via the new node.

Figure 4.26 shows the completion of the insert of key 40. The root now has three children; the last two are the split interior node. Notice that the key 40, which marks the lowest of the keys reachable via the second of the split nodes, has been installed in the root to separate the keys of the root's second and third children. □

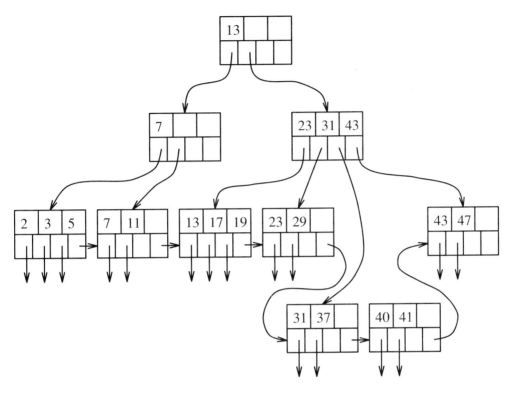

Figure 4.25: Beginning the insertion of key 40

4.3.6 Deletion From B-Trees

If we are to delete a record with a given key K, we must first locate that record and its key-pointer pair in a leaf of the B-tree. This part of the deletion process is essentially a lookup, as in Section 4.3.3. We then delete the record itself from the data file and we delete the key-pointer pair from the B-tree.

If the B-tree node from which a deletion occurred still has at least the minimum number of keys and pointers, then there is nothing more to be done.[7] However, it is possible that the node was right at the minimum occupancy before the deletion, so after deletion the constraint on the number of keys is violated. We then need to do one of two things for a node N whose contents are subminimum; one case requires a recursive deletion up the tree:

1. If one of the adjacent siblings of node N has more than the minimum number of keys and pointers, then one key-pointer pair can be moved to N, keeping the order of keys intact. Possibly, the keys at the parent of N

---

[7]If the data record with the least key at a leaf is deleted, then we have the option of raising the appropriate key at one of the ancestors of that leaf, but there is no requirement that we do so; all searches will still go to the appropriate leaf.

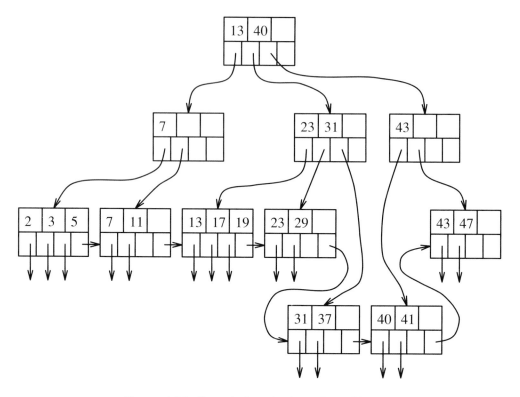

Figure 4.26: Completing the insertion of key 40

must be adjusted to reflect the new situation. For instance, if the right sibling of N, say node M, provides an extra key and pointer, then it must be the smallest key that is moved from M to N. At the parent of M and N, there is a key that represents the smallest key accessible via M; that key must be raised.

2. The hard case is when neither adjacent sibling can be used to provide an extra key for N. However, in that case, we have two adjacent nodes, N and one of its siblings M, one with the minimum number of keys and one with less than that. Therefore, together they have no more keys and pointers than are allowed in a single node (which is why half-full was chosen as the minimum allowable occupancy of B-tree nodes). We merge these two nodes, effectively deleting one of them. We need to adjust the keys at the parent, and then delete a key and pointer at the parent. If the parent is still full enough, then we are done. If not, then we recursively apply the deletion algorithm at the parent.

Example 4.26: Let us begin with the original B-tree of Fig. 4.23, before the insertion of key 40. Suppose we delete key 7. This key is found in the second leaf. We delete it, its associated pointer, and the record that pointer points to.

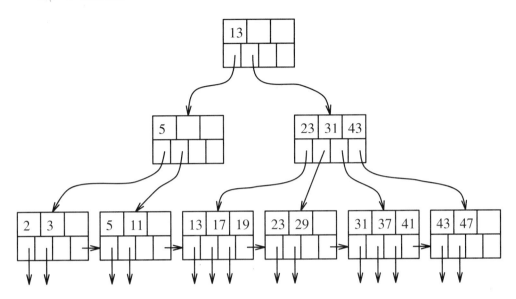

Figure 4.27: Deletion of key 7

Unfortunately, the second leaf now has only one key, and we need at least two in every leaf. But we are saved by the sibling to the left, the first leaf, because that leaf has an extra key-pointer pair. We may therefore move the highest key, 5, and its associated pointer to the second leaf. The resulting B-tree is shown in Fig. 4.27. Notice that because the lowest key in the second leaf is now 5, the key in the parent of the first two leaves has been changed from 7 to 5.

Next, suppose we delete key 11. This deletion has the same effect on the second leaf; it again reduces the number of its keys below the minimum. This time, however, we cannot borrow from the first leaf, because the latter is down to the minimum number of keys. Additionally, there is no sibling to the right from which to borrow.[8] Thus, we need to merge the second leaf with a sibling, namely the first leaf.

The three remaining key-pointer pairs from the first two leaves fit in one leaf, so we move 5 to the first leaf and delete the second leaf. The pointers and keys in the parent are adjusted to reflect the new situation at its children; specifically, the two pointers are replaced by one (to the remaining leaf) and the key 5 is no longer relevant and is deleted. The situation is now as shown in Fig. 4.28.

Unfortunately, the deletion of a leaf has adversely affected the parent, which is the left child of the root. That node, as we see in Fig. 4.28, now has no keys

---

[8]Notice that the leaf to the right, with keys 13, 17, and 19, is not a sibling, because it has a different parent. We could "borrow" from that node anyway, but then the algorithm for adjusting keys throughout the tree becomes more complex. We leave this enhancement as an exercise.

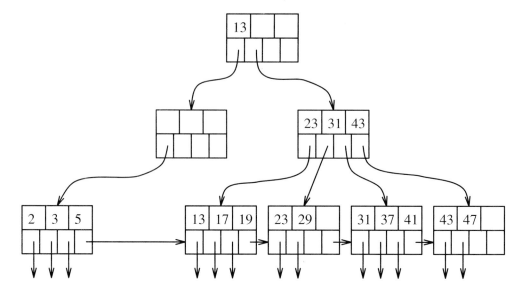

Figure 4.28: Beginning the deletion of key 11

and only one pointer. Thus, we try to obtain an extra key and pointer from an adjacent sibling. This time we have the easy case, since the other child of the root can afford to give up its smallest key and a pointer.

The change is shown in Fig. 4.29. The pointer to the leaf with keys 13, 17, and 19 has been moved from the second child of the root to the first child. We have also changed some keys at the interior nodes. The key 13, which used to reside at the root and represented the smallest key accessible via the pointer that was transferred, is now needed at the first child of the root. On the other hand, the key 23, which used to separate the first and second children of the second child of the root now represents the smallest key accessible from the second child of the root. It therefore is placed at the root itself.   □

4.3.7   Efficiency of B-Trees

B-trees allow lookup, insertion, and deletion of records using very few disk I/O's per file operation. First, we should observe that if n, the number of keys per block is reasonably large, say 10 or more, then it will be a rare event that calls for splitting or merging of blocks. Further, when such an operation is needed, it almost always is limited to the leaves, so only two leaves and their parent are affected. Thus, we can essentially neglect the I/O cost of B-tree reorganizations.

However, every search for the record(s) with a given search key requires us to go from the root down to a leaf, to find a pointer to the record. Since we are only reading B-tree blocks, the number of disk I/O's will be the number of levels the B-tree has, plus the one (for lookup) or two (for insert or delete)

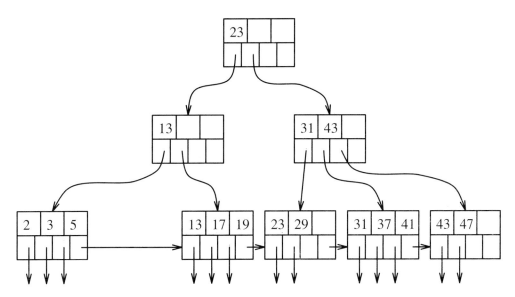

Figure 4.29: Completing the deletion of key 11

disk I/O's needed for manipulation of the record itself. We must thus ask: how many levels does a B-tree have? For the typical sizes of keys, pointers, and blocks, three levels are sufficient for all but the largest databases. Thus, we shall generally take 3 as the number of levels of a B-tree. The following example illustrates why.

Example 4.27: Recall our analysis in Example 4.19, where we determined that 340 key-pointer pairs could fit in one block for our example data. Suppose that the average block has an occupancy midway between the minimum and maximum, i.e., a typical block has 255 pointers. With a root, 255 children, and $255^2 = 65025$ leaves, we shall have among those leaves 255^3, or about 16.6 million pointers to records. That is, files with up to 16.6 million records can be accommodated by a 3-level B-tree. □

However, we can use even fewer than three disk I/O's per search through the B-tree. The root block of a B-tree is an excellent choice to keep permanently buffered in main memory. If so, then every search through a 3-level B-tree requires only two disk reads. In fact, under some circumstances it may make sense to keep second-level nodes of the B-tree buffered in main memory as sell, reducing the B-tree search to a single disk I/O, plus whatever is necessary to manipulate the blocks of the data file itself.

4.3.8 Exercises for Section 4.3

Exercise 4.3.1: Suppose that blocks can hold either ten records or 99 keys and 100 pointers. Also assume that the average B-tree node is 70% full; i.e., it

---

Should We Delete From B-Trees?

There are B-tree implementations that don't fix up deletions at all. If a leaf has too few keys and pointers, it is allowed to remain as it is. The rationale is that most files grow on balance, and while there might be an occasional deletion that makes a leaf become subminimum, the leaf will probably soon grow again and attain the minimum number of key-pointer pairs once again.

Further, if records have pointers from outside the B-tree index, then we need to replace the record by a "tombstone," and we don't want to delete its pointer from the B-tree anyway. In certain circumstances, when it can be guaranteed that all accesses to the deleted record will go through the B-tree, we can even leave the tombstone in place of the pointer to the record at a leaf of the B-tree. Then, space for the record can be reused.

---

will have 69 keys and 70 pointers. We can use B-trees as part of several different structures. For each structure described below, determine (i) the total number of blocks needed for a 1,000,000-record file, and (ii) the average number of disk I/O's to retrieve a record given its search key. You may assume nothing is in memory initially, and the search key is the primary key for the records.

* a) The data file is a sequential file, sorted on the search key, with 10 records per block. The B-tree is a dense index.

  b) The same as (a), but the data file consists of records in no particular order, packed 10 to a block.

  c) The same as (a), but the B-tree is a sparse index.

! d) Instead of the B-tree leaves having pointers to data records, the B-tree leaves hold the records themselves. A block can hold ten records, but on average, a leaf block is 70% full; i.e., there are seven records per leaf block.

* e) The data file is a sequential file, and the B-tree is a sparse index, but each primary block of the data file has one overflow block. On average, the primary block is full, and the overflow block is half full. However, records are in no particular order within a primary block and its overflow block.

Exercise 4.3.2: Repeat Exercise 4.3.1 in the case that the query is a range query that is matched by 1000 records.

Exercise 4.3.3: Suppose pointers are 4 bytes long, and keys are 12 bytes long. How many keys and pointers will a block of 16,384 bytes have?

Exercise 4.3.4 : What are the minimum numbers of keys and pointers in B-tree (*i*) interior nodes and (*ii*) leaves, when:

* a) $n = 10$; i.e., a block holds 10 keys and 11 pointers.

  b) $n = 11$; i.e., a block holds 11 keys and 12 pointers.

Exercise 4.3.5 : Execute the following operations on Fig. 4.23. Describe the changes for operations that modify the tree.

  a) Lookup the record with key 41.

  b) Lookup the record with key 40.

  c) Lookup all records in the range 20 to 30.

  d) Lookup all records with keys less than 30.

  e) Lookup all records with keys greater than 30.

  f) Insert a record with key 1.

  g) Insert records with keys 14 through 16.

  h) Delete the record with key 23.

  i) Delete all the records with keys 23 and higher.

! **Exercise 4.3.6 :** We mentioned that the leaf of Fig. 4.21 and the interior node of Fig. 4.22 could never appear in the same B-tree. Explain why.

Exercise 4.3.7 : When duplicate keys are allowed in a B-tree, there are some necessary modifications to the algorithms for lookup, insertion, and deletion that we described in this section. Give the changes for:

* a) Lookup.

  b) Insertion.

  c) Deletion.

! **Exercise 4.3.8 :** In Example 4.26 we suggested that it would be possible to borrow keys from a nonsibling to the right (or left) if we used a more complicated algorithm for maintaining keys at interior nodes. Describe a suitable algorithm that rebalances by borrowing from adjacent nodes at a level, regardless of whether they are siblings of the node that has too many or too few key-pointer pairs.

Exercise 4.3.9 : If we use the 3-key, 4-pointer nodes of our examples in this section, how many different B-trees are there when the data file has:

*! a) 6 records.

!! b) 10 records.

!! c) 15 records.

*! **Exercise 4.3.10 :** Suppose we have B-tree nodes with room for three keys and four pointers, as in the examples of this section. Suppose also that when we split a leaf, we divide the pointers 2 and 2, while when we split an interior node, the first 3 pointers go with the first (left) node, and the last 2 pointers go with the second (right) node. We start with a leaf containing pointers to records with keys 1, 2, and 3. We then add in order, records with keys 4, 5, 6, and so on. At the insertion of what key will the B-tree first reach four levels?

!! **Exercise 4.3.11 :** Consider an index organized as a B+ tree. The leaf nodes contain pointers to a total of N records, and each block that makes up the index has m pointers. We wish to choose the value of m that will minimize search times on a particular disk with the following characteristics:

> $i.$ The time to read a given block into memory can be approximated by $70+.05m$ milliseconds. The 70 milliseconds represent the seek and latency components of the read, and the $.05m$ milliseconds is the transfer time. That is, as m becomes larger, the block will be larger, and it will take more time to read it into memory.

> $ii.$ Once the block is in memory, a binary search is used to find the correct pointer. Thus, the time to process a block in main memory is $a + b \log_2 m$ milliseconds, for some constants a and b.

> $iii.$ The main memory time constant a is much smaller than the disk seek and latency time of 70 milliseconds.

> $iv.$ The index is full, so that the number of blocks that must be examined per search is $\log_m N$.

Answer the following:

a) What value of m minimizes the time to search for a given record?

b) What happens as the seek and latency constant (70ms) decreases? For instance, if this constant is cut in half, how does the optimum m value change?

4.4   Hash Tables

There are a number of data structures involving a hash table that are useful as indexes. We assume the reader has seen the hash table used as a main-memory data structure. In such a structure there is a *hash function* that takes a search key (which we may call the *hash key*) as an argument and computes from it an integer in the range 0 to $B - 1$, where B is the number of *buckets*. A *bucket array*, which is an array indexed from 0 to $B - 1$, holds the headers of B linked lists, one for each bucket of the array. If a record has search key K, then we store the record by linking it to the bucket list for the bucket numbered $h(K)$, where h is the hash function.

4.4.1 Secondary-Storage Hash Tables

A hash table that holds a very large number of records, so many that they must be kept mainly in secondary storage, differs from the main-memory version in small but important ways. First, the bucket array consists of blocks, rather than pointers to the headers of lists. Records that are hashed by the hash function h to a certain bucket are put in the block for that bucket. If a bucket *overflows*, meaning that it cannot hold all the records that belong in that bucket, then a chain of *overflow blocks* can be added to the bucket to hold more records.

We shall assume that the location of the first block for any bucket i can be found given i. For example, there might be a main-memory array of pointers to blocks, indexed by the bucket number. Another possibility is to put the first block for each bucket in fixed, consecutive disk locations, so we can compute the location of bucket i from the integer i.

Example 4.28 : Figure 4.30 shows a hash table. To keep our illustrations manageable, we assume that a block can hold only two records, and that $B = 4$; i.e., the hash function h returns values from 0 to 3. We show certain records populating the hash table. Keys are letters a through f in Fig. 4.30. We assume that $h(d) = 0$, $h(c) = h(e) = 1$, $h(b) = 2$, and $h(a) = h(f) = 3$. Thus, the six records are distributed into blocks as shown. $\square$

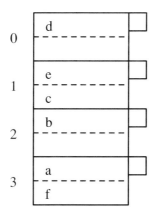

Figure 4.30: A hash table

Note that we show each block in Fig. 4.30 with a "nub" at the right end.

Choice of Hash Function

The hash function should "hash" the key so the resulting integer is a seemingly random function of the key. Thus, buckets will tend to have equal numbers of records, which improves the average time to access a record, as we shall discuss in Section 4.4.4. Also, the hash function should be easy to compute, since we shall compute it many times.

- A common choice of hash function when keys are integers is to compute the remainder of K/B, where K is the key value and B is the number of buckets. Often, B is chosen to be a prime, although there are reasons to make B a power of 2, as we discuss starting in Section 4.4.5.

- For character-string search keys, we may treat each character as an integer, sum these integers, and take the remainder when the sum is divided by B.

This nub represents additional information in the block's header. We shall use it to chain overflow blocks together, and starting in Section 4.4.5, we shall use it to keep other critical information about the block.

4.4.2 Insertion Into a Hash Table

When a new record with search key K must be inserted, we compute $h(K)$. If the bucket numbered $h(K)$ has space, then we insert the record into the block for this bucket, or into one of the overflow blocks on its chain if there is no room in the first block. If none of the blocks of the chain for bucket $h(K)$ has room, we add a new overflow block to the chain and store the new record there.

Example 4.29: Suppose we add to the hash table of Fig. 4.30 a record with key g, and $h(g) = 1$. Then we must add the new record to the bucket numbered 1, which is the second bucket from the top. However, the block for that bucket already has two records. Thus, we add a new block and chain it to the original block for bucket 1. The record with key g goes in that block, as shown in Fig. 4.31. □

4.4.3 Hash-Table Deletion

Deletion of the record (or records) with search key K follows the same pattern. We go to the bucket numbered $h(K)$ and search for records with that search key. Any that we find are deleted. If we are able to move records around among

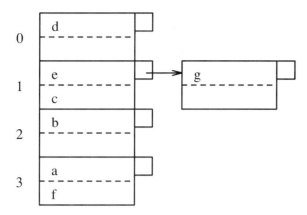

Figure 4.31: Adding an additional block to a hash-table bucket

blocks, then after deletion we may optionally consolidate the blocks of a chain into one fewer block.[9]

Example 4.30: Figure 4.32 shows the result of deleting the record with key c from the hash table of Fig. 4.31. Recall $h(c) = 1$, so we go to the bucket numbered 1 (i.e., the second bucket) and search all its blocks to find a record (or records if the search key were not the primary key) with key c. We find it in the first block of the chain for bucket 1. Since there is now room to move the record with key g from the second block of the chain to the first, we can do so and remove the second block.

We also so the deletion of the record with key a. For this key, we found our way to bucket 3, deleted it, and "consolidated" the remaining record at the beginning of the block. □

4.4.4 Efficiency of Hash Table Indexes

Ideally, there are enough buckets that most of the buckets consist of a single block. If so, then the typical lookup takes only one disk I/O, and insertion or deletion from the file takes only two disk I/O's. That number is significantly better than straightforward sparse or dense indexes, or B-tree indexes (although hash tables do not support range queries as B-trees do; see Section 4.3.4).

However, if the file grows, then we shall eventually reach a situation where there are many blocks in the chain for a typical bucket. If so, then we need to search long lists of buckets, taking at least one disk I/O per block. Thus, there is a good reason to try to keep the number of blocks per bucket low.

---

[9]A risk of consolidating blocks of a chain whenever possible is that an oscillation, where we alternately insert and delete records from a bucket will cause a block to be created or destroyed at each step.

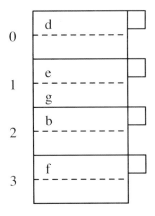

Figure 4.32: Result of deletions from a hash table

The hash tables we have examined so far are called *static hash tables*, because B, the number of buckets, never changes. However, there are several kinds of *dynamic hash tables*, where B is allowed to vary, so B approximates the number of records divided by the number of records that can fit on a block; i.e., there is about one block per bucket. We shall discuss two such methods:

1. Extensible hashing in Section 4.4.5, and

2. Linear hashing in Section 4.4.7.

The first grows B by doubling it whenever it is deemed too small, and the second grows B by 1 each time statistics of the file suggest some growth is needed.

4.4.5 Extensible Hash Tables

Our first approach to dynamic hashing is called *extensible hash tables*. The major additions to the simpler static hash table structure are:

1. There is a level of indirection introduced for the buckets. That is, an array of pointers to blocks represents the buckets, instead of the array consisting of the data blocks themselves.

2. The array of pointers can grow. Its length is always a power of 2, so in a growing step the number of buckets doubles.

3. However, there does not have to be a data block for each bucket; certain buckets can share a block if the total number of records in those buckets can fit in the block.

4. The hash function h computes for each key a sequence of k bits for some large k, say 32. However, the bucket numbers will at all times use some

smaller number of bits, say i bits, from the beginning of this sequence. That is, the bucket array will have 2^i entries when i is the number of bits used.

Example 4.31: Figure 4.33 shows a small extensible hash table. We suppose, for simplicity of the example, that $k = 4$; i.e., the hash function produces a sequence of only four bits. At the moment, only one of these bits is used, as indicated by $i = 1$ in the box above the bucket array. The bucket array therefore has only two entries, one for 0 and one for 1.

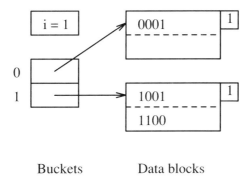

Buckets   Data blocks

Figure 4.33: An extensible hash table

The bucket array entries point to two blocks. The first holds all the current records whose search keys hash to a bit sequence that begins with 0, and the second holds all those whose search keys hash to a sequence beginning with 1. For convenience, we show the keys of records as if they were the entire bit sequence that the hash function converts them to. Thus, the first block holds a record whose key hashes to 0001, and the second holds records whose keys hash to 1001 and 1100. □

We should notice the number 1 appearing in the "nub" of each of the blocks in Fig. 4.33. This number, which would actually appear in the block header, indicates how many bits of the hash function's sequence is used to determine membership of records in this block. In the situation of Example 4.31, there is only one bit considered for all blocks and records, but as we shall see, the number of bits considered for various blocks can differ as the hash table grows. That is, the bucket array size is determined by the maximum number of bits we are now using, but some blocks may use fewer.

4.4.6 Insertion Into Extensible Hash Tables

Insertion into an extensible hash table begins like insertion into a static hash table. To insert a record with search key K, we compute $h(K)$, take the first i bits of this bit sequence, and go to the entry of the bucket array indexed by these i bits. Note that we can determine i because it is kept as part of the hash data structure.

We follow the pointer in this entry of the bucket array and arrive at a block B. If there is room to put the new record in block B, we do so and we are done. If there is no room, then there are two possibilities, depending on the number j, which indicates how many bits of the hash value are used to determine membership in block B (recall the value of j is found in the "nub" of each block in figures).

1. If $j < i$, then nothing needs to be done to the bucket array. We:

   (a) Split block B into two.

   (b) Distribute records in B to the two blocks, based on the value of their $(j+1)$st bit — records whose key has 0 in that bit stay in B and those with 1 there go to the new block.

   (c) Put $j+1$ in each block's "nub" to indicate the number of bits used to determine membership.

   (d) Adjust the pointers in the bucket array so entries that formerly pointed to B now point either to B or the new block, depending on their $(j+1)$st bit.

   Note that splitting block B may not solve the problem, since by chance all the records of B may go into one of the two blocks into which it was split. If so, we need to repeat the process with the next higher value of j and the block that is still overfull.

2. If $j = i$, then we must first increment i by 1. We double the length of the bucket array, so it now has 2^{i+1} entries. Suppose w is a sequence of i bits indexing one of the entries in the previous bucket array. In the new bucket array, the entries indexed by both $w0$ and $w1$ (i.e., the two numbers derived from w by extending it with 0 or 1) each point to the same block that the w entry used to point to. That is, the two new entries share the block, and the block itself does not change. Membership in the block is still determined by whatever number of bits was previously used. Finally, we proceed to split block B as in case 1. Since i is now greater than j, that case applies.

Example 4.32 : Suppose we insert into the table of Fig. 4.33 a record whose key hashes to the sequence 1010. Since the first bit is 1, this record belongs in the second block. However, that block is already full, so it needs to be split. We find that $j = i = 1$ in this case, so we first need to double the bucket array, as shown in Fig. 4.34. We have also set $i = 2$ in this figure.

Notice that the two entries beginning with 0 each point to the block for records whose hashed keys begin with 0, and that block still has the integer 1 in its "nub" to indicate that only the first bit determines membership in the block. However, the block for records beginning with 1 needs to be split, so we

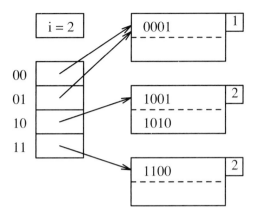

Figure 4.34: Now, two bits of the hash function are used

partition its records into those beginning 10 and those beginning 11. A 2 in each of these blocks indicates that two bits are used to determine membership. Fortunately, the split is successful; since each of the two new blocks gets at least one record, we do not have to split recursively.

Now suppose we insert records whose keys hash to 0000 and 0111. These both go in the first block of Fig. 4.34, which then overflows. Since only one bit is used to determine membership in this block, while $i = 2$, we do not have to adjust the bucket array. We simply split the block, with 0000 and 0001 staying, and 0111 going to the new block. The entry for 01 in the bucket array is made to point to the new block. Again, we have been fortunate that the records did not all go in one of the new blocks, so we have no need to split recursively.

Now suppose a record whose key hashes to 1000 is inserted. The block for 10 overflows. Since it already uses two bits to determine membership, it is time to split the bucket array again and set $i = 3$. Figure 4.35 shows the data structure at this point. Notice that the block for 10 has been split into blocks for 100 and 101, while the other blocks continue to use only two bits to determine membership.   □

4.4.7   Linear Hash Tables

Extensible hash tables have some important advantages. Most significant is the fact that when looking for a record, we never need to search more than one data block. We also have to examine an entry of the bucket array, but if the bucket array is small enough to be kept in main memory, then there is no disk I/O needed to access the bucket array. However, extensible hash tables also suffer from some defects:

   1. When the bucket array needs to be doubled in size, there is a substantial amount of work to be done (when i is large). This work interrupts access

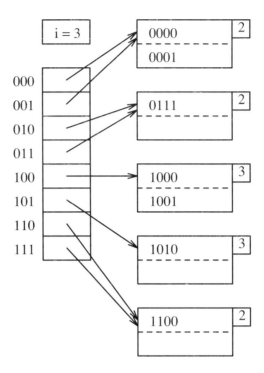

Figure 4.35: The hash table now uses three bits of the hash function

to the data file, or makes certain insertions appear to take a very large amount of time.

2. When the bucket array is doubled in size, it may no longer fit in main memory, or may crowd out other data that we would like to hold in main memory. As a result, a system that was performing well might suddenly start using many more disk I/O's per operation and exhibit a noticeably degraded performance.

3. If the number of records per block is small, then there is likely to be one block that needs to be split well in advance of the logical time to do so. For instance, if there are two records per block as in our running example, there might be one sequence of 20 bits with three records, even though the total number of records is much less than 2^{20}. In that case, we would have to use $i = 20$ and a million bucket-array entries, even though the number of blocks holding records was much smaller than a million.

Another strategy, called *linear hashing*, grows the number of buckets more slowly. The principal new elements we find in linear hashing are:

- The number of buckets n is always chosen so the average number of records per bucket is a fixed fraction, say 80%, of the number of records that fill one block.

- Since blocks cannot always be split, overflow blocks are permitted, although the average number of overflow blocks per bucket will be much less than 1.

- The number of bits used to number the entries of the bucket array is $\lceil \log_2 n \rceil$, where n is the current number of buckets. These bits are always taken from the *right* (low-order) end of the bit sequence that is produced by the hash function.

- Suppose i bits of the hash function are being used to number array entries, and a record with key K is intended for bucket $a_1 a_2 \cdots a_i$; that is, $a_1 a_2 \cdots a_i$ are the last i bits of $h(K)$. Then let $a_1 a_2 \cdots a_i$ be m, treated as an i-bit binary integer. If $m < n$, then the bucket numbered m exists, and we place the record in that bucket. If $n \leq m < 2^i$, then the bucket m does not yet exist, so we place the record in bucket $m - 2^{i-1}$, that is, the bucket we would get if we changed a_1 (which must be 1) to 0.

Example 4.33 : Figure 4.36 shows a linear hash table with $n = 2$. We currently are using only one bit of the hash value to determine the buckets of records. Following the pattern established in Example 4.31, we assume the hash function h produces 4 bits, and we represent records by the value produced by h when applied to the search key of the record.

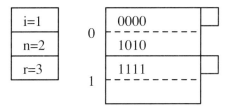

Figure 4.36: A linear hash table

We see in Fig. 4.36 the two buckets, each consisting of one block. The buckets are numbered 0 and 1. All records whose hash value ends in 0 go in the first bucket, and those whose hash value ends in 1 go in the second.

Also part of the structure are the parameters i (the number of bits of the hash function that currently are used), n (the current number of buckets), and r (the current number of records in the hash table). The ratio r/n will be limited so that the typical bucket will need about one disk block. We shall adopt the policy of choosing n, the number of buckets, so that there are no more than $1.7n$ records in the file; i.e., $r \leq 1.7n$. That is, since blocks hold two records, the average occupancy of a bucket does not exceed 85% of the capacity of a block. □

4.4.8   Insertion Into Linear Hash Tables

When we insert a new record, we determine its bucket by the algorithm outlined in Section 4.4.7. That is, we compute $h(K)$, where K is the key of the record, and determine the correct number of bits at the end of bit sequence $h(K)$ to use as the bucket number. We put the record either in that bucket, or (if the bucket number is n or greater) in the bucket with the leading bit changed from 1 to 0. If there is no room in the bucket, then we create an overflow block, add it to the chain for that bucket, and put the record there.

Each time we insert, we compare the current number of records r with the threshold ratio of r/n, and if the ratio is too high, we add the next bucket to the table. Note that the bucket we add bears no relationship to the bucket into which the insertion occurs! If the binary representation of the number of the bucket we add is $1a_2 \cdots a_i$, then we split the bucket numbered $0a_2 \cdots a_i$, putting records into one or the other bucket, depending on their last i bits. Note that all these records will have hash values that end in $a_2 \cdots a_i$, and only the ith bit from the right end will vary.

The last important detail is what happens when n exceeds 2^i. Then, i is incremented by 1. Technically, all the bucket numbers get an additional 0 in front of their bit sequences, but there is no need to make any physical change, since these bit sequences, interpreted as integers, remain the same.

Example 4.34: We shall continue with Example 4.33 and consider what happens when a record whose key hashes to 0101 is inserted. Since this bit sequence ends in 1, the record goes into the second bucket of Fig. 4.36. There is room for the record, so no overflow block is created.

However, since there are now 4 records in 2 buckets, we exceed the ratio 1.7, and we must therefore raise n to 3. Since $\lceil \log_2 3 \rceil = 2$, we should begin to think of buckets 0 and 1 as 00 and 01, but no change to the data structure is necessary. We add to the table the next bucket, which would have number 10. Then, we split the bucket 00, that bucket whose number differs from the added bucket only in the first bit. When we do the split, the record whose key hashes to 0000 stays in 00, since it ends with 00, while the record whose key hashes to 1010 goes to 10 because it ends that way. The resulting hash table is shown in Fig. 4.37.

Next, let us suppose we add a record whose search key hashes to 0001. The last two bits are 01, so we put it in this bucket, which currently exists. Unfortunately, the bucket's block is full, so we add an overflow block. The three records are distributed among the two blocks of the bucket; we chose to keep them in numerical order of their hashed keys, but order is not important. Since the ratio of records to buckets for the table as a whole is 5/3, and this ratio is less than 1.7, we do not create a new bucket. The result is seen in Fig. 4.38.

Finally, consider the insertion of a record whose search key hashes to 0111. The last two bits are 11, but bucket 11 does not yet exist. We therefore redirect this record to bucket 01, whose number differs by having a 0 in the first bit. The new record fits in the overflow block of this bucket.

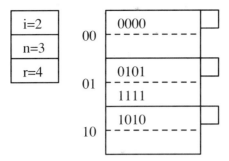

Figure 4.37: Adding a third bucket

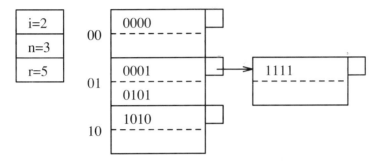

Figure 4.38: Overflow blocks are used if necessary

However, the ratio of the number of records to buckets has exceeded 1.7, so we must create a new bucket, numbered 11. Coincidentally, this bucket is the one we wanted for the new record. We split the four records in bucket 01, with 0001 and 0101 remaining, and 0111 and 1111 going to the new bucket. Since bucket 01 now has only two records, we can delete the overflow block. The hash table is now as shown in Fig. 4.39.

Notice that the next time we insert a record into Fig. 4.39, we shall exceed the 1.7 ratio of records to buckets. Then, we shall raise n to 5 and i becomes 3. □

Example 4.35 : Lookup in a linear hash table follows the procedure we described for selecting the bucket in which an inserted record belongs. If the record we wish to look up is not in that bucket, it cannot be anywhere. For illustration, consider the situation of Fig. 4.37, where we have $i = 2$ and $n = 3$.

First, suppose we want to look up a record whose key hashes to 1010. Since $i = 2$, we look at the last two bits, 10, which we interpret as a binary integer, namely $m = 2$. Since $m < n$, the bucket numbered 10 exists, and we look there. Notice that just because we find a record with hash value 1010 doesn't mean that this record is the one we want; we need to check the complete key of that record to be sure.

Second, consider the lookup of a record whose key hashes to 1011. Now, we

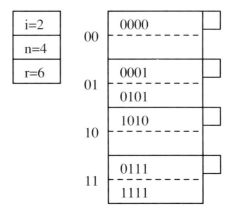

Figure 4.39: Adding a fourth bucket

must look in the bucket whose number is 11. Since that bucket number as a binary integer is $m = 3$, and $m \geq n$, the bucket 11 does not exist. We redirect to bucket 01 by changing the leading 1 to 0. However, bucket 01 has no record whose key has hash value 1011, and therefore surely our desired record is not in the hash table.   □

4.4.9   Exercises for Section 4.4

Exercise 4.4.1 : Show what happens to the buckets in Fig. 4.30 if the following insertions and deletions occur:

  i. Records g through j are inserted into buckets 0 through 3, respectively.

  ii. Records a and b are deleted.

  iii. Records k through n are inserted into buckets 0 through 3, respectively.

  iv. Records c and d are deleted.

Exercise 4.4.2 : We did not discuss how deletions can be carried out in a linear or extensible hash table. The mechanics of locating the record(s) to be deleted should be obvious. What method would you suggest for executing the deletion? In particular, what are the advantages and disadvantages of restructuring the table if its smaller size after deletion allows for compression of certain blocks?

! Exercise 4.4.3 : The material of this section assumes that search keys are unique. However, only small modifications are needed to allow the techniques to work for search keys with duplicates. Describe the necessary changes to insertion, deletion, and lookup algorithms, and suggest the major problems that arise when there are duplicates in:

  * a) A simple hash table.

b) An extensible hash table.

c) A linear hash table.

! **Exercise 4.4.4:** Some hash functions do not work as well as theoretically possible. Suppose that we use the hash function on integer keys i defined by $h(i) = i^2 \bmod B$.

* a) What is wrong with this hash function if $B = 10$?

b) How good is this hash function if $B = 16$?

c) Are there values of B for which this hash function is useful?

Exercise 4.4.5: In an extensible hash table with n records per block, what is the probability that an overflowing block will have to be handled recursively; i.e., all members of the block will go into the same one of the two blocks created in the split?

Exercise 4.4.6: Suppose keys are hashed to four-bit sequences, as in our examples of extensible and linear hashing in this section. However, also suppose that blocks can hold three records, rather than the two-record blocks of our examples. If we start with a hash table with two empty blocks (corresponding to 0 and 1), show the organization after we insert records with keys:

* a) $0000, 0001, \ldots, 1111$, and the method of hashing is extensible hashing.

b) $0000, 0001, \ldots, 1111$, and the method of hashing is linear hashing with a capacity threshold of 100%.

c) $1111, 1110, \ldots, 0000$, and the method of hashing is extensible hashing.

d) $1111, 1110, \ldots, 0000$, and the method of hashing is linear hashing with a capacity threshold of 75%.

* **Exercise 4.4.7:** Suppose we use a linear or extensible hashing scheme, but there are pointers to records from outside. These pointers prevent us from moving records between blocks, as is sometimes required by these hashing methods. Suggest several ways that we could modify the structure to allow pointers from outside.

!! **Exercise 4.4.8:** A linear-hashing scheme with blocks that hold k records uses a threshold constant c, such that the current number of buckets n and the current number of records r are related by $r = ckn$. For instance, in Example 4.33 we used $k = 2$ and $c = 0.85$, so there were 1.7 records per bucket; i.e., $r = 1.7n$.

a) Suppose for convenience that each key occurs exactly its expected number of times.[10] As a function of c, k, and n, how many blocks, including overflow blocks, are needed for the structure?

---

[10]This assumption does not mean all buckets have the same number of records, because some buckets represent twice as many keys as others.

b) Keys will not generally distribute equally, but rather the number of records with a given key (or suffix of a key) will be *Poisson distributed*. That is, if λ is the expected number of records with a given key suffix, then the actual number of such records will be i with probability $e^{-\lambda}\lambda^i/i!$. Under this assumption, calculate the expected number of blocks used, as a function of c, k, and n.

*! **Exercise 4.4.9 :** Suppose we have a file of 1,000,000 records that we want to hash into a table with 1000 buckets. 100 records will fit in a block, and we wish to keep blocks as full as possible, but not allow two buckets to share a block. What are the minimum and maximum number of blocks that we could need to store this hash table?

4.5 Summary of Chapter 4

✦ *Sequential Files*: Several simple file organizations begin by sorting the data file according to some search key and placing an index on top of this file.

✦ *Dense Indexes*: These indexes have a key-pointer pair for every record in the data file. The pairs are kept in sorted order of their key values.

✦ *Sparse Indexes*: These indexes have one key-pointer pair for each block of the data file. The key associated with a pointer to a block is the first key found on that block.

✦ *Multilevel Indexes*: It is sometimes useful to put an index on the index file itself, an index file on that, and so on. Higher levels of index must be sparse.

✦ *Expanding Files*: As a data file and its index file(s) grow, some provision for adding additional blocks to the file must be made. Adding overflow blocks to the original blocks is one possibility. Inserting additional blocks in the sequence for the data or index file may be possible, unless the file itself is required to be in sequential blocks of the disk.

✦ *Secondary Indexes*: An index on a search key K can be created even if the data file is not sorted by K. Such an index must be dense.

✦ *Inverted Indexes*: The relation between documents and the words they contain is often represented by an index structure with word-pointer pairs. The pointer goes to a place in a "bucket" file where is found a list of pointers to places where that word occurs.

✦ *B-trees*: These structures are essentially multilevel indexes, with graceful growth capabilities. Blocks with n keys and $n + 1$ pointers are organized in a tree, with the leaves pointing to records. All blocks are between half-full and completely full at all times.

✦ *Range Queries*: Queries in which we ask for all records whose search-key value lies in a given range are facilitated by indexed sequential files and B-tree indexes, although not by hash-table indexes.

✦ *Hash Tables*: We can create hash tables out of blocks in secondary memory, much as we can create main-memory hash tables. A hash function maps search-key values to buckets, effectively partitioning the records of a data file into many small groups (the buckets). Buckets are represented by a block and possible overflow blocks.

✦ *Dynamic Hashing*: Since performance of a hash table degrades if there are too many records in one bucket, the number of buckets may need to grow as time goes on. Two important methods of allowing graceful growth are extensible and linear hashing. Both begin by hashing search-key values to long bit-strings and use a varying number of those bits to determine the bucket for records.

✦ *Extensible Hashing*: This method allows the number of buckets to double whenever any bucket has too many records. It uses an array of pointers to blocks that represent the buckets. To avoid having too many blocks, several buckets can be represented by the same block.

✦ *Linear Hashing*: This method grows the number of buckets by 1 each time the ratio of records to buckets exceeds a threshold. Since the population of a single bucket cannot cause the table to expand, overflow blocks for buckets are needed in some situations.

4.6 References for Chapter 4

The B-tree was the original idea of Bayer and McCreight [2]. Unlike the B+ tree described here, this formulation had pointers to records at the interior nodes as well as at the leaves. [3] is a survey of B-tree varieties.

Hashing as a data structure goes back to Peterson [8]. Extensible hashing was developed by [4], while linear hashing is from [7]. The book by Knuth [6] contains much information on data structures, including techniques for selecting hash functions and designing hash tables, as well as a number of ideas concerning B-tree variants. The B+ tree formulation (without key values at interior nodes) appeared in the 1973 edition of [6].

Secondary indexes and other techniques for retrieval of documents are covered by [9]. Also, [5] and [1] are surveys of index methods for text documents.

1. R. Baeza-Yates, "Integrating contents and structure in text retrieval," *SIGMOD Record* **25**:1 (1996), pp. 67–79.

2. R. Bayer and E. M. McCreight, "Organization and maintenance of large ordered indexes," *Acta Informatica* **1**:3 (1972), pp. 173–189.

3. D. Comer, "The ubiquitous B-tree," *Computing Surveys* **11**:2 (1979), pp. 121–137.

4. R. Fagin, J. Nievergelt, N. Pippenger, and H. R. Strong, "Extendible hashing — a fast access method for dynamic files," *ACM Trans. on Database Systems* **4**:3 (1979), pp. 315–344.

5. C. Faloutsos, "Access methods for text," *Computing Surveys* **17**:1 (1985), pp. 49–74.

6. D. E. Knuth, *The Art of Computer Programming, Vol. III, Sorting and Searching, Third Edition*, Addison-Wesley, Reading MA, 1998.

7. W. Litwin, "Linear hashing: a new tool for file and table addressing," *Proc. Intl. Conf. on Very Large Databases* (1980) pp. 212–223.

8. W. W. Peterson, "Addressing for random access storage," *IBM J. Research and Development* **1**:2 (1957), pp. 130–146.

9. G. Salton, *Introduction to Modern Information Retrieval*, McGraw-Hill, New York, 1983.

Chapter 5

Multidimensional Indexes

All the index structures discussed so far are *one dimensional*; that is, they assume a single search key, and they retrieve records that match a given search-key value. We have imagined that the search key was a single attribute or field. However, an index whose search key is a combination of fields can still be one-dimensional. If we want a one-dimensional index whose search key is the fields $(F_1, F_2, \ldots, F_k)$, then we can take the search-key value to be the concatenation of values, the first from F_1, the second from F_2, and so on. We can separate these values by special marker symbols to make the association between search-key values and lists of values for the fields $F_1, \ldots, F_k$ unambiguous.

Example 5.1 : If fields F_1 and F_2 are a string and an integer, respectively, and # is a character that cannot appear in strings, then the combination of values $F_1 = $ 'abcd' and $F_2 = 123$ can be represented by the string 'abcd#123'. $\square$

In Chapter 4, we took advantage of a one-dimensional key space in several ways:

- Indexes on sequential files and B-trees both take advantage of having all keys in a single, sorted order.

- Hash tables require that the search key be completely known for any lookup. If a key consists of several fields, and even one is unknown, we cannot apply the hash function, but must instead search all the buckets.

There are a number of applications that require us to view data as existing in a 2-dimensional space, or sometimes in higher dimensions. Some of these applications can be supported by conventional DBMS's, but there are also some specialized systems designed for multidimensional applications. One important way in which these specialized systems distinguish themselves is by using data structures that support certain kinds of queries that are not common in SQL applications. Section 5.1 introduces us to the typical queries that benefit from an index that is designed to support multidimensional data and multidimensional queries. Then, in Sections 5.2 and 5.3 we discuss the following data structures:

1. *Grid files*, a multidimensional extension of one-dimensional hash-tables.

2. *Partitioned hash functions*, another way that brings hash-table ideas to multidimensional data.

3. *Multiple-key indexes*, in which the index on one attribute A leads to indexes on another attribute B for each possible value of A.

4. *kd-trees*, an approach to generalizing B-trees to sets of points.

5. *Quad trees*, which are multiway trees in which each child of a node represents a quadrant of a larger space.

6. *R-trees*, a B-tree generalization suitable for collections of regions.

Finally, Section 5.4 discusses an index structure called *bitmap indexes*. These indexes are succinct codes for the location of records with a given value in a given field. They are today beginning to appear in the major commercial DBMS's, and they sometimes are an excellent choice for a one-dimensional index. However, they also can be a powerful tool for answering certain kinds of multidimensional queries.

5.1   Applications Needing Multiple Dimensions

We shall consider two general classes of multidimensional applications. One is *geographic* in nature, where the data is elements in a two-dimensional world, or sometimes a three-dimensional world. The second involves more abstract notions of dimensions. Roughly, every attribute of a relation can be thought of as a dimension, and all tuples are points in a space defined by those dimensions.

Also in this section is an analysis of how conventional indexes, such as B-trees, could be used to support multidimensional queries. While in some cases they are adequate, there are also examples where they are clearly dominated by more specialized structures.

5.1.1   Geographic Information Systems

A *geographic information system* stores objects in a (typically) two-dimensional space. The objects may be points or shapes. Often, these databases are maps, where the stored objects could represent houses, roads, bridges, pipelines, and many other physical objects. A suggestion of such a map is in Fig. 5.1.

However, there are many other uses as well. For instance, an integrated-circuit design is a two-dimensional map of regions, often rectangles, composed of specific materials, called "layers." Likewise, we can think of the windows and icons on a screen as a collection of objects in two-dimensional space.

The queries asked of geographic information systems are not typical of SQL queries, although many can be expressed in SQL with some effort. Examples of these types of queries are:

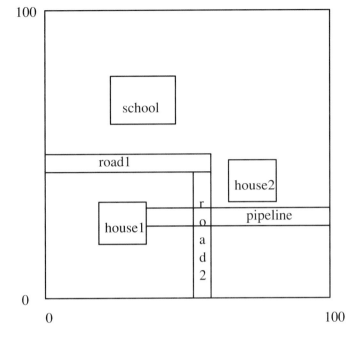

Figure 5.1: Some objects in 2-dimensional space

1. *Partial match queries.* We specify values for one or more dimensions and look for all points matching those values in those dimensions.

2. *Range queries.* We give ranges for one or more of the dimensions, and we ask for the set of points within those ranges, or if shapes are represented, then the set of shapes that are partially or wholly within the range. These queries generalize the one-dimensional range queries that we considered in Section 4.3.4.

3. *Nearest-neighbor queries.* We ask for the closest point to a given point. For instance, if points represent cities, we might want to find the city of over 100,000 population closest to a given small city.

4. *Where-am-I queries.* We are given a point and we want to know in which shape, if any, the point is located. A familiar example is what happens when you click your mouse, and the system determines which of the displayed elements you were clicking.

5.1.2 Data Cubes

A recent development is a family of DBMS's, sometimes called *data cube* systems, that see data as existing in a high-dimensional space. These are discussed in more detail in Section 11.4, but the following example suggests the main idea.

Multidimensional data is gathered by many corporations for *decision-support* applications, where they analyze information such as sales to better understand company operations. For example, a chain store may record each sale made, including:

1. The day and time.

2. The store at which the sale was made.

3. The item purchased.

4. The color of the item.

5. The size of the item.

and perhaps other properties of the sale.

It is common to view the data as a relation with an attribute for each property. These attributes can be seen as dimensions of a multidimensional space, the "data cube." Each tuple is a point in the space. Analysts then ask queries that typically group the data along some of the dimensions and summarize the groups by an aggregation. A typical example would be "give the sales of pink shirts for each store and each month of 1998."

5.1.3 Multidimensional Queries in SQL

It is possible to set up each of the applications suggested above as a conventional, relational database and to issue the suggested queries in SQL. Here are some examples.

Example 5.2 : Suppose we wish to answer nearest-neighbor queries about a set of points in two-dimensional space. We may represent the points as a relation consisting of a pair of reals:

        Points(x, y)

That is, there are two attributes, x and y, representing the x- and y-coordinates of the point. Other, unseen, attributes of relation Points may represent properties of the point.

Suppose we want the nearest point to the point $(10.0, 20.0)$. The query of Fig. 5.2 finds the nearest point, or points if there is a tie. It asks, for each point p, whether there exists another point q that is closer to $(10.0, 20.0)$. Comparison of distances is carried out by computing the sum of the squares of the differences in the x- and y-coordinates between the point $(10.0, 20.0)$ and the points in question. Notice that we do not have to take the square roots of the sums to get the actual distances; comparing the squares of the distances is the same as comparing the distances themselves.   □

```
SELECT *
FROM POINTS p
WHERE NOT EXISTS(
    SELECT *
    FROM POINTS q
    WHERE (q.x-10.0)*(q.x-10.0) + (q.y-20.0)*(q.y-20.0) <
          (p.x-10.0)*(p.x-10.0) + (p.y-20.0)*(p.y-20.0)
);
```

Figure 5.2: Finding the points with no point nearer to $(10.0, 20.0)$

Example 5.3: Rectangles are a common form of shape used in geographic systems. We can represent a rectangle in several ways; a popular one is to give the coordinates of the lower-left and upper-right corners. We then represent a collection of rectangles by a relation `Rectangles` with attributes for a rectangle-ID, the four coordinates that describe the rectangle, and any other properties of the rectangle that we wished to record. We shall use the relation

    Rectangles(id, xll, yll, xur, yur)

in this example. The attributes are the rectangle's ID, the x-coordinate of its lower-left corner, the y-coordinate of that corner, and the two coordinates of the upper-right corner, respectively.

Figure 5.3 is a query that asks for the rectangle(s) enclosing the point $(10.0, 20.0)$. The where-clause condition is straightforward. For the rectangle to enclose $(10.0, 20.0)$, the lower-left corner must have its x-coordinate at or to the left of 10.0, and its y-coordinate at or below 20.0. The upper right corner must also be at or to the right of $x = 10.0$ and at or above $y = 20.0$. □

```
SELECT id
FROM Rectangles
WHERE xll <= 10.0 AND yll <= 20.0 AND
      xur >= 10.0 AND yur >= 20.0;
```

Figure 5.3: Finding the rectangles that contain a given point

Example 5.4: Data suitable for a data-cube system is typically organized into a *fact table*, which gives the basic elements being recorded (e.g., each sale), and *dimension tables*, which give properties of the values along each dimension. For instance, if the store at which a sale was made is a dimension, the dimension table for stores might give the address, phone, and name of the store's manager.

In this example, we shall deal only with the fact table, which we assume has the dimensions suggested in Section 5.1.2. That is, the fact table is the relation

```
Sales(day, store, item, color, size)
```

The query "summarize the sales of pink shirts by day and store" is shown in Fig. 5.4. It uses grouping to organize sales by the dimensions day and store, while summarizing the other dimensions through the COUNT aggregation operator. We focus on only those points of the data cube that we care about by using the WHERE-clause to select only the tuples for pink shirts. □

```
SELECT day, store, COUNT(*) AS totalSales
FROM Sales
WHERE item = 'shirt' AND
      color = 'pink'
GROUP BY day, store;
```

Figure 5.4: Summarizing the sales of pink shirts

5.1.4 Executing Range Queries Using Conventional Indexes

Now, let us consider to what extent the indexes described in Chapter 4 would help in answering range queries. Suppose for simplicity that there are two dimensions. We could put a secondary index on each of the dimensions, x and y. Using a B+ tree for each would make it especially easy to get a range of values for each dimension.

Given ranges in both dimensions, we could begin by using the B-tree for x to get pointers to all of the records in the range for x. Next, we use the B-tree for y to get pointers to the records for all points whose y-coordinate is in the range for y. Finally, we intersect these pointers using the idea of Section 4.2.3. If the pointers fit in main memory, then the total number of disk I/O's is the number of leaf nodes of each B-tree that need to be examined, plus a few I/O's for finding our way down the B-trees (see Section 4.3.7). To this amount we must add the disk I/O's needed to retrieve all the matching records, however many they may be.

Example 5.5: Let us consider a hypothetical set of 1,000,000 points distributed randomly in a space in which both the x- and y-coordinates range from 0 to 1000. Suppose that 100 point records fit on a block, and an average B-tree leaf has about 200 key-pointer pairs (recall that not all slots of a B-tree block are necessarily occupied, at any given time). We shall assume there are B-tree indexes on both x and y.

Imagine we are given the range query asking for points in the square of side 100 surrounding the center of the space, that is, $450 \leq x \leq 550$ and $450 \leq y \leq 550$. Using the B-tree for x, we can find pointers to all the records with x in the range; there should be about 100,000 pointers, and this number of pointers should fit in main memory. Similarly, we use the B-tree for y to get the pointers to all the records with y in the desired range; again there are about 100,000 of them. Approximately 10,000 pointers will be in the intersection of these two sets, and it is the records reached by the 10,000 pointers in the intersection that form our answer.

Now, let us estimate the number of disk I/O's needed to answer the range query. First, as we pointed out in Section 4.3.7, it is generally feasible to keep the root of any B-tree in main memory. Since we are looking for a range of search-key values in each B-tree, and the pointers at the leaves are sorted by this search key, all we have to do to access the 100,000 pointers in either dimension is examine one intermediate-level node and all the leaves that contain the desired pointers. Since we assumed leaves have about 200 key-pointer pairs each, we shall have to look at about 500 leaf blocks in each of the B-trees. When we add in one intermediate node per B-tree, we have a total of 1002 disk I/O's.

Finally, we have to retrieve the blocks containing the 10,000 desired records. If they are stored randomly, we must expect that they will be on almost 10,000 different blocks. Since the entire file of a million records is assumed stored over 10,000 blocks, packed 100 to a block, we essentially have to look at every block of the data file anyway. Thus, in this example at least, conventional indexes have been little if any help in answering the range query. Of course, if the range were smaller, then constructing the intersection of the two pointer sets would allow us to limit the search to a fraction of the blocks in the data file. □

5.1.5 Executing Nearest-Neighbor Queries Using Conventional Indexes

Almost any data structure we use will allow us to answer a nearest-neighbor query by picking a range in each dimension, asking the range query, and selecting the point closest to the target within that range. Unfortunately, there are two things that could go wrong:

1. There is no point within the selected range.

2. The closest point within the range might not be the closest point overall.

Let us consider each of these problems in the context of the nearest-neighbor query of Example 5.2, using the hypothetical indexes on dimensions x and y introduced in Example 5.5. If we had reason to believe that a point within distance d of $(10.0, 20.0)$ existed, we could use the B-tree for x to get pointers to all the records for points whose x-coordinate is between $10 - d$ and $10 + d$. We could then use the B-tree for y to get pointers to all the records whose y-coordinate is between $20 - d$ and $20 + d$.

If we have one or more points in the intersection, and we have recorded with each pointer its x- or y-coordinate (whichever is the search key for the index), then we have the coordinates of all the points in the intersection. We can thus determine which of these points is closest to $(10.0, 20.0)$ and retrieve only its record. Unfortunately, we cannot be certain that there are any points within distance d of the given point, so we may have to repeat the entire process with a higher value of d.

However, even if there is a point in the range we have searched, there are some circumstances where the closest point in the range is further than distance d from the target point, e.g., $(10.0, 20.0)$ in our example. The situation is suggested by Fig. 5.5. If that is the case, then we must expand our range and search again, to make sure that no closer point exists. If the distance from the target to the closest point found so far is d', and $d' > d$, then we must repeat the search with d' in place of d.

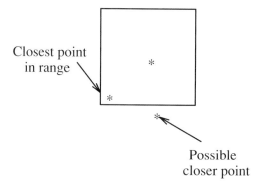

Figure 5.5: The point is in the range, but there could be a closer point outside the range

Example 5.6: Let us consider the same data and indexes as in Example 5.5. If we want the nearest neighbor to target point $P = (10.0, 20.0)$, we might pick $d = 1$. Then, there will be one point per unit of area on the average, and with $d = 1$ we find every point within a square of side 2.0 around the point P, wherein the expected number of points is 4.

If we examine the B-tree for the x-coordinate with the range query $9.0 \leq x \leq 11.0$, then we shall find about 2,000 points, so we need to traverse at least 10 leaves, and most likely 11 (since the points with $x = 9.0$ are unlikely to start just at the beginning of a leaf). As in Example 5.5, we can probably keep the roots of the B-trees in main memory, so we only need one disk I/O for an intermediate node and 11 disk I/O's for the leaves. Another 12 disk I/O's search the B-tree index on the y-coordinate for the points whose y-coordinate is between 19.0 and 21.0.

If we intersect the approximately 4000 pointers in main memory, we shall find about four records that are candidates for the nearest neighbor of point

$(10.0, 20.0)$. Assuming there is at least one, we can determine from the associated x- and y-coordinates of the pointers which is the nearest neighbor. One more disk I/O to retrieve the desired record, for a total of 23 disk I/O's, completes the query. However, if there is no point in the square with $d = 1$, or the closest point is more than distance 1 from the target, then we have to repeat the search with a larger value of d. □

The conclusion to draw from Example 5.6 is that conventional indexes might not be terrible for a nearest-neighbor query, but they use significantly more disk I/O's than would be used, say, to find a record given its key and a B-tree index on that key (which would probably take only two or three disk I/O's). The methods suggested in this chapter will generally provide better performance and are used in specialized DBMS's that support multidimensional data.

5.1.6 Other Limitations of Conventional Indexes

The previously mentioned structures fare no better for range queries than for nearest-neighbor queries. In fact, our approach to solving a nearest-neighbor query in Example 5.6 was really to convert it to a range-query with a small range in each dimension and hope the range was sufficient to include at least one point. Thus, if we were to tackle a range query with larger ranges, and the data structure were indexes in each dimension, then the number of disk I/O's necessary to retrieve the pointers to candidate records in each dimension would be even greater than what we found in Example 5.6.

The multidimensional aggregation of the query in Fig. 5.4 is likewise not well supported. If we have indexes on item and color, we can find all the records representing sales of pink shirts and intersect them, as we did in Example 5.6. However, queries in which other attributes besides item and color were specified would require indexes on those attributes instead.

Worse, while we can keep the data file sorted on one of the five attributes, we cannot keep it sorted on two attributes, let alone five. Thus, most queries of the form suggested by Fig. 5.4 would require that records from all or almost all of the blocks of the data file be retrieved. These queries of this type would be extremely expensive to execute if data was in secondary memory.

5.1.7 Overview of Multidimensional Index Structures

Most data structures for supporting queries on multidimensional data fall into one of two categories:

1. Hash-table-like approaches.

2. Tree-like approaches.

For each of these structures, we give up something that we have in the one-dimensional structures of Chapter 4.

- With the hash-bashed schemes — grid files and partitioned hash functions in Section 5.2 — we no longer have the advantage that the answer to our query is in exactly one bucket. However, each of these schemes limit our search to a subset of the buckets.

- With the tree-based schemes, we give up at least one of these important properties of B-trees:

  1. The balance of the tree, where all leaves are at the same level.

  2. The correspondence between tree nodes and disk blocks.

  3. The speed with which modifications to the data may be performed.

As we shall see in Section 5.3, trees will often be deeper in some parts than in others; often the deep parts correspond to regions that have many points. We shall also see that it is common that the information corresponding to a tree node is considerably smaller than what fits in one block. It is thus necessary to group nodes into blocks in some useful way.

5.1.8   Exercises for Section 5.1

Exercise 5.1.1: Write SQL queries using the relation

```
Rectangles(id, xll, yll, xur, yur)
```

from Example 5.3 to answer the following questions:

* a) Find the set of rectangles that intersect the rectangle whose lower-left corner is at $(10.0, 20.0)$ and whose upper-right corner is at $(40.0, 30.0)$.

  b) Find the pairs of rectangles that intersect.

  c) Find the rectangles that completely contain the rectangle mentioned in (a).

  d) Find the rectangles that are completely contained within the rectangle mentioned in (a).

! e) Find the "rectangles" in the relation `Rectangles` that are not really rectangles; i.e., they cannot exist physically.

For each of these queries, tell what indexes, if any, would help retrieve the desired tuples.

Exercise 5.1.2: Using the relation

```
Sales(day, store, item, color, size)
```

from Example 5.4, write the following queries in SQL:

 * a) List all colors of shirts and their total sales, provided there are more than 1000 sales for that color.

 b) List sales of shirts by store and color.

 c) List sales of all items by store and color.

 ! d) List for each item and color the store with the largest sales and the amount of those sales.

For each of these queries, tell what indexes, if any, would help retrieve the desired tuples.

Exercise 5.1.3 : Redo Example 5.5 under the assumption that the range query asks for a square in the middle that is $n \times n$ for some n between 1 and 1000. How many disk I/O's are needed? For which values of n do indexes help?

 * **Exercise 5.1.4 :** Repeat Exercise 5.1.3 if the file of records is sorted on x.

!! **Exercise 5.1.5 :** Suppose that we have points distributed randomly in a square, as in Example 5.6, and we want to perform a nearest neighbor query. We choose a distance d and find all points in the square of side $2d$ with the center at the target point. Our search is successful if we find within this square at least one point whose distance from the target point is d or less.

 * a) If there is on average one point per unit of area, give as a function of d the probability that we will be successful.

 b) If we are unsuccessful, we must repeat the search with a larger d. Assume for simplicity that each time we are unsuccessful, we double d and pay twice as much as we did for the previous search. Again assuming that there is one point per unit area, what initial value of d gives us the minimum expected search cost?

5.2 Hash-Like Structures for Multidimensional Data

In this section we shall consider two data structures that generalize hash tables built using a single key. In each case, the bucket for a point is a function of all the attributes or dimensions. One scheme, called the "grid file," usually doesn't "hash" values along the dimensions, but rather partitions the dimensions by sorting the values along that dimension. The other, called "partitioned hashing," does "hash" the various dimensions, with each dimension contributing to the bucket number.

5.2.1   Grid Files

One of the simplest data structures that often outperforms single-dimension indexes for queries involving multidimensional data is the *grid file*. Think of the space of points partitioned in a grid. In each dimension, *grid lines* partition the space into *stripes*. Points that fall on a grid line will be considered to belong to the stripe for which that grid line is the lower boundary. The number of grid lines in different dimensions may vary, and there may be different spacings between adjacent grid lines, even between lines in the same dimension.

Example 5.7: Let us introduce a running example for this chapter: the question "who buys gold jewelry?" We shall imagine a database of customers for gold jewelry that tells us many things about each customer — their name, address, and so on. However, to make things simpler, we assume that the only relevant attributes are the customer's age and salary. Our example database has twelve customers, which we can represent by the following age-salary pairs:

$$(25, 60) \quad (45, 60) \quad (50, 75) \quad (50, 100)$$
$$(50, 120) \quad (70, 110) \quad (85, 140) \quad (30, 260)$$
$$(25, 400) \quad (45, 350) \quad (50, 275) \quad (60, 260)$$

In Fig. 5.6 we see these twelve points located in a 2-dimensional space. We have also selected some grid lines in each dimension. For this simple example, we have chosen two lines in each dimension, dividing the space into nine rectangular regions, but there is no reason why the same number of lines must be used in each dimension. We have also allowed the spacing between the lines to vary. For instance, in the age dimension, the three regions into which the two vertical lines divide the space have width 40, 15, and 45.

In this example, no points are exactly on a grid line. But in general, a rectangle includes points on its lower and left boundaries, but not on its upper and right boundaries. For instance, the central rectangle in Fig. 5.6 represents points with $40 \leq age < 55$ and $90 \leq salary < 225$. □

5.2.2   Lookup in a Grid File

Each of the regions into which a space is partitioned can be thought of as a bucket of a hash table, and each of the points in that region has its record placed in a block belonging to that bucket. If needed, overflow blocks can be used to increase the size of a bucket.

Instead of a one-dimensional array of buckets, as is found in conventional hash tables, the grid file uses an array whose number of dimensions is the same as for the data file. To locate the proper bucket for a point, we need to know, for each dimension, the list of values at which the grid lines occur. Hashing a point is thus somewhat different from applying a hash function to the values of its components. Rather, we look at each component of the point and determine the position of the point in the grid for that dimension. The positions of the point in each of the dimensions together determine the bucket.

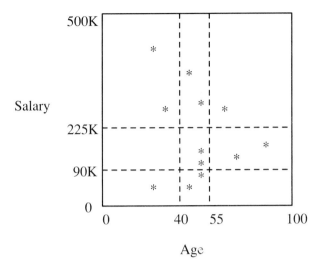

Figure 5.6: A grid file

Example 5.8 : Figure 5.7 shows the data of Fig. 5.6 placed in buckets. Since the grids in both dimensions divide the space into three regions, the bucket array is a 3×3 matrix. Two of the buckets:

1. Salary between $90K and $225K and age between 0 and 40, and

2. Salary below $90K and age above 55

are empty, and we do not show a block for that bucket. The other buckets are shown, with the artificially low maximum of two data points per block. In this simple example, no bucket has more than two members, so no overflow blocks are needed. □

5.2.3 Insertion Into Grid Files

When we insert a record into a grid file, we follow the procedure for lookup of the record, and we place the new record in that bucket. If there is room in the block for the bucket then there is nothing more to do. The problem occurs when there is no room in the bucket. There are two general approaches:

1. Add overflow blocks to the buckets, as needed. This approach works well as long as the chains of blocks for a bucket do not get too large. If they do, then the number of disk I/O's needed for lookup, insertion, or deletion eventually grows unacceptably large.

2. Reorganize the structure by adding or moving the grid lines. This approach is similar to the dynamic hashing techniques discussed in Section 4.4, but there are additional problems because the contents of buckets are linked across a dimension. That is, adding a grid line splits all the

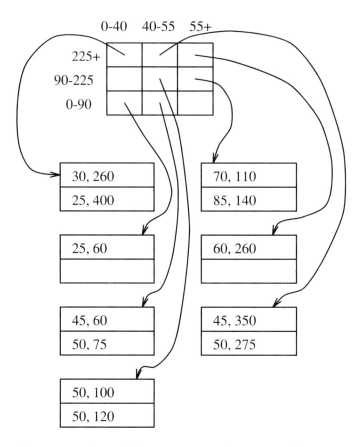

Figure 5.7: A grid file representing the points of Fig. 5.6

buckets along that line. As a result, it may not be possible to select a new grid line that does the best for all buckets. For instance, if one bucket is too big, we might not be able to choose either the dimension of the split or the point of the split without making many empty buckets or leaving several very full ones.

Example 5.9 : Suppose someone 52 years old with an income of $200K buys gold jewelry. This customer belongs in the central rectangle of Fig. 5.6. However, there are now three records in that bucket. We could simply add an overflow block. If we want to split the bucket, then we need to choose either the age or salary dimension, and we need to choose a new grid line to create the division. There are only three ways to introduce a grid line that will split the central bucket so two points are on one side and one on the other, which is the most even possible split in this case.

1. A vertical line, such as age = 51, that separates the two 50's from the 52. This line does nothing to split the buckets above or below, since both

---

Accessing Buckets of a Grid File

While finding the proper coordinates for a point in a three-by-three grid like Fig. 5.7 is easy, we should remember that the grid file may have a very large number of stripes in each dimension. If so, then we must create an index for each dimension. The search key for an index is the set of partition values in that dimension.

Given a value v in some coordinate, we search for the greatest key value w less than or equal to v. Associated with w in that index will be the row or column of the matrix into which v falls. Given values in each dimension, we can find where in the matrix the pointer to the bucket falls. We may then retrieve the block with that pointer directly.

In extreme cases, the matrix is so big, that most of the buckets are empty and we cannot afford to store all the empty buckets. Then, we must treat the matrix as a relation whose attributes are the corners of the nonempty buckets and a final attribute representing the pointer to the bucket. Lookup in this relation is itself a multidimensional search, but its size is smaller than the size of the data file itself.

---

points of each of the other buckets for age 40–55 will be to the left of the line age = 51.

2. A horizontal line that separates the point with salary = 200 from the other two points in the central bucket. We may as well choose a number like 130, which will also split the bucket to the right (that for age 55–100 and salary 90–225).

3. A horizontal line that separates the point with salary = 100 from the other two points. Again, we would be advised to pick a number like 115 that also splits the bucket to the right.

Choice (1) is probably not advised, since it doesn't split any other bucket; we are left with more empty buckets and have not reduced the size of any occupied buckets. Choices (2) and (3) are equally good, although we might pick (2) because it puts the horizontal grid line at salary = 130, which is closer to midway between the upper and lower limits of 90 and 225 than we get with choice (3). The resulting partition into buckets is shown in Fig. 5.8. □

5.2.4 Performance of Grid Files

Let us consider how many disk I/O's a grid file requires on various types of queries. We have been focusing on the two-dimensional version of grid files, although they can be used for any number of dimensions. One major problem

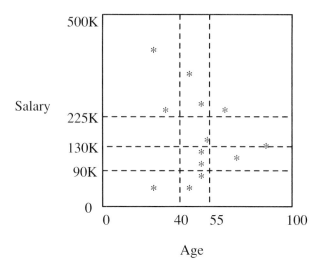

Figure 5.8: Insertion of the point $(52, 200)$ followed by splitting of buckets

in the high-dimensional case is that the number of buckets grows exponentially with the dimension. If large portions of a space are empty, then there will be many empty buckets. We can envision the problem even in two dimensions. Suppose that there were a high correlation between age and salary, so all points in Fig. 5.6 lay along the diagonal. then no matter where we placed the grid lines, the buckets off the diagonal would have to be empty.

However, if the data is well distributed, and the data file itself is not too large, then we can choose grid lines so that:

1. There are sufficiently few buckets that we can keep the bucket matrix in main memory, thus not incurring disk I/O to consult it, or to add rows or columns to the matrix when we introduce a new grid line.

2. We can also keep in memory indexes on the values of the grid lines in each dimension (see the box on "accessing buckets of a grid file"), or we can avoid the indexes altogether and use main-memory binary search of the values defining the grid lines in each dimension.

3. The typical bucket does not have more than a few overflow blocks, so we do not incur too many disk I/O's when we search through a bucket.

Under those assumptions, here is how the grid file behaves on some important classes of queries.

Lookup of Specific Points

We are directed to the proper bucket, so the only disk I/O is what is necessary to read the bucket. If we are inserting or deleting, then an additional disk write is needed. Inserts that require the creation of an overflow block cause an additional write.

Partial-Match Queries

Examples of this query would include "find all customers aged 50," or "find all customers with a salary of $200K." Now, we need to look at all the buckets in a row or column of the bucket matrix. The number of disk I/O's can be quite high if there are many buckets in these rows or columns.

Range Queries

A range query defines a rectangular region of the grid, and all points found in the buckets that cover that region will be answers to the query, with the exception of some of the points in buckets on the border of the search region. For example, if we want to find all customers aged 35–45 with a salary of 50–100, then we need to look in the four buckets in the lower left of Fig. 5.6. In this case, all buckets are on the border, so we may look at a good number of points that are not answers to the query. However, if the search region involves a large number of buckets, then most of them must be interior, and all their points are answers. For range queries, the number of disk I/O's may be large, as we may be required to examine many buckets. However, since range queries tend to produce large answer sets, we typically will examine not too many more blocks than the minimum number of blocks on which the answer could be placed by any organization whatsoever.

Nearest-Neighbor Queries

Given a point P, we start by searching the bucket in which that point belongs. If we find at least one point there, we have a candidate Q for the nearest neighbor. However, it is possible that there are points in adjacent buckets that are closer to P than Q is; the situation is like that suggested in Fig. 5.5. We have to consider whether the distance between P and a border of its bucket is less than the distance from P to Q. If there are such borders, then the adjacent buckets on the other side of each such border must be searched also. In fact, if buckets are severely rectangular — much longer in one dimension than the other — then it may be necessary to search even buckets that are not adjacent to the one containing point P.

Example 5.10 : Suppose we are looking in Fig. 5.6 for the point nearest $P = (45, 200)$. We find that $(50, 120)$ is the closest point in the bucket, at a distance of 80.2. No point in the lower three buckets can be this close to $(45, 200)$, because their salary component is at most 90, so we can omit searching them. However, the other five buckets must be searched, and we find that there are actually two equally close points: $(30, 260)$ and $(60, 260)$, at a distance of 61.8 from P. Generally, the search for a nearest neighbor can be limited to a few buckets, and thus a few disk I/O's. However, since the buckets nearest the point P may be empty, we cannot easily put an upper bound on how costly the search is.   □

5.2.5 Partitioned Hash Functions

Hash functions can take a list of attribute values as an argument, although typically they hash values from only one attribute. For instance, if a is an integer-valued attribute and b is a character-string-valued attribute, then we could add the value of a to the value of the ASCII code for each character of b, divide by the number of buckets, and take the remainder. The result could be used as the bucket number of a hash table suitable as an index on the pair of attributes (a, b).

However, such a hash table could only be used in queries that specified values for both a and b. A preferable option is to design the hash function so it produces some number of bits, say k. These k bits are divided among n attributes, so that we produce k_i bits of the hash value from the ith attribute, for $i = 1, 2, \ldots, n$, where $\sum_{i=1}^{n} k_i = k$. More precisely, the hash function h is actually a list of hash functions $(h_1, h_2, \ldots, h_n)$, such that h_i applies to a value for the ith attribute and produces a sequence of k_i bits. The bucket in which to place a tuple with values $(v_1, v_2, \ldots, v_n)$ in the n attributes that are involved in the hashing is computed by concatenating the bit sequences $h_1(v_1)h_2(v_2)\cdots h_n(v_n)$.

Example 5.11: If we have a hash table with 10-bit bucket numbers (1024 buckets), we could devote four bits to attribute a and the remaining six bits to attribute b. Suppose we have a tuple with a-value A and b-value B, perhaps with other attributes that are not involved in the hash. We hash A using a hash function h_a associated with attribute a to get four bits, say 0101. We then hash B, using a hash function h_b, perhaps receiving the six bits 111000. The bucket number for this tuple is thus 0101111000, the concatenation of the two bit sequences.

By partitioning the hash function this way, we get some advantage from knowing values for any one or more of the attributes that contribute to the hash function. For instance, if we are given a value A for attribute a, and we find that $h_a(A) = 0101$, then we know that the only tuples with a-value A are in the 64 buckets whose numbers are of the form $0101\cdots$, where the $\cdots$ represents any six bits. Similarly, if we are given the b-value B of a tuple, we can isolate the possible buckets of the tuple to the 16 buckets whose number ends in the six bits $h_b(B)$.   □

Example 5.12: Suppose we have the "gold jewelry" data of Example 5.7, which we want to store in a partitioned hash table with eight buckets (i.e., three bits for bucket numbers). We assume as before that two records are all that can fit in one block. We shall devote one bit to the age attribute and the remaining two bits to the salary attribute.

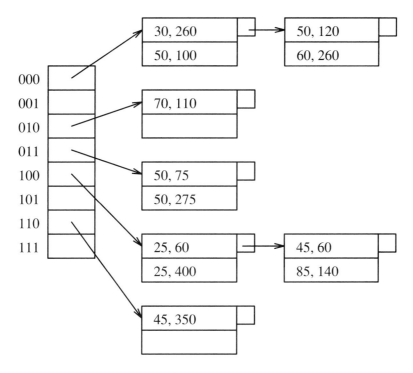

Figure 5.9: A partitioned hash table

For the hash function on age, we shall take the age modulo 2; that is, a record with an even age will hash into a bucket whose number is of the form $0xy$ for some bits x and y. A record with an odd age hashes to one of the buckets with a number of the form $1xy$. The hash function for salary will be the salary (in thousands) modulo 4. For example, a salary that leaves a remainder of 1 when divided by 4, such as 57K, will be in a bucket whose number is $z01$ for some bit z.

In Fig. 5.9 we see the data from Example 5.7 placed in this hash table. Notice that, because we have used mostly ages and salaries divisible by 10, the hash function does not distribute the points too well. Two of the eight buckets have four records each and need overflow blocks, while three other buckets are empty. □

5.2.6 Comparison of Grid Files and Partitioned Hashing

The performance of the two data structures discussed in this section are quite different. Here are the major points of comparison.

- Partitioned hash tables are actually quite useless for nearest-neighbor queries or range queries. The problem is that physical distance between points is not reflected by the closeness of bucket numbers. Of course we could design the hash function on some attribute a so the smallest values were assigned the first bit string (all 0's), the next values were assigned the next bit string ($00 \cdots 01$), and so on. If we do so, then we have reinvented the grid file.

- A well chosen hash function will randomize the buckets into which points fall, and thus buckets will tend to be equally occupied. However, grid files, especially when the number of dimensions is large, will tend to leave many buckets empty or nearly so. The intuitive reason is that when there are many attributes, there is likely to be some correlation among at least some of them, so large regions of the space are left empty. For instance, we mentioned in Section 5.2.4 that a correlation between age and salary would cause most points of Fig. 5.6 to lie near the diagonal, with most of the rectangle empty. As a consequence, we can use fewer buckets, and/or have fewer overflow blocks in a partitioned hash table than in a grid file.

Thus, if we are only required to support partial match queries, where we specify some attributes' values and leave the other attributes completely unspecified, then the partitioned hash function is likely to outperform the grid file. Conversely, if we need to do nearest-neighbor queries or range queries frequently, then we would prefer to use a grid file.

5.2.7 Exercises for Section 5.2

model	speed	ram	hard-disk
A	300	32	6.0
B	333	64	4.0
C	400	64	12.7
D	350	32	10.8
E	450	96	14.0
F	400	128	12.7
G	450	128	18.1
H	233	32	4.0
I	266	64	6.0
J	300	64	6.0
K	350	64	12.0
L	400	128	6.0

Figure 5.10: Some PC's and their characteristics

Exercise 5.2.1: In Fig. 5.10 are specifications for twelve PC's. Suppose we wish to design an index on speed and hard-disk size only.

* a) Choose five grid lines (total for the two dimensions), so that there are no more than two points in any bucket.

Handling Tiny Buckets

We generally think of buckets as containing about one block's worth of data. However, there are reasons why we might need to create so many buckets that the average bucket has only a small fraction of the number of records that will fit in a block. For example, high-dimensional data will require many buckets if we are to partition significantly along each dimension. Thus, in the structures of this section and also for the tree-based schemes of Section 5.3, we might choose to pack several buckets (or nodes of trees) into one block. If we do so, there are some important points to remember:

- The block must keep in its header information about where each record is, and to which bucket it belongs.

- If we insert a record into a bucket, we may not have room in the block containing that bucket. If so, we need to split the block in some way. We must decide which buckets go with each block, find the records of each bucket and put them in the proper block, and adjust the bucket table to point to the proper block.

! b) Can you separate the points with at most two per bucket if you use only four grid lines? Either show how or argue that it is not possible.

! c) Suggest a partitioned hash function that will partition these points into four buckets with at most four points per bucket.

! **Exercise 5.2.2:** Suppose we wish to place the data of Fig. 5.10 in a three-dimensional grid file, based on the speed, ram, and hard-disk attributes. Suggest a partition in each dimension that will divide the data well.

Exercise 5.2.3: Choose a partitioned hash function with one bit for each of the three attributes speed, ram, and hard-disk that divides the data of Fig. 5.10 well.

Exercise 5.2.4: Suppose we place the data of Fig. 5.10 in a grid file with dimensions for speed and ram only. The partitions are at speeds of 310, 375, and 425, and at ram of 40 and 75. Suppose also that only two points can fit in one bucket. Suggest good splits if we insert points at:

* a) Speed = 250 and ram = 48.

b) Speed = 333 and ram = 48.

Exercise 5.2.5: Suppose we store a relation $R(x, y)$ in a grid file. Both attributes have a range of values from 0 to 1000. The partitions of this grid file happen to be uniformly spaced; for x there are partitions every 20 units, at 20, 40, 60, and so on, while for y the partitions are every 50 units, at 50, 100, 150, and so on.

a) How many buckets do we have to examine to answer the range query

```
SELECT *
FROM R
WHERE 310 < x AND x < 400 AND 520 < y AND y < 730;
```

*! b) We wish to perform a nearest-neighbor query for the point $(110, 205)$. We begin by searching the bucket with lower-left corner at $(100, 200)$ and upper-right corner at $(120, 250)$, and we find that the closest point in this bucket is $(115, 220)$. What other buckets must be searched to verify that this point is the closest?

! **Exercise 5.2.6:** Suppose we have a grid file with three lines (i.e., four stripes) in each dimension. However, the points (x, y) happen to have a special property. Tell the largest possible number of nonempty buckets if:

* a) The points are on a line; i.e., there is are constants a and b such that $y = ax + b$ for every point (x, y).

b) The points are related quadratically; i.e., there are constants a, b, and c such that $y = ax^2 + bx + c$ for every point (x, y).

Exercise 5.2.7: Suppose we store a relation $R(x, y, z)$ in a partitioned hash table with 1024 buckets (i.e., 10-bit bucket addresses). Queries about R each specify exactly one of the attributes, and each of the three attributes is equally likely to be specified. If the hash function produces 5 bits based only on x, 3 bits based only on y, and 2 bits based only on z, what is the average number of buckets that need to be searched to answer a query?

!! **Exercise 5.2.8:** Suppose we have a hash table whose buckets are numbered 0 to $2^n - 1$; i.e., bucket addresses are n bits long. We wish to store in the table a relation with two attributes x and y. A query will either specify a value for x or y, but never both. With probability p, it is x whose value is specified.

a) Suppose we partition the hash function so that m bits are devoted to x and the remaining $n - m$ bits to y. As a function of m, n, and p, what is the expected number of buckets that must be examined to answer a random query?

b) For what value of m (as a function of n and p) is the expected number of buckets minimized? Do not worry that this m is unlikely to be an integer.

*! **Exercise 5.2.9:** Suppose we have a relation $R(x, y)$ with 1,000,000 points randomly distributed. The range of both x and y is 0 to 1000. We can fit 100 tuples of R in a block. We decide to use a grid file with uniformly spaced grid lines in each dimension, with m as the width of the stripes. we wish to select m in order to minimize the number of disk I/O's needed to read all the necessary buckets to ask a range query that is a square 50 units on each side. You may assume that the sides of this square *never* align with the grid lines. If we pick m too large, we shall have a lot of overflow blocks in each bucket, and many of the points in a bucket will be outside the range of the query. If we pick m too small, then there will be too many buckets, and blocks will tend not to be full of data. What is the best value of m?

5.3 Tree-Like Structures for Multidimensional Data

We shall now consider four more structures that are useful for range queries or nearest-neighbor queries on multidimensional data. In order, we shall consider:

1. Multiple-key indexes.

2. *kd*-trees.

3. Quad trees.

4. R-trees.

The first three are intended for sets of points. The R-tree is commonly used to represent sets of regions; it is also useful for points.

5.3.1 Multiple-Key Indexes

Suppose we have several attributes representing dimensions of our data points, and we want to support range queries or nearest-neighbor queries on these points. A simple tree-like scheme for accessing these points is an index of indexes, or more generally a tree in which the nodes at each level are indexes for one attribute.

The idea is suggested in Fig. 5.11 for the case of two attributes. The "root of the tree" is an index for the first of the two attributes. This index could be any type of conventional index, such as a B-tree or a hash table. The index associates with each of its search-key values — i.e., values for the first attribute — a pointer to another index. If V is a value of the first attribute, then the index we reach by following key V and its pointer is an index into the set of points that have V for their value in the first attribute and any value for the second attribute.

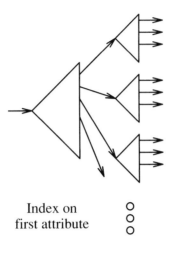

Index on
first attribute   o
                         o
                         o

Indexes on
second attribute

Figure 5.11: Using nested indexes on different keys

Example 5.13: Figure 5.12 shows a multiple-key index for our running "gold jewelry" example, where the first attribute is age, and the second attribute is salary. The root index, on age, is suggested at the left of Fig. 5.12. We have not indicated how the index works. For example, the key-pointer pairs forming the seven rows of that index might be spread among the leaves of a B-tree. However, what is important is that the only keys present are the ages for which there is one or more data point, and the index makes it easy to find the pointer associated with a given key value.

At the right of Fig. 5.12 are seven indexes that provide access to the points themselves. For example, if we follow the pointer associated with age 50 in the root index, we get to a smaller index where salary is the key, and the four key values in the index are the four salaries associated with points that have age 50. Again, we have not indicated in the figure how the index is implemented, just the key-pointer associations it makes. When we follow the pointers associated with each of these values (75, 100, 120, and 275), we get to the record for the individual represented. For instance, following the pointer associated with 100, we find the person whose age is 50 and whose salary is $100K. □

In a multiple-key index, some of the second or higher rank indexes may be very small. For example, Fig 5.12 has four second-rank indexes with but a single pair. Thus, it may be appropriate to implement these indexes as simple tables that are packed several to a block, in the manner suggested by the box "Handling Tiny Buckets" in Section 5.2.5.

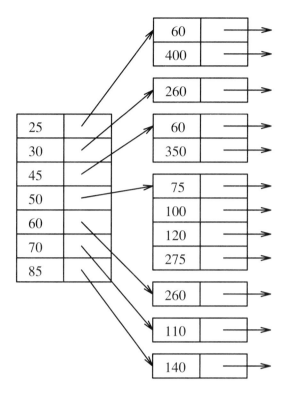

Figure 5.12: Multilevel indexes for age/salary data

5.3.2 Performance of Multiple-Key Indexes

Let us consider how a multiple key index performs on various kinds of multidimensional queries. We shall concentrate on the case of two attributes, although the generalization to more than two attributes is unsurprising.

Partial-Match Queries

If the first attribute is specified, then the access is quite efficient. e use the root index to find the one subindex that leads to the points we want. For example, if the root is a B-tree index, then we shall do two or three disk I/O's to get to the proper subindex, and then use whatever I/O's are needed to access all of that index and the points of the data file itself. On the other hand, if the first attribute does not have a specified value, then we must search every subindex, a potentially time-consuming process.

Range Queries

The multiple-key index works quite well for a range query, provided the individual indexes themselves support range queries on their attribute (e.g., if they are

B-tree indexes). To answer a range query, we use the root index and the range of the first attribute to find all of the subindexes that might contain answer points. We then search each of these subindexes, using the range specified for the second attribute.

Example 5.14 : Suppose we have the multiple-key index of Fig. 5.12 and we are asked the range query $35 \leq$ age ≤ 55 and $100 \leq$ salary ≤ 200. When we examine the root index, we find that the keys 45 and 50 are in the range for age. We follow the associated pointers to two subindexes on salary. The index for age 45 has no salary in the range 100 to 200, while the index for age 50 has two such salaries: 100 and 120. Thus, the only two points in the range are $(50, 100)$ and $(50, 120)$. $\square$

Nearest-Neighbor Queries

The answering of a nearest-neighbor query with a multiple-key index uses the same strategy as for almost all the data structures of this chapter. To find the nearest neighbor of point (x_0, y_0), we find a distance d such that we can expect to find several points within distance d of (x_0, y_0). We then ask the range query $x_0 - d \leq x \leq x_0 + d$ and $y_0 - d \leq y \leq y_0 + d$. If there turn out to be no points in this range, or if there is a point, but distance from (x_0, y_0) of the closest point is greater than d (and therefore there could be a closer point outside the range, as was discussed in Section 5.1.5), then we must increase the range and search again. However, we can order the search so the closest places are searched first.

5.3.3 kd-Trees

A kd-tree (k-dimensional search tree) is a main-memory data structure generalizing the binary search tree to multidimensional data. We shall present the idea and then discuss how the idea has been adapted to the block model of storage. A kd-tree is a binary tree in which interior nodes have an associated attribute a and a value V that splits the data points into two parts: those with a-value less than V and those with a-value equal to or greater than V. The attributes at different levels of the tree are different, with levels rotating among the attributes of all dimensions.

   In the classical kd-tree, the data points are placed at the nodes, just as in a binary search tree. However, we shall make two modifications in our initial presentation of the idea to take some limited advantage of the block model of storage.

   1. Interior nodes will have only an attribute, a dividing value for that attribute, and pointers to left and right children.

   2. Leaves will be blocks, with space for as many records as a block can hold.

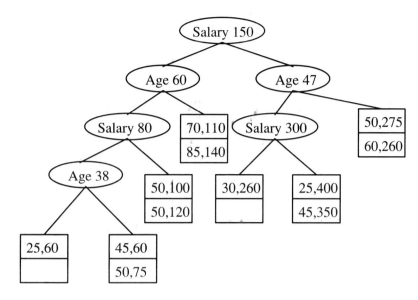

Figure 5.13: A kd-tree

Example 5.15: In Fig. 5.13 is a kd-tree for the twelve points of our running gold-jewelry example. We use blocks that hold only two records for simplicity; these blocks and their contents are shown as square leaves. The interior nodes are ovals with an attribute — either age or salary — and a value. For instance, the root splits by salary, with all records in the left subtree having a salary less than \$150K, and all records in the right subtree having a salary at least \$150K.

At the second level, the split is by age. The left child of the root splits at age 60, so everything in its left subtree will have age less than 60 and salary less than \$150K. Its right subtree will have age at least 60 and salary less than \$150K. Figure 5.14 suggests how the various interior nodes split the space of points into leaf blocks. For example, the horizontal line at salary = 150 represents the split at the root. The space below that line is split vertically at age 60, while the space above is split at age 47, corresponding to the decision at the right child of the root. □

5.3.4 Operations on kd-Trees

A lookup of a tuple given values for all dimensions proceeds as in a binary search tree. We make a decision which way to go at each interior node and are directed to a single leaf, whose block we search.

To perform an insertion, we proceed as for a lookup. We are eventually directed to a leaf, and if its block has room we put the new data point there. If there is no room, we split the block into two, and we divide its contents according to whatever attribute is appropriate at the level of the leaf being

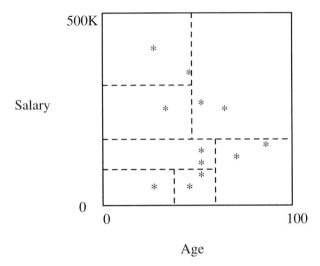

Figure 5.14: The partitions implied by the tree of Fig. 5.13

split. We create a new interior node whose children are the two new blocks, and we install at that interior node a splitting value that is appropriate for the split we have just made.[1]

Example 5.16: Suppose someone 35 years old with a salary of $500K buys gold jewelry. Starting at the root, we know the salary is at least $150K, so we go to the right. There, we compare the age 35 with the age 47 at the node, which directs us to the left. At the third level, we compare salaries again, and our salary is greater than the splitting value, $300K. We are thus directed to a leaf containing the points (25, 400) and (45, 350), along with the new point (35, 500).

There isn't room for three records in this block, so we must split it. The fourth level splits on age, so we have to pick some age that divides the records as evenly as possible. The median value, 35, is a good choice, so we replace the leaf by an interior node that splits on age = 35. To the left of this interior node is a leaf block with only the record (25, 400), while to the right is a leaf block with the other two records, as shown in Fig. 5.15. □

The more complex queries discussed in this chapter are also supported by a *kd*-tree. Here are the key ideas and synopses of the algorithms:

Partial-Match Queries

If we are given values for some of the attributes, then we can go one way when we are at a level belonging to an attribute whose value we know. When we don't

---

[1]One problem that might arise is a situation where there are so many points with the same value in a given dimension that the bucket has only one value in that dimension and cannot be split. We can try splitting along another dimension, or we can use an overflow block.

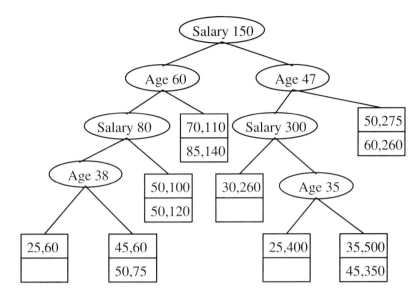

Figure 5.15: Tree after insertion of $(35, 500)$

know the value of the attribute at a node, we must explore both of its children. For example, if we ask for all points with age = 50 in the tree of Fig. 5.13, we must look at both children of the root, since the root splits on salary. However, at the left child of the root, we need go only to the left, and at the right child of the root we need only explore its right subtree. Suppose, for instance, that the tree were perfectly balanced, had a large number of levels, and had two dimensions, of which one was specified in the search. Then we would have to explore both ways at every other level, ultimately reaching about the square root of the total number of leaves.

Range Queries

Sometimes, a range will allow us to move to only one child of a node, but if the range straddles the splitting value at the node then we must explore both children. For example, given the range of ages 35 to 55 and the range of salaries from $100K to $200K, we would explore the tree of Fig. 5.13 as follows. The salary range straddles the $150K at the root, so we must explore both children. At the left child, the range is entirely to the left, so we move to the node with salary $80K. Now, the range is entirely to the right, so we reach the leaf with records $(50, 100)$ and $(50, 120)$, both of which meet the range query. Returning to the right child of the root, the splitting value age = 47 tells us to look at both subtrees. At the node with salary $300K, we can go only to the left, finding the point $(30, 260)$, which is actually outside the range. At the right child of the node for age = 47, we find two other points, both of which are outside the range.

Nothing Lasts Forever

Each of the data structures discussed in this chapter allow insertions and deletions that make local decisions about how to reorganize the structure. After many database updates, the effects of these local decisions may make the structure unbalanced in some way. For instance, a grid file may have too many empty buckets, or a kd-tree may be greatly unbalanced.

It is quite usual for any database to be restructured after a while. By reloading the database, we have the opportunity to create index structures that, at least for the moment, as as balanced and efficient as is possible for that type of index. The cost of such restructuring can be amortized over the large number of updates that led to the imbalance, so the cost per update is small. However, we do need to be able to "take the database down"; i.e., make it unavailable for the time it is being reloaded. That situation may or may not be a problem, depending on the application. For instance, many databases are taken down overnight, when no one is accessing them.

Nearest-Neighbor Queries

Use the same approach as was discussed in Section 5.3.2. Treat the problem as a range query with the appropriate range and repeat with a larger range if necessary.

5.3.5 Adapting kd-Trees to Secondary Storage

Suppose we store a file in a kd-tree with n leaves. Then the average length of a path from the root to a leaf will be about $\log_2 n$, as for any binary tree. If we store each node in a block, then as we traverse a path we must do one disk I/O per node. For example, if $n = 1000$, then we shall need about 10 disk I/O's, much more than the 2 or 3 disk I/O's that would be typical for a B-tree, even on a much larger file. In addition, since interior nodes of a kd-tree have relatively little information, most of the block would be wasted space.

We cannot solve the twin problems of long paths and unused space completely. However, here are two approaches that will make some improvement in performance.

Multiway Branches at Interior Nodes

Interior nodes of a kd-tree could look more like B-tree nodes, with many key-pointer pairs. If we had n keys at a node, we could split values of an attribute a into $n + 1$ ranges. If there were $n + 1$ pointers, we could follow the appropriate one to a subtree that contained only points with attribute a in that range.

Problems enter when we try to reorganize nodes, in order to keep distribution and balance as we do for a B-tree. For example, suppose we have a node that splits on age, and we need to merge two of its children, each of which splits on salary. We cannot simply make one node with all the salary ranges of the two children, because these ranges will typically overlap. Notice how much easier it would be if (as in a B-tree) the two children both further refined the range of ages.

Group Interior Nodes Into Blocks

We may, instead, retain the idea that tree nodes have only two children. We could pack many interior nodes into a single block. In order to minimize the number of blocks that we must read from disk while traveling down one path, we are best off including in one block a node and all its descendants for some number of levels. That way, once we retrieve the block with this node, we are sure to use some additional nodes on the same block, saving disk I/O's. For instance, suppose we can pack three interior nodes into one block. Then in the tree of Fig. 5.13, we would pack the root and its two children into one block. We could then pack the node for salary = 80 and its left child into another block, and we are left with the node salary = 300, which belongs on a separate block; perhaps it could share a block with the latter two nodes, although sharing requires us to do considerable work when the tree grows or shrinks. Thus, if we wanted to look up the record $(25, 60)$, we would need to traverse only two blocks, even though we travel through four interior nodes.

5.3.6 Quad Trees

In a *quad tree*, each interior node corresponds to a square region in two dimensions, or to a k-dimensional cube in k dimensions. As with the other data structures in this chapter, we shall consider primarily the two-dimensional case. If the number of points in a square is no larger than what will fit in a block, then we can think of this square as a leaf of the tree, and it is represented by the block that holds its points. If there are too many points to fit in one block, then we treat the square as an interior node, with children corresponding to its four quadrants.

Example 5.17: Figure 5.16 shows the gold-jewelry data points organized into regions that correspond to nodes of a quad tree. For ease of calculation, we have restricted the usual space so salary ranges between 0 and \$400K, rather than up to \$500K as in other examples of this chapter. We continue to make the assumption that only two records can fit in a block.

Figure 5.17 shows the tree explicitly. We use the compass designations for the quadrants and for the children of a node (e.g., SW stands for the southwest quadrant — the points to the left and below the center). The order of children is always as indicated at the root. Each interior node indicates the coordinates of the center of its region.

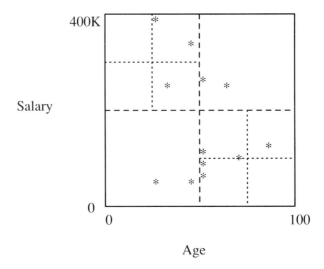

Figure 5.16: Data organized in a quad tree

Since the entire space has 12 points, and only two will fit in one block, we must split the space into quadrants, which we show by the dashed line in Fig. 5.16. Two of the resulting quadrants — the southwest and northeast — have only two points. They can be represented by leaves and need not be split further.

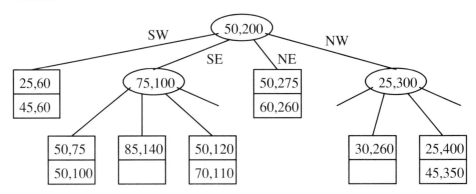

Figure 5.17: A quad tree

The remaining two quadrants each have more than two points. Both are split into subquadrants, as suggested by the dotted lines in Fig. 5.16. Each of the resulting quadrants has two or fewer points, so no more splitting is necessary. □

Since interior nodes of a quad tree in k dimensions have 2^k children, there is a range of k where nodes fit conveniently into blocks. For instance, if 128, or

2^7, pointers can fit in a block, then $k = 7$ is a convenient number of dimensions. However, for the 2-dimensional case, the situation is not much better than for *kd*-trees; an interior node has four children. Moreover, while we can choose the splitting point for a *kd*-tree node, we are constrained to pick the center of a quad-tree region, which may or may not divide the points in that region evenly. Especially when the number of dimensions is large, we expect to find many null pointers (corresponding to empty quadrants) in interior nodes. Of course we can be somewhat clever about how high-dimension nodes are represented, and keep only the non-null pointers and a designation of which quadrant the pointer represents, thus saving considerable space.

We shall not go into detail regarding the standard operations that we discussed in Section 5.3.4 for *kd*-trees. The algorithms for quad trees resemble those for *kd*-trees.

5.3.7 R-Trees

An *R-tree* (region tree) is a data structure that captures some of the spirit of a B-tree for multidimensional data. Recall that a B-tree node has a set of keys that divide a line into segments. Points along that line belong to only one segment, as suggested by Fig. 5.18. The B-tree thus makes it easy for us to find points; if we think the point is somewhere along the line represented by a B-tree node, we can determine a unique child of that node where the point could be found.

Figure 5.18: A B-tree node divides keys along a line into disjoint segments

An R-tree, on the other hand, represents data that consists of 2-dimensional, or higher-dimensional regions, which we call *data regions*. An interior node of an R-tree corresponds to some *interior region*, or just "region," which is not normally a data region. In principle, the region can be of any shape, although in practice it is usually a rectangle or other simple shape. The R-tree node has, in place of keys, subregions that represent the contents of its children. Figure 5.19 suggests a node of an R-tree that is associated with the large solid rectangle. The dotted rectangles represent the subregions associated with four of its children. Notice that the subregions do not cover the entire region, which is satisfactory as long as all the data regions that lie within the large region are wholly contained within one of the small regions. Further, the subregions are allowed to overlap, although it is desirable to keep the overlap small.

5.3.8 Operations on R-trees

A typical query for which an R-tree is useful is a "where-am-I" query, which specifies a point P and asks for the data region or regions in which the point lies.

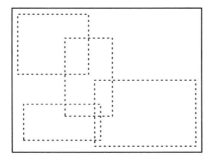

Figure 5.19: The region of an R-tree node and subregions of its children

We start at the root, with which the entire region is associated. We examine the subregions at the root and determine which children of the root correspond to interior regions that contain point P. Note that there may be zero, one, or several such regions.

If there are zero regions, then we are done; P is not in any data region. If there is at least one interior region that contains P, then we must recursively search for P at the child corresponding to *each* such region. When we reach one or more leaves, we shall find the actual data regions, along with either the complete record for each data region or a pointer to that record.

When we insert a new region R into an R-tree, we start at the root and try to find a subregion into which R fits. If there is more than one such region, then we pick one, go to its corresponding child, and repeat the process there. If there is no subregion that contains R, then we have to expand one of the subregions. Which one to pick may be a difficult decision. Intuitively, we want to expand regions as little as possible, so we might ask which of the children's subregions would have their area increased as little as possible, change the boundary of that region to include R, and recursively insert R at the corresponding child.

Eventually, we reach a leaf, where we insert the region R. However, if there is no room for R at that leaf, then we must split the leaf. How we split the leaf is subject to some choice. We generally want the two subregions to be as small as possible, yet they must, between them, cover all the data regions of the original leaf. Having split the leaf, we replace the region and pointer for the original leaf at the node above by a pair of regions and pointers corresponding to the two new leaves. If there is room at the parent, we are done. Otherwise, as in a B-tree, we recursively split nodes going up the tree.

Example 5.18 : Let us consider the addition of a new region to the map of Fig. 5.1. Suppose that leaves have room for six regions. Further suppose that the six regions of Fig. 5.1 are together on one leaf, whose region is represented by the outer (solid) rectangle in Fig. 5.20.

Now, suppose the local cellular phone company adds a POP (point of presence, or antenna) at the position shown in Fig. 5.20. Since the seven data regions do not fit on one leaf, we shall split the leaf, with four in one leaf and

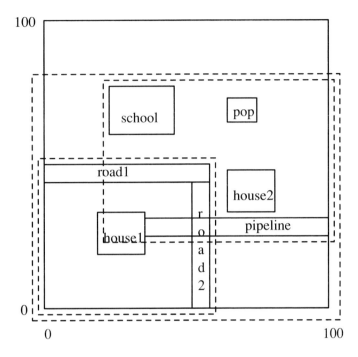

Figure 5.20: Splitting the set of objects

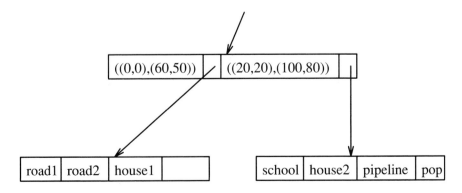

Figure 5.21: An R-tree

three in the other. Our options are many; we have picked in Fig. 5.20 the division (indicated by the inner, dashed rectangles) that minimizes the overlap, while splitting the leaves as evenly as possible.

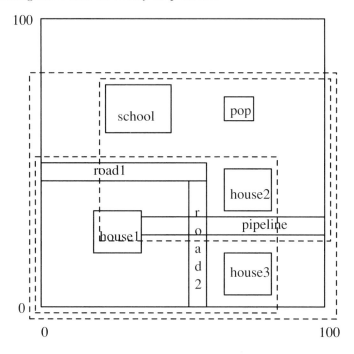

Figure 5.22: Extending a region to accommodate new data

We show in Fig. 5.21 how the two new leaves fit into the R-tree. The parent of these nodes has pointers to both leaves, and associated with the pointers are the lower-left and upper-right corners of the rectangular regions covered by each leaf. □

Example 5.19: Suppose we inserted another house below house2, with lower-left coordinates $(70, 5)$ and upper-right coordinates $(80, 15)$. Since this house is not wholly contained within either of the leaves' regions, we must choose which region to expand. If we expand the lower subregion, corresponding to the first leaf in Fig. 5.21, then we add 1000 square units to the region, since we extend it 20 units to the right. If we extend the other subregion by lowering its bottom by 15 units, then we add 1200 square units. We prefer the first, and the new regions are changed in Fig. 5.22. We also must change the description of the region in the top node of Fig. 5.21 from $((0, 0), (60, 50))$ to $((0, 0), (80, 50))$. □

5.3.9   Exercises for Section 5.3

Exercise 5.3.1: Show a multilevel index for the data of Fig. 5.10 if the indexes are on:

a) Speed, then ram.

b) Ram then hard-disk.

c) Speed, then ram, then hard-disk.

Exercise 5.3.2: Place the data of Fig. 5.10 in a kd-tree. Assume two records can fit in one block. At each level, pick a separating value that divides the data as evenly as possible. For an order of the splitting attributes choose:

a) Speed, then ram, alternating.

b) Speed, then ram, then hard-disk, alternating.

c) Whatever attribute produces the most even split at each node.

Exercise 5.3.3: Suppose we have a relation $R(x, y, z)$, where the pair of attributes x and y together form the key. Attribute x ranges from 1 to 100, and y ranges from 1 to 1000. For each x there are records with 100 different values of y, and for each y there are records with 10 different values of x. Note that there are thus 10,000 records in R. We wish to use a multiple-key index that will help us to answer queries of the form

```
SELECT z
FROM R
WHERE x = C AND y = D;
```

where C and D are constants. Assume that blocks can hold ten key-pointer pairs, and we wish to create dense indexes at each level, perhaps with sparse higher-level indexes above them, so that each index starts from a single block. Also assume that initially all index and data blocks are on disk.

* a) How many disk I/O's are necessary to answer a query of the above form if the first index is on x?

b) How many disk I/O's are necessary to answer a query of the above form if the first index is on y?

! c) Suppose you were allowed to buffer 11 blocks in memory at all times. Which blocks would you choose, and would you make x or y the first index, if you wanted to minimize the number of additional disk I/O's needed?

Exercise 5.3.4: For the structure of Exercise 5.3.3(a), how many disk I/O's are required to answer the range query in which $20 \le x \le 35$ and $200 \le y \le 350$. Assume data is distributed uniformly; i.e., the expected number of points will be found within any given range.

Exercise 5.3.5: In the tree of Fig. 5.13, what new points would be directed to:

* a) The block with point $(30, 260)$?

  b) The block with points $(50, 100)$ and $(50, 120)$?

Exercise 5.3.6: Show a possible evolution of the tree of Fig. 5.15 if we insert the points $(20, 110)$ and then $(40, 400)$.

! **Exercise 5.3.7:** We mentioned that if a kd-tree were perfectly balanced, and we execute a partial-match query in which one of two attributes has a value specified, then we wind up looking at about $\sqrt{n}$ out of the n leaves.

  a) Explain why.

  b) If the tree split alternately in d dimensions, and we specified values for m of those dimensions, what fraction of the leaves would we expect to have to search?

  c) How does the performance of (b) compare with a partitioned hash table?

Exercise 5.3.8: Place the data of Fig. 5.10 in a quad tree with dimensions speed and ram. Assume the range for speed is 100 to 500, and for ram it is 0 to 256.

Exercise 5.3.9: Repeat Exercise 5.3.8 with the addition of a third dimension, hard-disk, that ranges from 0 to 32.

*! **Exercise 5.3.10:** If we are allowed to put the central point in a quadrant of a quad tree wherever we want, can we always divide a quadrant into subquadrants with an equal number of points (or as equal as possible, if the number of points in the quadrant is not divisible by 4)? Justify your answer.

! **Exercise 5.3.11:** Suppose we have a database of 1,000,000 regions, which may overlap. Nodes (blocks) of an R-tree can hold 100 regions and pointers. The region represented by any node has 100 subregions, and the overlap among these regions is such that the total area of the 100 subregions is 150% of the area of the region. If we perform a "where-am-I" query for a given point, how many blocks do we expect to retrieve?

! **Exercise 5.3.12:** In the R-tree represented by Fig. 5.22, a new region might go into the subregion containing the school or the subregion containing house3. Describe the rectangular regions for which we would prefer to place the new region in the subregion with the school (i.e., that choice minimizes the increase in the subregion size).

5.4 Bitmap Indexes

Let us now turn to a type of index that is rather different from the kinds seen so far. We begin by imagining that records of a file have permanent numbers, $1, 2, \ldots, n$. Moreover, there is some data structure for the file that lets us find the ith record easily for any i.

A *bitmap index* for a field F is a collection of bit-vectors of length n, one for each possible value that may appear in the field F. The vector for value v has 1 in position i if the ith record has v in field F, and it has 0 there if not.

Example 5.20: Suppose a file consists of records with two fields, F and G, of type integer and string, respectively. The current file has six records, numbered 1 through 6, with the following values in order: $(30, \texttt{foo})$, $(30, \texttt{bar})$, $(40, \texttt{baz})$, $(50, \texttt{foo})$, $(40, \texttt{bar})$, $(30, \texttt{baz})$.

A bitmap index for the first field, F, would have three bit-vectors, each of length 6. The first, for value 30, is 110001, because the first, second, and sixth records have $F = 30$. The other two, for 40 and 50, respectively, are 001010 and 000100.

A bitmap index for G would also have three bit-vectors, because there are three different strings appearing there. The three bit-vectors are:

Value	Vector
foo	100100
bar	010010
baz	001001

In each case, the 1's indicate in which records the corresponding string appears. □

5.4.1 Motivation for Bitmap Indexes

It might at first appear that bitmap indexes require much too much space, especially when there are many different values for a field, since the total number of bits is the product of the number of records and the number of values. For example, if the field is a key, and there are n records, then n^2 bits are used among all the bit-vectors for that field. However, compression can be used to make the number of bits closer to n, independent of the number of different values, as we shall see in Section 5.4.2.

You might also suspect that there are problems managing the bitmap indexes. For example, they depend on the number of a record remaining the same throughout time. How do we find the ith record as the file adds and deletes records? Similarly, values for a field may appear or disappear. How do we find the bitmap for a value efficiently? These and related questions are discussed in Section 5.4.4.

The compensating advantage of bitmap indexes is that they allow us to answer partial-match queries very efficiently in many situations. In a sense they offer the advantages of buckets that we discussed in Example 4.16, where we found the Movie tuples with specified values in several attributes without first retrieving all the records that matched in each of the attributes. An example will illustrate the point.

Example 5.21 : Recall Example 4.16, where we queried the relation

        Movie(title, year, length, studioName)

with the query

        SELECT title
        FROM Movie
        WHERE studioName = 'Disney' AND
              year = 1995;

Suppose there are bitmap indexes on both attributes studioName and year. Then we can intersect the vectors for year = 1995 and studioName = 'Disney'; that is, we take the bitwise AND of these vectors, which will give us a vector with a 1 in position i if and only if the ith Movie tuple is for a movie made by Disney in 1995.

If we can retrieve tuples of Movie given their numbers, then we need to read only those blocks containing one or more of these tuples, just as we did in Example 4.16. To intersect the bit vectors, we must read them into memory, which requires a disk I/O for each block occupied by one of the two vectors. As mentioned, we shall later address both matters: accessing records given their numbers in Section 5.4.4 and making sure the bit-vectors do not occupy too much space in Section 5.4.2. □

Bitmap indexes can also help answer range queries. We shall consider an example next that both illustrates their use for range queries and shows in detail with short bit-vectors how the bitwise AND and OR of bit-vectors can be used to discover the answer to a query without looking at any records but the ones we want.

Example 5.22 : Consider the gold jewelry data first introduced in Example 5.7. Suppose that the twelve points of that example are records numbered from 1 to 12 as follows:

1:	$(25, 60)$	2:	$(45, 60)$	3:	$(50, 75)$	4:	$(50, 100)$
5:	$(50, 120)$	6:	$(70, 110)$	7:	$(85, 140)$	8:	$(30, 260)$
9:	$(25, 400)$	10:	$(45, 350)$	11:	$(50, 275)$	12:	$(60, 260)$

For the first component, age, there are seven different values, so the bitmap index for age consists of the following seven vectors:

25:	100000001000	30:	000000010000	45:	010000000100
50:	001110000010	60:	000000000001	70:	000001000000
85:	000000100000				

For the salary component, there are ten different values, so the salary bitmap index has the following ten bit-vectors:

60:	110000000000	75:	001000000000	100:	000100000000
110:	000001000000	120:	000010000000	140:	000000100000
260:	000000010001	275:	000000000010	350:	000000000100
400:	000000001000				

Suppose we want to find the jewelry buyers with an age in the range 45-55 and a salary in the range 100-200. We first find the bit-vectors for the age values in this range; in this example there are only two: 010000000100 and 001110000010, for 45 and 50, respectively. If we take their bitwise OR, we have a new bit-vector with 1 in position i if and only if the ith record has an age in the desired range. This bit-vector is 011110000110.

Next, we find the bit-vectors for the salaries between 100 and 200 thousand. There are four, corresponding to salaries 100, 110, 120, and 140; their bitwise OR is 000111100000.

The last step is to take the bitwise AND of the two bit-vectors we calculated by OR. That is:

$$011110000110 \text{ AND } 000111100000 = 000110000000$$

We thus find that only the fourth and fifth records, which are $(50, 100)$ and $(50, 120)$, are in the desired range. $\square$

5.4.2 Compressed Bitmaps

Suppose we have a bitmap index on field F of a file with n records, and there are m different values for field F that appear in the file. Then the number of bits in all the bit-vectors for this index is mn. If, say, blocks are 4096 bytes long, then we can fit 32,768 bits in one block, so the number of blocks needed is $mn/32768$. That number can be small compared to the number of blocks needed to hold the file itself, but the larger m is, the more space the bitmap index takes.

But if m is large, then 1's in a bit-vector will be very rare; precisely, the probability that any bit is 1 is $1/m$. If 1's are rare, then we have an opportunity to encode bit-vectors so that they take much fewer than n bits on the average. A common approach is called *run-length encoding*, where we represent a *run*, that is, a sequence of i 0's followed by a 1, by some suitable binary encoding of the integer i. We concatenate the codes for each run together, and that sequence of bits is the encoding of the entire bit-vector.

We might imagine that we could just represent integer i by expressing i as a binary number. However, that simple a scheme will not do, because it is not possible to break a sequence of codes apart to determine uniquely the lengths of the runs involved (see the box on "Binary Numbers Won't Serve as a Run-Length Encoding"). Thus, the encoding of integers i that represent a run length must be more complex than a simple binary representation.

Binary Numbers Won't Serve as a Run-Length Encoding

Suppose we represented a run of i 0's followed by a 1 with the integer i in binary. Then the bit-vector 000101 consists of two runs, of lengths 3 and 1, respectively. The binary representations of these integers are 11 and 1, so the run-length encoding of 000101 is 111. However, a similar calculation shows that the bit-vector 010001 is also encoded by 111; bit-vector 010101 is a third vector encoded by 111. Thus, 111 cannot be decoded uniquely into one bit-vector.

We shall use one of many possible schemes for encoding. There are some better, more complex schemes that can improve on the amount of compression achieved here, by almost a factor of 2, but only when typical runs are very long. In our scheme, we first need to determine how many bits the binary representation of i has. This number j, which is approximately $\log_2 i$, is represented in "unary," by $j - 1$ 1's and a single 0. Then, we can follow with i in binary.[2]

Example 5.23: If $i = 13$, then $j = 4$; that is, we need 4 bits in the binary representation of i. Thus, the encoding for i begins with 1110. We follow with i in binary, or 1101. Thus, the encoding for 13 is 11101101.

The encoding for $i = 1$ is 01, and the encoding for $i = 0$ is 00. In each case, $j = 1$, so we begin with a single 0 and follow that 0 with the one bit that represents i.   □

If we concatenate a sequence of integer codes, we can always recover the sequence of run lengths and therefore recover the original bit-vector. Suppose we have scanned some of the encoded bits, and we are now at the beginning of the sequence of bits that encodes some integer i. We scan forward to the first 0, to determine the value of j. That is, j equals the number of bits we must scan until we get to the first 0 (including that 0 in the count of bits). Once we know j, we look at the next j bits; i is the integer represented there in binary. Moreover, once we have scanned the bits representing i, we know where the next code for an integer begins, so we can repeat the process.

Example 5.24: Let us decode the sequence 11101101001011. Starting at the beginning, we find the first 0 at the 4th bit, so $j = 4$. The next 4 bits are 1101, so we determine that the first integer is 13. We are now left with 001011 to decode.

---

[2]Actually, except for the case that $j = 1$ (i.e., $i = 0$ or $i = 1$), we can be sure that the binary representation of i begins with 1. Thus, we can save about one bit per number if we omit this 1 and use only the remaining $j - 1$ bits.

Since the first bit is 0, we know the next bit represents the next integer by itself; this integer is 0. Thus, we have decoded the sequence 13, 0, and we must decode the remaining sequence 1011.

We find the first 0 in the second position, whereupon we conclude that the final two bits represent the last integer, 3. Our entire sequence of run-lengths is thus 13, 0, 3. From these numbers, we can reconstruct the actual bit-vector, 0000000000000110001. □

Technically, every bit-vector so decoded will end in a 1, and any trailing 0's will not be recovered. Since we presumably know the number of records in the file, the additional 0's can be added. However, since 0 in a bit-vector indicates the corresponding record is not in the described set, we don't even have to know the total number of records, and can ignore the trailing 0's.

Example 5.25: Let us convert some of the bit-vectors from Example 5.23 to our run-length code. The vectors for the first three ages, 25, 30, and 45, are 100000001000, 000000010000, and 010000000100, respectively. The first of these has the run-length sequence $(0, 7)$. The code for 0 is 00, and the code for 7 is 110111. Thus, the bit-vector for age 25 becomes 00110111.

Similarly, the bit-vector for age 30 has only one run, with seven 0's. Thus, its code is 110111. The bit-vector for age 45 has two runs, $(1, 7)$. Since 1 has the code 01, and we determined that 7 has the code 110111, the code for the third bit-vector is 01110111. □

The compression in Example 5.25 is not great. However, we cannot see the true benefits when n, the number of records, is small. To appreciate the value of the encoding, suppose that $m = n$, i.e., each value for the field on which the bitmap index is constructed, has a unique value. Notice that the code for a run of length i has about $2 \log_2 i$ bits. If each bit-vector has a single 1, then it has a single run, and the length of that run cannot be longer than n. Thus, $2 \log_2 n$ bits is an upper bound on the length of a bit-vector's code in this case.

Since there are n bit-vectors in the index (because $m = n$), the total number of bits to represent the index is at most $2n \log_2 n$. Notice that without the encoding, n^2 bits would be required. As long as $n > 4$, we have $2n \log_2 n < n^2$, and as n grows, $2n \log_2 n$ becomes arbitrarily smaller than n^2.

5.4.3 Operating on Run-Length-Encoded Bit-Vectors

When we need to perform bitwise AND or OR on encoded bit-vectors, we have little choice but to decode them and operate on the original bit-vectors. However, we do not have to do the decoding all at once. The compression scheme we have described lets us decode one run at a time, and we can thus determine where the next 1 is in each operand bit-vector. If we are taking the OR, we can produce a 1 at that position of the output, and if we are taking the AND we produce a 1 if and only if both operands have their next 1 at the same position. The algorithms involved are complex, but an example may make the idea adequately clear.

Example 5.26 : Consider the encoded bit-vectors we obtained in Example 5.25 for ages 25 and 30: 00110111 and 110111, respectively. We can decode their first runs easily; we find they are 0 and 7, respectively. That is, the first 1 of the bit-vector for 25 occurs in position 1, while the first 1 in the bit-vector for 30 occurs at position 8. We therefore generate 1 in position 1.

Next, we must decode the next run for age 25, since that bit-vector may produce another 1 before age 30's bit-vector produces a 1 at position 8. However, the next run for age 25 is 7, which says that this bit-vector next produces a 1 at position 9. We therefore generate six 0's and the 1 at position 8 that comes from the bit-vector for age 30. Now, that bit-vector contributes no more 1's to the output. The 1 at position 9 from age 25's bit-vector is produced, and that bit-vector too produces no subsequent 1's.

We conclude that the OR of these bit-vectors is 100000011. Referring to the original bit-vectors of length 12, we see that is almost right; there are three trailing 0's omitted. If we know that the number of records in the file is 12, we can append those 0's. However, it doesn't matter whether or not we append the 0's, since only a 1 can cause a record to be retrieved. In this example, we shall not retrieve any of records 10 through 12 anyway. □

5.4.4 Managing Bitmap Indexes

We have described operations on bitmap indexes without addressing three important issues:

1. When we want to find the bit-vector for a given value, or the bit-vectors corresponding to values in a given range, how do we find these efficiently?

2. When we have selected a set of records that answer our query, how do we retrieve those records efficiently?

3. When the data file changes by insertion or deletion of records, how do we adjust the bitmap index on a given field?

Finding Bit-Vectors

The first question can be answered based on techniques we have already learned. Think of each bit-vector as a record whose key is the value corresponding to this bit-vector (although the value itself does not appear in this "record"). Then any secondary index technique will take us efficiently from values to their bit-vectors. For example, we could use a B-tree, whose leaves contain key-pointer pairs; the pointer leads to the bit-vector for the key value. The B-tree is often a good choice, because it supports range queries easily, but hash tables or indexed-sequential files are other options.

We also need to store the bit-vectors somewhere. It is best to think of them as variable-length records, since they will generally grow as more records are added to the data file. If the bit-vectors, perhaps in compressed form, are typically shorter than blocks, then we can consider packing several to a block and moving them around as needed. If bit-vectors are typically longer than a block, we should consider using a chain of blocks to hold each one. The techniques of Section 3.4 are useful.

Finding Records

Now let us consider the second question: once we have determined that we need record k of the data file, how do we find it. Again, techniques we have already seen may be adapted. Think of the kth record as having search-key value k (although this key does not actually appear in the record). We may then create a secondary index on the data file, whose search key is the number of the record.

If there is no reason to organize the file any other way, we can even use the record number as the search key for a primary index, as discussed in Section 4.1. Then, the file organization is particularly simple, since record numbers never change (even as records are deleted), and we only have to add new records to the end of the data file. It is thus possible to pack blocks of the data file completely full, instead of leaving extra space for insertions into the middle of the file as we found necessary for the general case of an indexed-sequential file in Section 4.1.6.

Handling Modifications to the Data File

There are two aspects to the problem of reflecting data-file modifications in a bitmap index.

1. Record numbers must remain fixed once assigned.

2. Changes to the data file require the bitmap index to change as well.

The consequence of point (1) is that when we delete record i, it is easiest to "retire" its number. Its space is replaced by a "tombstone" in the data file. The bitmap index must also be changed, since the bit-vector that had a 1 in position i must have that 1 changed to 0. Note that we can find the appropriate bit-vector, since we know what value record i had before deletion.

Next consider insertion of a new record. We keep track of the next available record number and assign it to the new record. Then, for each bitmap index, we must determine the value the new record has in the corresponding field and modify the bit-vector for that value by appending a 1 at the end. Technically, all the other bit-vectors in this index get a new 0 at the end, but if we are using a compression technique such as that of Section 5.4.2, then no change to the compressed values is needed.

As a special case, the new record may have a value for the indexed field that has not been seen before. In that case, we need a new bit-vector for this value, and this bit-vector and its corresponding value need to be inserted into the secondary-index structure that is used to find a bit-vector given its corresponding value.

Last, let us consider a modification to a record i of the data file that changes the value of a field that has a bitmap index, say from value v to value w. We must find the bit-vector for v and change the 1 in position i to 0. If there is a bit-vector for value w, then we change its 0 in position i to 1. If there is not yet a bit-vector for w, then we create it as discussed in the paragraph above for the case when an insertion introduces a new value.

5.4.5   Exercises for Section 5.4

Exercise 5.4.1 : For the data of Fig. 5.10 show the bitmap indexes for the attributes:

* a) Speed,

  b) Ram, and

  c) Hard-disk,

both in (i) uncompressed form, and (ii) compressed form using the scheme of Section 5.4.2.

Exercise 5.4.2 : Using the bitmaps of Example 5.22, find the jewelry buyers with an age in the range 20–40 and a salary in the range 0–100.

Exercise 5.4.3 : Consider a file of 1,000,000 records, with a field F that has m different values.

  a) As a function of m, how many bytes does the bitmap index for F have?

! b) Suppose that the records numbered from 1 to 1,000,000 are given values for the field F in a round-robin fashion, so each value appears every m records. How many bytes would be consumed by a compressed index?

!! **Exercise 5.4.4 :** We suggested in Section 5.4.2 that it was possible to reduce the number of bits taken to encode number i from the $2 \log_2 i$ that we used in that section until it is close to $\log_2 i$. Show how to approach that limit as closely as you like, as long as i is large. *Hint*: We used a unary encoding of the length of the binary encoding that we used for i. Can you encode the length of the code in binary?

Exercise 5.4.5 : Encode, using the scheme of Section 5.4.2, the following bitmaps:

* a) 0110000000100000100.

  b) 10000010000001001101.

   c) 000100000000010000010000.

! **Exercise 5.4.6:** We pointed out that compressed bitmap indexes consume about $2n \log_2 n$ bits for a file of n records. How does this number of bits compare with the number of bits consumed by a B-tree index? Remember that the B-tree index's size depends on the size of keys and pointers, as well as (to a small extent) on the size of blocks. However, make some reasonable estimates of these parameters in your calculations. Why might we prefer a B-tree, even if it takes more space than compressed bitmaps?

5.5 Summary of Chapter 5

✦ *Multidimensional Data*: Many applications, such as geographic databases or sales and inventory data, can be thought of as points in a space of two or more dimensions.

✦ *Queries Needing Multidimensional Indexes*: The sorts of queries that need to be supported on multidimensional data include partial-match (all points with specified values in a subset of the dimensions), range queries (all points within a range in each dimension), nearest-neighbor (closest point to a given point), and where-am-i (region or regions containing a given point).

✦ *Executing Nearest-Neighbor Queries*: Many data structures allow nearest-neighbor queries to be executed by performing a range query around the target point, and expanding the range if there is no point in that range. We must be careful, because finding a point within a rectangular range may not rule out the possibility of a closer point outside that rectangle.

✦ *Grid Files*: The grid file slices the space of points in each of the dimensions. The grid lines can be spaced differently, and there can be different numbers of lines for each dimension. Grid files support range queries, partial-match queries, and nearest-neighbor queries well, as long as data is fairly uniform in distribution.

✦ *Partitioned Hash Tables*: A partitioned hash function constructs some bits of the bucket number from each dimension. They support partial-match queries well, and are not dependent on the data being uniformly distributed.

✦ *Multiple-Key Indexes*: A simple multidimensional structure has a root that is an index on one attribute, leading to a collection of indexes on a second attribute, which can lead to indexes on a third attribute, and so on. They are useful for range and nearest-neighbor queries.

✦ *kd-Trees*: These trees are like binary search trees, but they branch on different attributes at different levels. They support partial-match, range, and nearest-neighbor queries well. Some careful packing of tree nodes into blocks must be done to make the structure suitable for secondary-storage operations.

✦ *Quad Trees*: The quad tree divides a multidimensional cube into quadrants, and recursively divides the quadrants the same way if they have too many points. They support partial-match, range, and nearest-neighbor queries.

✦ *R-Trees*: This form of tree normally represents a collection of regions by grouping them into a hierarchy of larger regions. It helps with where-am-i queries and, if the atomic regions are actually points, will support the other types of queries studied in this chapter, as well.

✦ *Bitmap Indexes*: Multidimensional queries are supported by a form of index that orders the points or records and represents the positions of the records with a given value in an attribute by a bit vector. These indexes support range, nearest-neighbor, and partial-match queries.

✦ *Compressed Bitmaps*: In order to save space, the bitmap indexes, which tend to consist of vectors with very few 1's, are compressed by using a run-length encoding.

5.6   References for Chapter 5

Most of the data structures discussed in this section were the product of research in the 1970's or early 1980's. The *kd*-tree is from [2]. Modifications suitable for secondary storage appeared in [3] and [13]. Partitioned hashing and its use in partial-match retieval is from [12] and [5]. However, the design idea from Exercise 5.2.8 is from [14].

Grid files first appeared in [9]. The quad tree is in [6]. The R-tree is from [8], and two extensions [15] and [1] are well known.

The bitmap index has an interesting history. There was a company called Nucleus, founded by Ted Glaser, that patented the idea and developed a DBMS in which the bitmap index was both the index structure and the data representation. The company failed in the late 1980's, but the idea has recently been incorporated into several major commercial database systems. The first published work on the subject was [10]. [11] is a recent expansion of the idea.

There are a number of surveys of multidimensional storage structures. One of the earliest is [4]. More recent surveys are found in [16] and [7]. The former also includes surveys of several other important database topics.

1. N. Beekmann, H.-P. Kriegel, R. Schneider, and B. Seeger, "The R*-tree: an efficient and robust access method for points and rectangles," *Proc. ACM SIGMOD Intl. Conf. on Management of Data* (1990), pp. 322–331.

2. J. L. Bentley, "Multidimensional binary search trees used for associative searching," *Comm. ACM* **18**:9 (1975), pp. 509–517.

3. J. L. Bentley, "Multidimensional binary search trees in database applications," *IEEE Trans. on Software Engineering* **SE-5**:4 (1979), pp. 333-340.

4. J. L. Bentley and J. H. Friedman, "Data structures for range searching," *Computing Surveys* **13**:3 (1979), pp. 397–409.

5. W. A. Burkhard, "Hashing and trie algorithms for partial match retrieval," *ACM Trans. on Database Systems* **1**:2 (1976), pp. 175–187.

6. R. A. Finkel and J. L. Bentley, "Quad trees, a data structure for retrieval on composite keys," *Acta Informatica* **4**:1 (1974), pp. 1–9.

7. V. Gaede and O. Gunther, "Multidimensional access methods," *Computing Surveys* **30**:2 (1998), pp. 170–231.

8. A. Guttman, "R-trees: a dynamic index structure for spatial searching," *Proc. ACM SIGMOD Intl. Conf. on Management of Data* (1984), pp. 47–57.

9. J. Nievergelt, H. Hinterberger, and K. Sevcik, "The grid file: an adaptable, symmetric, multikey file structure," *ACM Trans. on Database Systems* **9**:1 (1984), pp. 38–71.

10. P. O'Neil, "Model 204 architecture and performance," *Proc. Second Intl. Workshop on High Performance Transaction Systems*, Springer-Verlag, Berlin, 1987.

11. P. O'Neil and D. Quass, "Improved query performance with variant indexes," *Proc. ACM SIGMOD Intl. Conf. on Management of Data* (1997), pp. 38–49.

12. R. L. Rivest, "Partial match retrieval algorithms," *SIAM J. Computing* **5**:1 (1976), pp. 19–50.

13. J. T. Robinson, "The K-D-B-tree: a search structure for large multidimensional dynamic indexes," *Proc. ACM SIGMOD Intl. Conf. on Mamagement of Data* (1981), pp. 10–18.

14. J. B. Rothnie Jr. and T. Lozano, "Attribute based file organization in a paged memory environment, *Comm. ACM* **17**:2 (1974), pp. 63–69.

15. T. K. Sellis, N. Roussopoulos, and C. Faloutsos, "The R+-tree: a dynamic index for multidimensional objects," *Proc. Intl. Conf. on Very Large Databases* (1987), pp. 507–518.

16. C. Zaniolo, S. Ceri, C. Faloutsos, R. T. Snodgrass, V. S. Subrahmanian, and R. Zicari, *Advanced Database Systems*, Morgan-Kaufmann, San Francisco, 1997.

Chapter 6

Query Execution

Previous chapters gave us data structures that help support basic database operations such as finding tuples given a search key. We are now ready to use these structures to support efficient algorithms for answering queries. The broad topic of query processing will be covered in this chapter and Chapter 7. The *query processor* is the group of components of a DBMS that turns user queries and data-modification commands into a sequence of operations on the database and executes those operations. Since SQL lets us express queries at a very high level, the query processor must supply a lot of detail regarding how the query is to be executed. Moreover, a naive execution strategy for a query may lead to an algorithm for executing the query that takes far more time than necessary.

Figure 6.1 suggests the division of topics between Chapters 6 and 7. In this chapter, we concentrate on query execution, that is, the algorithms that manipulate the data of the database. We shall begin with a review of relational algebra. This notation, or something similar, is used by most relational database systems to represent internally the queries that the user expresses in SQL. This algebra involves operations on relations, such as join and union, with which you may already be familiar. However, SQL uses a bag (multiset) model of data, rather than a set model. Also, there are operations in SQL, such as aggregation, grouping, and ordering (sorting), that are not part of the classical relational algebra. Thus, we need to reconsider this algebra in the light of its role as a representation for SQL queries.

One advantage of using relational algebra is that it makes alternative forms of a query easy to explore. The different algebraic expressions for a query are called *logical query plans*. Often, these plans are represented as expression trees, as we shall do in this book.

This chapter catalogs the principal methods for execution of the operations of relational algebra. These methods differ in their basic strategy; scanning, hashing, sorting, and indexing are the major approaches. The methods also differ on their assumption as to the amount of available main memory. Some

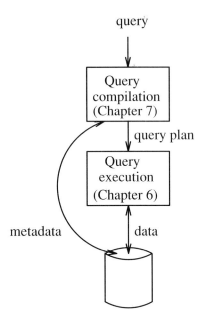

Figure 6.1: The major parts of the query processor

algorithms assume that enough main memory is available to hold at least one of the relations involved in an operation. Others assume that the arguments of the operation are too big to fit in memory, and these algorithms have significantly different costs and structures.

Preview of Query Compilation

Query compilation can be divided into three major steps, as sketched in Fig. 6.2.

a) *Parsing*, in which a *parse tree*, representing the query and its structure, is constructed.

b) *Query rewrite*, in which the parse tree is converted to an initial query plan, which is usually an algebraic representation of the query. This initial plan is then transformed into an equivalent plan that is expected to require less time to execute.

c) *Physical plan generation*, where the abstract query plan from (b), often called a *logical query plan*, is turned into a *physical query plan* by selecting algorithms to implement each of the operators of the logical plan, and by selecting an order of execution for these operators. The physical plan, like the result of parsing and the logical plan, is represented by an expression tree. The physical plan also includes details such as how the queried relations are accessed, and when and if a relation should be sorted.

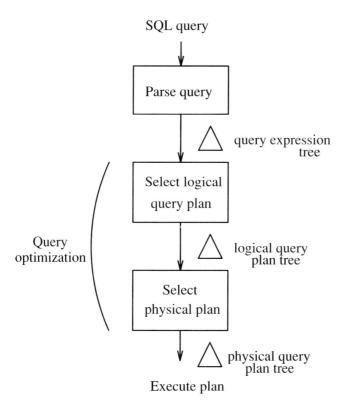

Figure 6.2: Outline of query compilation

Parts (b) and (c) are often called the *query optimizer*, and these are the hard parts of query compilation. Chapter 7 is devoted to query optimization; we shall learn there how to select a "query plan" that takes as little time as possible. To select the best query plan we need to decide:

1. Which of the algebraically equivalent forms of a query leads to the most efficient algorithm for answering the query?

2. For each operation of the selected form, what algorithm should we use to implement that operation?

3. How should the operations pass data from one to the other, e.g., in a pipelined fashion, in main-memory buffers, or via the disk?

Each of these choices depends on the metadata about the database. Typical metadata that is available to the query optimizer includes: the size of each relation; statistics such as the approximate number and frequency of different values for an attribute; the existence of certain indexes; and the layout of data on disk.

6.1   An Algebra for Queries

In order to talk about good algorithms for executing queries, we first need to develop a notation for the elementary actions of which queries are constructed. Many SQL queries are expressed with a few operators that form the classical "relational algebra," and even object-oriented query languages perform essentially the same operations as are found in relational algebra. However, there are also features of SQL and other query languages that are not expressed in the classical relational algebra, so after describing that algebra we shall add operators for SQL features such as group-by, order-by, and select-distinct.

Moreover, relational algebra was originally designed as if relations were sets. Yet relations in SQL are really *bags*, or *multisets*; that is, the same tuple can appear more than once in an SQL relation. Thus, we shall introduce relational algebra as an algebra on bags. The relational algebra operators are:

- *Union, intersection, and difference.* On sets, these are the usual set operators. On bags, there are some differences that we shall discuss in Section 6.1.1. These operators correspond to the SQL operators UNION, INTERSECT, and EXCEPT.

- *Selection.* This operator produces a new relation from an old one by selecting some of the rows of the old relation, based on some condition or predicate. It corresponds roughly to the WHERE clause of an SQL query.

- *Projection.* This operator produces a new relation from an old one by choosing some of the columns, like the SELECT clause of an SQL query. We shall extend this operator beyond classical relational algebra to allow renaming of attributes and construction of attributes by calculation with constants and attributes of the old relation, just as the SQL SELECT clause does.

- *Product.* This operator is the set-theoretic Cartesian product (or cross-product), which constructs tuples by pairing the tuples of two relations in all possible ways. It corresponds in SQL to the list of relations in a FROM clause, whose product forms the relation to which the condition of the WHERE clause and the projection of the SELECT clause are applied.

- *Join.* There are various types of join operators, which correspond to the operators such as JOIN, NATURAL JOIN, and OUTER JOIN in the SQL2 standard. We shall discuss these in Section 6.1.5.

In addition, we shall extend the relational algebra with the following operators, introduced for the purpose of discussing the optimization of the full range of possible SQL queries:

- *Duplicate elimination.* This operator turns a bag into a set, like the keyword DISTINCT in an SQL SELECT clause.

- *Grouping.* This operator is designed to mimic the effect of an SQL GROUP BY, as well as the aggregation operators (sum, average, and so on) that may appear in SQL SELECT clauses.

- *Sorting.* This operator represents the effect of the SQL ORDER BY clause. It is also used as part of certain sort-based algorithms for other operators such as join.

6.1.1 Union, Intersection, and Difference

If relations were sets, then the operators ∪, ∩, and − on relations would be the familiar operations. However, there are two major differences between SQL relations and sets:

a) Relations are bags.

b) Relations have schemas, i.e., sets of attributes that name their columns.

Problem (b) is easy to deal with. For union, intersection, and difference, we require that the schemas of the two argument relations must be the same. The schema of the resulting relation is thus the same as that of either argument.

However, (a) requires some new definitions, because the way union, intersection, and difference work on bags is somewhat different from the way they work on sets. The rules for constructing the results change to the following:

1. For $R \cup S$, a tuple t is in the result as many times as the number of times it is in R plus the number of times it is in S.

2. For $R \cap S$, a tuple t is in the result the minimum of the number of times it is in R and S.

3. For $R - S$, a tuple t is in the result the number of times it is in R minus the number of times it is in S, but not fewer than zero times.

Notice that if R and S happen to be sets, i.e., no element appears more than once in either, then the result of $R \cap S$ or $R - S$ will be exactly what we would expect from the definition of these operators on sets. However, even if R and S are sets, the bag-union $R \cup S$ can have a result that is not a set. Specifically, an element that appears in both R and S will appear twice in $R \cup S$, but only once if the set-union were taken.

Example 6.1 : Let $R = \{A, B, B\}$ and $S = \{C, A, B, C\}$ be two bags. Then:

- $R \cup S = \{A, A, B, B, B, C, C\}$.

- $R \cap S = \{A, B\}$.

- $R - S = \{B\}$.

The union contains A twice because each of R and S has one copy of A; it contains three B's because there are two in R and one in S. We have shown the members of the union in sorted order, but you should remember that order doesn't matter and we could have permuted the seven members of the bag in any way we wished.

The intersection has one A because each of R and S contains one A, so the minimum number of times A appears is 1. There is also one B, because while there are two B's in S, there is only one in R. C does not appear at all, because although it appears twice in S, it appears zero times in R.

Finally, the difference does not have an A, because although A appears in R, it appears at least as many times in S. The difference has one B, because it appears twice in R and once in S, and $2 - 1 = 1$. There is no C, because C does not appear in R. The fact that C appears in S is thus irrelevant as far as the difference $R - S$ is concerned. □

The rules above for operations on bags do not depend on whether the members of R and S are tuples, objects, or something else. However, for the relational algebra, we assume that R and S are relations, and therefore that they have schemas (i.e., lists of attributes labeling the columns of the relations). We require that the schemas of the two relations be the same, if we are to take their union, intersection, or difference. Moreover, we assign the same schema to the result, so the result too is a relation.

By default, the SQL operators `UNION`, `INTERSECT`, and `EXCEPT` eliminate duplicates from the result, even if the argument relations have duplicates. We can take the bag versions of these operations in SQL by using the keyword `ALL`, as in `UNION ALL` for example. Note that the default versions of these operators in SQL are not precisely the set operators; rather they are the bag versions of the operators followed by the duplicate-elimination operator δ introduced in Section 6.1.6.

In this chapter we shall offer algorithms for both the set and bag versions of the union, intersection, and difference operators. To avoid confusion, we distinguish these two kinds of operators by subscript S or B, for "set" or "bag," respectively. Thus, for example, $\cup_S$ is set-union, and $-_B$ is bag-difference. An unsubscripted operator is the bag version by default. As an exception, when we write algebraic laws (see Section 7.2), the intent is that the law holds for both versions of the operator if there is no subscript.

6.1.2 The Selection Operator

The *selection* $\sigma_C(R)$ takes a relation R and a condition C. The condition C may involve:

1. Arithmetic (e.g., $+$, $*$) or string operators (e.g., concatenation or `LIKE`) on constants and/or attributes,

2. Comparisons between terms constructed in (1), e.g., $a < b$ or $a + b = 10$, and

---

Subqueries in WHERE Clauses

The σ operator introduced here is more powerful than the conventional selection operator of relational algebra, since we allow logical operators AND, OR, and NOT in the subscript of the σ. However, even this σ operator is not as powerful as a WHERE clause in SQL, because there we can have subqueries and certain logical operators on relations, such as EXISTS. A condition involving a subquery must be expressed by an operator that works on whole relations, while the subscript of the σ operator is intended to be a test applied to individual tuples.

In relational algebra, all relations involved in an operation are explicit arguments of the operator, not parameters appearing in a subscript. Thus, it is necessary in relational algebra to handle subqueries by operators such as $\bowtie$ (join), in which the relation of the subquery and relation of the outer query are connected. We defer the matter to Section 7.1. We also discuss in Section 7.3.2 a variant of the selection operator that allows subqueries as explicit arguments.

---

3. Boolean connectives AND, OR, and NOT applied to the terms constructed in (2).

Selection $\sigma_C(R)$ produces the bag of those tuples in R that satisfy the condition C. The schema of the resulting relation is the same as the schema of R.

Example 6.2: Let $R(a, b)$ be the relation

a	b
0	1
2	3
4	5
2	3

The result of $\sigma_{a \geq 1}(R)$ is

a	b
2	3
4	5
2	3

Notice that a tuple meeting the condition appears as many times in the output as it does in the input, while a tuple such as $(0, 1)$ that does not meet the condition does not appear at all.

The result of $\sigma_{b \geq 3 \text{ AND } a+b \geq 6}(R)$ is

a	b
4	5

□

6.1.3   The Projection Operator

If R is a relation, then $\pi_L(R)$ is the *projection* of R onto the list L. In the classical relational algebra, L is a list of (some of the) attributes of R. We extend the projection operator to make it resemble the SELECT clause in SQL. Our projection lists can have the following kinds of elements:

1. A single attribute of R.

2. An expression $x \to y$, where x and y are names for attributes. The element $x \to y$ in the list L asks that we take the attribute x of R and *rename* it y; i.e., the name of this attribute in the schema of the result relation is y.

3. An expression $E \to z$, where E is an expression involving attributes of R, constants, arithmetic operators, and string operators, and z is a new name for the attribute that results from the calculation implied by E. For example, $a+b \to x$ as a list element represents the sum of the attributes a and b, renamed x. Element $c\,||\,d \to e$ means concatenate the (presumably string-valued) attributes c and d and call the result e.

The result of the projection is computed by considering each tuple of R in turn. We evaluate the list L by substituting the tuple's components for the corresponding attributes mentioned in L and applying any operators indicated by L to these values. The result is a relation whose schema is the names of the attributes on list L, with whatever renaming the list specifies. Each tuple of R yields one tuple of the result. Duplicate tuples in R surely yield duplicate tuples in the result, but the result can have duplicates even if R does not.

Example 6.3 : Let R be the relation

a	b	c
0	1	2
0	1	2
3	4	5

Then the result of $\pi_{a,b+c \to x}(R)$ is

a	x
0	3
0	3
3	9

The result's schema has two attributes. One is a, the first attribute of R, not renamed. The second is the sum of the second and third attributes of R, with the name x.

For another example, $\pi_{b-a\to x, c-b\to y}(R)$ is

x	y
1	1
1	1
1	1

Notice that the calculation required by this projection list happens to turn different tuples $(0, 1, 2)$ and $(3, 4, 5)$ into the same tuple $(1, 1)$. Thus, the latter tuple appears three times in the result.   □

6.1.4   The Product of Relations

If R and S are relations, the *product* $R \times S$ is a relation whose schema consists of the attributes of R and the attributes of S. Should there be an attribute name, say a, found in both schemas, then we use $R.a$ and $S.a$ as the names of the two attributes in the product schema.

The tuples of the product are all those that can be formed by taking a tuple of R and following its components by the components of any one tuple of S. If a tuple r appears n times in R, and a tuple s appears m times in S, then in the product, the tuple rs appears nm times.

Example 6.4: Let $R(a, b)$ be the relation

a	b
0	1
2	3
2	3

and let relation $S(b, c)$ be

b	c
1	4
1	4
2	5

Then $R \times S$ is the relation shown in Fig. 6.3. Note that each tuple of R is paired with each tuple of S, regardless of duplication. Thus, for example, tuple $(2, 3, 1, 4)$ appears four times, since it is composed of duplicated tuples from both R and S. Also notice that the schema of the product has two attributes called $R.b$ and $S.b$ corresponding to the attributes called b from the two relations.   □

a	$R.b$	$S.b$	c
0	1	1	4
0	1	1	4
0	1	2	5
2	3	1	4
2	3	1	4
2	3	2	5
2	3	1	4
2	3	1	4
2	3	2	5

Figure 6.3: The product of relations R and S

6.1.5   Joins

There are a number of useful "join" operators that are built from a product followed by a selection and projection. These operators are found explicitly in the SQL2 standard, as ways to combine relations in a FROM clause. However, joins also represent the effect of many common SQL queries whose FROM clause is a list of two or more relations and whose WHERE clause applies equalities or other comparisons to some attributes of these relations.

The simplest and most common is the *natural join*; we denote the natural join of relations R and S by $R \bowtie S$. This expression is a shorthand for $\pi_L\big(\sigma_C(R \times S)\big)$, where:

1. C is a condition that equates all pairs of attributes of R and S that have the same name.

2. L is a list of all the attributes of R and S, except that one copy of each pair of equated attributes is omitted. If $R.x$ and $S.x$ are equated attributes, then since in the result of the projection there is only one attribute x, we conventionally rename as x whichever of $R.x$ and $S.x$ is chosen.

Example 6.5: If $R(a, b)$ and $S(b, c)$ are the relations introduced in Example 6.4, then $R \bowtie S$ stands for $\pi_{a,R.b \to b,c}\big(\sigma_{R.b=S.b}(R \times S)\big)$. That is, since b is the only common attribute name of R and S, the selection equates these two attributes named b and no other pair of attributes. The projection list consists of one copy of each attribute name. We have chosen to get b from $R.b$ and renamed it b; we could have chosen $S.b$ had we wished.

The result of a natural join could be computed by applying the three operators $\times$, σ, and π, in turn. However, it is easier to compute the natural join "all at once." Several methods exist for finding those pairs of tuples, one from R and one from S, that agree on all pairs of attributes with the same name. For each such pair of tuples, we produce the result tuple that agrees with these tuples on all attributes. For instance, using the relations R and S from Example 6.4, we find that the only pairs of tuples that match on their b-values are $(0, 1)$ from R and the two $(1, 4)$ tuples from S. The result of $R \bowtie S$ is thus:

a	b	c
0	1	4
0	1	4

Note that there are two pairs of joining tuples; they happen to have identical tuples from S, which is why the tuple $(0, 1, 4)$ appears twice in the result. □

Another form of join is the *theta-join*. If R and S are relations, then $R \underset{C}{\bowtie} S$ is shorthand for $\sigma_C(R \times S)$. If the condition C is a single term of the form $x = y$, where x is an attribute of R and y is an attribute of S, then we call the join an *equijoin*. Notice that, unlike the natural join, an equijoin does not involve projecting out any attributes, even if the result has two or more identical columns.

Example 6.6: Let $R(a, b)$ and $S(b, c)$ be the relations from Examples 6.4 and 6.5. Then $R \underset{a+R.b<c+S.b}{\bowtie} S$ is the same as $\sigma_{a+R.b<c+S.b}(R \times S)$. That is, the joining condition requires the sum of the components from the tuple of R to be less than the sum of the components of the tuple from S. The result has all the tuples of $R \times S$, except those where the R-tuple is $(2, 3)$ and the S-tuple is $(1, 4)$, because here the sum from R is not less than the sum from S. The result relation is shown in Fig. 6.4.

a	$R.b$	$S.b$	c
0	1	1	4
0	1	1	4
0	1	2	5
2	3	2	5
2	3	2	5

Figure 6.4: The result of a theta-join

For another example, consider the equijoin $R \underset{b=b}{\bowtie} S$. By convention, the first of the equated attributes in a theta-join comes from the left argument and the second comes from the right argument, so this expression is the same as $R \underset{R.b=S.b}{\bowtie} S$. The result is the same as that of $R \bowtie S$, except the two equated b attributes remain. That is,

a	$R.b$	$S.b$	c
0	1	1	4
0	1	1	4

is the result of this equijoin. □

The Meaning of "Theta-Join"

Historically, all joins involved a simple condition that compared two attributes, one from each of the two argument relations. The generic form of such a join was written $R \underset{x\theta y}{\bowtie} S$, where x and y are attributes from R and S, respectively, and θ stands for any of the six arithmetic comparisons: $=$, $\neq$, $<$, $\leq$, $>$, or $\geq$. Since the comparison was represented by symbol θ, the operation came to be known as a "theta-join." Today, we retain the terminology, although the condition of our theta-join is no longer restricted to be a simple comparison between attributes; it can be any condition that could appear in a selection. Nevertheless, the theta-join that compares two attributes, especially the equijoin version that equates two attributes, is undoubtedly the predominant form of join in practice.

6.1.6 Duplicate Elimination

We need an operator that converts a bag to a set, corresponding to the keyword DISTINCT in SQL. For that purpose, we use $\delta(R)$ to return the set consisting of one copy of every tuple that appears one or more times in relation R.

Example 6.7: If R is the relation of that name from Example 6.4, then $\delta(R)$ is

a	b
0	1
2	3

Note that the tuple $(2, 3)$, which appeared twice in R, appears only once in $\delta(R)$. □

Recall that the UNION, INTERSECT, and EXCEPT operators of SQL eliminate duplicates by default, but we have defined the operators $\cup$, $\cap$, and $-$ to follow the bag definitions of these operators by default. Thus, if we want to translate an SQL expression like R UNION S to our algebra, we have to write $\delta(R \cup S)$.

6.1.7 Grouping and Aggregation

There is a family of features in SQL that work together to allow queries involving "grouping and aggregation":

1. *Aggregation operators.* The five operators AVG, SUM, COUNT, MIN, and MAX produce the average, sum, count, minimum, or maximum values, respectively, of the attribute to which they are applied. These operators appear in SELECT clauses.

2. *Grouping.* A `GROUP BY` clause in an SQL query causes the relation constructed by the `FROM` and `WHERE` clauses to be grouped according to the value of the attribute or attributes mentioned in the `GROUP BY` clause. Aggregations are then applied on a per-group basis.

3. *"Having".* A `HAVING` clause must follow a `GROUP BY` clause and provides a condition (which may involve aggregations and the attributes in the group-by) that a group must satisfy to contribute to the result of the query.

Grouping and aggregation generally need to be implemented and optimized together. We shall thus introduce into our extended relational algebra a single operator, γ, that represents the effect of grouping and aggregation. The γ operator also helps implement a `HAVING` clause, which is represented by following the γ with selection and projection.

The subscript used with the γ operator is a list L of elements, each of which is either:

a) An attribute of the relation to which the γ is applied; this attribute is one of the attributes of the `GROUP BY` list of the query. This element is said to be a *grouping* attribute.

b) An aggregation operator applied to an attribute of the relation. To provide a name for the attribute corresponding to this aggregation in the result, an arrow and new name are appended to the aggregation. This element represents one of the aggregations in the `SELECT` clause of the query. The underlying attribute is said to be an *aggregated* attribute.

The relation returned by the expression $\gamma_L(R)$ is constructed as follows:

1. Partition the tuples of R into *groups*. Each group consists of all tuples having one particular assignment of values to the grouping attributes in the list L. If there are no grouping attributes, the entire relation R is one group.

2. For each group, produce one tuple consisting of:

   i. The grouping attributes' values for that group and

   ii. The aggregations, over all tuples of that group, that are specified by the aggregated attributes on list L.

Example 6.8 : Suppose we have the relation

    StarsIn(title, year, starName)

and we wish to find, for each star who has appeared in at least three movies, the earliest year in which they appeared. The following SQL query does the job:

δ is a Special Case of γ

Technically, the δ operator is redundant. If $R(a_1, a_2, \ldots, a_n)$ is a relation, then $\delta(R)$ is equivalent to $\gamma_{a_1, a_2, \ldots, a_n}(R)$. That is, to eliminate duplicates, we group on all the attributes of the relation and do no aggregation. Then each group corresponds to a tuple that is found one or more times in R. Since the result of γ contains exactly one tuple from each group, the effect of this "grouping" is to eliminate duplicates. However, because δ is such a common and important operator, we shall continue to consider it separately when we study algebraic laws and algorithms for implementing the operators.

```
SELECT starName, MIN(year) AS minYear
FROM StarsIn
GROUP BY starName
HAVING COUNT(title) >= 3;
```

The equivalent algebraic expression will involve grouping, using `starName` as a grouping attribute. We clearly must compute for each group the `MIN(year)` aggregate. However, in order to decide which groups satisfy the `HAVING` clause, we must also compute the `COUNT(title)` aggregate for each group.

We begin with the grouping expression

$$\gamma_{starName,\ MIN(year)\rightarrow minYear,\ COUNT(title)\rightarrow ctTitle}(\texttt{StarsIn})$$

The first two columns of the result of this expression are needed for the query result. The third column is an auxiliary attribute, which we have named `ctTitle`; it is needed to apply to each tuple the test of the `HAVING` clause. That is, we continue the algebraic expression for the query by selecting for `ctTitle >= 3` and then projecting onto the first two columns. A representation for the query is shown in Fig. 6.5; it is a simple form of an expression tree (see Section 6.1.9), where four operators in cascade are shown, each above the previous operator. □

Even without a `HAVING` clause, there are SQL group-by queries that cannot be expressed entirely as a single γ operation. For example, the `FROM` clause may contain several relations, and these must first be combined with a product operator. If the query has a `WHERE` clause, then the condition of this clause must be expressed with a σ operation or possibly by turning the product of relations into a join. Additionally, there is the possibility that an attribute mentioned in the `GROUP BY` clause does not appear in the `SELECT` list. For instance, we could have omitted `starName` from the `SELECT` clause of Example 6.8, although the effect would have been strange: we'd get a list of years without an indication of which year corresponded to which star. In this situation, we mention all

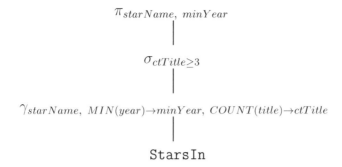

$$\pi_{starName,\ minYear}$$

$$\sigma_{ctTitle\geq3}$$

$$\gamma_{starName,\ MIN(year)\rightarrow minYear,\ COUNT(title)\rightarrow ctTitle}$$

StarsIn

Figure 6.5: Algebraic expression tree for the SQL query of Example 6.8

attributes of the GROUP BY in the list of the γ and follow that operator by a projection that removes the grouping attributes that do not appear in the SELECT clause.

6.1.8 The Sorting Operator

We shall use the operator τ to sort a relation. This operator can be used to implement an SQL ORDER BY clause. Sorting also plays a role as a physical-query-plan operator, since many of the other operators of relational algebra can be facilitated by first sorting one or more of the argument relations.

To be precise, the expression $\tau_L(R)$, where R is a relation and L a list of some of R's attributes, is the relation R, but with the tuples of R sorted in the order indicated by L. If L is the list $a_1, a_2, \ldots, a_n$, then the tuples of R are sorted first by their value of attribute a_1. Ties are broken according to the value of a_2; tuples that agree on both a_1 and a_2 are ordered according to their value of a_3, and so on. Ties that remain after attribute a_n is considered may be ordered arbitrarily. As with SQL, we shall assume that by default sorting is in ascending order but can be changed to descending order by following the attribute by DESC.

Example 6.9 : If R is a relation with schema $R(a, b, c)$, then $\tau_{c,b}(R)$ orders the tuples of R by their value of c, and tuples with the same c-value are ordered by their b value. Tuples that agree on both b and c may be ordered arbitrarily. $\square$

The operator τ is anomalous, in that it is the only operator in our relational algebra whose result is a list of tuples, rather than a set. Thus, it only makes sense to talk about τ as the final operator in an algebraic expression. If another operator of relational algebra is applied after τ, the result of the τ is treated as a set or bag, and no ordering of the tuples is implied. However, we shall often use τ in physical query plans, whose operators are not the same as the relational-algebra operators. Many of the latter operators take advantage of an argument or arguments that are sorted and may themselves produce sorted results.

6.1.9 Expression Trees

We can combine several relational-algebra operators into one expression by applying one operator to the result(s) of one or more other operators. Thus, as for any algebra, we can picture the application of several operators as an *expression tree*. The leaves of this tree are names of relations, and the interior nodes are each labeled with an operator that makes sense when applied to the relation(s) represented by its child or children. Figure 6.5 was an example of a simple expression tree representing the successive application of three unary operators. However, many expression trees involve binary operators and have several branches.

Example 6.10: Suppose we have available the relations

```
MovieStar(name, addr, gender, birthdate)
StarsIn(title, year, starName)
```

from which we ask for the birthdate and movie title for those female stars who appeared in movies in 1996:

```
SELECT title, birthdate
FROM MovieStar, StarsIn
WHERE year = 1996 AND
      gender = 'F' AND
      starName = name;
```

That is, we join the two relations MovieStar and StarsIn, using the condition that the name of the star in both relations is the same, and we select for the year of the movie being 1996 and the gender of the star being female.

A simple SQL query such as the one above will be translated by the parser (as in Fig. 6.2) into a logical query plan whose first step is to combine the relations in the FROM list using product operators. The next step is to perform a selection that represents the WHERE clause, and the last step is to project onto the list in the SELECT clause. The algebraic expression for the above query is shown as a tree in Fig. 6.6.

There are many other expressions *equivalent to* that of Fig. 6.6, in the sense that whatever instances of relations MovieStar and StarsIn one takes, the results of the two expressions are the same. We give one example of an equivalent expression in Fig. 6.7. This expression uses a significantly different plan from Fig. 6.6. First, we recognize that the condition starName = name in the WHERE clause, applied to the product of the two relations, is the same as an equijoin. In Fig. 6.7 this combination of a selection and a product into a join has been

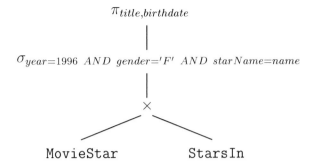

Figure 6.6: A logical query plan derived from the SQL query of Example 6.10

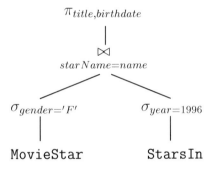

Figure 6.7: Another, probably better, logical query plan

performed. Generally, joins produce fewer tuples than products, so joins are preferable to products when we have a choice.

Second, the other two conditions of the WHERE clause have been separated into two σ operations, and these operations have each been "pushed" down the tree to the appropriate relation. For instance, the selection $\sigma_{year=1996}$ applies directly to the relation StarsIn, because that relation is the one that brought attribute year to the product in Fig. 6.6. There is a general rule that (usually) it makes sense to do selections as soon as possible. Since products and joins are typically more time-consuming than selections, cutting down the sizes of the relations quickly, by performing selections as far down the tree as we can as in Fig. 6.7, will tend to reduce the join time more than it increases the time required for selection. The general topic of improving logical query plans is taken up again in Section 7.2.   □

6.1.10   Exercises for Section 6.1

Exercise 6.1.1 : Here are two relations:

$$R(a,b): \{(0,1),\ (2,3),\ (0,1),\ (2,4),\ (3,4)\}$$

$$S(a,b): \{(0,1),\ (2,4),\ (2,5),\ (3,4),\ (0,2),\ (3,4)\}$$

Compute the following:

* a) $R \cup_S S$.

  b) $R \cup_B S$.

  c) $R \cap_S S$.

  d) $R \cap_B S$.

  e) $R -_S S$.

  f) $R -_B S$.

  g) $S -_S R$.

  h) $S -_B R$.

* i) $\pi_{a+b,a^2,b^2}(R)$.

  j) $\pi_{a+1,b-1}(S)$.

* k) $\sigma_{a<b\ \text{AND}\ (a+b>a\times b\ \text{OR}\ a+b\geq 6)}(R)$.

  l) $\sigma_{a<b\ \text{AND}\ (a+b>a\times b\ \text{OR}\ a+b\geq 6)}(S)$.

  m) $\sigma_{a>1\ \text{OR}\ b>4\ \text{OR}\ b=2}(R)$.

  n) $\sigma_{a>1\ \text{OR}\ b>4\ \text{OR}\ b=2}(S)$.

Exercise 6.1.2 : Here are three relations:

$$R(a,b): \{(0,1),\ (2,3),\ (0,1),\ (2,4),\ (3,4)\}$$

$$S(b,c): \{(1,2),\ (1,2),\ (2,5),\ (3,5),\ (4,5)\}$$

$$T(c,d): \{(2,3),\ (3,4),\ (4,5),\ (5,6)\}$$

Compute the following:

* a) $R \bowtie S$.

  b) $S \bowtie T$.

! c) $R \bowtie T$.

Join-Like Operators

There are several operators that are commonly viewed as varieties of join. Here are their symbols and definitions:

1. The *semijoin* of relations R and S, written $R \ltimes S$, is the bag of tuples t in R such that there is at least one tuple in S that agrees with t in all attributes that R and S have in common.

2. The *antisemijoin* $R \overline{\ltimes} S$ is the bag of tuples t in R that do *not* agree with any tuple of S in the attributes common to R and S.

3. The *outerjoin* $R \overset{\circ}{\bowtie} S$ is formed by starting with $R \bowtie S$, and adding any dangling tuples from R or S (a tuple is *dangling* if it did not join with any tuple from the other relation). The added tuples must be padded with a special *null* symbol (NULL in SQL, but $\perp$ will serve in these exercises) for all the attributes that they do not possess, but that appear in the join result.

4. The *left outerjoin* $R \overset{\circ}{\bowtie}_L S$ is like the outerjoin, but only dangling tuples of the left argument R are padded with $\perp$ and added to the result.

5. The *right outerjoin* $R \overset{\circ}{\bowtie}_R S$ is like the outerjoin, but only the dangling tuples of the right argument S are padded with $\perp$ and added to the result.

---

d) $R \underset{R.b < S.b}{\bowtie} S$.

* e) $R \underset{a+d=5}{\bowtie} T$.

f) $R \underset{b=c}{\bowtie} T$.

* g) $\gamma_{a,SUM(b)}(R)$.

h) $\gamma_{c,MIN(b)}(S)$.

i) $\delta(R)$.

j) $\tau_{b,a}(R)$.

! **Exercise 6.1.3:** Give expressions for the five operators defined in the box "Join-Like Operators" using only the standard operators of relational algebra defined in this section. For the outerjoin variants, you may use special "null relations" $N(a_1, a_2, \ldots a_k)$ that consist of one tuple, with $\perp$ in each component.

   * a) Semijoin.

     b) Antisemijoin.

   * c) Left outerjoin.

     d) Right outerjoin.

     e) Outerjoin.

Exercise 6.1.4: Write the following joins as expressions involving selection, projection, and product.

    a) $R(a,b,c,d) \bowtie S(b,d,e)$.

    b) $R(a,b,c) \underset{a+d=10 \ \text{OR} \ b=S.c}{\bowtie} S(c,d)$.

! Exercise 6.1.5: A unary operator f is said to be *idempotent* if for all relations R, $f\big(f(R)\big) = f(R)$. That is, applying f more than once is the same as applying it once. Which of the following operators are idempotent? Either explain why or give a counterexample.

   * a) δ.

   * b) π_L.

     c) σ_C.

     d) γ_L.

     e) τ.

Exercise 6.1.6: Using the following "movie" relations:

```
Movie(title, year, length, studioName)
MovieStar(name, address, gender, birthdate)
StarsIn(title, year, starName)
Studio(name, address)
```

turn the following queries into expression trees using the algebraic operators of this section.

a)
```
SELECT address
FROM Movie, Studio
WHERE studioName = name AND title = 'Gone With the Wind';
```

b)
```
(SELECT name FROM MovieStar)
    UNION
(SELECT starName FROM StarsIn);
```

c) (SELECT name FROM MovieStar)
        UNION ALL
    (SELECT starName FROM StarsIn);

d) SELECT starName, SUM(length)
    FROM Movie NATURAL JOIN StarsIn
    GROUP BY starName
    HAVING COUNT(*) >= 3;

6.2 Introduction to Physical-Query-Plan Operators

Physical query plans are built from operators, each of which implements one step of the plan. Often, the physical operators are particular implementations for one of the operators of relational algebra. However, we also need physical operators for other tasks that do not involve an operator of relational algebra. For example, we often need to "scan" a table, that is, bring into main memory each tuple of some relation that is an operand of a relational-algebra expression. In this section, we shall introduce the basic building blocks of physical query plans. Later sections cover the more complex algorithms that implement operators of relational algebra efficiently; these algorithms also form an essential part of physical query plans. We also introduce here the "iterator" concept, which is an important method by which the operators comprising a physical query plan can pass requests for tuples and answers among themselves.

6.2.1 Scanning Tables

Perhaps the most basic thing we can do in a physical query plan is to read the entire contents of a relation R. This step is necessary when, for example, we take the union or join of R with another relation. A variation of this operator involves a simple predicate, where we read only those tuples of the relation R that satisfy the predicate. There are two basic approaches to locating the tuples of a relation R.

1. In many cases, the relation R is stored in an area of secondary memory, with its tuples arranged in blocks. The blocks containing the tuples of R are known to the system, and it is possible to get the blocks one by one. This operation is called *table-scan*.

2. If there is an index on any attribute of R, we may be able to use this index to get all the tuples of R. For example, a sparse index on R, as discussed in Section 4.1.3, can be used to lead us to all the blocks holding R, even if we don't know otherwise which blocks these are. This operation is called *index-scan*.

We shall take up index-scan again in Section 6.7.2, when we talk about implementation of the σ operator. However, the important observation for now is that we can use the index not only to get *all* the tuples of the relation it indexes, but to get only those tuples that have a particular value (or sometimes a particular range of values) in the attribute or attributes that form the search key for the index.

6.2.2 Sorting While Scanning Tables

There are a number of reasons why we might want to sort a relation as we read its tuples. For one, the query could include an ORDER BY clause, requiring that a relation be sorted. For another, various algorithms for relational-algebra operations require one or both of their arguments to be sorted relations. These algorithms appear in Section 6.5 and elsewhere.

The physical-query-plan operator *sort-scan* takes a relation R and a specification of the attributes on which the sort is to be made, and produces R in that sorted order. There are several ways that sort-scan can be implemented:

a) If we are to produce a relation R sorted by attribute a, and there is a B-tree index on a, or R is stored as an indexed-sequential file ordered by a, then a scan of the index allows us to produce R in the desired order.

b) If the relation R that we wish to retrieve in sorted order is small enough to fit in main memory, then we can retrieve its tuples using a table scan or index scan, and then use one of many possible efficient, main-memory sorting algorithms. Main-memory sorting is covered in many books on the subject, and we shall not consider the matter here.

c) If R is too large to fit in main memory, then the multiway merging approach covered in Section 2.3.3 is a good choice. However, instead of storing the final sorted R back on disk, we produce one block of the sorted R at a time, as its tuples are needed.

6.2.3 The Model of Computation for Physical Operators

A query generally consists of several operations of relational algebra, and the corresponding physical query plan is composed of several physical operators. Often, a physical operator is an implementation of a relational-algebra operator, but as we saw in Section 6.2.1, other physical plan operators correspond to operations like scanning that may be invisible in relational algebra.

Since choosing physical plan operators wisely is an essential of a good query processor, we must be able to estimate the "cost" of each operator we use. We shall use the number of disk I/O's as our measure of cost for an operation. This measure is consistent with our view (see Section 2.3.1) that it takes longer to get data from disk than to do anything useful with it once the data is in main memory. The one major exception is when answering a query involves communicating data across a network. We discuss costs for distributed query processing in Sections 6.10 and 10.4.4.

When comparing algorithms for the same operations, we shall make an assumption that may be surprising at first:

- We assume that the arguments of any operator are found on disk, but the result of the operator is left in main memory.

If the operator produces the final answer to a query, and that result is indeed written to disk, then the cost of doing so depends only on the size of the answer, and not on how the answer was computed. We can simply add the final write-back cost to the total cost of the query. However, in many applications, the answer is not stored on disk at all, but printed or passed to some formatting program. Then, the disk I/O cost of the output either is zero or depends upon what some unknown application program does with the data.

Similarly, the result of an operator that forms part of a query (rather than the whole query) often is not written to disk. In Section 7.7.3 we shall discuss "pipelining," where the result of one operator is constructed in main memory, perhaps a small piece at a time, and passed as an argument to another operator. In this situation, we never have to write the result to disk, and moreover, we save the cost of reading from disk this argument of the operator that uses the result. This saving is an excellent opportunity for the query optimizer.

6.2.4 Parameters for Measuring Costs

Now, let us introduce the parameters that we use to express the cost of an operator. Estimates of cost are essential if the optimizer is to determine which of the many query plans is likely to execute fastest. Section 7.5 introduces the exploitation of these cost estimates.

We need a parameter to represent the portion of main memory that the operator uses, and we require other parameters to measure the size of its argument(s). Assume that main memory is divided into buffers, whose size is the same as the size of disk blocks. Then M will denote the number of main-memory buffers available to an execution of a particular operator. Remember that when evaluating the cost of an operator, we do not count the cost — either memory used or disk I/O's — of producing the output; thus M includes only the space used to hold the input and any intermediate results of the operator.

Sometimes, we can think of M as the entire main memory, or most of the main memory, as we did in Section 2.3.4. However, we shall also see situations where several operations share the main memory, so M could be much smaller than the total main memory. In fact, as we shall discuss in Section 6.8, the number of buffers available to an operation may not be a predictable constant, but may be decided during execution, based on what other processes are executing at the same time. If so, M is really an estimate of the number of buffers available to the operation. If the estimate is wrong, then the actual execution time will differ from the predicted time used by the optimizer. We could even find that the chosen physical query plan would have been different, had the query optimizer known what the true buffer availability would be during execution.

Next, let us consider the parameters that measure the cost of accessing argument relations. These parameters, measuring size and distribution of data in a relation, are often computed periodically to help the query optimizer choose physical operators.

We shall make the simplifying assumption that data is accessed one block at a time from disk. In practice, one of the techniques discussed in Section 2.4 might be able to speed up the algorithm if we are able to read many blocks of the relation at once, and they can be read from consecutive blocks on a track. There are three parameter families, B, T, and V:

- When describing the size of a relation R, we most often are concerned with the number of blocks that are needed to hold all the tuples of R. This number of blocks will be denoted $B(R)$, or just B if we know that relation R is meant. Usually, we assume that R is *clustered*; that is, it is stored in B blocks or in approximately B blocks. As discussed in Section 4.1.6, we may in fact wish to keep a small fraction of each block holding R empty for future insertions into R. Nevertheless, B will often be a good-enough approximation to the number of blocks that we must read from disk to see all of R, and we shall use B as that estimate uniformly.

- Sometimes, we also need to know the number of tuples in R, and we denote this quantity by $T(R)$, or just T if R is understood. If we need the number of tuples of R that can fit in one block, we can use the ratio T/B. Further, there are some instances where a relation is stored distributed among blocks that are also occupied by tuples of other relations. If so, then a simplifying assumption is that each tuple of R requires a separate disk read, and we shall use T as an estimate of the disk I/O's needed to read R in this situation.

- Finally, we shall sometimes want to refer to the number of distinct values that appear in a column of a relation. If R is a relation, and one of its attributes is a, then $V(R, a)$ is the number of distinct values of the column for a in R. More generally, if $[a_1, a_2, \ldots, a_n]$ is a list of attributes, then $V(R, [a_1, a_2, \ldots, a_n])$ is the number of distinct n-tuples in the columns of R for attributes $a_1, a_2, \ldots, a_n$. Put another way, it is the number of tuples in $\delta\left(\pi_{a_1,a_2,\ldots,a_n}(R)\right)$.

6.2.5 I/O Cost for Scan Operators

As a simple application of the parameters were have introduced, we can represent the number of disk I/O's needed for each of the table-scan operators discussed so far. If relation R is clustered, then the number of disk I/O's for the table-scan operator is approximately B. Likewise, if R fits in main-memory, then we can implement sort-scan by reading R into memory and performing an in-memory sort, again requiring only B disk I/O's.

If R is clustered but requires a two-phase multiway merge sort, then, as discussed in Section 2.3.4, we require about $3B$ disk I/O's, divided equally among the operations of reading R in sublists, writing out the sublists, and rereading the sublists. Remember that we do not charge for the final writing of the result. Neither do we charge memory space for accumulated output. Rather, we assume each output block is immediately consumed by some other operation; possibly it is simply written to disk.

However, if R is not clustered, then the number of required disk I/O's is generally much higher. If R is distributed among tuples of other relations, then a table-scan for R may require reading as many blocks as there are tuples of R; that is, the I/O cost is T. Similarly, if we want to sort R, but R fits in memory, then T disk I/O's are what we need to get all of R into memory. Finally, if R is not clustered and requires a two-phase sort, then it takes T disk I/O's to read the subgroups initially. However, we may store and reread the sublists in clustered form, so these steps require only $2B$ disk I/O's. The total cost for performing sort-scan on a large, unclustered relation is thus $T + 2B$.

Finally, let us consider the cost of an index-scan. Generally, an index on a relation R requires many fewer than $B(R)$ blocks. Therefore, a scan of the entire R, which takes at least B disk I/O's, will require significantly more I/O's than does examining the entire index. Thus, even though index-scan requires examining both the relation and its index,

- We continue to use B or T as an estimate of the cost of accessing a clustered or unclustered relation in its entirety, using an index.

However, if we only want part of R, we often are able to avoid looking at the entire index and the entire R. We shall defer analysis of these uses of indexes to Section 6.7.2.

6.2.6 Iterators for Implementation of Physical Operators

Many physical operators can be implemented as an *iterator*, which is a group of three functions that allows a consumer of the result of the physical operator to get the result one tuple at a time. The three functions forming the iterator for an operation are:

1. `Open`. This function starts the process of getting tuples, but does not get a tuple. It initializes any data structures needed to perform the operation and calls `Open` for any arguments of the operation.

2. `GetNext`. This function returns the next tuple in the result and adjusts data structures as necessary to allow subsequent tuples to be obtained. In getting the next tuple of its result, it typically calls `GetNext` one or more times on its argument(s). This function also sets a signal that tells

---

Why Iterators?

We shall see in Section 7.7 how iterators support efficient execution when they are composed within query plans. They contrast with a *materialization* strategy, where the result of each operator is produced in its entirety — and either stored on disk or allowed to take up space in main memory. When iterators are used, many operations are active at once. Tuples pass between operators as needed, thus reducing the need for storage. Of course, as we shall see, not all physical operators support the iteration approach, or "pipelining," in a useful way. In some cases, almost all the work would need to be done by the `Open` function, which is tantamount to materialization.

---

whether a tuple was produced, or whether there were no more tuples to be produced. We shall use `Found` as a boolean variable that is true if and only if a new tuple has been returned.

3. `Close`. This function ends the iteration after all tuples, or all tuples that the consumer wanted, have been obtained. Typically, it calls `Close` on any arguments of the operator.

When describing iterators and their functions, we shall regard `Open`, `GetNext`, and `Close` as overloaded names of methods. That is, these methods have many different implementations, depending on the "class" to which the method is applied. In particular, assume that for each physical operator there is a class whose objects are the relations that can be produced by this operator. If R is a member of such a class, then we use `R.Open()`, `R.GetNext()`, and `R.Close()` to apply the functions of the iterator for R.

Example 6.11 : Perhaps the simplest iterator is the one that implements the table-scan operator. Let us suppose that we want to perform `TableScan(R)`, where R is a relation clustered in some list of blocks, which we can access in a convenient way. Thus, we shall assume that the notion of "get the next block of R" is implemented by the storage system and need not be described in detail. Further, we assume that within a block there is a directory of records (tuples) so that it is easy to get the next tuple of a block or tell that the last tuple has been reached.

Figure 6.8 sketches the three functions for this iterator. We imagine a block pointer b and a tuple pointer t that points to a tuple within block b. We assume that both pointers can point "beyond" the last block or last tuple of a block, respectively, and that it is possible to identify when these conditions occur. Notice that `Close` in this case does nothing. In practice, a `Close` function for an iterator might clean up the internal structure of the DBMS in various ways. It might inform the buffer manager that certain buffers are no longer needed,

```
Open(R) {
    b := the first block of R;
    t := the first tuple of block b;
    Found := TRUE;
}

GetNext(R) {
    IF (t is past the last tuple on block b) {
        increment b to the next block;
        IF (there is no next block) {
            Found := FALSE;
            RETURN;
        }
        ELSE /* b is a new block */
            t := first tuple on block b;
    /* now we are ready to return t and increment */
    oldt := t;
    increment t to the next tuple of b;
    RETURN oldt;
}

Close(R) {
}
```

Figure 6.8: An iterator for the table-scan operator

or inform the concurrency manager that the read of a relation has completed.
□

Example 6.12 : Now, let us consider an example where the iterator does most of the work in its `Open` function. The operator is sort-scan, where we read the tuples of a relation R but return them in sorted order. Further, let us suppose that R is so large that we need to use a two-phase, multiway merge-sort, as in Section 2.3.4.

We cannot return even the first tuple until we have examined each tuple of R. Thus, `Open` must do at least the following:

1. Read all the tuples of R in main-memory-sized chunks, sort them, and store them on disk.

2. Initialize the data structure for the second (merge) phase, and load the first block of each sublist into the main-memory structure.

Then, `GetNext` can run a competition for the first remaining tuple at the heads of all the sublists. If the block from the winning sublist is exhausted, `GetNext` reloads its buffer.   □

Example 6.13 : Finally, let us consider a simple example of how iterators can be combined by calling other iterators. It is not a good example of how many iterators can be active simultaneously, but that will have to wait until we have considered algorithms for physical operators like selection and join, which exploit this capability of iterators better.

Our operation is the bag union $R \cup S$, in which we produce first all the tuples of R and then all the tuples of S, without regard for the existence of duplicates. We assume that there are functions R.Open, R.GetNext, and R.Close, that form the iterator for R, and analogous functions for relation S. These functions could be the functions for table-scan applied to R and S, if these are stored relations, or they could be iterators that call a network of other iterators to compute R and S. The iterator functions for this union are sketched in Fig. 6.9. One subtle point is that the functions use a shared variable CurRel that is either R or S, depending on which relation is being read from currently.   □

6.3   One-Pass Algorithms for Database Operations

We shall now begin our study of a very important topic in query optimization: how should we execute each of the individual steps — for example, a join or selection — of a logical query plan? The choice of an algorithm for each operator is an essential part of the process of transforming a logical query plan into a physical query plan. While many algorithms for operators have been proposed, they largely fall into three classes:

1. Sorting-based methods. These are covered primarily in Section 6.5.

2. Hash-based methods. These are mentioned in Section 6.6 and Section 6.10, among other places.

3. Index-based methods. These are emphasized in Section 6.7.

In addition, we can divide algorithms for operators into three "degrees" of difficulty and cost:

a) Some methods involve reading the data only once from disk. These are the *one-pass* algorithms, and they are the topic of this section. Usually, they work only when at least one of the arguments of the operation fits in main memory, although there are exceptions, especially for selection and projection as discussed in Section 6.3.1.

b) Some methods work for data that is too large to fit in available main memory but not for the largest imaginable data sets. An example of

```
Open(R,S) {
    R.Open();
    CurRel := R;
}

GetNext(R,S) {
    IF (CurRel = R) {
        t := R.GetNext();
        IF (Found) /* R is not exhausted */
            RETURN t;
        ELSE /* R is exhausted */ {
            S.Open();
            CurRel := S;
        }
    }
    /* here, we must read from S */
    RETURN S.GetNext();
    /* notice that if S is exhausted, Found will
       be set to FALSE by S.GetNext, which is the
       correct action for GetNext as well */
}

Close(R,S) {
    R.Close();
    S.Close();
}
```

Figure 6.9: Building a union iterator from its components

such an algorithm is the two-phase, multiway merge sort of Section 2.3.4. These *two-pass* algorithms are characterized by reading data a first time from disk, processing it in some way, writing all, or almost all of it to disk, and then reading it a second time for further processing during the second pass. We meet these algorithms in Sections 6.5 and 6.6.

c) Some methods work without a limit on the size of the data. These methods use three or more passes to do their jobs, and are natural, recursive generalizations of the two-pass algorithms; we shall study multipass methods in Section 6.9.

In this section, we shall concentrate on the one-pass methods. However, both in this section and subsequently, we shall classify operators into three broad groups:

1. *Tuple-at-a-time, unary operations.* These operations — selection and projection — do not require an entire relation, or even a large part of it, in
   memory at once. Thus, we can read a block at a time, use one main-
   memory buffer, and produce our output.

2. *Full-relation, unary operations.* These one-argument operations require
   seeing all or most of the tuples in memory at once, so one-pass algorithms
   are limited to relations that are approximately of size M or less. The
   operations of this class that we consider here are γ and δ.

3. *Full-relation, binary operations.* All the other operations are in this class:
   set and bag versions of union, intersection, and difference, joins, and products. We shall see that each of these operations requires at least one of the
   arguments to be limited to size M, if we are to use a one-pass algorithm.

6.3.1   One-Pass Algorithms for Tuple-at-a-Time Operations

The tuple-at-a-time operations $\sigma(R)$ and $\pi(R)$ have obvious algorithms, regardless of whether the relation fits in main memory. We read the blocks of R one
at a time into an input buffer, perform the operation on each tuple, and move
the selected tuples or the projected tuples to the output buffer, as suggested
by Fig. 6.10. Since the output buffer may be an input buffer of some other
operator, or may be sending data to a user or application, we do not count the
output buffer as needed space. Thus, we require only that $M \geq 1$ for the input
buffer, regardless of B.

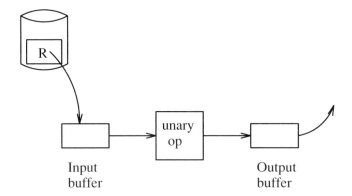

Figure 6.10: A selection or projection being performed on a relation R

The disk I/O requirement for this process depends only on how the argument
relation R is provided. If R is initially on disk, then the cost is whatever it
takes to perform a table-scan or index-scan of R. The cost was discussed in
Section 6.2.5; typically it is B if R is clustered and T if it is not clustered.
However, we should remind the reader again of the important exception when

---

Extra Buffers Can Speed Up Operations

Although tuple-at-a-time operations can get by with only one input buffer and one output buffer, as suggested by Fig. 6.10, we can often speed up processing if we allocate more input buffers. The idea appeared first in Section 2.4.1. If R is stored on consecutive blocks within cylinders, then we can read an entire cylinder into buffers, while paying for the seek time and rotational latency for only one block per cylinder. Similarly, if the output of the operation can be stored on full cylinders, we waste almost no time writing.

---

the operation being performed is a selection, and the condition compares a constant to an attribute that has an index. In that case, we can use the index to retrieve only a subset of the blocks holding R, thus improving performance, often markedly.

6.3.2 One-Pass Algorithms for Unary, Full-Relation Operations

Now, let us consider the unary operations that apply to relations as a whole, rather than to one tuple at a time: duplicate elimination (δ) and grouping (γ).

Duplicate Elimination

To eliminate duplicates, we can read each block of R one at a time, but for each tuple we need to make a decision as to whether:

1. It is the first time we have seen this tuple, in which case we copy it to the output, or

2. We have seen the tuple before, in which case we must not output this tuple.

To support this decision, we need to keep in memory one copy of every tuple we have seen, as suggested in Fig. 6.11. One memory buffer holds one block of R's tuples, and the remaining $M - 1$ buffers can be used to hold a single copy of every tuple seen so far.

When storing the already-seen tuples, we must be careful about the main-memory data structure we use. Naively, we might just list the tuples we have seen. When a new tuple from R is considered, we compare it with all tuples seen so far, and if it is not equal to any of these tuples we both copy it to the output and add it to the in-memory list of tuples we have seen.

However, if there are n tuples in main memory, each new tuple takes processor time proportional to n, so the complete operation takes processor time

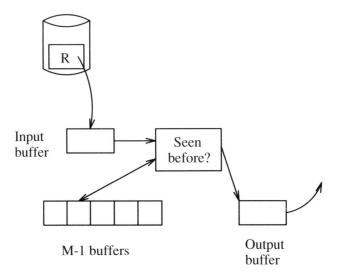

Figure 6.11: Managing memory for a one-pass duplicate-elimination

proportional to n^2. Since n could be very large, this amount of time calls into serious question our assumption that only the disk I/O time was significant. Thus, we need a main-memory structure that allows each of the operations:

1. Add a new tuple, and

2. Tell whether a given tuple is already there

to be done in time that is close to a constant, independent of the number of tuples n that we currently have in memory. There are many such structures known. For example, we could use a hash table with a large number of buckets, or some form of balanced binary search tree.[1] Each of these structures requires some overhead in addition to the space needed to store the tuples; for instance, a main-memory hash table needs a bucket array and space for pointers to link the tuples in a bucket. However, the extra space needed tends to be small compared with the space needed to store the tuples. We shall thus make the simplifying assumption that no extra space is needed and concentrate on the space needed to store the tuples in main memory.

On this assumption, we may store in the $M - 1$ available buffers of main memory as many tuples as will fit in $M - 1$ blocks of R. If we want one copy of each distinct tuple of R to fit in main memory, then $B(\delta(R))$ must be no larger than $M - 1$. Since we expect M to be much larger than 1, a simpler approximation to this rule, and the one we shall generally use, is:

---

[1] See Aho, A. V., J. E. Hopcroft, and J. D. Ullman *Data Structures and Algorithms*, Addison-Wesley, 1984 for discussions of suitable main-memory structures. In particular, hashing takes on average $O(n)$ time to process n items, and balanced trees take $O(n \log n)$ time; either is sufficiently close to linear for our purposes.

- $B\big(\delta(R)\big) \leq M$

Note that we cannot in general compute the size of $\delta(R)$ without computing $\delta(R)$ itself. Should we underestimate that size, so $B\big(\delta(R)\big)$ is actually larger than M, we shall pay a significant penalty due to thrashing, as the blocks holding the distinct tuples of R must be brought into and out of main memory frequently.

Grouping

A grouping operation γ_L gives us zero or more grouping attributes and presumably one or more aggregated attributes. If we create in main memory one entry for each group — that is, for each value of the grouping attributes — then we can scan the tuples of R, one block at a time. The *entry* for a group consists of values for the grouping attributes and an accumulated value or values for each aggregation. The accumulated value is, except in one case, obvious:

- For a `MIN(a)` or `MAX(a)` aggregate, record the minimum or maximum value, respectively, of attribute a seen for any tuple in the group so far. Change this minimum or maximum, if appropriate, each time a tuple of the group is seen.

- For any `COUNT` aggregation, add one for each tuple of the group that is seen.

- For `SUM(a)`, add the value of attribute a to the accumulated sum seen so far.

- `AVG(a)` is the hard case. We must maintain two accumulations: the count of the number of tuples in the group and the sum of the a-values of these tuples. Each is computed as we would for a `COUNT` and `SUM` aggregation, respectively. After all tuples of R are seen, we take the quotient of the sum and count to obtain the average.

When all tuples of R have been read into the input buffer and contributed to the aggregation(s) for their group, we can produce the output by writing the tuple for each group. Note that until the last tuple is seen, we cannot begin to create output for a γ operation. A consequence of this observation is that this algorithm does not fit the iterator framework very well; the entire grouping has to be done by the `Open` function before the first tuple can be retrieved by `GetNext`.

In order that the in-memory processing of each tuple be efficient, we need to use a main-memory data structure that lets us find the entry for each group, given values for the grouping attributes. As discussed above for the δ operation, common main-memory data structures such as hash tables or balanced trees will serve well. We should remember, however, that the search key for this structure is the grouping attributes only.

Operations on Nonclustered Data

Remember that all our calculations regarding the number of disk I/O's required for an operation are predicated on the assumption that the operand relations are clustered. In the (typically rare) event that an operand R is not clustered, then it may take us $T(R)$ disk I/O's, rather than $B(R)$ disk I/O's to read all the tuples of R. Note, however, that any relation that is the result of an operator may always be assumed clustered, since we have no reason to store a temporary relation in a nonclustered fashion.

The number of disk I/O's needed for this one-pass algorithm is B, as must be the case for any one-pass algorithm for a unary operator. The number of required memory buffers M is not related to B in any simple way, although typically M will be less than B. The problem is that the entries for the groups could be longer or shorter than tuples of R, and the number of groups could be anything equal to or less than the number of tuples of R. However, in most cases, group entries will be no longer than R's tuples, and there will be many fewer groups than tuples.

6.3.3   One-Pass Algorithms for Binary Operations

Let us now take up the binary operations: union, intersection, difference, product, and join. To simplify the discussion of joins, we shall consider only the natural join. An equijoin can be implemented the same way, after attributes are renamed appropriately, and theta-joins can be thought of as a product or equijoin followed by a selection for those conditions that cannot be expressed in an equijoin.

There is one exceptional operation — bag union — that can be computed by a very simple, one-pass algorithm. To compute $R \cup_B S$, we copy each tuple of R to the output and then copy every tuple of S, as we did in Example 6.13. The number of disk I/O's is $B(R)+B(S)$, as it must be for a one-pass algorithm on operands R and S, while $M = 1$ suffices regardless of how large R and S are.

Other binary operations require reading the smaller of the operands R and S into main memory and building a suitable data structure so tuples can be both inserted quickly and found quickly, as discussed in Section 6.3.2. As before, a hash table or balanced tree suffices. The structure requires a small amount of space (in addition to the space for the tuples themselves), which we shall neglect. Thus, the approximate requirement for a binary operation on relations R and S to be performed in one pass is:

- $\min(B(R), B(S)) \leq M$

This rule assumes that one buffer will be used to read the blocks of the larger relation, while approximately M buffers are needed to house the entire smaller relation and its main-memory data structure.

We shall now give the details of the various operations. In each case, we assume R is the larger of the relations, and we house S in main memory.

Set Union

We read S into $M - 1$ buffers of main memory and build a search structure where the search key is the entire tuple. All these tuples are also copied to the output. We then read each block of R into the Mth buffer, one at a time. For each tuple t of R, we see if t is in S, and if not, we copy t to the output. If t is also in S, we skip t.

Set Intersection

Read S into $M - 1$ buffers and build a search structure with full tuples as the search key. Read each block of R, and for each tuple t of R, see if t is also in S. If so, copy t to the output, and if not, ignore t.

Set Difference

Since the difference is not a commutative operator, we must distinguish between $R -_S S$ and $S -_S R$, continuing to assume that R is the larger relation. In each case, we read S into $M - 1$ buffers and build a search structure with full tuples as the search key.

To compute $R -_S S$, we read each block of R and examine each tuple t on that block. If t is in S, then ignore t; if it is not in S then copy t to the output.

To compute $S -_S R$, we again read the blocks of R and examine each tuple t in turn. If t is in S, then we delete t from the copy of S in main memory, while if t is not in S we do nothing. After considering each tuple of R, we copy to the output those tuples of S that remain.

Bag Intersection

We read S into $M - 1$ buffers, but we associate with each distinct tuple a *count*, which initially measures the number of times this tuple occurs in S. Multiple copies of a tuple t are not stored individually. Rather we store one copy of t and associate with it a count equal to the number of times t occurs.

This structure could take slightly more space than $B(S)$ blocks if there were few duplicates, although frequently the result is that S is compacted. Thus, we shall continue to assume that $B(S) \leq M - 1$ is sufficient for a one-pass algorithm to work, although the condition is only an approximation.

Next, we read each block of R, and for each tuple t of R we see whether t occurs in S. If not we ignore t; it cannot appear in the intersection. However, if t appears in S, and the count associated with t is still positive, then we output

t and decrement the count by 1. If t appears in S, but its count has reached 0, then we do not output t; we have already produced as many copies of t in the output as there were copies in S.

Bag Difference

To compute $S -_B R$, we read the tuples of S into main memory, and count the number of occurrences of each distinct tuple, as we did for bag intersection. When we read R, for each tuple t we see whether t occurs in S, and if so, we decrement its associated count. At the end, we copy to the output each tuple in main memory whose count is positive, and the number of times we copy it equals that count.

To compute $R -_B S$, we also read the tuples of S into main memory and count the number of occurrences of distinct tuples. We may think of a tuple t with a count of c as c reasons not to copy t to the output as we read tuples of R. That is, when we read a tuple t of R, we see if t occurs in S. If not, then we copy t to the output. If t does occur in S, then we look at the current count c associated with t. If $c = 0$, then copy t to the output. If $c > 0$, do not copy t to the output, but decrement c by 1.

Product

Read S into $M - 1$ buffers of main memory; no special data structure is needed. Then read each block of R, and for each tuple t of R concatenate t with each tuple of S in main memory. Output each concatenated tuple as it is formed.

Notice that this algorithm may take a considerable amount of processor time per tuple of R, because each such tuple must be matched with $M - 1$ blocks full of tuples. However, the output size is also large, and we would expect the time needed to write the result to disk or otherwise process the output to exceed the processor time needed to create the output.

Natural Join

In this and other join algorithms, let us take the convention that $R(X, Y)$ is being joined with $S(Y, Z)$, where Y represents all the attributes that R and S have in common, X is all attributes of R that are not in the schema of S, and Z is all attributes of S that are not in the schema of R. We continue to assume that S is the smaller relation. To compute the natural join, do the following:

1. Read all the tuples of S and form them into a main-memory search structure with the attributes of Y as the search key. As usual, a hash table or balanced tree are good examples of such structures. Use $M - 1$ blocks of memory for this purpose.

2. Read each block of R into the one remaining main-memory buffer. For each tuple t of R, find the tuples of S that agree with t on all attributes

---

What if M is not Known?

While we present algorithms as if M, the number of available memory blocks, were fixed and known in advance, remember that the available M is often unknown, except within some obvious limits like the total memory of the machine. Thus, a query optimizer, when choosing between a one-pass and a two-pass algorithm, might estimate M and make the choice based on this estimate. If the optimizer is wrong, the penalty is either thrashing of buffers between disk and memory (if the guess of M was too high), or unnecessary passes if M was underestimated.

There are also some algorithms that degrade gracefully when there is less memory than expected. For example, we can behave like a one-pass algorithm, unless we run out of space, and then start behaving like a two-pass algorithm. Sections 6.6.6 and 6.8.3 discuss some of these approaches.

---

of Y, using the search structure. For each matching tuple of S, form a tuple by joining it with t, and move the resulting tuple to the output.

Like all the one-pass, binary algorithms, this one takes $B(R) + B(S)$ disk I/O's to read the operands. It works as long as $B(S) \leq M - 1$, or approximately, $B(S) \leq M$. Also as for the other algorithms we have studied, the space required by the main-memory search structure is not counted but may lead to a small, additional memory requirement.

We shall not discuss joins other than the natural join. Remember that an equijoin is executed in essentially the same way as a natural join, but we must account for the fact that "equal" attributes from the two relations may have different names. A theta-join that is not an equijoin can be replaced by an equijoin or product followed by a selection.

6.3.4 Exercises for Section 6.3

Exercise 6.3.1: For each of the operations below, write an iterator that uses the algorithm described in this section.

* a) Projection.

* b) Distinct (δ).

  c) Grouping (γ_L).

* d) Set union.

  e) Set intersection.

f) Set difference.

g) Bag intersection.

h) Bag difference.

i) Product.

j) Natural join.

Exercise 6.3.2: For each of the operators in Exercise 6.3.1, tell whether the operator is *blocking*, by which we mean that the first output cannot be produced until all the input has been read. Put another way, a blocking operator is one whose only possible iterators have all the important work done by `Open`.

* **Exercise 6.3.3:** Show what the entries for groups would be if we implemented the γ operator for the query of Exercise 6.1.6(d).

Exercise 6.3.4: Figure 6.14 summarizes the memory and disk-I/O requirements of the algorithms of this section and the next. However, it assumes all arguments are clustered. How would the entries change if one or both arguments were not clustered?

! **Exercise 6.3.5:** In Exercise 6.1.3 we defined five join-like operators. Give one-pass algorithms for each of them:

* a) $R \bowtie S$, assuming R fits in memory.

* b) $R \bowtie S$, assuming S fits in memory.

c) $R \overline{\bowtie} S$, assuming R fits in memory.

d) $R \overline{\bowtie} S$, assuming S fits in memory.

* e) $R \overset{\circ}{\bowtie}_L S$, assuming R fits in memory.

f) $R \overset{\circ}{\bowtie}_L S$, assuming S fits in memory.

g) $R \overset{\circ}{\bowtie}_R S$, assuming R fits in memory.

h) $R \overset{\circ}{\bowtie}_R S$, assuming S fits in memory.

i) $R \overset{\circ}{\bowtie} S$, assuming R fits in memory.

6.4 Nested-Loop Joins

Before proceeding to the more complex algorithms in the next sections, we shall turn our attention to a family of algorithms for the join operator called "nested-loop" joins. These algorithms are, in a sense, "one-and-a-half" passes, since in each variation one of the two arguments has its tuples read only once, while the other argument will be read repeatedly. Nested-loop joins can be used for relations of any size; it is not necessary that one relation fit in main memory.

6.4.1 Tuple-Based Nested-Loop Join

We shall begin with the simplest variation of the nested-loop theme, where the loops range over individual tuples of the relations involved. In this algorithm, which we call *tuple-based nested-loop join*, we compute the join

$$R(X, Y) \bowtie S(Y, Z)$$

as follows:

```
FOR each tuple s in S DO
    FOR each tuple r in R DO
        IF r and s join to make a tuple t THEN
            output t;
```

If we are careless about how we buffer the blocks of relations R and S, then this algorithm could require as many as $T(R)T(S)$ disk I/O's. However, there are many situations where this algorithm can be modified to have much lower cost. One case is when we can use an index on the join attribute or attributes of R to find the tuples of R that match a given tuple of S, without having to read the entire relation R. We discuss index-based joins in Section 6.7.3. A second improvement looks much more carefully at the way tuples of R and S are divided among blocks, and uses as much of the memory as it can to reduce the number of disk I/O's as we go through the inner loop. We shall consider this block-based version of nested-loop join in Section 6.4.3.

6.4.2 An Iterator for Tuple-Based Nested-Loop Join

One advantage of a nested-loop join is that it fits well into an iterator framework, and thus, as we shall see in Section 7.7.3, allows us to avoid storing intermediate relations on disk in some situations. The iterator for $R \bowtie S$ is easy to build from the iterators for R and S, which we denote by R.Open, and so on, as in Section 6.2.6. The code for the three iterator functions for nested-loop join is in Fig. 6.12. It makes the assumption that neither relation R nor S is empty.

6.4.3 A Block-Based Nested-Loop Join Algorithm

We can improve on the tuple-based nested-loop join of Section 6.4.1 if we compute $R \bowtie S$ by:

1. Organizing access to both argument relations by blocks, and

2. Using as much main memory as we can to store tuples belonging to the relation S, the relation of the outer loop.

Point (1) makes sure that when we run through the tuples of R in the inner loop, we use as few disk I/O's as possible to read R. Point (2) enables us to join

```
Open(R,S) {
    R.Open();
    S.Open();
    s := S.GetNext();
}

GetNext(R,S) {
    REPEAT {
        r := R.GetNext();
        IF (NOT Found) { /* R is exhausted for
                the current s */
            R.Close();
            s := S.GetNext();
            IF (NOT Found) RETURN; /* both R and S
                    are exhausted */
            R.Open();
            r := R.GetNext();
        }
    }
    UNTIL(r and s join);
    RETURN the join of r and s;
}

Close(R,S) {
    R.Close();
    S.Close();
}
```

Figure 6.12: Iterator functions for tuple-based nested-loop join

each tuple of R that we read with not just one tuple of S, but with as many tuples of S as will fit in memory.

As in Section 6.3.3, let us assume $B(S) \leq B(R)$, but now let us also assume that $B(S) > M$; i.e., neither relation fits entirely in main memory. We repeatedly read $M - 1$ blocks of S into main-memory buffers. A search structure, with search key equal to the common attributes of R and S, is created for the tuples of S that are in main memory. Then we go through all the blocks of R, reading each one in turn into the last block of memory. Once there, we compare all the tuples of R's block with all the tuples in all the blocks of S that are currently in main memory. For those that join, we output the joined tuple. The nested-loop structure of this algorithm can be seen when we describe the algorithm more formally, in Fig. 6.13.

```
FOR each chunk of M-1 blocks of S DO BEGIN
    read these blocks into main-memory buffers;
    organize their tuples into a search structure whose
        search key is the common attributes of R and S;
    FOR each block b of R DO BEGIN
        read b into main memory;
        FOR each tuple t of b DO BEGIN
            find the tuples of S in main memory that
                join with t;
            output the join of t with each of these tuples;
        END;
    END;
END;
```

Figure 6.13: The nested-loop join algorithm

The program of Fig. 6.13 appears to have three nested loops. However, there really are only two loops if we look at the code at the right level of abstraction. The first, or outer loop, runs through the tuples of S. The other two loops run through the tuples of R. However, we expressed the process as two loops to emphasize that the order in which we visit the tuples of R is not arbitrary. Rather, we need to look at these tuples a block at a time (the role of the second loop), and within one block, we look at all the tuples of that block before moving on to the next block (the role of the third loop).

Example 6.14: Assume $B(R) = 1000$ and $B(S) = 500$, and let $M = 101$. we shall use 100 blocks of memory to buffer S in 100-block chunks, so the outer loop of Fig. 6.13 iterates five times. At each iteration, we do 100 disk I/O's to read the chunk of S, and we must read R entirely in the second loop, using 1000 disk I/O's. Thus, the total number of disk I/O's is 5500.

Notice that if we reversed the roles of R and S, the algorithm would use slightly more disk I/O's. We would iterate 10 times through the outer loop and do 600 disk I/O's at each iteration, for a total of 6000. In general, there is a slight advantage to using the smaller relation in the outer loop. $\square$

The algorithm of Fig. 6.13 is sometimes called "nested-block join." We shall continue to call it simply *nested-loop join*, since it is the variant of the nested-loop idea most commonly implemented in practice. If necessary to distinguish it from the tuple-based nested-loop join of Section 6.4.1, we can call Fig. 6.13 "block-based nested-loop join."

6.4.4 Analysis of Nested-Loop Join

The analysis of Example 6.14 can be repeated for any $B(R)$, $B(S)$, and M. Assuming S is the smaller relation, the number of chunks, or iterations of the outer loop is $B(S)/(M-1)$. At each iteration, we read $M-1$ blocks of S and $B(R)$ blocks of R. The number of disk I/O's is thus

$$\frac{B(S)}{M-1}\bigl(M-1+B(R)\bigr)$$

or

$$B(S) + \frac{B(S)B(R)}{M-1}$$

Assuming all of M, $B(S)$, and $B(R)$ are large, but M is the smallest of these, an approximation to the above formula is $B(S)B(R)/M$. That is, the cost is proportional to the product of the sizes of the two relations, divided by the amount of available main memory. We can do much better when both relations are large, although we should notice that for reasonably small examples such as Example 6.14, the cost of the nested-loop join is not much greater than the cost of a one-pass join, which would be 1500 disk I/O's. In fact, if $B(S) \leq M-1$, the nested-loop join becomes identical to the one-pass join algorithm of Section 6.3.3.

Although nested-loop join is generally not the most efficient join algorithm possible, we should note that in some early relational DBMS's, it was the only method available. Even today, it is needed as a subroutine in more efficient join algorithms in certain situations, such as when large numbers of tuples from each relation share a common value for the join attribute(s). For an example where nested-loop join is essential, see Section 6.5.5.

6.4.5 Summary of Algorithms so Far

The main-memory and disk I/O requirements for the algorithms we have discussed in Sections 6.3 and 6.4 are shown in Fig. 6.14. The memory requirements for γ and δ are actually more complex than shown, and $M = B$ is only a loose approximation. For γ, M grows with the number of groups, and for δ, M grows with the number of distinct tuples.

6.4.6 Exercises for Section 6.4

Exercise 6.4.1 : Give the three iterator functions for the block-based version of nested-loop join.

* **Exercise 6.4.2 :** Suppose $B(R) = B(S) = 10{,}000$, and $M = 1000$. Calculate the disk I/O cost of a nested-loop join.

Exercise 6.4.3 : For the relations of Exercise 6.4.2, what value of M would we need to compute $R \bowtie S$ using the nested-loop algorithm with no more than

Operators	Approximate M required	Disk I/O	Section
σ, π	1	B	6.3.1
γ, δ	B	B	6.3.2
$\cup$, $\cap$, $-$, $\times$, $\bowtie$	$\min(B(R), B(S))$	$B(R) + B(S)$	6.3.3
$\bowtie$	any $M \geq 2$	$B(R)B(S)/M$	6.4.3

Figure 6.14: Main memory and disk I/O requirements for one-pass and nested-loop algorithms

   a) 100,000

! b) 25,000

! c) 15,000

disk I/O's?

! **Exercise 6.4.4:** If R and S are both unclustered, it seems that nested-loop join would require about $T(R)T(S)/M$ disk I/O's.

   a) How can you do significantly better than this cost?

   b) If only one of R and S is unclustered, how would you perform a nested-loop join? Consider both the cases that the larger is unclustered and that the smaller is unclustered.

! **Exercise 6.4.5:** The iterator of Fig. 6.12 will not work properly if either R or S is empty. Rewrite the functions so they will work, even if one or both relations are empty.

6.5 Two-Pass Algorithms Based on Sorting

We shall now begin the study of multipass algorithms for performing relational-algebra operations on relations that are larger than what the one-pass algorithms of Section 6.3 can handle. We concentrate on *two-pass algorithms*, where data from the operand relations is read into main memory, processed in some way, written out to disk again, and then reread from disk to complete the operation. We can naturally extend this idea to any number of passes, where the data is read many times into main memory. However, we concentrate on two-pass algorithms because:

   a) Two passes are usually enough, even for very large relations,

b) Generalizing to more than two passes is not hard; we discuss these extensions in Section 6.9.

In this section, we consider sorting as a tool for implementing relational operations. The basic idea is as follows. If we have a large relation R, where $B(R)$ is larger than M, the number of memory buffers we have available, then we can repeatedly:

1. Read M blocks of R into main memory.

2. Sort these M blocks in main memory, using an efficient sorting algorithm. Such an algorithm will take an amount of processor time that is just slightly more than linear in the number of tuples in main memory, so we expect that the time to sort will not exceed the disk I/O time for step (1).

3. Write the sorted list into M blocks of disk. We shall refer to the contents of these blocks as one of the *sorted sublists* of R.

All the algorithms we shall discuss then use a second pass to "merge" the sorted sublists in some way to execute the desired operator.

6.5.1   Duplicate Elimination Using Sorting

To perform the $\delta(R)$ operation in two passes, we sort the tuples of R in sublists as described above. We then use the available main memory to hold one block from each sorted sublist, as we did for the multiway merge sort of Section 2.3.4. However, instead of sorting the tuples from these sublists, we repeatedly copy one to the output and ignore all tuples identical to it. The process is suggested by Fig. 6.15.

More precisely, we look at the first unconsidered tuple from each block, and we find among them the first in sorted order, say t. We make one copy of t in the output, and we remove from the fronts of the various input blocks all copies of t. If a block is exhausted, we bring into its buffer the next block from the same sublist, and if there are t's on that block we remove them as well.

Example 6.15: Suppose for simplicity that tuples are integers, and only two tuples fit on a block. Also, $M = 3$; i.e., there are three blocks in main memory. The relation R consists of 17 tuples:

$$2, 5, 2, 1, 2, 2, 4, 5, 4, 3, 4, 2, 1, 5, 2, 1, 3$$

We read the first six tuples into the three blocks of main memory, sort them, and write them out as the sublist R_1. Similarly, tuples seven through twelve are then read in, sorted and written as the sublist R_2. The last five tuples are likewise sorted and become the sublist R_3.

To start the second pass, we can bring into main memory the first block (two tuples) from each of the three sublists. The situation is now:

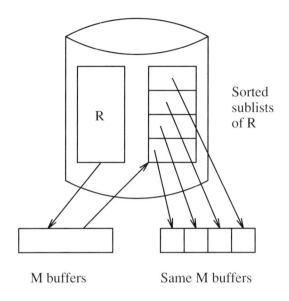

Figure 6.15: A two-pass algorithm for eliminating duplicates

Sublist	In memory	Waiting on disk
R_1:	1 2	2 2, 2 5
R_2:	2 3	4 4, 4 5
R_3:	1 1	2 3, 5

Looking at the first tuples of the three blocks in main memory, we find that 1 is the first tuple in sorted order. We therefore make one copy of 1 to the output, and we remove all 1's from the blocks in memory. When we do so, the block from R_3 is exhausted, so we bring in the next block, with tuples 2 and 3, from that sublist. Had there been more 1's on this block, we would eliminate them. The situation is now:

Sublist	In memory	Waiting on disk
R_1:	2	2 2, 2 5
R_2:	2 3	4 4, 4 5
R_3:	2 3	5

Now, 2 is the least tuple at the fronts of the lists, and in fact it happens to appear on each list. We write one copy of 2 to the output and eliminate 2's from the in-memory blocks. The block from R_1 is exhausted and the next block from that sublist is brought to memory. That block has 2's, which are eliminated, again exhausting the block from R_1. The third block from that sublist is brought to memory, and its 2 is eliminated. The present situation is:

Sublist	In memory	Waiting on disk
R_1:	5	
R_2:	3	4 4, 4 5
R_3:	3	5

Now, 3 is selected as the least tuple, one copy of 3 is written to the output, and the blocks from R_2 and R_3 are exhausted and replaced from disk, leaving:

Sublist	In memory	Waiting on disk
R_1:	5	
R_2:	4 4	4 5
R_3:	5	

To complete the example, 4 is next selected, consuming most of list R_2. At the final step, each list happens to consist of a single 5, which is output once and eliminated from the input buffers.   □

The number of disk I/O's performed by this algorithm, as always ignoring the handling of the output, is:

1. $B(R)$ to read each block of R when creating the sorted sublists.

2. $B(R)$ to write each of the sorted sublists to disk.

3. $B(R)$ to read each block from the sublists at the appropriate time.

Thus, the total cost of this algorithm is $3B(R)$, compared with $B(R)$ for the single-pass algorithm of Section 6.3.2.

On the other hand, we can handle much larger files using the two-pass algorithm than with the one-pass algorithm. Assuming M blocks of memory are available, we create sorted sublists of M blocks each. For the second pass, we need one block from each sublist in main memory, so there can be no more than M sublists, each M blocks long. Thus, $B \leq M^2$ is required for the two-pass algorithm to be feasible, compared with $B \leq M$ for the one-pass algorithm. Put another way, to compute $\delta(R)$ with the two-pass algorithm requires only $\sqrt{B(R)}$ blocks of memory, rather than $B(R)$ blocks of memory.

6.5.2   Grouping and Aggregation Using Sorting

The two-pass algorithm for $\gamma_L(R)$ is quite similar to the algorithm of Section 6.5.1 for $\delta(R)$. We summarize it as follows:

1. Read the tuples of R into memory, M blocks at a time. Sort each M blocks, using the grouping attributes of L as the sort key. Write each sorted sublist to disk.

2. Use one main-memory buffer for each sublist, and initially load the first block of each sublist into its buffer.

3. Repeatedly find the least value of the sort key (grouping attributes) present among the first available tuples in the buffers. This value, v, becomes the next group, for which we:

    (a) Prepare to compute all the aggregates on list L for this group. As in Section 6.3.2, use a count and sum in place of an average.

    (b) Examine each of the tuples with sort key v, and accumulate the needed aggregates.

    (c) If a buffer becomes empty, replace it with the next block from the same sublist.

    When there are no more tuples with sort key v available, output a tuple consisting of the grouping attributes of L and the associated values of the aggregations we have computed for the group.

As for the δ algorithm, this two-pass algorithm for γ takes $3B(R)$ disk I/O's, and will work as long as $B(R) \leq M^2$.

6.5.3 A Sort-Based Union Algorithm

When bag-union is wanted, the one-pass algorithm of Section 6.3.3, where we simply copy both relations, works regardless of the size of the arguments, so there is no need to consider a two-pass algorithm for $\cup_B$. However, the one-pass algorithm for $\cup_S$ only works when at least one relation is smaller than the available main memory, so we should consider a two-pass algorithm for set union. The methodology we present works for the set and bag versions of intersection and difference as well, as we shall see in Section 6.5.4. To compute $R \cup_S S$, we do the following:

1. Repeatedly bring M blocks of R into main memory, sort their tuples, and write the resulting sorted sublist back to disk.

2. Do the same for S, to create sorted sublists for relation S.

3. Use one main-memory buffer for each sublist of R and S. Initialize each with the first block from the corresponding sublist.

4. Repeatedly find the first remaining tuple t among all the buffers. Copy t to the output, and remove from the buffers all copies of t (if R and S are sets there should be at most two copies). If a buffer becomes empty, reload it with the next block from its sublist.

We observe that each tuple of R and S is read twice into main memory, once when the sublists are being created, and the second time as part of one of the sublists. The tuple is also written to disk once, as part of a newly formed sublist. Thus, the cost in disk I/O's is $3\big(B(R) + B(S)\big)$.

The algorithm works as long as the total number of sublists among the two relations does not exceed M, because we need one buffer for each sublist. Since each sublist is M blocks long, that says the sizes of the two relations must not exceed M^2; that is, $B(R) + B(S) \leq M^2$.

6.5.4   Sort-Based Algorithms for Intersection and Difference

Whether the set version or the bag version is wanted, the algorithms are essentially the same as that of Section 6.5.3, except that the way we handle the copies of a tuple t at the fronts of the sorted sublists differs. In general we create the sorted sublists of M blocks each for both argument relations R and S. We use one main-memory buffer for each sublist, initially loaded with the first block of the sublist.

We then repeatedly consider the least tuple t among the remaining tuples in all the buffers. We count the number of tuples of R that are identical to t and we also count the number of tuples of S that are identical to t. Doing so requires that we reload buffers from any sublists whose currently buffered block is exhausted. The following indicates how we determine whether t is output, and if so, how many times:

- If the operation is set intersection, output t if it appears in both R and S.

- If the operation is bag intersection, output t the minimum of the number of times it appears in R and in S. Note that t is not output if either of these counts is 0; that is, if t does not appear in both of the relations.

- If the operation is set difference, $R -_S S$, output t if and only if it appears in R but not in S.

- If the operation is bag difference, $R -_B S$, output t the number of times it appears in R minus the number of times it appears in S. Of course, if t appears in S at least as many times as it appears in R, then do not output t at all.

Example 6.16: Let us make the same assumptions as in Example 6.15: $M = 3$, tuples are integers, and two tuples fit in a block. The data will be almost the same as in that example as well. However, here we need two arguments, so we shall assume that R has 12 tuples and S has 5 tuples. Since main memory can fit six tuples, in the first pass we get two sublists from R, which we shall call R_1 and R_2, and only one sorted sublist from S, which we refer to as S_1.[2] After creating the sorted sublists (from unsorted relations similar to the data from Example 6.15), the situation is:

---

[2]Since S fits in main memory, we could actually use the one-pass algorithms of Section 6.3.3, but we shall use the two-pass approach for illustration.

Sublist	In memory	Waiting on disk
R_1:	1 2	2 2, 2 5
R_2:	2 3	4 4, 4 5
S_1:	1 1	2 3, 5

Suppose we want to take the bag difference $R -_B S$. We find that the least tuple among the main-memory buffers is 1, so we count the number of 1's among the sublists of R and among the sublists of S. We find that 1 appears once in R and twice in S. Since 1 does not appear more times in R than in S, we do not output any copies of tuple 1. Since the first block of S_1 was exhausted counting 1's, we loaded the next block of S_1, leaving the following situation:

Sublist	In memory	Waiting on disk
R_1:	2	2 2, 2 5
R_2:	2 3	4 4, 4 5
S_1:	2 3	5

We now find that 2 is the least remaining tuple, so we count the number of its occurrences in R, which is five occurrences, and we count the number of its occurrences in S, which is one. We thus output tuple 2 four times. As we perform the counts, we must reload the buffer for R_1 twice, which leaves:

Sublist	In memory	Waiting on disk
R_1:	5	
R_2:	3	4 4, 4 5
S_1:	3	5

Next, we consider tuple 3, and find it appears once in R and once in S. We therefore do not output 3 and remove its copies from the buffers, leaving:

Sublist	In memory	Waiting on disk
R_1:	5	
R_2:	4 4	4 5
S_1:	5	

Tuple 4 occurs three times in R and not at all in S, so we output three copies of 4. Last, 5 appears twice in R and once in S, so we output 5 once. The complete output is 2, 2, 2, 2, 4, 4, 4, 5. □

The analysis of this family of algorithms is the same as for the set-union algorithm described in Section 6.5.3:

- $3\big(B(R) + B(S)\big)$ disk I/O's.

- Approximately $B(R) + B(S) \leq M^2$ for the algorithm to work.

6.5.5   A Simple Sort-Based Join Algorithm

There are several ways that sorting can be used to join large relations. Before examining the join algorithms, let us observe one problem that can occur when we compute a join but was not an issue for the binary operations considered so far. When taking a join, the number of tuples from the two relations that share a common value of the join attribute(s), and therefore need to be in main memory simultaneously, can exceed what fits in memory. The extreme example is when there is only one value of the join attribute(s), and every tuple of one relation joins with every tuple of the other relation. In this situation, there is really no choice but to take a nested-loop join of the two sets of tuples with a common value in the join-attribute(s).

To avoid facing this situation, we can try to reduce main-memory use for other aspects of the algorithm, and thus make available a large number of buffers to hold the tuples with a given join-attribute value. In this section we shall discuss the algorithm that makes the greatest possible number of buffers available for joining tuples with a common value. In Section 6.5.7 we consider another sort-based algorithm that uses fewer disk I/O's, but can present problems when there are large numbers of tuples with a common join-attribute value.

Given relations $R(X, Y)$ and $S(Y, Z)$ to join, and given M blocks of main memory for buffers, we do the following:

1. Sort R, using a two-phase, multiway merge sort, with Y as the sort key.

2. Sort S similarly.

3. Merge the sorted R and S. We generally use only two buffers, one for the current block of R and the other for the current block of S. The following steps are done repeatedly:

    (a) Find the least value y of the join attributes Y that is currently at the front of the blocks for R and S.

    (b) If y does not appear at the front of the other relation, then remove the tuple(s) with sort key y.

    (c) Otherwise, identify all the tuples from both relations having sort key y. If necessary, read blocks from the sorted R and/or S, until we are sure there are no more y's in either relation. As many as M buffers are available for this purpose.

    (d) Output all the tuples that can be formed by joining tuples from R and S with a common Y-value y.

    (e) If either relation has no more unconsidered tuples in main memory, reload the buffer for that relation.

Example 6.17 : Let us consider the relations R and S from Example 6.14. Recall these relations occupy 1000 and 500 blocks, respectively, and there are $M = 101$ main-memory buffers. When we use two-phase, multiway merge sort on a relation, we do four disk I/O's per block, two in each of the two phases. Thus, we use $4(B(R) + B(S))$ disk I/O's to sort R and S, or 6000 disk I/O's.

When we merge the sorted R and S to find the joined tuples, we read each block of R and S a fifth time, using another 1500 disk I/O's. In this merge we generally need only two of the 101 blocks of memory. However, if necessary, we could use all 101 blocks to hold the tuples of R and S that share a common Y-value y. Thus, it is sufficient that for no y do the tuples of R and S that have Y-value y together occupy more than 101 blocks.

Notice that the total number of disk I/O's performed by this algorithm is 7500, compared with 5500 for nested-loop join in Example 6.14. However, nested-loop join is inherently a quadratic algorithm, taking time proportional to $B(R)B(S)$, while sort-join has linear I/O cost, taking time proportional to $B(R) + B(S)$. It is only the constant factors and the small size of the example (each relation is only 5 or 10 times larger than a relation that fits entirely in the allotted buffers) that make nested-loop join preferable. Moreover, we shall see in Section 6.5.7 that it is usually possible to perform a sort-join in $3(B(R) + B(S))$ disk I/O's, which would be 4500 in this example and which is below the cost of nested-loop join. □

If there is a Y-value y for which the number of tuples with this Y-value does not fit in M buffers, then we need to modify the above algorithm.

1. If the tuples from one of the relations, say R, that have Y-value y fit in $M - 1$ buffers, then load these blocks of R into buffers, and read the blocks of S that hold tuples with y, one at a time, into the remaining buffer. In effect, we do the one-pass join of Section 6.3.3 on only the tuples with Y-value y.

2. If neither relation has sufficiently few tuples with Y-value y that they all fit in $M - 1$ buffers, then use the M buffers to perform a nested-loop join on the tuples with Y-value y from both relations.

Note that in either case, it may be necessary to read blocks from one relation and then ignore them, having to read them later. For example, in case (1), we might first read the blocks of S that have tuples with Y-value y and find that there are too many to fit in $M - 1$ buffers. However, if we then read the tuples of R with that Y-value we find that they do fit in $M - 1$ buffers.

6.5.6 Analysis of Simple Sort-Join

As we noted in Example 6.17, our algorithm performs five disk I/O's for every block of the argument relation. The exception would be if there were so many tuples with a common Y-value that we needed to do one of the specialized joins on these tuples. In that case, the number of extra disk I/O's depends on whether one or both relations have so many tuples with a common Y-value that they require more than $M - 1$ buffers by themselves. We shall not go into all the detailed cases here; the exercises contain some examples to work out.

We also need to consider how big M needs to be in order for the simple sort-join to work. The primary constraint is that we need to be able to perform the two-phase, multiway merge sorts on R and S. As we observed in Section 2.3.4, we need $B(R) \leq M^2$ and $B(S) \leq M^2$ to perform these sorts. Once done, we shall not run out of buffers, although as discussed before, we may have to deviate from the simple merge if the tuples with a common Y-value cannot fit in M buffers. In summary, assuming no such deviations are necessary:

- The simple sort-join uses $5(B(R) + B(S))$ disk I/O's.

- It requires $B(R) \leq M^2$ and $B(S) \leq M^2$ to work.

6.5.7 A More Efficient Sort-Based Join

If we do not have to worry about very large numbers of tuples with a common value for the join attribute(s), then we can save two disk I/O's per block by combining the second phase of the sorts with the join itself. We call this algorithm *sort-join*; other names by which it is known include "merge-join" and "sort-merge-join." To compute $R(X, Y) \bowtie S(Y, Z)$ using M main-memory buffers we:

1. Create sorted sublists of size M, using Y as the sort key, for both R and S.

2. Bring the first block of each sublist into a buffer; we assume there are no more than M sublists in all.

3. Repeatedly find the least Y-value y among the first available tuples of all the sublists. Identify all the tuples of both relations that have Y-value y, perhaps using some of the M available buffers to hold them, if there are fewer than M sublists. Output the join of all tuples from R with all tuples from S that share this common Y-value. If the buffer for one of the sublists is exhausted, then replenish it from disk.

Example 6.18: Let us again consider the problem of Example 6.14: joining relations R and S of sizes 1000 and 500 blocks, respectively, using 101 buffers. We divide R into 10 sublists and S into 5 sublists, each of length 100, and sort them.[3] We then use 15 buffers to hold the current blocks of each of the sublists. If we face a situation in which many tuples have a fixed Y-value, we can use the remaining 86 buffers to store these tuples, but if there are more tuples than that we must use a special algorithm such as was discussed at the end of Section 6.5.5.

Assuming that we do not need to modify the algorithm for large groups of tuples with the same Y-value, then we perform three disk I/O's per block of

---

[3]Technically, we could have arranged for the sublists to have length 101 blocks each, with the last sublist of R having 91 blocks and the last sublist of S having 96 blocks, but the costs would turn out exactly the same.

data. Two of those are to create the sorted sublists. Then, every block of every sorted sublist is read into main memory one more time in the multiway merging process. Thus, the total number of disk I/O's is 4500. □

This sort-join algorithm is more efficient than the algorithm of Section 6.5.5 when it can be used. As we observed in Example 6.18, the number of disk I/O's is $3(B(R) + B(S))$. We can perform the algorithm on data that is almost as large as that of the previous algorithm. The sizes of the sorted sublists are M blocks, and there can be at most M of them among the two lists. Thus, $B(R) + B(S) \leq M^2$ is sufficient.

We might wonder whether we can avoid the trouble that arises when there are many tuples with a common Y-value. Some important considerations are:

1. Sometimes we can be sure the problem will not arise. For example, if Y is a key for R, then a given Y-value y can appear only once among all the blocks of the sublists for R. When it is y's turn, we can leave the tuple from R in place and join it with all the tuples of S that match. If blocks of S's sublists are exhausted during this process, they can have their buffers reloaded with the next block, and there is never any need for additional space, no matter how many tuples of S have Y-value y. Of course, if Y is a key for S rather than R, the same argument applies with R and S switched.

2. If $B(R) + B(S)$ is much less than M^2, we shall have many unused buffers for storing tuples with a common Y-value, as we suggested in Example 6.18.

3. If all else fails, we can use a nested-loop join on just the tuples with a common Y-value, using extra disk I/O's but getting the job done correctly. This option was discussed in Section 6.5.5.

6.5.8 Summary of Sort-Based Algorithms

In Fig. 6.16 is a table of the analysis of the algorithms we have discussed in Section 6.5. As discussed in Sections 6.5.5 and 6.5.7, modifications to the time and memory requirements are necessary if we join two relations that have many tuples with the same value in the join attribute(s).

6.5.9 Exercises for Section 6.5

Exercise 6.5.1: Using the assumptions of Example 6.15 (two tuples per block, etc.),

a) Show the behavior of the two-pass duplicate-elimination algorithm on the sequence of thirty one-component tuples in which the sequence 0, 1, 2, 3, 4 repeats six times.

Operators	Approximate M required	Disk I/O	Section
γ, δ	$\sqrt{B}$	$3B$	6.5.1, 6.5.2
$\cup, \cap, -$	$\sqrt{B(R)+B(S)}$	$3(B(R)+B(S))$	6.5.3, 6.5.4
$\bowtie$	$\sqrt{\max(B(R),B(S))}$	$5(B(R)+B(S))$	6.5.5
$\bowtie$	$\sqrt{B(R)+B(S)}$	$3(B(R)+B(S))$	6.5.7

Figure 6.16: Main memory and disk I/O requirements for sort-based algorithms

b) Show the behavior of the two-pass grouping algorithm computing the relation $\gamma_{a,AVG(b)}(R)$. Relation $R(a,b)$ consists of the thirty tuples t_0 through t_{29}, and the tuple t_i has i modulo 5 as its grouping component a, and i as its second component b.

Exercise 6.5.2: For each of the operations below, write an iterator that uses the algorithm described in this section.

* a) Distinct (δ).

  b) Grouping (γ_L).

* c) Set intersection.

  d) Bag difference.

  e) Natural join.

Exercise 6.5.3: If $B(R) = B(S) = 10{,}000$ and $M = 1000$, what are the disk I/O requirements of:

  a) Set union.

* b) Simple sort-join.

  c) The more efficient sort-join of Section 6.5.7.

! **Exercise 6.5.4:** Suppose that the second pass of an algorithm described in this section does not need all M buffers, because there are fewer than M sublists. How might we save disk I/O's by using the extra buffers?

! **Exercise 6.5.5 :** In Example 6.17 we discussed the join of two relations R and S, with 1000 and 500 blocks, respectively, and $M = 101$. However, we pointed out that there would be additional disk I/O's if there were so many tuples with a given value that neither relation's tuples could fit in main memory. Calculate the total number of disk I/O's needed if:

* a) There are only two Y-values, each appearing in half the tuples of R and half the tuples of S (recall Y is the join attribute or attributes).

  b) There are five Y-values, each equally likely in each relation.

  c) There are 10 Y-values, each equally likely in each relation.

! **Exercise 6.5.6 :** Repeat Exercise 6.5.5 for the more efficient sort-join of Section 6.5.7.

Exercise 6.5.7 : How much memory do we need to use a two-pass, sort-based algorithm for relations of 10,000 blocks each, if the operation is:

* a) δ.

  b) γ.

  c) A binary operation such as join or union.

Exercise 6.5.8 : Describe a two-pass, sort-based algorithm for each of the five join-like operators of Exercise 6.1.3.

! **Exercise 6.5.9 :** Suppose records could be larger than blocks, i.e., we could have spanned records. How would the memory requirements of two-pass, sort-based algorithms change?

!! **Exercise 6.5.10 :** Sometimes, it is possible to save some disk I/O's if we leave the last sublist in memory. It may even make sense to use sublists of fewer than M blocks to take advantage of this effect. How many disk I/O's can be saved this way?

!! **Exercise 6.5.11 :** OQL allows grouping of objects according to arbitrary, user-specified functions of the objects. For example, one could group tuples according to the sum of two attributes. How would we perform a sort-based grouping operation of this type on a set of objects?

6.6 Two-Pass Algorithms Based on Hashing

There is a family of hash-based algorithms that attack the same problems as in Section 6.5. The essential idea behind all these algorithms is as follows. If the data is too big to store in main-memory buffers, hash all the tuples of the argument or arguments using an appropriate hash key. For all the common

operations, there is a way to select the hash key so all the tuples that need
to be considered together when we perform the operation have the same hash
value.

We then perform the operation by working on one bucket at a time (or on
a pair of buckets with the same hash value, in the case of a binary operation).
In effect, we have reduced the size of the operand(s) by a factor equal to the
number of buckets. If there are M buffers available, we can pick M as the
number of buckets, thus gaining a factor of M in the size of the relations we
can handle. Notice that the sort-based algorithms of Section 6.5 also gain a
factor of M by preprocessing, although the sorting and hashing approaches
achieve their similar gains by rather different means.

6.6.1   Partitioning Relations by Hashing

To begin, let us review the way we would take a relation R and, using M buffers,
partition R into $M - 1$ buckets of roughly equal size. We shall assume that
h is the hash function, and that h takes complete tuples of R as its argument
(i.e., all attributes of R are part of the hash key). We associate one buffer with
each bucket. The last buffer holds blocks of R, one at a time. Each tuple t
in the block is hashed to bucket $h(t)$ and copied to the appropriate buffer. If
that buffer is full, we write it out to disk, and initialize another block for the
same bucket. At the end, we write out the last bucket of each block if it is not
empty. The algorithm is given in more detail in Fig. 6.17. Note that it assumes
that tuples, while they may be variable-length, are never too large to fit in an
empty buffer.

```
initialize M-1 buckets using M-1 empty buffers;
FOR each block b of relation R DO BEGIN
    read block b into the Mth buffer;
    FOR each tuple t in b DO BEGIN
        IF the buffer for bucket h(t) has no room for t THEN
            BEGIN
                copy the buffer to disk;
                initialize a new empty block in that buffer;
            END;
        copy t to the buffer for bucket h(t);
    END;
END;
FOR each bucket DO
    IF the buffer for this bucket is not empty THEN
        write the buffer to disk;
```

Figure 6.17: Partitioning a relation R into $M - 1$ buckets

6.6.2 A Hash-Based Algorithm for Duplicate Elimination

We shall now consider the details of hash-based algorithms for the various operations of relational algebra that might need two-pass algorithms. First, consider duplicate elimination, that is, the operation $\delta(R)$. We hash R to $M - 1$ buckets, as in Fig. 6.17. Note that two copies of the same tuple t will hash to the same bucket. Thus, δ has the essential property we need: we can examine one bucket at a time, perform δ on that bucket in isolation, and take as the answer the union of $\delta(R_i)$, where R_i is the portion of R that hashes to the ith bucket. The one-pass algorithm of Section 6.3.2 can be used to eliminate duplicates from each R_i in turn and write out the resulting unique tuples.

This method will work as long as the individual R_i's are sufficiently small to fit in main memory and thus allow a one-pass algorithm. Since we assume the hash function h partitions R into equal-sized buckets, each R_i will be approximately $B(R)/(M-1)$ blocks in size. If that number of blocks is no larger than M, i.e., $B(R) \leq M(M-1)$, then the two-pass, hash-based algorithm will work. In fact, as we discussed in Section 6.3.2, it is only necessary that the number of distinct tuples in one bucket fit in M buffers, but we cannot be sure that there are any duplicates at all. Thus, a conservative estimate, with a simple form in which M and $M - 1$ are considered the same, is $B(R) \leq M^2$, exactly as for the sort-based, two-pass algorithm for δ.

The number of disk I/O's is also similar to that of the sort-based algorithm. We read each block of R once as we hash its tuples, and we write each block of each bucket to disk. We then read each block of each bucket again in the one-pass algorithm that focuses on that bucket. Thus, the total number of disk I/O's is $3B(R)$.

6.6.3 A Hash-Based Algorithm for Grouping and Aggregation

To perform the $\gamma_L(R)$ operation, we again start by hashing all the tuples of R to $M - 1$ buckets. However, in order to make sure that all tuples of the same group wind up in the same bucket, we must choose a hash function that depends only on the grouping attributes of the list L.

Having partitioned R into buckets, we can then use the one-pass algorithm for γ from Section 6.3.2 to process each bucket in turn. As we discussed for δ in Section 6.6.2, we can process each bucket in main memory provided $B(R) \leq M^2$.

However, on the second pass, we only need one record per group as we process each bucket. Thus, even if the size of a bucket is larger than M, we can handle the bucket in one pass provided the records for all the groups in the bucket take no more than M buffers. Normally, a group's record will be no larger than a tuple of R. If so, then a better upper bound on $B(R)$ is M^2 times the average number of tuples per group.

As a consequence, if there are are few groups, then we may actually be able to handle much larger relations R than is indicated by the $B(R) \leq M^2$ rule. On the other hand, if M exceeds the number of groups, then we cannot fill all buckets. Thus, the actual limitation on the size of R as a function of M is complex, but $B(R) \leq M^2$ is a conservative estimate. Finally, we observe that the number of disk I/O's for γ, as for δ, is $3B(R)$.

6.6.4   Hash-Based Algorithms for Union, Intersection, and Difference

When the operation is binary, we must make sure that we use the same hash function to hash tuples of both arguments. For example, to compute $R \cup_S S$, we hash both R and S to $M - 1$ buckets each, say $R_1, R_2, \ldots, R_{M-1}$ and $S_1, S_2, \ldots, S_{M-1}$. We then take the set-union of R_i with S_i for all i, and output the result. Notice that if a tuple t appears in both R and S, then for some i we shall find t in both R_i and S_i. Thus, when we take the union of these two buckets, we shall output only one copy of t, and there is no possibility of introducing duplicates into the result. For $\cup_B$, the simple bag-union algorithm of Section 6.3.3 is preferable to any other approach for that operation.

To take the intersection or difference of R and S, we create the $2(M - 1)$ buckets exactly as for set-union and apply the appropriate one-pass algorithm to each pair of corresponding buckets. Notice that all these algorithms require $B(R) + B(S)$ disk I/O's. To this quantity we must add the two disk I/O's per block that are necessary to hash the tuples of the two relations and store the buckets on disk, for a total of $3\big(B(R) + B(S)\big)$ disk I/O's.

In order for the algorithms to work, we must be able to take the one-pass union, intersection, or difference of R_i and S_i, whose sizes will be approximately $B(R)/(M - 1)$ and $B(S)/(M - 1)$, respectively. Recall that the one-pass algorithms for these operations require that the smaller operand occupies at most $M - 1$ blocks. Thus, the two-pass, hash-based algorithms require that $\min\big(B(R), B(S)\big) \leq M^2$, approximately.

6.6.5   The Hash-Join Algorithm

To compute $R(X, Y) \bowtie S(Y, Z)$ using a two-pass, hash-based algorithm, we act almost as for the other binary operations discussed in Section 6.6.4. The only difference is that we must use as the hash key just the join attributes, Y. Then we can be sure that if tuples of R and S join, they will wind up in corresponding buckets R_i and S_i for some i. A one-pass join of all pairs of corresponding buckets completes this algorithm, which we call *hash-join*.[4]

Example 6.19: Let us renew our discussion of the two relations R and S from Example 6.14, whose sizes were 1000 and 500 blocks, respectively, and for which

---

[4]Sometimes, the term "hash-join" is reserved for the variant of the one-pass join algorithm of Section 6.3.3 in which a hash table is used as the main-memory search structure. Then, the two-pass hash-join algorithm described here is called "partition hash-join."

101 main-memory buffers are made available. We may hash each relation to 100 buckets, so the average size of a bucket is 10 blocks for R and 5 blocks for S. Since the smaller number, 5, is much less than the number of available buffers, we expect to have no trouble performing a one-pass join on each pair of buckets.

The number of disk I/O's is 1500 to read each of R and S while hashing into buckets, another 1500 to write all the buckets to disk, and a third 1500 to read each pair of buckets into main memory again while taking the one-pass join of corresponding buckets. Thus, the number of disk I/O's required is 4500, just as for the efficient sort-join of Section 6.5.7. □

We may generalize Example 6.19 to conclude that:

- Hash join requires $3\big(B(R) + B(S)\big)$ disk I/O's to perform its task.

- The two-pass hash-join algorithm will work as long as approximately $\min\big(B(R), B(S)\big) \leq M^2$.

The argument for the latter point is the same as for the other binary operations: one of each pair of buckets must fit in $M - 1$ buffers.

6.6.6 Saving Some Disk I/O's

If there is more memory available on the first pass than we need to hold one block per bucket, then we have some opportunities to save disk I/O's. One option is to use several blocks for each bucket, and write them out as a group, in consecutive blocks of disk. Strictly speaking, this technique doesn't save disk I/O's, but it makes the I/O's go faster, since we save seek time and rotational latency when we write.

However, there are several tricks that have been used to avoid writing some of the buckets to disk and then reading them again. The most effective of them, called *hybrid hash-join*, works as follows. In general, suppose we decide that to join $R \bowtie S$, with S the smaller relation, we need to create k buckets, where k is much less than M, the available memory. When we hash S, we can choose to keep m of the k buckets entirely in main memory, while keeping only one block for each of the other $k - m$ buckets. We can manage to do so provided the expected size of the buckets in memory, plus one block for each of the other buckets, does not exceed M; that is:

$$\frac{mB(S)}{k} + k - m \leq M \tag{6.1}$$

In explanation, the expected size of a bucket is $B(S)/k$, and there are m buckets in memory.

Now, when we read the tuples of the other relation, R, to hash that relation into buckets, we keep in memory:

1. The m buckets of S that were never written to disk, and

2. One block for each of the $k - m$ buckets of R whose corresponding buckets of S were written to disk.

If a tuple t of R hashes to one of the first m buckets, then we immediately join it with all the tuples of the corresponding S-bucket, as if this were a one-pass, hash-join. The result of any successful joins is immediately output. It is necessary to organize each of the in-memory buckets of S into an efficient search structure to facilitate this join, just as for the one-pass hash-join. If t hashes to one of the buckets whose corresponding S-bucket is on disk, then t is sent to the main-memory block for that bucket, and eventually migrates to disk, as for a two-pass, hash-based join.

On the second pass, we join the corresponding buckets of R and S as usual. However, there is no need to join the pairs of buckets for which the S-bucket was left in memory; these buckets have already been joined and their result output.

The savings in disk I/O's is equal to two for every block of the buckets of S that remain in memory, and their corresponding R-buckets. Since m/k of the buckets are in memory, the savings is $2(m/k)\big(B(R) + B(S)\big)$. We must thus ask how to maximize m/k, subject to the constraint of equation (6.1). While the solution of this problem can be done formally, there is an intuition that gives the surprising but correct answer: $m = 1$, while k is as small as possible.

The argument is that all but $k - m$ of the main-memory buffers can be used to hold tuples of S in main memory, and the more of these tuples, the fewer the disk I/O's. Thus, we want to minimize k, the total number of buckets. We do so by making each bucket about as big as can fit in main memory; that is, buckets are of size M, and therefore $k = B(S)/M$. If that is the case, then there is only room for one bucket in the extra main memory; i.e., $m = 1$.

In fact, we really need to make the buckets slightly smaller than $B(S)/M$, or else we shall not quite have room for one full bucket and one block for the other $k - 1$ buckets in memory at the same time. Assuming, for simplicity, that k is about $B(S)/M$ and $m = 1$, the savings in disk I/O's is

$$\left(\frac{2M}{B(S)}\right)\Big(B(R) + B(S)\Big)$$

and the total cost is

$$\left(3 - \frac{2M}{B(S)}\right)\Big(B(R) + B(S)\Big)$$

Example 6.20 : Consider the problem of Example 6.14, where we had to join relations R and S, of 1000 and 500 blocks, respectively, using $M = 101$. If we use a hybrid hash-join, then we want k, the number of buckets, to be about $500/101$. Suppose we pick $k = 5$. Then the average bucket will have 100 blocks of S's tuples. If we try to fit one of these buckets and four extra blocks for the other four buckets, we need 104 blocks of main memory, and we cannot take the chance that the in-memory bucket will overflow memory.

Thus, we are advised to choose $k = 6$. Now, when hashing S on the first pass, we have five buffers for five of the buckets, and we have up to 96 buffers for the in-memory bucket, whose expected size is 500/6 or 83. The number of disk I/O's we use for S on the first pass is thus 500 to read all of S, and $500 - 83 = 417$ to write five buckets to disk. When we process R on the first pass, we need to read all of R (1000 disk I/O's) and write 5 of its 6 buckets (833 disk I/O's).

On the second pass, we read all the buckets written to disk, or $417 + 833 = 1250$ additional disk I/O's. The total number of disk I/O's is thus 1500 to read R and S, 1250 to write 5/6 of these relations, and another 1250 to read those tuples again, or 4000 disk I/O's. This figure compares with the 4500 disk I/O's needed for the straightforward hash-join or sort-join. □

6.6.7 Summary of Hash-Based Algorithms

Figure 6.18 gives the memory requirements and disk I/O's needed by each of the algorithms discussed in this section. As with other types of algorithms, we should observe that the estimates for γ and δ may be conservative, since they really depend on the number of duplicates and groups, respectively, rather than on the number of tuples in the argument relation.

Operators	Approximate M required	Disk I/O	Section
γ, δ	$\sqrt{B}$	$3B$	6.6.2, 6.6.3
$\cup, \cap, -$	$\sqrt{B(S)}$	$3\big(B(R) + B(S)\big)$	6.6.4
$\bowtie$	$\sqrt{B(S)}$	$3\big(B(R) + B(S)\big)$	6.6.5
$\bowtie$	$\sqrt{B(S)}$	$\big(3 - 2M/B(S)\big)\big(B(R) + B(S)\big)$	6.6.6

Figure 6.18: Main memory and disk I/O requirements for hash-based algorithms; for binary operations, assume $B(S) \leq B(R)$

Notice that the requirements for sort-based and the corresponding hash-based algorithms are almost the same. The significant differences between the two approaches are:

1. Hash-based algorithms for binary operations have a size requirement that depends only on the smaller of two arguments rather than on the sum of the argument sizes, as for sort-based algorithms.

2. Sort-based algorithms sometimes allow us to produce a result in sorted order and take advantage of that sort later. The result might be used in

another sort-based algorithm later, or it could be the answer to a query that is required to be produced in sorted order.

3. Hash-based algorithms depend on the buckets being of equal size. Since there is generally at least a small variation in size, it is not possible to use buckets that, on average, occupy M blocks; we must limit them to a somewhat smaller figure. This effect is especially prominent if the number of different hash keys is small, e.g., performing a group-by on a relation with few groups or a join with very few values for the join attributes.

4. In sort-based algorithms, the sorted sublists may be written to consecutive blocks of the disk if we organize the disk properly. Thus, one of the three disk I/O's per block may require little rotational latency or seek time and therefore may be much faster than the I/O's needed for hash-based algorithms.

5. Moreover, if M is much larger than the number of sorted sublists, then we may read in several consecutive blocks at a time from a sorted sublist, again saving some latency and seek time.

6. On the other hand, if we can choose the number of buckets to be less than M in a hash-based algorithm, then we can write out several blocks of a bucket at once. We thus obtain the same benefit on the write step for hashing that the sort-based algorithms have for the second read, as we observed in (5). Similarly, we may be able to organize the disk so that a bucket eventually winds up on consecutive blocks of tracks. If so, buckets can be read with little latency or seek time, just as sorted sublists were observed in (4) to be writable efficiently.

6.6.8   Exercises for Section 6.6

Exercise 6.6.1: The hybrid-hash-join idea, storing one bucket in main memory, can also be applied to other operations. Show how to save the cost of storing and reading one bucket from each relation when implementing a two-pass, hash-based algorithm for:

* a) δ.

  b) γ.

  c) $\cap_B$.

  d) $-_S$.

Exercise 6.6.2: If $B(S) = B(R) = 10,000$ and $M = 1000$, what is the number of disk I/O's required for a hybrid hash join?

Exercise 6.6.3: Write iterators that implement the two-pass, hash-based algorithms for (a) δ (b) γ (c) $\cap_B$ (d) $-_S$ (e) $\bowtie$.

*! Exercise 6.6.4: Suppose we are performing a two-pass, hash-based grouping operation on a relation R of the appropriate size; i.e., $B(R) \leq M^2$. However, there are so few groups, that some groups are larger than M; i.e., they will not fit in main memory at once. What modifications, if any, need to be made to the algorithm given here?

! Exercise 6.6.5: Suppose that we are using a disk where the time to move the head to a block is 100 milliseconds, and it takes 1/2 millisecond to read one block. Therefore, it takes $k/2$ milliseconds to read k consecutive blocks, once the head is positioned. Suppose we want to compute a two-pass hash-join $R \bowtie S$, where $B(R) = 1000$, $B(S) = 500$, and $M = 101$. To speed up the join, we want to use as few buckets as possible (assuming tuples distribute evenly among buckets), and read and write as many blocks as we can to consecutive positions on disk. Counting 100.5 milliseconds for a random disk I/O and $100 + k/2$ milliseconds for reading or writing k consecutive blocks from or to disk:

a) How much time does the disk I/O take?

b) How much time does the disk I/O take if we use a hybrid hash-join as described in Example 6.20?

c) How much time does a sort-based join take under the same conditions, assuming we write sorted sublists to consecutive blocks of disk?

6.7 Index-Based Algorithms

The existence of an index on one or more attributes of a relation makes available some algorithms that would not be feasible without the index. Index-based algorithms are especially useful for the selection operator, but algorithms for join and other binary operators also use indexes to very good advantage. In this section, we shall introduce these algorithms. We also continue with the discussion of the index-scan operator for accessing a stored table with an index that we began in Section 6.2.1. To appreciate many of the issues, we first need to digress and consider "clustering" indexes.

6.7.1 Clustering and Nonclustering Indexes

Recall from Section 6.2.3 that a relation is "clustered" if its tuples are packed into roughly as few blocks as can possibly hold those tuples. All the analyses we have done so far assume that relations are clustered.

We may also speak of *clustering indexes*, which are indexes on an attribute or attributes such that all the tuples with a fixed value for the search key of this index appear on roughly as few blocks as can hold them. Note that a relation that isn't clustered cannot have a clustering index,[5] but even a clustered relation can have nonclustering indexes.

Example 6.21 : A relation $R(a, b)$ that is sorted on attribute a and stored in that order, packed into blocks, is surely clustered. An index on a is a clustering index, since for a given a-value a_1, all the tuples with that value for a are consecutive. They thus appear packed into blocks, except possibly for the first and last blocks that contain a-value a_1, as suggested in Fig. 6.19. However, an index on b is unlikely to be clustering, since the tuples with a fixed b-value will be spread all over the file unless the values of a and b are very closely correlated. □

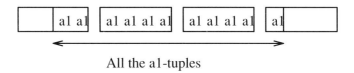

All the a1-tuples

Figure 6.19: A clustering index has all tuples with a fixed value packed into (close to) the minimum possible number of blocks

6.7.2   Index-Based Selection

In Section 6.2.1 we discussed implementing a selection $\sigma_C(R)$ by reading all the tuples of relation R, seeing which meet the condition C, and outputting those that do. If there are no indexes on R, then that is the best we can do; the number of disk I/O's used by the operation is $B(R)$, or even $T(R)$, the number of tuples of R, should R not be a clustered relation.[6] However, suppose that the condition C is of the form $a = v$, where a is an attribute for which an index exists, and v is a value. Then one can search the index with value v and get pointers to exactly those tuples of R that have a-value v. These tuples constitute the result of $\sigma_{a=v}(R)$, so all we have to do is retrieve them.

If the index on $R.a$ is clustering, then the number of disk I/O's to retrieve the set $\sigma_{a=v}(R)$ will be about $B(R)/V(R, a)$. The actual number may be somewhat higher, because:

1. Often, the index is not kept entirely in main memory, and therefore some disk I/O's are needed to support the index lookup.

---

[5]Technically, if the index is on a key for the relation, so only one tuple with a given value in the index key exists, then the index is always "clustering," even if the relation is not clustered. However, if there is only one tuple per index-key value, then there is no advantage from clustering, and the performance measure for such an index is the same as if it were considered nonclustering.

[6]Recall from Section 6.2.3 the notation we developed: $T(R)$ for the number of tuples in R and $V(R, L)$ for the number of distinct tuples in $\pi_L(R)$.

Notions of Clustering

We have seen three different, although related, concepts called "clustering" or "clustered."

1. In Section 4.2.2 we spoke of the "clustered-file organization," where tuples of one relation R are placed with a tuple of some other relation S with which they share a common value; the example was grouping movie tuples with the tuple of the studio that made the movie.

2. In Section 6.2.3 we spoke of a "clustered relation," meaning that the tuples of the relation are stored in blocks that are exclusively, or at least predominantly, devoted to storing that relation.

3. Here, we have introduced the notion of a clustering index — an index in which the tuples having a given value of the search key appear in blocks that are largely devoted to storing tuples with that search-key value. Typically, the tuples with a fixed value will be stored consecutively, and only the first and last blocks with tuples of that value will also have tuples of another search-key value.

The clustered-file organization is one example of a way to have a clustered relation that is not packed into blocks which are exclusively its own. Suppose that one tuple of the relation S is associated with many R-tuples in a clustered file. Then, while the tuples of R are not packed in blocks exclusively devoted to R, these blocks are "predominantly" devoted to R, and we call R clustered. On the other hand, S will typically *not* be a clustered relation, since its tuples are usually on blocks devoted predominantly to R-tuples rather than S-tuples.

---

2. Even though all the tuples with $a = v$ might fit in b blocks, they could be spread over $b + 1$ blocks because they don't start at the beginning of a block.

3. Although the index is clustering, the tuples with $a = v$ may be spread over several extra blocks. Two reasons why that situation might occur are:

   (a) We might not pack blocks of R as tightly as possible because we want to leave room for growth of R, as discussed in Section 4.1.6.

   (b) R might be stored with some other tuples that do not belong to R, say in a clustered-file organization.

Moreover, we of course must round up if the ratio $B(R)/V(R,a)$ is not an integer. Most significant is that should a be a key for R, then $V(R,a) = T(R)$, which is presumably much bigger than $B(R)$, yet we surely require one disk I/O to retrieve the tuple with key value v, plus whatever disk I/O's are needed to access the index.

Now, let us consider what happens when the index on $R.a$ is nonclustering. To a first approximation, each tuple we retrieve will be on a different block, and we must access $T(R)/V(R,a)$ tuples. Thus, $T(R)/V(R,a)$ is an estimate of the number of disk I/O's we need. The number could be higher because we may also need to read some index blocks from disk; it could be lower because fortuitously some retrieved tuples appear on the same block, and that block remains buffered in memory.

Example 6.22: Suppose $B(R) = 1000$, and $T(R) = 20{,}000$. That is, R has 20,000 tuples that are packed 20 to a block. Let a be one of the attributes of R, suppose there is an index on a, and consider the operation $\sigma_{a=0}(R)$. Here are some possible situations and the worst-case number of disk I/O's required. We shall ignore the cost of accessing the index blocks in all cases.

1. If R is clustered, but we do not use the index, then the cost is 1000 disk I/O's. That is, we must retrieve every block of R.

2. If R is not clustered and we do not use the index, then the cost is 20,000 disk I/O's.

3. If $V(R,a) = 100$ and the index is clustering, then the index-based algorithm uses $1000/100 = 10$ disk I/O's.

4. If $V(R,a) = 100$ and the index is nonclustering, then the index-based algorithm uses $20{,}000/100 = 2000$ disk I/O's. Notice that this cost is higher than scanning the entire relation R, if R is clustered but the index is not.

5. If $V(R,a) = 20{,}000$, i.e., a is a key, then the index-based algorithm takes 1 disk I/O plus whatever is needed to access the index, regardless of whether the index is clustering or not.

□

Index-scan as an access method can help in several other kinds of selection operations.

a) An index such as a B-tree lets us access the search-key values in a given range efficiently. If such an index on attribute a of relation R exists, then we can use the index to retrieve just the tuples of R in the desired range for selections such as $\sigma_{a\geq 10}(R)$, or even $\sigma_{a\geq 10 \text{ AND } a\leq 20}(R)$.

b) A selection with a complex condition C can sometimes be implemented by an index-scan followed by another selection on only those tuples retrieved by the index-scan. If C is of the form $a = v$ AND C', where C' is any condition, then we can split the selection into a cascade of two selections, the first checking only for $a = v$, and the second checking condition C'. The first is a candidate for use of the index-scan operator. This splitting of a selection operation is one of many improvements that a query optimizer may make to a logical query plan; it is discussed particularly in Section 7.7.1.

6.7.3 Joining by Using an Index

All the binary operations we have considered, and the unary full-relation operations of γ and δ as well, can use certain indexes profitably. We shall leave most of these algorithms as exercises, while we focus on the matter of joins. In particular, let us examine the natural join $R(X, Y) \bowtie S(Y, Z)$; recall that X, Y, and Z can stand for sets of attributes, although it is adequate to think of them as single attributes.

For our first index-based join algorithm, suppose that S has an index on the attribute(s) Y. Then one way to compute the join is to examine each block of R, and within each block consider each tuple t. Let t_Y be the component or components of t corresponding to the attribute(s) Y. Use the index to find all those tuples of S that have t_Y in their Y-component(s). These are exactly the tuples of S that join with tuple t of R, so we output the join of each of these tuples with t.

The number of disk I/O's depends on several factors. First, assuming R is clustered, we shall have to read $B(R)$ blocks to get all the tuples of R. If R is not clustered, then up to $T(R)$ disk I/O's may be required.

For each tuple t of R we must read an average of $T(S)/V(S, Y)$ tuples of S. If S has a nonclustered index on Y, then the number of disk I/O's required is $T(R)T(S)/V(S, Y)$, but if the index is clustered, then only $T(R)B(S)/V(S, Y)$ disk I/O's suffice.[7] In either case, we may have to add a few disk I/O's per Y-value, to account for the reading of the index itself.

Regardless of whether or not R is clustered, the cost of accessing tuples of S dominates, so we may take $T(R)T(S)/V(S, Y)$ or $T(R)\big(\max(1, B(S)/V(S, Y))\big)$ as the cost of this join method, for the cases of nonclustered and clustered indexes on S, respectively.

Example 6.23: Let us consider our running example, relations $R(X, Y)$ and $S(Y, Z)$ covering 1000 and 500 blocks, respectively. Assume ten tuples of either relation fit on one block, so $T(R) = 10,000$ and $T(S) = 5000$. Also, assume $V(S, Y) = 100$; i.e., there are 100 different values of Y among the tuples of S.

Suppose that R is clustered, and there is a clustering index on Y for S. Then the approximate number of disk I/O's, excluding what is needed to access the index itself, is 1000 to read the blocks of R (neglected in the formulas above) plus $10,000 \times 500 / 100 = 50,000$ disk I/O's. This number is considerably above

---

[7]But remember that $B(S)/V(S, Y)$ must be replaced by 1 if it is less, as discussed in Section 6.7.2.

the cost of other methods for the same data discussed previously. If either R or the index on S is not clustered, then the cost is even higher. □

While Example 6.23 makes it look as if an index-join is a very bad idea, there are other situations where the join $R \bowtie S$ by this method makes much more sense. Most common is the case where R is very small compared with S, and $V(S, Y)$ is large. We discuss in Exercise 6.7.5 a typical query in which selection before a join makes R tiny. In that case, most of S will never be examined by this algorithm, since most Y-values don't appear in R at all. However, both sort- and hash-based join methods will examine every tuple of S at least once.

6.7.4 Joins Using a Sorted Index

When the index is a B-tree or other structure from which we can easily extract the tuples of a relation in sorted order, then we have a number of other opportunities to use the index. Perhaps the simplest is when we want to compute $R(X, Y) \bowtie S(Y, Z)$, and we have a sorted index on Y for either R or S. We can then perform an ordinary sort-join, but we do not have to perform the intermediate step of sorting one of the relations on Y.

As an extreme case, if we have sorting indexes on Y for both R and S, then we need to perform only the final step of the simple sort-based join of Section 6.5.5. This method is sometimes called *zig-zag join*, because we jump back and forth between the indexes finding Y-values that they share in common. Notice that tuples from R with a Y-value that does not appear in S need never be retrieved, and similarly, tuples of S whose Y-value does not appear in R need not be retrieved.

Example 6.24 : Suppose that we have relations $R(X, Y)$ and $S(Y, Z)$ with indexes on Y for both relations. In a tiny example, let the search keys (Y-values) for the tuples of R be in order $1, 3, 4, 4, 4, 5, 6$, and let the search key values for S be $2, 2, 4, 4, 6, 7$. We start with the first keys of R and S, which are 1 and 2, respectively. Since $1 < 2$, we skip the first key of R and look at the second key, 3. Now, the current key of S is less than the current key of R, so we skip the two 2's of S to reach 4.

At this point, the key 3 of R is less than the key of S, so we skip the key of R. Now, both current keys are 4. We follow the pointers associated with all the keys 4 from both relations, retrieve the corresponding tuples, and join them. Notice that until we met the common key 4, no tuples of the relation were retrieved.

Having dispensed with the 4's, we go to key 5 of R and key 6 of S. Since $5 < 6$, we skip to the next key of R. Now the keys are both 6, so we retrieve the corresponding tuples and join them. Since R is now exhausted, we know there are no more pairs of tuples from the two relations that join. □

If the indexes are B-trees, then we can scan the leaves of the two B-trees in order from the left, using the pointers from leaf to leaf that are built into the structure, as suggested in Fig. 6.20. If R and S are clustered, then retrieval of all the tuples with a given key will result in a number of disk I/O's proportional to the fractions of these two relations read. Note that in extreme cases, where there are so many tuples from R and S that neither fits in the available main memory, we shall have to use a fixup like that discussed in Section 6.5.5. However, in typical cases, the step of joining all tuples with a common Y-value can be carried out with only as many disk I/O's as it takes to read them.

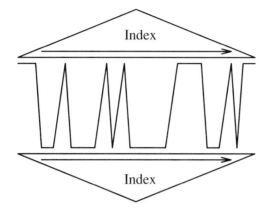

Figure 6.20: A zig-zag join using two indexes

Example 6.25 : Let us continue with Example 6.23, to see how joins using a combination of sorting and indexing would typically perform on this data. First, assume that there is an index on Y for S that allows us to retrieve the tuples of S sorted by Y. We shall, in this example, also assume both relations and the index are clustered. For the moment, we assume there is no index on R.

Assuming 101 available blocks of main memory, we may use them to create 10 sorted sublists for the 1000-block relation R. The number of disk I/O's is 2000 to read and write all of R. We next use 11 blocks of memory — 10 for the sublists of R and one for a block of S's tuples, retrieved via the index. We neglect disk I/O's and memory buffers needed to manipulate the index, but if the index is a B-tree, these numbers will be small anyway. In this second pass, we read all the tuples of R and S, using a total of 1500 disk I/O's, plus the small amount needed for reading the index blocks once each. We thus estimate the total number of disk I/O's at 3500, which is less than that for other methods considered so far.

Now, assume that both R and S have indexes on Y. Then there is no need to sort either relation. We use just 1500 disk I/O's to read the blocks of R and S through their indexes. In fact, if we determine from the indexes alone that a large fraction of R or S cannot match tuples of the other relation, then the total cost could be considerably less than 1500 disk I/O's. However, in any event we should add the small number of disk I/O's needed to read the indexes themselves.   □

6.7.5   Exercises for Section 6.7

Exercise 6.7.1: Suppose there is an index on attribute $R.a$. Describe how this index could be used to improve the execution of the following operations. Under what circumstances would the index-based algorithm be more efficient than sort- or hash-based algorithms?

* a) $R \cup_S S$ (assume that R and S have no duplicates, although they may have tuples in common).

  b) $R \cap_S S$ (again, with R and S sets).

  c) $\delta(R)$.

Exercise 6.7.2: Suppose $B(R) = 10{,}000$ and $T(R) = 500{,}000$. Let there be an index on $R.a$, and let $V(R, a) = k$ for some number k. Give the cost of $\sigma_{a=0}(R)$, as a function of k, under the following circumstances. You may neglect disk I/O's needed to access the index itself.

* a) The index is clustering.

  b) The index is not clustering.

  c) R is clustered, and the index is not used.

Exercise 6.7.3: Repeat Exercise 6.7.2 if the operation is the range query $\sigma_{C \leq a \text{ AND } a \leq D}(R)$. You may assume that C and D are constants such that $k/10$ of the values are in the range.

! **Exercise 6.7.4:** If R is clustered, but the index on $R.a$ is *not* clustering, then depending on k we may prefer to implement a query by performing a table-scan of R or using the index. For what values of k would we prefer to use the index if the relation and query are as in:

  a) Exercise 6.7.2.

  b) Exercise 6.7.3.

* **Exercise 6.7.5:** Consider the SQL query:

```
SELECT birthdate
FROM StarsIn, MovieStar
WHERE title = 'King Kong' AND starName = name;
```

This query uses the "movie" relations:

```
StarsIn(title, year, starName)
MovieStar(name, address, gender, birthdate)
```

If we translate it to relational algebra, the heart is an equijoin between

$$\sigma_{title=\text{'King Kong'}}(\texttt{StarsIn})$$

and MovieStar, which can be implemented much as a natural join $R \bowtie S$. Since there were only two movies named "King Kong," $T(R)$ is very small. Suppose that S, the relation MovieStar, has an index on name. Compare the cost of an index-join for this $R \bowtie S$ with the cost of a sort- or hash-based join.

! **Exercise 6.7.6:** In Example 6.25 we discussed the disk-I/O cost of a join $R \bowtie S$ in which one or both of R and S had sorting indexes on the join attribute(s). However, the methods described in that example can fail if there are too many tuples with the same value in the join attribute(s). What are the limits (in number of blocks occupied by tuples with the same value) under which the methods described will not need to do additional disk I/O's?

6.8 Buffer Management

We have assumed that operators on relations have available some number M of main-memory buffers that they can use to store needed data. In practice, these buffers are rarely allocated in advance to the operator, and the value of M may vary depending on system conditions. The central task of making main-memory buffers available to processes, such as queries, that act on the database is given to the *buffer manager*. It is the responsibility of the buffer manager to allow processes to get the memory they need, while minimizing the delay and unsatisfiable requests. The role of the buffer manager is illustrated in Fig. 6.21.

6.8.1 Buffer Management Architecture

There are two broad architectures for a buffer manager:

1. The buffer manager controls main memory directly, as in many relational DBMS's, or

2. The buffer manager allocates buffers in virtual memory, allowing the operating system to decide which buffers are actually in main memory at any time and which are in the "swap space" on disk that the operating system manages. Many "main-memory" DBMS's and "object-oriented" DBMS's operate this way.

Whichever approach a DBMS uses, the same problem arises: the buffer manager should limit the number of buffers in use so they fit in the available

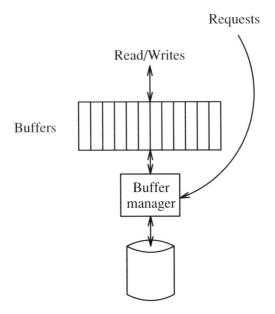

Figure 6.21: The buffer manager responds to requests for main-memory access to disk blocks

main memory. When the buffer manager controls main memory directly, and requests exceed available space, it has to select a buffer to empty, by returning its contents to disk. If the buffered block has not been changed, then it may simply be erased from main memory, but if the block has changed it must be written back to its place on the disk. When the buffer manager allocates space in virtual memory, it has the option to allocate more buffers than can fit in main memory. However, if all these buffers are really in use, then there will be "thrashing," a common operating-system problem, where many blocks are moved in and out of the disk's swap space. In this situation, the system spends most of its time swapping blocks, while very little useful work gets done.

Normally, the number of buffers is a parameter set when the DBMS is initialized. We would expect that this number is set so that the buffers occupy the available main memory, regardless of whether the buffers are allocated in main or virtual memory. In what follows, we shall not concern ourselves with which mode of buffering is used, and simply assume that there is a fixed-size *buffer pool*, a set of buffers available to queries and other database actions.

6.8.2   Buffer Management Strategies

The critical choice that the buffer manager must make is what block to throw out of the buffer pool when a buffer is needed for a newly requested block. The *buffer-replacement strategies* in common use may be familiar to you from other applications of scheduling policies, such as in operating systems. These include:

- *Least-Recently Used* (LRU). The LRU rule is to throw out the block that has not been read or written for the longest time. This method requires that the buffer manager maintain a table indicating the last time the block in each buffer was accessed. It also requires that each database access make an entry in this table, so there is significant effort in maintaining this information. However, LRU is an effective strategy; intuitively, buffers that have not been used for a long time are less likely to be accessed sooner than those that have been accessed recently.

- *First-In-First-Out* (FIFO). When a buffer is needed, under the FIFO policy the buffer that has been occupied the longest by the same block is emptied and used for the new block. In this approach, the buffer manager needs to know only the time at which the block currently occupying a buffer was loaded into that buffer. An entry into a table can thus be made when the block is read from disk, and there is no need to modify the table when the block is accessed. FIFO requires less maintenance than LRU, but it can make more mistakes. A block that is used repeatedly, say the root block of a B-tree index, will eventually become the oldest block in a buffer. It will be written back to disk, only to be reread shortly thereafter into another buffer.

- *The "Clock" Algorithm.* This algorithm is a commonly implemented, efficient approximation to LRU. Think of the buffers as arranged in a circle, as suggested by Fig. 6.22. A "hand" points to one of the buffers, and will rotate clockwise if it needs to find a buffer in which to place a disk block. Each buffer has an associated "flag," which is either 0 or 1. Buffers with a 0 flag are vulnerable to having their contents sent back to disk; buffers with a 1 are not. When a block is read into a buffer, its flag is set to 1. Likewise, when the contents of a buffer is accessed, its flag is set to 1. When the buffer manager needs a buffer for a new block, it looks for the first 0 it can find, rotating clockwise. If it passes 1's, it sets them to 0. Thus, a block is only thrown out of its buffer if it remains unaccessed for the time it takes the hand to make a complete rotation to set its flag to 0 and then make another complete rotation to find the buffer with its 0 unchanged. For instance, in Fig. 6.22, the hand will set to 0 the 1 in the buffer to its left, and then move clockwise to find the buffer with 0, whose block it will replace and whose flag it will set to 1.

- *System Control.* The query processor or other components of a DBMS can give advice to the buffer manager in order to avoid some of the mistakes that would occur with a strict policy such as LRU, FIFO, or Clock. Recall from Section 3.3.5 that there are sometimes technical reasons why a block in main memory can *not* be moved to disk without first modifying certain other blocks that point to it. These blocks are called "pinned," and any

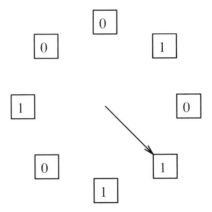

Figure 6.22: The clock algorithm visits buffers in a round-robin fashion and replaces the first one with a 0 flag

---

More Tricks Using the Clock Algorithm

The "clock" algorithm for choosing buffers to free is not limited to the scheme described in Section 6.8.2, where flags had values 0 and 1. For instance, one can start an important page with a number higher than 1 as its flag, and decrement the flag by 1 each time the "hand" passes that page. In fact, one can incorporate the concept of pinning blocks by giving the pinned block an infinite value for its flag, and then having the system release the pin at the appropriate time by setting the flag to 0.

---

buffer manager has to modify its buffer-replacement strategy to avoid expelling pinned blocks. This fact gives us the opportunity to force other blocks to remain in main memory by declaring them "pinned," even if there is no technical reason why they could not be written to disk. For example, a cure for the problem with FIFO mentioned above regarding the root of a B-tree is to "pin" the root, forcing it to remain in memory at all times. Similarly, for an algorithm like a one-pass hash-join, the query processor may "pin" the blocks of the smaller relation in order to assure that it will remain in main memory during the entire time.

6.8.3   The Relationship Between Physical Operator Selection and Buffer Management

The query optimizer will eventually select a set of physical operators that will be used to execute a given query. This selection of operators may assume that a certain number of buffers M is available for execution of each of these operators.

However, as we have seen, the buffer manager may not be willing or able to guarantee the availability of these M buffers when the query is executed. There are thus two related questions to ask about the physical operators:

1. Can the algorithm adapt to changes in the value of M, the number of main-memory buffers available?

2. When the expected M buffers are not available, and some blocks that are expected to be in memory have actually been moved to disk by the buffer manager, how does the buffer-replacement strategy used by the buffer manager impact the number of additional I/O's that must be performed?

Example 6.26 : As an example of the issues, let us consider the block-based nested-loop join of Fig. 6.13. The basic algorithm does not really depend on the value of M, although its performance depends on M. Thus, it is sufficient to find out what M is just before execution begins.

It is even possible that M will change at different iterations of the outer loop. That is, each time we load main memory with a portion of the relation S (the relation of the outer loop), we can use all but one of the buffers available at that time; the remaining buffer is reserved for a block of R, the relation of the inner loop. Thus, the number of times we go around the outer loop depends on the average number of buffers available at each iteration. However, as long as M buffers are available *on average*, then the cost analysis of Section 6.4.4 will hold. In the extreme, we might have the good fortune to find that at the first iteration, enough buffers are available to hold all of S, in which case nested-loop join gracefully becomes the one-pass join of Section 6.3.3.

If we pin the $M - 1$ blocks we use for S on one iteration of the outer loop, then we shall not lose their buffers during the round. On the other hand, more buffers may become available during that iteration. These buffers allow more than one block of R to be kept in memory at the same time, but unless we are careful, the extra buffers will not improve the running time of the nested-loop join.

For instance, suppose that we use an LRU buffer-replacement strategy, and there are k buffers available to hold blocks of R. As we read each block of R, in order, the blocks that remain in buffers at the end of this iteration of the outer loop will be the last k blocks of R. We next reload the $M - 1$ buffers for S with new blocks of S and start reading the blocks of R again, in the next iteration of the outer loop. However, if we start from the beginning of R again, then the k buffers for R will need to be replaced, and we do not save disk I/O's just because $k > 1$.

A better implementation of nested-loop join will visit the blocks of R in an order that alternates: first-to-last and then last-to-first. In that way, if there are k buffers available to R, we save k disk I/O's on each iteration of the outer loop except the first. That is, the second and subsequent iterations require only $B(R) - k$ disk I/O's for R. Notice that even if $k = 1$ (i.e., no *extra* buffers are available to R), we save one disk I/O per iteration. □

Other algorithms are also impacted by the fact that M can vary and by the buffer-replacement strategy used by the buffer manager. Here are some useful observations.

- If we use a sort-based algorithm for some operator, then it is possible to adapt to changes in M. If M shrinks, we can change the size of a sublist, since the sort-based algorithms we discussed do not depend on the sublists being the same size. The major limitation is that as M shrinks, we could be forced to create so many sublists that we cannot then allocate a buffer for each sublist in the merging process.

- The main-memory sorting of sublists can be performed by a number of different algorithms. Since algorithms like merge-sort and quicksort are recursive, most of the time is spent on rather small regions of memory. Thus, either LRU or FIFO will perform well for this part of a sort-based algorithm.

- If the algorithm is hash-based, we can reduce the number of buckets if M shrinks, as long as the buckets do not then become so large that they do not fit in allotted main memory. However, unlike sort-based algorithms, we cannot respond to changes in M while the algorithm runs. Rather, once the number of buckets is chosen, it remains fixed throughout the first pass, and if buffers become unavailable, the blocks belonging to some of the buckets will have to be swapped out.

6.8.4   Exercises for Section 6.8

Exercise 6.8.1: Suppose that we wish to execute a join $R \bowtie S$, and the available memory will vary between M and $M/2$. In terms of M, $B(R)$, and $B(S)$, give the conditions under which we can guarantee that the following algorithms can be executed:

* a) A one-pass join.

* b) A two-pass, hash-based join.

  c) A two-pass, sort-based join.

! **Exercise 6.8.2:** How would the number of disk I/O's taken by a nested-loop join improve if extra buffers became available and the buffer-replacement policy were:

  a) First-in-first-out.

  b) The clock algorithm.

!! **Exercise 6.8.3:** In Example 6.26, we suggested that it was possible to take advantage of extra buffers becoming available during the join by keeping more than one block of R buffered and visiting the blocks of R in reverse order on even-numbered iterations of the outer loop. However, we could also maintain only one buffer for R and increase the number of buffers used for S. Which strategy yields the fewest disk I/O's?

6.9 Algorithms Using More Than Two Passes

While two passes are enough for operations on all but the largest relations, we should observe that the principal techniques discussed in Sections 6.5 and 6.6 generalize to algorithms that, by using as many passes as necessary, can process relations of arbitrary size. In this section we shall consider the generalization of both sort- and hash-based approaches.

6.9.1 Multipass Sort-Based Algorithms

In Section 2.3.5 we alluded to how the two-phase multiway merge sort could be extended to a three-pass algorithm. In fact, there is a simple recursive approach to sorting that will allow us to sort a relation, however large, completely, or if we prefer, to create n sorted sublists for any particular n.

Suppose we have M main-memory buffers available to sort a relation R, which we shall assume is stored clustered. Then do the following:

BASIS: If R fits in M blocks (i.e., $B(R) \leq M$), then read R into main memory, sort it using your favorite main-memory sorting algorithm, and write the sorted relation to disk.

INDUCTION: If R does not fit into main memory, partition the blocks holding R into M groups, which we shall call $R_1, R_2, \ldots, R_M$. Recursively sort R_i for each $i = 1, 2, \ldots, M$. Then, merge the M sorted sublists, as in Section 2.3.4.

If we are not merely sorting R, but performing a unary operation such as γ or δ on R, then we modify the above so that at the final merge we perform the operation on the tuples at the front of the sorted sublists. That is,

- For a δ, output one copy of each distinct tuple, and skip over copies of the tuple.

- For a γ, sort on the grouping attributes only, and combine the tuples with a given value of these grouping attributes in the appropriate manner, as discussed in Section 6.5.2.

When we want to perform a binary operation, such as intersection or join, we use essentially the same idea, except that the two relations are first divided into a total of M sublists. Then, each sublist is sorted by the recursive algorithm above. Finally, we read each of the M sublists, each into one buffer, and we perform the operation in the manner described by the appropriate subsection of Section 6.5.

We can divide the M buffers between relations R and S as we wish. However, to minimize the total number of passes, we would normally divide the buffers in proportion to the number of blocks taken by the relations. That is, R gets $M \times B(R)/\big(B(R) + B(S)\big)$ of the buffers, and S gets the rest.

6.9.2   Performance of Multipass, Sort-Based Algorithms

Now, let us explore the relationship between the number of disk I/O's required, the size of the relation(s) operated upon, and the size of main memory. Let $s(M, k)$ be the maximum size of a relation that we can sort using M buffers and k passes. Then we can compute $s(M, k)$ as follows:

BASIS: If $k = 1$, i.e., one pass is allowed, then we must have $B(R) \le M$. Put another way, $s(M, 1) = M$.

INDUCTION: Suppose $k > 1$. Then we partition R into M pieces, each of which must be sortable in $k - 1$ passes. If $B(R) = s(M, k)$, then $s(M, k)/M$, which is the size of each of the M pieces of R, cannot exceed $s(M, k - 1)$. That is: $s(M, k) = Ms(M, k - 1)$.

If we expand the above recursion, we find

$$s(M, k) = Ms(M, k - 1) = M^2 s(M, k - 2) = \cdots = M^{k-1} s(M, 1)$$

Since $s(M, 1) = M$, we conclude that $s(M, k) = M^k$. That is, using k passes, we can sort a relation R if $B(R) \le s(M, k)$, which says that $B(R) \le M^k$. Put another way, if we want to sort R in k passes, then the minimum number of buffers we can use is $M = \big(B(R)\big)^{1/k}$.

Each pass of a sorting algorithm reads all the data from disk and writes it out again. Thus, a k-pass sorting algorithm requires $2kB(R)$ disk I/O's.

Now, let us consider the cost of a multipass join $R(X, Y) \bowtie S(Y, Z)$, as representative of a binary operation on relations. Let $j(M, k)$ be the largest number of blocks such that in k passes, using M buffers, we can join relations of $j(M, k)$ or fewer total blocks. That is, the join can be accomplished provided $B(R) + B(S) \le j(M, k)$.

On the final pass, we merge M sorted sublists from the two relations. Each of the sublists is sorted using $k - 1$ passes, so they can be no longer than $s(M, k - 1) = M^{k-1}$ each, or a total of $Ms(M, k - 1) = M^k$. That is, $B(R) + B(S)$ can be no larger than M^k, or put another way, $j(M, k) = M^k$. Reversing the role of the parameters, we can also state that to compute the join in k passes requires $\big(B(R) + B(S)\big)^{1/k}$ buffers.

To calculate the number of disk I/O's needed in the multipass algorithms, we should remember that, unlike for sorting, we do not count the cost of writing the final result to disk for joins or other relational operations. Thus, we use $2(k-1)\big(B(R)+B(S)\big)$ disk I/O's to sort the sublists, and another $B(R)+B(S)$

disk I/O's to read the sorted sublists in the final pass. The result is a total of $(2k-1)\big(B(R) + B(S)\big)$ disk I/O's.

6.9.3 Multipass Hash-Based Algorithms

There is a corresponding recursive approach to using hashing for operations on large relations. We hash the relation or relations into $M-1$ buckets, where M is the number of available memory buffers. We then apply the operation to each bucket individually, in the case of a unary operation. If the operation is binary, such as a join, we apply the operation to each pair of corresponding buckets, as if they were the entire relations. For the common relational operations we have considered — duplicate-elimination, grouping, union, intersection, difference, natural join, and equijoin — the result of the operation on the entire relation(s) will be the union of the results on the bucket(s). We can describe this approach recursively as:

BASIS: For a unary operation, if the relation fits in M buffers, read it into memory and perform the operation. For a binary operation, if either relation fits in $M-1$ buffers, perform the operation by reading this relation into main memory and then read the second relation, one block at a time, into the Mth buffer.

INDUCTION: If no relation fits in main memory, then hash each relation into $M-1$ buckets, as discussed in Section 6.6.1. Recursively perform the operation on each bucket or corresponding pair of buckets, and accumulate the output from each bucket or pair.

6.9.4 Performance of Multipass Hash-Based Algorithms

In what follows, we shall make the assumption that when we hash a relation, the tuples divide as evenly as possible among the buckets. In practice, this assumption will be met approximately if we choose a truly random hash function, but there will always be some unevenness in the distribution of tuples among buckets.

First, consider a unary operation, like γ or δ on a relation R using M buffers. Let $u(M, k)$ be the number of blocks in the largest relation that a k-pass hashing algorithm can handle. We can define u recursively by:

BASIS: $u(M, 1) = M$, since the relation R must fit in M buffers; i.e., $B(R) \leq M$.

INDUCTION: We assume that the first step divides the relation R into $M-1$ buckets of equal size. Thus, we can compute $u(M, k)$ as follows. The buckets for the next pass must be sufficiently small that they can be handled in $k-1$ passes; that is, the buckets are of size $u(M, k-1)$. Since R is divided into $M-1$ buckets, we must have $u(M, k) = (M-1)u(M, k-1)$.

If we expand the recurrence above, we find that $u(M, k) = M(M-1)^{k-1}$, or approximately, assuming M is large, $u(M, k) = M^k$. Equivalently, we can perform one of the unary relational operations on relation R in k passes with M buffers, provided $M \leq \left(B(R)\right)^{1/k}$.

We may perform a similar analysis for binary operations. As in Section 6.9.2, let us consider the join. Let $j(M, k)$ be an upper bound on the size of the smaller of the two relations R and S involved in $R(X, Y) \bowtie S(Y, Z)$. Here, as before, M is the number of available buffers and k is the number of passes we can use.

BASIS: $j(M, 1) = M - 1$; that is, if we use the one-pass algorithm to join, then either R or S must fit in $M - 1$ blocks, as we discussed in Section 6.3.3.

INDUCTION: $j(M, k) = (M - 1)j(M, k - 1)$; that is, on the first of k passes, we can divide each relation into $M - 1$ buckets, and we may expect each bucket to be $1/(M - 1)$ of its entire relation, but we must then be able to join each pair of corresponding buckets in $M - 1$ passes.

By expanding the recurrence for $j(M, k)$, we conclude that $j(M, k) = (M-1)^k$. Again assuming M is large, we can say approximately $j(M, k) = M^k$. That is, we can join $R(X, Y) \bowtie S(Y, Z)$ using k passes and M buffers provided $M^k \geq \min\left(B(R), B(S)\right)$.

6.9.5   Exercises for Section 6.9

Exercise 6.9.1: Suppose $B(R) = 20{,}000$, $B(S) = 50{,}000$, and $M = 101$. Describe the behavior of the following algorithms to compute $R \bowtie S$:

* a) A three-pass, sort-based algorithm.

  b) A three-pass, hash-based algorithm.

! **Exercise 6.9.2:** There are several "tricks" we have discussed for improving the performance of two-pass algorithms. For the following, tell whether the trick could be used in a multipass algorithm, and if so, how?

  a) The hybrid-hash-join trick of Section 6.6.6.

  b) Improving a sort-based algorithm by storing blocks consecutively on disk (Section 6.6.7).

  c) Improving a hash-based algorithm by storing blocks consecutively on disk (Section 6.6.7).

6.10 Parallel Algorithms for Relational Operations

Database operations, frequently being time-consuming and involving a lot of data, can generally profit from parallel processing. In this section, we shall review the principal architectures for parallel machines. We then concentrate on the "shared-nothing" architecture, which appears to be the most cost effective for database operations, although it may not be superior for other parallel applications. There are simple modifications of the standard algorithms for most relational operations that will exploit parallelism almost perfectly. That is, the time to complete an operation on a p-processor machine is about $1/p$ of the time it takes to complete the operation on a uniprocessor.

6.10.1 Models of Parallelism

At the heart of all parallel machines is a collection of processors. Often the number of processors p is large, in the hundreds or thousands. We shall assume that each processor has its own local cache, which we do not show explicitly in our diagrams. In most organizations, each processor also has local memory, which we do show. Of great importance to database processing is the fact that along with these processors are many disks, perhaps one or more per processor, or in some architectures a large collection of disks accessible to all processors directly.

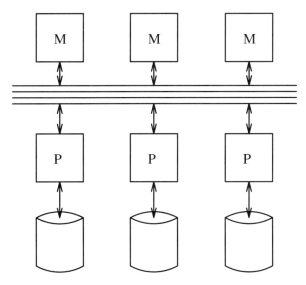

Figure 6.23: A shared-memory machine

Additionally, parallel computers all have some communications facility for passing information among processors. In our diagrams, we show the communication as if there were a shared bus for all the elements of the machine. However, in practice a bus cannot interconnect as many processors or other elements as are found in the largest machines, so the interconnection system is in many architectures a powerful switch, perhaps augmented by busses that connect subsets of the processors in local *clusters*.

The three most important classes of parallel machines are:

1. *Shared Memory.* In this architecture, illustrated in Fig. 6.23, each processor has access to all the memory of all the processors. That is, there is a single physical address space for the entire machine, rather than one address space for each processor. The diagram of Fig. 6.23 is actually too extreme, suggesting that processors have no private memory at all. Rather, each processor has some local memory, which it typically uses whenever it can. However, it has direct access to the memory of other processors when it needs to. Large machines of this class are of the *NUMA* (nonuniform memory access) type, meaning that it takes somewhat more time for a processor to access data in a memory that "belongs" to some other processor than it does to access its "own" memory, or the memory of processors in its local cluster. However, the difference in memory-access times are not great in current architectures. Rather, all memory accesses, no matter where the data is, take much more time than a cache access, so the critical issue is whether or not the data a processor needs is in its own cache.

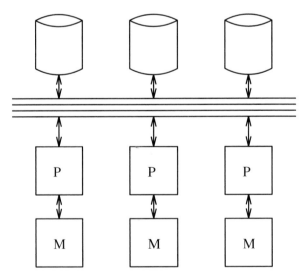

Figure 6.24: A shared-disk machine

2. *Shared Disk.* In this architecture, suggested by Fig. 6.24, every processor has its own memory, which is not accessible directly from other processors.

However, the disks are accessible from any of the processors through the communication network. Disk controllers manage the potentially competing requests from different processors. The number of disks and processors need not be identical, as it might appear from Fig. 6.24.

3. *Shared Nothing.* Here, all processors have their own memory and their own disk or disks, as in Fig. 6.25. All communication is via the communication network, from processor to processor. For example, if one processor P wants to read tuples from the disk of another processor Q, then processor P sends a message to Q asking for the data. Then, Q obtains the tuples from its disk and ships them over the network in another message, which is received by P.

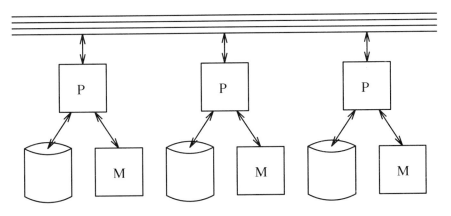

Figure 6.25: A shared-nothing machine

As we mentioned in the introduction to this section, the shared-nothing architecture is the most commonly used architecture for "database machines," that is, parallel computers designed specifically for supporting a database. Shared-nothing machines are relatively inexpensive to build, but when we design algorithms for these machines we must be aware that it is costly to send data from one processor to another.

Normally, data must be sent between processors in a message, which has considerable overhead associated with it. Both processors must execute a program that supports the message transfer, and there may be contention or delays associated with the communication network as well. Typically, the cost of a message can be broken into a large fixed overhead plus a small amount of time per byte transmitted. Thus, there is a significant advantage to designing a parallel algorithm so that communications between processors involve large amounts of data sent at once. For instance, we might buffer several blocks of data at processor P, all bound for processor Q. If Q does not need the data immediately, it may be much more efficient to wait until we have a long message at P and then send it to Q.

Algorithms on Other Parallel Architectures

The shared-disk machine favors long messages, just like the shared-nothing machine does. If all communication is via a disk, then we need to move data in block-sized chunks, and if we can organize the data to be moved so it is together on one track or cylinder, then we can save much of the latency, as discussed in Section 2.4.1.

On the other hand, a shared-memory machine allows communication to occur between any two processors via the memory. There is no extensive software needed to send a message, and the cost of reading or writing main memory is proportional to the number of bytes involved. Thus, shared-memory machines would be able to take advantage of algorithms that required fast, frequent, and short communications between processors. It is interesting that, while such algorithms are known in other domains, database processing does not seem to require such algorithms.

6.10.2 Tuple-at-a-Time Operations in Parallel

Let us begin our discussion of parallel algorithms for a shared-nothing machine by considering the selection operator. First, we must consider how data is best stored. As first suggested by Section 2.4.2, it is useful to distribute our data across as many disks as possible. For convenience, we shall assume there is one disk per processor. Then if there are p processors, divide any relation R's tuples evenly among the p processor's disks.

Suppose we want to perform $\sigma_C(R)$. We may use each processor to examine the tuples of R present on its own disk. For each, it finds those tuples satisfying condition C and copies those to the output. To avoid communication among processors, we store those tuples t in $\sigma_C(R)$ at the same processor that has t on its disk. Thus, the result relation $\sigma_C(R)$ is divided among the processors, just like R is.

Since $\sigma_C(R)$ may be the input relation to another operation, and since we want to minimize the elapsed time and keep all the processors busy all the time, we would like $\sigma_C(R)$ to be divided evenly among the processors. If we were doing a projection, rather than a selection, then the number of tuples in $\pi_L(R)$ at each processor would be the same as the number of tuples of R at that processor. Thus, if R is distributed evenly, so would its projection. However, a selection could radically change the distribution of tuples in the result, compared to the distribution of R.

Example 6.27: Suppose the selection is $\sigma_{a=10}(R)$, that is, find all the tuples of R whose value in the attribute a (assumed to be one of R's attributes) is 10. Suppose also that we have divided R according to the value of the attribute a. Then all the tuples of R with $a = 10$ are at one of the processors, and the entire relation $\sigma_{a=10}(R)$ is at one processor. □

To avoid the problem suggested by Example 6.27, we need to think carefully about the policy for partitioning our stored relations among the processors. Probably the best we can do is to use a hash function h that involves all the components of a tuple in such a way that changing one component of a tuple t can change $h(t)$ to be any possible bucket number.[8] For example, if we want B buckets, we might convert each component somehow to an integer between 0 and $B - 1$, add the integers for each component, divide the result by B, and take the remainder as the bucket number. If B is also the number of processors, then we can associate each processor with a bucket and give that processor the contents of its bucket.

6.10.3   Parallel Algorithms for Full-Relation Operations

First, let us consider the operation $\delta(R)$, which is somewhat atypical of the full-relation operations. If we use a hash function to distribute the tuples of R as suggested in Section 6.10.2, then we shall place duplicate tuples of R at the same processor. If so, then we can produce $\delta(R)$ in parallel by applying a standard, uniprocessor algorithm (as in Section 6.5.1 or 6.6.2, e.g.) to the portion of R at each processor. Likewise, if we use the same hash functions to distribute the tuples of both R and S, then we can take the union, intersection, or difference of R and S by working in parallel on the portions of R and S at each processor.

However, suppose that R and S are not distributed using the same hash function, and we wish to take their union.[9] In this case, we must first make copies of all the tuples of R and S and distribute them according to a single hash function h.[10]

In parallel, we hash the tuples of R and S at each processor, using hash function h. The hashing proceeds as described in Section 6.6.1, but when the buffer corresponding to a bucket i at one processor j is filled, instead of moving it to the disk at j, we ship the contents of the buffer to processor i. If we have room for several blocks per bucket in main memory, then we may wait to fill several buffers with tuples of bucket i before shipping them to processor i.

Thus, processor i receives all the tuples of R and S that belong in bucket i. In the second stage, each processor performs the union of the tuples from R and S belonging to its bucket. As a result, the relation $R \cup S$ will be distributed over all the processors. If hash function h truly randomizes the placement of

---

[8] In particular, we do *not* want to use a partitioned hash function (which was discussed in Section 5.2.5), because that would place all the tuples with a given value of an attribute, say $a = 10$, among only a small subset of the buckets.

[9] In principle, this union could be either a set- or bag-union. But the simple bag-union technique from Section 6.3.3 of copying all the tuples from both arguments works in parallel, so we probably would not want to use the algorithm described here for a bag-union.

[10] If the hash function used to distribute tuples of R or S is known, we can use that hash function for the other and not distribute both relations.

tuples in buckets, then we expect approximately the same number of tuples of $R \cup S$ to be at each processor.

The operations of intersection and difference may be performed just like a union; it does not matter whether these are set or bag versions of these operations. Moreover:

- To take a join $R(X, Y) \bowtie S(Y, Z)$, we hash the tuples of R and S to a number of buckets equal to the number of processors. However, the hash function h we use must depend only on the attributes of Y, not all the attributes, so that joining tuples are always sent to the same bucket. As with union, we ship tuples of bucket i to processor i. We may then perform the join at each processor using any of the uniprocessor join algorithms we have discussed in this chapter.

- To perform grouping and aggregation $\gamma_L(R)$, we distribute the tuples of R using a hash function h that depends only on the grouping attributes in list L. If each processor has all the tuples corresponding to one of the buckets of h, then we can perform the γ_L operation on these tuples locally, using any uniprocessor γ algorithm.

6.10.4   Performance of Parallel Algorithms

Now, let us consider how the running time of a parallel algorithm on a p-processor machine compares with the time to execute an algorithm for the same operation on the same data, using a uniprocessor. The total work — disk I/O's and processor cycles — cannot be smaller for a parallel machine than a uniprocessor. However, because there are p processors working with p disks, we can expect the elapsed, or wall-clock, time to be much smaller for the multiprocessor than for the uniprocessor.

A unary operation such as $\sigma_C(R)$ can be completed in $1/p$th of the time it would take to perform the operation at a single processor, provided relation R is distributed evenly, as was supposed in Section 6.10.2. The number of disk I/O's is essentially the same as for a uniprocessor selection. The only difference is that there will, on average, be p half-full blocks of R, one at each processor, rather than a single half-full block of R had we stored all of R on one processor's disk.

Now, consider a binary operation, such as join. We use a hash function on the join attributes that sends each tuple to one of p buckets, where p is the number of processors. To send the tuples of bucket i to processor i, for all i, we must read each tuple from disk to memory, compute the hash function, and ship all tuples except the one out of p tuples that happens to belong to the bucket at its own processor. If we are computing $R(X, Y) \bowtie S(Y, Z)$, then we need to do $B(R) + B(S)$ disk I/O's to read all the tuples of R and S and determine their buckets.

We then must ship $\left(\frac{p-1}{p}\right)(B(R) + B(S))$ blocks of data across the network to their proper processors; only the $(1/p)$th of the tuples already at the right processor need not be shipped. The cost of shipment can be greater or less than the cost of the same number of disk I/O's, depending on the architecture of the machine. However, we shall assume that shipment across the network is significantly cheaper than movement of data between disk and memory, because no physical motion is involved in shipment across a network, while it is for disk I/O.

In principle, we might suppose that the receiving processor has to store the data on its own disk, then execute a local join on the tuples received. For example, if we used a two-pass sort-join at each processor, a naive parallel algorithm would use $3\big(B(R) + B(S)\big)/p$ disk I/O's at each processor, since the sizes of the relations in each bucket would be approximately $B(R)/p$ and $B(S)/p$, and this type of join takes three disk I/O's per block occupied by each of the argument relations. To this cost we would add another $2\big(B(R) + B(S)\big)/p$ disk I/O's per processor, to account for the first read of each tuple and the storing away of each tuple by the processor receiving the tuple during the hash and distribution of tuples. We should also add the cost of shipping the data, but we have elected to consider that cost negligible compared with the cost of disk I/O for the same data.

The above comparison demonstrates the value of the multiprocessor. While we do more disk I/O in total — five disk I/O's per block of data, rather than three — the elapsed time, as measured by the number of disk I/O's performed at each processor has gone down from $3\big(B(R) + B(S)\big)$ to $5\big(B(R) + B(S)\big)/p$, a significant win for large p.

Moreover, there are ways to improve the speed of the parallel algorithm so that the total number of disk I/O's is not greater than what is required for a uniprocessor algorithm. In fact, since we operate on smaller relations at each processor, we may be able to use a local join algorithm that uses fewer disk I/O's per block of data. For instance, even if R and S were so large that we need a two-pass algorithm on a uniprocessor, we may be able to use a one-pass algorithm on $(1/p)$th of the data.

We can avoid two disk I/O's per block if, when we ship a block to the processor of its bucket, that processor can use the block immediately as part of its join algorithm. Most of the algorithms known for join and the other relational operators allow this use, in which case the parallel algorithm looks just like a multipass algorithm in which the first pass uses the hashing technique of Section 6.9.3.

Example 6.28: Consider our running example $R(X, Y) \bowtie S(Y, Z)$, where R and S occupy 1000 and 500 blocks, respectively. Now, let there be 101 buffers at each processor of a 10-processor machine. Also, assume that R and S are distributed uniformly among these 10 processors.

We begin by hashing each tuple of R and S to one of 10 "buckets," using a hash function h that depends only on the join attributes Y. These 10 "buckets" represent the 10 processors, and tuples are shipped to the processor corresponding to their "bucket." The total number of disk I/O's needed to read

---

Biiig Mistake

When using hash-based algorithms to distribute relations among processors and to execute operations, as in Example 6.28, we must be careful not to overuse one hash function. For instance, suppose we used a hash function h to hash the tuples of relations R and S among processors, in order to take their join. We might be tempted to use h to hash the tuples of S locally into buckets as we perform a one-pass hash-join at each processor. But if we do so, all those tuples will go to the same bucket, and the main-memory join suggested in Example 6.28 will be extremely inefficient.

---

the tuples of R and S is 1500, or 150 per processor. Each processor will have about 15 blocks worth of data for each other processor, so it ships 135 blocks to the other nine processors. The total communication is thus 1350 blocks.

We shall arrange that the processors ship the tuples of S before the tuples of R. Since each processor receives about 50 blocks of tuples from S, it can store those tuples in a main-memory data structure, using 50 of its 101 buffers. Then, when processors start sending R-tuples, each one is compared with the local S-tuples, and any resulting joined tuples are output.

In this way, the only cost of the join is 1500 disk I/O's, much less than for any other method discussed in this chapter. Moreover, the elapsed time is primarily the 150 disk I/O's performed at each processor, plus the time to ship tuples between processors and perform the main-memory computations. Note that 150 disk I/O's is less than 1/10th of the time to perform the same algorithm on a uniprocessor; we have not only gained because we had 10 processors working for us, but the fact that there are a total of 1010 buffers among those 10 processors gives us additional efficiency.

Of course, one might argue that had there been 1010 buffers at a single processor, then our example join could have been done in one pass, using 1500 disk I/O's. However, since multiprocessors usually have memory in proportion to the number of processors, we have only exploited two advantages of multiprocessing simultaneously to get two independent speedups: one in proportion to the number of processors and one because the extra memory allows us to use a more efficient algorithm.   □

6.10.5   Exercises for Section 6.10

Exercise 6.10.1: Suppose that a disk I/O takes 100 milliseconds. Let $B(R) = 100$, so the disk I/O's for computing $\sigma_C(R)$ on a uniprocessor machine will take about 10 seconds. What is the speedup if this selection is executed on a parallel machine with p processors, where:

* a) $p = 8$.

 b) $p = 100$.

 c) $p = 1000$.

! **Exercise 6.10.2:** In Example 6.28 we described an algorithm that computed the join $R \bowtie S$ in parallel by first hash-distributing the tuples among the processors and then performing a one-pass join at the processors. In terms of $B(R)$ and $B(S)$, the sizes of the relations involved, p (the number of processors), and M (the number of blocks of main memory at each processor), give the condition under which this algorithm can be executed successfully.

6.11 Summary of Chapter 6

◆ *Query Processing*: Queries are compiled, which involves extensive optimization, and then executed. The study of query execution involves knowing methods for executing operations of relational algebra with some extensions to match the capabilities of SQL.

◆ *Query Plans*: Queries are compiled first into logical query plans, which are often like expressions of relational algebra, and then converted to a physical query plan by selecting an implementation for each operator, ordering joins and making other decisions, as will be discussed in Chapter 7.

◆ *Extended Relational Algebra*: The usual operators of relational algebra — union, intersection, difference, selection, projection, product, and various forms of join — must be modified for a relational query processor by using bag (rather than set) forms of these operators. We must additionally add operators corresponding to the SQL operations of duplicate elimination, grouping and aggregation, and ordering.

◆ *Table Scanning*: To access the tuples of a relation, there are several possible physical operators. The table-scan operator simply reads each block holding tuples of the relation. Index-scan uses an index to find tuples, and sort-scan produces the tuples in sorted order.

◆ *Cost Measures for Physical Operators*: Commonly, the number of disk I/O's taken to execute an operation is the dominant component of the time. In our model, we count only disk I/O time, and we charge for the time and space needed to read arguments, but not to write the result.

◆ *Iterators*: Several operations involved in the execution of a query can be meshed conveniently if we think of their execution as performed by an iterator. This mechanism consists of three functions, to open the construction of a relation, to get the next tuple of the relation, and to close the construction.

✦ *One-Pass Algorithms*: As long as one of the arguments of a relational-algebra operator can fit in main memory, we can execute the operator by reading the smaller relation to memory, and reading the other argument one block at a time.

✦ *Nested-Loop Join*: This simple join algorithm works even when neither argument fits in main memory. It reads as much as it can of the smaller relation into memory, and compares that with the entire other argument; this process is repeated until all of the smaller relation has had its turn in memory.

✦ *Two-Pass Algorithms*: Except for nested-loop join, most algorithms for arguments that are too large to fit into memory are either sort-based, hash-based, or index-based.

✦ *Sort-Based Algorithms*: These partition their argument(s) into main-memory-sized, sorted sublists. The sorted sublists are then merged appropriately to produce the desired result.

✦ *Hash-Based Algorithms*: These use a hash function to partition the argument(s) into buckets. The operation is then applied to the buckets individually (for a unary operation) or in pairs (for a binary operation).

✦ *Hashing Versus Sorting*: Hash-based algorithms are often superior to sort-based algorithms, since they require only one of their arguments to be "small." Sort-based algorithms, on the other hand, work well when there is another reason to keep some of the data sorted.

✦ *Index-Based Algorithms*: The use of an index is an excellent way to speed up a selection whose condition equates the indexed attribute to a constant. Index-based joins are also excellent when one of the relations is small, and the other has an index on the join attribute(s).

✦ *The Buffer Manager*: The availability of blocks of memory is controlled by the buffer manager. When a new buffer is needed in memory, the buffer manager uses one of the familiar replacement policies, such as least-recently-used, to decide which buffer is returned to disk.

✦ *Coping With Variable Numbers of Buffers*: Often, the number of main-memory buffers available to an operation cannot be predicted in advance. If so, the algorithm used to implement an operation needs to degrade gracefully as the number of available buffers shrinks.

✦ *Multipass Algorithms*: The two-pass algorithms based on sorting or hashing have natural recursive analogs that take three or more passes and will work for larger amounts of data.

✦ *Parallel Machines*: Today's parallel machines can be characterized as shared-memory, shared-disk, or shared-nothing. For database applications, the shared-nothing architecture is generally the most cost-effective.

✦ *Parallel Algorithms*: The operations of relational algebra can generally be sped up on a parallel machine by a factor close to the number of processors. The preferred algorithms start by hashing the data to buckets that correspond to the processors, and shipping data to the appropriate processor. Each processor then performs the operation on its local data.

6.12 References for Chapter 6

Two surveys of query optimization are [7] and [2]. An early study of join methods is in [6]. Buffer-pool management was analyzed, surveyed, and improved by [3].

The relational algebra dates from Codd's original paper on the relational model [4]. Our extension to the grouping operator and the generalization of Codd's projection are from [8].

The use of sort-based techniques was pioneered by [1]. The advantage of hash-based algorithms for join was expressed by [9] and [5]; the latter is the origin of the hybrid hash-join. The use of hashing in parallel join and other operations has been proposed several times. The earliest source we know of is [10].

1. M. W. Blasgen and K. P. Eswaran, "Storage access in relational databases," *IBM Systems J.* **16**:4 (1977), pp. 363–378.

2. S. Chaudhuri, "An overview of query optimization in relational systems," *Proc. Seventeenth Annual ACM Symposium on Principles of Database Systems*, pp. 34–43, June, 1998.

3. H.-T. Chou and D. J. DeWitt, "An evaluation of buffer management strategies for relational database systems," *Proc. Intl. Conf. on Very Large Databases* (1985), pp. 127–141.

4. E. F. Codd, "A relational model for shared data banks," *Comm. ACM* **13**:6 (1970), pp. 377–387.

5. D. J. DeWitt, R. H. Katz, F. Olken, L. D. Shapiro, M. Stonebraker, and D. Wood, "Implementation techniques for main-memory database systems," *Proc. ACM SIGMOD Intl. Conf. on Management of Data* (1984), pp. 1–8.

6. L. R. Gotlieb, "Computing joins of relations," *Proc. ACM SIGMOD Intl. Conf. on Management of Data* (1975), pp. 55–63.

7. G. Graefe, "Query evaluation techniques for large databases," *Computing Surveys* **25**:2 (June, 1993), pp. 73–170.

8. A. Gupta, V. Harinarayan, and D. Quass, "Aggregate-query processing in data warehousing environments," *Proc. Intl. Conf. on Very Large Databases* (1995), pp. 358–369.

9. M. Kitsuregawa, H. Tanaka, and T. Moto-oka, "Application of hash to data base machine and its architecture," *New Generation Computing* **1**:1 (1983), pp. 66–74.

10. D. E. Shaw, "Knowledge-based retrieval on a relational database machine," Ph. D. thesis, Dept. of CS, Stanford Univ. (1980).

Chapter 7

The Query Compiler

Having seen the basic algorithms for executing physical-query-plan operators in Chapter 6, we shall now take up the architecture of the query compiler and its optimizer. As we noted in Fig. 6.2, there are three broad steps that the query processor must take:

1. The query, written in a language like SQL, is *parsed*, that is, turned into a parse tree representing the structure of the query in a useful way.

2. The parse tree is transformed into an expression tree of relational algebra (or a similar notation), which we term a *logical query plan*.

3. The logical query plan must be turned into a *physical query plan*, which indicates not only the operations performed, but the order in which they are performed, the algorithm used to perform each step, and the ways in which stored data is obtained and data is passed from one operation to another.

The first step, parsing, is the subject of Section 7.1. The result of this step is a parse tree for the query. The other two steps involve a number of choices. In picking a logical query plan, we have opportunities to apply many different algebraic operations, with the goal of producing the best logical query plan. Section 7.2 discusses the algebraic laws for relational algebra in the abstract. Then, Section 7.3 discusses the conversion of parse trees to initial logical query plans and shows how the algebraic laws from Section 7.2 can be used in strategies to improve the initial logical plan.

When producing a physical query plan from a logical plan, we must evaluate the predicted cost of each possible option. Cost estimation is a science of its own, which we discuss in Section 7.4. We show how to use cost estimates to evaluate plans in Section 7.5, and the special problems that come up when we order the joins of several relations are the subject of Section 7.6. Finally, Section 7.7 covers additional issues and strategies for selecting the physical query plan: algorithm choice and pipelining versus materialization.

7.1   Parsing

The first stages of query compilation are illustrated in Fig. 7.1. The four boxes in that figure correspond to the first two stages of Fig. 6.2. We have isolated a "preprocessing" step, which we shall discuss in Section 7.1.3, between parsing and conversion to the initial logical query plan.

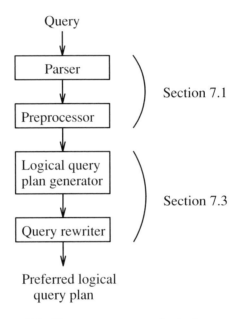

Figure 7.1: From a query to a logical query plan

In this section, we discuss parsing of SQL and give rudiments of a grammar that can be used for that language. Section 7.2 is a digression from the line of query-compilation steps, where we consider extensively the various laws or transformations that apply to expressions of relational algebra. In Section 7.3, we resume the query-compilation story. First, we consider how a parse tree is turned into an expression of relational algebra, which becomes our initial logical query plan. Then, we consider ways in which certain transformations of Section 7.2 can be applied in order to improve the query plan, rather than simply to change the plan into an equivalent plan of ambiguous merit.

7.1.1   Syntax Analysis and Parse Trees

The job of the parser is to take text written in a language such as SQL and convert it to a *parse tree*, which is a tree whose nodes correspond to either:

1. *Atoms*, which are lexical elements such as keywords (e.g., SELECT), names of attributes or relations, constants, parentheses, operators such as + or <, and other schema elements, or

2. *Syntactic categories*, which are names for families of query subparts that all play a similar role in a query. We shall represent syntactic categories by triangular brackets around a descriptive name. For example, <SFW> will be used to represent any query in the common select-from-where form, and <Condition> will represent any expression that is a condition; i.e., it can follow WHERE in SQL.

If a node is an atom, then it has no children. However, if the node is a syntactic category, then its children are described by one of the *rules* of the grammar for the language. We shall present these ideas by example. The details of how one designs grammars for a language, and how one "parses," i.e., turns a program or query into the correct parse tree, is properly the subject of a course on compiling.[1]

7.1.2　A Grammar for a Simple Subset of SQL

We shall illustrate the parsing process by giving some rules that could be used for a query language that is a subset of SQL. We shall include some remarks about what additional rules would be necessary to produce a complete grammar for SQL.

Queries

The syntactic category <Query> is intended to represent all well-formed queries of SQL. Some of its rules are:

```
<Query> ::= <SFW>
<Query> ::= ( <Query> )
```

Note that we use the symbol ::= conventionally to mean "can be expressed as." The first of these rules says that a query can be a select-from-where form; we shall see the rules that describe <SFW> next. The second rule says that a query can be a pair of parentheses surrounding another query. In a full SQL grammar, we would also need rules that allowed a query to be a single relation or an expression involving relations and operations of various types, such as UNION and JOIN.

Select-From-Where Forms

We give the syntactic category <SFW> one rule:

```
<SFW> ::= SELECT <SelList> FROM <FromList> WHERE <Condition>
```

---

[1] Those unfamiliar with the subject may wish to examine A. V. Aho, R. Sethi, and J. D. Ullman, *Compilers: Principles, Techniques, and Tools*, Addison-Wesley, Reading MA, 1986, although the examples of Section 7.1.2 should be sufficient to place parsing in the context of the query processor.

This rule allows a limited form of SQL query. It does not provide for the various optional clauses such as GROUP BY, HAVING, or ORDER BY, nor for options such as DISTINCT after SELECT. Remember that a real SQL grammar would have a much more complex structure for queries, including the above variations on select-from-where, queries built from operators like UNION, NATURAL JOIN, and many others.

Note our convention that keywords are capitalized. The syntactic categories <SelList> and <FromList> represent lists that can follow SELECT and FROM, respectively. We shall describe limited forms of such lists shortly. The syntactic category <Condition> represents SQL conditions (expressions that are either true or false); we shall give some simplified rules for this category later.

Select-Lists

```
<SelList> ::= <Attribute> , <SelList>
<SelList> ::= <Attribute>
```

These two rules say that a select-list can be any comma-separated list of attributes: either a single attribute or an attribute, a comma, and any list of one or more attributes. Note that in a full SQL grammar we would also need provision for expressions and aggregation functions in the select-list and for aliasing of attributes and expressions.

From-Lists

```
<FromList> ::= <Relation> , <FromList>
<FromList> ::= <Relation>
```

Here, a from-list is defined to be any comma-separated list of relations. For simplification, we omit the possibility that elements of a from-list can be expressions, e.g., R JOIN S, or even a select-from-where expression. Likewise, a full SQL grammar would have to provide for aliasing of relations mentioned in the from-list; here, we do not allow a relation to be followed by the name of a tuple variable representing that relation.

Conditions

The rules we shall use are:

```
<Condition> ::= <Condition> AND <Condition>
<Condition> ::= <Tuple> IN <Query>
<Condition> ::= <Attribute> = <Attribute>
<Condition> ::= <Attribute> LIKE <Pattern>
```

Although we have listed more rules for conditions than for other categories, these rules only scratch the surface of the forms of conditions. We have omitted rules introducing operators OR, NOT, and EXISTS, comparisons other than equality and LIKE, constant operands, and a number of other structures that are needed in a full SQL grammar. In addition, although there are several forms that a tuple may take, we shall introduce only the one rule for syntactic category <Tuple> that says a tuple can be a single attribute:

```
<Tuple> ::= <Attribute>
```

Base Syntactic Categories

Syntactic categories <Attribute>, <Relation>, and <Pattern> are special, in that they are not defined by grammatical rules, but by rules about the atoms for which they can stand. For example, in a parse tree, the one child of <Attribute> can be any string of characters that can be interpreted as the name of an attribute in whatever database schema the query is issued. Similarly, <Relation> can be replaced by any string of characters that makes sense as a relation in the current schema, and <Pattern> can be replaced by any quoted string that is a legal SQL pattern.

Example 7.1: Our study of the parsing and query rewriting phase will center around two versions of a query about relations of the running movies example:

```
StarsIn(title, year, starName)
MovieStar(name, address, gender, birthdate)
```

Both variations of the query ask for the titles of movies that have at least one star born in 1960. We identify stars born in 1960 by asking if their birthdate (an SQL string) ends in '1960', using the LIKE operator.

One way to ask this query is to construct the set of names of those stars born in 1960 as a subquery, and ask about each StarsIn tuple whether the starName in that tuple is a member of the set returned by this subquery. The SQL for this variation of the query is shown in Fig. 7.2.

The parse tree for the query of Fig. 7.2, according to the grammar we have sketched, is shown in Fig. 7.3. At the root is the syntactic category <Query>, as must be the case for any parse tree of a query. Working down the tree, we see that this query is a select-from-where form; the select-list consists of only the attribute title, and the from-list is only the one relation StarsIn.

The condition in the outer WHERE-clause is more complex. It has the form of tuple-IN-query, and the query itself is a parenthesized subquery, since all subqueries must be surrounded by parentheses in SQL. The subquery itself is another select-from-where form, with its own singleton select- and from-lists and a simple condition involving a LIKE operator.   □

Example 7.2: Now, let us consider another version of the query of Fig. 7.2, this time without using a subquery. We may instead equijoin the relations StarsIn and MovieStar, using the condition starName = name, to require that the star mentioned in both relations be the same. Note that starName is an

```
SELECT title
FROM StarsIn
WHERE starName IN (
    SELECT name
    FROM MovieStar
    WHERE birthdate LIKE '%1960'
);
```

Figure 7.2: Find the movies with stars born in 1960

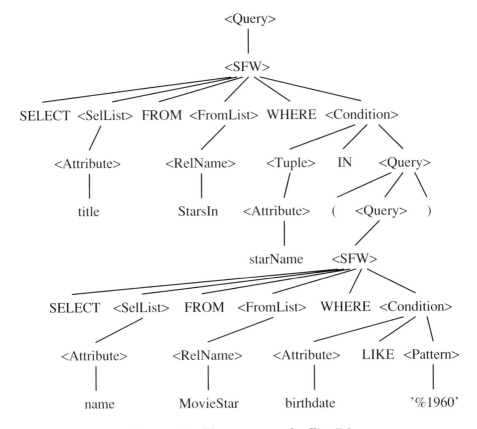

Figure 7.3: The parse tree for Fig. 7.2

```
SELECT title
FROM StarsIn, MovieStar
WHERE starName = name AND
    birthdate LIKE '%1960';
```

Figure 7.4: Another way to ask for the movies with stars born in 1960

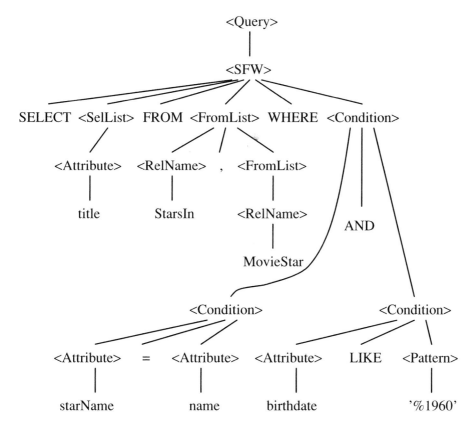

Figure 7.5: The parse tree for Fig. 7.4

attribute of relation `StarsIn`, while `name` is an attribute of `MovieStar`. This form of the query of Fig. 7.2 is shown in Fig. 7.4.[2]

The parse tree for Fig. 7.4 is seen in Fig. 7.5. Many of the rules used in this parse tree are the same as in Fig. 7.3. However, notice how a from-list with more than one relation is expressed in the tree, and also observe how a condition can be several smaller conditions connected by an operator, `AND` in this case.   □

7.1.3   The Preprocessor

What we termed the *preprocessor* in Fig. 7.1 has several important functions. If a relation used in the query is actually a view, then each use of this relation in the from-list must be replaced by a parse tree that describes the view. This parse tree is obtained from the definition of the view, which is essentially a query.

The preprocessor is also responsible for *semantic checking*. Even if the query is valid syntactically, it actually may violate one or more semantic rules on the use of names. For instance, the preprocessor must:

1. *Check relation uses.* Every relation mentioned in a `FROM`-clause must be a relation or view in the schema against which the query is executed. For instance, the preprocessor applied to the parse tree of Fig. 7.3 will check that the two relations `StarsIn` and `MovieStar`, mentioned in the two from-lists, are legitimate relations in the schema.

2. *Check and resolve attribute uses.* Every attribute that is mentioned in the `SELECT`- or `WHERE`-clause must be an attribute of some relation in the current scope; if not, the parser must signal an error. For instance, attribute `title` in the first select-list of Fig. 7.3 is in the scope of only relation `StarsIn`. Fortunately, `title` is an attribute of `StarsIn`, so the preprocessor validates this use of `title`. The typical query processor would at this point *resolve* each attribute by attaching to it the relation to which it refers, if that relation was not attached explicitly in the query (e.g., `StarsIn.title`). It would also check ambiguity, signaling an error if the attribute is in the scope of two or more relations with that attribute.

3. *Check types.* All attributes must be of a type appropriate to their uses. For instance, `birthdate` in Fig. 7.3 is used in a `LIKE` comparison, which requires that `birthdate` be a string or a type that can be coerced to a string. Since `birthdate` is a date, and dates in SQL can normally be treated as strings, this use of an attribute is validated. Likewise, operators are checked to see that they apply to values of appropriate and compatible types.

---

[2]There is a small difference between the two queries in that Fig. 7.4 can produce duplicates if a movie has more than one star born in 1960. Strictly speaking, we should add `DISTINCT` to Fig. 7.4, but our example grammar was simplified to the extent of omitting that option.

If the parse tree passes all these tests, then it is said to be *valid*, and the tree, modified by possible view expansion, and with attribute uses resolved, is given to the logical query-plan generator. If the parse tree is not valid, then an appropriate diagnostic is issued, and no further processing occurs.

7.1.4 Exercises for Section 7.1

Exercise 7.1.1: Add to or modify the rules for <SFW> to include simple versions of the following features of SQL select-from-where expressions:

* a) The ability to produce a set with the DISTINCT keyword.

   b) A GROUP BY clause and a HAVING clause.

   c) Sorted output with the ORDER BY clause.

   d) A query with no where-clause.

Exercise 7.1.2: Add to the rules for <Condition> to allow the following features of SQL conditionals:

* a) Logical operators OR and NOT.

   b) Comparisons other than =.

   c) Parenthesized conditions.

   d) EXISTS expressions.

Exercise 7.1.3: Using the simple SQL grammar exhibited in this section, give parse trees for the following queries about relations $R(a, b)$ and $S(b, c)$:

```
a)    SELECT a, c
      FROM R, S
      WHERE R.b = S.b;
```

```
b)    SELECT a FROM R WHERE b IN (
          SELECT a FROM R, S WHERE R.b = S.b
      );
```

7.2 Algebraic Laws for Improving Query Plans

We resume our discussion of the query compiler in Section 7.3, where we first transform the parse tree into an expression that is wholly or mostly operators of the extended relational algebra that we introduced in Section 6.1. Also in that section, we see how to apply heuristics that we hope will improve the algebraic expression of the query, using some of the many algebraic laws that hold for relational algebra. As a preliminary, this section catalogs algebraic laws that turn one expression tree into an equivalent expression tree that may have a more efficient physical query plan.

The result of applying these algebraic transformations is the logical query plan that is the output of the query-rewrite phase. The logical query plan is then converted to a physical query plan, as the optimizer makes a series of decisions about implementation of operators. Physical query-plan generation is taken up starting with Section 7.4. An alternative (not much used in practice) is for the query-rewrite phase to generate several good logical plans, and for physical plans generated from each of these to be considered when choosing the best overall physical plan.

7.2.1   Commutative and Associative Laws

The most common algebraic laws, used for simplifying expressions of all kinds, are commutative and associative laws. A *commutative law* about an operator says that it does not matter in which order you present the arguments of the operator; the result will be the same. For instance, $+$ and $\times$ are commutative operators of arithmetic. More precisely, $x + y = y + x$ and $x \times y = y \times x$ for any numbers x and y. On the other hand, $-$ is not a commutative arithmetic operator: $x - y \neq y - x$.

An *associative law* about an operator says that we may group two uses of the operator either from the left or the right. For instance, $+$ and $\times$ are associative arithmetic operators, meaning that $(x + y) + z = x + (y + z)$ and $(x \times y) \times z = x \times (y \times z)$. On the other hand, $-$ is not associative: $(x - y) - z \neq x - (y - z)$. When an operator is both associative and commutative, then any number of operands connected by this operator can be grouped and ordered as we wish without changing the result. For example, $((w + x) + y) + z = (y + x) + (z + w)$.

Several of the operators of relational algebra are both associative and commutative. Particularly:

- $R \times S = S \times R$; $(R \times S) \times T = R \times (S \times T)$.

- $R \bowtie S = S \bowtie R$; $(R \bowtie S) \bowtie T = R \bowtie (S \bowtie T)$.

- $R \cup S = S \cup R$; $(R \cup S) \cup T = R \cup (S \cup T)$.

- $R \cap S = S \cap R$; $(R \cap S) \cap T = R \cap (S \cap T)$.

Note that the laws for union and intersection hold for both sets and bags.

We shall not prove each of these laws, although we give one example of a proof, below. The general method for verifying an algebraic law involving relations is to check that every tuple produced by the expression on the left must also be produced by the expression on the right, and also that every tuple produced on the right is likewise produced on the left.

Example 7.3: Let us verify the commutative law for $\bowtie$: $R \bowtie S = S \bowtie R$. First, suppose a tuple t is in the result of $R \bowtie S$, the expression on the left.

Then there must be a tuple r in R and a tuple s in S that agree with t on every attribute that each shares with t. Thus, when we evaluate the expression on the right, $S \bowtie R$, the tuples s and r will again combine to form t.

We might imagine that the order of components of t will be different on the left and right, but formally, tuples in relational algebra have no fixed order of attributes. Rather, we are free to reorder components, as long as we carry the proper attributes along in the column headers. More precisely, a tuple like

a	b	c
0	1	2

is exactly the same tuple as

b	c	a
1	2	0

or any of the other four permutations of its columns.

We are not done yet with the proof. Since our relational algebra is an algebra of bags, not sets, we must also verify that if t appears n times on the left, then it appears at least n times on the right, and conversely, if it appears n times on the right then it appears at least n times on the left. Suppose t appears n times on the left. Then it must be that the tuple r from R that agrees with t appears some number of times n_R, and the tuple s from S that agrees with t appears some n_S times, where $n_R n_S = n$. Then when we evaluate the expression $S \bowtie R$ on the right, we have s appearing n_S times and r appearing n_R times, so we get $n_S n_R$ copies of t, which is n copies.

We are still not done. We have finished the half of the proof that says everything on the left appears on the right, but we must show that everything on the right appears on the left. Because of the obvious symmetry, the argument is essentially the same, and we shall not go through the details here. $\square$

Example 7.4: Proofs of the associative laws are somewhat more complex. However, let us consider as an example the associative law for $\bowtie$:

$$(R \bowtie S) \bowtie T = R \bowtie (S \bowtie T)$$

To prove this law, we argue that the tuples appearing on the left are exactly those tuples we get by searching for tuples r from R, s from S, and t from T that mutually agree on all the attributes they have in common. We then argue that exactly these tuples are also produced on the right, and that they will be produced as many times as on the left. $\square$

We did not include the theta-join among the associative-commutative operators. True, this operator is commutative:

- $R \underset{C}{\bowtie} S = S \underset{C}{\bowtie} R.$

Laws for Bags and Sets Can Differ

We should be careful about trying to apply familiar laws about sets to relations that are bags. For instance, you may have learned set-theoretic laws such as $A \cap_S (B \cup_S C) = (A \cap_S B) \cup_S (A \cap_S C)$, which is formally the "distributive law of intersection over union." This law holds for sets, but not for bags.

   As an example, suppose bags A, B, and C were each $\{x\}$. Then $B \cup_B C = \{x, x\}$, and $A \cap_B (B \cup_B C) = \{x\}$, since intersection of bags takes the minimum of the numbers of occurrences. However, $A \cap B$ and $A \cap C$ are both $\{x\}$, so the right-hand-side expression $(A \cap_B B) \cup_B (A \cap_B C) = \{x, x\}$, which differs from the left-hand-side, $\{x\}$.

Moreover, if the conditions involved make sense where they are positioned, then the theta-join is associative. However, there are examples, such as the following, where we cannot apply the associative law because the conditions do not apply to attributes of the relations being joined.

Example 7.5: Suppose we have three relations $R(a, b)$, $S(b, c)$, and $T(c, d)$. The expression

$$(R \underset{R.b > S.b}{\bowtie} S) \underset{a < d}{\bowtie} T$$

would be transformable by a hypothetical associative law into

$$R \underset{R.b > S.b}{\bowtie} (S \underset{a < d}{\bowtie} T)$$

However, we cannot join S and T using the condition $a < d$, because a is an attribute of neither S nor T. Thus, the associative law for theta-join cannot be applied arbitrarily.   □

7.2.2   Laws Involving Selection

Selections are crucial operations from the point of view of query optimization. Since selections tend to reduce the size of relations markedly, one of the most important rules of efficient query processing is to move the selections down the tree as far as they will go without changing what the expression does. Indeed early query optimizers used variants of this transformation as their primary strategy for selecting good logical query plans. As we shall point out shortly, the transformation of "push selections down the tree" is not quite general enough, but the idea of "pushing selections" is still a major tool for the query optimizer.

   In this section we shall study the laws involving the σ operator. To start, when the condition of a selection is complex (i.e., it involves conditions connected by AND or OR), it helps to break the condition into its constituent parts.

The motivation is that one part, involving fewer attributes than the whole condition, may be moved to a convenient place that the entire condition cannot go. Thus, our first two laws for σ are the *splitting laws*:

- $\sigma_{C_1 \text{ AND } C_2}(R) = \sigma_{C_1}\big(\sigma_{C_2}(R)\big)$.

- $\sigma_{C_1 \text{ OR } C_2}(R) = \big(\sigma_{C_1}(R)\big) \cup_S \big(\sigma_{C_2}(R)\big)$.

However, the second law, for OR, works only if the relation R is a set. Notice that if R were a bag, the set-union would have the effect of eliminating duplicates incorrectly.

Notice that the order of C_1 and C_2 is flexible. For example, we could just as well have written the first law above with C_2 applied after C_1, as $\sigma_{C_2}\big(\sigma_{C_1}(R)\big)$. In fact, more generally, we can swap the order of any sequence of σ operators:

- $\sigma_{C_1}\big(\sigma_{C_2}(R)\big) = \sigma_{C_2}\big(\sigma_{C_1}(R)\big)$.

Example 7.6: Let $R(a, b, c)$ be a relation. Then $\sigma_{(a=1 \text{ OR } a=3) \text{ AND } b<c}(R)$ can be split as $\sigma_{a=1 \text{ OR } a=3}\big(\sigma_{b<c}(R)\big)$. We can then split this expression at the OR into $\sigma_{a=1}\big(\sigma_{b<c}(R)\big) \cup \sigma_{a=3}\big(\sigma_{b<c}(R)\big)$. In this case, because it is impossible for a tuple to satisfy both $a = 1$ and $a = 3$, this transformation holds regardless of whether or not R is a set, as long as $\cup_B$ is used for the union. However, in general the splitting of an OR requires that the argument be a set and that $\cup_S$ be used.

Alternatively, we could have started to split by making $\sigma_{b<c}$ the outer operation, as $\sigma_{b<c}\big(\sigma_{a=1 \text{ OR } a=3}(R)\big)$. When we then split the OR, we would get $\sigma_{b<c}\big(\sigma_{a=1}(R) \cup \sigma_{a=3}(R)\big)$, an expression that is equivalent to, but somewhat different from the first expression we derived. $\Box$

The next family of laws involving σ allow us to push selections through the binary operators: product, union, intersection, difference, and join. There are three types of laws, depending on whether it is optional or required to push the selection to each of the arguments:

1. For a union, the selection *must* be pushed to both arguments.

2. For a difference, the selection must be pushed to the first argument and optionally may be pushed to the second.

3. For the other operators it is only required that the selection be pushed to one argument. For joins and products, it may not make sense to push the selection to both arguments, since an argument may or may not have the attributes that the selection requires. When it is possible to push to both, it may or may not improve the plan to do so; see Exercise 7.2.1.

Thus, the law for union is:

- $\sigma_C(R \cup S) = \sigma_C(R) \cup \sigma_C(S)$.

Here, it is mandatory to move the selection down both branches of the tree.
    For difference, one version of the law is:

- $\sigma_C(R - S) = \sigma_C(R) - S.$

However, it is also permissible to push the selection to both arguments, as:

- $\sigma_C(R - S) = \sigma_C(R) - \sigma_C(S).$

    The next laws allow the selection to be pushed to one or both arguments.
If the selection is σ_C, then we can only push this selection to a relation that
has all the attributes mentioned in C, if there is one. We shall show the laws
below assuming that the relation R has all the attributes mentioned in C.

- $\sigma_C(R \times S) = \sigma_C(R) \times S.$

- $\sigma_C(R \bowtie S) = \sigma_C(R) \bowtie S.$

- $\sigma_C(R \underset{D}{\bowtie} S) = \sigma_C(R) \underset{D}{\bowtie} S.$

- $\sigma_C(R \cap S) = \sigma_C(R) \cap S.$

If C has only attributes of S, then we can instead write:

- $\sigma_C(R \times S) = R \times \sigma_C(S).$

and similarly for the other three operators $\bowtie$, $\underset{D}{\bowtie}$, and $\cap$. Should relations R
and S both happen to have all attributes of C, then we can use laws such as:

- $\sigma_C(R \bowtie S) = \sigma_C(R) \bowtie \sigma_C(S).$

Note that it is impossible for this variant to apply if the operator is $\times$ or $\underset{D}{\bowtie}$,
since in those cases R and S have no shared attributes. On the other hand, for
$\cap$ the law always applies since the schemas of R and S must then be the same.

Example 7.7 : Consider relations $R(a, b)$ and $S(b, c)$ and the expression

$$\sigma_{(a=1 \text{ OR } a=3) \text{ AND } b<c}(R \bowtie S)$$

The condition $b < c$ can be applied to S alone, and the condition $a = 1$ OR $a = 3$
can be applied to R alone. We thus begin by splitting the AND of the two
conditions as we did in the first alternative of Example 7.6:

$$\sigma_{a=1 \text{ OR } a=3}\big(\sigma_{b<c}(R \bowtie S)\big)$$

Next, we can push the selection $\sigma_{b<c}$ to S, giving us the expression:

$$\sigma_{a=1 \text{ OR } a=3}\big(R \bowtie \sigma_{b<c}(S)\big)$$

Lastly, we push the first condition to R, yielding: $\sigma_{a=1 \text{ OR } a=3}(R) \bowtie \sigma_{b<c}(S)$.
Optionally, we can split the OR of two conditions as we did in Example 7.6.
However, it may or may not be advantageous to do so. $\square$

Some Trivial Laws

We are not going to state every true law for the relational algebra. The reader should be alert, in particular, for laws about extreme cases: a relation that is empty, a selection or theta-join whose condition is always true or always false, or a projection onto the list of all attributes, for example. A few of the many possible special-case laws:

- Any selection on an empty relation is empty.

- If C is an always-true condition (e.g., $x > 10$ OR $x \leq 10$ on a relation that forbids $x = $ NULL), then $\sigma_C(R) = R$.

- If R is empty, then $R \cup S = S$.

7.2.3 Pushing Selections

As we have mentioned, pushing a selection down an expression tree — that is, replacing the left side of one of the rules in Section 7.2.2 by its right side — is one of the most powerful tools of the query optimizer. It was long assumed that we could optimize by applying the laws for σ only in that direction. However, when systems that supported the use of views became common, it was found that in some situations it was essential first to move a selection as far *up* the tree as it would go, and *then* push the selections down all possible branches. An example should illustrate the proper selection-pushing approach.

Example 7.8: Suppose we have the relations

```
StarsIn(title, year, starName)
Movie(title, year, length, studioName)
```

and the view defined in SQL by:

```
CREATE VIEW MoviesOf1996 AS
    SELECT *
    FROM Movie
    WHERE year = 1996;
```

We can ask the query "which stars worked for which studios in 1996?" by the SQL query:

```
SELECT starName, studioName
FROM MoviesOf1996 NATURAL JOIN StarsIn
```

The view MoviesOf1996 is defined by the relational-algebra expression

$\sigma_{year=1996}(\texttt{Movie})$

Thus, the query, which is the natural join of this expression with `StarsIn`, followed by a projection onto attributes `starName` and `studioName`, has the expression, or "logical query plan," shown in Fig. 7.6.

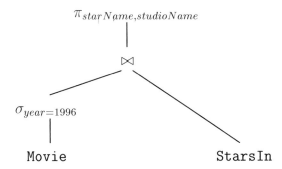

Figure 7.6: Logical query plan constructed from definition of a query and view

In this expression, the one selection is already as far down the tree as it will go, so there is no way to "push selections down the tree." However, the rule $\sigma_C(R \bowtie S) = \sigma_C(R) \bowtie S$ can be applied "backwards," to bring the selection $\sigma_{year=1996}$ above the join in Fig. 7.6. Then, since *year* is an attribute of both `Movie` and `StarsIn`, we may push the selection down to *both* children of the join node. The resulting logical query plan is shown in Fig. 7.7. It is likely to be an improvement, since we reduce the size of the relation `StarsIn` before we join it with the movies of 1996.   □

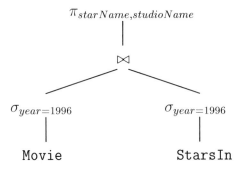

Figure 7.7: Improving the query plan by moving selections up and down the tree

7.2.4 Laws Involving Projection

Projections, like selections, can be "pushed down" through many other operators. Pushing projections differs from pushing selections in that when we push projections, it is quite usual for the projection also to remain where it is. Put another way, "pushing" projections really involves introducing a new projection somewhere below an existing projection.

Pushing projections is useful, but generally less so than pushing selections. The reason is that while selections often reduce the size of a relation by a large factor, projection keeps the number of tuples the same and only reduces the length of tuples. In fact, as we observed in Section 6.1.3, sometimes a projection actually increases the length of tuples.

To describe the transformations using the general form of projection introduced in Section 6.1.3, we need to introduce some terminology. Consider a term $E \to x$ on the list for a projection, where E is an attribute or an expression involving attributes and constants. We say all attributes mentioned in E are *input* attributes of the projection, and x is an *output* attribute. If a term is a single attribute, then it is both an input and output attribute. Note that it is not possible to have an expression other than a single attribute without an arrow and renaming, so we have covered all the cases.

If a projection list consists only of attributes, with no renaming or expressions other than a single attribute, then we say the projection is *simple*. In the classical relational algebra, all projections are simple.

Example 7.9: Projection $\pi_{a,b,c}(R)$ is simple; a, b, and c are both its input attributes and its output attributes. On the other hand, $\pi_{a+b\to x,\ c}(R)$ is not simple. It has input attributes a, b, and c, and its output attributes are x and c. $\square$

The principle behind laws for projection is that:

- We may introduce a projection anywhere in an expression tree, as long as it eliminates only attributes that are never used by any of the operators above, and are not in the result of the entire expression.

In the most basic form of these laws, the introduced projections are always simple:

- $\pi_L(R \bowtie S) = \pi_L\big(\pi_M(R) \bowtie \pi_N(S)\big)$, where M is the list of all attributes of R that are either join attributes (in the schema of both R and S) or are input attributes of L, and N is the list of attributes of S that are either join attributes or input attributes of L.

- $\pi_L(R \underset{C}{\bowtie} S) = \pi_L\big(\pi_M(R) \underset{C}{\bowtie} \pi_N(S)\big)$, where M is the list of all attributes of R that are either join attributes (i.e., are mentioned in condition C) or are input attributes of L, and N is the list of attributes of S that are either join attributes or input attributes of L.

- $\pi_L(R \times S) = \pi_L\big(\pi_M(R) \times \pi_N(S)\big)$, where M and N are the lists of all attributes of R and S, respectively, that are input attributes of L.

Example 7.10: Let $R(a, b, c)$ and $S(c, d, e)$ be two relations. Consider the expression $\pi_{a+e \to x,\ b \to y}(R \bowtie S)$. The input attributes of the projection are a, b, and e, and c is the only join attribute. We may apply the law for pushing projections below joins to get the equivalent expression:

$$\pi_{a+e \to x,\ b \to y}\big(\pi_{a,b,c}(R) \bowtie \pi_{c,e}(S)\big)$$

Notice that the projection $\pi_{a,b,c}(R)$ is trivial; it projects onto all the attributes of R. We may thus eliminate this projection and get a third equivalent expression: $\pi_{a+e \to x,\ b \to y}\big(R \bowtie \pi_{c,e}(S)\big)$. That is, the only change from the original is that we remove the attribute d from S before the join. $\Box$

In addition, we can perform a projection entirely before a bag union. That is:

- $\pi_L(R \cup_B S) = \pi_L(R) \cup_B \pi_L(S)$.

On the other hand, projections cannot be pushed below set unions or either the set or bag versions of intersection or difference at all.

Example 7.11: Let $R(a, b)$ consist of the one tuple $\{(1, 2)\}$ and $S(a, b)$ consist of the one tuple $\{(1, 3)\}$. Then $\pi_a(R \cap S) = \pi_a(\emptyset) = \emptyset$. However, $\pi_a(R) \cap \pi_a(S) = \{(1)\} \cap \{(1)\} = \{(1)\}$. $\Box$

If the projection involves some computations, and the input attributes of a term on the projection list belong entirely to one of the arguments of a join or product below the projection, then we have the option, although not the obligation, to perform the computation directly on that argument. An example should help illustrate the point.

Example 7.12: Again let $R(a, b, c)$ and $S(c, d, e)$ be relations, and consider the join and projection $\pi_{a+b \to x,\ d+e \to y}(R \bowtie S)$. We can move the sum $a + b$ and its renaming to x directly onto the relation R, and move the sum $d + e$ to S similarly. The resulting equivalent expression is $\pi_{x,y}\big(\pi_{a+b \to x,\ c}(R) \bowtie \pi_{d+e \to y,\ c}(S)\big)$.

One special case to handle is if x or y were c. Then, we could not rename a sum to c, because a relation cannot have two attributes named c. Thus, we would have to invent a temporary name and do another renaming in the projection above the join. For example, $\pi_{a+b \to c,\ d+e \to y}(R \bowtie S)$ could become $\pi_{z \to x,\ y}\big(\pi_{a+b \to z,\ c}(R) \bowtie \pi_{d+e \to y,\ c}(S)\big)$. $\Box$

It is also possible to push a projection below a selection.

- $\pi_L\big(\sigma_C(R)\big) = \pi_L\Big(\sigma_C\big(\pi_M(R)\big)\Big)$, where M is the list of all attributes that are either input attributes of L or mentioned in condition C.

As in Example 7.12, we have the option of performing computations on the list L in the list M instead, provided the condition C does not need the input attributes of L that are involved in a computation.

Often, we wish to push projections down expression trees, even if we have to leave another projection above, because projections tend to reduce the size of tuples and therefore to reduce the number of blocks occupied by an intermediate relation. However, we must be careful when doing so, because there are some common examples where pushing a projection down costs time.

Example 7.13: Consider the query asking for those stars that worked in 1996.

```
SELECT starName
FROM StarsIn
WHERE year = 1996;
```

about the relation `StarsIn(title, year, starName)`. The direct translation of this query to a logical query plan is shown in Fig. 7.8.

Figure 7.8: Logical query plan for the query of Example 7.13

We can add below the selection a projection onto the attributes

1. `starName`, because that attribute is needed in the result, and

2. `year`, because that attribute is needed for the selection condition.

The result is shown in Fig. 7.9.

If `StarsIn` were not a stored relation, but a relation that was constructed by another operation, such as a join, then the plan of Fig. 7.9 makes sense. We can "pipeline" the projection (see Section 7.7.3) as tuples of the join are generated, by simply dropping the useless `title` attribute.

However, in this case `StarsIn` is a stored relation. The lower projection in Fig. 7.9 could actually waste a lot of time, especially if there were an index on `year`. Then a physical query plan based on the logical query plan of Fig. 7.8 would first use the index to get only those tuples of `StarsIn` that have `year` equal to 1996, presumably a small fraction of the tuples. If we do the projection first, as in Fig. 7.9, then we have to read every tuple of `StarsIn` and project it.

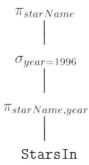

Figure 7.9: Result of introducing a projection

To make matters worse, the index on year is probably useless in the projected relation $\pi_{starName,year}(\text{StarsIn})$, so the selection now involves a scan of all the tuples that result from the projection.   □

7.2.5   Laws About Joins and Products

We saw in Section 7.2.1 many of the important laws involving joins and products: their commutative and associative laws. However, there are a few additional laws that follow directly from the definition of the join.

- $R \underset{C}{\bowtie} S = \sigma_C(R \times S)$.

- $R \bowtie S = \pi_L\big(\sigma_C(R \times S)\big)$, where C is the condition that equates each pair of attributes from R and S with the same name, and L is a list that includes one attribute from each equated pair and all the other attributes of R and S.

Examples 6.5 and 6.6 in Section 6.1.5 gave examples of the use of these rules. In practice, we usually want to apply these rules from right to left. That is, we identify a product followed by a selection as a join of some kind. The reason for doing so is that the algorithms for computing joins are generally much faster than algorithms that compute a product followed by a selection on the (very large) result of the product.

7.2.6   Laws Involving Duplicate Elimination

The operator δ, which eliminates duplicates from a bag, can be pushed through many, but not all operators. In general, moving a δ down the tree reduces the size of intermediate relations and may therefore be beneficial. Moreover, we can sometimes move the δ to a position where it can be eliminated altogether, because it is applied to a relation that is known not to possess duplicates:

- $\delta(R) = R$ if R has no duplicates. Important cases of such a relation R include

    a) A stored relation with a declared primary key, and

    b) A relation that is the result of a γ operation, since grouping creates a relation with no duplicates.

Several laws that "push" δ through other operators are:

- $\delta(R \times S) = \delta(R) \times \delta(S)$.

- $\delta(R \bowtie S) = \delta(R) \bowtie \delta(S)$.

- $\delta(R \underset{C}{\bowtie} S) = \delta(R) \underset{C}{\bowtie} \delta(S)$.

- $\delta\big(\sigma_C(R)\big) = \sigma_C\big(\delta(R)\big)$.

We can also move the δ to either or both of the arguments of an intersection:

- $\delta(R \cap_B S) = \delta(R) \cap_B S = R \cap_B \delta(S) = \delta(R) \cap_B \delta(S)$.

On the other hand, δ cannot be moved across the operators $\cup_B$, $-_B$, or π in general.

Example 7.14: Let R have two copies of the tuple t and S have one copy of t. Then $\delta(R \cup_B S)$ has one copy of t, while $\delta(R) \cup_B \delta(S)$ has two copies of t. Also, $\delta(R -_B S)$ has one copy of t, while $\delta(R) -_B \delta(S)$ has no copy of t.

Now, consider relation $T(a,b)$ with one copy each of the tuples $(1,2)$ and $(1,3)$, and no other tuples. Then $\delta\big(\pi_a(T)\big)$ has one copy of the tuple (1), while $\pi_a\big(\delta(T)\big)$ has two copies of (1). $\square$

Finally, note that commuting δ with $\cup_S$, $\cap_S$, or $-_S$ makes no sense. Since producing a set is one way to guarantee there are no duplicates, we can eliminate the δ instead. For example:

- $\delta(R \cup_S S) = R \cup_S S$.

Note, however, that an implementation of $\cup_S$ or the other set operators involves a duplicate-elimination process that is tantamount to applying δ; see Section 6.3.3, for example.

7.2.7 Laws Involving Grouping and Aggregation

When we consider the operator γ, we find that the applicability of many transformations depends on the details of the aggregate operators used. Thus, we cannot state laws in the generality that we used for the other operators. One exception is the law, mentioned in Section 7.2.6, that a γ absorbs a δ. Precisely:

- $\delta\big(\gamma_L(R)\big) = \gamma_L(R)$.

Another general rule is that we may project useless attributes from the argument should we wish, prior to applying the γ operation. This law can be written:

- $\gamma_L(R) = \gamma_L\big(\pi_M(R)\big)$ if M is a list of all those attributes of R that are mentioned in L.

The reason that other transformations depend on the aggregation(s) involved in a γ is that some aggregations — MIN and MAX in particular — are not affected by the presence or absence of duplicates. The other aggregations — SUM, COUNT, and AVG — generally produce different values if duplicates are eliminated prior to application of the aggregation.

Thus, let us call an operator γ_L *duplicate-impervious* if the only aggregations in L are MIN and/or MAX. Then:

- $\gamma_L(R) = \gamma_L\big(\delta(R)\big)$ provided γ_L is duplicate-impervious.

Example 7.15 : Suppose we have the relations

```
MovieStar(name, addr, gender, birthdate)
StarsIn(title, year, starName)
```

and we want to know for each year the birthdate of the youngest star to appear in a movie that year. We can express this query as

```
SELECT year, MAX(birthdate)
FROM MovieStar, StarsIn
WHERE name = starName
GROUP BY year;
```

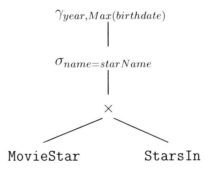

Figure 7.10: Initial logical query plan for the query of Example 7.15

An initial logical query plan constructed directly from the query is shown in Fig. 7.10. The FROM list is expressed by a product, and the WHERE clause by a selection above it. The grouping and aggregation are expressed by the γ operator above those. Some transformations that we could apply to Fig. 7.10 if we wished are:

1. Combine the selection and product into an equijoin.

2. Generate a δ below the γ, since the γ is duplicate-impervious.

3. Generate a π between the γ and the introduced δ to project onto year and birthdate, the only attributes relevant to the γ.

The resulting plan is shown in Fig. 7.11.

We can now push the δ below the $\bowtie$ and introduce π's below that if we wish. This new query plan is shown in Fig. 7.12. If name is a key for MovieStar, the δ can be eliminated along the branch leading to that relation. □

7.2.8 Exercises for Section 7.2

* **Exercise 7.2.1:** When it is possible to push a selection to both arguments of a binary operator, we need to decide whether or not to do so. How would the existence of indexes on one of the arguments affect our choice? Consider, for instance, an expression $\sigma_C(R \cap S)$, where there is an index on S.

Exercise 7.2.2: Give examples to show that:

* a) Projection cannot be pushed below set union.

b) Projection cannot be pushed below set or bag difference.

c) Duplicate elimination (δ) cannot be pushed below projection.

d) Duplicate elimination cannot be pushed below bag union or difference.

! **Exercise 7.2.3:** Prove that we can always push a projection below both branches of a bag union.

! **Exercise 7.2.4:** Some laws that hold for sets hold for bags; others do not. For each of the laws below that are true for sets, tell whether or not it is true for bags. Either give a proof the law for bags is true, or give a counterexample.

* a) $R \cup R = R$ (the idempotent law for union).

b) $R \cap R = R$ (the idempotent law for intersection).

c) $R - R = \emptyset$.

d) $R \cup (S \cap T) = (R \cup S) \cap (R \cup T)$ (distribution of union over intersection).

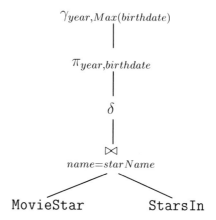

Figure 7.11: Another query plan for the query of Example 7.15

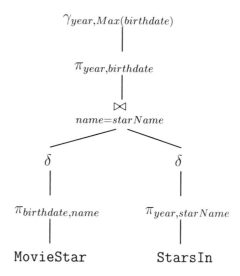

Figure 7.12: A third query plan for Example 7.15

! Exercise 7.2.5: We can define $\subseteq$ for bags by: $R \subseteq S$ if and only if for every element x, the number of times x appears in R is less than or equal to the number of times it appears in S. Tell whether the following statements (which are all true for sets) are true for bags; give either a proof or a counterexample:

    a) If $R \subseteq S$, then $R \cup S = S$.

    b) If $R \subseteq S$, then $R \cap S = R$.

    c) If $R \subseteq S$ and $S \subseteq R$, then $R = S$.

Exercise 7.2.6: Starting with an expression $\pi_L\big(R(a,b,c) \bowtie S(b,c,d,e)\big)$, push the projection down as far as it can go if L is:

    * a) $b + c \to x$, $c + d \to y$.

    b) a, b, $a + d \to z$.

! Exercise 7.2.7: We mentioned in Example 7.15 that none of the plans we showed is necessarily the best plan. Can you think of a better plan?

! Exercise 7.2.8: The following are possible equalities involving operations on a relation $R(a,b)$. Tell whether or not they are true; give either a proof or a counterexample.

    a) $\gamma_{MIN(a)\to y,\ x}\big(\gamma_{a,\ SUM(b)\to x}(R)\big) = \gamma_{y, SUM(b)\to x}\big(\gamma_{MIN(a)\to y,\ b}(R)\big)$.

    b) $\gamma_{MIN(a)\to y,\ x}\big(\gamma_{a,\ MAX(b)\to x}(R)\big) = \gamma_{y, MAX(b)\to x}\big(\gamma_{MIN(a)\to y,\ b}(R)\big)$.

!! Exercise 7.2.9: The join-like operators of Exercise 6.1.3 obey some of the familiar laws, and others do not. Tell whether each of the following is or is not true. Give either a proof that the law holds or a counterexample.

    * a) $\sigma_C(R \ltimes S) = \sigma_C(R) \ltimes S$.

    * b) $\sigma_C(R \mathbin{\overset{\circ}{\bowtie}} S) = \sigma_C(R) \mathbin{\overset{\circ}{\bowtie}} S$.

    c) $\sigma_C(R \mathbin{\overset{\circ}{\bowtie}}_L S) = \sigma_C(R) \mathbin{\overset{\circ}{\bowtie}}_L S$, where C involves only attributes of R.

    d) $\sigma_C(R \mathbin{\overset{\circ}{\bowtie}}_L S) = R \mathbin{\overset{\circ}{\bowtie}}_L \sigma_C(S)$, where C involves only attributes of S.

    e) $\pi_L(R \overline{\ltimes} S) = \pi_L(R) \overline{\ltimes} S$.

    * f) $(R \mathbin{\overset{\circ}{\bowtie}} S) \mathbin{\overset{\circ}{\bowtie}} T = R \mathbin{\overset{\circ}{\bowtie}} (S \mathbin{\overset{\circ}{\bowtie}} T)$.

    g) $R \mathbin{\overset{\circ}{\bowtie}} S = S \mathbin{\overset{\circ}{\bowtie}} R$.

    h) $R \mathbin{\overset{\circ}{\bowtie}}_L S = S \mathbin{\overset{\circ}{\bowtie}}_L R$.

    i) $R \ltimes S = S \ltimes R$.

7.3   From Parse Trees to Logical Query Plans

We now resume our discussion of the query compiler. Having constructed a parse tree for a query in Section 7.1, we next need to turn the parse tree into the preferred logical query plan. There are two steps, as was suggested in Fig. 7.1.

The first step is to replace the nodes and structures of the parse tree, in appropriate groups, by an operator or operators of relational algebra. We shall suggest some of these rules and leave some others for exercises. The second step is to take the relational-algebra expression produced by the first step and to turn it into an expression that we expect can be converted to the most efficient physical query plan.

7.3.1   Conversion to Relational Algebra

We shall now describe informally some rules for transforming SQL parse trees to algebraic logical query plans. The first rule, perhaps the most important, allows us to convert all "simple" select-from-where constructs to relational algebra directly. Its informal statement:

- If we have a <Query> that is a <SFW> construct, and the <Condition> in this construct has no subqueries, then we may replace the entire construct — the select-list, from-list, and condition — by a relational-algebra expression consisting, from bottom to top, of:

    1. The product of all the relations mentioned in the <FromList>, which is the argument of:

    2. A selection σ_C, where C is the <Condition> expression in the construct being replaced, which in turn is the argument of:

    3. A projection π_L, where L is the list of attributes in the <SelList>.

Example 7.16: Let us consider the parse tree of Fig. 7.5. The select-from-where transformation applies to the entire tree of Fig. 7.5. We take the product of the two relations StarsIn and MovieStar of the from-list, select for the condition in the subtree rooted at <Condition>, and project onto the select-list, title. The resulting relational-algebra expression is seen in Fig. 7.13.

The same transformation does not apply to the outer query of Fig. 7.3. The reason is that the condition involves a subquery. We shall discuss in Section 7.3.2 how to deal with conditions that have subqueries, and you should examine the box on "Limitations on Selection Conditions" for an explanation of why we make the distinction between conditions that have subqueries and those that do not.

However, we could apply the select-from-where rule to the subquery in Fig. 7.3. The expression of relational algebra that we get from the subquery is $\pi_{name}\left(\sigma_{birthdate\ \text{LIKE}\ \text{'%1960'}}(\text{MovieStar})\right)$.   □

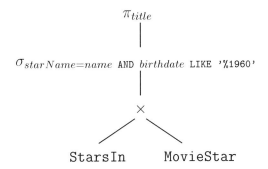

Figure 7.13: Translation of a parse tree to an algebraic expression tree

7.3.2 Removing Subqueries From Conditions

For parse trees with a <Condition> that has a subquery, we shall introduce an intermediate form of operator, between the syntactic categories of the parse tree and the relational-algebra operators that apply to relations. This operator is often called *two-argument selection*. We shall represent a two-argument selection in a transformed parse tree by a node labeled σ, with no parameter. Below this node is a left child that represents the relation R upon which the selection is being performed, and a right child that is an expression for the condition applied to each tuple of R. Both arguments may be represented as parse trees, as expression trees, or as a mixture of the two.

Example 7.17: In Fig. 7.14 is a rewriting of the parse tree of Fig. 7.3 that uses a two-argument selection. Several transformations have been made to construct Fig. 7.14 from Fig. 7.3:

1. The subquery in Fig. 7.3 has been replaced by an expression of relational algebra, as discussed at the end of Example 7.16.

2. The outer query has also been replaced, using the rule for select-from-where expressions from Section 7.3.1. However, we have expressed the necessary selection as a two-argument selection, rather than by the conventional σ operator of relational algebra. As a result, the upper node of the parse tree labeled <Condition> has not been replaced, but remains as an argument of the selection, with part of *its* expression replaced by relational algebra, per point (1).

This tree needs further transformation, which we discuss next. □

We need rules that allow us to replace a two-argument selection by a one-argument selection and other operators of relational algebra. Each form of

---

Limitations on Selection Conditions

One might wonder why we do not allow C, in a selection operator σ_C, to involve a subquery. It is conventional in relational algebra for the *arguments* of an operator — the elements that do not appear in subscripts — to be expressions that yield relations. On the other hand, *parameters* — the elements that appear in subscripts — have a type other than relations. For instance, parameter C in σ_C is a boolean-valued condition, and parameter L in π_L is a list of attributes or formulas.

If we follow this convention, then whatever calculation is implied by a parameter can be applied to each tuple of the relation argument(s). That limitation on the use of parameters simplifies query optimization. Suppose, in contrast, that we allowed an operator like $\sigma_C(R)$, where C involves a subquery. Then the application of C to each tuple of R involves computing the subquery. Do we compute it anew for every tuple of R? That would be unnecessarily expensive, unless the subquery were *correlated*, i.e., its value depends on something defined outside the query, as the subquery of Fig. 7.3 depends on the value of `starName`. Even correlated subqueries can be evaluated without recomputation for each tuple, in most cases, provided we organize the computation correctly.

---

condition may require its own rule. In common situations, it is possible to remove the two-argument selection and reach an expression that is pure relational algebra. However, in extreme cases, the two-argument selection can be left in place and considered part of the logical query plan.

We shall give, as an example, the rule that lets us deal with the condition in Fig. 7.14 involving the IN operator. Note that the subquery in this condition is uncorrelated; that is, the relation can be computed once and for all, independent of the tuple being tested. The rule for eliminating such a condition is stated informally as follows:

- Suppose we have a two-argument selection in which the first argument represents some relation R and the second argument is a <Condition> of the form t IN S, where expression S is an uncorrelated subquery, and t is a tuple composed of (some) attributes of R. We transform the tree as follows:

    a) Replace the <Condition> by the tree that is the expression for S. If S may have duplicates, then it is necessary to include a δ operation at the root of the expression for S, so the expression being formed does not produce more copies of tuples than the original query does.

    b) Replace the two-argument selection by a one-argument selection σ_C, where C is the condition that equates each component of the tuple

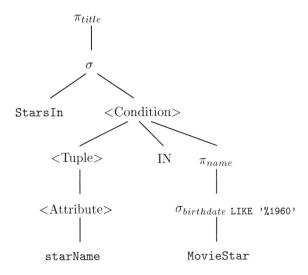

Figure 7.14: An expression using a two-argument σ, midway between a parse tree and relational algebra

> t to the corresponding attribute of the relation S.

> c) Give σ_C an argument that is the product of R and S.

Figure 7.15 illustrates this transformation.

Example 7.18: Consider the tree of Fig. 7.14, to which we shall apply the rule for IN conditions described above. In this figure, relation R is StarsIn, and relation S is the result of the relational-algebra expression consisting of the subtree rooted at π_{name}. The tuple t has one component, the attribute starName.

The two-argument selection is replaced by $\sigma_{starName=name}$; its condition C equates the one component of tuple t to the attribute of the result of query S. The child of the σ node is a $\times$ node, and the arguments of the $\times$ node are the node labeled StarsIn and the root of the expression for S. Notice that, because name is the key for MovieStar, there is no need to introduce a duplicate-eliminating δ in the expression for S. The new expression is shown in Fig. 7.16. It is completely in relational algebra, and is equivalent to the expression of Fig. 7.13, although its structure is quite different. □

The strategy for translating subqueries to relational algebra is more complex when the subquery is correlated. Since correlated subqueries involve unknown values defined outside themselves, they cannot be translated in isolation. Rather, we need to translate the subquery so that it produces a relation in which certain extra attributes appear — the attributes that must later be compared

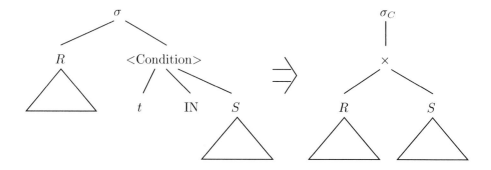

Figure 7.15: This rule handles a two-argument selection with a condition involving IN

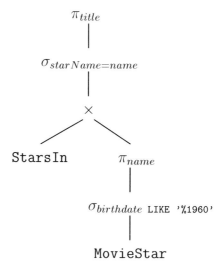

Figure 7.16: Applying the rule for IN conditions

with the externally defined attributes. The conditions that relate attributes from the subquery to attributes outside are then applied to this relation, and the extra attributes that are no longer necessary can then be projected out. During this process, we must be careful about accidentally introducing duplicate tuples, if the query does not eliminate duplicates at the end. The following example illustrates this technique.

Example 7.19 : Using the same relations as were introduced in Example 7.1, consider the query "find the movies where the average age of the stars was at most 40 when the movie was made." Figure 7.17 is an SQL rendition of this query. To simplify, we treat `birthdate` as a birth year, so we can take its average and get a value that can be compared with the `year` attribute of `StarsIn`. We have also written the query so that each of the three references to relations has its own tuple variable, in order to help remind us where the various attributes come from.

Fig. 7.18 shows the result of parsing the query and performing a partial translation to relational algebra. During this initial translation, we split the `WHERE`-clause of the subquery in two, and used part of it to convert the product of relations to an equijoin. We have retained the aliases m1, m2, and s in the nodes of this tree, in order to make clearer the origin of each attribute. Alternatively, we could have used projections to rename attributes and thus avoid conflicting attribute names, but the result would be harder to follow.

In order to remove the <Condition> node and eliminate the two-argument σ, we need to create an expression that describes the relation in the right branch of the <Condition>. However, because the subquery is correlated, there is no way to obtain the attributes `m1.title` or `m1.year` from the relations mentioned in the subquery, which are `StarsIn` (with alias m2) and `MovieStar`. Thus, we need to defer the selection $\sigma_{m2.title=m1.title \text{ AND } m2.year=m1.year}$ until after the relation from the subquery is combined with the copy of `StarsIn` from the outer query (the copy aliased m1). To transform the logical query plan in this way, we need to modify the γ to group by the attributes `m2.title` and `m2.year`, so these attributes will be available when needed by the selection. The net effect is that we compute for the subquery a relation consisting of movies, each represented by its title and year, and the average star birth year for that movie.

The modified group-by operator appears in Fig. 7.19; in addition to the two grouping attributes, we need to rename the average `abd` (average birthdate) so we can refer to it later. Figure 7.19 also shows the complete translation to relational algebra. Above the γ, the `StarsIn` from the outer query is joined with the result of the subquery. The selection from the subquery is then applied to the product of `StarsIn` and the result of the subquery; we show this selection as a theta-join, which it would become after normal application of algebraic laws. Above the theta-join is another selection, this one corresponding to the selection of the outer query, in which we compare the movie's year to the average birth year of its stars. The algebraic expression finishes at the top like the expression of Fig. 7.18, with the projection onto the desired attributes and the elimination

```
SELECT DISTINCT m1.title, m1.year
FROM StarsIn m1
WHERE m1.year - 40 <= (
    SELECT AVG(birthdate)
    FROM StarsIn m2, MovieStar s
    WHERE m2.starName = s.name AND
        m1.title = m2.title AND
        m1.year = m2.year
);
```

Figure 7.17: Finding movies with high average star age

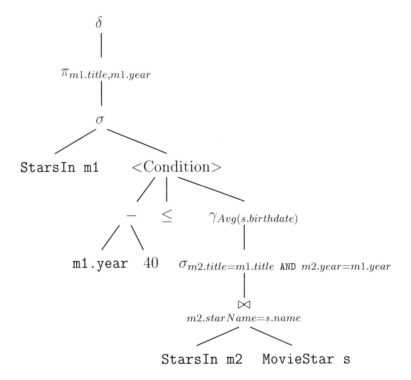

Figure 7.18: Partially transformed parse tree for Fig. 7.17

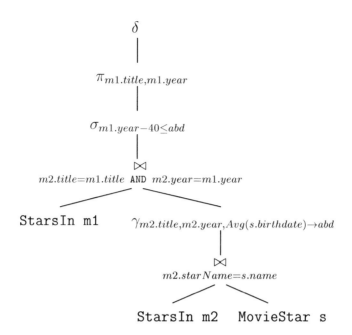

Figure 7.19: Translation of Fig. 7.18 to a logical query plan

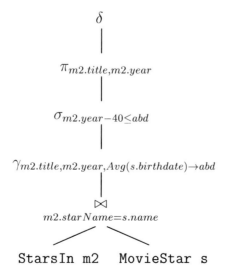

Figure 7.20: Simplification of Fig. 7.19

of duplicates.

As we shall see in Section 7.3.3, there is much more that a query optimizer can do to improve the query plan. This particular example satisfies three conditions that let us improve the plan considerably. The conditions are:

1. Duplicates are eliminated at the end,

2. Star names from `StarsIn m1` are projected out, and

3. The join between `StarsIn m1` and the rest of the expression equates the title and year attributes from `StarsIn m1` and `StarsIn m2`.

Because these conditions hold, we can replace all uses of `m1.title` and `m1.year` by `m2.title` and `m2.year`, respectively. Thus, the upper join in Fig. 7.19 is unnecessary, as is the argument `StarsIn m1`. This logical query plan is shown in Fig. 7.20. □

7.3.3 Improving the Logical Query Plan

When we convert our query to relational algebra we obtain one possible logical query plan. The next step is to rewrite the plan using the algebraic laws outlined in Section 7.2. Alternatively, we could generate more than one logical plan, representing different orders or combinations of operators. But in this book we shall assume that the query rewriter chooses a single logical query plan that it believes is "best," meaning that it is likely to result ultimately in the cheapest physical plan.

We do, however, leave open the matter of what is known as "join ordering," so a logical query plan that involves joining relations can be thought of as a family of plans, corresponding to the different ways a join could be ordered and grouped. We discuss choosing a join order in Section 7.6. Similarly, a query plan involving three or more relations that are arguments to the other associative and commutative operators, such as union, should be assumed to allow reordering and regrouping as we convert the logical plan to a physical plan. We begin discussing the issues regarding ordering and physical plan selection in Section 7.4.

There are a number of algebraic laws from Section 7.2 that tend to improve logical query plans. The following are most commonly used in optimizers:

- Selections can be pushed down the expression tree as far as they can go. If a selection condition is the `AND` of several conditions, then we can split the condition and push each piece down the tree separately. This strategy is probably the most effective improvement technique, but we should recall the discussion in Section 7.2.3, where we saw that in some circumstances it was necessary to push the selection up the tree first.

- Similarly, projections can be pushed down the tree, or new projections can be added. As with selections, the pushing of projections should be done with care, as discussed in Section 7.2.4.

- Duplicate eliminations can sometimes be removed, or moved to a more convenient position in the tree, as discussed in Section 7.2.6.

- Certain selections can be combined with a product below to turn the pair of operations into an equijoin, which is generally much more efficient to evaluate than are the two operations separately. We discussed these laws in Section 7.2.5.

Example 7.20 : Let us consider the query of Fig. 7.13. First, we may split the two parts of the selection into $\sigma_{starName=name}$ and $\sigma_{birthdate}$ LIKE '%1960'. The latter can be pushed down the tree, since the only attribute involved, `birthdate`, is from the relation `MovieStar`. The first condition involves attributes from both sides of the product, but they are equated, so the product and selection is really an equijoin. The effect of these transformations is shown in Fig. 7.21. □

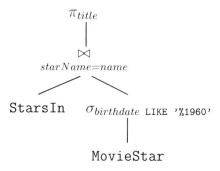

Figure 7.21: The effect of query rewriting

Example 7.21 : The expression tree of Fig. 7.16 can also be improved. However, the only useful transformation is one of those we mentioned in Example 7.20: replace a selection and a product below it by an equijoin. The resulting query plan, in Fig. 7.22, looks almost like Fig. 7.21, but it has an additional projection, onto `name`. When we perform a selection on `MovieStar`, to find the stars born in 1960, we may as well produce only the `name` component, because that is what we use in later operations. Notice that the plan of Fig. 7.22 can be obtained from the plan of Fig. 7.21 by pushing the projection down the right branch of the tree. We could also push the projection down the left branch (while still leaving π_{title} at the root), but projecting a stored relation like `StarsIn` might be costly if we could then no longer use an index to access those tuples of `StarsIn` that were needed in the join. □

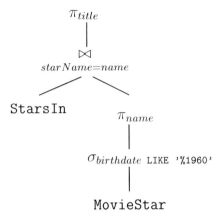

Figure 7.22: An improvement on Fig. 7.16

7.3.4 Grouping Associative/Commutative Operators

Conventional parsers do not produce trees whose nodes can have an unlimited number of children. Thus, it is normal for operators to appear only in their unary or binary form. However, associative and commutative operators may be thought of as having any number of operands. Moreover, thinking of an operator such as join as a multiway operator offers us opportunities to reorder the operands so that when the join is executed as a sequence of binary joins, they take less time than if we had executed the joins in the order implied by the parse tree. We discuss ordering multiway joins in Section 7.6.

Thus, we shall perform a last step before producing the final logical query plan: for each portion of the subtree that consists of nodes with the same associative and commutative operator, we group the nodes with these operators into a single node with many children. Recall that the usual associative/commutative operators are natural join, union, and intersection. Natural joins and theta-joins can also be combined with each other under certain circumstances:

1. We must replace the natural joins with theta-joins that equate the attributes of the same name.

2. We must add a projection to eliminate duplicate copies of attributes involved in a natural join that has become a theta-join.

3. The theta-join conditions must be associative. Recall there are cases, as discussed in Section 7.2.1, where theta-joins are not associative.

In addition, products can be considered as a special case of natural join and combined with joins if they are adjacent in the tree. Figure 7.23 illustrates this transformation in a situation where the logical query plan has a cluster of two union operators and a cluster of three natural join operators. Note that the letters R through W stand for any expressions, not necessarily for stored relations.

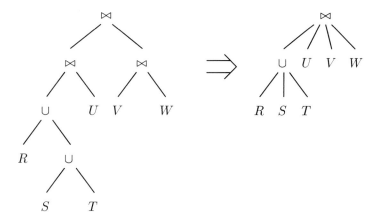

Figure 7.23: Final step in producing the logical query plan: group the associative and commutative operators

7.3.5 Exercises for Section 7.3

Exercise 7.3.1: Replace the natural joins in the following expressions by equivalent theta-joins and projections. Tell whether the resulting theta-joins form a commutative and associative group.

* a) $\big(R(a,b) \bowtie S(b,c)\big) \underset{S.c > T.c}{\bowtie} T(c,d)$.

  b) $\big(R(a,b) \bowtie S(b,c)\big) \bowtie \big(T(c,d) \bowtie U(d,e)\big)$.

  c) $\big(R(a,b) \bowtie S(b,c)\big) \bowtie \big(T(c,d) \bowtie U(a,d)\big)$.

Exercise 7.3.2: Convert to relational algebra your parse trees from Exercise 7.1.3(a) and (b). For (b), show both the form with a two-argument selection and its eventual conversion to a one-argument (conventional σ_C) selection.

! Exercise 7.3.3: Give a rule for converting each of the following forms of <Condition> to relational algebra. All conditions may be assumed to be applied (by a two-argument selection) to a relation R. You may assume that the subquery is not corollated with R. Be careful that you do not introduce or eliminate duplicates in opposition to the formal definition of SQL.

* a) A condition of the form EXISTS(<Query>).

b) A condition of the form $a = $ ANY $<$Query$>$, where a is an attribute of R.

c) A condition of the form $a = $ ALL $<$Query$>$, where a is an attribute of R.

!! **Exercise 7.3.4:** Repeat Exercise 7.3.3, but allow the subquery to be corollated with R. For simplicity, you may assume that the subquery has the simple form of select-from-where expression described in this section, with *no* further subqueries.

!! **Exercise 7.3.5:** From how many different expression trees could the grouped tree on the right of Fig. 7.23 have come? Remember that the order of children after grouping is not necessarily reflective of the ordering in the original expression tree.

7.4   Estimating the Cost of Operations

Suppose we have parsed a query and transformed it into a logical query plan. Suppose further that whatever transformations we choose have been applied to construct the preferred logical query plan. We must next turn our logical plan into a physical plan. We normally do so by considering many different physical plans that are derived from the logical plan, and evaluating or estimating the cost of each. After this evaluation, often called *cost-based enumeration*, we pick the physical query plan with the least estimated cost; that plan is the one passed to the query-execution engine. When enumerating possible physical plans derivable from a given logical plan, we select for each physical plan:

1. An order and grouping for associative-and-commutative operations like joins, unions, and intersections.

2. An algorithm for each operator in the logical plan, for instance, deciding whether a nested-loop join or a hash-join should be used.

3. Additional operators — scanning, sorting, and so on — that are needed for the physical plan but that were not present explicitly in the logical plan.

4. The way in which arguments are passed from one operator to the next, for instance, by storing the intermediate result on disk or by using iterators and passing an argument one main-memory buffer at a time.

We shall consider each of these issues subsequently. However, in order to answer the questions associated with each of these choices, we need to understand what the costs of the various physical plans are. We cannot know these costs exactly without executing the plan, and we surely don't want to execute more than one plan for one query. Thus, we are forced to estimate the cost of any plan without executing it.

Preliminary to our discussion of physical plan enumeration, then, is a consideration of how to estimate costs of such plans accurately. Such estimates are based on parameters of the data (see the box on "Review of Notation") that must be either computed exactly from the data or estimated by a process of "statistics gathering" that we discuss in Section 7.5.1. Given values for these parameters, we may make a number of reasonable estimates of relation sizes that can be used to predict the cost of a complete physical plan.

7.4.1 Estimating Sizes of Intermediate Relations

The physical plan is selected to minimize the cost of evaluating the query. The principal cost is usually disk I/O's, although in some cases processor time or communication time (if the query is being evaluated on a parallel machine or collection of interconnected machines) is also important.

When the expression of the logical plan involves several operators, we know something about how the intermediate relations will be represented. That is, while the stored relations that are arguments of the expression may be stored in various ways — clustered or nonclustered, indexed or not — any relation we compute during the execution of the query, and choose to store on disk, can be stored clustered on as few blocks as possible. Further, such a relation will not have any indexes unless we explicitly create them as part of the physical query plan.

As a consequence, the number of disk I/O's needed to manage intermediate relations will be a function of only their size: the number of tuples in the intermediate relation times the number of bytes per tuple. We can deduce from the attributes of the intermediate relation and their types how many bytes a tuple will occupy, so the only mystery is how many tuples the intermediate relation will have. Since we generally cannot tell exactly how many tuples an intermediate relation has without computing it, we shall introduce some reasonable rules for estimating these sizes.

Ideally, we want rules for estimating the number of tuples in an intermediate relation so that the rules:

1. Give accurate estimates.

2. Are easy to compute.

3. Are logically consistent; that is, the size estimate for an intermediate relation should not depend on how that relation is computed. For instance, the size estimate for a join of several relations should not depend on the order in which we join the relations.

There is no universally agreed-upon way to meet these three conditions. We shall give some simple rules that serve in most situations. Fortunately, the goal of size estimation is not to predict the exact size; it is to help select a physical query plan. Even an inaccurate size-estimation method will serve that purpose

---

Review of Notation

Recall from Section 6.2.3 the conventions we use for representing sizes of relations:

- $B(R)$ is the number of blocks needed to hold all the tuples of relation R.

- $T(R)$ is the number of tuples of relation R.

- $V(R, a)$ is the *value count* for attribute a of relation R, that is, the number of distinct values relation R has in attribute a. Also, $V(R, [a_1, a_2, \ldots, a_n])$ is the number of distinct values R has when all of attributes $a_1, a_2, \ldots, a_n$ are considered together, that is, the number of distinct tuples in $\pi_{a_1, a_2, \ldots, a_n}(R)$.

---

well if it errs consistently, that is, if the size estimator assigns the least cost to the best physical query plan, even if the actual cost of that plan turns out to be different from what was predicted.

7.4.2   Estimating the Size of a Projection

The projection is different from the other operators, in that the size of the result is computable. Since a projection produces a result tuple for every argument tuple, the only change in the output size is the change in the lengths of the tuples. Recall that the projection operator used here is a bag operator and does not eliminate duplicates; if we want to eliminate duplicates produced during a projection, we need to follow with the δ operator.

Normally, tuples shrink during a projection, as some components are eliminated. However, the general form of projection we introduced in Section 6.1.3 allows the creation of new components that are combinations of attributes, and so there are situations where a π operator actually increases the size of the relation.

Example 7.22: Suppose $R(a, b, c)$ is a relation, where a and b are integers of four bytes each, and c is a string of 100 bytes. Let tuple headers require 12 bytes. Then each tuple of R requires 120 bytes. Let blocks be 1024 bytes long, with block headers of 24 bytes. We can thus fit 8 tuples in one block. Suppose $T(R) = 10,000$; i.e., there are 10,000 tuples in R. Then $B(R) = 1250$.

Consider $S = \pi_{a+b,c}(R)$; that is, we replace a and b by their sum. Tuples of S require 116 bytes: 12 for header, 4 for the sum, and 100 for the string. Although tuples of S are slightly smaller than tuples of R, we can still fit only 8 tuples in a block. Thus, $T(S) = 10,000$ and $B(S) = 1250$.

Now consider $U = \pi_{a,b}(R)$, where we eliminate the string component. Tuples of U are only 20 bytes long. $T(U)$ is still 10,000. However, we can now pack 50 tuples of U into one block, so $B(U) = 200$. This projection thus shrinks the relation by a factor slightly more than 6. □

7.4.3 Estimating the Size of a Selection

When we perform a selection, we generally reduce the number of tuples, although the sizes of tuples remain the same. In the simplest kind of selection, where an attribute is equated to a constant, there is an easy way to estimate the size of the result, provided we know, or can estimate, the number of different values the attribute has. Let $S = \sigma_{A=c}(R)$, where A is an attribute of R and c is a constant. Then we recommend as an estimate:

- $T(S) = T(R)/V(R, A)$

The rule above surely holds if all values of attribute A occur equally often in the database. However, as discussed in the box on "The Zipfian Distribution," the formula above is still the best estimate on the average, even if values of A are not uniformly distributed in the database; we require, however, that all values of A are equally likely to appear in queries that specify the value of A.

The size estimate is more problematic when the selection involves an inequality comparison, for instance, $S = \sigma_{a<10}(R)$. One might think that on the average, half the tuples would satisfy the comparison and half not, so $T(R)/2$ would estimate the size of S. However, there is an intuition that queries involving an inequality tend give a small fraction of the possible tuples.[3] Thus, we propose a rule that acknowledges this tendency, and assumes the typical inequality will return about one third of the tuples, rather than half the tuples. If $S = \sigma_{a<c}(R)$, then our estimate for $T(S)$ is:

- $T(S) = T(R)/3$

The case of a "not equals" comparison is rare. However, should we encounter a selection like $S = \sigma_{a\neq 10}(R)$, we recommend assuming that essentially all tuples will satisfy the condition. That is, take $T(S) = T(R)$ as an estimate. Alternatively, we may use $T(S) = T(R)(V(R, a) - 1)/V(R, a)$, which is slightly less, as an estimate. This approach acknowledges that about $1/V(R, a)$ tuples of R will fail to meet the condition because their a-value *does* equal the constant.

When the selection condition C is the AND of several equalities and inequalities, we can treat the selection $\sigma_C(R)$ as a cascade of simple selections, each of which checks for one of the conditions. Note that the order in which we place these selections doesn't matter. The effect will be that the size estimate for the result is the size of the original relation multiplied by the *selectivity* factor for each condition. That factor is $1/3$ for any inequality, 1 for $\neq$, and $1/V(R, A)$ for any attribute A that is compared to a constant in the condition C.

---

[3]For instance, if you had data about faculty salaries, would you be more likely to query for those faculty who made *less* than \$200,000 or *more* than \$200,000?

The Zipfian Distribution

When we assume that one out of $V(R, a)$ tuples of R will satisfy a condition like $a = 10$, we appear to be making the tacit assumption that all values of attribute a are equally likely to appear in a given tuple of R. We also assume that 10 is one of these values, but that is a reasonable assumption, since most of the time one looks in a database for things that actually exist. However, the assumption that values distribute equally is rarely upheld, even approximately.

Many attributes have values whose occurrences follow a *Zipfian distribution*, where the frequencies of the ith most common values are in proportion to $1/\sqrt{i}$. For example, if the most common value appears 1000 times, then the second most common value would be expected to appear about $1000/\sqrt{2}$ times, or 707 times, and the third most common value would appear about $1000/\sqrt{3}$ times, or 577 times. Originally postulated as a way to describe the relative frequencies of words in English sentences, this distribution has been found to appear in many sorts of data. For example, in the US, state populations follow an approximate Zipfian distribution, with, say, the second most populous state, New York, having about 70% of the population of the most populous, California. Thus, if state were an attribute of a relation describing US people, say a list of magazine subscribers, we would expect the values of state to distribute in the Zipfian, rather than uniform manner.

As long as the constant in the selection condition is chosen randomly, it doesn't matter whether the values of the attribute involved have a uniform, Zipfian, or other distribution; the *average* size of the matching set will still be $T(R)/V(R, a)$. However, if the constants are also chosen with a Zipfian distribution, then we would expect the average size of the selected set to be somewhat larger than $T(R)/V(R, a)$.

Example 7.23: Let $R(a, b, c)$ be a relation, and $S = \sigma_{a=10 \text{ AND } b<20}(R)$. Also, let $T(R) = 10{,}000$, and $V(R, a) = 50$. Then our best estimate of $T(S)$ is $T(R)/(50 \times 3)$, or 67. That is, 1/50th of the tuples of R will survive the $a = 10$ filter, and 1/3 of those will survive the $b < 20$ filter.

An interesting special case where our analysis breaks down is when the condition is contradictory. For instance, consider $S = \sigma_{a=10 \text{ AND } a>20}(R)$. According to our rule, $T(S) = T(R)/3V(R, a)$, or 67 tuples. However, it should be clear that no tuple can have both $a = 10$ and $a > 20$, so the correct answer is $T(S) = 0$. When rewriting the logical query plan, the query optimizer can look for instances of many special-case rules. In the above instance, the optimizer can apply a rule that finds the selection condition logically equivalent to FALSE and replaces the expression for S by the empty set. $\square$

When a selection involves an OR of conditions, say $S = \sigma_{C_1 \text{ OR } C_2}(R)$, then we have less certainty about the size of the result. One simple assumption is that no tuple will satisfy both conditions, so the size of the result is the sum of the number of tuples that satisfy each. That measure is generally an overestimate, and in fact can sometimes lead us to the absurd conclusion that there are more tuples in S than in the original relation R. Thus, another simple approach is to take the smaller of the size of R and the sum of the number of tuples satisfying C_1 and those satisfying C_2.

A less simple, but possibly more accurate estimate of the size of

$$S = \sigma_{C_1 \text{ OR } C_2}(R)$$

is to assume that C_1 and C_2 are independent. Then, if R has n tuples, m_1 of which satisfy C_1 and m_2 of which satisfy C_2, we would estimate the number of tuples in S as

$$n\left(1 - (1 - \frac{m_1}{n})(1 - \frac{m_2}{n})\right)$$

In explanation, $1 - m_1/n$ is the fraction of tuples that do not satisfy C_1, and $1 - m_2/n$ is the fraction that do not satisfy C_2. The product of these numbers is the fraction of R's tuples that are *not* in S, and 1 minus this product is the fraction that are in S.

Example 7.24 : Suppose $R(a,b)$ has $T(R) = 10{,}000$ tuples, and

$$S = \sigma_{a=10 \text{ OR } b<20}(R)$$

Let $V(R,a) = 50$. Then the number of tuples that satisfy $a = 10$ we estimate at 200, i.e., $T(R)/V(R,a)$. The number of tuples that satisfy $b < 20$ we estimate at $T(R)/3$, or 3333.

The simplest estimate for the size of S is the sum of these numbers, or 3533. The more complex estimate based on independence of the conditions $a = 10$ and $b < 20$ gives

$$10000\left(1 - (1 - \frac{200}{10000})(1 - \frac{3333}{10000})\right)$$

or 3466. There is little difference between the two estimates, and it is very unlikely that choosing one over the other would change our estimate of the best physical query plan. $\square$

The final operator that could appear in a selection condition is NOT. If a relation R has n tuples, then the estimated number of tuples of R that satisfy condition NOT C is n minus the estimated number that satisfy C.

7.4.4 Estimating the Size of a Join

We shall consider here only the natural join. Other joins can be handled according to the following outline:

1. The number of tuples in the result of an equijoin can be computed exactly as for a natural join, after accounting for the change in variable names. Example 7.26 will illustrate this point.

2. Other theta-joins can be estimated as if they were a selection following a product, with the following additional observations:

   (a) The number of tuples in a product is the product of the number of tuples in the relations involved.

   (b) An equality comparison can be estimated using the techniques to be developed for natural joins.

   (c) An inequality comparison between two attributes, such as $R.a < S.b$, can be handled as for the inequality comparisons of the form $R.a < 10$ that we discussed in Section 7.4.3. That is, we can assume this condition has selectivity factor $1/3$ (if you believe that queries tend to ask for rare conditions) or $1/2$ (if you do not make that assumption).

We shall begin our study with the assumption that the natural join of two relations involves only the equality of two attributes. That is, we study the join $R(X, Y) \bowtie S(Y, Z)$, but initially we assume that Y is a single attribute although X and Z can represent any set of attributes.

The problem is that we don't know how the Y-values in R and S relate. For instance:

1. The two relations could have disjoint sets of Y-values, in which case the join is empty and $T(R \bowtie S) = 0$.

2. Y might be the key of S and a foreign key of R, so each tuple of R joins with exactly one tuple of S, and $T(R \bowtie S) = T(R)$.

3. Almost all the tuples of R and S could have the same Y-value, in which case $T(R \bowtie S)$ is about $T(R)T(S)$.

To focus on the most common situations, we shall make two simplifying assumptions:

- *Containment of Value Sets.* If Y is an attribute appearing in several relations, then each relation chooses its values from the front of a fixed list of values $y_1, y_2, y_3, \ldots$ and has all the values in that prefix. As a consequence, if R and S are two relations with an attribute Y, and $V(R, Y) \leq V(S, Y)$, then every Y-value of R will be a Y-value of S.

- *Preservation of Value Sets.* If we join a relation R with another relation, then an attribute A that is not a join attribute (i.e., not present in both relations) does not lose values from its set of possible values. More precisely, if A is an attribute of R but not of S, then $V(R \bowtie S, A) = V(R, A)$. Note that the order of joining R and S is not important, so we could just as well have said that $V(S \bowtie R, A) = V(R, A)$.

Assumption (1), containment of value sets, clearly might be violated, but it *is* satisfied when Y is a key in S and a foreign key in R. It also is approximately true in many other cases, since we would intuitively expect that if S has many Y-values, then a given Y-value that appears in R has a good chance of appearing in S.

Assumption (2), preservation of value sets, also might be violated, but it is true when the join attribute(s) of $R \bowtie S$ are a key for S and a foreign key for R. In fact, (2) can only be violated when there are "dangling tuples" in R, that is, tuples of R that join with no tuple of S; and even if there *are* dangling tuples in R, the assumption might still hold.

Under these assumptions, we can estimate the size of $R(X, Y) \bowtie S(Y, Z)$ as follows. Let $V(R, Y) \leq V(S, Y)$. Then every tuple t of R has a chance $1/V(S, Y)$ of joining with a given tuple of S. Since there are $T(S)$ tuples in S, the expected number of tuples that t joins with is $T(S)/V(S, Y)$. As there are $T(R)$ tuples of R, the estimated size of $R \bowtie S$ is $T(R)T(S)/V(S, Y)$. If $V(R, Y) \geq V(S, Y)$, then a symmetric argument gives us estimate $T(R \bowtie S) = T(R)T(S)/V(R, Y)$. In general, we divide by whichever of $V(R, Y)$ and $V(S, Y)$ is larger. That is:

- $T(R \bowtie S) = T(R)T(S)/\max\big(V(R, Y), V(S, Y)\big)$

Example 7.25: Let us consider the following three relations and their important statistics:

$R(a, b)$	$S(b, c)$	$U(c, d)$
$T(R) = 1000$	$T(S) = 2000$	$T(U) = 5000$
$V(R, b) = 20$	$V(S, b) = 50$	
	$V(S, c) = 100$	$V(U, c) = 500$

Suppose we want to compute the natural join $R \bowtie S \bowtie U$. One way is to group R and S first, as $(R \bowtie S) \bowtie U$. Our estimate for $T(R \bowtie S)$ is $T(R)T(S)/\max\big(V(R, b), V(S, b)\big)$, which is $1000 \times 2000/50$, or 40,000.

We then need to join $R \bowtie S$ with U. Our estimate for the size of the result is $T(R \bowtie S)T(U)/\max\big(V(R \bowtie S, c), V(U, c)\big)$. By our assumption that value sets are preserved, $V(R \bowtie S, c)$ is the same as $V(S, c)$, or 100; that is no values of attribute c disappear when we performed the join. In that case, we get as our estimate for the number of tuples in $R \bowtie S \bowtie U$ the value $40,000 \times 5000/\max(100, 500)$, or 400,000.

We could also start by joining S and U. If we do, then we get the estimate $T(S \bowtie U) = T(S)T(U)/\max\big(V(S, c), V(U, c)\big) = 2000 \times 5000/500 = 20,000$. By our assumption that value sets are preserved, $V(S \bowtie U, b) = V(S, b) = 50$, so the estimated size of the result is

$$T(R)T(S \bowtie U)/\max\big(V(R, b), V(S \bowtie U, b)\big)$$

which is $1000 \times 20,000/50$, or 400,000. $\quad\square$

It is no coincidence that in Example 7.25 the estimate of the size of the join $R \bowtie S \bowtie U$ is the same whether we start by joining $R \bowtie S$ or by joining $S \bowtie U$. Recall that one of our desiderata of Section 7.4.1 is that the estimate for the result of an expression should not depend on order of evaluation. It can be shown that the two assumptions we have made — containment and preservation of value sets — guarantee that the estimate of any natural join is the same, regardless of how we order the joins.

7.4.5 Natural Joins With Multiple Join Attributes

Now, let us see what happens when Y represents several attributes in the join $R(X, Y) \bowtie S(Y, Z)$. For a specific example, suppose we want to join $R(x, y_1, y_2) \bowtie S(y_1, y_2, z)$. Consider a tuple r in R. The probability that r joins with a given tuple s of S can be calculated as follows.

First, what is the probability that r and s agree on attribute y_1? Suppose that $V(R, y_1) \geq V(S, y_1)$. Then the y_1-value of s is surely one of the y_1 values that appear in R, by the containment-of-value-sets assumption. Hence, the chance that r has the same y_1-value as s is $1/V(R, y_1)$. Similarly, if $V(R, y_1) < V(S, y_1)$, then the value of y_1 in r will appear in S, and the probability is $1/V(S, y_1)$ that r and s will share the same y_1-value. In general, we see that the probability of agreement on the y_1 value is $1/\max\big(V(R, y_1), V(S, y_1)\big)$.

A similar argument about the probability of r and s agreeing on y_2 tells us this probability is $1/\max\big(V(R, y_2), V(S, y_2)\big)$. As the values of y_1 and y_2 are independent, the probability that tuples will agree on both y_1 and y_2 is the product of these fractions. Thus, of the $T(R)T(S)$ pairs of tuples from R and S, the expected number of pairs that match in both y_1 and y_2 is

$$\frac{T(R)T(S)}{\max\big(V(R, y_1), V(S, y_1)\big) \max\big(V(R, y_2), V(S, y_2)\big)}$$

In general, the following rule can be used to estimate the size of a natural join when there are any number of attributes shared between the two relations.

- The estimate of the size of $R \bowtie S$ is computed by multiplying $T(R)$ by $T(S)$ and dividing by the larger of $V(R, y)$ and $V(S, y)$ for each attribute y that is common to R and S.

Example 7.26: The following example uses the rule above. It also illustrates that the analysis we have been doing for natural joins applies to any equijoin. Consider the join

$$R(a, b, c) \underset{R.b=S.d \text{ AND } R.c=S.e}{\overset{\bowtie}{}} S(d, e, f)$$

Suppose we have the following size parameters:

$R(a, b, c)$	$S(d, e, f)$
$T(R) = 1000$	$T(S) = 2000$
$V(R, b) = 20$	$V(S, d) = 50$
$V(R, c) = 100$	$V(S, e) = 50$

Numbers of Tuples is not Enough

Although our analysis of relation sizes has focused on the number of tuples in the result, we also have to take into account the size of each tuple. For instance, joins of relations produce tuples that are longer than the tuples of either relation. As an example, joining two relations $R \bowtie S$, each with 1000 tuples, might yield a result that also has 1000 tuples. However, the result would occupy more blocks than either R or S.

Example 7.26 is an interesting case in point. Although we can use natural-join techniques to estimate the number of tuples in a theta-join, as we did there, the tuples in a theta-join have more components than tuples of the corresponding natural join. Specifically, the theta-join $R(a,b,c) \underset{R.b=S.d \text{ AND } R.c=S.e}{\bowtie} S(d,e,f)$ produces tuples with six components, one each for a through f, while the natural join $R(a,b,c) \bowtie S(b,c,d)$ produces the same number of tuples, but each tuple has only four components.

We can think of this join as a natural join if we regard $R.b$ and $S.d$ as the same attribute and also regard $R.c$ and $S.e$ as the same attribute. Then the rule given above tells us the estimate for the size of $R \bowtie S$ is the product 1000×2000 divided by the larger of 20 and 50 and also divided by the larger of 100 and 50. Thus, the size estimate for the join is $1000 \times 2000/(50 \times 100) = 400$ tuples. □

Example 7.27: Let us reconsider Example 7.25, but consider the third possible order for the joins, where we first take $R(a,b) \bowtie U(c,d)$. This join is actually a product, and the number of tuples in the result is $T(R)T(U) = 1000 \times 5000 = 5,000,000$. Note that the number of different b's in the product is $V(R,b) = 20$, and the number of different c's is $V(U,c) = 500$.

When we join this product with $S(b,c)$, we multiply the numbers of tuples and divide by both $\max(V(R,b), V(S,b))$ and $\max(V(U,c), V(S,c))$. This quantity is $2000 \times 5,000,000/(50 \times 500) = 400,000$. Note that this third way of joining gives the same estimate for the size of the result that we found in Example 7.25. □

7.4.6 Joins of Many Relations

Finally, let us consider the general case of a natural join:

$$S = R_1 \bowtie R_2 \bowtie \cdots \bowtie R_n$$

Suppose that attribute A appears in k of the R_i's, and the numbers of its sets of values in these k relations — that is, the various values of $V(R_i, A)$ for

$i = 1, 2, \ldots, k$ — are $v_1 \le v_2 \le \cdots \le v_k$, in order from smallest to largest. Suppose we pick a tuple from each relation. What is the probability that all tuples selected agree on attribute A?

In answer, consider the tuple t_1 chosen from the relation that has the smallest number of A-values, v_1. By the containment-of-value-sets assumption, each of these v_1 values is among the A-values found in the other relations that have attribute A. Consider the relation that has v_i values in attribute A. Its selected tuple t_i has probability $1/v_i$ of agreeing with t_1 on A. Since this claim is true for all $i = 2, 3, \ldots, k$, the probability that all k tuples agree on A is the product $1/v_2 v_3 \cdots v_k$. This analysis gives us the rule for estimating the size of any join.

- Start with the product of the number of tuples in each relation. Then, for each attribute A appearing at least twice, divide by all but the least of the $V(R, A)$'s.

Likewise, we can estimate the number of values that will remain for attribute A after the join. By the preservation-of-value-sets assumption, it is the least of these $V(R, A)$'s.

Example 7.28: Consider the join $R(a, b, c) \bowtie S(b, c, d) \bowtie U(b, e)$, and suppose the important statistics are as given in Fig. 7.24. To estimate the size of this join, we begin by multiplying the relation sizes; $1000 \times 2000 \times 5000$. Next, we look at the attributes that appear more than once; these are b, which appears three times, and c, which appears twice. We divide by the two largest of $V(R, b)$, $V(S, b)$, and $V(U, b)$; these are 50 and 200. Finally, we divide by the larger of $V(R, c)$ and $V(S, c)$, which is 200. The resulting estimate is

$$1000 \times 2000 \times 5000 / (50 \times 200 \times 100)$$

or 10,000.

$R(a, b, c)$	$S(b, c, d)$	$U(b, e)$
$T(R) = 1000$	$T(S) = 2000$	$T(U) = 5000$
$V(R, a) = 100$		
$V(R, b) = 20$	$V(S, b) = 50$	$V(U, b) = 200$
$V(R, c) = 200$	$V(S, c) = 100$	
	$V(S, d) = 400$	
		$V(U, e) = 500$

Figure 7.24: Parameters for Example 7.28

We can also estimate the number of values for each of the attributes in the join. Each estimate is the least value count for the attribute among all the relations in which it appears. These numbers are, for a, b, c, d, e respectively: 100, 20, 100, 400, and 500. □

Why is the Join Size Estimate Independent of Order?

A formal proof of this claim is by induction on the number of relations involved in the join. We shall not give this proof, but this box contains the intuition. Suppose we join some relations, and the final step is

$$(R_1 \bowtie \cdots \bowtie R_n) \bowtie (S_1 \bowtie \cdots \bowtie S_m)$$

We may assume that no matter how the joins of the R's was taken, the size estimate for this join is the product of the sizes of the R's divided by all but the smallest value count for each attribute that appears more than once among the R's. Further, the estimated value count for each attribute is the smallest of its value counts among the R's. Similar statements apply to the S's.

When we apply the rule for estimating the size of the join of two relations (from Section 7.4.4) to the two relations that are the join of the R's and the join of the S's, the estimate will be the product of the two estimates, divided by the larger of the value counts for each attribute that appears among both the R's and S's. Thus, this estimate will surely have one factor that is the size of each relation $R_1, \ldots, R_n, S_1, \ldots, S_m$. In addition, the estimate will have a divisor for each attribute value count that is *not* the smallest for its attribute. Either that divisor is already present in the estimate for the R's or the S's, or it is introduced at the last step, because its attribute A appears among both the R's and S's, and it is the larger of the two value counts that are the smallest of the $V(R_i, A)$'s and smallest of the $V(S_j, A)$'s, respectively.

Based on the two assumptions we have made — containment and preservation of value sets — we have a surprising and convenient property of the estimating rule given above.

- No matter how we group and order the terms in a natural join of n relations, the estimation rules, applied to each join individually, yield the same estimate for the size of the result. Moreover, this estimate is the same that we get if we apply the rule for the join of all n relations as a whole.

Examples 7.25 and 7.27 form an illustration of this rule in action for the three groupings of a three-relation join, including the grouping where one of the "joins" is actually a product.

7.4.7 Estimating Sizes for Other Operations

We have seen two operations with an exact formula for the number of tuples in the result:

1. Projections do not change the number of tuples in a relation.

2. Products produce a result with a number of tuples equal to the product of the numbers of tuples in the argument relations.

There are two other operations — selection and join — where we have developed reasonable estimating techniques. However, for the remaining operations, the size of the result is not easy to determine. We shall review the other relational-algebra operators and give some suggestions as to how this estimation could be done.

Union

If the bag union is taken, then the size is exactly the sum of the sizes of the arguments. A set union can be as large as the sum of the sizes or as small as the larger of the two arguments. We suggest that something in the middle be chosen, e.g., the average of the sum and the larger (which is the same as the larger plus half the smaller).

Intersection

The result can have as few as 0 tuples or as many as the smaller of the two arguments, regardless of whether set- or bag-intersection is taken. One approach is to take the average of the extremes, which is half the smaller.

   Another approach is to recognize that the intersection is an extreme case of the natural join and use the formula of Section 7.4.4. When a set intersection is meant, this formula is guaranteed to produce a result that is no greater than the smaller of the two relations. However, in the case of a bag intersection, there can be some anomalies, where the estimate is larger than either argument. For instance, consider $R(a, b) \cap_B S(a, b)$, where R consists of two copies of tuple $(0, 1)$ and S consists of three copies of the same tuple. Then

$$V(R, a) = V(S, a) = V(R, b) = V(S, b) = 1$$

$T(R) = 2$, and $T(S) = 3$. The estimate is $2 \times 3/(1 \times 1 \times 1 \times 1) = 6$ from the rule for joins, but clearly there can be no more than $\min(T(R), T(S)) = 2$ tuples in the result.

Difference

When we compute $R - S$, the result can have between $T(R)$ and $T(R) - T(S)$ tuples. We suggest the average as an estimate: $T(R) - \frac{1}{2}T(S)$.

Duplicate Elimination

If $R(a_1, a_2, \ldots, a_n)$ is a relation, then $V(R, [a_1, a_2, \ldots, a_n])$ is the size of $\delta(R)$. However, often we shall not have this statistic available, so it must be approximated. In the extremes, the size of $\delta(R)$ could be the same as the size of R (no duplicates) or as small as 1 (all tuples in R are the same).[4] Another upper limit on the number of tuples in $\delta(R)$ is the maximum number of distinct tuples that could exist: the product of $V(R, a_i)$ for $i = 1, 2, \ldots, n$. That number could be smaller than other estimates of $T(R)$. There are several rules that could be used to estimate $T(\delta(R))$. One reasonable one is to take the smaller of $\frac{1}{2}T(R)$ and the product of all the $V(R, a_i)$'s.

Grouping and Aggregation

Suppose we have an expression $\gamma_L(R)$, the size of whose result we need to estimate. If the statistic $V(R, [g_1, g_2, \ldots, g_k])$, where the g_i's are the grouping attributes in L, is available, then that is our answer. However, that statistic may well not be obtainable, so we need another way to estimate the size of $\gamma_L(R)$. The number of tuples in $\gamma_L(R)$ is the same as the number of groups. There could be as few as one group in the result or as many groups as there are tuples in R. As with δ, we can also upper-bound the number of groups by a product of $V(R, A)$'s, but here attribute A ranges over only the grouping attributes of L. We again suggest an estimate that is the smaller of $\frac{1}{2}T(R)$ and this product.

7.4.8 Exercises for Section 7.4

Exercise 7.4.1 : Below are the vital statistics for four relations, W, X, Y, and Z:

$W(a, b)$	$X(b, c)$	$Y(c, d)$	$Z(d, e)$
$T(W) = 100$	$T(X) = 200$	$T(Y) = 300$	$T(Z) = 400$
$V(W, a) = 20$	$V(X, b) = 50$	$V(Y, c) = 50$	$V(Z, d) = 40$
$V(W, b) = 60$	$V(X, c) = 100$	$V(Y, d) = 50$	$V(Z, e) = 100$

Estimate the sizes of relations that are the results of the following expressions:

* a) $W \bowtie X \bowtie Y \bowtie Z$.

* b) $\sigma_{a=10}(W)$.

  c) $\sigma_{c=20}(Y)$.

  d) $\sigma_{c=20}(Y) \bowtie Z$.

  e) $W \times Y$.

---

[4]Strictly speaking, if R is empty there are no tuples in either R or $\delta(R)$, so the lower bound is 0. However, we are rarely interested in this special case.

f) $\sigma_{d>10}(Z)$.

* g) $\sigma_{a=1 \text{ AND } b=2}(W)$.

h) $\sigma_{a=1 \text{ AND } b>2}(W)$.

i) $X \underset{X.c<Y.c}{\bowtie} Y$.

* **Exercise 7.4.2:** Here are the statistics for four relations E, F, G, and H:

$E(a,b,c)$	$F(a,b,d)$	$G(a,c,d)$	$H(b,c,d)$
$T(E)=1000$	$T(F)=2000$	$T(G)=3000$	$T(H)=4000$
$V(E,a)=1000$	$V(F,a)=50$	$V(G,a)=50$	$V(H,b)=40$
$V(E,b)=50$	$V(F,b)=100$	$V(G,c)=300$	$V(H,c)=100$
$V(E,c)=20$	$V(F,d)=200$	$V(G,d)=500$	$V(H,d)=400$

How many tuples does the join of these tuples have, using the techniques for estimation from this section?

! **Exercise 7.4.3:** How would you estimate the size of a semijoin?

!! **Exercise 7.4.4:** Suppose we compute $R(a,b) \bowtie S(a,c)$, where R and S each have 1000 tuples. The a attribute of each relation has 100 different values, and they are the *same* 100 values. If the distribution of values was uniform; i.e., each a-value appeared in exactly 10 tuples of each relation, then there would be 10,000 tuples in the join. Suppose instead that the 100 a-values have the same Zipfian distribution in each relation. Precisely, let the values be $a_1, a_2, \ldots, a_{100}$. Then the number of tuples of both R and S that have a-value a_i is proportional to $1/\sqrt{i}$. Under these circumstances, how many tuples does the join have? You should ignore the fact that the number of tuples with a given a-value may not be an integer.

7.5　Introduction to Cost-Based Plan Selection

Whether selecting a logical query plan or constructing a physical query plan from a logical plan, the query optimizer needs to estimate the cost of evaluating certain expressions. We study the issues involved in cost-based plan selection here, and in Section 7.6 we consider in detail one of the most important and difficult problems in cost-based plan selection: the selection of a join order for several relations.

As before, we shall assume that the "cost" of evaluating an expression is approximated well by the number of disk I/O's performed. The number of disk I/O's, in turn, is influenced by:

1. The particular logical operators chosen to implement the query, a matter decided when we choose the logical query plan.

2. The sizes of intermediate relations, whose estimation we discussed in Section 7.4.

3. The physical operators used to implement logical operators, e.g., the choice of a one-pass or two-pass join, or the choice to sort or not sort a given relation; this matter is discussed in Section 7.7.

4. The ordering of similar operations, especially joins as discussed in Section 7.6.

5. The method of passing arguments from one physical operator to the next, which is also discussed in Section 7.7.

Many issues need to be resolved in order to perform effective cost-based plan selection. In this section, we first consider how the size parameters, which were so essential for estimating relation sizes in Section 7.4, can be obtained from the database efficiently. We then revisit the algebraic laws we introduced to find the preferred logical query plan. Cost-based analysis justifies the use of many of the common heuristics for transforming logical query plans, such as pushing selections down the tree. Finally, we consider the various approaches to enumerating all the physical query plans that can be derived from the selected logical plan. Especially important are methods for reducing the number of plans that need to be evaluated, while making it likely that the least-cost plan is still considered.

7.5.1 Obtaining Estimates for Size Parameters

The formulas of Section 7.4 were predicated on knowing certain important parameters, especially $T(R)$, the number of tuples in a relation R, and $V(R,a)$, the number of different values in the column of relation R for attribute a. A modern DBMS generally allows the user or administrator explicitly to request the gathering of statistics. These statistics are then used in subsequent query optimizations to estimate the cost of operations. Changes in values for the statistics due to subsequent database modifications are considered only after the next statistics-gathering command.

By scanning an entire relation R, it is straightforward to count the number of tuples $T(R)$ and also to discover the number of different values $V(R,A)$ for each attribute A. The number of blocks in which R can fit, $B(R)$, can be estimated either by counting the actual number of blocks used (if R is clustered), or by dividing $T(R)$ by the length of a tuple (or by the average length of a tuple, if R's tuples are stored in a variable-length format). Note that these two estimates of $B(R)$ may not be the same, but they are usually "close enough" for comparisons of costs, as long as we consistently choose one approach or the other.

In addition, a DBMS may compute a *histogram* of the values for a given attribute. If $V(R,A)$ is not too large, then the histogram may consist of the number (or fraction) of the tuples having each of the values of attribute A. If there are a great many values of this attribute, then only the most frequent values may be recorded individually, while other values are counted in groups. The most common types of histograms are:

1. *Equal-width.* A width w is chosen, along with a constant v_0. Counts are provided of the number of tuples with values v in the ranges $v_0 \leq v < v_0 + w$, $v_0 + w \leq v < v_0 + 2w$, and so on. The value v_0 may be the lowest possible value or the current minimum value seen. In the latter case, should a new, lower value be seen, we can lower the value of v_0 by w and add a new count to the histogram.

2. *Equal-height.* These are the common "percentiles." We pick some fraction p, and list the lowest value, the value that is fraction p from the lowest, the fraction $2p$ from the lowest, and so on, up to the highest value.

3. *Most-frequent-values.* We may list the most common values and their numbers of occurrences. This information may be provided along with a count of occurrences for all the other values as a group, or we may record frequent values in addition to an equal-width or equal-height histogram for the other values.

One advantage of keeping a histogram is that the sizes of joins can be estimated more accurately than by the simplified methods of Section 7.4. In particular, if a value of the join attribute appears explicitly in the histograms of both relations being joined, then we know exactly how many tuples of the result will have this value. For those values of the join attribute that do not appear explicitly in the histogram of one or both relations, we estimate their effect on the join as in Section 7.4. However, if we use an equal-width histogram, with the same bands for the join attributes of both relations, then we can estimate the size of the joins of corresponding bands, and sum those estimates. The result will be correct, because only tuples in corresponding bands can join. The following examples will suggest how to carry out histogram-based estimation; we shall not use histograms in estimates subsequently.

Example 7.29 : Consider histograms that mention the three most frequent values and their counts, and group the remaining values. Suppose we want to compute the join $R(a, b) \bowtie S(b, c)$. Let the histogram for $R.b$ be:

$$1: 200, \quad 0: 150, \quad 5: 100, \quad \text{others: } 550$$

That is, of the 1000 tuples in R, 200 of them have b-value 1, 150 have b-value 0, and 100 have b-value 5. In addition, 550 tuples have b-values other than 0, 1, or 5, and none of these other values appears more than 100 times.

Let the histogram for $S.b$ be:

$$0: 100, \quad 1: 80, \quad 2: 70, \quad \text{others: } 250$$

Suppose also that $V(R, b) = 14$ and $V(S, b) = 13$. That is, the 550 tuples of R with unknown b-values are divided among eleven values, for an average of 50 tuples each, and the 250 tuples of S with unknown b-values are divided among ten values, each with an average of 25 tuples each.

Values 0 and 1 appear explicitly in both histograms, so we can calculate that the 150 tuples of R with $b = 0$ join with the 100 tuples of S having the same b-value, to yield 15,000 tuples in the result. Likewise, the 200 tuples of R with $b = 1$ join with the 80 tuples of S having $b = 1$ to yield 16,000 more tuples in the result.

The estimate of the effect of the remaining tuples is more complex. We shall continue to make the assumption that every value appearing in the relation with the smaller set of values (S in this case) will also appear in the set of values of the other relation. Thus, among the eleven remaining b-values of S, we know one of those values is 2, and we shall assume another of the values is 5, since that is one of the most frequent values in R. We estimate that 2 appears 50 times in R, and 5 appears 25 times in S. These estimates are each obtained by assuming that the value is one of the "other" values for its relation's histogram. The number of additional tuples from b-value 2 is thus $70 \times 50 = 3500$, and the number of additional tuples from b-value 5 is $100 \times 25 = 2500$.

Finally, there are nine other b-values that appear in both relations, and we estimate that each of them appears in 50 tuples of R and 25 tuples of S. Each of the nine values thus contributes $50 \times 25 = 1250$ tuples to the result. The estimate of the output size is thus:

$$15000 + 16000 + 3500 + 2500 + 9 \times 1250$$

or 48,250 tuples. Note that the simpler estimate from Section 7.4 would be $1000 \times 500/14$, or 35,714, based on the assumptions of equal numbers of occurrences of each value in each relation. $\square$

Example 7.30: In this example, we shall assume an equal-width partition, and we shall demonstrate how knowing that values of two relations are almost disjoint can impact the estimate of a join size. Our relations are:

```
Jan(day, temp)
July(day, temp)
```

and the query is:

```
SELECT Jan.day, July.day
FROM Jan, July
WHERE Jan.temp = July.temp;
```

That is, find pairs of days in January and July that had the same temperature. The query plan is to equijoin Jan and July on the temperature, and project onto the two day attributes.

Suppose the histogram of temperatures for the relations Jan and July are as given in the table of Fig. 7.25.[5] In general, if both join attributes have equal-

---

[5] Our friends south of the equator should reverse the columns for January and July.

width histograms with the same set of bands (perhaps with some bands empty for one of the relations), then we can estimate the size of the join by estimating the size of the join of each pair of corresponding bands and summing.

Range	Jan	July
0–9	40	0
10–19	60	0
20–29	80	0
30–39	50	0
40–49	10	5
50–59	5	20
60–69	0	50
70–79	0	100
80–89	0	60
90–99	0	10

Figure 7.25: Histograms of temperature

If two corresponding bands have T_1 and T_2 tuples, respectively, and the number of values in a band is V, then the estimate for the number of tuples in the join of those bands is $T_1 T_2 / V$, following the principles laid out in Section 7.4.4. For the histograms of Fig. 7.25, many of these products are 0, because one or the other of T_1 and T_2 is 0. The only bands for which neither is 0 are 40–49 and 50–59. Since $V = 10$ is the width of a band, the 40–49 band contributes $10 \times 5/10 = 5$ tuples, and the the 50–59 band contributes $5 \times 20/10 = 10$ tuples.

Thus our estimate for the size of this join is $5 + 10 = 15$ tuples. If we had no histogram, and knew only that each relation had 245 tuples distributed among 100 values from 0 to 99, then our estimate of the join size would be $245 \times 245/100 = 600$ tuples. □

7.5.2 Incremental Computation of Statistics

The periodic computation of statistics is preferred in query optimizers because these statistics tend not to change radically in a short time. Also, as we have mentioned, even inaccurate statistics are useful as long as they are applied to all the plans that compete for the title of "best." However, examining entire relations even periodically is expensive, and an alternative to periodic recomputation of statistics is *incremental evaluation*. In this mode, estimates of the parameters are maintained and updated each time the database is modified. Here are some of the ways that the system can do so:

- To maintain $T(R)$, the system adds 1 every time a tuple is inserted and subtracts one every time a tuple is deleted. Note that doing so requires a modification to the functions that insert and delete tuples. It adds to the cost of every such operation, but the extra cost is normally negligible.

- If there is a B-tree index on any attribute of R, then we can estimate $T(R)$ by counting only the number of blocks in the B-tree. We might, for example, assume that each block is 3/4 full, and use knowledge of the number of keys and pointers that fit on a block to estimate the number of tuples pointed to by the leaves of the B-tree. This approach is less accurate than counting $T(R)$ directly, but requires effort only when the structure of the B-tree changes, which is relatively rare compared with the rate of insertions and deletions.

- If there is an index on attribute a of relation R, then we can maintain $V(R, a)$ exactly. On insert into R, we must find the a-value for the new tuple in the index anyway, and as we do so we determine whether there was another tuple with the same a-value. If not, we increment our count of $V(R, a)$. Similarly, on deletion from R we check whether we are deleting the last tuple of R with that a-value, and if so we decrement $V(R, a)$.

- If we know that a is a key for R, then we know $V(R, a) = T(R)$ without consulting an index or maintaining $V(R, a)$ directly.

- If there is no index on $R.a$, the system could, in effect, create a rudimentary index by keeping a data structure (e.g., a hash table or B-tree) that holds every value of a.

A final option regarding the computation of statistics for $V(R, A)$ is to obtain a statistical estimate of this quantity when needed, by sampling a small fraction of the data. This sort of calculation is complex, and depends on a number of assumptions, such as whether values for an attribute are distributed uniformly, according to a Zipfian distribution, or according to some other distribution. However, the intuition is as follows. If we look at a small sample of R, say 1% of its tuples, and we find that most of the a-values we see are different, then it is likely that $V(R, a)$ is close to $T(R)$. If we find that the sample has very few different values of a, then it is likely that we have seen most of the a-values that exist in the current relation.

7.5.3 Heuristics for Reducing the Cost of Logical Query Plans

One important use of cost estimates for queries or subqueries is in the application of heuristic transformations of the query. We have already observed in Section 7.3.3 how certain heuristics applied independent of cost estimates can be expected almost certainly to improve the cost of a logical query plan. Pushing selections down the tree is the canonical example of such a transformation. However, there are other points in the query optimization process where estimating the cost both before and after a transformation will allow us to apply a transformation where it appears to reduce cost and avoid the transformation

---

Why Measure Size Instead of Disk I/O's?

When considering logical query plans, we have not yet made decisions about the physical operators that will be used to implement the operators of relational algebra. Thus, we cannot be sure of the numbers of disk I/O's that will be used to execute a plan. However, we may follow the useful heuristic that a plan with the smaller sum of sizes of the intermediate relations is likely to be the better plan. Recall that the justification for this heuristic is that the smaller relations are, the fewer disk I/O's needed to read or write them, and the more efficient the algorithms are that we can use to implement operations on these relations.

In fact, numbers of disk I/O's is in turn an estimate of the true cost of a query. A more detailed analysis would consider CPU time, and still more detailed analysis would consider the motion of the disk head, taking into account the possible locality of blocks accessed on the disk. In practice, even the simplest measure — sizes of the intermediate relations — is generally good enough, especially since the query optimizer needs only to compare query plans, not to predict exact execution time.

---

otherwise. In particular, when the preferred logical query plan is being generated, we may consider a number of optional transformations and the costs before and after. One example will serve to illustrate the issues and process.

Example 7.31: Consider the initial logical query plan of Fig. 7.26, and let the statistics for the relations R and S be as follows:

$R(a,b)$	$S(b,c)$
$T(R) = 5000$	$T(S) = 2000$
$V(R,a) = 50$	
$V(R,b) = 100$	$V(S,b) = 200$
	$V(S,c) = 100$

To generate a final logical query plan from Fig. 7.26, we shall insist that the selection be pushed down as far as possible. However, we are not sure whether it makes sense to push the δ below the join or not. Thus, we generate from Fig. 7.26 the two query plans shown in Fig. 7.27; they differ in whether we have chosen to eliminate duplicates before or after the join. Notice that in plan (a) the δ is pushed down both branches of the tree. If R and/or S is known to have no duplicates, then the δ along its branch could be eliminated.

We know how to estimate the size of the result of the selections, from Section 7.4.3; we divide by $V(R,a) = 50$. We also know how to estimate the size of the joins; we multiply the sizes of the arguments and divide by $\max(V(R,b), V(S,b))$, which is 200. What we don't know is how to estimate the size of the relations with duplicates eliminated.

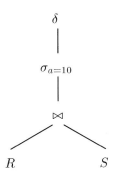

Figure 7.26: Logical query plan for Example 7.31

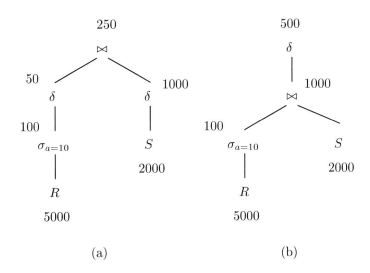

Figure 7.27: Two candidates for the best logical query plan

Estimates for Result Sizes Need Not Be the Same

Notice that in Fig. 7.27 the estimates at the roots of the two trees are different: 250 in one case and 500 in the other. Because estimation is an inexact science, these sorts of anomalies will occur. In fact, it is the exception when we can offer a guarantee of consistency, as we did in Section 7.4.6.

Intuitively, the estimate for plan (b) is higher because if there are duplicates in both R and S, these duplicates will be multiplied in the join; e.g., for tuples that appear 3 times in R and twice in S, their join will appear six times in $R \bowtie S$. Our simple formula for estimating the size of the result of a δ does not take into account the possibility that the effect of duplicates has been amplified by previous operations.

First, consider the size estimate for $\delta\big(\sigma_{a=10}(R)\big)$. Since $\sigma_{a=10}(R)$ has only one value for a and up to 100 values for b, and there are an estimated 100 tuples in this relation, the rule from Section 7.4.7 tells us that the product of the value counts for each of the attributes is not a limiting factor. Thus, we estimate the size of the result of δ as half the tuples in $\sigma_{a=10}(R)$. Thus, Fig. 7.27(a) shows an estimate of 50 tuples for $\delta\big(\sigma_{a=10}(R)\big)$.

Now, consider the estimate of the result of the δ in Fig. 7.27(b). The join has one value for a, an estimated $\min\big(V(R,b), V(S,b)\big) = 100$ values for b, and an estimated $V(S,c) = 100$ values for c. Thus again the product of the value counts does not limit how big the result of the δ can be. We estimate this result as 500 tuples, or half the number of tuples in the join.

To compare the two plans of Fig. 7.27, we add the estimated sizes for all the nodes except the root and the leaves. We exclude the root and leaves, because these sizes are not dependent on the plan chosen. For plan (a) this cost, the sum of the estimated sizes of the interior nodes, is $100 + 50 + 1000 = 1150$, while for plan (b) the sum is $100 + 1000 = 1100$. Thus, by a small margin we conclude that deferring the duplicate elimination to the end is a better plan. We would come to the opposite conclusion if, say, R or S had fewer b-values. Then the join size would be greater, making the cost of plan (b) greater. □

7.5.4 Approaches to Enumerating Physical Plans

Now, let us consider the use of cost estimates in the conversion of a logical query plan to a physical query plan. The baseline approach, called *exhaustive*, is to consider all combinations of choices for each of the issues outlined at the beginning of Section 7.4 (order of joins, physical implementation of operators, and so on). Each possible physical plan is assigned an estimated cost, and the one with the smallest cost is selected.

However, there are a number of other approaches to selection of a physical plan. In this section, we shall outline various approaches that have been used, while Section 7.6 illustrates the major ideas in the context of the important problem of selecting a join order. Before proceeding, let us comment that there are two broad approaches to exploring the space of possible physical plans:

- *Top-down*: Here, we work down the tree of the logical query plan from the root. For each possible implementation of the operation at the root, we consider each possible way to evaluate its argument(s), and compute the cost of each combination, taking the best.[6]

- *Bottom-up*: For each subexpression of the logical-query-plan tree, we compute the costs of all possible ways to compute that subexpression. The possibilities and costs for a subexpression E are computed by considering the options for the subexpressions for E, and combining them in all possible ways with implementations for the root operator of E.

There is actually not much difference between the two approaches in their broadest interpretations, since either way, all possible combinations of ways to implement each operator in the query tree are considered. When limiting the search, a top-down approach may allow us to eliminate certain options that could not be eliminated bottom-up. However, bottom-up strategies that limit choices effectively have also been developed, so we shall concentrate on bottom-up methods in what follows.

You may, in fact, have noticed that there is an apparent simplification of the bottom-up method, where we consider only the *best* plan for each subexpression when we compute the plans for a larger subexpression. This approach, called *dynamic programming* in the list of methods below, is not guaranteed to yield the best plan, although often it does. The approach called *Selinger-style* (or *System-R-style*) optimization, also listed below, exploits additional properties that some of the plans for a subexpression may have, in order to produce optimal overall plans from plans that are not optimal for certain subexpressions.

Heuristic Selection

One option is to use the same approach to selecting a physical plan that is generally used for selecting a logical plan: make a sequence of choices based on heuristics. In Section 7.6.6, we shall discuss a "greedy" heuristic for join ordering, where we start by joining the pair of relations whose result has the smallest estimated size, then repeat the process for the result of that join and the other relations in the set to be joined. There are many other heuristics that may be applied; here are some of the most commonly used ones:

---

[6]Remember from Section 7.3.4 that a single node of the logical-query-plan tree may represent many uses of a single commutative and associative operator, such as join. Thus, the consideration of all possible plans for a single node may itself involve enumeration of very many choices.

1. If the logical plan calls for a selection $\sigma_{A=c}(R)$, and stored relation R has an index on attribute A, then perform an indexed scan to obtain only the tuples of R with A-value equal to c.

2. More generally, if the selection involves one condition like $A = c$ above, and other conditions as well, we can implement the selection by an indexed scan followed by a further selection on the tuples, which we shall represent by the physical operator *filter*. This matter is discussed further in Section 7.7.1.

3. If an argument of a join has an index on the join attribute(s), then use an index-join with that relation in the inner loop.

4. If one argument of a join is sorted on the join attribute(s), then prefer a sort-join to a hash-join, although not necessarily to an index-join if one is possible.

5. When computing the union or intersection of three or more relations, group the smallest relations first.

Branch-and-Bound Plan Enumeration

This approach, often used in practice, begins by using heuristics to find a good physical plan for the entire logical query plan. Let the cost of this plan be C. Then as we consider other plans for subqueries, we can eliminate any plan for a subquery that has a cost greater than C, since that plan for the subquery could not possibly participate in a plan for the complete query that is better than what we already know. Likewise, if we construct a plan for the complete query that has cost less than C, we replace C by the cost of this better plan in subsequent exploration of the space of physical query plans.

An important advantage of this approach is that we can choose when to cut off the search and take the best plan found so far. For instance, if the cost C is small, then even if there are much better plans to be found, the time spent finding them may exceed C, so it does not make sense to continue the search. However, if C is large, then investing time in the hope of finding a faster plan is wise.

Hill Climbing

This approach, in which we really search for a "valley" in the space of physical plans and their costs, starts with a heuristically selected physical plan. We can then make small changes to the plan, e.g., replacing one method for an operator by another, or reordering joins by using the associative and/or commutative laws, to find "nearby" plans that have lower cost. When we find a plan such that no small modification yields a plan of lower cost, we make that plan our chosen physical query plan.

Dynamic Programming

In this variation of the general bottom-up strategy, we keep for each subexpression only the plan of least cost. As we work up the tree, we consider possible implementations of each node, assuming the best plan for each subexpression is also used. We examine this approach extensively in Section 7.6.

Selinger-Style Optimization

This approach improves upon the dynamic-programming approach by keeping for each subexpression not only the plan of least cost, but certain other plans that have higher cost but produce a result that is sorted in an order that may be useful higher up in the expression tree. Examples of such *interesting* orders are when the result of the subexpression is sorted on one of:

1. The attribute(s) specified in a sort (τ) operator at the root.

2. The grouping attribute(s) of a later group-by (γ) operator.

3. The join attribute(s) of a later join.

If we take the cost of a plan to be the sum of the sizes of the intermediate relations, then there appears to be no advantage to having an argument sorted. However, if we use the more accurate measure, disk I/O's, as the cost, then the advantage of having an argument sorted becomes clear if we can use one of the sort-based algorithms of section 6.5, and save the work of the first pass for the argument that is sorted already.

7.5.5 Exercises for Section 7.5

Exercise 7.5.1: Estimate the size of the join $R(a, b) \bowtie S(b, c)$ using histograms for $R.b$ and $S.b$. Assume $V(R, b) = V(S, b) = 20$, and the histograms for both attributes give the frequency of the four most common values, as tabulated below:

	0	1	2	3	4	others
$R.b$	5	6	4	5		32
$S.b$	10	8	5		7	48

How does this estimate compare with the simpler estimate, assuming that all 20 values are equally likely to occur, with $T(R) = 52$ and $T(S) = 78$?

* **Exercise 7.5.2:** Estimate the size of the join $R(a, b) \bowtie S(b, c)$ if we have the following histogram information:

	$b < 0$	$b = 0$	$b > 0$
R	500	100	400
S	300	200	500

! Exercise 7.5.3: In Example 7.31 we suggested that reducing the number of values that either attribute named b had could make plan (a) better than plan (b) of Fig. 7.27. For what values of:

* *** a)** $V(R, b)$

   b) $V(S, b)$

will plan (a) have a lower estimated cost than plan (b)?

! Exercise 7.5.4: Consider four relations R, S, T, and V. Respectively, they have 200, 300, 400, and 500 tuples, chosen randomly and independently from the same pool of 1000 tuples. For instance, the probability of finding any given tuple in R is 1/5, and for S is 3/10. The probability that a tuple is in both R and S is 3/50.

* *** a)** What is the expected size of $R \cup S \cup T \cup V$?

   b) What is the expected size of $R \cap S \cap T \cap V$?

* *** c)** What order of unions gives the least cost (estimated sum of the sizes of the intermediate relations)?

   d) What order of intersections gives the least cost (estimated sum of the sizes of the intermediate relations)?

! Exercise 7.5.5: Repeat Exercise 7.5.4 if all four relations have 500 of the 1000 tuples, at random.[7]

!! Exercise 7.5.6: Suppose we wish to compute the expression

$$\tau_b \big(R(a, b) \bowtie S(b, c) \bowtie T(c, d) \big)$$

That is, we join the three relations and produce the result sorted on attribute b. Let us make the simplifying assumptions:

   i. We shall not "join" R and T first, because that is a product.

   ii. Any other join can be performed with a two-pass sort-join or hash-join, but in no other way.

   iii. Any relation, or the result of any expression, can be sorted by a two-phase, multiway merge-sort, but in no other way.

   iv. The result of the first two relations to be joined will be passed as an argument to the last join one block at a time and not stored temporarily on disk.

---

[7]Solutions to corresponding parts of this exercise are *not* published on the Web.

     v. Each relation occupies 1000 blocks, and the result of either join of two relations occupies 5000 blocks.

Answer the following based on these assumptions:

* a) What are all the subexpressions and orders that a Selinger-style optimization would consider?

  b) Using disk I/O's as the measure of cost,[8] tell which query plan yields the least cost.

!! **Exercise 7.5.7:** Give an example of a logical query plan of the form $E \bowtie F$, for some expressions E and F (which you may choose), where using the best plans to evaluate E and F does not allow any choice of algorithm for the final join that minimizes the total cost of evaluating the entire expression. Make whatever assumptions you wish about the number of available main-memory buffers and the sizes of relations mentioned in E and F.

7.6 Choosing an Order for Joins

In this section we focus on a critical problem in cost-based optimization: selecting an order for the (natural) join of three or more relations. Similar ideas can be applied to other binary operations like union or intersection, but these operations are less important in practice, because they typically take less time to execute than joins, and they more rarely appear in clusters of three or more.

7.6.1 Significance of Left and Right Join Arguments

When ordering a join, we should remember that many of the join methods discussed in Chapter 6 are asymmetric, in the sense that the roles played by the two argument relations are different, and the cost of the join depends on which relation plays which role. Perhaps most important, the one-pass join of Section 6.3.3 reads one relation — preferably the smaller — into main memory, creating a structure such as a hash table to facilitate matching of tuples from the other relation. It then reads the other relation, one block at a time, to join its tuples with the tuples stored in memory.

    Suppose that when we select a physical plan, we decide to use a one-pass join. Then we shall treat the left argument of the join as the (smaller) relation to be stored in a main-memory data structure (this relation is called the *build relation*), while the right argument of the join is read a block at a time and its tuples matched with the stored relation (the *probe relation*). Other join algorithms that distinguish between their arguments include:

---

[8] Notice that, because we have made some very specific assumptions about the join methods to be used, we can estimate disk I/O's, instead of relying on the simpler, but less accurate, counts of tuples as our cost measure.

1. Nested-loop join, where we assume the left argument is the relation of the outer loop.

2. Index-join, where we assume the right argument has the index.

7.6.2 Join Trees

When we have the join of two relations, we need to order the arguments. We shall conventionally select the one whose estimated size is the smaller as the left argument. Notice that the algorithms mentioned above — one-pass, nested-loop, and indexed — each work best if the left argument is the smaller. More precisely, one-pass and nested-loop joins each assign a special role to the smaller relation (build relation, or outer loop), and index-joins typically are reasonable choices only if one relation is small and the other has an index. It is quite common for there to be a significant and discernible difference in the sizes of arguments, because a query involving joins very often also involves a selection on at least one attribute, and that selection reduces the estimated size of one of the relations greatly.

Example 7.32 : Recall the query

```
SELECT title
FROM StarsIn, MovieStar
WHERE starName = name AND
    birthdate LIKE '%1960';
```

from Fig. 7.4, which leads to the preferred logical query plan of Fig. 7.21, in which we take the join of relation `StarsIn` and the result of a selection on relation `MovieStar`. We have not given estimates for the sizes of relations `StarsIn` or `MovieStar`, but we can assume that selecting for stars born in a single year will produce about 1/50th of the tuples in `MovieStar`. Since there are generally several stars per movie, we expect `StarsIn` to be larger than `MovieStar` to begin with, so the second argument of the join, $\sigma_{birthdate}$ LIKE '%1960' (`MovieStar`), is much smaller than the first argument `StarsIn`. We conclude that the order of arguments in Fig. 7.21 should be reversed, so that the selection on `MovieStar` is the left argument.   □

There are only two choices for a join tree when there are two relations — take either of the two relations to be the left argument. When the join involves more than two relations, the number of possible join trees grows rapidly. For example, Fig. 7.28 shows the three possible shapes of trees in which four relations R, S, T, and U, are joined. However, the three trees shown all have these four relations in alphabetical order from the left. Since order of arguments matters, and there are $n!$ ways to order n things, each tree represents $4! = 24$ different trees when the possible labelings of the leaves are considered.

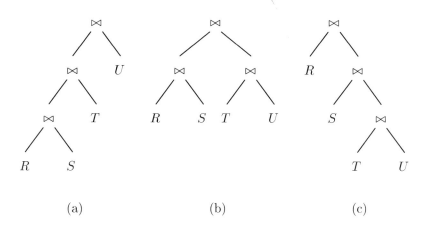

Figure 7.28: Ways to join four relations

7.6.3 Left-Deep Join Trees

Figure 7.28(a) is an example of what is called a *left-deep* tree. In general, a binary tree is left-deep if all right children are leaves. Similarly, a tree like Fig. 7.28(c), all of whose left children are leaves, is called a *right-deep* tree. A tree like Fig. 7.28(b) that is neither left-deep nor right-deep is called *bushy*. We shall argue below that there is a two-fold advantage to considering only left-deep trees as possible join orders.

1. The number of possible left-deep trees with a given number of leaves is large, but not nearly as large as the number of all trees. Thus, searches for query plans can be used for larger queries if we limit the search to left-deep trees.

2. Left-deep trees for joins interact well with common join algorithms — nested-loop joins and one-pass joins in particular. Query plans based on left-deep trees plus these algorithms will tend to be more efficient than the same algorithms used with non-left-deep trees.

The "leaves" in a left- or right-deep join tree can actually be interior nodes, with operators other than a join. Thus, for instance, Fig. 7.21 is technically a left-deep join tree with one join operator. The fact that a selection is applied to the right operand of the join does not take the tree out of the left-deep class.

The number of left-deep trees does not grow nearly as fast as the number of all trees for the multiway join of a given number of relations. For n relations, there is only one left-deep tree shape, to which we may assign the relations in $n!$ ways. There are the same number of right-deep trees for n relations. However, the total number of tree shapes $T(n)$ for n relations is given by the recurrence:

$$T(1) = 1$$
$$T(n) = \sum_{i=1}^{n-1} T(i)T(n-i)$$

The explanation for the second equation is that we may pick any number i between 1 and $n-1$ to be the number of leaves in the left subtree of the root, and those leaves may be arranged in any of the $T(i)$ ways that trees with i leaves can be arranged. Similarly, the remaining $n-i$ leaves in the right subtree can be arranged in any of $T(n-i)$ ways.

The first few values of $T(n)$ are $T(1) = 1$, $T(2) = 1$, $T(3) = 2$, $T(4) = 5$, $T(5) = 14$, and $T(6) = 42$. To get the total number of trees once relations are assigned to the leaves, we multiply $T(n)$ by $n!$. Thus, for instance, the number of leaf-labeled trees of 6 leaves is $42 \times 6!$ or 30,240, of which $6!$, or 720, are left-deep trees and another 720 are right-deep trees.

Now, let us consider the second advantage mentioned for left-deep join trees: their tendency to produce efficient plans. We shall give two examples:

1. If one-pass joins are used, and the build relation is on the left, then the amount of memory needed at any one time tends to be smaller than if we used a right-deep tree or a bushy tree for the same relations.

2. If we use nested-loop joins, implemented by iterators, then we avoid having to construct any intermediate relation more than once.

Example 7.33: Consider the left-deep tree in Fig. 7.28(a), and suppose that we are going to use a simple one-pass join for each of the three $\bowtie$ operators, with the left argument as the build relation; i.e., left arguments will be held in main memory. To compute $R \bowtie S$, we need to keep R in main memory, and as we compute $R \bowtie S$ we need to keep the result in main memory as well. Thus, we need $B(R) + B(R \bowtie S)$ main-memory buffers. If we pick R to be the smallest of the relations, and a selection has made R be rather small, then there is likely to be no problem making this number of buffers available.

Having computed $R \bowtie S$, we must join this relation with T. However, the buffers used for R are no longer needed and can be reused to hold (some of) the result of $(R \bowtie S) \bowtie T$. Similarly, when we join this relation with U, the relation $R \bowtie S$ is no longer needed and its buffers can be reused by the result of the final join. In general, a left-deep tree of joins that is computed by one-pass joins requires that space for at most two of the temporary relations be found in main memory at any time.

Now, consider a similar implementation of the right-deep tree of Fig. 7.28(c). The first thing we need to do is load R into main-memory buffers, since left arguments are always the build relation. Then, we need to construct $S \bowtie (T \bowtie U)$ and use that as the probe relation for the join at the root. To compute $S \bowtie (T \bowtie U)$ we need to bring S into buffers and then compute $T \bowtie U$ as the probe relation for S. But $T \bowtie U$ requires that we first bring T into buffers. Now we have all three of R, S, and T in memory at the same time. In general, if we try to compute a right-deep join tree with n leaves, we shall have to bring $n-1$ relations into memory simultaneously.

Role of the Buffer Manager

The reader may notice a difference between our approach in the series of examples such as Example 6.14 and 6.17, where we assumed that there was a fixed limit on the number of main-memory buffers available for a join, and the more flexible assumption taken here, where we assume that as many buffers as necessary are available, but we try not to use "too many." Recall from Section 6.8 that the buffer manager has significant flexibility to allocate buffers to operations. However, if too many buffers are allocated at once, there will be thrashing, thus degrading the assumed performance of the algorithm being used.

Of course it is possible that the total size $B(R) + B(S) + B(T)$ is less than the amount of space we need at either of the two intermediate stages of the computation of the left-deep tree, which are $B(R) + B(R \bowtie S)$ and $B(R \bowtie S) + B\big((R \bowtie S) \bowtie T\big)$, respectively.[9] However, as we pointed out in Example 7.32, queries with several joins often will have a small relation with which we can start as the leftmost argument in a left-deep tree. If R is small, we might expect $R \bowtie S$ to be significantly smaller than S and $(R \bowtie S) \bowtie T$ to be smaller than T, further justifying the use of a left-deep tree. $\quad\square$

Example 7.34 : Now, let us suppose we are going to implement the four-way join of Fig. 7.28 by nested-loop joins, and that we use an iterator for each of the three joins involved. Also, assume for simplicity that each of the relations R, S, T, and U are stored relations, rather than expressions. If we use the left-deep tree of Fig. 7.28(a), then the iterator at the root gets a main-memory-sized chunk of its left argument $(R \bowtie S) \bowtie T$. It then joins the chunk with all of U, but as long as U is a stored relation, it is only necessary to scan U, not to construct it. When the next chunk of the left argument is obtained and put in memory, U will be read again, but nested-loop join requires that repetition, which cannot be avoided if both arguments are large.

Similarly, to get a chunk of $(R \bowtie S) \bowtie T$, we get a chunk of $R \bowtie S$ into memory and scan T. Several scans of T may eventually be necessary, but cannot be avoided. Finally, to get a chunk of $R \bowtie S$ requires reading a chunk of R and comparing it with S, perhaps several times. However, in all this action, only stored relations are read multiple times, and this repeated reading is an artifact of the way nested-loop join works when the main memory is insufficient to hold an entire relation.

Now, compare the behavior of iterators on the left-deep tree with the behavior of iterators on the right-deep tree of Fig. 7.28(c). The iterator at the

---

[9]Note that as always we do not count the cost of storing the result of an expression tree when measuring costs.

root starts by reading a chunk of R. It must then construct the entire relation $S \bowtie (T \bowtie U)$ and compare it with that chunk of R. When we read the next chunk of R into memory, $S \bowtie (T \bowtie U)$ must be constructed again. Each subsequent chunk of R likewise requires constructing this same relation.

Of course, we could construct $S \bowtie (T \bowtie U)$ once and store it, either in memory on on disk. If we store it on disk, we are using extra disk I/O's compared with the left-deep tree's plan, and if we store it in memory, then we run into the same problem with overuse of memory that we discussed in Example 7.33. □

7.6.4 Dynamic Programming to Select a Join Order and Grouping

To pick an order for the join of many relations we have three choices:

1. Consider them all.

2. Consider a subset.

3. Use a heuristic to pick one.

We shall here consider a sensible approach to enumeration called *dynamic programming*. It can be used either to consider all orders, or to consider certain subsets only, such as orders restricted to left-deep trees. In Section 7.6.6 we consider a reasonable heuristic for selecting a single ordering. Dynamic programming is a common algorithmic paradigm.[10] The idea behind dynamic programming is that we fill in a table of costs, remembering only the minimum information we need to proceed to a conclusion.

Suppose we want to join $R_1 \bowtie R_2 \bowtie \cdots \bowtie R_n$. In a dynamic programming algorithm, we construct a table with an entry for each subset of one or more of the n relations. In that table we put:

1. The estimated size of the join of these relations. For this quantity we may use the formula of Section 7.4.6.

2. The least cost of computing the join of these relations. We shall use in our examples the sum of the sizes of the intermediate relations (not including the R_i's themselves or the join of the full set of relations associated with this table entry). Recall that the sizes of intermediate relations is the simplest measure we can use to estimate the true cost of disk I/O's, CPU utilization, or other factors. However, other, more complex estimates, such as total disk I/O's, could be used if we were willing and able to do the extra calculation involved. If we use disk I/O's or another measure of running time, then we also have to consider the algorithm used for the join

_____

[10]See Aho, Hopcroft and Ullman, *Data Structures and Algorithms*, Addison-Wesley, 1984, for a general treatment of dynamic programming.

in question, since different algorithms will have different costs. We shall discuss these issues after learning the basics of dynamic-programming techniques.

3. The expression that yields the least cost. This expression joins the set of relations in question, with some grouping. We can optionally restrict ourselves to left-deep expressions, in which case the expression is just an ordering of the relations.

The construction of this table is an induction on the subset size. There are two variations, depending on whether we wish to consider all possible tree shapes or only left-deep trees. There is a difference in the way the table is constructed; we explain the difference when we discuss the inductive step of table construction, below.

BASIS: The entry for a single relation R consists of the size of R, a cost of 0, and a formula that is just R itself. The entry for a pair of relations $\{R_i, R_j\}$ is also easy to compute. The cost is 0, since there are no intermediate relations involved, and the size estimate is given by the rule of Section 7.4.6; it is the product of the sizes of R_i and R_j divided by the larger value-set size for each attribute shared by R_i and R_j, if any. The formula is either $R_i \bowtie R_j$ or $R_j \bowtie R_i$. Following the idea introduced in Section 7.6.1, we pick the smaller of R_i and R_j as the left argument.

INDUCTION: Now, we can build the table, computing entries for all subsets of size 3, 4, and so on, until we get an entry for the one subset of size n. That entry tells us the best way to compute the join of all the relations; it also gives us the estimated cost of that method, which is needed as we compute later entries. We need to see how to compute the entry for a set of k relations $\mathcal{R}$.

If we wish to consider only left-deep trees, then for each of the k relations R in $\mathcal{R}$ we consider the possibility that we compute the join for $\mathcal{R}$ by first computing the join of $\mathcal{R} - \{R\}$ and then joining it with R. The cost of the join for $\mathcal{R}$ is the cost of $\mathcal{R} - \{R\}$ plus the size of the latter join. We pick whichever R yields the least cost. The expression for $\mathcal{R}$ has the best join expression for $\mathcal{R} - \{R\}$ as the left argument of a final join, and R as the right argument. The size for $\mathcal{R}$ is whatever the formula from Section 7.4.6 gives.

If we wish to consider all trees, then computing the entry for a set of relations $\mathcal{R}$ is somewhat more complex. We need to consider all ways to partition $\mathcal{R}$ into disjoint sets $\mathcal{R}_1$ and $\mathcal{R}_2$. For each such subset, we consider the sum of:

1. The best costs of $\mathcal{R}_1$ and $\mathcal{R}_2$.

2. The sizes of $\mathcal{R}_1$ and $\mathcal{R}_2$.

For whichever partition gives the best cost, we use this sum as the cost for $\mathcal{R}$, and the formula for $\mathcal{R}$ is the join of the best join orders for $\mathcal{R}_1$ and $\mathcal{R}_2$.

Example 7.35: Consider the join of four relations R, S, T, and U. For simplicity, we shall assume they each have 1000 tuples. Their attributes and the estimated sizes of values sets for the attributes in each relation are summarized in Fig. 7.29.

$R(a,b)$	$S(b,c)$	$T(c,d)$	$U(d,a)$
$V(R,a) = 100$			$V(U,a) = 50$
$V(R,b) = 200$	$V(S,b) = 100$		
	$V(S,c) = 500$	$V(T,c) = 20$	
		$V(T,d) = 50$	$V(U,d) = 1000$

Figure 7.29: Parameters for Example 7.35

For the singleton sets, the sizes, costs and best plans are as in the table of Fig. 7.30. That is, for each single relation, the size is as given, 1000 for each, the cost is 0 since there are no intermediate relations needed, and the best (and only) expression is the relation itself.

	$\{R\}$	$\{S\}$	$\{T\}$	$\{U\}$
Size	1000	1000	1000	1000
Cost	0	0	0	0
Best Plan	R	S	T	U

Figure 7.30: The table for singleton sets

Now, consider the pairs of relations. The cost for each is 0, since there are still no intermediate relations in a join of two. There are two possible plans, since either of the two relations can be the left argument, but since the sizes happen to be the same for each relation we have no basis on which to choose between the plans. We shall take the first, in alphabetical order, to be the left argument in each case. The sizes of the resulting relations are computed by the usual formula. The results are summarized in Fig. 7.31. Note that 1M stands for 1,000,000, the size of those "joins" that are actually a product.

	$\{R,S\}$	$\{R,T\}$	$\{R,U\}$	$\{S,T\}$	$\{S,U\}$	$\{T,U\}$
Size	5000	1M	10,000	2000	1M	1000
Cost	0	0	0	0	0	0
Best Plan	$R \bowtie S$	$R \bowtie T$	$R \bowtie U$	$S \bowtie T$	$S \bowtie U$	$T \bowtie U$

Figure 7.31: The table for pairs of relations

Now, consider the table for joins of three out of the four relations. The only way to compute a join of three relations is to pick two to join first. The size estimate for the result is computed by the standard formula, and we omit the details of this calculation; remember that we'll get the same size regardless of which way we compute the join.

The cost estimate for each triple of relations is the size of the one intermediate relation — the join of the first two chosen. Since we want this cost to be as small as possible, we consider each pair of two out of the three relations and take the pair with the smallest size.

For the formula, we group the two chosen relations first, but these could be either the left or right argument. Let us suppose that we are only interested in left-deep trees, so we always use the join of the first two relations as the left argument. Since in all cases the estimated size for the join of two of our relations is at least 1000 (the size of each individual relation), were we to allow non-left-deep trees we would always select the single relation as the left argument in this example. The summary table for the triples is shown in Fig. 7.32.

	$\{R,S,T\}$	$\{R,S,U\}$	$\{R,T,U\}$	$\{S,T,U\}$
Size	10,000	50,000	10,000	2,000
Cost	2,000	5,000	1,000	1,000
Best Plan	$(S \bowtie T) \bowtie R$	$(R \bowtie S) \bowtie U$	$(T \bowtie U) \bowtie R$	$(T \bowtie U) \bowtie S$

Figure 7.32: The table for triples of relations

Let us consider $\{R,S,T\}$ as an example of the calculation. We must consider each of the three pairs in turn. If we start with $R \bowtie S$, then the cost is the size of this relation, which is 5000, as we learned from the table for the pairs in Fig. 7.31. Starting with $R \bowtie T$ gives us a cost of 1,000,000 for the intermediate relation, and starting with $S \bowtie T$ has a cost of 2000. Since the latter is the smallest cost of the three options, we choose that plan. The choice is reflected not only in the cost entry of the $\{R,S,T\}$ column, but in the best-plan row, where the plan that groups S and T first appears.

Now, we must consider the situation for the join of all four relations. The size estimate for this relation is 100 tuples, so the true cost is essentially all in the construction of intermediate relations. However, recall that we never charge for the size of the result anyway when comparing plans.

There are two general ways we can compute the join of all four:

1. Pick three to join in the best possible way, and then join in the fourth.

2. Divide the four relations into two pairs of two, join the pairs and then join the results.

Of course, if we only consider left-deep trees then the second type of plan is excluded, because it yields bushy trees. The table of Fig. 7.33 summarizes the

seven possible ways to group the joins, based on the preferred groupings from
Figs. 7.31 and 7.32.

Grouping	Cost
$((S \bowtie T) \bowtie R) \bowtie U$	12,000
$((R \bowtie S) \bowtie U) \bowtie T$	55,000
$((T \bowtie U) \bowtie R) \bowtie S$	11,000
$((T \bowtie U) \bowtie S) \bowtie R$	3,000
$(T \bowtie U) \bowtie (R \bowtie S)$	6,000
$(R \bowtie T) \bowtie (S \bowtie U)$	2,000,000
$(S \bowtie T) \bowtie (R \bowtie U)$	12,000

Figure 7.33: Join groupings and their costs

For instance, consider the first formula in Fig. 7.33. It represents joining
R, S, and T first, and then joining that result with U. From Fig. 7.32, we
know that the best way to join R, S, and T is to join S and T first. We have
used the left-deep form of this expression, and joined U on the right to continue
the left-deep form. If we consider only left-deep trees, then this expression and
relation order is the only option. If we allowed bushy trees, we would join U
on the left, since it is smaller than the join of the other three. The cost of this
join is 12,000, which is the sum of the cost and size of $(S \bowtie T) \bowtie R$, which are
2000 and 10,000, respectively.

The last three expressions in Fig. 7.33 represent additional options if we
include bushy trees. These are formed by joining relations first in two pairs.
For example, the last line represents the strategy of joining $R \bowtie U$ and $S \bowtie T$,
and then joining the result. The cost of this expression is the sum of the sizes
and costs of the two pairs. The costs are 0, as must be the case for any pair, and
the sizes are 10,000 and 2000, respectively. Since we generally select the smaller
relation to be the left argument, we show the expression as $(S \bowtie T) \bowtie (R \bowtie U)$.

In this example, we see that the least of all costs is associated with the fourth
formula: $((T \bowtie U) \bowtie S) \bowtie R$. This formula is the one we select for computing
the join; its cost is 3000. Since it is a left-deep tree, it is the selected logical
query plan regardless of whether our dynamic-programming strategy considers
all plans or just left-deep plans.   □

7.6.5 Dynamic Programming With More Detailed Cost Functions

Using relation sizes as the cost estimate simplifies the calculations in a dynamic-
programming algorithm. However, a disadvantage of this simplification is that
it does not involve the actual costs of the joins in the calculation. As an extreme
example, if one possible join $R(a, b) \bowtie S(b, c)$ involves a relation R with one
tuple and another relation S that has an index on the join attribute b, then the

join takes almost no time. On the other hand, if S has no index, then we must scan it, taking $B(S)$ disk I/O's, even when R is a singleton. A cost measure that only involved the sizes of R, S, and $R \bowtie S$ cannot distinguish these two cases, so the cost of using $R \bowtie S$ in the grouping will be either overestimated or underestimated.

However, modifying the dynamic programming algorithm to take join algorithms into account is not hard. First, the cost measure we use becomes disk I/O's, or whatever running-time units we prefer. When computing the cost of $\mathcal{R}_1 \bowtie \mathcal{R}_2$, we sum the cost of $\mathcal{R}_1$, the cost of $\mathcal{R}_2$, and the least cost of joining these two relations using the best available algorithm. Since the latter cost usually depends on the sizes of $\mathcal{R}_1$ and $\mathcal{R}_2$, we must also compute estimates for these sizes as we did in Example 7.35.

An even more powerful version of dynamic programming is based on the Selinger-style optimization mentioned in Section 7.5.4. Now, for each set of relations that might be joined, we keep not only one cost, but several costs. Recall that Selinger-style optimization considers not only the least cost of producing the result of the join, but also the least cost of producing that relation sorted in any of a number of "interesting" orders. These interesting sorts include any that might be used to advantage in a later sort-join or that could be used to produce the output of the entire query in the sorted order desired by the user. When sorted relations must be produced, the use of sort-join, either one-pass or multipass, must be considered as an option, while without considering the value of sorting a result, hash-joins are always at least as good as the corresponding sort-join.

7.6.6 A Greedy Algorithm for Selecting a Join Order

As Example 7.35 suggests, even the carefully limited search of dynamic programming leads to an exponential number of calculations, as a function of the number of relations joined. It is reasonable to use an exhaustive method like dynamic programming or branch-and-bound search to find optimal join orders of five or six relations. However, when the number of joins grows beyond that, or if we choose not to invest the necessary time in an exhaustive search, then we can use a join-order heuristic in our query optimizer.

The most common choice of heuristic is a *greedy* algorithm, where we make one decision at a time about the order of joins and never backtrack or reconsider decisions once made. We shall consider a greedy algorithm that only selects a left-deep tree. The "greediness" is based on the idea that we want to keep the intermediate relations as small as possible at each level of the tree.

BASIS: Start with the pair of relations whose estimated join size is the smallest. The join of these relations becomes the *current tree*.

INDUCTION: Find, among all those relations not yet included in the current tree, the relation that, when joined with the current tree, yields the relation of

---

Join Selectivity

A useful way to view heuristics such as the greedy algorithm for selecting a left-deep join tree is that each relation R, when joined with the current tree, has a *selectivity*, which is the ratio

$$\frac{\text{size of the join result}}{\text{size of the current tree's result}}$$

Since we usually do not have the exact sizes of either relation, we estimate these sizes as we have done previously. A greedy approach to join ordering is to pick that relation with the smallest selectivity.

For example, if a join attribute is a key for R, then the selectivity is at most 1, which is usually a favorable situation. Notice that, judging from the statistics of Fig. 7.29, attribute d is a key for U, and there are no keys for other relations, which suggests why joining T with U is the best way to start the join.

---

smallest estimated size. The new current tree has the old current tree as its left argument and the selected relation as its right argument.

Example 7.36 : Let us apply the greedy algorithm to the relations of Example 7.35. The basis step is to find the pair of relations that have the smallest join. Consulting Fig. 7.31, we see that this honor goes to the join $T \bowtie U$, with a cost of 1000. Thus, $T \bowtie U$ is the "current tree."

We now consider whether to join R or S into the tree next. Thus we compare the sizes of $(T \bowtie U) \bowtie R$ and $(T \bowtie U) \bowtie S$. Figure 7.32 tells us that the latter, with a size of 2000 is better than the former, with a size of 10,000. Thus, we pick as the new current tree $(T \bowtie U) \bowtie S$.

Now there is no choice; we must join R at the last step, leaving us with a total cost of 3000, the sum of the sizes of the two intermediate relations. Note that the tree resulting from the greedy algorithm is the same as that selected by the dynamic-programming algorithm in Example 7.35. However, there are examples where the greedy algorithm fails to find the best solution, while the dynamic-programming algorithm guarantees to find the best; see Exercise 7.6.4. $\square$

7.6.7   Exercises for Section 7.6

Exercise 7.6.1 : For the relations of Exercise 7.4.1, give the dynamic-programming table entries that evaluates all possible join orders allowing:

a) Left-deep trees only.

b) All trees.

What is the best choice in each case?

Exercise 7.6.2: Repeat Exercise 7.6.1 with the following modifications:

  i. The schema for Z is changed to $Z(d, a)$.

  ii. $V(Z, a) = 100$.

Exercise 7.6.3: Repeat Exercise 7.6.1 with the relations of Exercise 7.4.2.

* **Exercise 7.6.4:** Consider the join of relations $R(a, b)$, $S(b, c)$, $T(c, d)$, and $U(a, d)$, where R and U each have 1000 tuples, while S and T each have 100 tuples. Further, there are 100 values of all attributes of all relations, except for attribute c, where $V(S, c) = V(T, c) = 10$.

  a) What is the order selected by the greedy algorithm? What is its cost?

  b) What is the optimum join ordering and its cost?

Exercise 7.6.5: How many trees are there for the join of:

* a) Seven relations.

  b) Eight relations.

How many of these are neither left-deep nor right-deep?

! **Exercise 7.6.6:** Suppose we wish to join the relations R, S, T, and U in one of the tree structures of Fig. 7.28, and we want to keep all intermediate relations in memory until they are no longer needed. Following our usual assumption, the result of the join of all four will be consumed by some other process as it is generated, so no memory is needed for that relation. In terms of the number of blocks required for the stored relations and the intermediate relations [e.g., $B(R)$ or $B(R \bowtie S)$], give a lower bound on M, the number of blocks of memory needed, for:

* a) The left-deep tree of Fig. 7.28(a).

  b) The bushy tree of Fig. 7.28(b).

  c) The right-deep of Fig. 7.28(c).

What assumptions let us conclude that one tree is certain to use less memory than another?

*! **Exercise 7.6.7:** If we use dynamic programming to select an order for the join of k relations, how many entries of the table do we have to fill?

7.7 Completing the Physical-Query-Plan Selection

We have parsed the query, converted it to an initial logical query plan, and improved that logical query plan with transformations described in Section 7.3. Part of the process of selecting the physical query plan is enumeration and cost-estimation for all of our options, which we discussed in Section 7.5. Section 7.6 focused on the question of enumeration, cost estimation, and ordering for joins of several relations. By extension, we can use similar techniques to order groups of unions, intersections, or any associative/commutative operation.

There are still several steps needed to turn the logical plan into a complete physical query plan. The principal issues that we must yet cover in this section are:

1. Selection of algorithms to implement the operations of the query plan, when algorithm-selection was not done as part of some earlier step such as selection of a join order by dynamic programming.

2. Decisions regarding when intermediate results will be *materialized* (created whole and stored on disk), and when they will be *pipelined* (created only in main memory, and not necessarily kept in their entirety at any one time).

3. Notation for physical-query-plan operators, which must include details regarding access methods for stored relations and algorithms for implementation of relational-algebra operators.

We shall not discuss the subject of selection of algorithms for operators in its entirety. Rather, we sample the issues by discussing two of the most important operators: selection in Section 7.7.1 and joins in Section 7.7.2. Then, we consider the choice between pipelining and materialization in Sections 7.7.3 through 7.7.5. A notation for physical query plans is presented in Section 7.7.6.

7.7.1 Choosing a Selection Method

One of the important steps in choosing a physical query plan is to pick algorithms for each selection operator. In Section 6.3.1 we mentioned the obvious implementation of a $\sigma_C(R)$ operator, where we access the entire relation R and see which tuples satisfy condition C. Then in Section 6.7.2 we considered the possibility that C was of the form "attribute equals constant," and we had an index on that attribute. If so, then we can find the tuples that satisfy condition C without looking at all of R. Now, let us consider the generalization of this problem, where we have a selection condition that is the AND of several conditions, some of which are of the form "attribute equals constant" or another comparison between an attribute and a constant, such as $<$.

Assuming there are no multidimensional indexes on several of the attributes, then the strategy we must use involves choosing one or more attributes that each:

a) Have an index, and

b) Are compared to a constant in one of the terms of the selection.

We then use these indexes to identify the sets of tuples that satisfy each of the conditions. Sections 4.2.3 and 5.1.5 discussed how we could use pointers to the tuples obtained from these indexes to find only the tuples that satisfied all the conditions before we read these tuples from disk.

For simplicity, we shall not consider the use of several indexes in this way. Rather, we limit our discussion to algorithms that:

1. Use one comparison of the form $A\theta c$, where A is an attribute with an index, c is a constant, and θ is a comparison operator such as $=$ or $<$.

2. Retrieve all tuples that satisfy the comparison from (1), using the index-scan physical operator discussed in Section 6.2.1.

3. Consider each tuple selected in (2) to decide whether it satisfies the rest of the selection condition. We shall call the physical operator that performs this step `Filter`; it takes the condition used to select tuples as a parameter, much as the σ operator of relational algebra does.

In addition to algorithms of this form, we must also consider an algorithm that uses no index but reads the entire relation (using the table-scan physical operator) and passes each tuple to the `Filter` operator to check for satisfaction of the selection condition.

We decide among algorithms with which to implement a given selection by estimating the cost of reading data for each possible option. To compare costs of alternative algorithms we cannot continue using the simplified cost estimate of intermediate-relation size. The reason is that we are now considering implementations of a single step of the logical query plan, and intermediate relations are independent of implementation.

Thus, we shall refocus our attention and resume counting disk I/O's, as we did when we discussed algorithms and their costs in Chapter 6. To simplify as before, we shall count only the cost of accessing the data blocks, not the index blocks. Recall that the number of index blocks needed is generally much smaller than the number of data blocks needed, this approximation to disk I/O cost is usually accurate enough.

The following is an outline of how costs for the various algorithms are estimated. We assume that the operation is $\sigma_C(R)$, where condition C is the AND of one or more terms. We use the example terms $a = 10$ and $b < 20$ to represent equality conditions and inequality conditions, respectively.

1. The cost of the table-scan algorithm coupled with a filter step is:

(a) $B(R)$ if R is clustered, and

(b) $T(R)$ if R is not clustered.

2. The cost of an algorithm that picks an equality term such as $a = 10$ for which an index on attribute a exists, uses index-scan to find the matching tuples, and then filters the retrieved tuples to see if they satisfy the full condition C is:

(a) $B(R)/V(R,a)$ if the index is clustering, and

(b) $T(R)/V(R,a)$ if the index is not clustering.

3. The cost of an algorithm that picks an inequality term such as $b < 20$ for which an index on attribute b exists, uses index-scan to retrieve the matching tuples, and then filters the retrieved tuples to see if they satisfy the full condition C is:

(a) $B(R)/3$ if the index is clustering,[11] and

(b) $T(R)/3$ if the index is not clustering.

Example 7.37: Consider selection $\sigma_{x=1 \text{ AND } y=2 \text{ AND } z<5}(R)$, where $R(x,y,z)$ has the following parameters: $T(R) = 5000$, $B(R) = 200$, $V(R,x) = 100$, and $V(R,y) = 500$. Further, suppose R is clustered, and there are indexes on all of x, y, and z, but only the index on z is clustering. The following are the options for implementing this selection:

1. Table-scan followed by filter. The cost is $B(R)$, or 200 disk I/O's, since R is clustered.

2. Use the index on x and the index-scan operator to find those tuples with $x = 1$, then use the filter operator to check that $y = 2$ and $z < 5$. Since there are about $T(R)/V(R,x) = 50$ tuples with $x = 1$, and the index is not clustering, we require about 50 disk I/O's.

3. Use the index on y and index-scan to find those tuples with $y = 2$, then filter these tuples to see that $x = 1$ and $z < 5$. The cost for using this nonclustering index is about $T(R)/V(R,y)$, or 10 disk I/O's.

4. Use the clustering index on z and index-scan to find those tuples with $z < 5$, then filter these tuples to see that $x = 1$ and $y = 2$. The number of disk I/O's is about $B(R)/3 = 67$.

We see that the least cost algorithm is the third, with an estimated cost of 10 disk I/O's. Thus, the preferred physical plan for this selection retrieves all tuples with $y = 2$ and then filters for the other two conditions. □

---

[11] Recall that we assume the typical inequality retrieves only 1/3 the tuples, for reasons discussed in Section 7.4.3.

7.7.2 Choosing a Join Method

We saw in Chapter 6 the costs associated with the various join algorithms. On the assumption that we know (or can estimate) how many buffers are available to perform the join, we can apply the formulas in Section 6.5.8 for sort-joins, Section 6.6.7 for hash-joins, and Sections 6.7.3 and 6.7.4 for indexed joins.

However, if we are not sure of, or cannot know, the number of buffers that will be available during the execution of this query (because we do not know what else the DBMS is doing at the same time), or if we do not have estimates of important size parameters such as the $V(R, a)$'s, then there are still some principles we can apply to choosing a join method. Similar ideas apply to other binary operations such as unions, and to the full-relation, unary operators, γ and δ.

- One approach is to call for the one-pass join, hoping that the buffer manager can devote enough buffers to the join, or that the buffer manager can come close, so thrashing is not a major cost. An alternative (for joins only, not for other binary operators) is to choose a nested-loop join, hoping that if the left argument cannot be granted enough buffers to fit in memory at once, then that argument will not have to be divided into too many pieces, and the resulting join will still be reasonably efficient.

- A sort-join is a good choice when either:

    1. One or both arguments are already sorted on their join attribute(s), or

    2. There are two or more joins on the same attribute, such as

    $$\big(R(a, b) \bowtie S(a, c)\big) \bowtie T(a, d)$$

    where sorting R and S on a will cause the result of $R \bowtie S$ to be sorted on a and used directly in a second sort-join.

- If there is an index opportunity such as a join $R(a, b) \bowtie S(b, c)$, where R is expected to be small (perhaps the result of a selection on a key that must yield only one tuple), and there is an index on the join attribute $S.b$, then we should choose an index-join.

- If there is no opportunity to use already-sorted relations or indexes, and a multipass join is needed, then hashing is probably the best choice, because the number of passes it requires depends on the size of the smaller argument rather than on both arguments.

7.7.3 Pipelining Versus Materialization

The last major issue we shall discuss in connection with choice of a physical query plan is pipelining of results. The naive way to execute a query plan is

---

Materialization in Memory

One might imagine that there is an intermediate approach, between pipelining and materialization, where the entire result of one operation is stored in main-memory buffers (not on disk) before being passed to the consuming operation. We regard this possible mode of operation as pipelining, where the first thing that the consuming operation does is organize the entire relation, or a large portion of it, in memory. An example of this sort of behavior is a selection, whose result is pipelined as the left (build) argument to one of several join algorithms, including the simple one-pass join, multipass hash-join, or sort-join.

---

to order the operations appropriately (so an operation is not performed until the argument(s) below it have been performed), and store the result of each operation on disk until it is needed by another operation. This strategy is called *materialization*, since each intermediate relation is materialized on disk.

A more subtle, and generally more efficient, way to execute a query plan is to have several operations running at once. The tuples produced by one operation are passed directly to the operation that uses it, without ever storing the intermediate tuples on disk. This approach is called *pipelining*, and it typically is implemented by a network of iterators (see Section 6.2.6), whose functions call each other at appropriate times. Since it saves disk I/O's, there is an obvious advantage to pipelining, but there is a corresponding disadvantage. Since several operations must share main memory at any time, there is a chance that algorithms with higher disk-I/O requirements must be chosen, or thrashing will occur, thus giving back all the disk-I/O savings that were gained by pipelining, and possibly more.

7.7.4 Pipelining Unary Operations

Unary operations — selection and projection — are excellent candidates for pipelining. Since these operations are tuple-at-a-time, we never need to have more than one block for input, and one block for the output. This mode of operation was suggested by Fig. 6.10.

We may implement a pipelined unary operation by iterators, as discussed in Section 6.2.6. The consumer of the pipelined result calls GetNext() each time another tuple is needed. In the case of a projection, it is only necessary to call GetNext() once on the source of tuples, project that tuple appropriately, and return the result to the consumer. For a selection σ_C (technically, the physical operator Filter(C)), it may be necessary to call GetNext() several times at the source, until one tuple that satisfies condition C is found. Figure 7.34 illustrates this process.

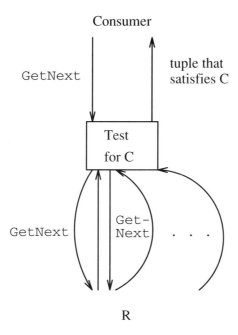

Figure 7.34: Execution of a pipelined selection using iterators

7.7.5 Pipelining Binary Operations

The results of binary operations can also be pipelined. We use one buffer to pass the result to its consumer, one block at a time. However, the number of other buffers needed to compute the result and to consume the result varies, depending on the size of the result and the sizes of other relations involved in the query. We shall use an extended example to illustrate the tradeoffs and opportunities.

Example 7.38 : Let us consider physical query plans for the expression

$$\bigl(R(w,x) \bowtie S(x,y)\bigr) \bowtie U(y,z)$$

We make the following assumptions:

1. R occupies 5000 blocks; S and U each occupy 10,000 blocks.

2. The intermediate result $R \bowtie S$ occupies k blocks for some k. We can estimate k, based on the number of x-values in R and S and the size of (w,x,y) tuples compared to the (w,x) tuples of R and the (x,y) tuples of S. However, we want to see what happens as k varies, so we leave this constant open.

3. Both joins will be implemented as hash-joins, either one-pass or two-pass, depending on k.

4. There are 101 buffers available. This number, as usual, is set artificially low.

A sketch of the expression with key parameters is in Fig. 7.35.

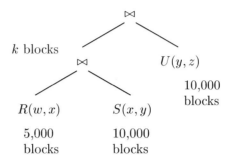

Figure 7.35: Logical query plan and parameters for Example 7.38

First, consider the join $R \bowtie S$. Neither relation fits in main memory, so we need a two-pass hash-join. To limit the buckets of the smaller relation R to 100 blocks each, we need at least 50 buckets.[12] If we use exactly 50 buckets, then the second pass of the hash-join $R \bowtie S$ uses 51 buffers, leaving 50 buffers to use for the join of the result of $R \bowtie S$ with U.

Now, suppose that $k \leq 49$; that is, the result of $R \bowtie S$ occupies at most 49 blocks. Then we can pipeline the result of $R \bowtie S$ into 49 buffers, organize them for lookup as a hash table, and we have one buffer left to read each block of U in turn. We may thus execute the second join as a one-pass join. The total number of disk I/O's is:

a) 45,000 to perform the two-pass hash join of R and S.

b) 10,000 to read U in the one-pass hash-join of $(R \bowtie S) \bowtie U$.

The total is 55,000 disk I/O's.

Now, suppose $k > 49$, but $k \leq 5000$. We can still pipeline the result of $R \bowtie S$, but we need to use another strategy, in which this relation is joined with U in a 50-bucket, two-pass hash-join.

1. Before we start on $R \bowtie S$, we hash U into 50 buckets of 200 blocks each.

---

[12]We shall assume for convenience that all buckets wind up with exactly their fair share of tuples. If there are variations, as there surely will be, then some extra buffers will be needed occasionally, and we rely on the buffer manager to make them available, perhaps by moving some buffers to swap space on disk, temporarily. We do not, however, consider the additional cost of disk I/O's for swapping, as we can expect that cost to be a small fraction of the total cost.

2. Next, we perform a two-pass hash join of R and S using 51 buckets as before, but as each tuple of $R \bowtie S$ is generated, we place it in one of the 50 remaining buffers that is used to help form the 50 buckets for the join of $R \bowtie S$ with U. These buffers are written to disk when they get full, as is normal for a two-pass hash-join.

3. Finally, we join $R \bowtie S$ with U bucket by bucket. Since $k \leq 5000$, the buckets of $R \bowtie S$ will be of size at most 100 blocks, so this join is feasible. The fact that buckets of U are of size 200 blocks is not a problem, since we are using buckets of $R \bowtie S$ as the build relation and buckets of U as the probe relation in the one-pass joins of buckets.

The number of disk I/O's for this pipelined join is:

a) 20,000 to read U and write its tuples into buckets.

b) 45,000 to perform the two-pass hash-join $R \bowtie S$.

c) k to write out the buckets of $R \bowtie S$.

d) $k + 10,000$ to read the buckets of $R \bowtie S$ and U in the final join.

The total cost is thus $75,000 + 2k$. Note that there is an apparent discontinuity as k grows from 49 to 50, since we had to change the final join from one-pass to two-pass. In practice, the cost would not change so precipitously, since we could use the one-pass join even if there were not enough buffers and a small amount of thrashing occurred.

Last, let us consider what happens when $k > 5000$. Now, we cannot perform a two-pass join in the 50 buffers available if the result of $R \bowtie S$ is pipelined. We could use a three-pass join, but that would require an extra 2 disk I/O's per block of either argument, or $20,000 + 2k$ more disk I/O's. We can do better if we instead decline to pipeline $R \bowtie S$. Now, an outline of the computation of the joins is:

1. Compute $R \bowtie S$ using a two-pass hash join and store the result on disk.

2. Join $R \bowtie S$ with U, also using a two-pass hash-join. Note that since $B(U) = 10,000$, we can perform a two-pass hash-join using 100 buckets, regardless of how large k is. Technically, U should appear as the left argument of its join in Fig. 7.35 if we decide to make U the build relation for the hash join.

The number of disk I/O's for this algorithm is:

a) 45,000 for the two-pass join of R and S.

b) k to store $R \bowtie S$ on disk.

c) $30,000 + 3k$ for the two-pass hash-join of U with $R \bowtie S$.

The total cost is thus $75{,}000 + 4k$, which is less than the cost of going to a three-pass join at the final step. The three complete algorithms are summarized in the table of Fig. 7.36.   □

Range of k	Pipeline or Materialize	Algorithm for final join	Total Disk I/O's
$k \leq 49$	Pipeline	one-pass	55,000
$50 \leq k \leq 5000$	Pipeline	50-bucket, two-pass	$75{,}000 + 2k$
$5000 < k$	Materialize	100-bucket, two-pass	$75{,}000 + 4k$

Figure 7.36: Costs of join algorithms as a function of the size of $R \bowtie S$

7.7.6 Notation for Physical Query Plans

We have seen many examples of the operators that can be used to form a physical query plan. In general, each operator of the logical plan becomes one or more operators of the physical plan, and leaves (stored relations) of the logical plan become, in the physical plan, one of the scan operators applied to that relation. In addition, materialization would be indicated by a `Store` operator applied to the intermediate result that is to be materialized, followed by a suitable scan operator (usually `TableScan`, since there is no index on the intermediate relation unless one is constructed explicitly) when the materialized result is accessed by its consumer. However, for simplicity, in our physical-query-plan trees we shall indicate that a certain intermediate relation is materialized by a double line crossing the edge between that relation and its consumer. All other edges are assumed to represent pipelining between the supplier and consumer of tuples.

We shall now catalog the various operators that are typically found in physical query plans. Unlike the relational algebra, whose notation is fairly standard, each DBMS will use its own internal notation for physical query plans.

Operators for Leaves

Each relation R that is a leaf operand of the logical-query-plan tree will be replaced by a scan operator. The options are:

1. `TableScan(R)`: All blocks holding tuples of R are read in arbitrary order.

2. `SortScan(R,L)`: Tuples of R are read in order, sorted according to the attribute(s) on list L.

3. `IndexScan(R,C)`: Here, C is a condition of the form $A\theta c$, where A is an attribute of R, θ is a comparison such as $=$ or $<$, and c is a constant. Tuples of R are accessed through an index on attribute A. If the comparison θ is not $=$, then the index must be one, such as a B-tree, that supports range queries.

4. `IndexScan(R,A)`: Here A is an attribute of R. The entire relation R is retrieved via an index on $R.A$. This operator behaves like `TableScan`, but may be more efficient in certain circumstances, if R is not clustered and/or its blocks are not easily found.

Physical Operators for Selection

A logical operator $\sigma_C(R)$ is often combined, or partially combined, with the access method for relation R, when R is a stored relation. Other selections, where the argument is not a stored relation or an appropriate index is not available, will be replaced by the corresponding physical operator we have called `Filter`. Recall the strategy for choosing a selection implementation, which we discussed in Section 7.7.1. The notation we shall use for the various selection implementations are:

1. We may simply replace $\sigma_C(R)$ by the operator `Filter(C)`. This choice makes sense if there is no index on R, or no index on an attribute that condition C mentions. If R, the argument of the selection, is actually an intermediate relation being pipelined to the selection, then no other operator besides `Filter` is needed. If R is a stored or materialized relation, then we must use an operator, `TableScan` or perhaps `SortScan(L)`, to access R. We might prefer sort-scan if the result of $\sigma_C(R)$ will later be passed to an operator that requires its argument sorted.

2. If condition C can be expressed as $A\theta c$ `AND` D for some other condition D, and there is an index on $R.A$, then we may:

   (a) Use the operator `IndexScan(R,A`θ`c)` to access R, and

   (b) Use `Filter(D)` in place of the selection $\sigma_C(R)$.

Physical Sort Operators

Sorting of a relation can occur at any point in the physical query plan. We have already introduced the `SortScan(R,L)` operator, which reads a stored relation R and produces it sorted according to the list of attributes L. When we apply a sort-based algorithm for operations such as join or grouping, there is an initial phase in which we sort the argument according to some list of attributes. It is common to use an explicit physical operator `Sort(L)` to perform this sort on an operand relation that is not stored. This operator can also be used at the top of the physical-query-plan tree if the result needs to be sorted because of an ORDER BY clause in the original query, thus playing the same role as the τ operator we introduced into our version of relational algebra.

Other Relational-Algebra Operations

All other operations are replaced by a suitable physical operator. These operators can be given designations that indicate:

1. The operation being performed, e.g., join or grouping.

2. Necessary parameters, e.g., the condition in a theta-join or the list of elements in a grouping.

3. A general strategy for the algorithm: sort-based, hash-based, or in some joins, index-based.

4. A decision about the number of passes to be used: one-pass, two-pass, or multipass (recursive, using as many passes as necessary for the data at hand). Alternatively, this choice may be left until run-time.

5. An anticipated number of buffers the operation will require.

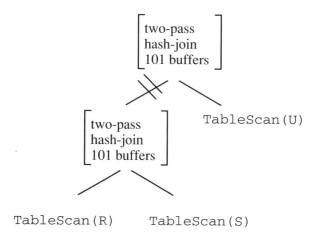

Figure 7.37: A physical plan from Example 7.38

Example 7.39 : Figure 7.37 shows the physical plan developed in Example 7.38 for the case $k > 5000$. In this plan, we access each of the three relations by a table-scan. We use a two-pass hash-join for the first join, materialize it, and use a two-pass hash-join for the second join. By implication of the double-line symbol for materialization, the left argument of the top join is also obtained by a table-scan, and the result of the first join is stored using the Store operator.

In contrast, if $k \le 49$, then the physical plan developed in Example 7.38 is that shown in Fig. 7.38. Notice that the second join uses a different number of

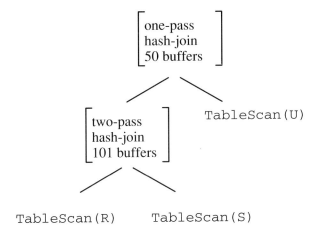

Figure 7.38: Another physical plan for the case where $R \bowtie S$ is expected to be very small

passes, a different number of buffers, and a left argument that is pipelined, not materialized.   □

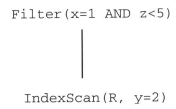

Figure 7.39: Annotating a selection to use the most appropriate index

Example 7.40: Consider the selection operation in Example 7.37, where we decided that the best of options was to use the index on y to find those tuples with $y = 2$, then check these tuples for the other conditions $x = 1$ and $z < 5$. Figure 7.39 shows the physical query plan. The leaf indicates that R will be accessed through its index on y, retrieving only those tuples with $y = 2$. The filter operator says that we complete the selection by further selecting those of the retrieved tuples that have both $x = 1$ and $z < 5$.   □

7.7.7 Ordering of Physical Operations

Our final topic regarding physical query plans is the matter of order of operations. The physical query plan is generally represented as a tree, and trees imply something about order of operations, since data must flow up the tree. However, since bushy trees may have interior nodes that are neither ancestors nor descendants of one another, the order of evaluation of interior nodes may not always be clear. Moreover, since iterators can be used to implement operations in a pipelined manner, it is possible that the times of execution for various nodes overlap, and the notion of "ordering" nodes makes no sense.

If materialization is implemented in the obvious store-and-later-retrieve way, and pipelining is implemented by iterators, then we may establish a fixed sequence of events whereby each operation of a physical query plan is executed. The following rules summarize the ordering of events implicit in a physical-query-plan tree:

1. Break the tree into subtrees at each edge that represents materialization. The subtrees will be executed one-at-a-time.

2. Order the execution of the subtrees in a bottom-up, left-to-right manner. To be precise, perform a preorder traversal of the entire tree. Order the subtrees in the order in which the preorder traversal exits from the subtrees.

3. Execute all nodes of each subtree using a network of iterators. Thus, all the nodes in one subtree are executed simultaneously, with GetNext calls among their operators determining the exact order of events.

Following this strategy, the query optimizer can now generate executable code, perhaps a sequence of function calls, for the query.

7.7.8   Exercises for Section 7.7

Exercise 7.7.1: Consider a relation $R(a, b, c, d)$ that has a clustering index on a and nonclustering indexes on each of the other attributes. The relevant parameters are: $B(R) = 1000$, $T(R) = 5000$, $V(R, a) = 20$, $V(R, b) = 1000$, $V(R, c) = 5000$, and $V(R, d) = 500$. Give the best query plan (index-scan or table-scan followed by a filter step) and the disk-I/O cost for each of the following selections:

* a) $\sigma_{a=1 \text{ AND } b=2 \text{ AND } d=3}(R)$.

  b) $\sigma_{a=1 \text{ AND } b=2 \text{ AND } c\geq3}(R)$.

  c) $\sigma_{a=1 \text{ AND } b\leq2 \text{ AND } c\geq3}(R)$.

! **Exercise 7.7.2:** In terms of $B(R)$, $T(R)$, $V(R, x)$, and $V(R, y)$, express the following conditions about the cost of implementing a selection on R:

* a) It is better to use index-scan with a nonclustering index on x and a term that equates x to a constant than a nonclustering index on y and a term that equates y to a constant.

b) It is better to use index-scan with a nonclustering index on x and a term that equates x to a constant than a clustering index on y and a term that equates y to a constant.

c) It is better to use index-scan with a nonclustering index on x and a term that equates x to a constant than a clustering index on y and a term of the form $y > C$ for some constant C.

Exercise 7.7.3 : How would the conclusions about when to pipeline in Example 7.38 change if the size of relation R were not 5000 blocks, but:

a) 2000 blocks.

! b) 10,000 blocks.

! c) 100 blocks.

! **Exercise 7.7.4 :** Suppose we want to compute $\big(R(a,b) \bowtie S(a,c)\big) \bowtie T(a,d)$ in the order indicated. We have $M = 101$ main-memory buffers, and $B(R) = B(S) = 2000$. Because the join attribute a is the same for both joins, we decide to implement the first join $R \bowtie S$ by a two-pass sort-join, and we shall use the appropriate number of passes for the second join, first dividing T into some number of sublists sorted on a, and merging them with the sorted and pipelined stream of tuples from the join $R \bowtie S$. For what values of $B(T)$ should we choose for the join of T with $R \bowtie S$:

* a) A one-pass join; i.e., we read T into memory, and compare its tuples with the tuples of $R \bowtie S$ as they are generated.

b) A two-pass join; i.e., we create sorted sublists for T and keep one buffer in memory for each sorted sublist, while we generate tuples of $R \bowtie S$.

7.8 Summary of Chapter 7

✦ *Compilation of Queries*: Compilation turns a query into a physical query plan, which is a sequence of operations that can be implemented by the query-execution engine. The principal steps of query compilation are parsing, semantic checking, selection of the preferred logical query plan (algebraic expression), and generation from that of the best physical plan.

✦ *The Parser*: The first step in processing an SQL query is to parse it, as one would for code in any programming language. The result of parsing is a parse tree with nodes corresponding to SQL constructs.

✦ *Semantic Checking*: A preprocessor examines the parse tree, checks that the attributes, relation names, and types make sense, and resolves attribute references when there are several relations with the same attribute name.

✦ *Conversion to a Logical Query Plan*: The query processor must convert the semantically checked parse tree to an algebraic expression. Much of the conversion to relational algebra is straightforward, but subqueries present a problem. The usual approach is to introduce a two-argument selection that puts the subquery in the condition of the selection, and then apply appropriate transformations that cover the common special cases.

✦ *Algebraic Transformations*: There are many ways that a logical query plan can be transformed to a better plan by using algebraic transformations. Section 7.2 enumerates the principal ones.

✦ *Choosing a Logical Query Plan*: The query processor must select that query plan that is most likely to lead to an efficient physical plan. In addition to applying algebraic transformations, it is useful to group associative and commutative operators, especially joins, so the physical query plan can choose the best order and grouping for these operations.

✦ *Estimating Sizes of Relations*: When selecting the best logical plan, or when ordering joins or other associative-commutative operations, we use the estimated size of intermediate relations as a surrogate for the true running time or disk-I/O cost of the physical plan that we shall ultimately select. Knowing, or estimating, both the size (number of tuples) of relations and the number of distinct values for each attribute of each relation helps us get good estimates of the sizes of intermediate relations.

✦ *Histograms*: Some systems keep histograms of the values for a given attribute. This information can be used to obtain better estimates of intermediate-relation sizes than the simple methods stressed in this chapter.

✦ *Cost-Based Optimization*: When selecting the best physical plan, one needs to be able to estimate the cost of each possible plan. Various strategies are used to generate all or some of the possible physical plans that implement a given logical plan.

✦ *Plan-Enumeration Strategies*: The common approaches to searching the space of physical plans for the best include dynamic programming (tabularizing the best plan for each subexpression of the given logical plan), Selinger-style dynamic programming (which includes the sort-order of results as part of the table, giving best plans for each sort-order and for an unsorted result), greedy approaches (making a series of locally optimal decisions, given the choices for the physical plan that have been made so far), and branch-and-bound (enumerating only plans that are not immediately known to be worse than the best plan found so far).

✦ *Left-Deep Join Trees*: When picking a grouping and order for the join of several relations, it is common to restrict the search to left-deep trees, which are binary trees with a single spine down the left edge, with only leaves as right children. This form of join expression tends to yield efficient plans and also limits significantly the number of physical plans that need to be considered.

◆ *Physical Plans for Selection*: If possible, a selection should be broken into an index-scan of the relation to which the selection is applied (typically using a condition in which the indexed attribute is equated to a constant), followed by a filter operation. The filter examines the tuples retrieved by the index-scan and passes through only those that meet the portions of the selection condition other than that on which the index scan is based.

◆ *Pipelining Versus Materialization*: Ideally, the result of each physical operator is consumed by another operator, with the result being passed between the two in main memory ("pipelining"), perhaps using an iterator to control the flow of data from one to the other. However, sometimes there is an advantage to storing ("materializing") the result of one operator to save space in main memory for other operators. Thus, the physical-query-plan generator should consider both pipelining and materialization of intermediates.

7.9 References for Chapter 7

The surveys mentioned in the bibliographic notes to Chapter 6 also contain material relevant to query compilation. In addition, we recommend the survey [1], which contains material on the query optimizers of commercial systems.

Three of the earliest studies of query optimization are [4], [5], and [3]. Paper [7], another early study, incorporates the idea of pushing selections down the tree with the greedy algorithm for join-order choice. The paper [2] is the source for "Selinger-style optimization" as well as describing the System R optimizer, which was one of the most ambitious attempts at query optimization of its day.

The reader who wishes to see the complete grammar for SQL2 should look at [6].

1. G. Graefe (ed.), *Data Engineering* **16**:4 (1993), special issue on query processing in commercial database management systems, IEEE.

2. P. Griffiths-Selinger, M. M. Astrahan, D. D. Chamberlin, R. A. Lorie, and T. G. Price, "Access path selection in a relational database system," *Proc. ACM SIGMOD Intl. Conf. on Management of Data* (1979), pp. 23–34.

3. P. A. V. Hall, "Optimization of a single relational expression in a relational database system," *IBM J. Research and Development* **20**:3 (1976), pp. 244–257.

4. F. P. Palermo, "A database search problem," in: J. T. Tou (ed.) *Information Systems COINS IV*, Plenum, New York, 1974.

5. J. M. Smith and P. Y. Chang, "Optimizing the performance of a relational algebra database interface," *Comm. ACM* **18**:10 (1975), pp. 568–579.

6. `ftp://jerry.ece.umassd.edu/isowg3/dbl/BASEdocs/public/sql-92.bnf`

7. E. Wong and K. Youssefi, "Decomposition — a strategy for query processing," *ACM Trans. on Database Systems* **1**:3 (1976), pp. 223–241.

Chapter 8

Coping With System Failures

Starting with this chapter, we focus our attention on the parts of a database management system that control access to data. There are two major issues that must be addressed:

1. Data must be protected in the face of a system failure. This chapter deals with techniques for supporting the goal of *resilience*, that is, integrity of the data when the system fails in some way.

2. Data must not be corrupted simply because several error-free queries or database modifications are being done at once. This matter is addressed in Chapters 9 and 10.

   The principal technique for supporting resilience is a *log* that records the history of changes to the database in a secure way. We shall discuss three different styles of logging, called "undo," "redo," and "undo/redo." We also discuss *recovery*, the process whereby the log is used to reconstruct what has happened to the database when there has been a failure. An important aspect of logging and recovery is avoidance of the situation where the log must be examined into the distant past. Thus, we shall learn the important technique called "checkpointing," which limits the length of log that must be examined during recovery.

   In a final section, we discuss "archiving," which allows the database to survive not only temporary system failures, but situations where the entire database is lost. Then, we must rely on a recent copy of the database (the archive) plus whatever log information survives, to reconstruct the database as it existed at some point in the recent past.

8.1 Issues and Models for Resilient Operation

We shall begin our discussion of coping with failures by reviewing the kinds of things that can go wrong, and what a database management system can and should do about them. We initially focus on "system failures" or "crashes," the kinds of errors that the logging and recovery methods are designed to fix. We also introduce in Section 8.1.4 the model for buffer management that underlies all discussions of recovery from system errors. The same model is needed in the next chapter as we discuss concurrent access to the database by several transactions.

8.1.1 Failure Modes

There are many things that can go wrong as a database is queried and modified. Problems range from the keyboard entry of incorrect data to an explosion in the room where the database is stored on disk. The following items are a catalog of the most important failure modes and what the DBMS can do about them.

Erroneous Data Entry

Some data errors are impossible to detect. For example, if a clerk mistypes one digit of your phone number, the data will still look like a phone number that *could* be yours. On the other hand, if the clerk omits a digit from your phone number, then the data is evidently in error, since it does not have the form of a phone number.

A modern DBMS provides a number of software mechanisms for catching those data-entry errors that are detectable. For example, the SQL2 and SQL3 standards, as well as all popular implementations of SQL, include a way for the database designer to introduce into the database schema constraints such as key constraints, foreign key constraints, and constraints on values (e.g., a phone number must be 10 digits long). Triggers, which are programs that execute whenever a modification of a certain type (e.g., insertion of a tuple into relation R) occurs, are used to check that the data just entered meets any constraint that the database designer believes it should satisfy.

Media Failures

A local failure of a disk, one that changes only a bit or a few bits, can normally be detected by parity checks associated with the sectors of the disk, as we discussed in Section 2.2.5. Major failures of a disk, principally head crashes, where the entire disk becomes unreadable, are generally handled by one or both of the following approaches:

1. Use one of the RAID schemes discussed in Section 2.6, so the lost disk can be restored.

2. Maintain an *archive*, a copy of the database on a medium such as tape or optical disk. The archive is periodically created, either fully or incrementally, and stored at a safe distance from the database itself. We shall discuss archiving in Section 8.5.

3. Instead of an archive, one could keep redundant copies of the database on-line, distributed among several sites. These copies are kept consistent by mechanisms we shall discuss in Section 10.6.

Catastrophic Failure

In this category are a number of situations in which the media holding the database is completely destroyed. Examples would include explosions or fires at the site of the database and vandalism or viruses. RAID will not help, since all the data disks and their parity check disks become useless simultaneously. However, the other approaches that can be used to protect against media failure — archiving and redundant, distributed copies — will also protect against a catastrophic failure.

System Failures

The processes that query and modify the database are called *transactions*. A transaction, like any program, executes a number of steps in sequence; often, several of these steps will modify the database. Each transaction has a *state*, which represents what has happened so far in the transaction. The state includes the current place in the transaction's code being executed and the values of any local variables of the transaction that will be needed later on.

System failures are problems that cause the state of a transaction to be lost. Typical system failures are power loss and software errors. To see why problems such as power outages cause loss of state, observe that, like any program, the steps of a transaction initially occur in main memory. Unlike disk, main memory is "volatile," as we discussed in Section 2.1.6. That is, a power failure will cause the contents of main memory to disappear, while a disk's (nonvolatile) data remains intact. Similarly, a software error may overwrite part of main memory, possibly including values that were part of the state of the program.

When main memory is lost, the transaction state is lost; that is, we can no longer tell what parts of the transaction, including its database modifications, were made. Running the transaction again may not fix the problem. For example, if the transaction must add 1 to a value in the database, we do not know whether to repeat the addition of 1 or not. The principal remedy for the problems that arise due to a system error is logging of all database changes in a separate, nonvolatile log, coupled with recovery when necessary. However, the mechanisms whereby such logging can be done in a fail-safe manner are surprisingly intricate, as we shall see starting in Section 8.2.

Transactions and Triggers

The extent of a transaction can be affected by the existence of triggers or other active elements in the database schema. If a transaction includes a modification action, and that action causes one or more triggers to be invoked, then the triggers' actions are also part of the transaction. In some systems, triggers may cascade, with the effect of one causing another to be triggered. If so, then all these actions form part of the transaction that initiated the sequence of triggers.

8.1.2   More About Transactions

Before proceeding to our study of database resilience and recovery from failures, we need to discuss the fundamental notion of a transaction in more detail. The transaction is the unit of execution of database operations. For example, if we are issuing ad-hoc commands to an SQL system, then each query or database modification statement is a transaction. When we are using an embedded SQL interface, then the programmer controls the extent of a transaction, which may include several queries or modifications, as well as operations performed in the host language. In the typical embedded SQL system, transactions begin as soon as operations on the database are executed and end with an explicit COMMIT or ROLLBACK ("abort") command.

As we shall discuss in Section 8.1.3, a transaction must execute atomically, that is, all-or-nothing and as if it were executed at an instant in time. Assuring that transactions are executed correctly is the job of a *transaction manager*, a subsystem that performs several functions, including:

1. Issuing signals to the log manager (described below) so that necessary information in the form of "log records" can be stored on the log.

2. Assuring that concurrently executing transactions do not interfere with each other in ways that introduce errors ("scheduling"; see Section 9.1).

The transaction manager and its interactions are suggested by Fig. 8.1. The transaction manager will send messages about actions of transactions to the log manager, to the buffer manager about when it is possible or necessary to copy the buffer back to disk, and to the query processor to execute the queries and other database operations that comprise the transaction.

The log manager maintains the log. It must deal with the buffer manager, since space for the log initially appears in main-memory buffers, and at certain times these buffers must be copied to disk. The log, as well as the data, occupies space on the disk, as we suggest in Fig. 8.1.

Finally, we show in Fig. 8.1 the role of the recovery manager. When there is a crash, the recovery manager is activated. It examines the log and uses it to

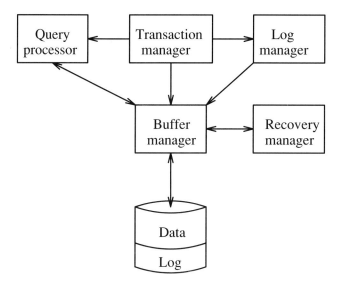

Figure 8.1: The log manager and transaction manager

repair the data, if necessary. As always, access to the disk is through the buffer manager.

8.1.3   Correct Execution of Transactions

Before we can deal with correcting system errors, we need to understand what it means for a transaction to be executed "correctly." To begin, we assume that the database is composed of "elements." We shall not specify precisely what an "element" is, except to say it has a value and can be accessed or modified by transactions. Different database systems use different notions of elements, but they are usually chosen from one or more of the following:

1. Relations, or their object-oriented equivalent: the extent of a class.

2. Disk blocks or pages.

3. Individual tuples of a relation, or their object-oriented equivalent: objects.

In examples to follow, one can imagine that database elements are tuples, or in many examples, simply integers. However, there are several good reasons in practice to use choice (2) — disk blocks or pages — as the database element. In this way, buffer-contents become single elements, allowing us to avoid some serious problems with logging and transactions that we shall explore periodically as we learn various techniques. Avoiding database elements that are bigger than disk blocks also prevents a situation where part but not all of an element has been placed in nonvolatile storage when a crash occurs.

Is the Correctness Principle Believable?

Given that a database transaction could be an ad-hoc modification command issued at a terminal, perhaps by someone who doesn't understand the implicit constraints in the mind of the database designer, is it plausible to assume all transactions take the database from a consistent state to another consistent state? Explicit constraints are enforced by the database, so any transaction that violates them will be rejected by the system and not change the database at all. As for implicit constraints, one cannot characterize them exactly under any circumstances. Our position, justifying the correctness principle, is that if someone is given authority to modify the database, then they also have the authority to judge what the implicit constraints are.

A database has a *state*, which is a value for each of its elements.[1] Intuitively, we regard certain states as *consistent*, and others as inconsistent. Consistent states satisfy all constraints of the database schema, such as key constraints or constraints on values. However, consistent states must also satisfy implicit constraints that are in the mind of the database designer. The implicit constraints may be maintained by triggers that are part of the database schema, but they might also be maintained only by policy statements concerning the database, or warnings associated with the user interface through which updates are made.

Example 8.1: Suppose our database consists of the relations

```
StarsIn(title, year, starName)
MovieStar(name, address, gender, birthdate)
```

We might assert a foreign-key constraint such as "every value of `starName` appears as a value of `name` in `MovieStar`," or a value-constraint such as "the value of `gender` can be only 'M' or 'F'." The state of the database is consistent if and only if all such constraints are satisfied by the current values of the two relations. □

A fundamental assumption about transactions is:

- *The Correctness Principle*: If a transaction executes in the absence of any other transactions or system errors, and it starts with the database in a consistent state, then the database is also in a consistent state when the transaction ends.

---

[1] We should not confuse the database state with the state of a transaction; the latter is values for the transaction's local variables, not database elements.

There is a converse to the correctness principle that forms the motivation for both the logging techniques discussed in this chapter and the concurrency control mechanisms discussed in Chapter 9. This converse involves two points:

1. A transaction is *atomic*; that is, it must be executed as a whole or not at all. If only part of a transaction executes, then there is a good chance that the resulting database state will not be consistent.

2. Transactions that execute simultaneously are likely to lead to an inconsistent state unless we take steps to control their interactions, as we shall in Chapter 9.

8.1.4 The Primitive Operations of Transactions

Let us now consider in detail how transactions interact with the database. There are three address spaces that interact in important ways:

1. The space of disk blocks holding the database elements.

2. The virtual or main memory address space that is managed by the buffer manager.

3. The local address space of the transaction.

For a transaction to read a database element, that element must first be brought to a main-memory buffer or buffers, if it is not already there. Then, the contents of the buffer(s) can be read by the transaction into its own address space. Writing of a new value for a database element by a transaction follows the reverse route. The new value is first created by the transaction in its own space. Then, this value is copied to the appropriate buffer(s).

The buffer may or may not be copied to disk immediately; that decision is the responsibility of the buffer manager in general. As we shall soon see, one of the principal steps of using a log to assure resilience in the face of system errors is forcing the buffer manager to write the block in a buffer back to disk at appropriate times. However, in order to reduce the number of disk I/O's, database systems can and will allow a change to exist only in volatile main-memory storage, at least for certain periods of time and under the proper set of conditions.

In order to study the details of logging algorithms and other transaction-management algorithms, we need a notation that describes all the operations that move data between address spaces. The primitives we shall use are:

1. `INPUT(X)`: Copy the disk block containing database element X to a memory buffer.

2. `READ(X,t)`: Copy the database element X to the transaction's local variable t. More precisely, if the block containing database element X is not in a memory buffer then first execute `INPUT(X)`. Next, assign the value of X to local variable t.

Buffers in Query Processing and in Transactions

If you got used to the analysis of buffer utilization in the chapters on query processing, you may notice a change in viewpoint here. In Chapters 6 and 7 we were interested in buffers principally as they were used to compute temporary relations during the evaluation of a query. That is one important use of buffers, but there is never a need to preserve a temporary value, so these buffers do not generally have their values logged. On the other hand, those buffers that hold data retrieved from the database *do* need to have those values preserved, especially when the transaction updates them.

---

3. WRITE(X,t): Copy the value of local variable t to database element X in a memory buffer. More precisely, if the block containing database element X is not in a memory buffer then execute INPUT(X). Next, copy the value of t to X in the buffer.

4. OUTPUT(X): Copy the buffer containing X to disk.

The above operations make sense as long as database elements reside within a single disk block, and therefore within a single buffer. That would be the case for database elements that *are* blocks. It would also be true for database elements that are tuples, as long as the relation schema does not allow tuples that are bigger than the space available in one block. If database elements occupy several blocks, then we shall imagine that each block-sized portion of the element is an element by itself. The logging mechanism to be used will assure that the transaction cannot complete without the write of X being atomic; i.e., either all blocks of X are written to disk, or none are. Thus, we shall assume for the entire discussion of logging that

- A database element is no larger than a single block.

It is important to observe that the components issuing these commands differ. READ and WRITE are issued by transactions. INPUT and OUTPUT are issued by the buffer manager, although OUTPUT can also be initiated by the log manager under certain conditions, as we shall see.

Example 8.2: To see how the above primitive operations relate to what a transaction might do, let us consider a database that has two elements A and B with the constraint that they must be equal in all consistent states.[2]

Transaction T consists logically of the following two steps:

---

[2]One reasonably might ask why we should bother to have two different elements that are constrained to be equal, rather than maintaining only one element. However, this simple numerical constraint captures the spirit of many more realistic constraints, e.g., the number of seats sold on a flight must not exceed the number of seats on the plane by more than 10%, or the sum of the loan balances at a bank must equal the total debt of the bank.

```
A := A*2;
B := B*2;
```

Notice that if the only consistency requirement for the database is that $A = B$, and if T starts in a correct state and completes its activities without interference from another transaction or system error, then the final state must also be consistent. That is, T doubles two equal elements to get new, equal elements.

Execution of T involves reading A and B from disk, performing arithmetic in the local address space of T, and writing the new values of A and B to their buffers. We could express T as the sequence of six relevant steps:

```
READ(A,t); t := t*2; WRITE(A,t);
READ(B,t); t := t*2; WRITE(B,t);
```

In addition, the buffer manager will eventually execute the OUTPUT steps to write these buffers back to disk. Figure 8.2 shows the primitive steps of T, followed by the two OUTPUT commands from the buffer manager. We assume that initially $A = B = 8$. The values of the memory and disk copies of A and B and the local variable t in the address space of transaction T are indicated for each step.

Action	t	Mem A	Mem B	Disk A	Disk B
READ(A,t)	8	8		8	8
t := t*2	16	8		8	8
WRITE(A,t)	16	16		8	8
READ(B,t)	8	16	8	8	8
t := t*2	16	16	8	8	8
WRITE(B,t)	16	16	16	8	8
OUTPUT(A)	16	16	16	16	8
OUTPUT(B)	16	16	16	16	16

Figure 8.2: Steps of a transaction and its effect on memory and disk

At the first step, T reads A, which causes an INPUT(A) command to the buffer manager if A's block is not already in a buffer. The value of A is also copied by the READ command into local variable t of T's address space. The second step doubles t; it has no affect on A, either in a buffer or on disk. The third step writes t into A of the buffer; it does not affect A on disk. The next three steps do the same for B, and the last two steps copy A and B to disk.

Observe that as long as all these steps execute, consistency of the database is preserved. If a system error occurs before OUTPUT(A) is executed, then there is no effect to the database stored on disk; it is as if T never ran, and consistency is preserved. However, if there is a system error after OUTPUT(A) but before OUTPUT(B), then the database is left in an inconsistent state. We cannot prevent this situation from ever occurring, but we can arrange that when it does occur, the problem can be repaired — either both A and B will be reset to 8, or both will be advanced to 16.   □

8.1.5   Exercises for Section 8.1

Exercise 8.1.1: Suppose that the consistency constraint on the database is $0 \leq A \leq B$. Tell whether each of the following transactions preserves consistency.

* a) `A := A+B; B := A+B;`

  b) `B := A+B; A := A+B;`

  c) `A := B+1; B := A+1;`

Exercise 8.1.2: For each of the transactions of Exercise 8.1.1, add the read- and write-actions to the computation and show the effect of the steps on main memory and disk. Assume that initially $A = 5$ and $B = 10$. Also, tell whether it is possible, with the appropriate order of OUTPUT actions, to assure that consistency is preserved even if there is a crash while the transaction is executing.

8.2   Undo Logging

We shall now begin our study of logging as a way to assure that transactions are atomic — they appear to the database either to have executed in their entirety or not to have executed at all. A *log* is a sequence of *log records*, each telling something about what some transaction has done. The actions of several transactions can "interleave," so that a step of one transaction may be executed and its effect logged, then the same happens for a step of another transaction, then for a second step of the first transaction or a step of a third transaction, and so on. This interleaving of transactions complicates logging; it is not sufficient simply to log the entire story of a transaction after that transaction completes.

    If there is a system crash, the log is consulted to reconstruct what transactions were doing when the crash occurred. The log also may be used, in conjunction with an archive, if there is a media failure of a disk that does not store the log. Generally, to repair the effect of the crash, some transactions will have their work done again, and the new values they wrote into the database are written again. Other transactions will have their work undone, and the database restored so that it appears that they never executed.

    Our first style of logging, which is called *undo logging*, makes only repairs of the second type. If it is not absolutely certain that the effects of a transaction have been completed and stored on disk, then any database changes that the transaction may have made to the database are undone, and the database state is restored to what existed prior to the transaction.

    In this section we shall introduce the basic idea of log records, including the *commit* (successful completion of a transaction) action and its effect on the

---

Why Might a Transaction Abort?

One might wonder why a transaction would abort rather than commit. There are actually several reasons. The simplest is when there is some error condition in the code of the transaction itself, for example an attempted division by zero that is handled by "canceling" the transaction. The DBMS may also need to abort a transaction for one of several reasons. For instance, a transaction may be involved in a deadlock, where it and one or more other transactions each hold some resource (e.g., the privilege to write a new value of some database element) that the other wants. We shall see in Section 10.3 that in such a situation one or more transactions must be forced by the system to abort.

---

database state and log. We shall also consider how the log itself is created in main memory and copied to disk by a "flush-log" operation. Finally, we examine the undo log specifically, and learn how to use it in recovery from a crash. In order to avoid having to examine the entire log during recovery, we introduce the idea of "checkpointing," which allows old portions of the log to be thrown away. The checkpointing method for an undo log is considered explicitly in this section.

8.2.1 Log Records

Imagine the log as a file opened for appending only. As transactions execute, the *log manager* has the job of recording in the log each important event. One block of the log at a time is filled with log records, each representing one of these events. Log blocks are initially created in main memory and are allocated by the buffer manager like any other blocks that the DBMS needs. The log blocks are written to nonvolatile storage on disk as soon as is feasible; we shall have more to say about this matter in Section 8.2.2.

There are several forms of log record that are used with each of the types of logging we discuss in this chapter. These are:

1. <START T>: This record indicates that transaction T has begun.

2. <COMMIT T>: Transaction T has completed successfully and will make no more changes to database elements. Any changes to the database made by T should appear on disk. However, because we cannot control when the buffer manager chooses to copy blocks from memory to disk, we cannot in general be sure that the changes are already on disk when we see the <COMMIT T> log record. If we insist that the changes already be on disk, this requirement must be enforced by the log manager (as is the case for undo logging).

How Big Is an Update Record?

If database elements are disk blocks, and an update record includes the old value of a database element (or both the old and new values of the database element as we shall see in Section 8.4 for undo/redo logging), then it appears that a log record can be bigger than a block. That is not necessarily a problem, since like any conventional file, we may think of a log as a sequence of disk blocks, with bytes covering blocks without any concern for block boundaries. However, there are ways to compress the log. For instance, under some circumstances, we can log only the change, e.g., the name of the attribute of some tuple that has been changed by the transaction, and its old value. The matter of "logical logging" of changes is discussed in Section 10.1.5.

---

3. $<$ABORT $T>$: Transaction T could not complete successfully. If transaction T aborts, no changes it made can have been copied to disk, and it is the job of the transaction manager to make sure that such changes never appear on disk, or that their effect on disk is cancelled if they do. We shall discuss the matter of repairing the effect of aborted transactions in Section 10.1.1.

For an undo log, the only other kind of log record we need is an *update record*, which is a triple $<T, X, v>$. The meaning of this record is: transaction T has changed database element X, and its former value was v. The change reflected by an update record normally occurs in memory, not disk; i.e., the log record is a response to a WRITE action, not an OUTPUT action (see Section 8.1.4 to recall the distinction between these operations). Notice also that an undo log does not record the new value of a database element, only the old value. As we shall see, should recovery be necessary in a system using undo logging, the only thing the recovery manager will do is cancel the possible effect of a transaction on disk by restoring the old value.

8.2.2 The Undo-Logging Rules

There are two rules that transactions must obey in order that an undo log allows us to recover from a system failure. These rules affect what the buffer manager can do and also requires that certain actions be taken whenever a transaction commits. We summarize them here.

U_1: If transaction T modifies database element X, then the log record of the form $<T, X, v>$ must be written to disk *before* the new value of X is written to disk.

Preview of Other Logging Methods

In "redo logging" (Section 8.3), on recovery we redo any transaction that has started but not committed. Rules for redo logging assure that there is never a need to redo a transaction if we see its COMMIT record on the log. "Undo/redo logging" (Section 8.4) will, on recovery, undo any transaction that has not committed, and will redo those transactions that have committed. Again, rules about management of the log and buffers will assure that these steps successfully repair any damage to the database.

U_2: If a transaction commits, then its COMMIT log record must be written to disk only *after* all database elements changed by the transaction have been written to disk, but as soon thereafter as possible.

To summarize rules U_1 and U_2, material associated with one transaction must be written to disk in the following order:

a) The log records indicating changed database elements.

b) The changed database elements themselves.

c) The COMMIT log record.

However, the order of (a) and (b) applies to each database element individually, not to the group of update records for a transaction as a whole.

In order to force log records to disk, the log manager needs a *flush-log* command that tells the buffer manager to copy to disk any log blocks that have not previously been copied to disk or that have been changed since they were last copied. In sequences of actions, we shall show FLUSH LOG explicitly. The transaction manager also needs to have a way to tell the buffer manager to perform an OUTPUT action on a database element. We shall continue to show the OUTPUT action in sequences of transaction steps.

Example 8.3: Let us reconsider the transaction of Example 8.2 in the light of undo logging. Figure 8.3 expands on Fig. 8.2 to show the log entries and flush-log actions that have to take place along with the actions of the transaction T. Note we have shortened the headers to M-A for "the copy of A in a memory buffer" or D-B for "the copy of B on disk," and so on.

In line (1) of Fig. 8.3, transaction T begins. The first thing that happens is that the <START T> record is written to the log. Line (2) represents the read of A by T. Line (3) is the local change to t, which affects neither the database stored on disk nor any portion of the database in a memory buffer. Neither lines (2) nor (3) require any log entry, since they have no affect on the database.

Line (4) is the write of the new value of A to the buffer. This modification to A is reflected by the log entry <$T, A, 8$> which says that A was changed by

Step	Action	t	M-A	M-B	D-A	D-B	Log
1)							$<$START $T>$
2)	READ(A,t)	8	8		8	8	
3)	t := t*2	16	8		8	8	
4)	WRITE(A,t)	16	16		8	8	$<T, A, 8>$
5)	READ(B,t)	8	16	8	8	8	
6)	t := t*2	16	16	8	8	8	
7)	WRITE(B,t)	16	16	16	8	8	$<T, B, 8>$
8)	FLUSH LOG						
9)	OUTPUT(A)	16	16	16	16	8	
10)	OUTPUT(B)	16	16	16	16	16	
11)							$<$COMMIT $T>$
12)	FLUSH LOG						

Figure 8.3: Actions and their log entries

T and its former value was 8. Note that the new value, 16, is not mentioned in an undo log.

Lines (5) through (7) perform the same three steps with B instead of A. At this point, T has completed and must commit. It would like the changed A and B to migrate to disk, but in order to follow the two rules for undo logging, there is a fixed sequence of events that must happen.

First, A and B cannot be copied to disk until the log records for the changes are on disk. Thus, at step (8) the log is flushed, assuring that these records appear on disk. Then, steps (9) and (10) copy A and B to disk. The transaction manager requests these steps from the buffer manager in order to commit T.

Now, it is possible to commit T, and the $<$COMMIT $T>$ record is written to the log, which is step (11). Finally, we must flush the log again at step (12) to make sure that the $<$COMMIT $T>$ record of the log appears on disk. Notice that without writing this record to disk, we could have a situation where a transaction has committed, but for a long time a review of the log does not tell us that it has committed. That situation could cause strange behavior if there were a crash, because, as we shall see in Section 8.2.3, a transaction that appeared to the user to have committed and written its changes to disk would then be undone and effectively aborted. □

8.2.3 Recovery Using Undo Logging

Suppose now that a system failure occurs. It is possible that certain database changes made by a given transaction may have been written to disk, while other changes made by the same transaction never reached the disk. If so, the transaction was not executed atomically, and there may be an inconsistent

Background Activity Affects the Log and Buffers

As we look at a sequence of actions and log entries like Fig. 8.3, it is tempting to imagine that these actions occur in isolation. However, the DBMS may be processing many transactions simultaneously. Thus, the four log records for transaction T may be interleaved on the log with records for other transactions. Moreover, if one of these transactions flushes the log, then the log records from T may appear on disk earlier than is implied by the flush-log actions of Fig. 8.3. There is no harm if log records reflecting a database modification appear earlier than necessary, and we don't write the <COMMIT T> record until the OUTPUT actions for T are completed, thus assuring that the changed values appear on disk before the COMMIT record.

A trickier situation occurs if two database elements A and B share a block. Then, writing one of them to disk writes the other as well. In the worst case, we can violate rule U_1 by writing one of these elements prematurely. It may be necessary to adopt additional constraints on transactions in order to make undo logging work. For instance, we might use a locking scheme where database elements are disk blocks, as described in Section 9.3, to prevent two transactions from accessing the same block at the same time. This and other problems that appear when database elements are fractions of a block motivate our suggestion that blocks *be* the database elements.

database state. It is the job of the *recovery manager* to use the log to restore the database state to some consistent state.

In this section we consider only the simplest form of recovery manager, one that looks at the entire log, no matter how long, and makes database changes as a result of its examination. In Section 8.2.4 we consider a more sensible approach, where the log is periodically "checkpointed," to limit the distance back in history that the recovery manager must go.

The first task of the recovery manager is to divide the transactions into committed and uncommitted transactions. If there is a log record <COMMIT T>, then by undo rule U_2 all changes made by transaction T were previously written to disk. Thus, T by itself could not have left the database in an inconsistent state when the system failure occurred.

However, suppose that we find a <START T> record on the log but no <COMMIT T> record. Then there could have been some changes to the database made by T that got written to disk before the crash, while other changes by T either were not made, even in the main-memory buffers, or were made in the buffers but not copied to disk. In this case, T is an *incomplete transaction* and must be *undone*. That is, whatever changes T made must be reset to their previous value. Fortunately, rule U_1 assures us that if T changed X on disk before the crash, then there will be a $<T, X, v>$ record on the log, and that record will have been copied to disk before the crash. Thus, during the recovery, we must write the value v for database element X. Note that this rule begs the question whether X had value v in the database anyway; we don't even bother to check.

Since there may be several uncommitted transactions in the log, and there may even be several uncommitted transactions that modified X, we have to be systematic about the order in which we restore values. Thus, the recovery manager must scan the log from the end (i.e., from the most recently written record to the earliest written). As it travels, it remembers all those transactions T for which it has seen a $<$COMMIT $T>$ record or an $<$ABORT $T>$ record. Also as it travels backward, if it sees a record $<T, X, v>$, then:

1. If T is a transaction whose COMMIT record has been seen, then do nothing. T is committed and need not be undone.

2. Otherwise, T is an incomplete transaction, or an aborted transaction. The recovery manager must change the value of X in the database to v.[3]

After making these changes, the recovery manager must write a log record $<$ABORT $T>$ for each incomplete transaction T that was not previously aborted, and then flush the log. Now, normal operation of the database may resume, and new transactions may begin executing.

Example 8.4: Let us consider the sequence of actions from Fig. 8.3 and Example 8.3. There are several different times that the system crash could have occurred; let us consider each significantly different one.

1. The crash occurs after step (12). Then we know the $<$COMMIT $T>$ record got to disk before the crash. When we recover, there is no need to undo the results of T, and all log records concerning T are ignored by the recovery manager.

2. The crash occurs between steps (11) and (12). It is possible that the log record containing the COMMIT got flushed to disk; for instance, the buffer manager may have needed the buffer containing the end of the log for another transaction, or some other transaction may have asked for a log flush. If so, then the recovery is the same as in case (1) as far as T is concerned. However, if the COMMIT record never reached disk, then the recovery manager considers T incomplete. When it scans the log backward, it comes first to the record $<T, B, 8>$. It therefore stores 8 as the value of B on disk. It then comes to the record $<T, A, 8>$ and makes A have value 8 on disk. Finally, the record $<$ABORT $T>$ is written to the log, and the log is flushed.

---

[3]If T aborted, then the effect on the database should have been restored anyway.

Crashes During Recovery

Suppose the system again crashes while we are recovering from a previous crash. Because of the way undo-log records are designed, giving the old value rather than, say, the change in the value of a database element, the recovery steps are *idempotent*; that is, repeating them many times has exactly the same effect as performing them once. We have already observed that if we find a record $<T, X, v>$, it does not matter whether the value of X is already v — we may write v for X regardless. Similarly, if we have to repeat the recovery process, it will not matter whether the first, incomplete recovery restored some old values; we simply restore them again. Incidentally, the same reasoning holds for the other logging methods we discuss in this chapter. Since the recovery operations are idempotent, we can recover a second time without worrying about changes made the first time.

---

3. The crash occurs between steps (10) and (11). Now, the COMMIT record surely was not written, so T is incomplete and is undone as in case (2).

4. The crash occurs between steps (8) and (10). Again as in case (3), T is undone. The only difference is that now the change to A and/or B may not have reached disk. Nevertheless, the proper value, 8, is stored for each of these database elements.

5. The crash occurs prior to step (8). Now, it is not certain whether any of the log records concerning T have reached disk. However, it doesn't matter, because we know by rule U_1 that if the change to A and/or B reached disk, then the corresponding log record reached disk, and therefore if there were changes to A and/or B made on disk by T, then the corresponding log record will cause the recovery manager to undo those changes.

$\square$

8.2.4 Checkpointing

As we observed, recovery requires that the entire log be examined, in principle. When logging follows the undo style, once a transaction has its COMMIT log record written to disk, the log records of that transaction are no longer needed during recovery. We might imagine that we could delete the log prior to a COMMIT, but sometimes we cannot. The reason is that often many transactions execute at once. If we truncated the log after one transaction committed, log records pertaining to some other active transaction T might be lost and could not be used to undo T if recovery were necessary.

The simplest way to untangle potential problems is to *checkpoint* the log periodically. In a simple checkpoint, we:

1. Stop accepting new transactions.

2. Wait until all currently active transactions commit or abort and have written a COMMIT or ABORT record on the log.

3. Flush the log to disk.

4. Write a log record <CKPT>, and flush the log again.

5. Resume accepting transactions.

Any transaction that executed prior to the checkpoint will have finished, and by rule U_2 its changes will have reached the disk. Thus, there will be no need to undo any of these transactions during recovery. During a recovery, we scan the log backwards from the end, identifying incomplete transactions as in Section 8.2.3. However, when we find a <CKPT> record, we know that we have seen all the incomplete transactions. Since no transactions may begin until the checkpoint ends, we must have seen every log record pertaining to the incomplete transactions already. Thus, there is no need to scan prior to the <CKPT>, and in fact the log before that point can be deleted or overwritten safely.

Example 8.5 : Suppose the log begins:

$$<\text{START } T_1>$$
$$<T_1, A, 5>$$
$$<\text{START } T_2>$$
$$<T_2, B, 10>$$

At this time, we decide to do a checkpoint. Since T_1 and T_2 are the active (incomplete) transactions, we shall have to wait until they complete before writing the <CKPT> record on the log.

A possible continuation of the log is shown in Fig. 8.4. Suppose a crash occurs at this point. Scanning the log from the end, we identify T_3 as the only incomplete transaction, and restore E and F to their former values 25 and 30, respectively. When we reach the <CKPT> record, we know there is no need to examine prior log records and the restoration of the database state is complete. □

8.2.5 Nonquiescent Checkpointing

A problem with the checkpointing technique described in Section 8.2.4 is that effectively we must shut down the system while the checkpoint is being made. Since the active transactions may take a long time to commit or abort, the system may appear to users to be stalled. Thus, a more complex technique

---

Finding the Last Log Record

The log is essentially a file, whose blocks hold the log records. A space in a block that has never been filled can be marked "empty." If records were never overwritten, then the recovery manager could find the last log record by searching for the first empty record and taking the previous record as the end of the file.

However, if we overwrite old log records, then we need to keep a serial number, which only increases, with each record, as suggested by:

| ~~1~~ | ~~2~~ | ~~3~~ | 4 | 5 | 6 | 7 | 8 |
| 9 | 10 | 11 | | | | | |

Then, we can find the record whose serial number is greater than than of the next record; the latter record will be the current end of the log, and the entire log is found by ordering the current records by their present serial numbers.

In practice, a large log may be composed of many files, with a "top" file whose records indicate the files that comprise the log. Then, to recover, we find the last record of the top file, go to the file indicated, and find the last record there.

---

known as *nonquiescent ckeckpointing*, which allows new transactions to enter the system during the checkpoint, is usually preferred. The steps in a nonquiescent checkpoint are:

1. Write a log record <START CKPT $(T_1, \ldots, T_k)$> and flush the log. Here, $T_1, \ldots, T_k$ are the names or identifiers for all the *active* transactions (i.e., transactions that have not yet committed and written their changes to disk).

2. Wait until all of $T_1, \ldots, T_k$ commit or abort, but do not prohibit other transactions from starting.

3. When all of $T_1, \ldots, T_k$ have completed, write a log record <END CKPT> and flush the log.

With a log of this type, we can recover from a system crash as follows. As usual, we scan the log from the end, finding all incomplete transactions as we go, and restoring old values for database elements changed by these transactions. There are two cases, depending on whether, scanning backwards, we first meet an <END CKPT> record or a <START CKPT $(T_1, \ldots, T_k)$> record.

- If we first meet an <END CKPT> record, then we know that all incomplete transactions began after the previous <START CKPT $(T_1, \ldots, T_k)$> record.

$$<\text{START } T_1>$$
$$<T_1, A, 5>$$
$$<\text{START } T_2>$$
$$<T_2, B, 10>$$
$$<T_2, C, 15>$$
$$<T_1, D, 20>$$
$$<\text{COMMIT } T_1>$$
$$<\text{COMMIT } T_2>$$
$$<\text{CKPT}>$$
$$<\text{START } T_3>$$
$$<T_3, E, 25>$$
$$<T_3, F, 30>$$

Figure 8.4: An undo log

We may thus scan backwards as far as the next `START CKPT`, and then stop; previous log is useless and may as well have been discarded.

- If we first meet a record <`START CKPT` $(T_1, \ldots, T_k)$>, then the crash occurred during the checkpoint. However, the only incomplete transactions are those we met scanning backwards before we reached the `START CKPT` and those of $T_1, \ldots, T_k$ that did not complete before the crash. Thus, we need scan no further back than the start of the earliest of these incomplete transactions. The previous `START CKPT` record is certainly prior to any of these transaction starts, but often we shall find the starts of the incomplete transactions long before we reach the previous checkpoint.[4] Moreover, if we use pointers to chain together the log records that belong to the same transaction, then we need not search the whole log for records belonging to active transactions; we just follow their chains back through the log.

As a general rule, once an <`END CKPT`> record has been written to disk, we can delete the log prior to the previous `START CKPT` record.

Example 8.6: Suppose that, as in Example 8.5, the log begins:

$$<\text{START } T_1>$$
$$<T_1, A, 5>$$
$$<\text{START } T_2>$$
$$<T_2, B, 10>$$

Now, we decide to do a nonquiescent checkpoint. Since T_1 and T_2 are the active (incomplete) transactions at this time, we write a log record

---

[4]Notice, however, that because the checkpoint is nonquiescent, one of the incomplete transactions could have begun between the start and end of the previous checkpoint.

$$<\text{START CKPT } (T_1, T_2)>$$

Suppose that while waiting for T_1 and T_2 to complete, another transaction, T_3, initiates. A possible continuation of the log is shown in Fig. 8.5.

$$<\text{START } T_1>$$
$$<T_1, A, 5>$$
$$<\text{START } T_2>$$
$$<T_2, B, 10>$$
$$<\text{START CKPT } (T_1, T_2)>$$
$$<T_2, C, 15>$$
$$<\text{START } T_3>$$
$$<T_1, D, 20>$$
$$<\text{COMMIT } T_1>$$
$$<T_3, E, 25>$$
$$<\text{COMMIT } T_2>$$
$$<\text{END CKPT}>$$
$$<T_3, F, 30>$$

Figure 8.5: An undo log using nonquiescent checkpointing

Suppose that at this point there is a system crash. Examining the log from the end, we find that T_3 is an incomplete transaction and must be undone. The final log record tells us to restore database element F to the value 30. When we find the $<\text{END CKPT}>$ record, we know that all incomplete transactions began after the previous START CKPT. Scanning further back, we find the record $<T_3, E, 25>$, which tells us to restore E to value 25. Between that record, and the START CKPT there are no other transactions that started but did not commit, so no further changes to the database are made.

$$<\text{START } T_1>$$
$$<T_1, A, 5>$$
$$<\text{START } T_2>$$
$$<T_2, B, 10>$$
$$<\text{START CKPT } (T_1, T_2)>$$
$$<T_2, C, 15>$$
$$<\text{START } T_3>$$
$$<T_1, D, 20>$$
$$<\text{COMMIT } T_1>$$
$$<T_3, E, 25>$$

Figure 8.6: Undo log with a system crash during checkpointing

Now, let us consider a situation where the crash occurs during the checkpoint. Suppose the end of the log after the crash is as shown in Fig. 8.6. Scanning backwards, we identify T_3 and then T_2 as incomplete transactions and undo changes they have made. When we find the <START CKPT (T_1, T_2)> record, we know that the only other possible incomplete transaction is T_1. However, we have already scanned the <COMMIT T_1> record, so we know that T_1 is *not* incomplete. Also, we have already seen the <START T_3> record. Thus, we need only to continue backwards until we meet the START record for T_2, restoring database element B to value 10 as we go.   □

8.2.6 Exercises for Section 8.2

Exercise 8.2.1: Show the undo-log records for each of the transactions (call each T) of Exercise 8.1.1, assuming that initially $A = 5$ and $B = 10$.

Exercise 8.2.2: For each of the sequences of log records representing the actions of one transaction T, tell all the sequences of events that are legal according to the rules of undo logging, where the events of interest are the writing to disk of the blocks containing database elements, and the blocks of the log containing the update and commit records. You may assume that log records are written to disk in the order shown; i.e., it is not possible to write one log record to disk while a previous record is not written to disk.

* a) <START T>; <$T, A, 10$>; <$T, B, 20$>; <COMMIT T>;

  b) <START T>; <$T, A, 10$>; <$T, B, 20$>; <$T, C, 30$><COMMIT T>;

! **Exercise 8.2.3:** The pattern introduced in Exercise 8.2.2 can be extended to a transaction that writes new values for n database elements. How many legal sequences of events are there for such a transaction, if the undo-logging rules are obeyed?

Exercise 8.2.4: The following is a sequence of undo-log records written by two transactions T and U: <START T>; <$T, A, 10$>; <START U>; <$U, B, 20$>; <$T, C, 30$>; <$U, D, 40$>; <COMMIT U>; <$T, E, 50$>; <COMMIT T>. Describe the action of the recovery manager, including changes to both disk and the log, if there is a crash and the last log record to appear on disk is:

  a) <START U>.

* b) <COMMIT U>.

  c) <$T, E, 50$>.

  d) <COMMIT T>.

Exercise 8.2.5: For each of the situations described in Exercise 8.2.4, what values written by T and U *must* appear on disk? Which values *might* appear on disk?

*! **Exercise 8.2.6:** Suppose that the transaction U in Exercise 8.2.4 is changed so that the record $<U, D, 40>$ becomes $<U, A, 40>$. What is the effect on the disk value of A if there is a crash at some point during the sequence of events? What does this example say about the ability of logging by itself to preserve atomicity of transactions?

Exercise 8.2.7: Consider the following sequence of log records: $<$START $S>$; $<S, A, 60>$; $<$COMMIT $S>$; $<$START $T>$; $<T, A, 10>$; $<$START $U>$; $<U, B, 20>$; $<T, C, 30>$; $<$START $V>$; $<U, D, 40>$; $<V, F, 70>$; $<$COMMIT $U>$; $<T, E, 50>$; $<$COMMIT $T>$; $<V, B, 80>$; $<$COMMIT $V>$. Suppose that we begin a nonquiescent checkpoint immediately after one of the following log records has been written (in memory):

   a) $<S, A, 60>$.

 * b) $<T, A, 10>$.

   c) $<U, B, 20>$.

   d) $<U, D, 40>$.

   e) $<T, E, 50>$.

For each, tell:

   i. When the $<$CKPT$>$ record is written, and

   ii. For each possible point at which a crash could occur, how far back in the log we must look to find all possible incomplete transactions.

8.3 Redo Logging

While undo logging provides a natural and simple strategy for maintaining a log and recovering from a system failure, it is not the only possible approach. Undo logging has a potential problem that we cannot commit a transaction without first writing all its changed data to disk. Sometimes, we can save disk I/O's if we let changes to the database reside only in main memory for a while; as long as there is a log to fix things up in the event of a crash, it is safe to do so.

    The requirement for immediate backup of database elements to disk can be avoided if we use a logging mechanism called *redo logging*. The principal differences between redo and undo logging are:

  1. While undo logging cancels the effect of incomplete transactions and ignores committed ones during recovery, redo logging ignores incomplete transactions and repeats the changes made by committed transactions.

2. While undo logging requires us to write changed database elements to disk before the COMMIT log record reaches disk, redo logging requires that the COMMIT record appear on disk before any changed values reach disk.

3. While the old values of changed database elements are exactly what we need to recover when the undo rules U_1 and U_2 are followed, to recover using redo logging, we need the new values. Thus, redo-log records have a different meaning, although the same form, as undo-log records.

8.3.1 The Redo-Logging Rule

Redo logging represents changes to database elements by a log record that gives the new value, rather than the old value, which undo logging uses. These records look the same as for undo logging: $<T, X, v>$. The difference is that the meaning of this record is "transaction T wrote new value v for database element X." There is no indication of the old value of X in this record. Every time a transaction T modifies a database element X, a record of the form $<T, X, v>$ must be written to the log.

In addition, the order in which data and log entries reach disk can be described by a single "redo rule," called the *write-ahead logging rule*.

R_1: Before modifying any database element X on disk, it is necessary that all log records pertaining to this modification of X, including both the update record $<T, X, v>$ and the $<\text{COMMIT } T>$ record, must appear on disk.

Since the COMMIT record for a transaction can only be written to the log when the transaction completes, and therefore the commit record must follow all the update log records, we can summarize the effect of rule R_1 by asserting that when redo logging is in use, the order in which material associated with one transaction gets written to disk is:

1. The log records indicating changed database elements.

2. The COMMIT log record.

3. The changed database elements themselves.

Example 8.7: Let us consider the same transaction T as in Example 8.3. Figure 8.7 shows a possible sequence of events for this transaction.

The major differences between Figs. 8.7 and 8.3 are as follows. First, we note in lines (4) and (7) of Fig. 8.7 that the log records reflecting the changes have the new values of A and B, rather than the old values. Second, we see that the $<\text{COMMIT } T>$ record comes earlier, at step (8). Then, the log is flushed, so all log records involving the changes of transaction T appear on disk. Only then can the new values of A and B be written to disk. We show these values written immediately, at steps (10) and (11), although in practice they might occur much later.   □

Step	Action	t	M-A	M-B	D-A	D-B	Log
1)							$<$START $T>$
2)	READ(A,t)	8	8		8	8	
3)	t := t*2	16	8		8	8	
4)	WRITE(A,t)	16	16		8	8	$<T, A, 16>$
5)	READ(B,t)	8	16	8	8	8	
6)	t := t*2	16	16	8	8	8	
7)	WRITE(B,t)	16	16	16	8	8	$<T, B, 16>$
8)							$<$COMMIT $T>$
9)	FLUSH LOG						
10)	OUTPUT(A)	16	16	16	16	8	
11)	OUTPUT(B)	16	16	16	16	16	

Figure 8.7: Actions and their log entries using redo logging

8.3.2 Recovery With Redo Logging

An important consequence of the redo rule R_1 is that unless the log has a $<$COMMIT $T>$ record, we know that no changes to the database made by transaction T have been written to disk. Thus, incomplete transactions may be treated during recovery as if they had never occurred. However, the committed transactions present a problem, since we do not know which of their database changes have been written to disk. Fortunately, the redo log has exactly the information we need: the new values, which we may write to disk regardless of whether they were already there. To recover, using a redo log, after a system crash, we do the following.

1. Identify the committed transactions.

2. Scan the log forward from the beginning. For each log record $<T, X, v>$ encountered:

   (a) If T is not a committed transaction, do nothing.

   (b) If T is committed, write value v for database element X.

3. For each incomplete transaction T, write an $<$ABORT $T>$ record to the log and flush the log.

Example 8.8 : Let us consider the log written in Fig. 8.7 and see how recovery would be performed if the crash occurred after different steps in that sequence of actions.

1. If the crash occurs any time after step (9), then the $<$COMMIT $T>$ record has been flushed to disk. The recovery system identifies T as a committed

---

Order of Redo Matters

Since several committed transactions may have written new values for the same database element X, we have required that during a redo recovery, we scan the log from earliest to latest. Thus, the final value of X in the database will be the one written last, as it should be. Similarly, when describing undo recovery, we required that the log be scanned from latest to earliest. Thus, the final value of X will be the value that it had before any of the undone transactions changed it.

However, if the DBMS enforces atomicity, then we would not expect to find, in an undo log, two uncommitted transactions, each of which had written the same database element. In contrast, with redo logging we focus on the committed transactions, as these need to be redone. It is quite normal, for there to be two *committed* transactions, each of which changed the same database element at different times. Thus, order of redo is always important, while order of undo might not be if the right kind of concurrency control were in effect.

---

transaction. When scanning the log forward, the log records $<T, A, 16>$ and $<T, B, 16>$ cause the recovery manager to write values 16 for A and B. Notice that if the crash occurred between steps (10) and (11), then the write of A is redundant, but the write of B had not occurred and changing B to 16 is essential to restore the database state to consistency. If the crash occurred after step (11), then both writes are redundant but harmless.

2. If the crash occurs between steps (8) and (9), then although the record $<$COMMIT $T>$ was written to the log, it may not have gotten to disk (depending on whether the log was flushed for some other reason). If it did get to disk, then the recovery proceeds as in case (1), and if it did not get to disk, then recovery is as in case (3), below.

3. If the crash occurs prior to step (8), then $<$COMMIT $T>$ surely has not reached disk. Thus, T is treated as an incomplete transaction. No changes to A or B on disk are made on behalf of T, and eventually an $<$ABORT $T>$ record is written to the log.

□

8.3.3 Checkpointing a Redo Log

We can insert checkpoints into a redo log as well as an undo log. However, redo logs present a new problem: Since the changes of a committed transaction can be copied to disk much later than the time at which the transaction commits, we cannot limit our concern to transactions that are active at the time we decide to create a checkpoint. Regardless of whether the checkpoint is quiescent (transactions are not allowed to begin) or nonquiescent, the key action we must take between the start and end of the checkpoint is to write to disk all database elements that have been modified by committed transactions but not yet written to disk. To do so requires that the buffer manager keep track of which buffers are *dirty*, that is, they have been changed but not written to disk. It is also required to know which transactions modified which buffers.

On the other hand, we can complete the checkpoint without waiting for the active transactions to commit or abort, since they are not allowed to write their pages to disk at that time anyway. The steps to be taken to perform a nonquiescent checkpoint of a redo log are as follows:

1. Write a log record <START CKPT $(T_1, \ldots, T_k)$>, where $T_1, \ldots, T_k$ are all the active (uncommitted) transactions, and flush the log.

2. Write to disk all database elements that were written to buffers but not yet to disk by transactions that had already committed when the START CKPT record was written to the log.

3. Write an <END CKPT> record to the log and flush the log.

$$<\text{START } T_1>$$
$$<T_1, A, 5>$$
$$<\text{START } T_2>$$
$$<\text{COMMIT } T_1>$$
$$<T_2, B, 10>$$
$$<\text{START CKPT } (T_2)>$$
$$<T_2, C, 15>$$
$$<\text{START } T_3>$$
$$<T_3, D, 20>$$
$$<\text{END CKPT}>$$
$$<\text{COMMIT } T_2>$$
$$<\text{COMMIT } T_3>$$

Figure 8.8: A redo log

Example 8.9 : Figure 8.8 shows a possible redo log, in the middle of which a checkpoint occurs. When we start the checkpoint, only T_2 is active, but the value of A written by T_1 may have reached disk. If not, then we must copy A to disk before the checkpoint can end. We suggest the end of the checkpoint occurring after several other events have occurred: T_2 wrote a value for database element C, and a new transaction T_3 started and wrote a value of D. After the end of the checkpoint, the only things that happen are that T_2 and T_3 commit. □

8.3.4 Recovery With a Checkpointed Redo Log

As for an undo log, the insertion of records to mark the start and end of a checkpoint helps us limit our examination of the log when a recovery is necessary. Also as with undo logging, there are two cases, depending on whether the last checkpoint record is START or END.

- Suppose first that the last checkpoint record on the log before a crash is <END CKPT>. Now, we know that every value written by a transaction that committed before the corresponding <START CKPT $(T_1, \ldots, T_k)$> has had its changes written to disk, so we need not concern ourselves with recovering the effects of these transactions. However, any transaction that is either among the T_i's or that started after the beginning of the checkpoint can still have changes it made not yet migrated to disk, even though the transaction has committed. Thus, we must perform recovery as described in Section 8.3.2, but may limit our attention to the transactions that are either one of the T_i's mentioned in the last <START CKPT $(T_1, \ldots, T_k)$> or that started after that log record appeared in the log. In searching the log, we do not have to look further back than the earliest of the <START T_i> records. Notice, however, that these START records could appear prior to any number of checkpoints. Linking backwards all the log records for a given transaction helps us to find the necessary records, as it did for undo logging.

- Now, let us suppose that the last checkpoint record on the log is a <START CKPT $(T_1, \ldots, T_k)$> record. We cannot be sure that committed transactions prior to the start of this checkpoint had their changes written to disk. Thus, we must search back to the previous <END CKPT> record, find its matching <START CKPT $(S_1, \ldots, S_m)$> record,[5] and redo all those committed transactions that either started after that START CKPT or are among the S_i's.

Example 8.10 : Consider again the log of Fig. 8.8. If a crash occurs at the end, we search backwards, finding the <END CKPT> record. We thus know that it is sufficient to consider as candidates to redo all those transactions that either started after the <START CKPT (T_2)> record was written or that are on its list (i.e., T_2). Thus, our candidate set is $\{T_2, T_3\}$. We find the records <COMMIT T_2> and <COMMIT T_3>, so we know that each must be redone. We search the log as far back as the <START T_2> record, and find the update records <$T_2, B, 10$>, <$T_2, C, 15$>, and <$T_3, D, 20$> for the committed transactions. Since we don't know whether these changes reached disk, we rewrite the values 10, 15, and 20 for B, C, and D, respectively.

Now, suppose the crash occurred between the records <COMMIT T_2> and <COMMIT T_3>. The recovery is similar to the above, except that T_3 is no longer

---

[5]There is a small technicality that there could be a START CKPT record that, because of a previous crash, has no matching <END CKPT> record. That is why we must look not just for the previous START CKPT, but first for an <END CKPT> and then the previous START CKPT.

a committed transaction. Thus, its change $<T_3, D, 20>$ must *not* be redone, and no change is made to D during recovery, even though that log record is in the range of records that is examined. Also, we write an $<$ABORT $T_3>$ record to the log after recovery.

Finally, suppose that the crash occurs just prior to the $<$END CKPT$>$ record. in principal, we must search back to the next-to-last START CKPT record and get its list of active transactions. However, in this case there is no previous checkpoint, and we must go all the way to the beginning of the log. Thus, we identify T_1 as the only committed transaction, redo its action $<T_1, A, 5>$, and write records $<$ABORT $T_2>$ and $<$ABORT $T_3>$ to the log after recovery. □

Since transactions may be active during several checkpoints, it is convenient to include in the $<$START CKPT $(T_1, \ldots, T_k)>$ records not only the names of the active transactions, but pointers to the place on the log where they started. By doing so, we know when it is safe to delete early portions of the log. When we write an $<$END CKPT$>$, we know that we shall never need to look back further than the earliest of the $<$START $T_i>$ records for the active transactions T_i. Thus, anything prior to that START record may be deleted.

8.3.5 Exercises for Section 8.3

Exercise 8.3.1: Show the redo-log records for each of the transactions (call each T) of Exercise 8.1.1, assuming that initially $A = 5$ and $B = 10$.

Exercise 8.3.2: Repeat Exercise 8.2.2 for redo logging.

Exercise 8.3.3: Repeat Exercise 8.2.4 for redo logging.

Exercise 8.3.4: Repeat Exercise 8.2.5 for redo logging.

Exercise 8.3.5: Using the data of Exercise 8.2.7, answer for each of the positions (a) through (e) of that exercise:

i. At what points could the $<$END CKPT$>$ record be written, and

ii. For each possible point at which a crash could occur, how far back in the log we must look to find all possible incomplete transactions. Consider both the case that the $<$END CKPT$>$ record was or was not written prior to the crash.

8.4 Undo/Redo Logging

We have seen two different approaches to logging, differentiated by whether the log holds old values or new values when a database element is updated. Each has certain drawbacks:

- Undo logging requires that data be written to disk immediately after a transaction finishes, perhaps increasing the number of disk I/O's that need to be performed.

- On the other hand, redo logging requires us to keep all modified blocks in buffers until the transaction commits and the log records have been flushed, perhaps increasing the average number of buffers required by transactions.

- Both undo and redo logs may put contradictory requirements on how buffers are handled during a checkpoint, unless the database elements are complete blocks or sets of blocks. For instance, if a buffer contains one database element A that was changed by a committed transaction and another database element B that was changed in the same buffer by a transaction that has not yet had its COMMIT record written to disk, then we are required to copy the buffer to disk because of A but also forbidden to do so, because rule R_1 applies to B.

We shall now see a kind of logging called *undo/redo logging*, that provides increased flexibility to order actions, at the expense of maintaining more information on the log.

8.4.1   The Undo/Redo Rules

An undo/redo log has the same sorts of log records as the other kinds of log, with one exception. The update log record that we write when a database element changes value has four components. Record $<T, X, v, w>$ means that transaction T changed the value of database element X; its former value was v, and its new value is w. The constraints that an undo/redo logging system must follow are summarized by the following rule:

UR_1 Before modifying any database element X on disk because of changes made by some transaction T, it is necessary that the update record $<T, X, v, w>$ appear on disk.

Rule UR_1 for undo/redo logging thus enforces only the constraints enforced by *both* undo logging and redo logging. In particular, the $<\text{COMMIT } T>$ log record can precede or follow any of the changes to the database elements on disk.

Example 8.11 : Figure 8.9 is a variation in the order of the actions associated with the transaction T that we last saw in Example 8.7. Notice that the log records for updates now have both the old and the new values of A and B. In this sequence, we have written the $<\text{COMMIT } T>$ log record in the middle of the output of database elements A and B to disk. Step (10) could also have appeared before step (9) or after step (11).   □

Step	Action	t	M-A	M-B	D-A	D-B	Log
1)							$<$START $T>$
2)	READ(A,t)	8	8		8	8	
3)	t := t*2	16	8		8	8	
4)	WRITE(A,t)	16	16		8	8	$<T, A, 8, 16>$
5)	READ(B,t)	8	16	8	8	8	
6)	t := t*2	16	16	8	8	8	
7)	WRITE(B,t)	16	16	16	8	8	$<T, B, 8, 16>$
8)	FLUSH LOG						
9)	OUTPUT(A)	16	16	16	16	8	
10)							$<$COMMIT $T>$
11)	OUTPUT(B)	16	16	16	16	16	

Figure 8.9: A possible sequence of actions and their log entries using undo/redo logging

8.4.2 Recovery With Undo/Redo Logging

When we need to recover using an undo/redo log, we have the information in the update records either to undo a transaction T, by restoring the old values of the database elements that T changed, or to redo T by repeating the changes it has made. The undo/redo recovery policy is:

1. Redo all the committed transactions in the order earliest-first, and

2. Undo all the incomplete transactions in the order latest-first.

Notice that it is necessary for us to do both. Because of the flexibility allowed by undo/redo logging regarding the relative order in which COMMIT log records and the database changes themselves are copied to disk, we could have either a committed transaction with some or all of its changes not on disk, or an uncommitted transaction with some or all of its changes on disk.

Example 8.12: Consider the sequence of actions in Fig. 8.9. Here are the different ways that recovery would take place on the assumption that there is a crash at various points in the sequence.

1. Suppose the crash occurs after the $<$COMMIT $T>$ record is flushed to disk. Then T is identified as a committed transaction. We write the value 16 for both A and B to the disk. Because of the actual order of events, A already has the value 16, but B may not, depending on whether the crash occurred before or after step (11).

2. If the crash occurs prior to the $<$COMMIT $T>$ record reaching disk, then T is treated as an incomplete transaction. The previous values of A and

---

A Problem With Delayed Commitment

Like undo logging, a system using undo/redo logging can exhibit a behavior where a transaction appears to the user to have been completed (e.g., they booked an airline seat over the Web and disconnected), and yet because the <COMMIT T> record was not flushed to disk, a subsequent crash causes the transaction to be undone rather than redone. If this possibility is a problem, we suggest the use of an additional rule for undo/redo logging:

UR_2 A <COMMIT T> record must be flushed to disk as soon as it appears in the log.

For instance, we would add FLUSH LOG after step (10) of Fig. 8.9.

B, 8 in each case, are written to disk. If the crash occurs between steps (9) and (10), then the value of A was 16 on disk, and the restoration to value 8 is necessary. In this example, the value of B does not need to be undone, and if the crash occurs before step (9) then neither does the value of A. However, in general we cannot be sure whether restoration is necessary, so we always perform the undo operation.

□

8.4.3 Checkpointing an Undo/Redo Log

A nonquiescent checkpoint is somewhat simpler for undo/redo logging than for the other logging methods. We have only to do the following:

1. Write a <START CKPT $(T_1, \ldots, T_k)$> record to the log, where $T_1, \ldots, T_k$ are all the active transactions, and flush the log.

2. Write to disk all the buffers that are *dirty*; i.e., they contain one or more changed database elements. Unlike redo logging, we flush all buffers, not just those written by committed transactions.

3. Write an <END CKPT> record to the log, and flush the log.

Notice in connection with point (2) that, because of the flexibility undo/redo logging offers regarding when data reaches disk, we can tolerate the writing to disk of data written by incomplete transactions. Therefore we can tolerate database elements that are smaller than complete blocks and thus may share buffers. The only requirement we must make on transactions is:

- A transaction must not write any values (even to memory buffers) until it is certain not to abort.

Strange Behavior of Transactions During Recovery

The astute reader may have noticed that we did not specify whether undo's or redo's are done first during recovery using an undo/redo log. In fact, whether we perform the redo's or undo's first, we are open to the following situation: A transaction T that has committed and is redone read a value X written by some transaction U that has not committed and is undone. The problem is not whether we redo first, and leave X with its value prior to U, or we undo first and leave X with its value written by T. The situation makes no sense either way, because the final database state does not correspond to the effect of any sequence of atomic transactions.

In reality, the DBMS must do more than log changes. It must assure that such situations do not occur by some mechanisms. Chapter refconcurrency-ch talks about the means to isolate transactions like T and U, so the interaction between them through database element X cannot occur. In Section 10.1, we explicitly address means for preventing this situation where T reads a "dirty" value of X — one that has not been committed.

As we shall see in Section 10.1, this constraint is almost certainly needed anyway, in order to avoid inconsistent interactions between transactions. Notice that under redo logging, the above condition is not sufficient, since even if the transaction that wrote B is certain to commit, rule R_1 requires that the transaction's COMMIT record be written to disk before B is written to disk.

Example 8.13 : Figure 8.10 shows an undo/redo log analogous to the redo log of Fig. 8.8. We have only changed the update records, giving them an old value as well as a new value. For simplicity, we have assumed that in each case the old value is one less than the new value.

As in Example 8.9, T_2 is identified as the only active transaction when the checkpoint begins. Since this log is an undo/redo log, it is possible that T_2's new B-value 10 has been written to disk, which was not possible under redo logging. However, it is irrelevant whether or not that disk write has occurred. During the checkpoint, we shall surely flush B to disk if it is not already there, since we flush all dirty buffers. Likewise, we shall flush A, written by the committed transaction T_1, if it is not already on disk.

If the crash occurs at the end of this sequence of events, then T_2 and T_3 are identified as committed transactions. Transaction T_1 is prior to the checkpoint. Since we find the <END CKPT> record on the log, T_1 is correctly assumed to have both completed and had its changes written to disk. We therefore redo both T_2 and T_3, as in Example 8.9, and ignore T_1. However, when we redo a transaction such as T_2, we do not need to look prior to the <START CKPT (T_2)> record, even though T_2 was active at that time, because we know that T_2's changes prior to

$$<\text{START } T_1>$$
$$<T_1, A, 4, 5>$$
$$<\text{START } T_2>$$
$$<\text{COMMIT } T_1>$$
$$<T_2, B, 9, 10>$$
$$<\text{START CKPT } (T_2)>$$
$$<T_2, C, 14, 15>$$
$$<\text{START } T_3>$$
$$<T_3, D, 19, 20>$$
$$<\text{END CKPT}>$$
$$<\text{COMMIT } T_2>$$
$$<\text{COMMIT } T_3>$$

Figure 8.10: An undo/redo log

the start of the checkpoint were flushed to disk during the checkpoint.

For another instance, suppose the crash occurs just before the <COMMIT T_3> record is written to disk. Then we identify T_2 as committed but T_3 as incomplete. We redo T_2 by setting C to 15 on disk; it is not necessary to set B to 10 since we know that change reached disk before the <END CKPT>. However, unlike the situation with a redo log, we also undo T_3; that is, we set D to 19 on disk. If T_3 had been active at the start of the checkpoint, we would have had to look prior to the START-CKPT record to find if there were more actions by T_3 that may have reached disk and need to be undone.   □

8.4.4 Exercises for Section 8.4

Exercise 8.4.1: Show the undo/redo-log records for each of the transactions (call each T) of Exercise 8.1.1, assuming that initially $A = 5$ and $B = 10$.

Exercise 8.4.2: For each of the sequences of log records representing the actions of one transaction T, tell all the sequences of events that are legal according to the rules of undo logging, where the events of interest are the writing to disk of the blocks containing database elements, and the blocks of the log containing the update and commit records. You may assume that log records are written to disk in the order shown; i.e., it is not possible to write one log record to disk while a previous record is not written to disk.

* a) <START T>; <$T, A, 10, 11$>; <$T, B, 20, 21$>; <COMMIT T>;

  b) <START T>; <$T, A, 10, 21$>; <$T, B, 20, 21$>; <$T, C, 30, 31$><COMMIT T>;

Exercise 8.4.3: The following is a sequence of undo/redo-log records written by two transactions T and U: <START T>; <$T, A, 10, 11$>; <START U>;

$<U, B, 20, 21>$; $<T, C, 30, 31>$; $<U, D, 40, 41>$; $<$COMMIT $U>$; $<T, E, 50, 51>$; $<$COMMIT $T>$. Describe the action of the recovery manager, including changes to both disk and the log, if there is a crash and the last log record to appear on disk is:

a) $<$START $U>$.

* b) $<$COMMIT $U>$.

c) $<T, E, 50, 51>$.

d) $<$COMMIT $T>$.

Exercise 8.4.4: For each of the situations described in Exercise 8.4.3, what values written by T and U *must* appear on disk? Which values *might* appear on disk?

Exercise 8.4.5: Consider the following sequence of log records: $<$START $S>$; $<S, A, 60, 61>$; $<$COMMIT $S>$; $<$START $T>$; $<T, A, 61, 62>$; $<$START $U>$; $<U, B, 20, 21>$; $<T, C, 30, 31>$; $<$START $V>$; $<U, D, 40, 41>$; $<V, F, 70, 71>$; $<$COMMIT $U>$; $-<T, E, 50, 51>$; $<$COMMIT $T>$; $<V, B, 21, 22>$; $<$COMMIT $V>$. Suppose that we begin a nonquiescent checkpoint immediately after one of the following log records has been written (in memory):

a) $<S, A, 60, 61>$.

* b) $<T, A, 61, 62>$.

c) $<U, B, 20, 21>$.

d) $<U, D, 40, 41>$.

e) $<T, E, 50, 51>$.

For each, tell:

i. At what points could the $<$END CKPT$>$ record be written, and

ii. For each possible point at which a crash could occur, how far back in the log we must look to find all possible incomplete transactions. Consider both the case that the $<$END CKPT$>$ record was or was not written prior to the crash.

8.5 Protecting Against Media Failures

The log can protect us against system failures, where nothing is lost from disk, but temporary data in main memory is lost. However, as we discussed in Section 8.1.1, more serious failures involve the loss of one or more disks. We could, in principle, reconstruct the database from the log if:

a) The log were on a disk other than the disk(s) that hold the data,

b) The log were never thrown away after a checkpoint, and

c) The log were of the redo or the undo/redo type, so new values are stored on the log.

However, as we mentioned, the log will usually grow faster than the database, so it is not practical to keep the log forever.

8.5.1 The Archive

To protect against media failures, we are thus led to a solution involving *archiving* — maintaining a copy of the database separate from the database itself. If it were possible to shut down the database for a while, we could make a backup copy on some storage medium such as tape or optical disk, and store them remote from the database in some secure location. The backup would preserve the database state as it existed at this time, and if there were a media failure, the database could be restored to the state that existed then.

To advance to a more recent state, we could use the log, provided the log had been preserved since the archive copy was made, and the log itself survived the failure. In order to protect against losing the log, we could transmit a copy of the log, almost as soon as it is created, to the same remote site as the archive. Then, if the log as well as the data is lost, we can use the archive plus remotely stored log to recover, at least up to the point that the log was last transmitted to the remote site.

Since writing an archive is a lengthy process if the database is large, one generally tries to avoid copying the entire database at each archiving step. Thus, we distinguish between two levels of archiving:

1. A *full dump*, in which the entire database is copied.

2. An *incremental dump*, in which only those database elements changed since the previous full or incremental dump are copied.

It is also possible to have several levels of dump, with a full dump thought of as a "level 0" dump, and a "level i" dump copying everything changed since the last dump at level i or less.

We can restore the database from a full dump and its subsequent incremental dumps, in a process much like the way a redo or undo/redo log can be used to repair damage due to a system failure. We copy the full dump back to the database, and then in an earliest-first order, make the changes recorded by the later incremental dumps. Since incremental dumps will tend to involve only a small fraction of the data changed since the last dump, they take less space and can be done faster than full dumps.

Why Not Just Back Up the Log?

We might question the need for an archive, since we have to back up the log in a secure place anyway if we are not to be stuck at the state the database was in when the previous archive was made. While it may not be obvious, the answer lies in the typical rate of change of a large database. While only a small fraction of the database may change in a day, the changes, each of which must be logged, will over the course of a year become much larger than the database itself. If we never archived, then the log could never be truncated, and the cost of storing the log would soon exceed the cost of storing a copy of the database.

8.5.2 Nonquiescent Archiving

The problem with the simple view of archiving in Section 8.5.1 is that most databases cannot shut down for the period of time (possibly hours) that it takes to make a backup copy. We thus need to consider *nonquiescent archiving*, which is analogous to nonquiescent checkpointing. Recall that a nonquiescent checkpoint attempts to make a copy on the disk of the (approximate) database state that existed when the checkpoint started. We can rely on a small portion of the log around the time of the checkpoint to fix up any deviations from that database state, due to the fact that during the checkpoint, new transactions may have started and written to disk.

Similarly, a nonquiescent dump tries to make a copy of the database that existed when the dump began, but database activity may change many database elements on disk during the minutes or hours that the dump takes. If it is necessary to restore the database from the archive, the log entries made during the dump can be used to sort things out and get the database to a consistent state. The analogy is suggested by Fig. 8.11.

A nonquiescent dump copies the database elements in some fixed order, possibly while those elements are being changed by executing transactions. As a result, the value of a database element that is copied to the archive may or may not be the value that existed when the dump began. As long as the log for the duration of the dump is preserved, the discrepancies can be corrected from the log.

Example 8.14: For a very simple example, suppose that our database consists of four elements, A, B, C, and D, which have the values 1 through 4, respectively when the dump begins. During the dump, A is changed to 5, C is changed to 6, and B is changed to 7. However, the database elements are copied in order, and the sequence of events shown in Fig. 8.12 occurs. Then although the database at the beginning of the dump has values $(1, 2, 3, 4)$, and the database at the end of the dump has values $(5, 7, 6, 4)$, the copy of the

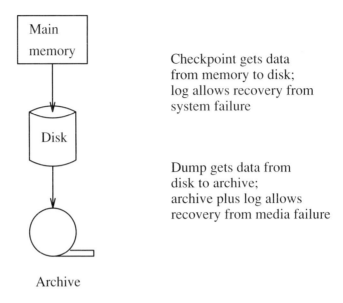

Checkpoint gets data
from memory to disk;
log allows recovery from
system failure

Dump gets data from
disk to archive;
archive plus log allows
recovery from media failure

Figure 8.11: The analogy between checkpoints and dumps

database in the archive has values $(1, 2, 6, 4)$, a database state that existed at no time during the dump. □

Disk	Archive
	Copy A
A := 5	
	Copy B
C := 6	
	Copy C
B := 7	
	Copy D

Figure 8.12: Events during a nonquiescent dump

In more detail, the process of making an archive can be broken into the following steps. We assume that the logging method is either redo or undo/redo; an undo log is not suitable for use with archiving.

1. Write a log record <START DUMP>.

2. Perform a checkpoint appropriate for whichever logging method is being used.

3. Perform a full or incremental dump of the data disk(s), as desired, making sure that the copy of the data has reached the secure, remote site.

4. Make sure that enough of the log has been copied to the secure, remote site that at least the prefix of the log up to and including the checkpoint in item (2) will survive a media failure of the database.

5. Write a log record <END DUMP>.

At the completion of the dump, it is safe to throw away log prior to the beginning of the checkpoint *previous* to the one performed in item (2) above.

Example 8.15 : Suppose that the changes to the simple database in Example 8.14 were caused by two transactions T_1 (which writes A and B) and T_2 (which writes C) that were active when the dump began. Figure 8.13 shows a possible undo/redo log of the events during the dump.

<START DUMP>
<START CKPT (T_1, T_2)>
<$T_1, A, 1, 5$>
<$T_2, C, 3, 6$>
<COMMIT T_2>
<$T_1, B, 2, 7$>
<END CKPT>
Dump completes
<END DUMP>

Figure 8.13: Log taken during a dump

Notice that we did not show T_1 committing. It would be unusual that a transaction remained active during the entire time a full dump was in progress, but that possibility doesn't affect the correctness of the recovery method that we discuss next. □

8.5.3 Recovery Using an Archive and Log

Suppose that a media failure occurs, and we must reconstruct the database from the most recent archive and whatever prefix of the log has reached the remote site and has not been lost in the crash. We perform the following steps:

1. Restore the database from the archive.

   (a) Find the most recent full dump and reconstruct the database from it (i.e., copy the archive into the database).

   (b) If there are later incremental dumps, modify the database according to each, earliest first.

2. Modify the database using the surviving log. Use the method of recovery appropriate to the log method being used.

Example 8.16: Suppose there is a media failure after the dump of Example 8.15 completes, and the log shown in Fig. 8.13 survives. Assume, to make the process interesting, that the surviving portion of the log does not include a <COMMIT T_1> record, although it does include the <COMMIT T_2> record shown in that figure. The database is first restored to the values in the archive, which is, for database elements A, B, C, and D, respectively, $(1, 2, 6, 4)$.

Now, we must look at the log. Since T_2 has completed, we redo the step that sets C to 6. In this example, C already had the value 6, but it might be that:

a) The archive for C was made before T_2 changed C, or

b) The archive actually captured a later value of C, which may or may not have been written by a transaction whose commit record survived. Later in the recovery, C will be restored to the value found in the archive *if* the transaction was committed.

Since T_1 presumably does not have a COMMIT record, we must undo T_1. We use the log records for T_1 to determine that A must be restored to value 1 and B to 2. It happens that they had these values in the archive, but the actual archive value could have been different because the modified A and/or B had been included in the archive.   □

8.5.4   Exercises for Section 8.5

Exercise 8.5.1: If a redo log, rather than an undo/redo log, were used in Examples 8.15 and 8.16:

a) What would the log look like?

*! b) If we had to recover using the archive and this log, what would be the consequence of T_1 not having committed?

c) What would be the state of the database after recovery?

8.6   Summary of Chapter 8

✦ *Transaction Management*: The two principal tasks of the transaction manager are assuring recoverability of database actions through logging, and assuring correct, concurrent behavior of transactions through the scheduler (not discussed in this chapter).

✦ *Database Elements*: The database is divided into elements, which are typically disk blocks, but could be tuples, extents of a class, or many other units. Database elements are the units for both logging and scheduling.

✦ *Logging*: A record of every important action of a transaction — beginning, changing a database element, committing, or aborting — is stored on a log. The log must be backed up on disk at a time that is related to when the corresponding database changes migrate to disk, but that time depends on the particular logging method used.

✦ *Recovery*: When a system crash occurs, the log is used to repair the database, restoring it to a consistent state.

✦ *Logging Methods*: The three principal methods for logging are undo, redo, and undo/redo, named for the way(s) that they are allowed to fix the database during recovery.

✦ *Undo Logging*: This method logs only the old value, each time a database element is changed. With undo logging, a new value of a database element can only be written to disk after the log record for the change has reached disk, but before the commit record for the transaction performing the change reaches disk. Recovery is done by restoring the old value for every uncommitted transaction.

✦ *Redo Logging*: Here, only the new value of database elements is logged. With this form of logging, values of a database element can only be written to disk after both the log record of its change and the commit record for its transaction have reached disk. Recovery involves rewriting the new value for every committed transaction.

✦ *Undo/Redo Logging* In this method, both old and new values are logged. Undo/redo logging is more flexible than the other methods, since it requires only that the log record of a change appear on the disk before the change itself does. There is no requirement about when the commit record appears. Recovery is effected by redoing committed transactions and undoing the uncommitted transactions.

✦ *Checkpointing*: Since all methods require, in principle, looking at the entire log from the dawn of history when a recovery is necessary, the DBMS must occasionally checkpoint the log, to assure that no log records prior to the checkpoint will be needed during a recovery. Thus, old log records can eventually be thrown away and its disk space reused.

✦ *Nonquiescent Checkpointing*: To avoid shutting down the system while a checkpoint is made, techniques associated with each logging method allow the checkpoint to be made while the system is in operation and database changes are occurring. The only cost is that some log records prior to the nonquiescent checkpoint may need to be examined during recovery.

✦ *Archiving*: While logging protects against system failures involving only the loss of main memory, archiving is necessary to protect against failures where the contents of disk are lost. Archives are copies of the database stored in a safe place.

✦ *Incremental Backups*: Instead of copying the entire database to an archive periodically, a single complete backup can be followed by several incremental backups, where only the changed data is copied to the archive.

✦ *Nonquiescent Archiving*: Techniques for making a backup of the data while the database is in operation exist. They involve making log records of the beginning and end of the archiving, as well as performing a checkpoint for the log during the archiving.

✦ *Recovery From Media Failures*: When a disk is lost, it may be restored by starting with a full backup of the database, modifying it according to any later incremental backups, and finally recovering to a consistent database state by using an archived copy of the log.

8.7   References for Chapter 8

The major textbook on all aspects of transaction processing, including logging and recovery, is by Gray and Reuter [5]. This book was partially fed by some informal notes on transaction processing by Jim Gray [3] that were widely circulated; the latter, along with [4] and [8] are the primary sources for much of the logging and recovery technology.

[2] is an earlier, more concise description of transaction-processing technology. [7] is a more recent treatment of the subject.

Two early surveys, [1] and [6] both represent much of the fundamental work in recovery and organized the subject in the undo-redo-undo/redo tricotomy that we followed here.

1. P. A. Bernstein, N. Goodman, and V. Hadzilacos, "Recovery algorithms for database systems," *Proc. 1983 IFIP Congress*, North Holland, Amsterdam, pp. 799–807.

2. P. A. Bernstein, V. Hadzilacos, and N. Goodman, *Concurrency Control and Recovery in Database Systems*, Addison-Wesley, Reading MA, 1987.

3. J. N. Gray, "Notes on database operating systems," in *Operating Systems: an Advanced Course*, pp. 393–481, Springer-Verlag, 1978.

4. J. N. Gray, P. R. McJones, and M. Blasgen, "The recovery manager of the System R database manager," *Computing Surveys* **13**:2 (1981), pp. 223–242.

5. J. N. Gray and A. Reuter, *Transaction Processing: Concepts and Techniques*, Morgan-Kaufmann, San Francisco, 1993.

6. T. Haerder and A. Reuter, "Principles of transaction-oriented database recovery — a taxonomy," *Computing Surveys* **15**:4 (1983), pp. 287–317.

7. V. Kumar and M. Hsu, *Recovery Mechanisms in Database Systems*, Prentice-Hall, Englewood Cliffs NJ, 1998.

8. C. Mohan, D. J. Haderle, B. G. Lindsay, H. Pirahesh, and P. Schwarz, "ARIES: a transaction recovery method supporting fine-granularity locking and partial rollbacks using write-ahead logging," *ACM Trans. on Database Systems* **17**:1 (1992), pp. 94–162.

Chapter 9

Concurrency Control

Interactions among transactions can cause the database state to become inconsistent, even when the transactions individually preserve correctness of the state, and there is no system failure. Thus, the order in which the individual steps of different transactions occur needs to be regulated in some manner. The function of controlling these steps is given to the *scheduler* component of the DBMS, and the general process of assuring that transactions preserve consistency when executing simultaneously is called *concurrency control*. The role of the scheduler is suggested by Fig. 9.1.

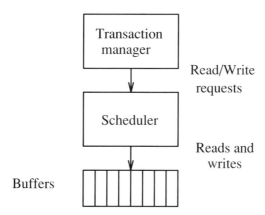

Figure 9.1: The scheduler takes read/write requests from transactions and either executes them in buffers or delays them

As transactions request reads and writes of database elements, these requests are passed to the scheduler. In most situations, the scheduler will execute the reads and writes directly, first calling on the buffer manager if the desired database element is not in a buffer. However, in some situations, it is not safe for the request to be executed immediately. The scheduler must delay the request; in some concurrency-control techniques, the scheduler may even abort the transaction that issued the request.

We begin by studying how to assure that concurrently executing transactions preserve correctness of the database state. The abstract requirement is called *serializability*, and there is an important, stronger condition called *conflict-serializability* that most schedulers actually enforce. We consider the most important techniques for implementing schedulers: locking, timestamping, and validation.

Our study of lock-based schedulers includes the important concept of "two-phase locking," which is a requirement widely used to assure serializability of schedules. We also find that there are many different sets of lock modes that a scheduler can use, each with a different application. Among the locking schemes we study are those for nested and tree-structured collections of lockable elements.

9.1 Serial and Serializable Schedules

To begin our study of concurrency control, we must examine the conditions under which a collection of concurrently executing transactions will preserve consistency of the database state. Our fundamental assumption, which we called the "correctness principle" in Section 8.1.3, is: every transaction, if executed in isolation (without any other transactions running concurrently), will transform any consistent state to another consistent state. However, in practice, transactions often run concurrently with other transactions, so the correctness principle doesn't apply directly. Thus, we need to consider "schedules" of actions that can be guaranteed to produce the same result as if the transactions executed one-at-a-time. The major theme of this entire chapter is methods for forcing transactions to execute concurrently only in ways that make them appear to run one-at-a-time.

9.1.1 Schedules

A *schedule* is a time-ordered sequence of the important actions taken by one or more transactions. When studying concurrency control, the important read and write actions take place in the main-memory buffers, not the disk. That is, a database element A that is brought to a buffer by some transaction T may be read or written in that buffer not only by T but by other transactions that access A. Recall from Section 8.1.4 that the READ and WRITE actions first call INPUT to get a database element from disk if it is not already in a buffer, but otherwise READ and WRITE actions access the element in the buffer directly. Thus, only the READ and WRITE actions, and their orders, are important when considering concurrency, and we shall ignore the INPUT and OUTPUT actions.

Example 9.1: Let us consider two transactions and the effect on the database when their actions are executed in certain orders. The important actions of the

T_1	T_2
READ(A,t)	READ(A,s)
t := t+100	s := s*2
WRITE(A,t)	WRITE(A,s)
READ(B,t)	READ(B,s)
t := t+100	s := s*2
WRITE(B,t)	WRITE(B,s)

Figure 9.2: Two transactions

transactions T_1 and T_2 are shown in Fig. 9.2. The variables t and s are local variables of T_1 and T_2, respectively; they are *not* database elements.

We shall assume that the only consistency constraint on the database state is that $A = B$. Since T_1 adds 100 to both A and B, and T_2 multiplies both A and B by 2, we know that each transaction, run in isolation, will preserve consistency. □

T_1	T_2	A	B
		25	25
READ(A,t)			
t := t+100			
WRITE(A,t)		125	
READ(B,t)			
t := t+100			
WRITE(B,t)			125
	READ(A,s)		
	s := s*2		
	WRITE(A,s)	250	
	READ(B,s)		
	s := s*2		
	WRITE(B,s)		250

Figure 9.3: Serial schedule in which T_1 precedes T_2

9.1.2 Serial Schedules

We say a schedule is *serial* if its actions consist of all the actions of one transaction, then all the actions of another transaction, and so on, with no mixing of the actions. More precisely, a schedule S is serial if for any two transactions T and T', if any action of T precedes any action of T', then all actions of T precede all actions of T'.

T_1	T_2	A	B
		25	25
	READ(A,s)		
	s := s*2		
	WRITE(A,s)	50	
	READ(B,s)		
	s := s*2		
	WRITE(B,s)		50
READ(A,t)			
t := t+100			
WRITE(A,t)		150	
READ(B,t)			
t := t+100			
WRITE(B,t)			150

Figure 9.4: Serial schedule in which T_2 precedes T_1

Example 9.2: For the transactions of Fig. 9.2, there are two serial schedules, one in which T_1 precedes T_2 and the other in which T_2 precedes T_1. Figure 9.3 shows the sequence of events when T_1 precedes T_2, and the initial state is $A = B = 25$. We shall take the convention that when displayed vertically, time proceeds down the page. Also, the values of A and B shown refer to their values in main-memory buffers, not necessarily to their values on disk.

Then, Fig. 9.4 shows another serial schedule in which T_2 precedes T_1; the initial state is again assumed to be $A = B = 25$. Notice that the final values of A and B are different for the two schedules; they both have value 250 when T_1 goes first and 150 when T_2 goes first. However, the final result is not the central issue, as long as consistency is preserved. In general, we would not expect the final state of a database to be independent of the order of transactions. □

We can represent a serial schedule as in Fig. 9.3 or Fig. 9.4, listing each of the actions in the order they occur. However, since the order of actions in a serial schedule depends only on the order of the transactions themselves, we shall sometimes represent a serial schedule by the list of transactions. Thus, the schedule of Fig. 9.3 is represented (T_1, T_2), and that of Fig. 9.4 is (T_2, T_1).

9.1.3 Serializable Schedules

The correctness principle for transactions tells us that every serial schedule will preserve consistency of the database state. But are there any other schedules that also are guaranteed to preserve consistency? There are, as the following example shows. In general, we say a schedule is *serializable* if its effect on the database state is the same as that of some serial schedule, regardless of what the initial state of the database is.

T_1	T_2	A	B
		25	25
READ(A,t)			
t := t+100			
WRITE(A,t)		125	
	READ(A,s)		
	s := s*2		
	WRITE(A,s)	250	
READ(B,t)			
t := t+100			
WRITE(B,t)			125
	READ(B,s)		
	s := s*2		
	WRITE(B,s)		250

Figure 9.5: A serializable, but not serial, schedule

Example 9.3 : Figure 9.5 shows a schedule of the transactions from Example 9.1 that is serializable but not serial. In this schedule, T_2 acts on A after T_1 does, but before T_1 acts on B. However, we see that the effect of the two transactions scheduled in this manner is the same as for the serial schedule (T_1, T_2) that we saw in Fig. 9.3. To convince ourselves of the truth of this statement, we must consider not only the effect from the database state $A = B = 25$, which we show in Fig. 9.5, but from any consistent database state. Since all consistent database states have $A = B = c$ for some constant c, it is not hard to deduce that in the schedule of Fig. 9.5, both A and B will be left with the value $2(c + 100)$, and thus consistency is preserved from any consistent state.

On the other hand, consider the schedule of Fig. 9.6. Clearly it is not serial, but more significantly, it is not serializable. The reason we can be sure it is not serializable is that it takes the consistent state $A = B = 25$ and leaves the database in an inconsistent state, where $A = 250$ and $B = 150$. Notice that in this order of actions, where T_1 operates on A first, but T_2 operates on B first, we have in effect applied different computations to A and B, that is $A := 2(A + 100)$ versus $B := 2B + 100$. The schedule of Fig. 9.6 is the sort of behavior that concurrency control mechanisms must avoid.   □

9.1.4   The Effect of Transaction Semantics

In our study of serializability so far, we have considered in detail the operations performed by the transactions, to determine whether or not a schedule is serializable. The details of the transactions do matter, as we can see from the following example.

T_1	T_2	A	B
		25	25
READ(A,t)			
t := t+100			
WRITE(A,t)		125	
	READ(A,s)		
	s := s*2		
	WRITE(A,s)	250	
	READ(B,s)		
	s := s*2		
	WRITE(B,s)		50
READ(B,t)			
t := t+100			
WRITE(B,t)			150

Figure 9.6: A nonserializable schedule

T_1	T_2	A	B
		25	25
READ(A,t)			
t := t+100			
WRITE(A,t)		125	
	READ(A,s)		
	s := s*1		
	WRITE(A,s)	125	
	READ(B,s)		
	s := s*1		
	WRITE(B,s)		25
READ(B,t)			
t := t+100			
WRITE(B,t)			125

Figure 9.7: A schedule that is serializable only because of the detailed behavior of the transactions

Example 9.4: Consider the schedule of Fig. 9.7, which differs from Fig. 9.6 only in the computation that T_2 performs. That is, instead of multiplying A and B by 2, T_2 multiplies them by 1.[1] Now, the values of A and B at the end of this schedule are equal, and one can easily check that regardless of the consistent initial state, the final state will be consistent. In fact, the final state is the one that results from either of the serial schedules (T_1, T_2) or (T_2, T_1). □

Unfortunately, it is not realistic for the scheduler to concern itself with the details of computation undertaken by transactions. Since transactions often involve code written in a general-purpose programming language as well as SQL or other high-level-language statements, it is sometimes very hard to answer questions like "does this transaction multiply A by a constant other than 1?" However, the scheduler does get to see the read and write requests from the transactions, so it can know what database elements each transaction reads, and what elements it *might* change. To simplify the job of the scheduler, it is conventional to assume that:

- Any database element A that a transaction T writes is given a value that depends on the database state in such a way that no arithmetic coincidences occur.

Put another way, if there is something that T could have done to A that will make the database state inconsistent, then T will do that. We shall make this assumption more precise in Section 9.2, when we talk about sufficient conditions to guarantee serializability.

9.1.5 A Notation for Transactions and Schedules

If we accept that the exact computations performed by a transaction can be arbitrary, then we do not need to consider the details of local computation steps such as t := t+100. Only the reads and writes performed by the transaction matter. Thus, we shall represent transactions and schedules by a shorthand notation, in which the actions are $r_T(X)$ and $w_T(X)$, meaning that transaction T reads, or respectively writes, database element X. Moreover, since we shall usually name our transactions $T_1, T_2, \ldots$, we adopt the convention that $r_i(X)$ and $w_i(X)$ are synonyms for $r_{T_i}(X)$ and $w_{T_i}(X)$, respectively.

Example 9.5: The transactions of Fig. 9.2 can be written:

T_1: $r_1(A)$; $w_1(A)$; $r_1(B)$; $w_1(B)$;

---

[1] One might reasonably ask why a transaction would behave that way, but let us ignore the matter for the sake of an example. In fact, there are many plausible transactions we could substitute for T_2 that would leave A and B unchanged; for instance, T_2 might simply read A and B and print their values. Or, T_2 might ask the user for some data, compute a factor F with which to multiply A and B, and find for some user inputs that $F = 1$.

T_2: $r_2(A)$; $w_2(A)$; $r_2(B)$; $w_2(B)$;

Notice that there is no mention of the local variables t and s anywhere, and no indication of what has happened to A and B after they were read. Intuitively, we shall "assume the worst," regarding the ways in which these database elements change.

As another example, consider the serializable schedule of T_1 and T_2 from Fig. 9.5. This schedule is written:

$$r_1(A); w_1(A); r_2(A); w_2(A); r_1(B); w_1(B); r_2(B); w_2(B);$$

□

To make the notation precise:

1. An *action* is an expression of the form $r_i(X)$ or $w_i(X)$, meaning that transaction T_i reads or writes, respectively, the database element X.

2. A *transaction* T_i is a sequence of actions with subscript i.

3. A *schedule* S of a set of transactions $\mathcal{T}$ is a sequence of actions, in which for each transaction T_i in $\mathcal{T}$, the actions of T_i appear in S in the same order that they appear in the definition of T_i itself. We say that S is an *interleaving* of the actions of the transactions of which it is composed.

For instance, the schedule of Example 9.5 has all the actions with subscript 1 appearing in the same order that they have in the definition of T_1, and the actions with subscript 2 appear in the same order that they appear in the definition of T_2.

9.1.6 Exercises for Section 9.1

* **Exercise 9.1.1:** A transaction T_1, executed by an airline-reservation system, performs the following steps:

   i. The customer is queried for a desired flight time and cities. Information about the desired flights is located in database elements (perhaps disk blocks) A and B, which the system retrieves from disk.

   ii. The customer is told about the options, and selects a flight whose data, including the number of reservations for that flight is in B. A reservation on that flight is made for the customer.

   iii. The customer selects a seat for the flight; seat data for the flight is in database element C.

   iv. The system gets the customer's credit-card number and appends the bill for the flight to a list of bills in database element D.

    v. The customer's phone and flight data is added to another list on database element E for a fax to be sent confirming the flight.

Express transaction T_1 as a sequence of r and w actions.

*! Exercise 9.1.2: If two transactions consist of 4 and 6 actions, respectively, how many interleavings of these transactions are there?

9.2 Conflict-Serializability

We shall now develop a condition that is sufficient to assure that a schedule is serializable. Schedulers in commercial systems generally assure this stronger condition, which we shall call "conflict-serializability," when they want to assure that transactions behave in a serializable manner. It is based on the idea of a *conflict*: a pair of consecutive actions in a schedule such that, if their order is interchanged, then the behavior of at least one of the transactions involved can change.

9.2.1 Conflicts

To begin, let us observe that most pairs of actions do *not* conflict in the sense above. In what follows, we assume that T_i and T_j are different transactions; i.e., $i \neq j$.

1. $r_i(X); r_j(Y)$ is never a conflict, even if $X = Y$. The reason is that neither of these steps change any value.

2. $r_i(X); w_j(Y)$ is not a conflict provided $X \neq Y$. The reason is that should T_j write Y before T_i reads X, the value of X is not changed. Also, the read of X by T_i has no effect on T_j, so it does not affect the value T_j writes for Y.

3. $w_i(X); r_j(Y)$ is not a conflict if $X \neq Y$, for the same reason as (2).

4. Also similarly, $w_i(X); w_j(Y)$ is not a conflict as long as $X \neq Y$.

On the other hand, there are three situations where we may not swap the order of actions:

a) Two actions of the same transaction, e.g., $r_i(X); w_i(Y)$, conflict. The reason is that the order of actions of a single transaction are fixed and may not be reordered by the DBMS.

b) Two writes of the same database element by different transactions conflict. That is, $w_i(X); w_j(X)$ is a conflict. The reason is that as written, the value of X remains afterward as whatever T_j computed it to be. If we swap the order, as $w_j(X); w_i(X)$, then we leave X with the value computed by

T_i. Our assumption of "no coincidences" tells us that the values written by T_i and T_j might be different, and therefore will be different for some initial state of the database.

c) A read and a write of the same database element by different transactions also conflict. That is, $r_i(X); w_j(X)$ is a conflict, and so is $w_i(X); r_j(X)$. If we move $w_j(X)$ ahead of $r_i(X)$, then the value of X read by T_i will be that written by T_j, which we assume is not necessarily the same as the previous value of X. Thus, swapping the order of $r_i(X)$ and $w_j(X)$ affects the value T_i reads for X and could therefore affect what T_i does.

The conclusion we draw is that any two actions of different transactions may be swapped in order, unless

1. They involve the same database element, and

2. At least one is a write.

Extending this idea, we may take any schedule and make as many nonconflicting swaps as we wish, with the goal of turning the schedule into a serial schedule. If we can do so, then the original schedule is serializable, because its effect on the database state remains the same as we perform each of the nonconflicting swaps.

We say that two schedules are *conflict-equivalent* if they can be turned one into the other by a sequence of nonconflicting swaps of adjacent actions. We shall call a schedule *conflict-serializable* if it is conflict-equivalent to a serial schedule. Note that conflict-serializability is a sufficient condition for serializability; i.e., a conflict-serializable schedule is a serializable schedule. Conflict-serializability is not required for a schedule to be serializable, but it is the condition that the schedulers in commercial systems generally use when they need to guarantee serializability.

Example 9.6 : Consider the schedule

$$r_1(A); w_1(A); r_2(A); w_2(A); r_1(B); w_1(B); r_2(B); w_2(B);$$

from Example 9.5. We claim this schedule is conflict-serializable. Figure 9.8 shows the sequence of swaps in which this schedule is converted to the serial schedule (T_1, T_2), where all of T_1's actions precede all those of T_2. We have underlined the pair of adjacent actions about to be swapped at each step.   □

9.2.2   Precedence Graphs and a Test for Conflict-Serializability

It is relatively simple to examine a schedule S and decide whether or not it is conflict-serializable. The idea is that when there are conflicting actions that

$$r_1(A); \; w_1(A); \; r_2(A); \; \underline{w_2(A)}; \; r_1(B); \; w_1(B); \; r_2(B); \; w_2(B);$$
$$r_1(A); \; w_1(A); \; r_2(A); \; \underline{r_1(B)}; \; w_2(A); \; w_1(B); \; r_2(B); \; w_2(B);$$
$$r_1(A); \; w_1(A); \; \underline{r_1(B)}; \; \underline{r_2(A)}; \; w_2(A); \; w_1(B); \; r_2(B); \; w_2(B);$$
$$r_1(A); \; w_1(A); \; r_1(B); \; r_2(A); \; \underline{w_1(B)}; \; \underline{w_2(A)}; \; r_2(B); \; w_2(B);$$
$$r_1(A); \; w_1(A); \; r_1(B); \; \underline{w_1(B)}; \; \underline{r_2(A)}; \; w_2(A); \; r_2(B); \; w_2(B);$$

Figure 9.8: Converting a conflict-serializable schedule to a serial schedule by swaps of adjacent actions

appear anywhere in S, the transactions performing those actions must appear in the same order in any conflict-equivalent serial schedule as the actions appear in S. Thus, conflicting pairs of actions put constraints on the order of transactions in the hypothetical, conflict-equivalent serial schedule. If these constraints are not contradictory, we can find a conflict-equivalent serial schedule. If they are contradictory, we know that no such serial schedule exists.

Given a schedule S, involving transactions T_1 and T_2, perhaps among other transactions, we say that T_1 *takes precedence over* T_2, written $T_1 <_S T_2$, if there are actions A_1 of T_1 and A_2 of T_2, such that:

1. A_1 is ahead of A_2 in S,

2. Both A_1 and A_2 involve the same database element, and

3. At least one of A_1 and A_2 is a write action.

Notice that these are exactly the conditions under which we cannot swap the order of A_1 and A_2. Thus, A_1 will appear before A_2 in any schedule that is conflict-equivalent to S. As a result, if one of these schedules is a serial schedule, then it must have T_1 before T_2.

We can summarize these precedences in a *precedence graph*. The nodes of the precedence graph are the transactions of a schedule S. When the transactions are T_i for various i, we shall label the node for T_i by only the integer i. There is an arc from node i to node j if $T_i <_S T_j$.

Example 9.7: The following schedule S involves three transactions, T_1, T_2, and T_3.

S: $r_2(A); \; r_1(B); \; w_2(A); \; r_3(A); \; w_1(B); \; w_3(A); \; r_2(B); \; w_2(B);$

If we look at the actions involving A, we find several reasons why $T_2 <_S T_3$. For example, $r_2(A)$ comes ahead of $w_3(A)$ in S, and $w_2(A)$ comes ahead of both $r_3(A)$ and $w_3(A)$. Any one of these three observations is sufficient to justify the arc in the precedence graph of Fig. 9.9 from 2 to 3.

Similarly, if we look at the actions involving B, we find that there are several reasons why $T_1 <_S T_2$. For instance, the action $r_1(B)$ comes before $w_2(B)$.

Why Conflict-Serializability is not Necessary for Serializability

One example has already been seen in Fig. 9.7. We saw there how the particular computation performed by T_2 made the schedule serializable. However, the schedule of Fig. 9.7 is not conflict-serializable, because A is written first by T_1 and B is written first by T_2. Since neither the writes of A nor the writes of B can be reordered, there is no way we can get all the actions of T_1 ahead of all actions of T_2, or vice-versa.

However, there are examples of serializable but not conflict-serializable schedules that do not depend on the computations performed by the transactions. For instance, consider three transactions T_1, T_2, and T_3 that each write a value for X. T_1 and T_2 also write values for Y before they write values for X. One possible schedule, which happens to be serial, is

S_1: $w_1(Y)$; $w_1(X)$; $w_2(Y)$; $w_2(X)$; $w_3(X)$

S_1 leaves X with the value written by T_3 and Y with the value written by T_2. However, so does the schedule

S_2: $w_1(Y)$; $w_2(Y)$; $w_2(X)$; $w_1(X)$; $w_3(X)$

Intuitively, the values of X written by T_1 and T_2 have no effect, since T_3 overwrites their values. Thus S_1 and S_2 leave both X and Y with the same value. Since S_1 is serial, and S_2 has the same effect as S_1 on any database state, we know that S_2 is serializable. However, since we cannot swap $w_1(Y)$ with $w_2(Y)$, and we cannot swap $w_1(X)$ with $w_2(X)$, therefore we cannot convert S_2 to any serial schedule by swaps. That is, S_2 is serializable, but not conflict-serializable.

Thus, the precedence graph for S also has an arc from 1 to 2. However, these are the only arcs we can justify from the order of actions in schedule S.   □

There is a simple rule for telling whether a schedule S is conflict-serializable:

- Construct the precedence graph for S and ask if there are any cycles.

If so, then S is not conflict-serializable. But if the graph is acyclic, then S is conflict-serializable, and moreover, any topological order of the nodes[2] is a conflict-equivalent serial order.

---

[2]A *topological order* of an acyclic graph is any order of the nodes such that for every arc $a \rightarrow b$, node a precedes node b in the topological order. We can find a topological order for any acyclic graph by repeatedly removing nodes that have no predecessors among the remaining nodes.

Figure 9.9: The precedence graph for the schedule S of Example 9.7

Example 9.8: Figure 9.9 is acyclic, so the schedule S of Example 9.7 is conflict-serializable. There is only one order of the nodes or transactions consistent with the arcs of that graph: (T_1, T_2, T_3). Notice that it is indeed possible to convert S into the schedule in which all actions of each of the three transactions occur in this order; this serial schedule is:

S': $r_1(B)$; $w_1(B)$; $r_2(A)$; $w_2(A)$; $r_2(B)$; $w_2(B)$; $r_3(A)$; $w_3(A)$;

To see that we can get from S to S' by swaps of adjacent elements, first notice we can move $r_1(B)$ ahead of $r_2(A)$ without conflict. Then, by three swaps we can move $w_1(B)$ just after $r_1(B)$, because each of the intervening actions involves A and not B. We can then move $r_2(B)$ and $w_2(B)$ to a position just after $w_2(A)$, moving through only actions involving A; the result is S'. □

Example 9.9: Consider the schedule

S_1: $r_2(A)$; $r_1(B)$; $w_2(A)$; $r_2(B)$; $r_3(A)$; $w_1(B)$; $w_3(A)$; $w_2(B)$;

which differs from S only in that action $r_2(B)$ has been moved forward three positions. Examination of the actions involving A still give us only the precedence $T_2 <_{S_1} T_3$. However, when we examine B we get not only $T_1 <_{S_1} T_2$ [because $r_1(B)$ and $w_1(B)$ appear before $w_2(B)$], but also $T_2 <_{S_1} T_1$ [because $r_2(B)$ appears before $w_1(B)$]. Thus, we have the precedence graph of Fig. 9.10 for schedule S_1.

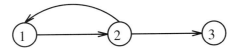

Figure 9.10: A cyclic precedence graph; its schedule is not conflict-serializable

This graph evidently has a cycle. We conclude that S_1 is not conflict-serializable. Intuitively, any conflict-equivalent serial schedule would have to have T_1 both ahead of and behind T_2, so therefore no such schedule exists. □

9.2.3 Why the Precedence-Graph Test Works

As we have seen, a cycle in the precedence graph puts too many constraints on the order of transactions in a hypothetical conflict-equivalent serial schedule. That is, if there is a cycle involving n transactions $T_1 \to T_2 \to \ldots \to T_n \to T_1$, then in the hypothetical serial order, the actions of T_1 must precede those of

T_2, which precede those of T_3, and so on, up to T_n. But the actions of T_n, which therefore come after those of T_1, are also required to precede those of T_1 because of the arc $T_n \to T_1$. Thus, we conclude that if there is a cycle in the precedence graph, then the schedule is not conflict-serializable.

The converse is a bit harder. We must show that whenever the precedence graph has no cycles, then we can reorder the schedule's actions using legal swaps of adjacent actions, until the schedule becomes a serial schedule. If we can do so, then we have our proof that every schedule with an acyclic precedence graph is conflict-serializable. The proof is an induction on the number of transactions involved in the schedule.

BASIS: If $n = 1$, i.e., there is only one transaction in the schedule, then the schedule is already serial, and therefore surely conflict-serializable.

INDUCTION: Let the schedule S consist of the actions of n transactions

$$T_1, T_2, \ldots, T_n$$

We suppose that S has an acyclic precedence graph. If a finite graph is acyclic, then there is at least one node that has no arcs in; let the node i corresponding to transaction T_i be such a node. Since there are no arcs into node i, there can be no action A in S that:

1. Involves any transaction T_j other than T_i,

2. Precedes some action of T_i, and

3. Conflicts with that action.

For if there were, we should have put an arc from node j to node i in the precedence graph.

It is thus possible to swap all the actions of T_i, keeping them in order, but moving them to the front of S. The schedule has now taken the form

$$(\text{Actions of } T_i)(\text{Actions of the other } n - 1 \text{ transactions})$$

Let us now consider the tail of S — the actions of all transactions other than T_i. Since these actions maintain the same relative order that they did in S, the precedence graph for the tail is the same as the precedence graph for S, except that the node for T_i and any arcs out of that node are missing.

Since the original precedence graph was acyclic, and deleting nodes and arcs cannot make it cyclic, we conclude that the tail's precedence graph is acyclic. Moreover, since the tail involves $n - 1$ transactions, the inductive hypothesis applies to it. Thus, we know we can reorder the actions of the tail using legal swaps of adjacent actions to turn it into a serial schedule. Now, S itself has been turned into a serial schedule, with the actions of T_i first and the actions of the other transactions following in some serial order. The induction is complete, and we conclude that every schedule with an acyclic precedence graph is conflict-serializable.

9.2.4 Exercises for Section 9.2

Exercise 9.2.1: Below are two transactions, described in terms of their effect on two database elements A and B, which we may assume are integers.

T_1: READ(A,t); t:=t+2; WRITE(A,t); READ(B,t); t:=t*3; WRITE(B,t);

T_2: READ(B,s); s:=s*2; WRITE(B,s); READ(A,s); s:=s+3; WRITE(A,s);

We assume that, whatever consistency constraints there are on the database, these transactions preserve them in isolation. Note that $A = B$ is *not* the consistency constraint.

a) It turns out that both serial orders have the same effect on the database; that is, (T_1, T_2) and (T_2, T_1) are equivalent. Demonstrate this fact by showing the effect of the two transactions on an arbitrary initial database state.

b) Give examples of a serializable schedule and a nonserializable schedule of the 12 actions above.

c) How many serial schedules of the 12 actions are there?

*!! d) How many serializable schedules of the 12 actions are there?

Exercise 9.2.2: The two transactions of Exercise 9.2.1 can be written in our notation that shows read- and write-actions only, as:

T_1: $r_1(A)$; $w_1(A)$; $r_1(B)$; $w_1(B)$;

T_2: $r_2(B)$; $w_2(B)$; $r_2(A)$; $w_2(A)$;

Answer the following:

*! a) Among the possible schedules of the eight actions above, how many are conflict-equivalent to the serial order (T_1, T_2)?

b) How many schedules of the eight actions are equivalent to the serial order (T_2, T_1)?

!! c) How many schedules of the eight actions are equivalent (not necessarily conflict-equivalent) to the serial schedule (T_1, T_2), assuming the transactions have the effect on the database described in Exercise 9.2.1?

! d) Why are the answers to (c) above and Exercise 9.2.1(d) different?

! **Exercise 9.2.3:** Suppose the transactions of Exercise 9.2.2 are changed to be:

T_1: $r_1(A)$; $w_1(A)$; $r_1(B)$; $w_1(B)$;

T_2: $r_2(A)$; $w_2(A)$; $r_2(B)$; $w_2(B)$;

That is, the transactions retain their semantics from Exercise 9.2.1, but T_2 has been changed so A is processed before B. Give:

a) The number of conflict-serializable schedules.

b) The number of serializable schedules, assuming the transactions have the same effect on the database state as in Exercise 9.2.1.

Exercise 9.2.4 : For each of the following schedules:

* a) $r_1(A)$; $r_2(A)$; $r_3(B)$; $w_1(A)$; $r_2(C)$; $r_2(B)$; $w_2(B)$; $w_1(C)$;

b) $r_1(A)$; $w_1(B)$; $r_2(B)$: $w_2(C)$; $r_3(C)$; $w_3(A)$;

c) $w_3(A)$; $r_1(A)$; $w_1(B)$; $r_2(B)$: $w_2(C)$; $r_3(C)$;

d) $r_1(A)$; $r_2(A)$; $w_1(B)$; $w_2(B)$; $r_1(B)$; $r_2(B)$; $w_2(C)$; $w_1(D)$;

e) $r_1(A)$; $r_2(A)$; $r_1(B)$; $r_2(B)$; $r_3(A)$; $r_4(B)$; $w_1(A)$; $w_2(B)$;

Answer the following questions:

  i. What is the precedence graph for the schedule?

 ii. Is the schedule conflict-serializable? If so, what are all the equivalent serial schedules?

! *iii.* Are there any serial schedules that must be equivalent (regardless of what the transactions do to the data), but are not conflict-equivalent?

!! **Exercise 9.2.5 :** Say that a transaction T *precedes* a transaction U in a schedule S if every action of T precedes every action of U in S. Note that if T and U are the only transactions in S, then saying T precedes U is the same as saying that S is the serial schedule (T, U). However, if S involves transactions other than T and U, then S might not be serializable, and in fact, because of the effect of other transactions, might note even be conflict-serializable. Give an example of a schedule S such that:

  i. In S, T_1 precedes T_2, and

 ii. S is conflict-serializable, but

iii. In every serial schedule conflict-equivalent to S, T_2 precedes T_1.

! **Exercise 9.2.6 :** Explain how, for any $n > 1$, one can find a schedule whose precedence graph has a cycle of length n, but no smaller cycle.

9.3 Enforcing Serializability by Locks

Imagine a collection of transactions performing their actions in an unconstrained manner. These actions will form some schedule, but it is unlikely that the schedule will be serializable. It is the job of the scheduler to prevent orders of actions that lead to an unserializable schedule. In this section we consider the most common architecture for a scheduler, one in which "locks" are maintained on database elements to prevent unserializable behavior. Intuitively, a transaction obtains locks on the database elements it accesses to prevent other transactions from accessing these elements at roughly the same time and thereby incurring the risk of unserializability.

In this section, we introduce the concept of locking with an (overly) simple locking scheme. In this scheme, there is only one kind of lock, which transactions must obtain on a database element if they want to perform any operation whatsoever on that element. In Section 9.4, we shall learn more realistic locking schemes, with several kinds of lock, including the common shared/exclusive locks that correspond to the privileges of reading and writing, respectively.

9.3.1 Locks

In Fig. 9.11 we see a scheduler that uses a lock table to help perform its job. Recall that the responsibility of the scheduler is to take requests from transactions and either allow them to operate on the database or defer them until such time as it is safe to allow them to execute. A lock table will be used to guide this decision in a manner that we shall discuss at length.

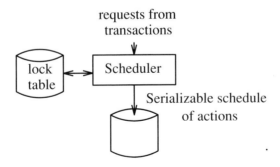

Figure 9.11: A scheduler that uses a lock table to guide decisions

Ideally, a scheduler would forward a request if and only if its execution cannot possibly lead to an inconsistent database state after all active transactions commit or abort. It is much too hard to decide this question in real time, however. Thus, all schedulers use a simple test that guarantees serializability but may forbid some actions that could not by themselves lead to inconsistency. A locking scheduler, like most types of scheduler, instead enforces conflict-serializability, which as we learned is a more stringent condition than serializability.

When a scheduler uses locks, transactions must request and release locks, in addition to reading and writing database elements. The use of locks must be proper in two senses, one applying to the structure of transactions, and the other to the structure of schedules.

- *Consistency of Transactions*: Actions and locks must relate in the expected ways:

  1. A transaction can only read or write an element if it previously requested a lock on that element and hasn't yet released the lock.

  2. If a transaction locks an element, it must later unlock that element.

- *Legality of Schedules*: Locks must have their intended meaning: no two transactions may have locked the same element without one having first released the lock.

We shall extend our notation for actions to include locking and unlocking actions:

$l_i(X)$: Transaction T_i requests a lock on database element X.

$u_i(X)$: Transaction T_i releases its lock ("unlocks") database element X.

Thus, the consistency condition for transactions can be stated as: "Whenever a transaction T_i has an action $r_i(X)$ or $w_i(X)$, then there is a previous action $l_i(X)$ with no intervening action $u_i(X)$, and there is a subsequent $u_i(X)$." The legality of schedules is stated: "If there are actions $l_i(X)$ followed by $l_j(X)$ in a schedule, then somewhere between these actions there must be an action $u_i(X)$."

Example 9.10: Let us consider the two transactions T_1 and T_2 that we introduced in Example 9.1. Recall that T_1 adds 100 to database elements A and B, while T_2 doubles them. Here are specifications for these transactions, in which we have included lock actions as well as arithmetic actions to help us remember what the transactions are doing.[3]

T_1: $l_1(A)$; $r_1(A)$; A := A+100; $w_1(A)$; $u_1(A)$; $l_1(B)$; $r_1(B)$; B := B+100; $w_1(B)$; $u_1(B)$;

T_2: $l_2(A)$; $r_2(A)$; A := A*2; $w_2(A)$; $u_2(A)$; $l_2(B)$; $r_2(B)$; B := B*2; $w_2(B)$; $u_2(B)$;

Each of these transactions is consistent. They each release the locks on A and B that they take. Moreover, they each operate on A and B only in steps where they have previously requested a lock on that element and have not yet released the lock.

---

[3]Remember that the actual computations of the transaction usually are not represented in our current notation, since they are not considered by the scheduler when deciding whether to grant or deny transaction requests.

T_1	T_2	A	B
		25	25
$l_1(A); r_1(A);$			
A := A+100;			
$w_1(A); u_1(A);$		125	
	$l_2(A); r_2(A);$		
	A := A*2;		
	$w_2(A); u_2(A);$	250	
	$l_2(B); r_2(B);$		
	B := B*2;		
	$w_2(B); u_2(B);$		50
$l_1(B); r_1(B);$			
B := B+100;			
$w_1(B); u_1(B);$			150

Figure 9.12: A legal schedule of consistent transactions; unfortunately it is not serializable

Figure 9.12 shows one legal schedule of these two transactions. To save space we have put several actions on one line. The schedule is legal because the two transactions never hold a lock on A at the same time, and likewise for B. Specifically, T_2 does not execute $l_2(A)$ until after T_1 executes $u_1(A)$, and T_1 does not execute $l_1(B)$ until after T_2 executes $u_2(B)$. As we see from the trace of the values computed, the schedule, although legal, is not serializable. We shall see in Section 9.3.3 the additional condition, "two-phase locking," that we need to assure that legal schedules are conflict-serializable. □

9.3.2 The Locking Scheduler

It is the job of a scheduler based on locking to grant requests if and only if the request will result in a legal schedule. To aid this decision, it has a lock table, which tells, for every database element, the transaction, if any, that currently holds a lock on that element. We shall discuss the structure of a lock table in more detail in Section 9.5.2. However, when there is only one kind of lock, as we have assumed so far, the table may be thought of as a relation Locks(element, transaction), consisting of pairs (X, T) such that transaction T currently has a lock on database element X. The scheduler has only to query this relation and modify it with simple INSERT and DELETE statements.

Example 9.11 : The schedule of Fig. 9.12 is legal, as we mentioned, so the locking scheduler would grant every request in the order of arrival shown. However, sometimes it is not possible to grant requests. Here are T_1 and T_2 from

Example 9.10, with simple (but important, as we shall see in Section 9.3.3) changes, in which T_1 and T_2 each lock B before releasing the lock on A.

T_1: $l_1(A)$; $r_1(A)$; A := A+100; $w_1(A)$; $l_1(B)$; $u_1(A)$; $r_1(B)$; B := B+100; $w_1(B)$; $u_1(B)$;

T_2: $l_2(A)$; $r_2(A)$; A := A*2; $w_2(A)$; $l_2(B)$; $u_2(A)$; $r_2(B)$; B := B*2; $w_2(B)$; $u_2(B)$;

T_1	T_2	A	B
		25	25
$l_1(A)$; $r_1(A)$;			
A := A+100;			
$w_1(A)$; $l_1(B)$; $u_1(A)$;		125	
	$l_2(A)$; $r_2(A)$;		
	A := A*2;		
	$w_2(A)$;	250	
	$l_2(B)$ **Denied**		
$r_1(B)$; B := B+100;			
$w_1(B)$; $u_1(B)$;			125
	$l_2(B)$; $u_2(A)$; $r_2(B)$;		
	B := B*2;		
	$w_2(B)$; $u_2(B)$;		250

Figure 9.13: The locking scheduler delays requests that would result in an illegal schedule

In Fig. 9.13, when T_2 requests a lock on B, the scheduler must deny the lock, because T_1 still holds a lock on B. Thus, T_2 stalls, and the next actions are from T_1. Eventually, T_1 executes $u_1(B)$, which unlocks B. Now, T_2 can get its lock on B, which is executed at the next step. Notice that because T_2 was forced to wait, it wound up multiplying B by 2 after T_1 added 100, resulting in a consistent database state.   □

9.3.3   Two-Phase Locking

There is a surprising condition under which we can guarantee that a legal schedule of consistent transactions is conflict-serializable. This condition, which is widely followed in commercial locking systems, is called *two-phase locking* or *2PL*. The 2PL condition is:

- In every transaction, all lock requests precede all unlock requests.

The "two phases" referred to by 2PL are thus the first phase, where locks are obtained and the second phase, where locks are relinquished. Two-phase locking is a condition, like consistency, on the order of actions in a transaction. A transaction that obeys the 2PL condition is said to be a *two-phase-locked transaction*, or 2PL transaction.

Example 9.12: In Example 9.10, the transactions do not obey the two-phase locking rule. For instance, T_1 unlocks A before it locks B. However, the versions of the transactions found in Example 9.11 *do* obey the 2PL condition. Notice that T_1 locks both A and B within the first five actions and unlocks them within the next five actions; T_2 behaves similarly. If we compare Figs. 9.12 and 9.13, we see how the two-phase-locked transactions interact properly with the scheduler to assure consistency, while the non-2PL transactions allow inconsistent (and therefore not-conflict-serializable) behavior. □

9.3.4 Why Two-Phase Locking Works

It is true, but far from obvious, that the benefit from 2PL that we observed in our examples holds in general. Intuitively, each two-phase-locked transaction may be thought to execute in its entirety at the instant it issues its first unlock request, as suggested by Fig. 9.14. The conflict-equivalent serial schedule for a schedule S of 2PL transactions is the one in which the transactions are ordered in the same order as their first unlocks.[4]

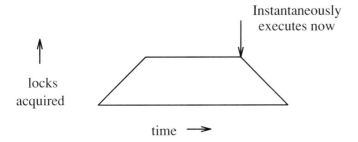

Figure 9.14: Every two-phase-locked transaction has a point at which it may be thought to execute instantaneously

We shall show how to convert any legal schedule S of consistent, two-phase-locked transactions to a conflict-equivalent serial schedule. The conversion is best described as an induction on n, the number of transactions in S. In what follows, it is important to remember that the issue of conflict-equivalence refers to the read and write actions only. As we swap the order of reads and writes, we ignore the lock and unlock actions. Once we have the read and write actions ordered serially, we can place the lock and unlock actions around them as the various transactions require. Since each transaction releases all locks before its end, we know that the serial schedule is legal.

---

[4]In some schedules, there are other conflict-equivalent serial schedules as well.

BASIS: If $n = 1$, there is nothing to do; S is already a serial schedule.

INDUCTION: Suppose S involves n transactions $T_1, T_2, \ldots, T_n$, and let T_i be the transaction with the first unlock action in the entire schedule S, say $u_i(X)$. We claim it is possible to move all the read and write actions of T_i forward to the beginning of the schedule without passing any conflicting actions.

Consider some action of T_i, say $w_i(Y)$. Could it be preceded in S by some conflicting action, say $w_j(Y)$? If so, then in schedule S, actions $u_j(Y)$ and $l_i(Y)$ must intervene, in a sequence of actions

$$\cdots w_j(Y); \cdots; \; u_j(Y); \cdots; \; l_i(Y); \cdots : \; w_i(Y); \cdots$$

Since T_i is the first to unlock, $u_i(X)$ precedes $u_j(Y)$ in S; that is, S might look like:
$$\cdots; \; w_j(Y); \cdots; \; u_i(X); \cdots; \; u_j(Y); \cdots; \; l_i(Y); \cdots; \; w_i(Y); \cdots$$

or $u_i(X)$ could even appear before $w_j(Y)$. In any case, $u_i(X)$ appears before $l_i(Y)$, which means that T_i is *not* two-phase-locked, as we assumed. While we have only argued the nonexistence of conflicting pairs of writes, the same argument applies to any pair of potentially conflicting actions, one from T_i and the other from another T_j.

We conclude that it is indeed possible to move all the actions of T_i forward to the beginning of S, using swaps of nonconflicting read and write actions, followed by restoration of the lock and unlock actions of T_i. That is, S can be written in the form

$$(\text{Actions of } T_i)(\text{Actions of the other } n - 1 \text{ transactions})$$

The tail of $n - 1$ transactions is still a legal schedule of consistent, 2PL transactions, so the inductive hypothesis applies to it. We convert the tail to a conflict-equivalent serial schedule, and now all of S has been shown conflict-serializable.

9.3.5 Exercises for Section 9.3

Exercise 9.3.1: Below are two transactions, with lock requests and the semantics of the transactions indicated. Recall from Exercise 9.2.1 that these transactions have the unusual property that they can be scheduled in ways that are not conflict-serializable, but, because of the semantics, are serializable.

T_1: $l_1(A)$; $r_1(A)$; A := A+2; $w_1(A)$; $u_1(A)$; $l_1(B)$; $r_1(B)$; B := B*3; $w_1(B)$; $u_1(B)$;

T_2: $l_2(B)$; $r_2(B)$; B := B*2; $w_2(B)$; $u_2(B)$; $l_2(A)$; $r_2(A)$; A := A+3; $w_2(A)$; $u_2(A)$;

In the questions below, consider only schedules of the read and write actions, not the lock, unlock, or assignment steps.

A Risk of Deadlock

One problem that is not solved by two-phase locking is the potential for deadlocks, where several transactions are forced by the scheduler to wait for a lock held by another transaction. For instance, consider the 2PL transactions from Example 9.11, but with T_2 changed to work on B first:

T_1: $l_1(A)$; $r_1(A)$; A := A+100; $w_1(A)$; $l_1(B)$; $u_1(A)$; $r_1(B)$; B := B+100; $w_1(B)$; $u_1(B)$;

T_2: $l_2(B)$; $r_2(B)$; B := B*2; $w_2(B)$; $l_2(A)$; $u_2(B)$; $r_2(A)$; A := A*2; $w_2(A)$; $u_2(A)$;

A possible interleaving of the actions of these transactions is:

T_1	T_2	A	B
		25	25
$l_1(A)$; $r_1(A)$;			
	$l_2(B)$; $r_2(B)$;		
A := A+100;			
	B := B*2;		
$w_1(A)$;		125	
	$w_2(B)$;		50
$l_1(B)$ **Denied**	$l_2(A)$ **Denied**		

Now, neither transaction can proceed, and they wait forever. In Section 10.3, we shall discuss methods to remedy this situation. However, observe that it is not possible to allow both transactions to proceed, since if we do so the final database state cannot possibly have $A = B$.

---

* a) Give an example of a schedule that is prohibited by the locks.

! b) Of the $\binom{8}{4} = 70$ orders of the eight read and write actions, how many are legal schedules (i.e., they are permitted by the locks)?

! c) Of the legal schedules, how many are serializable (according to the semantics of the transactions given)?

! d) Of those schedules that are legal and serializable, how many are conflict-serializable?

!! e) Since T_1 and T_2 are not two-phase-locked, we would expect that some nonserializable behaviors would occur. Are there any legal schedules that are unserializable? If so, give an example, and if not, explain why.

*! **Exercise 9.3.2:** Here are the transactions of Exercise 9.3.1, with all unlocks moved to the end so they are two-phase-locked.

T_1: $l_1(A)$; $r_1(A)$; A := A+2; $w_1(A)$; $l_1(B)$; $r_1(B)$; B := B*3; $w_1(B)$; $u_1(A)$; $u_1(B)$;

T_2: $l_2(B)$; $r_2(B)$; B := B*2; $w_2(B)$; $l_2(A)$; $r_2(A)$; A := A+3; $w_2(A)$; $u_2(B)$; $u_2(A)$;

How many legal schedules of all the read and write actions of these transactions are there?

Exercise 9.3.3: For each of the schedules of Exercise 9.2.4, assume that each transaction takes a lock on each database elements immediately before it reads or writes the element, and that each transaction releases its locks immediately after the last time it accesses an element. Tell what the locking scheduler would do with each of these schedules; i.e., what requests would get delayed, and when would they be allowed to resume?

! **Exercise 9.3.4:** For each of the transactions described below, suppose that we insert one lock and one unlock action for each database element that is accessed.

* a) $r_1(A)$; $w_1(B)$;

  b) $r_2(A)$; $w_2(A)$; $w_2(B)$;

Tell how many orders of the lock, unlock, read, and write actions are:

  i. Consistent and two-phase locked.

  ii. Consistent, but not two-phase locked.

  iii. Inconsistent, but two-phase locked.

  iv. Neither consistent nor two-phase locked.

9.4 Locking Systems With Several Lock Modes

The locking scheme of Section 9.3 illustrates the important ideas behind locking, but it is too simple to be a practical scheme. The main problem is that a transaction T must take a lock on a database element X even if it only wants to read X and not write it. We cannot avoid taking the lock, because if we didn't, then another transaction might write a new value for X while T was active and cause unserializable behavior. On the other hand, there is no reason why several transactions could not read X at the same time, as long as none is allowed to write X.

We are thus motivated to introduce the first, and most common, locking scheme, where there are two different kinds of locks, one for reading (called a "shared lock" or "read lock"), and one for writing (called an "exclusive lock" or "write lock"). We then examine an improved scheme where transactions are allowed to take a shared lock and "upgrade" it to an exclusive lock later. We also consider "increment locks," which treat specially write actions that increment a database element; the important distinction is that increment operations commute, while general writes do not. These examples lead us to the general notion of a lock scheme described by a "compatibility matrix" that indicates what locks on a database element may be granted when other locks are held.

9.4.1 Shared and Exclusive Locks

Since two read actions on the same database element do not create a conflict, there is no need to use locking or any other concurrency-control mechanism to force the read actions to occur in one particular order. As suggested in the introduction, we still need to lock an element we are about to read, since a writer of that element must be inhibited. However, the lock we need for writing is "stronger" than the lock we need to read, since it must prevent both reads and writes.

Let us therefore consider a locking scheduler that uses two different kinds of locks: *shared locks* and *exclusive locks*. Intuitively, for any database element X there can be either one exclusive lock on X, or no exclusive locks but any number of shared locks. If we want to write X, we need to have an exclusive lock on X, but if we wish only to read X we may have either a shared or exclusive lock on X. Presumably, if we want to read X but not write it, then we prefer to take only a shared lock.

We shall use $sl_i(X)$ to mean "transaction T_i requests a shared lock on database element X" and $xl_i(X)$ for "T_i requests an exclusive lock on X." We continue to use $u_i(X)$ to mean that T_i unlocks X; i.e., it relinquishes whatever lock(s) it has on X.

The three kinds of requirements — consistency and 2PL for transactions, and legality for schedules — each have their counterpart for a shared/exclusive lock system. We summarize these requirements here:

1. *Consistency of transactions*: You may not write without holding an exclusive lock, and you may not read without holding some lock. More precisely, in any transaction T_i,

   (a) A read action $r_i(X)$ must be preceded by $sl_i(X)$ or $xl_i(X)$, with no intervening $u_i(X)$.

   (b) A write action $w_i(X)$ must be preceded by $xl_i(X)$, with no intervening $u_i(X)$.

   All locks must be followed by an unlock of the same element.

2. *Two-phase locking of transactions*: Locking must precede unlocking. To be more precise, in any two-phase locked transaction T_i, no action $sl_i(X)$ or $xl_i(X)$ can be preceded by an action $u_i(X)$.

3. *Legality of schedules*: An element may either be locked exclusively by one transaction or by several in shared mode, but not both. More precisely:

   (a) If $xl_i(X)$ appears in a schedule, then there cannot be a following $xl_j(X)$ or $sl_j(X)$, for some j other than i, without an intervening $u_i(X)$.

   (b) If $sl_i(X)$ appears in a schedule, then there cannot be a following $xl_j(X)$, for $j \neq i$, without an intervening $u_i(X)$.

Note that we *do* allow one transaction request and hold both shared and exclusive locks on the same element, provided its doing so does not conflict with the lock(s) of other transactions. If transactions know in advance their needs for locks, then surely only the exclusive lock would be requested, but if lock needs are unpredictable, then it is possible that one transaction would request both shared and exclusive locks at different times.

Example 9.13 : Let us examine a possible schedule of the following two transactions, using shared and exclusive locks:

T_1: $sl_1(A)$; $r_1(A)$; $xl_1(B)$; $r_1(B)$; $w_1(B)$; $u_1(A)$; $u_1(B)$;

T_2: $sl_2(A)$; $r_2(A)$; $sl_2(B)$; $r_2(B)$; $u_2(A)$; $u_2(B)$;

Both T_1 and T_2 read A and B, but only T_1 writes B. Neither writes A.

In Fig. 9.15 is an interleaving of the actions of T_1 and T_2 in which T_1 begins by getting a shared lock on A. Then, T_2 follows by getting shared locks on both A and B. Now, T_1 needs an exclusive lock on B, since it will both read and write B. However, it cannot get the exclusive lock because T_2 already has a shared lock on B. Thus, the scheduler forces T_1 to wait. Eventually, T_2 releases the lock on B. At that time, T_1 may complete. □

T_1	T_2
$sl_1(A)$; $r_1(A)$;	
	$sl_2(A)$; $r_2(A)$;
	$sl_2(B)$; $r_2(B)$;
$xl_1(B)$ **Denied**	
	$u_2(A)$; $u_2(B)$
$xl_1(B)$; $r_1(B)$; $w_1(B)$;	
$u_1(A)$; $u_2(B)$;	

Figure 9.15: A schedule using shared and exclusive locks

Notice that the resulting schedule in Fig 9.15 is conflict-serializable. The conflict-equivalent serial order is (T_2, T_1), even though T_1 started first. While we do not prove it here, the argument we gave in Section 9.3.4 to show that legal schedules of consistent, 2PL transactions are conflict-serializable applies to systems with shared and exclusive locks as well. In Fig. 9.15, T_2 unlocks before T_1, so we would expect T_2 to precede T_1 in the serial order. Equivalently, we may examine the read and write actions of Fig. 9.15 and notice that we can swap $r_1(A)$ back, past all the actions of T_2, while we cannot move $w_1(B)$ ahead of $r_2(B)$, which would be necessary if T_1 could precede T_2 in a conflict-equivalent serial schedule.

9.4.2 Compatibility Matrices

If we use several lock modes, then the scheduler needs a policy about when it can grant a lock request, given the other locks that may already be held on the same database element. While the shared/exclusive system is simple, we shall see that there are considerably more complex systems of lock modes in use. We shall therefore introduce the following notation for describing lock-granting policies in the context of the simple shared/exclusive system.

A *compatibility matrix* has a row and column for each lock mode. The rows correspond to a lock that is already held on an element X by another transaction, and the columns correspond to the mode of a lock on X that is requested. The rule for using a compatibility matrix for lock-granting decisions is:

- We can grant the lock in mode C if and only if for every row R such that there is already a lock on X in mode R by some other transaction, there is a "Yes" in column C.

		Lock	requested
		S	X
Lock held	S	Yes	No
in mode	X	No	No

Figure 9.16: The compatibility matrix for shared and exclusive locks

Example 9.14: Figure 9.16 is the compatibility matrix for shared (S) and exclusive (X) locks. The column for S says that we can grant a shared lock on an element if the only locks held on that element currently are shared locks. The column for X says that we can grant an exclusive lock only if there are no other locks held currently. Notice how these rules reflect the definition of legality of schedules for this system of locks. □

9.4.3 Upgrading Locks

A transaction T that takes a shared lock on X is being "friendly" toward other transactions, since they are allowed to read X at the same time T is. Thus, we might wonder whether it would be friendlier still if a transaction T that wants to read and write a new value of X were to first take a shared lock on X, and only later, when T was ready to write the new value, *upgrade* the lock to exclusive (i.e., request an exclusive lock on X in addition to its already held shared lock on X). There is nothing that prevents a transaction from issuing requests for locks on the same database element in different modes. We adopt the convention that $u_i(X)$ releases all locks on X held by transaction T_i, although we could introduce mode-specific unlock actions if there were a use for them.

Example 9.15 : In the following example, transaction T_1 is able to perform its computation concurrently with T_2, which would not be possible had T_1 taken an exclusive lock on B initially. The two transactions are:

T_1: $sl_1(A)$; $r_1(A)$; $sl_1(B)$; $r_1(B)$; $xl_1(B)$; $w_1(B)$; $u_1(A)$; $u_1(B)$;

T_2: $sl_2(A)$; $r_2(A)$; $sl_2(B)$; $r_2(B)$; $u_2(A)$; $u_2(B)$;

Here, T_1 reads A and B and performs some (possibly lengthy) calculation with them, eventually using the result to write a new value of B. Notice that T_1 takes a shared lock on B first, and later, after its calculation involving A and B is finished, requests an exclusive lock on B. Transaction T_2 only reads A and B, and does not write.

T_1	T_2
$sl_1(A)$; $r_1(A)$;	
	$sl_2(A)$; $r_2(A)$;
	$sl_2(B)$; $r_2(B)$;
$sl_1(B)$; $r_1(B)$;	
$xl_1(B)$ **Denied**	
	$u_2(A)$; $u_2(B)$
$xl_1(B)$; $w_1(B)$;	
$u_1(A)$; $u_2(B)$;	

Figure 9.17: Upgrading locks allows more concurrent operation

Figure 9.17 shows a possible schedule of actions. T_2 gets a shared lock on B before T_1 does, but on the fourth line, T_1 is also able to lock B in shared mode. Thus, T_1 has both A and B and can perform its computation using their values. It is not until T_1 tries to upgrade its lock on B to exclusive that the scheduler must deny the request and force T_1 to wait until T_2 releases its lock on B. At that time, T_1 gets its exclusive lock on B, writes B, and finishes.

Notice that had T_1 asked for an exclusive lock on B initially, before reading B, then the request would have been denied, because T_2 already had a shared lock on B. T_1 could not perform its computation without reading B, and so T_1 would have more to do after T_2 releases its locks. As a result, T_1 finishes later using only an exclusive lock on B than it would if it used the upgrading strategy. □

Example 9.16: Unfortunately, indiscriminate use of upgrading introduces a new and potentially serious source of deadlocks. Suppose, that T_1 and T_2 each read database element A and write a new value for A. If both transactions use an upgrading approach, first getting a shared lock on A and then upgrading it to exclusive, the sequence of events suggested in Fig. 9.18 will happen whenever T_1 and T_2 initiate at approximately the same time.

T_1	T_2
$sl_1(A)$	
	$sl_2(A)$
$xl_1(A)$ **Denied**	
	$xl_2(A)$ **Denied**

Figure 9.18: Upgrading by two transactions can cause a deadlock

T_1 and T_2 are both able to get shared locks on A. Then, they each try to upgrade to exclusive, but the scheduler forces each to wait because the other has a shared lock on A. Thus, neither can make progress, and they will each wait forever, or until the system discovers that there is a deadlock, aborts one of the two transactions, and gives the other the exclusive lock on A. □

9.4.4 Update Locks

There is a way to avoid the deadlock problem of Example 9.16 by using a third lock mode, called *update locks*. An update lock $ul_i(X)$ gives transaction T_i only the privilege to read X, not to write X. However, only the update lock can be upgraded to a write lock later; a read lock cannot be upgraded. We can grant an update lock on X when there are already shared locks on X, but once there is an update lock on X we prevent additional locks of any kind — shared, update, or exclusive — from being taken on X. The reason is that if we don't deny such locks, then the updater might never get a chance to upgrade to exclusive, since there would always be other locks on X.

This rule leads to an asymmetric compatibility matrix, because the update (U) lock looks like a shared lock when we are requesting it and looks like an exclusive lock when we already have it. Thus, the columns for U and S locks are the same, and the rows for U and X locks are the same. The matrix is shown in Fig. 9.19.[5]

	S	X	U
S	Yes	No	Yes
X	No	No	No
U	No	No	No

Figure 9.19: Compatibility matrix for shared, exclusive, and update locks

Example 9.17 : The use of update locks would have no effect on Example 9.15. As its third action, T_1 would take an update lock on B, rather than a shared lock. But the update lock would be granted, since only shared locks are held on B, and the same sequence of actions shown in Fig. 9.17 would occur.

However, update locks fix the problem shown in Example 9.16. Now, both T_1 and T_2 first request update locks on A and only later take exclusive locks. Possible descriptions of T_1 and T_2 are:

T_1: $ul_1(A)$; $r_1(A)$; $xl_1(A)$; $w_1(A)$; $u_1(A)$;

T_2: $ul_2(A)$; $r_2(A)$; $xl_2(A)$; $w_2(A)$; $u_2(A)$;

The sequence of events corresponding to Fig. 9.18 is shown in Fig. 9.20. Now, T_2, the second to request an update lock on A, is denied. T_1 is allowed to finish, and then T_2 may proceed. The lock system has effectively prevented concurrent execution of T_1 and T_2, but in this example, any significant amount of concurrent execution will result in either a deadlock or an inconsistent database state. $\square$

T_1	T_2
$ul_1(A)$; $r_1(A)$;	
	$ul_2(A)$ **Denied**
$xl_1(A)$; $w_1(A)$; $u_1(A)$;	
	$ul_2(A)$; $r_2(A)$;
	$xl_2(A)$; $w_2(A)$; $u_2(A)$;

Figure 9.20: Correct execution using update locks

---

[5]Remember, however, that there is an additional condition regarding legality of schedules that is not reflected by this matrix: a transaction holding a shared lock but not an update lock on an element X cannot be given an exclusive lock on X, even though we do not in general prohibit a transaction from holding multiple locks on an element.

9.4.5 Increment Locks

Another interesting kind of lock that is useful in some situations is an "increment lock." Many transactions operate on the database only by incrementing or decrementing stored values. Examples are:

1. A transaction that transfers money from one bank account to another.

2. A transaction that sells an airplane ticket and decrements the count of available seats on that flight.

The interesting property of increment actions is that they commute with each other, since if two transactions add constants to the same database element, it does not matter which goes first, as the diagram of database state transitions in Fig. 9.21 suggests. On the other hand, incrementation commutes with neither reading nor writing; If you read A before or after it is incremented, you get different values, and if you increment A before or after some other transaction writes a new value for A, you get different values of A in the database.

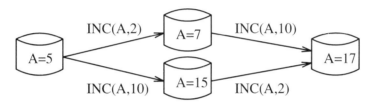

Figure 9.21: Two increment actions commute, since the final database state does not depend on which went first

Let us introduce as a possible action in transactions the *increment* action, written INC(A,c). Informally, this action adds constant c to database element A, which we assume is a single number. Note that c could be negative, in which case we are really decrementing A. In practice, we might apply INC to a component of a tuple, while the tuple itself, rather than one of its components, is the lockable element.

More formally, we use INC(A,c) to stand for the atomic execution of the following steps: READ(A,t); t := t+c; WRITE(A,t);. We shall not discuss the hardware and/or software mechanism that would be used to make this operation atomic, but we should note that this form of atomicity is on a lower level than the atomicity of transactions that we support by locking.

Corresponding to the increment action, we need an *increment lock*. We shall denote the action of T_i requesting an increment lock on X by $il_i(X)$. We also use shorthand $inc_i(X)$ for the action in which transaction T_i increments database element X by some constant; the exact constant doesn't matter.

The existence of increment actions and locks requires us to make several modifications to our definitions of consistent transactions, conflicts, and legal schedules. These changes are:

a) A consistent transaction can only have an increment action on X if it holds an increment lock on X at the time. An increment lock does not enable either read or write actions, however.

b) In a legal schedule, any number of transactions can hold an increment lock on X at any time. However, if an increment lock on X is held by some transaction, then no other transaction can hold either a shared or exclusive lock on X at the same time. These requirements are expressed by the compatibility matrix of Fig. 9.22, where I represents a lock in increment mode.

c) The action $inc_i(X)$ conflicts with both $r_j(X)$ and $w_j(X)$, for $j \neq i$, but does not conflict with $inc_j(X)$.

	S	X	I
S	Yes	No	No
X	No	No	No
I	No	No	Yes

Figure 9.22: Compatibility matrix for shared, exclusive, and increment locks

Example 9.18: Consider two transactions, each of which read database element A and then increment B. Perhaps they add A to B, or the constant by which they increment B may depend in some other way on A.

T_1: $sl_1(A)$; $r_1(A)$; $il_1(B)$; $inc_1(B)$; $u_1(A)$; $u_1(B)$;

T_2: $sl_2(A)$; $r_2(A)$; $il_2(B)$; $inc_2(B)$; $u_2(A)$; $u_2(B)$;

Notice that the transactions are consistent, since they only perform an incrementation while they have an increment lock, and they only read while they have a shared lock. Figure 9.23 shows a possible interleaving of T_1 and T_2. T_1 reads A first, but then T_2 both reads A and increments B. However, T_1 is then allowed to get its increment lock on B and proceed.

Notice that the scheduler did not have to delay any requests in Fig. 9.23. Suppose, for instance, that T_1 increments B by A, and T_2 increments B by $2A$. They can execute in either order, since the value of A does not change, and the incrementations may also be performed in either order.

Put another way, we may look at the sequence of non-lock actions in the schedule of Fig. 9.23; they are:

S: $r_1(A)$; $r_2(A)$; $inc_2(B)$; $inc_1(B)$;

T_1	T_2
$sl_1(A)$; $r_1(A)$;	
	$sl_2(A)$; $r_2(A)$;
	$il_2(B)$; $inc_2(B)$;
$il_1(B)$; $inc_1(B)$;	
	$u_2(A)$; $u_2(B)$;
$u_1(A)$; $u_1(B)$;	

Figure 9.23: A schedule of transactions with increment actions and locks

We may move the last action, $inc_1(B)$, to the second position, since it does not conflict with another increment of the same element, and surely does not conflict with a read of a different element. This sequence of swaps shows that S is conflict-equivalent to the serial schedule $r_1(A)$; $inc_1(B)$; $r_2(A)$; $inc_2(B)$;. Similarly, we can move the first action, $r_1(A)$ to the third position by swaps, giving a serial schedule in which T_2 precedes T_1. □

9.4.6 Exercises for Section 9.4

Exercise 9.4.1: For each of the schedules of transactions T_1, T_2, and T_3 below:

a) $r_1(A)$; $r_2(B)$; $r_3(C)$; $w_1(B)$; $w_2(C)$; $w_3(D)$;

b) $r_1(A)$; $r_2(B)$; $r_3(C)$; $w_1(B)$; $w_2(C)$; $w_3(A)$;

c) $r_1(A)$; $r_2(B)$; $r_3(C)$; $r_1(B)$; $r_2(C)$; $r_3(D)$; $w_1(C)$; $w_2(D)$; $w_3(E)$;

* d) $r_1(A)$; $r_2(B)$; $r_3(C)$; $r_1(B)$; $r_2(C)$; $r_3(D)$; $w_1(A)$; $w_2(B)$; $w_3(C)$;

e) $r_1(A)$; $r_2(B)$; $r_3(C)$; $r_1(B)$; $r_2(C)$; $r_3(A)$; $w_1(A)$; $w_2(B)$; $w_3(C)$;

do each of the following:

i. Insert shared and exclusive locks, and insert unlock actions. Place a shared lock immediately in front of each read action that is not followed by a write action of the same element by the same transaction. Place an exclusive lock in front of every other read or write action. Place the necessary unlocks at the end of every transaction.

ii. Tell what happens when each schedule is run by a scheduler that supports shared and exclusive locks.

iii. Insert shared and exclusive locks in a way that allows upgrading. Place a shared lock in front of every read, an exclusive lock in front of every write, and place the necessary unlocks at the ends of the transactions.

iv. Tell what happens when each schedule from (*iii*) is run by a scheduler that supports shared locks, exclusive locks, and upgrading.

v. Insert shared, exclusive, and update locks, along with unlock actions. Place a shared lock in front of every read action that is not going to be upgraded, place an update lock in front of every read action that will be upgraded, and place an exclusive lock in front of every write action. Place unlocks at the ends of transactions, as usual.

vi. Tell what happens when each schedule from (*v*) is run by a scheduler that supports shared, exclusive, and update locks.

! Exercise 9.4.2 : Consider the two transactions:

T_1: $r_1(A)$; $r_1(B)$; $inc_1(A)$; $inc_1(B)$;

T_2: $r_2(A)$; $r_2(B)$; $inc_2(A)$; $inc_2(B)$;

Answer the following:

* a) How many interleavings of these transactions are serializable?

 b) If the order of incrementation in T_2 were reversed [i.e., $inc_2(B)$ followed by $inc_2(A)$], how many serializable interleavings would there be?

Exercise 9.4.3 : For each of the following schedules, insert appropriate locks (read, write, or increment) before each action, and unlocks at the ends of transactions. Then tell what happens when the schedule is run by a scheduler that supports these three types of locks.

 a) $r_1(A)$; $r_2(B)$; $inc_1(B)$; $inc_2(C)$; $w_1(C)$; $w_2(D)$;

 b) $r_1(A)$; $r_2(B)$; $inc_1(B)$; $inc_2(A)$; $w_1(C)$; $w_2(D)$;

 c) $inc_1(A)$; $inc_2(B)$; $inc_1(B)$; $inc_2(C)$; $w_1(C)$; $w_2(D)$;

Exercise 9.4.4 : In Exercise 9.1.1, we discussed a hypothetical transaction involving an airline reservation. If the transaction manager had available to it shared, exclusive, update, and increment locks, what lock would you recommend for each of the steps of the transaction?

Exercise 9.4.5 : The action of multiplication by a constant factor can be modeled by an action of its own. Suppose `MC(X,c)` stands for an atomic execution of the steps `READ(X,t);` `t := c*t;` `WRITE(X,t);`. We can also introduce a lock mode that allows only multiplication by a constant factor.

 a) Show the compatibility matrix for read, write, and multiplication-by-a-constant locks.

! b) Show the compatibility matrix for read, write, incrementation, and mult-iplication-by-a-constant locks.

! **Exercise 9.4.6 :** Suppose for sake of argument that database elements are two-dimensional vectors. There are four operations we can perform on vectors, and each will have its own type of lock.

- *i*. Change the value along the x-axis (an X-lock).

- *ii*. Change the value along the y-axis (a Y-lock).

- *iii*. Change the angle of the vector (an A-lock).

- *iv*. Change the magnitude of the vector (an M-lock).

Answer the following questions.

* a) Which pairs of operations commute? For example, if we rotate the vector so it's angle is 120° and then change the x-coordinate to be 10, is that the same as first changing the x-coordinate to 10 and then changing the angle to 120°?

b) Based on your answer to (a), what is the compatibility matrix for the four types of locks?

!! c) Suppose we changed the four operations so that instead of giving new values for a measure, the operations incremented the measure (e.g., "add 10 to the x-coordinate," or "rotate the vector 30° clockwise"). What would the compatibility matrix then be?

! **Exercise 9.4.7 :** Here is a schedule with one action missing:

$$r_1(A); r_2(B); ???; w_1(C); w_2(A);$$

Your problem is to figure out what actions of certain types could replace the ??? and make the schedule not be serializable. Tell all possible nonserializable replacements for each of the following types of action:

* a) Read actions.

b) Write actions.

c) Update actions.

d) Increment actions.

9.5   An Architecture for a Locking Scheduler

Having seen a number of different locking schemes, we next need to consider
how a scheduler that uses one of these schemes operates. We shall consider here
only a simple scheduler architecture based on several principles:

1. The transactions themselves do not request locks, or cannot be relied
   upon to do so. It is the job of the scheduler to insert lock actions into the
   stream of reads, writes, and other actions that access data.

2. Transactions do not release locks. Rather, the scheduler releases the locks
   when the transaction manager tells it that the transaction will commit or
   abort.

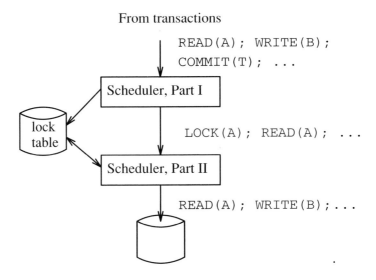

Figure 9.24: A scheduler that inserts lock requests into the transactions' request
stream

9.5.1   A Scheduler That Inserts Lock Actions

Figure 9.24 shows a two-part scheduler that accepts requests such as read,
write, commit, and abort, from transactions. The scheduler maintains a lock
table, which, although it is shown as secondary-storage data, may be partially
or completely in main memory. Normally, the main memory used by the lock
table is not part of the buffer pool that us used for query execution and logging.
Rather, the lock table is just another component of the DBMS, and will be
allocated space by the operating system like other code and internal data of the
DBMS.

Actions requested by a transaction are generally transmitted through the scheduler and executed on the database. However, under some circumstances a transaction is *delayed*, waiting for a lock, and its requests are not (yet) transmitted to the database. The two parts of the scheduler perform the following actions:

1. Part I takes the stream of requests generated by the transactions and inserts appropriate lock actions ahead of all database-access operations, such as read, write, increment, or update. The database access actions are then transmitted to Part II. Part I of the scheduler must select an appropriate lock mode from whatever set of lock modes the scheduler is using.

2. Part II takes the sequence of lock and database-access actions passed to it by Part I, and executes each appropriately. If a lock or database-access request is received by Part II, it determines whether the issuing transaction T is delayed because a lock has not been granted. If so, then the action is itself delayed and added to a list of actions that must eventually be performed for transaction T. If T is *not* delayed (i.e., all locks it previously requested have been granted already), then

   (a) If the action is a database access, it is transmitted to the database and executed.

   (b) If a lock action is received by Part II, it examines the lock table to see if the lock can be granted.

      i. If so, the lock table is modified to include the lock just granted.

      ii. If not, then an entry must be made in the lock table to indicate that the lock has been requested. Part II of the scheduler then delays further actions for transaction T, until such time as the lock is granted.

3. When a transaction T commits or aborts, Part I is notified by the transaction manager, and releases all locks held by T. If any transactions are waiting for any of these locks, Part I notifies Part II.

4. When Part II is notified that a lock on some database element X is available, it determines the next transaction or transactions that can now be given a lock on X. The transaction(s) that receive a lock are allowed to execute as many of their delayed actions as can execute, until either they complete or reach another lock request that cannot be granted.

Example 9.19: If there is only one kind of lock, as in Section 9.3, then the task of Part I of the scheduler is simple. If it sees any action on database element X, and it has not already inserted a lock request on X for that transaction, then it inserts the request. When a transaction commits or aborts, Part I can forget about that transaction after releasing its locks, so the memory required for Part I does not grow indefinitely.

When there are several kinds of locks, the scheduler may require advance notice of what future actions on the same database element will occur. Let us reconsider the case of shared-exclusive-update locks, using the transactions of Example 9.15, which we now write without any locks at all:

T_1: $r_1(A)$; $r_1(B)$; $w_1(B)$;

T_2: $r_2(A)$; $r_2(B)$;

The messages sent to Part I of the scheduler must include not only the read or write request, but an indication of future actions on the same element. In particular, when $r_1(B)$ is sent, the scheduler needs to know that there will be a later $w_1(B)$ action (or might be such an action, if transaction T_1 involves branching in its code). There are several ways the information might be made available. For example, if the transaction is a query, we know it will not write anything. If the transaction is an SQL database modification command, then the query processor can determine in advance the database elements that might be both read and written. If the transaction is a program with embedded SQL, then the compiler has access to all the SQL statements (which are the only ones that can write to the database) and can determine the potential database elements written.

In our example, suppose that events occur in the order suggested by Fig. 9.17. Then T_1 first issues $r_1(A)$. Since there will be no future upgrading of this lock, the scheduler inserts $sl_1(A)$ ahead of $r_1(A)$. Next, the requests from T_2 — $r_2(A)$ and $r_2(B)$ — arrive at the scheduler. Again there is no future upgrade, so the sequence of actions $sl_2(A)$; $r_2(A)$; $sl_2(B)$; $r_2(B)$ are issued by Part I.

Then, the action $r_1(B)$ arrives at the scheduler, along with a warning that this lock may be upgraded. The scheduler Part I thus emits $ul_1(B)$; $r_1(B)$ to Part II. The latter consults the lock table and finds that it can grant the update lock on B to T_1, because there are only shared locks on B.

When the action $w_1(B)$ arrives at the scheduler, Part I emits $xl_1(B)$; $w_1(B)$. However, Part II cannot grant the $xl_1(B)$ request, because there is a shared lock on B for T_2. This and any subsequent actions from T_1 are delayed, stored by Part II for future execution. Eventually, T_2 commits, and Part I releases the locks on A and B that T_2 held. At that time, it is found that T_1 is waiting for a lock on B. Part II of the scheduler is notified, and it finds the lock $xl_1(B)$ is now available. It enters this lock into the lock table and proceeds to execute stored actions from T_1 to the extent possible. In this case, T_1 completes. □

9.5.2 The Lock Table

Abstractly, the lock table is a relation that associates database elements with locking information about that element, as suggested by Fig. 9.25. The table might, for instance, be implemented with a hash table, using (addresses of) database elements as the hash key. Any element that is not locked does not

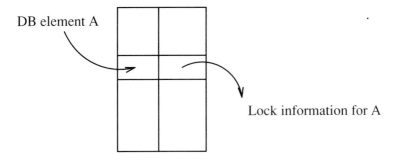

Figure 9.25: A lock table is a mapping from database elements to their lock information

appear in the table, so the size is proportional to the number of locked elements only, not to the size of the entire database.

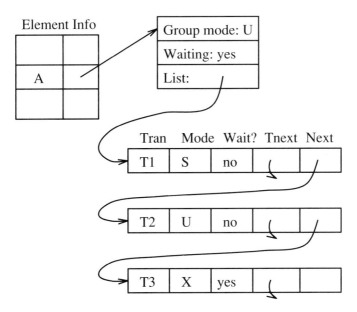

Figure 9.26: Structure of lock-table entries

In Fig. 9.26 is an example of the sort of information we would find in a lock-table entry. This example structure assumes that the shared-exclusive-update lock scheme of Section 9.4.4 is used by the scheduler. The entry shown for a typical database element A is a tuple with the following components:

1. The *group mode* is a summary of the most stringent conditions that a transaction requesting a new lock on A faces. Rather than comparing the lock request with every lock held by another transaction on the same

element, we can simplify the grant/deny decision by comparing the request with only the group mode.[6] For the shared-exclusive-update (SXU) lock scheme, the rule is simple: a group mode of

(a) S means that only shared locks are held.

(b) U means that there is one update lock and perhaps one or more shared locks.

(c) X means there is one exclusive lock and no other locks.

For other lock schemes, there is usually an appropriate system of summaries by a group mode; we leave examples as exercises.

2. The *waiting* bit tells that there is at least one transaction waiting for a lock on A.

3. A list describing all those transactions that either currently hold locks on A or are waiting for a lock on A. Useful information that each list entry has might include:

(a) The name of the transaction holding or waiting for a lock.

(b) The mode of this lock.

(c) Whether the transaction is holding or waiting for the lock.

We also show in Fig. 9.26 two links for each entry. One links the entries themselves, and the other links all entries for a particular transaction (`Tnext` in the figure). The latter link would be used when a transaction commits or aborts, so that we can easily find all the locks that must be released.

Handling Lock Requests

Suppose transaction T requests a lock on A. If there is no lock-table entry for A, then surely there are no locks on A, so the entry is created and the request is granted. If the lock-table entry for A exists, we use it to guide the decision about the lock request. We find the group mode, which in Fig. 9.26 is U, or "update." Once there is an update lock on an element, no other lock can be granted (except in the case that T itself holds the U lock and other locks are compatible with T's request). Thus, this request by T is denied, and an entry will be placed on the list saying T requests a lock (in whatever mode was requested), and `Wait? = 'yes'`.

---

[6]The lock manager must, however, deal with the possibility that the requesting transaction already has a lock in another mode on the same element. For instance, in the SXU lock system discussed, the lock manager may be able to grant an X-lock request if the requesting transaction is the one that holds a U lock on the same element. For systems that do not support multiple locks held by one transaction on one element, the group mode always tells what the lock manager needs to know.

If the group mode had been X (exclusive), then the same thing would happen, but if the group mode were S (shared), then another shared or update lock could be granted. In that case, the entry for T on the list would have `Wait? = 'no'`, and the group mode would be changed to U if the new lock were an update lock; otherwise, the group mode would remain S. Whether or not the lock is granted, the new list entry is linked properly, through its `Tnext` and `Next` fields. Notice that whether or not the lock is granted, the entry in the lock table tells the scheduler what it needs to know without having to examine the list of locks.

Handling Unlocks

Now suppose transaction T unlocks A. T's entry on the list for A is deleted. If the lock held by T is not the same as the group mode (e.g., T held an S lock, while the group mode was U), then there is no reason to change the group mode. On the other hand, if T's lock is in the group mode, we may have to examine the entire list to find the new group mode. In the example of Fig. 9.26, we know there can be only one U lock on an element, so if that lock is released, the new group mode could be only S (if there are shared locks remaining) or nothing (if no other locks are currently held).[7] If the group mode is X, we know there are no other locks, and if the group mode is S, we need to determine whether there are other shared locks.

If the value of `Waiting` is `'yes'`, then we need to grant one or more locks from the list of requested locks. There are several different approaches, each with its advantages:

1. *First-come-first-served*: Grant the lock request that has been waiting the longest. This strategy guarantees no *starvation*, the situation where a transaction can wait forever for a lock.

2. *Priority to shared locks*: First grant all the shared locks waiting. Then, grant one update lock, if there are any waiting. Only grant an exclusive lock if no others are waiting. This strategy can allow starvation, if a transaction is waiting for a U or X lock.

3. *Priority to upgrading*: If there is a transaction with a U lock waiting to upgrade it to an X lock, grant that first. Otherwise, follow one of the other strategies mentioned.

9.5.3 Exercises for Section 9.5

Exercise 9.5.1: What are suitable group modes for a lock table if the lock modes used are:

a) Shared and exclusive locks.

---

[7]We would never actually see a group mode of "nothing," since if there are no locks and no lock requests on an element, then there is no lock-table entry for that element.

*! b) Shared, exclusive, and increment locks.

!! c) The lock modes of Exercise 9.4.6.

Exercise 9.5.2: For each of the schedules of Exercise 9.2.4, tell the steps that the locking scheduler described in this section would execute.

9.6 Managing Hierarchies of Database Elements

Let us now return to the exploration of different locking schemes that we began in Section 9.4. In particular, we shall focus on two problems that come up when there is a tree structure to our data.

1. The first kind of tree structure we encounter is a hierarchy of lockable elements. We shall discuss in this section how to allow locks on both large elements, e.g., relations, and smaller elements contained within these, such as blocks holding several tuples of the relation, or individual tuples.

2. The second kind of hierarchy that is important in concurrency-control systems is data that is itself organized in a tree. A major example is B-tree indexes. We may view nodes of the B-tree as database elements, but if we do, then as we shall see in Section 9.7, the locking schemes studied so far perform poorly, and we need to use a new approach.

9.6.1 Locks With Multiple Granularity

Recall that the term "database element" was purposely left undefined, because different systems use different sizes of database elements to lock, such as tuples, pages or blocks, and relations. Some applications profit from small database elements, such as tuples, while others are best off with large elements.

Example 9.20: Consider a database for a bank. If we treated relations as database elements, and therefore had only one lock for an entire relation such as the one giving account balances, then the system would allow very little concurrency. Since most transactions will change the account balance either positively or negatively, most transactions would need an exclusive lock on the accounts relation. Thus, only one deposit or withdrawal could take place at any time, no matter how many processors we had available to execute these transactions. A better approach is to lock individual pages or data blocks. Thus, two accounts whose tuples are on different blocks can be updated at the same time, offering almost all the concurrency that is possible in the system. The extreme would be to provide a lock for every tuple, so any set of accounts whatsoever could be updated at once, but this fine a grain of locks is probably not worth the extra effort.

In contrast, consider a database of documents. These documents may be edited from time to time, but most transactions will retrieve whole documents.

The sensible choice of database element is a complete document. Since most transactions are *read-only* (i.e., they do not perform any write actions), locking is only necessary to avoid the reading of a document that is in the middle of being edited. Were we to use smaller-granularity locks, such as paragraphs, sentences, or words, there would be essentially no benefit but added expense. The only activity a smaller granularity lock would support is the ability to read parts of a document during the time that other parts of the same document are being edited. □

Some applications could use both large- and small-grained locks. For instance, the bank database discussed in Example 9.20 clearly needs block- or tuple-level locking, but might also at some time need a lock on the entire accounts relation in order to audit accounts (e.g., check that the sum of the accounts is correct). However, taking a shared lock on the accounts relation, in order to compute some aggregation on the relation, while at the same time there are exclusive locks on individual account tuples can easily lead to unserializable behavior, because the relation is actually changing while a supposedly frozen copy of it is being read by the aggregation query.

9.6.2 Warning Locks

The solution to the problem of managing locks at different granularities involves a new kind of lock called a "warning." These locks are useful when the database elements form a nested or hierarchical structure, as suggested in Fig. 9.27. There, we see three levels of database elements:

1. Relations are the largest lockable elements.

2. Each relation is composed of one or more block or pages, on which its tuples are stored.

3. Each block contains one or more tuples.

The rules for managing locks on a hierarchy of database elements constitute the *warning protocol*, which involves both "ordinary" locks and "warning" locks. We shall describe the lock scheme where the ordinary locks are S and X (shared and exclusive). The warning locks will be denoted by prefixing I (for "intention to") to the ordinary locks; for example IS represents the intention to obtain a shared lock on a subelement. The rules of the warning protocol are:

1. To place an ordinary S or X lock on any element, we must begin at the root of the hierarchy.

2. If we are at the element that we want to lock, we need look no further. We request an S or X lock on that element.

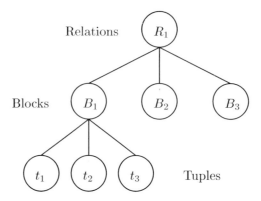

Figure 9.27: Database elements organized in a hierarchy

3. If the element we wish to lock is further down the hierarchy, then we place a warning at this node; that is, if we want to get a shared lock on a subelement we request an IS lock at this node, and if we want an exclusive lock on a subelement, we request an IX lock on this node. When the lock on the current node is granted, we proceed to the appropriate child (the one whose subtree contains the node we wish to lock). We then repeat step (2) or step (3), as appropriate, until we reach the desired node.

	IS	IX	S	X
IS	Yes	Yes	Yes	No
IX	Yes	Yes	No	No
S	Yes	No	Yes	No
X	No	No	No	No

Figure 9.28: Compatibility matrix for shared, exclusive, and intention locks

In order to decide whether or not one of these locks can be granted, we use the compatibility matrix of Fig. 9.28. To see why this matrix makes sense, consider first the IS column. When we request an IS lock on a node N, we intend to read a descendant of N. The only time this intent could create a problem is if some other transaction has already claimed the right to write a new copy of the entire database element represented by N; thus we see "No" in the row for X. Notice that if some other transaction plans to write only a subelement, indicated by an IX lock at N, then we can afford to grant the IS lock at N, and allow the conflict to be resolved at a lower level, if indeed the intent to write and the intent to read happen to involve a common element.

Now consider the column for IX. If we intend to write a subelement of node N, then we must prevent either reading or writing of the entire element represented by N. Thus, we see "No" in the entries for lock modes S and X. However, per our discussion of the IS column, another transaction that reads or writes a subelement can have potential conflicts dealt with at that level, so IX does not conflict with another IX at N or with an IS at N.

Next, consider the column for S. Reading the element corresponding to node N cannot conflict with either another read lock on N or a read lock on some subelement of N, represented by IS at N. Thus, we see "Yes" in the rows for both S and IS. However, either an X or an IX means that some other transaction will write at least a part of the element represented by N. Thus, we cannot grant the right to read all of N, which explains the "No" entries in the column for S.

Finally, the column for X has only "No" entries. We cannot allow writing of all of node N if any other transaction already has the right to read or write N, or to acquire that right on a subelement.

Example 9.21: Consider the relation

```
Movie(title, year, length, studioName)
```

Let us postulate a lock on the entire relation and locks on individual tuples. Then transaction T_1, which consists of the query

```
SELECT *
FROM Movie
WHERE title = 'King Kong';
```

starts by getting an IS lock on the entire relation. It then moves to the individual tuples (there are two movies with the title *King Kong*), and gets S locks on each of them.

Now, suppose that while we are executing the first query, transaction T_2, which changes the year component of a tuple, begins:

```
UPDATE Movie
SET year = 1939
WHERE title = 'Gone With the Wind';
```

T_2 needs an IX lock on the relation, since it plans to write a new value for one of the tuples. T_1's IS lock on the relation is compatible, so the lock is granted. When T_2 goes to the tuple for *Gone With the Wind*, it finds no lock there, and so gets its X lock and rewrites the tuple. Had T_2 tried to write a new value in the tuple for one of the *King Kong* movies, it would have had to wait until T_1 released its S lock, since S and X are not compatible. The collection of locks is suggested by Fig. 9.29. ☐

Group Modes for Intention Locks

The compatibility matrix of Fig. 9.28 exhibits a situation we have not seen before regarding the power of lock modes. In prior lock schemes, whenever it was possible for a database element to be locked in both modes M and N at the same time, one of these modes *dominates* the other, in the sense that its row and column each has "No" in whatever positions the other mode's row or column, respectively, has "No." For example, in Fig. 9.19 we see that U dominates S, and X dominates both S and U. An advantage of knowing that there is always one dominant lock on an element is that we can summarize the effect of many locks with a "group mode," as discussed in Section 9.5.2.

As we see from Fig. 9.28, neither of modes S and IX dominate the other. Moreover, it is possible for an element to be locked in both modes S and IX at the same time, provided the locks are requested by the same transaction (recall that the "No" entries in a compatibility matrix only apply to locks held by some *other* transaction). A transaction might request both locks if it wanted to read an entire element and then write a small subset of its subelements. If a transaction has both S and IX locks on an element, then it restricts other transactions to the extent that either lock does. That is, we can imagine another lock mode SIX, whose row and column have "No" everywhere except in the entry for IS. The lock mode SIX serves as the group mode if there is a transaction with locks in S and IX modes, but not X mode.

Incidentally, we might imagine that the same situation occurs in the matrix of Fig 9.22 for increment locks. That is, one transaction could hold locks in both S and I modes. However, this situation is equivalent to holding a lock in X mode, so we could use X as the group mode in that situation.

9.6.3 Phantoms and Handling Insertions Correctly

When transactions create new subelements of a lockable element, there are some opportunities to go wrong. The problem is that we can only lock existing items; there is no easy way to lock database elements that do not exist but might later be inserted. The following example illustrates the point.

Example 9.22 : Suppose we have the same Movie relation as in Example 9.21, and the first transaction to execute is T_3, which is the query

```
SELECT SUM(length)
FROM Movie
WHERE studioName = 'Disney';
```

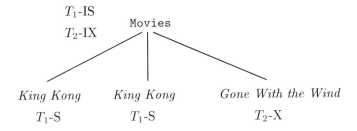

Figure 9.29: Locks granted to two transactions accessing `Movie` tuples

T_3 needs to read the tuples of all the Disney movies, so it might start by getting an *IS* lock on the relation and *S* locks on each of the tuples for Disney movies.[8]

Now, a transaction T_4 comes along and inserts a new Disney movie. It seems that T_4 needs no locks, but it has made the result of T_3 incorrect. That fact by itself is not a concurrency problem, since the serial order (T_3, T_4) is equivalent to what actually happened. However, there could also be some other element X that both T_3 and T_4 write, with T_4 writing first, so there *could* be an unserializable behavior of more complex transactions.

To be more precise, suppose that D_1 and D_2 are pre-existing Disney movies, and D_3 is the new Disney movie inserted by T_4. Let L be the sum of the lengths of the Disney movies computed by T_3, and assume the consistency constraint on the database is that L should be equal to the sum of all the lengths of the Disney movies. that existed the last time L it was computed. Then the following is a sequence of events that is legal under the warning protocol:

$$r_3(D_1); r_3(D_2); w_4(D_3); w_4(X); w_3(L); w_3(X);$$

Here, we have used $w_4(D_3)$ to represent the creation of D_3 by transaction T_4. The schedule above is not serializable. In particular, the value of L is not the sum of the lengths of D_1, D_2, and D_3, which are the current Disney movies. Moreover, the fact that X has the value written by T_3 and not T_4 rules out the possibility that T_3 was ahead of T_4 in a supposed equivalent serial order. □

The problem in Example 9.22 is that the new Disney movie has a *phantom* tuple, one that should have been locked but wasn't, because it didn't exist at the time the locks were taken. There is, however, a simple way to avoid the occurrence of phantoms. We must regard the insertion or deletion of a tuple as a write operation on the relation as a whole. Thus, transaction T_4 in Example 9.22 must obtain an X lock on the relation `Movie`. Since T_3 has already locked this relation in mode *IS*, and that mode is not compatible with mode X, T_4 would have to wait until after T_3 completes.

---

[8]However, if there were many Disney movies, it might be more efficient just to get an *S* lock on the entire relation.

9.6.4   Exercises for Section 9.6

Exercise 9.6.1: Consider, for variety, an object-oriented database. The objects of class C are stored on two blocks, B_1 and B_2. Block B_1 contains objects O_1 and O_2, while block B_2 contains objects O_3, O_4, and O_5. Class extents, blocks, and objects form a hierarchy of lockable database elements. Tell the sequence of lock requests and the response of a warning-protocol-based scheduler to the following sequences of requests. You may assume all requests occur just before they are needed, and all unlocks occur at the end of the transaction.

* a) $r_1(O_1); w_2(O_2); r_2(O_3); w_1()_4);$

 b) $r_1(O_5); w_2(O_5); r_2(O_3); w_1()_4);$

 c) $r_1(O_1); r_1(O_3); r_2(O_1); w_2(O_4); w_2(O_5);$

 d) $r_1(O_1); r_2(O_2); r_3(O_1); w_1(O_3); w_2(O_4); w_3(O_5); w_1(O_2);$

Exercise 9.6.2: Change the sequence of actions in Example 9.22 so that the $w_4(D_3)$ action becomes a write by T_4 of the entire relation Movie. Then, show the action of a warning-protocol-based scheduler on this sequence of requests.

!! **Exercise 9.6.3:** Show how to add increment locks to a warning-protocol-based scheduler.

9.7   The Tree Protocol

In this section we consider another problem involving trees of elements. Section 9.6 dealt with trees that are formed by the nesting structure of the database elements, with the children being subparts of the parent. Now, we deal with tree structures that are formed by the link pattern of the elements themselves. Database elements are disjoint pieces of data, but the only way to get to a node is through its parent; B-trees are an important example of this sort of data. Knowing that we must traverse a particular path to an element gives us some important freedom to manage locks differently from the two-phase locking approaches we have seen so far.

9.7.1   Motivation for Tree-Based Locking

Let us consider a B-tree index, in a system that treats individual nodes (i.e., blocks) as lockable database elements. The node is the right level of lock granularity, because treating smaller pieces as elements offers no benefit, and treating the entire B-tree as one database element prevents the sort of concurrent use of the index that can be achieved via the mechanisms that form the subject of Section 9.7.

   If we use a standard set of lock modes, like shared, exclusive, and update locks, and we use two-phase locking, then concurrent use of the B-tree is almost impossible. The reason is that every transaction using the index must begin by locking the root node of the B-tree. If the transaction is 2PL, then it cannot unlock the root until it has acquired all the locks it needs, both on B-tree nodes and other database elements.[9] Moreover, since in principle any transaction that inserts or deletes could wind up rewriting the root of the B-tree, the transaction needs at least an update lock on the root node, or an exclusive lock if update mode is not available. Thus, only one transaction that is not read-only can access the B-tree at any time.

However, in most situations, we can deduce almost immediately that a B-tree node will not be rewritten, even if the transaction inserts or deletes a tuple. For example, if the transaction inserts a tuple, but the child of the root that we visit is not completely full, then we know the insertion cannot propagate up to the root. Similarly, if the transaction deletes a single tuple, and the child of the root we visit has more than the minimum number of keys and pointers, then we can be sure the root will not change.

Thus, as soon as a transaction moves to a child of the root and observes the (quite usual) situation that rules out a rewrite of the root, we would like to release the lock on the root. The same observation applies to the lock on any interior node of the B-tree, although most of the opportunity for concurrent B-tree access comes from releasing locks on the root early. Unfortunately, releasing the lock on the root early will violate 2PL, so we cannot be sure that the schedule of several transactions accessing the B-tree will be serializable. The solution is a specialized protocol for transactions that access tree-structured data like B-trees. The protocol violates 2PL, but uses the fact that accesses to elements must proceed down the tree to assure serializability.

9.7.2 Rules for Access to Tree-Structured Data

The following restrictions on locks form the *tree protocol*. We assume that there is only one kind of lock, represented by lock requests of the form $l_i(X)$, but the idea generalizes to any set of lock modes. We assume that transactions are consistent, and schedules must be legal (i.e., the scheduler will enforce the expected restrictions by granting locks only when they do not conflict with locks already at a node), but there is no two-phase locking requirement on transactions.

1. A transaction's first lock may be at any node of the tree.[10]

2. Subsequent locks may only be acquired if the transaction currently has a lock on the parent node.

3. Nodes may be unlocked at any time.

---

[9]Additionally, there are good reasons why a transaction will hold all its locks until it is ready to commit; see Section 10.1.

[10]In the B-tree example of Section 9.7.1, the first lock would always be at the root.

4. A transaction may not relock a node on which it has released a lock, even if it still holds a lock on the node's parent.

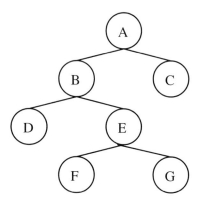

Figure 9.30: A tree of lockable elements

Example 9.23 : Figure 9.30 shows a hierarchy of nodes, and Fig. 9.31 indicates the action of three transactions on this data. T_1 starts at the root A, and proceeds downward to B, C, and D. T_2 starts at B and tries to move to E, but its move is initially denied because of the lock by T_3 on E. Transaction T_3 starts at E and moves to F and G. Notice that T_1 is not a 2PL transaction, because the lock on A is relinquished before the lock on D is acquired. Similarly, T_3 is not a 2PL transaction, although T_2 happens to be 2PL. □

9.7.3 Why the Tree Protocol Works

The tree protocol forces a serial order on the transactions involved in a schedule. We can define an order of precedence as follows. Say that $T_i <_S T_j$ if in schedule S, the transactions T_i and T_j lock a node in common, and T_i locks the node first.

Example 9.24 : In the schedule S of Fig 9.31, we find T_1 and T_2 lock B in common, and T_1 locks it first. Thus, $T_1 <_S T_2$. We also find that T_2 and T_3 lock E in common, and T_3 locks it first; thus $T_3 <_S T_2$. However, there is no precedence between T_1 and T_3, because they lock no node in common. Thus, the precedence graph derived from these precedence relations is as shown in Fig. 9.32. □

If the precedence graph drawn from the precedence relations that we defined above has no cycles, then we claim that any topological order of the transactions is an equivalent serial schedule. For example, either (T_1, T_3, T_2) or (T_3, T_1, T_2) is an equivalent serial schedule for Fig. 9.31. The reason is that in such a serial

T_1	T_2	T_3
$l_1(A); r_1(A);$		
$l_1(B); r_1(B);$		
$l_1(C); r_1(C);$		
$w_1(A); u_1(A);$		
$l_1(D); r_1(D);$		
$w_1(B); u_1(B);$		
	$l_2(B); r_2(B);$	
		$l_3(E); r_3(E);$
$w_1(D); u_1(D);$		
$w_1(C); u_1(C);$		
	$l_2(E)$ **Denied**	
		$l_3(F); r_3(F);$
		$w_3(F); u_3(F);$
		$l_3(G); r_3(G)$
		$w_3(E); u_3(E);$
	$l_2(E); r_2(E);$	
		$w_3(G); u_3(G)$
	$w_2(B); u_2(B);$	
	$w_2(E); u_2(E);$	

Figure 9.31: Three transactions following the tree protocol

schedule, all nodes are touched in the same order as they are in the original schedule.

To understand why the precedence graph described above must always be acyclic, let us first observe the following:

- If two transactions lock several elements in common, then they are all locked in the same order.

Consider some transactions T and U, which lock two or more items in common. First, notice that each transaction locks a set of elements that form a tree, and the intersection of two trees is itself a tree. Thus, there is some one highest element X that both T and U lock. Suppose that T locks X first, but that there is some other element Y that U locks before T. Then there is a path in the tree of elements from X to Y, and both T and U must lock each element along the path, because neither can lock a node without having a lock on its parent.

Consider the first element along this path, say Z, that U locks first, as suggested by Fig. 9.33. Then T locks the parent P of Z before U does. But then T is still holding the lock on P when it locks Z, so U has not yet locked P when it locks Z. It cannot be that Z is the first element U locks in common with T, since they both lock ancestor X (which could also be P, but not Z).

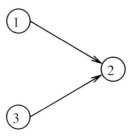

Figure 9.32: Precedence graph derived from the schedule of Fig. 9.31

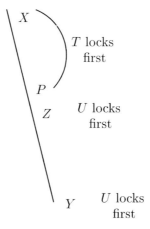

Figure 9.33: A path of elements locked by two transactions

Thus, U cannot lock Z until after it has acquired a lock on P, which is after T locks Z. We conclude that T precedes U at every node they lock in common.

Now, consider an arbitrary set of transactions $T_1, T_2, \ldots, T_n$ that obey the tree protocol and lock some of the nodes of a tree according to schedule S. First, among those that lock the root, they do so in some order, and by the rule just observed:

- If T_i locks the root before T_j, then T_i locks every node in common with T_j before T_j does. That is, $T_i <_S T_j$, but not $T_j <_S T_i$.

We can show by induction on the number of nodes of the tree that there is some serial order equivalent to S for the complete set of transactions.

BASIS: If there is only one node, the root, then as we just observed, the order in which the transactions lock the root serves.

INDUCTION: If there is more than one node in the tree, consider for each subtree of the root the set of transactions that lock one or more nodes in that subtree. Note that transactions locking the root may belong to more than one subtree, but a transaction that does not lock the root will belong to only one of the subtrees. For instance, among the transactions of Fig. 9.31, only T_1 locks the root, and it belongs to both subtrees — the tree rooted at B and the tree rooted at C. However, T_2 and T_3 belong only to the tree rooted at B.

By the inductive hypothesis, there is a serial order for all the transactions that lock nodes in any one subtree. We have only to blend the serial orders for the various subtrees. Since the only transactions these lists of transactions have in common are the transactions that lock the root, and we established that these transactions lock every node in common in the same order that they lock the root, it is not possible that two transactions locking the root appear in different orders in two of the sublists. Specifically, if T_i and T_j appear on the list for some child C of the root, then they lock C in the same order as they lock the root and therefore appear on the list in that order. Thus, we can build a serial order for the full set of transactions by starting with the transactions that lock the root, in their appropriate order, and interspersing those transactions that do not lock the root in any order consistent with the serial order of their subtrees.

Example 9.25 : Suppose there are 10 transactions $T_1, T_2, \ldots, T_{10}$, and of these, T_1, T_2, and T_3 lock the root in that order. Suppose also that there are two children of the root, the first locked by T_1 through T_7 and the second locked by T_2, T_3, T_8, T_9, and T_{10}. Hypothetically, let the serial order for the first subtree be $(T_4, T_1, T_5, T_2, T_6, T_3, T_7)$; note that this order must include T_1, T_2, and T_3 in that order. Also, let the serial order for the second subtree be $(T_8, T_2, T_9, T_{10}, T_3)$. As must be the case, the transactions T_2 and T_3, which locked the root, appear in this sequence in the order in which they locked the root.

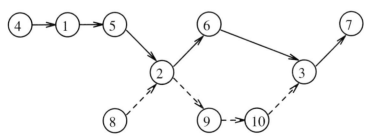

Figure 9.34: Combining serial orders for the subtrees into a serial order for all transactions

The constraints imposed on the serial order of these transactions are as shown in Fig. 9.34. Solid lines represent constraints due to the order at the first child of the root, while dashed lines represent the order at the second child. $(T_4, T_8, T_1, T_5, T_2, T_9, T_6, T_{10}, T_3, T_7)$ is one of the many topological sorts of this graph. □

9.7.4   Exercises for Section 9.7

Exercise 9.7.1 : Suppose we perform the following actions on the B-tree of Fig. 4.23. If we use the tree protocol, when can we release a write-lock on each of the nodes searched?

* a) Insert 10.

  b) Insert 20.

  c) Delete 5.

  d) Delete 23.

! **Exercise 9.7.2 :** Consider the following transactions that operate on the tree of Fig. 9.30.

T_1: $r_1(A)$; $r_1(B)$; $r_1(E)$;

T_2: $r_2(A)$; $r_2(C)$; $r_2(B)$;

T_3: $r_3(B)$; $r_3(E)$; $r_3(F)$;

Answer the following:

* a) In how many ways can T_1 and T_2 be interleaved, if they follow the tree protocol?

  b) In how many ways can T_1 and T_3 be interleaved, if they follow the tree protocol?

!! c) In how many ways can all three be interleaved, if they follow the tree protocol?

! **Exercise 9.7.3 :** Suppose there are eight transactions $T_1, T_2, \ldots, T_8$, of which the odd-numbered transactions, T_1, T_3, T_5, and T_7, lock the root of a tree, in that order. There are three children of the root, the first locked by T_1, T_2, T_3, and T_4 in that order. The second child is locked by T_3, T_6, and T_5, in that order, and the third child is locked by T_8 and T_7, in that order. How many serial orders of the transactions are consistent with these statements?

!! **Exercise 9.7.4 :** Suppose we use the tree protocol with shared and exclusive locks for reading and writing, respectively. Rule (2), which requires a lock on the parent to get a lock on a node, must be changed to prevent unserializable behavior. What is the proper rule (2) for shared and exclusive locks? *Hint*: Does the lock on the parent have to be of the same type as the lock on the child?

9.8 Concurrency Control by Timestamps

Next, we shall consider two methods other than locking that are used in some systems to assure serializability of transactions:

1. *Timestamping.* We assign a "timestamp" to each transaction, record the timestamps of the transactions that last read and write each database element, and compare these values to assure that the serial schedule according to the transactions' timestamps is equivalent to the actual schedule of the transactions. This approach is the subject of the present section.

2. *Validation.* We examine timestamps of the transaction and the database elements when a transaction is about to commit; this process is called "validation" of the transaction. The serial schedule that orders transactions according to their validation time must be equivalent to the actual schedule. The validation approach is discussed in Section 9.9.

Both these approaches are *optimistic*, in the sense that they assume that no unserializable behavior will occur and only fix things up when a violation is apparent. In contrast, all locking methods assume that things will go wrong unless transactions are prevented in advance from engaging in nonserializable behavior. The optimistic approaches differ from locking in that the only remedy when something does go wrong is to abort and restart a transaction that tries to engage in unserializable behavior. In contrast, locking schedulers delay transactions, but do not abort them.[11] Generally, optimistic schedulers are better than locking when many of the transactions are read-only, since those transactions can never by themselves cause unserializable behavior.

9.8.1 Timestamps

In order to use timestamping as a concurrency-control method, the scheduler needs to assign to each transaction T a unique number, its *timestamp* TS(T). Timestamps must be issued in ascending order, at the time that a transaction first notifies the scheduler that it is beginning. Two approaches to generating timestamps are:

a) One possible way to create timestamps is to use the system clock, provided the scheduler does not operate so fast that it could assign timestamps to two transactions on one tick of the clock.

b) Another approach is for the scheduler to maintain a counter. Each time a transaction starts, the counter is incremented by 1, and the new value becomes the timestamp of the transaction. In this approach, timestamps

---

[11]That is not to say that a system using a locking scheduler will never abort a transaction; for instance, Section 10.3 discusses aborting transactions to fix deadlocks. However, a locking scheduler never uses a transaction abort simply as a response to a lock request that it cannot grant.

have nothing to do with "time," but they have the important property that we need for any timestamp-generating system: a transaction that starts later has a higher timestamp than a transaction that starts earlier.

Whatever method of generating timestamps is used, the scheduler must maintain a table of currently active transactions and their timestamps.

To use timestamps as a concurrency-control method, we need to associate with each database element X two timestamps and an additional bit:

1. $\text{RT}(X)$, the *read time* of X, which is the highest timestamp of a transaction that has read X.

2. $\text{WT}(X)$, the *write time* of X, which is the highest timestamp of a transaction that has written X.

3. $\text{C}(X)$, the *commit bit* for X, which is true if and only if the most recent transaction to write X has already committed. The purpose of this bit is to avoid a situation where one transaction T reads data written by another transaction U, and U then aborts. This problem, where T makes a "dirty read" of uncommitted data, certainly can cause the database state to become inconsistent, and any scheduler needs a mechanism to prevent dirty reads.[12]

9.8.2 Physically Unrealizable Behaviors

In order to understand the architecture and rules of a timestamp-based scheduler, we need to remember that the scheduler assumes that the timestamp order of transactions is also the serial order in which they must appear to execute. Thus, the job of the scheduler, in addition to assigning timestamps and updating RT, WT, and C for the database elements, is to check that whenever a read or write occurs, what happens in real time *could* have happened if each transaction had executed instantaneously at the moment of its timestamp. If not, we say the behavior is *physically unrealizable*. There are two kinds of problems that can occur:

1. *Read too late*: Transaction T tries to read database element X, but the write time of X indicates that the current value of X was written after T theoretically executed; that is, $\text{TS}(T) < \text{WT}(X)$. Figure 9.35 illustrates the problem. The horizontal axis represents the real time at which events occur. Dotted lines link the actual events to the times at which they theoretically occur — the timestamp of the transaction that performs the event. Thus, we see a transaction U that started after transaction T, but wrote a value for X before T reads X. T should not be able to read the value written by U, because theoretically, U executed after T did. However, T has no choice, because U's value of X is the one that T now sees. The solution is to abort T when the problem is encountered.

---

[12]Although commercial systems generally give the user an option to allow dirty reads.

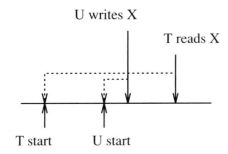

Figure 9.35: Transaction T tries to read too late

2. *Write too late*: Transaction T tries to write database element X, but the read time of X indicates that some other transaction should have read the value written by T but read some other value instead. That is, $\text{WT}(X) < \text{TS}(T) < \text{RT}(X)$. The problem is shown in Fig. 9.36. There we see a transaction U that started after T, but read X before T got a chance to write X. When T tries to write X, we find $\text{RT}(X) > \text{TS}(T)$, meaning that X has already been read by a transaction U that theoretically executed later than T. We also find $\text{WT}(X) < \text{TS}(T)$, which means that no other transaction wrote into X a value that would have overwritten T's value, thus, negating T's responsibility to get its value into X so transaction U could read it.

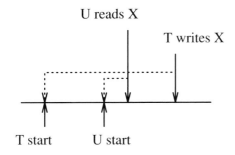

Figure 9.36: Transaction T tries to write too late

9.8.3 Problems With Dirty Data

There is a class of problems that the commit bit is designed to help deal with. One of these problems, a "dirty read," is suggested in Fig. 9.37. There, transaction T reads X, and X was last written by U. The timestamp of U is less than that of T, and the read by T occurs after the write by U in real time, so the event seems to be physically realizable. However, it is possible that after

T reads the value of X written by U, transaction U will abort; perhaps U encounters an error condition in its own data, such as a division by 0, or as we shall see in Section 9.8.4, the scheduler forces U to abort because it tries to do something physically unrealizable. Thus, although there is nothing physically unrealizable about T reading X, it is better to delay T's read until U commits or aborts. We can tell that U is not committed because the committed bit $\text{C}(X)$ will be false.

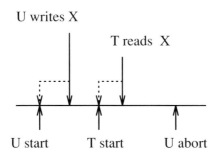

Figure 9.37: T could perform a dirty read if it reads X when shown

A second potential problem is suggested by Fig. 9.38. Here, U, a transaction with a later timestamp than T, has written X first. When T tries to write, the appropriate action is to do nothing. Evidently no other transaction V that should have read T's value of X got U's value instead, because if V tried to read X it would have aborted because of a too-late read. Future reads of X will want U's value or a later value of X, not T's value. This idea, that writes can be skipped when a write with a later write-time is already in place, is called the *Thomas write rule*.

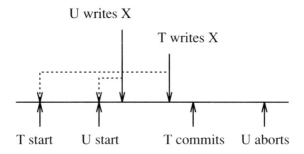

Figure 9.38: A write is cancelled because of a write with a later timestamp, but the writer then aborts

There is a potential problem with the Thomas write rule, however. If U later aborts, as is suggested in Fig. 9.38, then its value of X should be removed and the previous value and write-time restored. Since T is committed, it would seem that the value of X should be the one written by T for future reading.

However, we already skipped the write by T and it is too late to repair the damage.

While there are many ways to deal with the problems just described, we shall adopt a relatively simple policy based on the following assumed capability of the timestamp-based scheduler.

- When a transaction T writes a database element X, the write is "tentative" and may be undone if T aborts. The commit bit $C(X)$ is set to false, and the scheduler makes a copy of the old value of X and its previous $\text{WT}(X)$.

9.8.4 The Rules for Timestamp-Based Scheduling

We can now summarize the rules that a scheduler using timestamps must follow to make sure that nothing physically unrealizable may occur. The scheduler, in response to a read or write request from a transaction T has the choice of:

a) Granting the request,

b) Aborting T (if T would violate physical reality) and restarting T with a new timestamp (abort followed by restart is often called *rollback*), or

c) Delaying T and later deciding whether to abort T or to grant the request (if the request is a read, and the read might be dirty, as in Section 9.8.3).

The rules are as follows:

1. Suppose the scheduler receives a request $r_T(X)$.

   (a) If $\text{TS}(T) \geq \text{WT}(X)$, the read is physically realizable.

      i. If $\text{C}(X)$ is true, grant the request. If $\text{TS}(T) > \text{RT}(X)$, set $\text{RT}(X) := \text{TS}(T)$; otherwise do not change $\text{RT}(X)$.

      ii. If $\text{C}(X)$ is false, delay T until $\text{C}(X)$ becomes true or the transaction that wrote X aborts.

   (b) If $\text{TS}(T) < \text{WT}(X)$, the read is physically unrealizable. Rollback T; that is, abort T and restart it with a new, larger timestamp.

2. Suppose the scheduler receives a request $w_T(X)$.

   (a) If $\text{TS}(T) \geq \text{RT}(X)$ and $\text{TS}(T) \geq \text{WT}(X)$, the write is physically realizable and must be performed.

      i. Write the new value for X,

      ii. Set $\text{WT}(X) := \text{TS}(T)$, and

      iii. Set $\text{C}(X) := \texttt{false}$.

  (b) If $\text{TS}(T) \geq \text{RT}(X)$, but $\text{TS}(T) < \text{WT}(X)$, then the write is physically realizable, but there is already a later value in X. If $C(X)$ is true, then the previous writer of X is committed, and we simply ignore the write by T; we allow T to proceed and make no change to the database. However, if $C(X)$ is false, then we must delay T as in point 1(a)ii.

  (c) If $\text{TS}(T) < \text{RT}(X)$, then the write is physically unrealizable, and T must be rolled back.

3. Suppose the scheduler receives a request to commit T. It must find (using a list the scheduler maintains) all the database elements X written by T, and set $C(X) := \text{true}$. If any transactions are waiting for X to be committed (found from another scheduler-maintained list), these transactions are allowed to proceed.

4. Suppose the scheduler receives a request to abort T or decides to rollback T as in 1b or 2c. Then any transaction that was waiting on an element X that T wrote must repeat its attempt to read or write, and see whether the action is now legal after the aborted transaction's writes are cancelled.

Example 9.26 : Figure 9.39 shows a schedule of three transactions, T_1, T_2, and T_3 that access three database elements, A, B, and C. The real time at which events occur increases down the page, as usual. However, we have also indicated the timestamps of the transactions and the read and write times of the elements. We assume that at the beginning, each of the database elements has both a read and write time of 0. The timestamps of the transactions are acquired when they notify the scheduler that they are beginning. Notice that even though T_1 executes the first data access, it does not have the least timestamp. Presumably T_2 was the first to notify the scheduler of its start, and T_3 did so next, with T_1 last to start.

T_1	T_2	T_3	A	B	C
200	150	175	RT=0	RT=0	RT=0
			WT=0	WT=0	WT=0
$r_1(B)$;				RT=200	
	$r_2(A)$;		RT=150		
		$r_3(C)$;			RT=175
$w_1(B)$;				WT=200	
$w_1(A)$;			WT=200		
	$w_2(C)$;				
	Abort;				
		$w_3(A)$;			

Figure 9.39: Three transactions executing under a timestamp-based scheduler

In the first action, T_1 reads B. Since the write time of B is less than the timestamp of T_1, this read is physically realizable and allowed to happen. The read time of B is set to 200, the timestamp of T_1. The second and third read actions similarly are legal and result in the read time of each database element being set to the timestamp of the transaction that read it.

At the fourth step, T_1 writes B. Since the read time of B is not bigger than the timestamp of T_1, the write is physically realizable. Since the write time of B is no larger than the timestamp of T_1, we must actually perform the write. When we do, the write time of B is raised to 200, the timestamp of the writing transaction T_1.

Next, T_2 tries to write C. However, C was already read by transaction T_3, which theoretically executed at time 175, while T_2 would have written its value at time 150. Thus, T_2 is trying to do something that would result in physically unrealizable behavior, and T_2 must be rolled back.

The last step is the write of A by T_3. Since the read time of A, 150, is less than the timestamp of T_3, 175, the write is legal. However, there is already a later value of A stored in that database element, namely the value written by T_1, theoretically at time 200. Thus, T_3 is not rolled back, but neither does it write its value. □

9.8.5 Multiversion Timestamps

An important variation of timestamping maintains old versions of database elements in addition to the current version that is stored in the database itself. The purpose is to allow reads $r_T(X)$ that otherwise would cause transaction T to abort (because the current version of X was written in T's future) to proceed by reading the version of X that is appropriate for a transaction with T's timestamp. The method is especially useful if database elements are disk blocks or pages, since then all that must be done is for the buffer manager to keep in memory certain blocks that might be useful for some currently active transaction.

Example 9.27: Consider the set of transactions accessing database element A shown in Fig. 9.40. These transactions are operating under an ordinary timestamp-based scheduler, and when T_3 tries to read A, it finds $\text{WT}(A)$ to be greater than its own timestamp, and must abort. However, there is an old value of A written by T_1 and overwritten by T_2 that would have been suitable for T_3 to read; this version of A had a write time of 150, which is less than T_3's timestamp of 175. If this old value of A were available, T_3 could be allowed to read it, even though it is not the "current" value of A. □

A multiversion timestamping scheduler differs from the scheduler described in Section 9.8.4 in the following ways:

1. When a new write $w_T(X)$ occurs, if it is legal, then a new version of database element X is created. Its write time is $\text{TS}(T)$, and we shall refer to it as X_t, where $t = \text{TS}(T)$.

T_1	T_2	T_3	T_4	A
150	200	175	225	RT=0
				WT=0
$r_1(A)$				RT=150
$w_1(A)$				WT=150
	$r_2(A)$			RT=200
	$w_2(A)$			WT=200
		$r_3(A)$		
		Abort		
			$r_4(A)$	RT=225

Figure 9.40: T_3 must abort because it cannot access an old value of A

2. When a read $r_T(X)$ occurs, the scheduler finds the version X_t of X such that $t \leq \text{TS}(T)$, but there is no other version $X_{t'}$ with $t < t' \leq \text{TS}(T)$. That is, the version of X written immediately before T theoretically executed is the version that T reads.

3. Write times are associated with *versions* of an element, and they never change.

4. Read times are also associated with versions. They are used to reject certain writes, namely one whose time is less than the read time of the previous version. Figure 9.41 suggests the problem, where X has versions X_{50} and X_{100}, the former was read at time 80, and a new write by a transaction T whose timestamp is 60 occurs. This write must cause T to abort, because its value of X should have been read by the transaction with timestamp 80, had T been allowed to execute.

5. When a version X_t has a write time t such that no active transaction has a timestamp less than t, then we may delete any version of X *previous* to X_t.

Example 9.28 : Let us reconsider the actions of Fig. 9.40 if multiversion timestamping is used. First, there are three versions of A: A_0, which exists before these transactions start, A_{150}, written by T_1, and A_{200}, written by T_2. Figure 9.42 shows the sequence of events, when the versions are created, and when they are read. Notice in particular that T_3 does not have to abort, because it can read an earlier version of A.   □

9.8.6   Timestamps and Locking

Generally, timestamping is superior in situations where either most transactions are read-only, or it is rare that concurrent transactions will try to read and

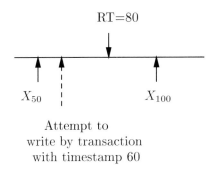

Figure 9.41: A transaction tries to write a version of X that would make events physically unrealizable

T_1	T_2	T_3	T_4	A_0	A_{150}	A_{200}
150	200	175	225			
$r_1(A)$				Read		
$w_1(A)$					Create	
	$r_2(A)$				Read	
	$w_2(A)$					Create
		$r_3(A)$			Read	
			$r_4(A)$			Read

Figure 9.42: Execution of transactions using multiversion concurrency control

write the same element. In high-conflict situations, locking performs better. The argument for this rule-of-thumb is:

- Locking will frequently delay transactions as they wait for locks, and can even lead to deadlocks, where several transactions wait for a long time, and then one has to be rolled back.

- But if concurrent transactions frequently read and write elements in common, then rollbacks will be frequent, introducing even more delay than a locking system.

There is an interesting compromise used in several commercial systems. The scheduler divides the transactions into read-only transactions and read/write transactions. Read/write transactions are executed using two-phase locking, to keep both each other and read-only transactions from accessing the elements they lock.

Read-only transactions are executed using multiversion timestamping. As the read/write transactions create new versions of a database element, those versions are managed as in Section 9.8.5. A read-only transaction is allowed to read whatever version of a database element is appropriate for its timestamp. A read-only transaction thus never has to abort, and will only rarely be delayed.

9.8.7 Exercises for Section 9.8

Exercise 9.8.1 : Below are several sequences of events, including *start* events, where st_i means that transaction T_i starts. These sequences represent real time, and the timestamp-based scheduler will allocate timestamps to transactions in the order of their starts. Tell what happens as each executes.

* a) st_1; st_2; $r_1(A)$; $r_2(B)$; $w_2(A)$; $w_1(B)$;

  b) st_1; $r_1(A)$; st_2; $w_2(B)$; $r_2(A)$; $w_1(B)$;

  c) st_1; st_2; st_3; $r_1(A)$; $r_2(B)$; $w_1(C)$; $r_3(B)$; $r_3(C)$; $w_2(B)$; $w_3(A)$;

  4) st_1; st_3; st_2; $r_1(A)$; $r_2(B)$; $w_1(C)$; $r_3(B)$; $r_3(C)$; $w_2(B)$; $w_3(A)$;

Exercise 9.8.2 : Tell what happens during the following sequences of events if a multiversion, timestamp-based scheduler is used. What happens instead, if the scheduler does not maintain multiple versions?

* a) st_1; st_2; st_3; st_4; $w_1(A)$; $w_2(A)$; $w_3(A)$; $r_2(A)$; $r_4(A)$;

  b) st_1; st_2; st_3; st_4; $w_1(A)$; $w_3(A)$; $r_4(A)$; $r_2(A)$;

  c) st_1; st_2; st_3; st_4; $w_1(A)$; $w_4(A)$; $r_3(A)$; $w_2(A)$;

!! **Exercise 9.8.3 :** We observed in our study of lock-based schedulers that there are several reasons why transactions that obtain locks could deadlock. Can a timestamp-based scheduler using the commit bit $C(X)$ have a deadlock?

9.9 Concurrency Control by Validation

Validation is another type of optimistic concurrency control, where we allow transactions to access data without locks, and at the appropriate time we check that the transaction has behaved in a serializable manner. Validation differs from timestamping principally in that the scheduler maintains a record of what active transactions are doing, rather than keeping read and write times for all database elements. Just before a transaction starts to write values of database elements, it goes through a "validation phase," where the sets of elements it has read and will write are compared with the write sets of other active transactions. Should there be a risk of physically unrealizable behavior, the transaction is rolled back.

9.9.1 Architecture of a Validation-Based Scheduler

When validation is used as the concurrency-control mechanism, the scheduler must be told for each transaction T the set of database elements T reads and the set of elements T writes. These sets are the *read set*, RS(T), and the *write set*, WS(T), respectively. Transactions are executed in three phases:

1. *Read.* In the first phase, the transaction reads from the database all the elements in its read set. The transaction also computes in its local address space all the results it is going to write.

2. *Validate.* In the second phase, the scheduler validates the transaction by comparing its read and write sets with those of other transactions. We shall describe the validation process in Section 9.9.2. If validation fails, then the transaction is rolled back; otherwise it proceeds to the third phase.

3. *Write.* In the third phase, the transaction writes to the database its values for the elements in its write set.

Intuitively, we may think of each transaction that successfully validates as executing at the moment that it validates. Thus, the validation-based scheduler has an assumed serial order of the transactions to work with, and it bases its decision to validate or not on whether the transactions' behaviors are consistent with this serial order.

To support the decision whether to validate a transaction, the scheduler maintains three sets:

1. *START*, the set of transactions that have started, but not yet completed validation. For each transaction T in this set, the scheduler maintains START(T), the time at which T started.

2. *VAL*, the set of transactions that have been validated but not yet finished the writing of phase 3. For each transaction T in this set, the scheduler maintains both START(T) and VAL(T), the time at which T validated. Note that VAL(T) is also the time at which T is imagined to execute in the hypothetical serial order of execution.

3. *FIN*, the set of transactions that have completed phase 3. For these transactions T, the scheduler records START(T), VAL(T), and FIN(T), the time at which T finished. In principle this set grows, but as we shall see, we do not have to remember transaction T if FIN(T) < START(U) for any active transaction U (i.e., for any U in *START* or *VAL*). The scheduler may thus periodically purge the *FIN* set to keep its size from growing beyond bounds.

9.9.2   The Validation Rules

If maintained by the scheduler, the information of Section 9.9.1 is enough for
it to detect any potential violation of the assumed serial order of the transactions — the order in which the transactions validate. To understand the rules,
let us first consider what can be wrong when we try to validate a transaction
T.

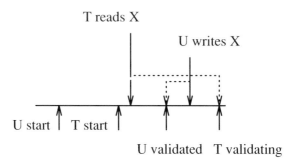

Figure 9.43: T cannot validate if an earlier transaction is now writing something
that T should have read

1. Suppose there is a transaction U such that:

   (a) U is in *VAL* or *FIN*; that is, U has validated.

   (b) $\text{FIN}(U) > \text{START}(T)$; that is, U did not finish before T started.[13]

   (c) $\text{RS}(T) \cap \text{WS}(U)$ is not empty; in particular, let it contain database
       element X.

   Then it is possible that U wrote X after T read X. In fact, U may not
   even have written X yet. A situation where U wrote X, but not in time
   is shown in Fig. 9.43. To interpret the figure, note that the dotted lines
   connect the events in real time with the time at which they would have
   occurred had transactions been executed at the moment they validated.
   Since we don't know whether or not T got to read U's value, we must
   rollback T to avoid a risk that the actions of T and U will not be consistent
   with the assumed serial order.

2. Suppose there is a transaction U such that:

   (a) U is in *VAL*; i.e., U has successfully validated.

   (b) $\text{FIN}(U) > \text{VAL}(T)$; that is, U did not finish before T entered its
       validation phase.

---

[13]Note that if U is in *VAL*, then U has not yet finished when T validates. In that case,
$\text{FIN}(U)$ is technically undefined. However, we know it must be larger than $\text{START}(T)$ in this
case.

(c) $\mathrm{WS}(T) \cap \mathrm{WS}(U) \neq \emptyset$; in particular, let X be in both write sets.

Then the potential problem is as shown in Fig. 9.44. T and U must both write values of X, and if we let T validate, it is possible that it will write X before U does. Since we cannot be sure, we rollback T to make sure it does not violate the assumed serial order in which it follows U.

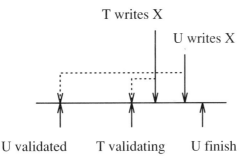

Figure 9.44: T cannot validate if it could then write something ahead of an earlier transaction

The two problems described above are the only situations in which a write by T could be physically unrealizable. In Fig. 9.43, if U finished before T started, then surely T would read the value of X that either U or some later transaction wrote. In Fig. 9.44, if U finished before T validated, then surely U wrote X before T did. We may thus summarize these observations with the following rule for validating a transaction T:

- Compare $\mathrm{RS}(T)$ with $\mathrm{WS}(U)$ and check that $\mathrm{RS}(T) \cap \mathrm{WS}(U) = \emptyset$ for any U that did not finish before T started, i.e., if $\mathrm{FIN}(U) > \mathrm{START}(T)$.

- Compare $\mathrm{WS}(T)$ with $WS(U)$ and check that $\mathrm{WS}(T) \cap \mathrm{WS}(U) = \emptyset$ for any U that did not finish before T validated, i.e., if $\mathrm{FIN}(U) > \mathrm{VAL}(T)$.

Example 9.29: Figure 9.45 shows a time line during which four transactions T, U, V, and W attempt to execute and validate. The read and write sets for each transaction are indicated on the diagram. T starts first, although U is the first to validate.

1. Validation of U: When U validates there are no other validated transactions, so there is nothing to check. U validates successfully and writes a value for database element D.

2. Validation of T: When T validates, U is validated but not finished. Thus, we must check that neither the read nor write set of T has anything in common with $\mathrm{WS}(U) = \{D\}$. Since $\mathrm{RS}(T) = \{A, B\}$, and $\mathrm{WS}(T) = \{A, C\}$, both checks are successful, and T validates.

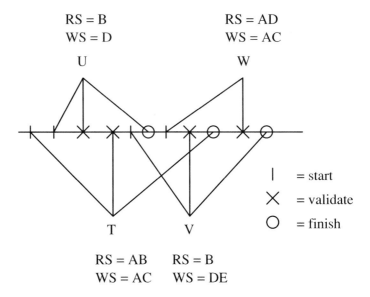

Figure 9.45: Four transactions and their validation

3. Validation of V: When V validates, U is validated and finished, and T is validated but not finished. Also, V started before U finished. Thus, we must compare both $RS(V)$ and $WS(V)$ against $WS(T)$, but only $RS(V)$ needs to be compared against $WS(U)$. we find:

   - $RS(V) \cap WS(T) = \{B\} \cap \{A, C\} = \emptyset$.
   - $WS(V) \cap WS(T) = \{D, E\} \cap \{A, C\} = \emptyset$.
   - $RS(V) \cap WS(U) = \{B\} \cap \{D\} = \emptyset$.

   Thus, V also validates successfully.

4. Validation of W: When W validates, we find that U finished before W started, so no comparison between W and U is performed. T is finished before W validates but did not finish before W started, so we compare only $RS(W)$ with $WS(T)$. V is validated but not finished, so we need to compare both $RS(W)$ and $WS(W)$ with $WS(T)$. These tests are:

   - $RS(W) \cap WS(T) = \{A, D\} \cap \{A, C\} = \{A\}$.
   - $RS(W) \cap WS(V) = \{A, D\} \cap \{D, E\} = \{D\}$.
   - $WS(W) \cap WS(V) = \{A, C\} \cap \{D, E\} = \emptyset$.

   Since the intersections are not all empty, W is not validated. Rather, W is rolled back and does not write values for A or C.

   $\square$

Just a Moment

You may have been concerned with a tacit notion that validation takes place in a moment, or indivisible instant of time. For example, we imagine that we can decide whether a transaction U has already validated before we start to validate transaction T. Could U perhaps finish validating while we are validating T?

If we are running on a uniprocessor system, and there is only one scheduler process, we can indeed think of validation and other actions of the scheduler as taking place in an instant of time. The reason is that if the scheduler is validating T, then it cannot also be validating U, so all during the validation of T, the validation status of U cannot change.

If we are running on a multiprocessor, and there are several scheduler processes, then it might be that one is validating T while the other is validating U. If so, then we need to rely on whatever synchronization mechanism the multiprocessor system provides to make validation an atomic action.

9.9.3 Comparison of Three Concurrency-Control Mechanisms

The three approaches to serializability that we have considered — locks, timestamps, and validation — each have their advantages. First, they can be compared for their storage utilization:

- *Locks*: Space in the lock table is proportional to the number of database elements locked.

- *Timestamps*: In a naive implementation, space is needed for read- and write-times with every database element, whether or not it is currently accessed. However, a more careful implementation will treat all timestamps that are prior to the earliest active transaction as "minus infinity" and not record them. In that case, we can store read- and write-times in a table analogous to a lock table, in which only those database elements that have been accessed recently are mentioned at all.

- *Validation*: Space is used for timestamps and read/write sets for each currently active transaction, plus a few more transactions that finished after some currently active transaction began.

Thus, the amounts of space used by each approach is approximately proportional to the sum over all active transactions of the number of database elements the transaction accesses. Timestamping and validation may use slightly more space because they keep track of certain accesses by recently committed transactions that a lock table would not record. A potential problem with validation is that the write set for a transaction must be known before the writes occur (but after the transaction's local computation has been completed).

We can also compare the methods for their effect on the ability of transactions to complete without delay. The performance of the three methods depends on whether *interaction* among transactions (the likelihood that a transaction will access an element that is also being accessed by a concurrent transaction) is high or low.

- Locking delays transactions but avoids rollbacks, even when interaction is high. Timestamps and validation do not delay transactions, but can cause them to rollback, which is a more serious form of delay and also wastes resources.

- If interference is low, then neither timestamps nor validation will cause many rollbacks, and may be preferable to locking because they generally have lower overhead than a locking scheduler.

- When a rollback is necessary, timestamps catch some problems earlier than validation, which always lets a transaction do all its internal work before considering whether the transaction must rollback.

9.9.4 Exercises for Section 9.9

Exercise 9.9.1: In the following sequences of events, we use $R_i(X)$ to mean "transaction T_i starts, and its read set is the list of database elements X." Also, V_i means "T_i attempts to validate," and $W_i(X)$ means that "T_i finishes, and its write set was X." Tell what happens when each sequence is processed by a validation-based scheduler.

* a) $R_1(A, B)$; $R_2(B, C)$; V_1; $R_3(C, D)$; V_3; $W_1(A)$; V_2; $W_2(A)$; $W_3(B)$;

   b) $R_1(A, B)$; $R_2(B, C)$; V_1; $R_3(C, D)$; V_3; $W_1(A)$; V_2; $W_2(A)$; $W_3(D)$;

   c) $R_1(A, B)$; $R_2(B, C)$; V_1; $R_3(C, D)$; V_3; $W_1(C)$; V_2; $W_2(A)$; $W_3(D)$;

   d) $R_1(A, B)$; $R_2(B, C)$; $R_3(C)$; V_1; V_2; V_3; $W_1(A)$; $W_2(B)$; $W_3(C)$;

   e) $R_1(A, B)$; $R_2(B, C)$; $R_3(C)$; V_1; V_2; V_3; $W_1(C)$; $W_2(B)$; $W_3(A)$;

   f) $R_1(A, B)$; $R_2(B, C)$; $R_3(C)$; V_1; V_2; V_3; $W_1(A)$; $W_2(C)$; $W_3(B)$;

9.10 Summary of Chapter 9

✦ *Consistent Database States*: Database states that obey whatever implied or declared constraints the designers intended are called consistent. It is essential that operations on the database preserve consistency, that is, they turn one consistent database state into another.

✦ *Consistency of Concurrent Transactions*: It is normal for several transactions to have access to a database at the same time. Transactions, run in isolation, are assumed to preserve consistency of the database. It is the job of the scheduler to assure that concurrently operating transactions also preserve the consistency of the database.

✦ *Schedules*: Transactions are broken into actions, mainly reading and writing from the database. A sequence of these actions from one or more transactions is called a schedule.

✦ *Serial Schedules*: If transactions execute one at a time, the schedule is said to be serial.

✦ *Serializable Schedules*: A schedule that is equivalent in its effect on the database to some serial schedule is said to be serializable. Interleaving of actions from several transactions is possible in a serializable schedule that is not itself serial, but we must be very careful what sequences of actions we allow, or an interleaving will leave the database in an inconsistent state.

✦ *Conflict-Serializability*: A simple-to-test, sufficient condition for serializability is that the schedule can be made serial by a sequence of swaps of adjacent actions without conflicts. Such a schedule is called conflict-serializable. A conflict occurs if we try to swap two actions of the same transaction, or to swap two actions that access the same database element, at least one of which actions is a write.

✦ *Precedence Graphs*: An easy test for conflict-serializability is to construct a precedence graph for the schedule. Nodes correspond to transactions, and there is an arc $T \to U$ if some action of T in the schedule conflicts with a later action of U. A schedule is conflict-serializable if and only if the precedence graph is acyclic.

✦ *Locking*: The most common approach to assuring serializable schedules is to lock database elements before accessing them, and to release the lock after finishing access to the element. Locks on an element prevent other transactions from accessing the element.

✦ *Two-Phase Locking*: Locking by itself does not assure serializability. However, two-phase locking, in which all transactions first enter a phase where they only acquire locks, and then enter a phase where they only release locks, will guarantee serializability.

✦ *Lock Modes*: To avoid locking out transactions unnecessarily, systems usually use several lock modes, with different rules for each mode about when a lock can be granted. Most common is the system with shared locks for read-only access and exclusive locks for accesses that include writing.

✦ *Compatibility Matrices*: A compatibility matrix is a useful summary of when it is legal to grant a lock in a certain lock mode, given that there may be other locks, in the same or other modes, on the same element.

✦ *Update Locks*: A scheduler can allow a transaction that plans to read and then write an element first to take an update lock, and later to upgrade the lock to exclusive. Update locks can be granted when there are already shared locks on the element, but once there, an update lock prevents other locks from being granted on that element.

✦ *Increment Locks*: For the common case where a transaction wants only to add or subtract a constant from an element, an increment lock is suitable. Increment locks on the same element do not conflict with each other, although they conflict with shared and exclusive locks.

✦ *Locking Elements With a Granularity Hierarchy*: When both large and small elements — relations, disk blocks, and tuples, perhaps — may need to be locked, a warning system of locks enforces serializability. Transactions place intention locks on large elements to warn other transactions that they plan to access one or more of its subelements.

✦ *Locking Elements Arranged in a Tree*: If database elements are only accessed by moving down a tree, as in a B-tree index, then a non-two-phase locking strategy can enforce serializability. The rules require a lock to be held on the parent while obtaining a lock on the child, although the lock on on the parent can then be released and additional locks taken later.

✦ *Optimistic Concurrency Control*: Instead of locking, a scheduler can assume transactions will be serializable, and abort a transaction if some potentially nonserializable behavior is seen. This approach, called optimistic, is divided into timestamp-based, and validation-based scheduling.

✦ *Timestamp-Based Schedulers*: This type of scheduler assigns timestamps to transactions as they begin. Database elements have associated read- and write-times, which are the timestamps of the transactions that most recently performed those actions. If an impossible situation, such as a read by one transaction of a value that was written in that transaction's future is detected, the violating transaction is rolled back, i.e., aborted and restarted.

✦ *Validation-Based Schedulers*: These schedulers validate transactions after they have read everything they need, but before they write. Transactions that have read, or will write, an element that some other transaction is in the process of writing, will have an ambiguous result, so the transaction is not validated. A transaction that fails to validate is rolled back.

✦ *Multiversion Timestamps*: A common technique in practice is for read-only transactions to be scheduled by timestamps, but with multiple versions, where a write of an element does not overwrite earlier values of that element until all transactions that could possibly need the earlier value have finished. Writing transactions are scheduled by conventional locks.

9.11 References for Chapter 9

The book [6] is an important source for material on scheduling, as well as locking. [3] is another important source. Two recent surveys of concurrency control are [12] and [11].

Probably the most significant paper in the field of transaction processing is [4] on two-phase locking. The warning protocol for hierarchies of granularity is from [5]. Non-two-phase locking for trees is from [10]. The compatibility matrix was introduced to study behavior of lock modes in [7].

Timestamps as a concurrency control method appeared in [2] and [1]. Scheduling by validation is from [8]. The use of multiple versions was studied by [9].

1. P. A. Bernstein and N. Goodman, "Timestamp-based algorithms for concurrency control in distributed database systems," *Proc. Intl. Conf. on Very Large Databases* (1980), pp. 285–300.

2. P. A. Bernstein, N. Goodman, J. B. Rothnie, Jr., and C. H. Papadimitriou, "Analysis of serializability in SDD-1: a system of distributed databases (the fully redundant case)," *IEEE Trans. on Software Engineering* **SE-4**:3 (1978), pp. 154–168.

3. P. A. Bernstein, V. Hadzilacos, and N. Goodman, *Concurrency Control and Recovery in Database Systems*, Addison-Wesley, Reading MA, 1987.

4. K. P. Eswaran, J. N. Gray, R. A. Lorie, and I. L. Traiger, "The notions of consistency and predicate locks in a database system," *Comm. ACM* **19**:11 (1976), pp. 624–633.

5. J. N. Gray, F. Putzolo, and I. L. Traiger, "Granularity of locks and degrees of consistency in a shared data base," in G. M. Nijssen (ed.), *Modeling in Data Base Management Systems*, North Holland, Amsterdam, 1976.

6. J. N. Gray and A. Reuter, *Transaction Processing: Concepts and Techniques*, Morgan-Kaufmann, San Francisco, 1993.

7. H. F. Korth, "Locking primitives in a database system," *J. ACM* **30**:1 (1983), pp. 55–79.

8. H.-T. Kung and J. T. Robinson, "Optimistic concurrency control," *ACM Trans. on Database Systems* **6**:2 (1981), pp. 312–326.

9. C. H. Papadimitriou and P. C. Kanellakis, "On concurrency control by multiple versions," *ACM Trans. on Database Systems* **9**:1 (1984), pp. 89–99.

10. A. Silberschatz and Z. Kedem, "Consistency in hierarchical database systems," *J. ACM* **27**:1 (1980), pp. 72–80.

11. A. Thompson, "Concurrency control: methods, performance, and analysis," *Computing Surveys* **30**:1 (1998), pp. 170–231.

12. B. Thuraisingham and H.-P. Ko, "Concurrency control in trusted database management systems: a survey," *SIGMOD Record* **22**:4 (1993), pp. 52–60.

Chapter 10

More About Transaction Management

In this chapter we cover several issues about transaction management that were not addressed in Chapters 8 or 9. We begin by reconciling the points of view of these two chapters: how do the needs to recover from errors, to allow transactions to abort, and to maintain serializability interact? Then, we discuss the management of deadlocks among transactions, which typically result from several transactions each having to wait for a resource, such as a lock, that is held by another transaction.

This chapter also includes an introduction to distributed databases. We focus on how to lock elements that are distributed among several sites, perhaps with replicated copies. We also consider how the decision to commit or abort a transaction can be made when the transaction itself involves actions at several sites.

Finally, we consider the problems that arise due to "long transactions." There are applications, such as CAD systems or "workflow" systems, in which human and computer processes interact, perhaps over a period of days. These systems, like short-transaction systems such as banking or airline reservations, need to preserve consistency of the database state. However, the concurrency-control methods discussed in Chapter 9 do not work reasonably when locks are held for days, or decisions to validate are based on events that happened days in the past.

10.1 Transactions that Read Uncommitted Data

In Chapter 8 we discussed the creation of a log and its use to recover the database state when a system crash occurs. We introduced the view of database computation in which values move between nonvolatile disk, volatile main-memory, and the local address space of transactions. The guarantee the various logging methods give is that, should a crash occur, it will be able to reconstruct the actions of the committed transactions (and only the committed transactions) on the disk copy of the database. A logging system makes no attempt to support serializability; it will blindly reconstruct a database state, even if it is the result of a nonserializable schedule of actions. In fact, commercial database systems do not always insist on serializability, and in some systems, serializability is enforced only on explicit request of the user.

On the other hand, Chapter 9 talked about serializability only. Schedulers designed according to the principles of that chapter may do things that the log manager cannot tolerate. For instance, there is nothing in the serializability definition that forbids a transaction with a lock on an element A from writing a new value of A into the database before committing, and thus violating a rule of the logging policy. Worse, a transaction might write into the database and then abort, which could easily result in an inconsistent database state, even though there is no system crash, and the scheduler theoretically maintains serializability.

10.1.1 The Dirty-Data Problem

Recall that data is "dirty" if it has been written by a transaction that is not yet committed. The dirty data could appear either in the buffers, or on disk, or both; either can cause trouble.

T_1	T_2	A	B
		25	25
$l_1(A)$; $r_1(A)$;			
A := A+100;			
$w_1(A)$; $l_1(B)$; $u_1(A)$;		125	
	$l_2(A)$; $r_2(A)$;		
	A := A*2;		
	$w_2(A)$;	250	
	$l_2(B)$ **Denied**		
$r_1(B)$;			
Abort; $u_1(B)$;			
	$l_2(B)$; $u_2(A)$; $r_2(B)$;		
	B := B*2;		
	$w_2(B)$; $u_2(B)$;		50

Figure 10.1: T_1 writes dirty data and then aborts

Example 10.1 : Let us reconsider the serializable schedule from Fig. 9.13, but suppose that after reading B, T_1 has to abort for some reason. Then the sequence of events is as in Fig. 10.1. After T_1 aborts, the scheduler releases the lock on B that T_1 obtained; that step is essential, or else the lock on B would be unavailable to any other transaction, forever.

However, T_2 has now read data that does not represent a consistent state of the database. That is, T_2 read the value of A that T_1 changed, but read the value of B that existed prior to T_1's actions. It doesn't matter in this case whether or not the value 125 for A that T_1 created was written to disk or not; T_2 gets that value from a buffer, regardless. As a result of reading an inconsistent state, T_2 leaves the database (on disk) with an inconsistent state, where $A \neq B$.

The problem in Fig. 10.1 is that A written by T_1 is dirty data, whether it is in a buffer or on disk. The fact that T_2 read A and used it in its own calculation makes T_2's actions questionable. As we shall see in Section 10.1.2, it is necessary, if such a situation is allowed to occur, to abort and roll back T_2 as well as T_1. Additionally, allowing T_1's A to get to disk is quite expensive to repair; we must use the log to undo the changes. Thus, we need to develop rules that will prevent dirty data from ever getting to disk. □

T_1	T_2	T_3	A	B	C
200	150	175	RT=0	RT=0	RT=0
			WT=0	WT=0	WT=0
	$w_2(B)$;			WT=150	
$r_1(B)$;					
	$r_2(A)$;		RT=150		
		$r_3(C)$;			RT=175
	$w_2(C)$;				
	Abort;			WT=0	
		$w_3(A)$;	WT=175		

Figure 10.2: T_1 has read dirty data from T_2 and must abort when T_2 does

Example 10.2 : Now, consider Fig. 10.2, which shows a sequence of actions under a timestamp-based scheduler as in Section 9.8. However, we imagine that this scheduler does not use the commit bit that was introduced in Section 9.8.1. Recall that the purpose of this bit is to prevent a value that was written by an uncommitted transaction to be read by another transaction. Thus, when T_1 reads B at the second step, there is no commit-bit check to tell T_1 to delay. T_1 can proceed and could even write to disk and commit; we have not shown further details of what T_1 does.

Eventually, T_2 tries to write C in a physically unrealizable way, and T_2 aborts. The effect of T_2's prior write of B is cancelled; the value and write-time of B is reset to what it was before T_2 wrote. Yet T_1 has been allowed to use this cancelled value of B and can do anything with it, such as using it to compute new values of A, B, and/or C and writing them to disk. Thus, T_1, having read

---

Isolation Levels in SQL

The SQL2 standard does not assume that every transaction runs in a serializable manner, and commercial systems likewise permit the user to specify the degree of concurrency control desired. In SQL2, the highest "isolation level" is *serializable*, which means exactly what the word implies: a transaction with this isolation level must run as if it occurred at an instant, and all other transactions occurred either completely before or completely after.

The isolation level "read committed" does not require serializability, but does forbid the transaction to read dirty data. It is possible, however, that a transaction T operating at this level will read element A twice and get different values, each written by some committed transaction. A related level, "repeatable read" is a slightly stronger condition, saying that not only will whatever T gets for A not be dirty, but if A is a relation, then successive reads of A can only get supersets; i.e., no part of A goes away while T is active.

The fourth level is "read uncommitted." Here, there are no constraints at all on what a transaction operating at this level can see. Only at this level is it permitted for the transaction to read dirty data.

---

a dirty value of B, can cause an inconsistent database state. Note that, had the commit bit been recorded and used, the read $r_1(B)$ at step (2) would have been delayed, and not allowed to occur until after T_2 aborted and the value of B had been restored to its previous (presumably committed) value. □

10.1.2 Cascading Rollback

As we see from the examples above, if dirty data is available to transactions, then we sometimes have to perform a *cascading rollback*. That is, when a transaction T aborts, we must determine which transactions have read data written by T, abort them, and recursively abort any transactions that have read data written by an aborted transaction. That is, we must find each transaction U that read dirty data written by T, abort U, find any transaction V that read dirty data from U, abort V, and so on. To cancel the effect of an aborted transaction, we can use the log, if it is one of the types (undo or undo/redo) that provides former values. We may also be able to restore the data from the disk copy of the database, if the effect of the dirty data has not migrated to disk. These approaches are considered in the next section.

As we have noted, a timestamp-based scheduler with a commit bit prevents a transaction that may have read dirty data from proceeding, so there is no possibility of cascading rollback with such a scheduler. A validation-based scheduler avoids cascading rollback, because writing to the database (even in buffers) occurs only after it is determined that the transaction will commit.

10.1.3 Managing Rollbacks

Let us now consider how the problem of cascading rollbacks can be managed in a lock-based scheduler. There is a simple way to guarantee that there are no cascading rollbacks:

- *Strict Locking*: A transaction must not release any write locks (or other locks, such as increment locks that allow values to be changed) until the transaction has either committed or aborted, and the commit or abort log record has been flushed to disk.

Notice that the condition that the commit action be flushed to disk before unlocking assures that if there is a crash after a transaction T releases its locks, and some transaction has read data written by T, that data cannot become dirty because T is aborted by the recovery process. A schedule of transactions that obey the strict locking rule is called *recoverable*.

Clearly, in a recoverable schedule, it is not possible for a transaction to read dirty data, since data written to a buffer by an uncommitted transaction remains locked until the transaction commits. However, we still have the problem of fixing the data in buffers when a transaction aborts, since these changes must have their effects cancelled. How difficult it is to fix buffered data depends on whether database elements are blocks or something smaller. We shall consider each.

Rollback for Blocks

If the lockable database elements are blocks, then there is a simple rollback method that never requires us to use the log. Suppose that a transaction T has obtained an exclusive lock on block A, written a new value for A in a buffer, and then had to abort. Since A has been locked since T wrote its value, no other transaction has read A. It is easy to restore the old value of A provided the following rule is followed:

- Blocks written by uncommitted transactions are pinned in main memory; that is, their buffers are not allowed to be written to disk.

In this case, we "roll back" T when it aborts by telling the buffer manager to ignore the value of A. That is, the buffer occupied by A is not written anywhere, and its buffer is added to the pool of available buffers. We can be sure that the value of A on disk is the most recent value written by a committed transaction, which is exactly the value we want A to have.

There is also a simple rollback method if we are using a multiversion system as in Sections 9.8.5 and 9.8.6. We must again assume that blocks written by uncommitted transactions are pinned in memory. Then, we simply remove the value of A that was written by T from the list of available values of A. Note that because T was a writing transaction, its value of A was locked from the time the value was written to the time it aborted (assuming the timestamp/lock scheme of Section 9.8.6 is used).

Rollback for Small Database Elements

When lockable database elements are fractions of a block (e.g., tuples or objects), then the simple approach to restoring buffers that have been modified by aborted transactions will not work. The problem is that a buffer may contain data changed by two or more transactions; if one of them aborts, we still must preserve the changes made by the other. We have several choices when we must restore the old value of a small database element A that was written by the transaction that has aborted:

1. We can read the original value of A from the database stored on disk and modify the buffer contents appropriately.

2. If the log is an undo or undo/redo log, then we can obtain the former value from the log itself.

3. We can keep a separate main-memory log of the changes made by each transaction, preserved for only the time that transaction is active. The old value can be found from this "log."

None of these approaches is ideal. The first surely involves a disk access. The second (examining the log) might not involve a disk access, if the relevant portion of the log is still in a buffer. However, it could also involve extensive examination of portions of the log on disk, searching for the update record that tells the correct former value. The last approach does not require disk accesses, but may consume a large fraction of memory for the main-memory "logs."

10.1.4   Group Commit

Under some circumstances, we can avoid reading dirty data even if we do not flush every commit record on the log to disk immediately. As long as we flush log records in the order that they are written, we can release locks as soon as the commit record is written to the log in a buffer.

Example 10.3: Suppose transaction T_1 writes X, finishes, writes its COMMIT record on the log, but the log record remains in a buffer. Even though T_1 has not committed in the sense that its commit record can survive a crash, we shall release T_1's locks. Then T_2 reads X and "commits," but its commit record, which follows that of T_1, also remains in a buffer. Since we are flushing log records in the order written, T_2 cannot be perceived as committed by a recovery manager (because its commit record reached disk) unless T_1 is also perceived as committed. Thus, there are three cases that the recovery manager could find:

When is a Transaction Really Committed?

The subtlety of group commit reminds us that a completed transaction can be in several different states between when it finishes its work and when it is truly "committed," in the sense that under no circumstances, including the occurrence of a system failure, will the effect of that transaction be lost. As we noted in Chapter 8, it is possible for a transaction to finish its work and even write its COMMIT record to the log in a main-memory buffer, yet have the effect of that transaction lost if there is a system crash and the COMMIT record has not yet reached disk. Moreover, we saw in Section 8.5 that even if the COMMIT record is on disk but not yet backed up in the archive, a media failure can cause the transaction to be undone and its effect to be lost.

 In the absence of failure, all these states are equivalent, in the sense that all transactions will surely advance from being finished to having its effects survive even a media failure. However, when we need to take failures and recovery into account, it is important to recognize the differences among these states, which otherwise could all be referred to informally as "committed."

---

1. Neither T_1 nor T_2 has its commit record on disk. Then both are aborted by the recovery manager, and the fact that T_2 read X from an uncommitted T_1 is irrelevant.

2. T_1 is committed, but T_2 is not. There is no problem for two reasons: T_2 did not read X from an uncommitted transaction, and it aborted anyway, with no effect on the database.

3. Both are committed. Then the read of X by T_2 was not dirty.

 On the other hand, suppose that the buffer containing T_2's commit record got flushed to disk (say because the buffer manager decided to use the buffer for something else), but the buffer containing T_1's commit record did not. If there is a crash at that point, it will look to the recovery manager that T_1 did not commit, but T_2 did. The effect of T_2 will be permanently reflected in the database, but this effect was based on the dirty read of X by T_2.   □

 Our conclusion from Example 10.3 is that we can release locks earlier than the time that the transaction's commit record is flushed to disk. This policy, often called *group commit*, is:

- Do not release locks until the transaction finishes, and the commit log record at least appears in a buffer.

- Flush log blocks in the order that they were created.

Concurrency and Recoverability

You may have noticed that the three logging approaches of Chapter 8 do not always meet the requirements for recoverable schedules. Systems that support all the requirements of both concurrency and recoverability are often called ACID (Atomic, Concurrent, Isolated, Durable); see the box on the subject in Section 1.2.4. Thus, it is a good time to remember that logging and locking (or another concurrency control mechanism) are orthogonal issues.

For example, we could have a system that logs transactions to assure atomicity of those transactions even if we have no desire to assure serializability or the absence of dirty reads. In fact, commercial systems often give the user the opportunity to declare that transactions do not have to be run in a serializable manner, or that dirty reads are allowable, as we mentioned in the box on SQL2 "isolation levels" in Section 10.1.1. Conversely, it is possible in common DBMS's to turn off logging, and yet have all or some of your transactions run in a serializable way. The consequence is that should there be a crash, serializability and database consistency are not guaranteed, but a user may have in mind some alternative way to restore consistency in the event of a crash.

Group commit, like the policy of requiring "recoverable schedules" as discussed in Section 10.1.3, guarantees that there is never a read of dirty data.

10.1.5 Logical Logging

We saw in Section 10.1.3 that dirty reads are easier to fix up when the unit of locking is the block or page. However, there are at least two problems presented when database elements are blocks.

1. All logging methods require either the old or new value of a database element, or both, to be recorded in the log. When the change to a block is small, e.g., a rewritten attribute of one tuple, or an inserted or deleted tuple, then there is a great deal of redundant information written on the log.

2. The requirement that the schedule be recoverable, releasing its locks only after commit, can inhibit concurrency severely. For example, recall our discussion in Section 9.7.1 of the advantage of early lock release as we access data through a B-tree index. If we require that locks be held until commit, then this advantage cannot be obtained, and we effectively allow only one writing transaction to access a B-tree at any time.

Both these concerns motivate the use of *logical logging*, where only the changes to the blocks are described. There are several degrees of complexity, depending on the nature of the change.

1. A small number of bytes of the database element are changed, e.g., the update of a fixed-length field. This situation can be handled in a straightforward way, where we record only the changed bytes and their positions. Example 10.4 will show this situation and an appropriate form of update record.

2. The change to the database element is simply described, and easily restored, but it has the effect of changing most or all of the bytes in the database element. One common situation, discussed in Example 10.5, is when a variable-length field is changed and much of its record, and even other records must slide within the block. The new and old values of the block look very different unless we realize and indicate the simple cause of the change.

3. The change affects many bytes of a database element, and further changes can prevent this change from ever being undone. This situation is true "logical" logging, since we cannot even see the undo/redo process as occurring on the database elements themselves, but rather on some higher-level "logical" structure that the database elements represent. We shall, in Example 10.6, take up the matter of B-trees, a logical structure represented by database elements that are disk blocks, to illustrate this complex form of logical logging.

Example 10.4: Suppose database elements are blocks that each contain a set of tuples from some relation. We can express the update of an attribute by a log record that says something like "tuple t had its attribute a changed from value v_1 to v_2." An insertion of a new tuple into empty space on the block can be expressed as "a tuple t with value $(a_1, a_2, \ldots, a_k)$ was inserted beginning at offset position p." Unless the attribute changed or the tuple inserted are comparable in size to a block, the amount of space taken by these records will be much smaller than the entire block. Moreover, they serve for both undo and redo operations.

Notice that both these operations are idempotent; if you perform them several times on a block, the result is the same as performing them once. Likewise, their implied inverses, where the value of $t[a]$ is restored from v_2 back to v_1, or the tuple t is removed, are also idempotent. Thus, records of these types can be used for recovery in exactly the same way that update log records were used throughout Chapter 8. □

Example 10.5: Again assume database elements are blocks holding tuples, but the tuples have some variable-length fields. If a change to a field such as was described in Example 10.4 occurs, we may have to slide large portions of the block to make room for a longer field, or to preserve space if a field becomes smaller. In extreme cases, we could have to create an overflow block (recall Section 3.5) to hold part of the contents of the original block, or we could remove an overflow block if a shorter field allows us to combine the contents of two blocks into one.

As long as the block and its overflow block(s) are considered part of one database element, then it is straightforward to use the old and/or new value of the changed field to undo or redo the change. However, the block-plus-overflow-block(s) must be thought of as holding certain tuples at a "logical" level. We may not even be able to restore the bytes of these blocks to their original state after an undo or redo, because there may have been reorganization of the blocks due to other changes that varied the length of other fields. However, if we think of a database element as being a collection of blocks that together represent certain tuples, then a redo or undo can indeed restore the logical "state" of the element. □

However, it may not be possible, as we suggested in Example 10.5, to treat blocks as expandable through the mechanism of overflow blocks. We may thus be able to undo or redo actions only at a level higher than blocks. The next example discusses the important case of B-tree indexes, where the management of blocks does not permit overflow blocks, and we must think of undo and redo as occurring at the "logical" level of the B-tree itself, rather than the blocks.

Example 10.6: Let us consider the problem of logical logging for B-tree nodes. Instead of writing the old and/or new value of an entire node (block) on the log, we write a short record that describes the change. These changes include:

1. Insertion or deletion of a key/pointer pair for a child.

2. Change of the key associated with a pointer.

3. Splitting or merging of nodes.

Each of these changes can be indicated with a short log record. Even the splitting operation requires only telling where the split occurs, and where the new nodes are. Likewise, merging requires only a reference to the nodes involved, since the manner of merging is determined by the B-tree management algorithms used.

Using logical update records of these types allows us to release locks earlier than would otherwise be required for a recoverable schedule. The reason is that dirty reads of B-tree blocks are never a problem for the transaction that reads them, provided its only purpose is to use the B-tree to locate the data the transaction needs to access.

For instance, suppose that transaction T reads a leaf node N, but the transaction U that last wrote N later aborts, and some change made to N (e.g., the insertion of a new key/pointer pair into N due to an insertion of a tuple by U) needs to be undone. If T has also inserted a key/pointer pair into N, then it is not possible to restore N to the way it was before U modified it. However, the effect of U on N can be undone; in this example we would delete the key/pointer pair that U had inserted. The resulting N is not the same as that which existed before U operated; it has the insertion made by T. However, there is no database inconsistency, since the B-tree as a whole continues to reflect only the changes made by committed transactions. That is, we have restored the B-tree at a logical level, but not at the physical level. □

10.1.6   Exercises for Section 10.1

* **Exercise 10.1.1:** Consider all ways to insert locks (of a single type only, as in Section 9.3) into the sequence of actions

$$r_1(A); \ r_1(B); \ w_1(A); \ w_1(B);$$

so that the transaction T_1 is:

a) Two-phase locked, and strict.

b) Two-phase locked, but not strict.

Exercise 10.1.2: Suppose that each of the sequences of actions below is followed by an abort action for transaction T_1. Tell which transactions need to be rolled back.

* a) $r_1(A); \ r_2(B); \ w_1(B); \ w_2(C); \ r_3(B); \ r_3(C); \ w_3(D);$

b) $r_1(A); \ w_1(B); \ r_2(B); \ w_2(C); \ r_3(C); \ w_3(D);$

c) $r_2(A); \ r_3(A); \ r_1(A); \ w_1(B); \ r_2(B); \ r_3(B); \ w_2(C); \ r_3(C);$

d) $r_2(A); \ r_3(A); \ r_1(A); \ w_1(B); \ r_3(B); \ w_2(C); \ r_3(C);$

Exercise 10.1.3: Consider each of the sequences of actions in Exercise 10.1.2, but now suppose that all three transactions commit and write their commit record on the log immediately after their last action. However, a crash occurs, and a tail of the log was not written to disk before the crash and is therefore lost. Tell, depending on where the lost tail of the log begins:

i. What transactions could be considered uncommitted?

ii. Are any dirty reads created during the recovery process? If so, what transactions need to be rolled back?

iii. What additional dirty reads could have been created if the portion of the log lost was not a tail, but rather some potions in the middle?

10.2   View Serializability

Recall our discussion in Section 9.1.4 of how our true goal in the design of a scheduler is to allow only schedules that are serializable. We also saw how differences in what operations transactions apply to the data can affect whether or not a given schedule is serializable. We also learned in Section 9.2 that schedulers normally enforce "conflict serializability," which guarantees serializability regardless of what the transactions do with their data.

However, there are weaker conditions than conflict-serializability that also guarantee serializability. In this section we shall consider one such condition, called "view-serializability." Intuitively, view-serializability considers all the connections between transactions T and U such that T writes a database element whose value U reads. The key difference between view- and conflict-serializability appears when a transaction T writes a value A that no other transaction reads (because some other transaction later writes its own value for A). In that case, the $w_T(A)$ action can be placed in certain other positions of the schedule (where A is likewise never read) that would not be permitted under the definition of conflict-serializability. In this section, we shall define view-serializability precisely and give a test for it.

10.2.1   View Equivalence

Suppose we have two schedules S_1 and S_2 of the same set of transactions. Imagine that there is a hypothetical transaction T_0 that wrote initial values for each database element read by any transaction in the schedules, and another hypothetical transaction T_f that reads every element written by one or more transactions after each schedule ends. Then for every read action $r_i(A)$ in one of the schedules, we can find the write action $w_j(A)$ that most closely preceded the read in question.[1] We say T_j is the *source* of the read action $T_i(A)$. Note that transaction T_j could be the hypothetical initial transaction T_0, and T_i could be T_f.

If for every read action in one of the schedules, its source is the same in the other schedule, we say that S_1 and S_2 are *view-equivalent*. Surely, view-equivalent schedules are truly equivalent; they each do the same when executed on any one database state. If a schedule S is view-equivalent to a serial schedule, we say S is *view-serializable*.

Example 10.7 : Consider the schedule S defined by:

T_1: $r_1(A)$ $w_1(B)$
T_2: $r_2(B)$ $w_2(A)$ $w_2(B)$
T_3: $r_3(A)$ $w_3(B)$

---

[1] While we have not previously prevented a transaction from writing an element twice, there is generally no need for it to do so, and in this study it is useful to assume that a transaction only writes a given element once.

Notice that we have separated the actions of each transaction vertically, to indicate better which transaction does what; you should read the schedule from left-to-right, as usual.

In S, both T_1 and T_2 write values of B that are lost; only the value of B written by T_3 survives to the end of the schedule and is "read" by the hypothetical transaction T_f. S is not conflict-serializable. To see why, first note that T_2 writes A before T_1 reads A, so T_2 must precede T_1 in a hypothetical conflict-equivalent serial schedule. The fact that the action $w_1(B)$ precedes $w_2(B)$ also forces T_1 to precede T_2 in any conflict-equivalent serial schedule. Yet neither $w_1(B)$ nor $w_2(B)$ has any long-term affect on the database. It is these sorts of irrelevant writes that view-serializability is able to ignore, when determining the true constraints on an equivalent serial schedule.

More precisely, let us consider the sources of all the reads in S:

1. The source of $r_2(B)$ is T_0, since there is no prior write of B in S.

2. The source of $r_1(A)$ is T_2, since T_2 most recently wrote A before the read.

3. Likewise, the source of $r_3(A)$ is T_2.

4. The source of the hypothetical read of A by T_f is T_2.

5. The source of the hypothetical read of B by T_f is T_3, the last writer of B.

Of course, T_0 appears before all real transactions in any schedule, and T_f appears after all transactions. If we order the real transactions (T_2, T_1, T_3), then the sources of all reads are the same as in schedule S. That is, T_2 reads B, and surely T_0 is the previous "writer." T_1 reads A, but T_2 already wrote A, so the source of $r_1(A)$ is T_2, as in S. T_3 also reads A, but since the prior T_2 wrote A, that is the source of $r_3(A)$, as in S. Finally, the hypothetical T_f reads A and B, but the last writers of A and B in the schedule (T_2, T_1, T_3) are T_2 and T_3 respectively, also as in S. We conclude that S is a view-serializable schedule, and the schedule represented by the order (T_2, T_1, T_3) is a view-equivalent schedule. $\square$

10.2.2 Polygraphs and the Test for View-Serializability

There is a generalization of the precedence graph, which we used to test conflict serializability in Section 9.2.2, that reflects all the precedence constraints required by the definition of view serializability. We define the *polygraph* for a schedule to consist of the following:

1. A node for each transaction and additional nodes for the hypothetical transactions T_0 and T_f.

2. For each action $r_i(X)$ with source T_j, place an arc from T_j to T_i.

3. Suppose T_j is the source of a read $r_i(X)$, and T_k is another writer of X. It is not allowed for T_k to intervene between T_j and T_i, so it must appear either before T_j or after T_i. We represent this condition by an *arc pair* (shown dashed) from T_k to T_j and from T_i to T_k. Intuitively, one or the other of an arc pair is "real," but we don't care which, and when we try to make the polygraph acyclic, we can pick whichever of the pair helps to make it acyclic. However, there are important special cases where the arc pair becomes a single arc:

   (a) If T_j is T_0, then it is not possible for T_k to appear before T_j, so we use an arc $T_i \to T_k$ in place of the arc pair.

   (b) If T_i is T_f, then T_k cannot follow T_i, so we use an arc $T_k \to T_j$ in place of the arc pair.

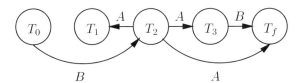

Figure 10.3: Beginning of polygraph for Example 10.8

Example 10.8 : Consider the schedule S from Example 10.7. We show in Fig. 10.3 the beginning of the polygraph for S, where only the nodes and the arcs from rule (2) have been placed. We have also indicated the database element causing each arc. That is, A is passed from T_2 to T_1, T_3, and T_f, while B is passed from T_0 to T_2 and from T_3 to T_f.

Now, we must consider what transactions might interfere with each of these five connections by writing the same element between them. These potential interferences are ruled out by the arc pairs from rule (3), although as we shall see, in this example each of the arc pairs involves a special case and becomes a single arc.

Consider the arc $T_2 \to T_1$ based on element A. The only writers of A are T_0 and T_2, and neither of them can get in the middle of this arc, since T_0 cannot move its position, and T_2 is already an end of the arc. Thus, no additional arcs are needed. A similar argument tells us no additional arcs are needed to keep writers of A outside the arcs $T_2 \to T_3$ and $T_2 \to T_f$.

Now consider the arcs based on B. Note that T_0, T_1, T_2, and T_3 all write B. Consider the arc $T_0 \to T_2$ first. T_1 and T_3 are other writers of B; T_0 and T_2 also write B, but as we saw, the arc ends cannot cause interference, so we need not consider them. As we cannot place T_1 between T_0 and T_2, in principle we need the arc pair $(T_1 \to T_0, T_2 \to T_1)$. However, nothing can precede T_0, so the option $T_1 \to T_0$ is not possible. We may in this special case just add the arc $T_2 \rightarrow T_1$ to the polygraph. But this arc is already there because of A, so in effect, we make no change to the polygraph to keep T_1 outside the arc $T_0 \rightarrow T_2$.

We also cannot place T_3 between T_0 and T_2. Similar reasoning tells us to add the arc $T_2 \rightarrow T_3$, rather than an arc pair. However, this arc too is already in the polygraph because of A, so we make no change.

Next, consider the arc $T_3 \rightarrow T_f$. Since T_0, T_1, and T_2 are other writers of B, we must keep them each outside the arc. T_0 cannot be moved between T_3 and T_f, but T_1 or T_2 could. Since neither could be moved after T_f, we must constrain T_1 and T_2 to appear before T_3. There is already an arc $T_2 \rightarrow T_3$, but we must add to the polygraph the arc $T_1 \rightarrow T_3$. This change is the only arc we must add to the polygraph, whose final set of arcs is shown in Fig. 10.4. $\Box$

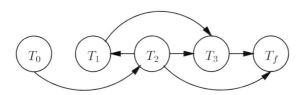

Figure 10.4: Complete polygraph for Example 10.8

Example 10.9 : In Example 10.8, all the arc pairs turned out to be single arcs as a special case. Figure 10.5 is an example of a schedule of four transactions where there is a true arc pair in the polygraph.

T_1	T_2	T_3	T_4
	$r_2(A)$;		
$r_1(A)$; $w_1(C)$;			
		$r_3(C)$;	
$w_1(B)$;			
			$r_4(B)$;
		$w_3(A)$;	
			$r_4(C)$;
	$w_2(D)$; $r_2(B)$;		
			$w_4(A)$; $w_4(B)$;

Figure 10.5: Example of transactions whose polygraph requires an arc pair

Figure 10.6 shows the polygraph, with only the arcs that come from the source-to-reader connections. As in Fig. 10.3 we label each arc by the element(s) that require it. We must then consider the possible ways that arc pairs could be added. As we saw in Example 10.8, there are several simplifications we can make. When avoiding interference with the arc $T_j \rightarrow T_i$, the only transactions that need be considered as T_k (the transaction that cannot be in the middle) are:

- Writers of an element that caused this arc $T_j \rightarrow T_i$,

- But not T_0 or T_f, which can never be T_k, and

- Not T_i or T_j, the ends of the arc itself.

With these rules in mind, let us consider the arcs due to database element A, which is written by T_0, T_3, and T_4. We need not consider T_0 at all. T_3 must not get between $T_4 \rightarrow T_f$, so we add arc $T_3 \rightarrow T_4$; remember that the other arc in the pair, $T_f \rightarrow T_3$ is not an option. Likewise, T_3 must not get between $T_0 \rightarrow T_1$ or $T_0 \rightarrow T_2$, which results in the arcs $T_1 \rightarrow T_3$ and $T_2 \rightarrow T_3$.

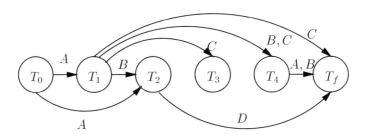

Figure 10.6: Beginning of polygraph for Example 10.9

Now, consider the fact that T_4 also must not get in the middle of an arc due to A. It is an end of $T_4 \rightarrow T_f$, so that arc is irrelevant. T_4 must not get between $T_0 \rightarrow T_1$ or $T_0 \rightarrow T_2$, which results in the arcs $T_1 \rightarrow T_4$ and $T_2 \rightarrow T_4$.

Next, let us consider the arcs due to B, which is written by T_0, T_1, and T_4. Again we need not consider T_0. The only arcs due to B are $T_1 \rightarrow T_2$, $T_1 \rightarrow T_4$, and $T_4 \rightarrow T_f$. T_1 cannot get in the middle of the first two, but the third requires arc $T_1 \rightarrow T_4$.

T_4 can get in the middle of $T_1 \rightarrow T_2$ only. This arc has neither end at T_0 or T_f, so it really requires an arc pair: $(T_4 \rightarrow T_1, T_2 \rightarrow T_4)$. We show this arc pair, as well as all the other arcs added, in Fig. 10.7.

Next, consider the writers of C: T_0 and T_1. As before, T_0 cannot present a problem. Also, T_1 is part of every arc due to C, so it cannot get in the middle. Similarly, D is written only by T_0 and T_2, so we can determine that no more arcs are necessary. The final polygraph is thus the one in Fig. 10.7.   □

10.2.3   Testing for View-Serializability

Since we must choose only one of each arc pair, we can find an equivalent serial order for schedule S if and only if there is some selection from each arc pair that turns S's polygraph into an acyclic graph. To see why, notice that if there

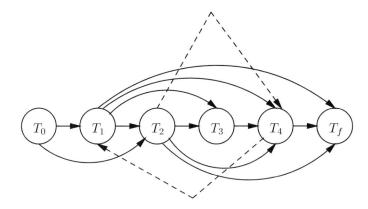

Figure 10.7: Complete polygraph for Example 10.9

is such an acyclic graph, then any topological sort of the graph gives an order in which no writer may appear between a reader and its source, and every writer appears before its readers. Thus, the reader-source connections in the serial order are exactly the same as in S; the two schedules are view-equivalent, and therefore S is view-serializable.

Conversely, if S is view-serializable, then there is a view-equivalent serial order S'. Every arc pair $(T_k \rightarrow T_j, T_i \rightarrow T_k)$ in S's polygraph must have T_k either before T_j or after T_i in S'; otherwise the writing by T_k breaks the connection from T_j to T_i, which means that S and S' are not view-equivalent. Likewise, every arc in the polygraph must be respected by the transaction order of S'. We conclude that there is a choice of arcs from each arc pair that makes the polygraph into a graph for which the serial order S' is consistent with each arc of the graph. Thus, this graph is acyclic.

Example 10.10: Consider the polygraph of Fig. 10.4. It is already a graph, and it is acyclic. The only topological order is (T_2, T_1, T_3), which is therefore a view-equivalent serial order for the schedule of Example 10.8.

Now consider the polygraph of Fig. 10.7. We must consider each choice from the one arc pair. If we choose $T_4 \rightarrow T_1$, then there is a cycle. However, if we choose $T_2 \rightarrow T_4$, the result is an acyclic graph. The sole topological order for this graph is (T_1, T_2, T_3, T_4). This order yields a view-equivalent serial order and shows that the original schedule is view-serializable. $\square$

10.2.4 Exercises for Section 10.2

Exercise 10.2.1: Draw the polygraph and find all view-equivalent serial orders for the following schedules:

* a) $r_1(A); r_2(A); r_3(A); w_1(B); w_2(B); w_3(B);$

  b) $r_1(A); r_2(A); r_3(A); r_4(A); w_1(B); w_2(B); w_3(B); w_4(B);$

    c) $r_1(A)$; $r_3(D)$; $w_1(B)$; $r_2(B)$; $w_3(B)$; $r_4(B)$; $w_2(C)$; $r_5(C)$; $w_4(E)$; $r_5(E)$; $w_5(B)$;

    d) $w_1(A)$; $r_2(A)$; $w_3(A)$; $r_4(A)$; $w_5(A)$; $r_6(A)$;

! **Exercise 10.2.2:** Below are some serial schedules. Tell how many schedules are (*i*) conflict-equivalent and (*ii*) view-equivalent to these serial schedules.

  * a) $r_1(A)$; $w_1(B)$; $r_2(A)$; $w_2(B)$; $r_3(A)$; $w_3(B)$; that is, three transactions each read A and then write B.

    b) $r_1(A)$; $w_1(B)$; $w_1(C)$; $r_2(A)$; $w_2(B)$; $w_2(C)$; that is, two transactions each read A and then write B and C.

10.3 Resolving Deadlocks

Several times we have observed that concurrently executing transactions can compete for resources and thereby reach a state where there is a *deadlock*: each of several transactions is waiting for a resource held by one of the others, and none can make progress.

- In Section 9.3.4 we saw how ordinary operation of two-phase-locked transactions can still lead to a deadlock, because each has locked something that another transaction also needs to lock.

- In Section 9.4.3 we saw how the ability to upgrade locks from shared to exclusive can cause a deadlock because each transaction holds a shared lock on the same element and wants to upgrade the lock.

There are two broad approaches to dealing with deadlock. We can detect deadlocks and fix them, or we can manage transactions in such a way that deadlocks are never able to form.

10.3.1 Deadlock Detection by Timeout

When a deadlock exists, it is generally impossible to repair the situation so that all transactions involved can proceed. Thus, at least one of the transactions will have to be rolled back — aborted and restarted.

    The simplest way to detect and resolve deadlocks is with a *timeout*. Put a limit on how long a transaction may be active, and if a transaction exceeds this time, roll it back. For example, in a simple transaction system, where typical transactions execute in milliseconds, a timeout of one minute would affect only transactions that are caught in a deadlock. If some transactions are more complex, we might want the timeout to occur after a longer interval, however.

    Notice that when one transaction involved in the deadlock times out, it releases its locks or other resources. Thus, there is a chance that the other transactions involved in the deadlock will complete before reaching their timeout limits. However, since transactions involved in a deadlock are likely to have started at approximately the same time (or else, one would have completed before another started), it is also possible that spurious timeouts of transactions that are no longer involved in a deadlock will occur.

10.3.2 The Waits-For Graph

Deadlocks that are caused by transactions waiting for locks held by another can be addressed by a *waits-for graph*, indicating which transactions are waiting for locks held by another transaction. This graph can be used either to detect deadlocks after they have formed or to prevent deadlocks from ever forming. We shall assume the latter, which requires us to maintain the waits-for graph at all times, refusing to allow an action that creates a cycle in the graph.

Recall from Section 9.5.2 that a lock table maintains for each database element X a list of the transactions that are waiting for locks on X, as well as transactions that currently hold locks on X. The waits-for graph has a node for each transaction that currently holds a lock or is waiting for one. There is an arc from node (transaction) T to node U if there is some database element A such that:

1. U holds a lock on A,

2. T is waiting for a lock on A, and

3. T cannot get a lock on A in its desired mode unless U first releases its lock on A.[2]

If there are no cycles in the waits-for graph, then each transaction can eventually complete. There will be at least one transaction waiting for no other transaction, and this transaction surely can complete. At that time, there will be at least one other transaction that is not waiting, which can complete, and so on.

However, if there is a cycle, then no transaction in the cycle can ever make progress, so there is a deadlock. Thus, a strategy for deadlock avoidance is to roll back any transaction that makes a request that would cause a cycle in the waits-for graph.

Example 10.11: Suppose we have the following four transactions, each of which reads one element and writes another:

T_1: $l_1(A)$; $r_1(A)$; $l_1(B)$; $w_1(B)$; $u_1(A)$; $u_1(B)$;

---

[2]In common situations, such as shared and exclusive locks, every waiting transaction will have to wait until *all* current lock holders release their locks, but there are examples of systems of lock modes where a transaction can get its lock after only some of the current locks are released; see Exercise 10.3.6.

T_2: $l_2(C)$; $r_2(C)$; $l_2(A)$; $w_2(A)$; $u_2(C)$; $u_2(A)$;

T_3: $l_3(B)$; $r_3(B)$; $l_3(C)$; $w_3(C)$; $u_3(B)$; $u_3(C)$;

T_4: $l_4(D)$; $r_4(D)$; $l_4(A)$; $w_4(A)$; $u_4(D)$; $u_4(A)$;

We use a simple locking system with only one lock mode, although the same effect would be noted if we were to use a shared/exclusive system and took locks in the appropriate mode: shared for a read and exclusive for a write.

	T_1	T_2	T_3	T_4
1)	$l_1(A)$; $r_1(A)$;			
2)		$l_2(C)$; $r_2(C)$;		
3)			$l_3(B)$; $r_3(B)$;	
4)				$l_4(D)$; $r_4(D)$;
5)		$l_2(A)$; **Denied**		
6)			$l_3(C)$; **Denied**	
7)				$l_4(A)$; **Denied**
8)	$l_1(B)$; **Denied**			

Figure 10.8: Beginning of a schedule with a deadlock

In Fig. 10.8 is the beginning of a schedule of these four transactions. In the first four steps, each transaction obtains a lock on the element it wants to read. At step (5), T_2 tries to lock A, but the request is denied because T_1 already has a lock on A. Thus, T_2 waits for T_1, and we draw an arc from the node for T_2 to the node for T_1.

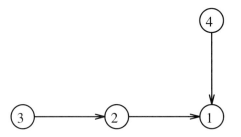

Figure 10.9: Waits-for graph after step (7) of Fig. 10.8

Similarly, at step (6) T_3 is denied a lock on C because of T_2, and at step (7), T_4 is denied a lock on A because of T_1. The waits-for graph at this point is as shown in Fig. 10.9. There is no cycle in this graph,

At step (8), T_1 must wait for the lock on B held by T_3. If we allowed T_1 to wait, then there would be a cycle in the waits-for graph involving T_1, T_2, and T_3, as suggested by Fig. 10.10. Since they are each waiting for another to finish,

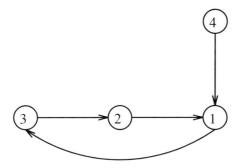

Figure 10.10: Waits-for graph with a cycle caused by step (8) of Fig. 10.8

none can make progress, and therefore there is a deadlock involving these three transactions. Incidentally, T_4 could not finish either, although it is not in the cycle, because T_4's progress depends on T_1 making progress.

Figure 10.11: Waits-for graph after T_1 is rolled back

Since we roll back any transaction that would cause a cycle, then T_1 must be rolled back, yielding the waits-for graph of Fig. 10.11. T_1 relinquishes its lock on A, which may be given to either T_2 or T_4. Suppose it is given to T_2. Then T_2 can complete, whereupon it relinquishes its locks on A and C. Now T_3, which needs a lock on C, and T_4, which needs a lock on A, can both complete. At some time, T_1 is restarted, but it cannot get locks on A and B until T_2, T_3, and T_4 have completed. □

10.3.3 Deadlock Prevention by Ordering Elements

Now, let us consider several more methods for deadlock prevention. The first requires us to order database elements in some arbitrary but fixed order. For instance, if database elements are blocks, we could order them lexicographically by their physical address. Recall from Section 3.3.1 that the physical address of a block is normally represented by a sequence of bytes describing its location within the storage system.

If every transaction is required to request locks on elements in order (a condition that is not realistic in most applications), then there can be no deadlock due to transactions waiting for locks. For suppose T_2 is waiting for a lock on A_1 held by T_1; T_3 is waiting for a lock on A_2 held by T_2, and so on, while T_n is waiting for a lock on A_{n-1} held by T_{n-1}, and T_1 is waiting for a lock on A_n held by T_n. Since T_2 has a lock on A_2 but is waiting for A_1, it must be that $A_2 < A_1$ in the order of elements. Similarly, $A_i < A_{i-1}$ for $i = 3, 4, \ldots, n$. But since T_1 has a lock on A_1 while it is waiting for A_n, it also follows that $A_1 < A_n$. We now have $A_1 < A_n < A_{n-1} < \cdots < A_2 < A_1$, which is impossible, since it implies $A_1 < A_1$.

Example 10.12 : Let us suppose elements are ordered alphabetically. Then if the four transactions of Example 10.11 are to lock elements in alphabetical order, T_2 and T_4 must be rewritten to lock elements in the opposite order. Thus, the four transactions are now:

T_1: $l_1(A)$; $r_1(A)$; $l_1(B)$; $w_1(B)$; $u_1(A)$; $u_1(B)$;

T_2: $l_2(A)$; $l_2(C)$; $r_2(C)$; $w_2(A)$; $u_2(C)$; $u_2(A)$;

T_3: $l_3(B)$; $r_3(B)$; $l_3(C)$; $w_3(C)$; $u_3(B)$; $u_3(C)$;

T_4: $l_4(A)$; $l_4(D)$; $r_4(D)$; $w_4(A)$; $u_4(D)$; $u_4(A)$;

Figure 10.12 shows what happens if the transactions execute with the same timing as Fig. 10.8. T_1 begins and gets a lock on A. T_2 tries to begin next by getting a lock on A, but must wait for T_1. Then, T_3 begins by getting a lock on B, but T_4 is unable to begin because it too needs a lock on A, for which it must wait.

	T_1	T_2	T_3	T_4
1)	$l_1(A)$; $r_1(A)$;			
2)		$l_2(A)$; **Denied**		
3)			$l_3(B)$; $r_3(B)$;	
4)				$l_4(A)$; **Denied**
5)			$l_3(C)$; $w_3(C)$;	
6)			$u_3(B)$; $u_3(C)$;	
7)	$l_1(B)$; $w_1(B)$;			
8)	$u_1(A)$; $u_1(B)$;			
9)		$l_2(A)$; $l_2(C)$;		
10)		$r_2(C)$; $w_2(A)$;		
11)		$u_2(A)$; $u_2(C)$;		
12)				$l_4(A)$; $l_4(D)$;
13)				$r_4(D)$; $w_4(A)$;
14)				$u_4(A)$; $u_4(D)$;

Figure 10.12: Locking elements in alphabetical order prevents deadlock

Since T_2 is stalled, it cannot proceed, and following the order of events in Fig. 10.8, T_3 gets a turn next. It is able to get its lock on C, whereupon it completes at step (6). Now, with T_3's locks on B and C released, T_1 is able to complete, which it does at step (8). At this point, the lock on A becomes available, and we suppose that it is given on a first-come-first-served basis to T_2. Then, T_2 can get both locks that it needs and completes at step (11). Finally, T_4 can get its locks and completes. □

10.3.4 Detecting Deadlocks by Timestamps

We can detect deadlocks by maintaining the waits-for graph, as we discussed in Section 10.3.2. However, this graph can be large, and analyzing it for cycles each time a transaction has to wait for a lock can be time-consuming. An alternative to maintaining the waits-for graph is to associate with each transaction a timestamp. This timestamp:

- Is for deadlock detection only; it is not the same as the timestamp used for concurrency control in Section 9.8, even if timestamp-based concurrency control is in use.

- In particular, if a transaction it rolled back, it restarts with a new, later concurrency timestamp, but its timestamp for deadlock detection never changes.

The timestamp is used when a transaction T has to wait for a lock that is held by another transaction U. Two different things happen, depending on whether T or U is *older* (has the earlier timestamp). There are two different policies that can be used to manage transactions and detect deadlocks.

1. The *Wait-Die Scheme*:

    (a) If T is older than U (i.e., the timestamp of T is smaller than U's timestamp), then T is allowed to wait for the lock(s) held by U.

    (b) If U is older than T, then T "dies"; it is rolled back.

2. The *Wound-Wait Scheme*:

    (a) If T is older than U, it "wounds" U. Usually, the "wound" is fatal: U must roll back and relinquish to T the lock(s) that T needs from U. There is an exception if, by the time the "wound" takes effect, U has already finished and released its locks. In that case, U survives and need not be rolled back.

    (b) If U is older than T, then T waits for the lock(s) held by U.

Example 10.13: Let us consider the wait-die scheme, using the transactions of Example 10.12. We shall assume that T_1, T_2, T_3, T_4 is the order of times; i.e., T_1 is the oldest transaction. We also assume that when a transaction rolls back,

	T_1	T_2	T_3	T_4
1)	$l_1(A); r_1(A);$			
2)		$l_2(A);$ **Dies**		
3)			$l_3(B); r_3(B);$	
4)				$l_4(A);$ **Dies**
5)			$l_3(C); w_3(C);$	
6)			$u_3(B); u_3(C);$	
7)	$l_1(B); w_1(B);$			
8)	$u_1(A); u_1(B);$			
9)				$l_4(A); l_4(D);$
10)		$l_2(A);$ **Waits**		
11)				$r_4(D); w_4(A);$
12)				$u_4(A); u_4(D);$
13)		$l_2(A); l_2(C);$		
14)		$r_2(C); w_2(A);$		
15)		$u_2(A); u_2(C);$		

Figure 10.13: Actions of transactions detecting deadlock under the wait-die scheme

	T_1	T_2	T_3	T_4
1)	$l_1(A); r_1(A);$			
2)		$l_2(A);$ **Waits**		
3)			$l_3(B); r_3(B);$	
4)				$l_4(A);$ **Waits**
5)	$l_1(B); w_1(B);$		**Wounded**	
6)	$u_1(A); u_1(B);$			
7)		$l_2(A); l_2(C);$		
8)		$r_2(C); w_2(A);$		
9)		$u_2(A); u_2(C);$		
10)				$l_4(A); l_4(D);$
11)				$r_4(D); w_4(A);$
12)				$u_4(A); u_4(D);$
13)			$l_3(B); r_3(B);$	
14)			$l_3(C); w_3(C);$	
15)			$u_3(B); u_3(C);$	

Figure 10.14: Actions of transactions detecting deadlock under the wound-wait scheme

---

Why Timestamp-Based Deadlock Detection Works

We claim that in either the wait-die or wound-wait scheme, there can be no cycle in the waits-for graph, and hence no deadlock. Suppose otherwise; that is, there is a cycle such as $T_1 \rightarrow T_2 \rightarrow T_3 \rightarrow T_1$. One of the transactions is the oldest, say T_2.

In the wait-die scheme, you can only wait for younger transactions. Thus, it is not possible that T_1 is waiting for T_2, since T_2 is surely older than T_1. In the wound-wait scheme, you can only wait for older transactions. Thus, there is no way T_2 could be waiting for the younger T_3. We conclude that the cycle cannot exist, and therefore there is no deadlock.

---

it does not restart soon enough to become active before the other transactions finish.

Figure 10.13 shows a possible sequence of events under the wait-die scheme. T_1 gets the lock on A first. When T_2 asks for a lock on A, it dies, because T_1 is older than T_2. In step (3), T_3 gets a lock on B, but in step (4), T_4 asks for a lock on A and dies because T_1, the holder of the lock on A, is older than T_4. Next, T_3 gets its lock on C and completes. When T_1 continues, it finds the lock on B available and also completes at step (8).

Now, the two transactions that rolled back — T_2 and T_4 — start again. Their timestamps as far as deadlock is concerned, do not change; T_2 is still older than T_4. However, we assume that T_4 restarts first, at step (9), and when the older transaction T_2 requests a lock on A at step (10), it is forced to wait, but does not abort. T_4 completes at step (12), and then T_2 is allowed to run to completion, as shown in the last three steps. □

Example 10.14: Next, let us consider the same transactions running under the wound-wait policy, as shown in Fig. 10.14. As in Fig. 10.13, T_1 begins by locking A. When T_2 requests a lock on A at step (2), it waits, since T_1 is older than T_2. After T_3 gets its lock on B at step (3), T_4 is also made to wait for the lock on A.

Then, suppose that T_1 continues at step (5) with its request for the lock on B. That lock is already held by T_3, but T_1 is older than T_3. Thus, T_1 "wounds" T_3. Since T_3 is not yet finished, the wound is fatal: T_3 relinquishes its lock and rolls back. Thus, T_1 is able to complete.

When T_1 makes the lock on A available, suppose it is given to T_2, which is then able to proceed. After T_2, the lock is given to T_4, which proceeds to completion. Finally, T_3 restarts and completes without interference. □

10.3.5   Comparison of Deadlock-Management Methods

In both the wait-die and wound-wait schemes, older transactions kill off newer transactions. Since transactions restart with their old timestamp, eventually each transaction becomes the oldest in the system and is sure to complete. This guarantee, that every transaction eventually completes, is called *no starvation*. Notice that other schemes described in this section do not necessarily prevent starvation; if extra measures are not taken, a transaction could repeatedly start, get involved in a deadlock, and be rolled back. See Exercise 10.3.7.

There is, however, a subtle difference in the way wait-die and wound-wait behave. In wound-wait, a newer transaction is killed whenever an old transaction asks for a lock held by the newer transaction. If we assume that transactions take their locks near the time that they begin, it will be rare that an old transaction was beaten to a lock by a new transaction. Thus, we expect rollback to be rare in wound-wait.

On the other hand, when a rollback does occur, wait-die rolls back a transaction that is still in the stage of gathering locks, presumably the earliest phase of the transaction. Thus, although wait-die may roll back more transactions than wound-wait, these transactions tend to have done little work. In contrast, when wound-wait does roll back a transaction, it is likely to have acquired its locks and for substantial processor time to have been invested in its activity. Thus, either scheme may turn out to cause more wasted work, depending on the population of transactions processed.

We should also consider the advantages and disadvantages of both wound-wait and wait-die when compared with a straightforward construction and use of the waits-for graph. The important points are:

- Both wound-wait and wait-die are easier to implement than a system that maintains or periodically constructs the waits-for graph. The disadvantage of constructing the waits-for graph is even more extreme when the database is distributed, and the waits-for graph must be constructed from a collection of lock tables at different sites. See Section 10.6 for a discussion.

- Using the waits-for graph minimizes the number of times we must abort a transaction because of deadlock. We never abort a transaction unless there really is a deadlock. On the other hand, either wound-wait or wait-die will sometimes roll back a transaction when there was no deadlock, and no deadlock would have occurred had the transaction be allowed to survive.

10.3.6   Exercises for Section 10.3

Exercise 10.3.1: For each of the sequences of actions below, assume that shared locks are requested immediately before each read action, and exclusive locks are requested immediately before every write action. Also, unlocks occur immediately after the final action that a transaction executes. Tell what actions are denied, and whether deadlock occurs. Also tell how the waits-for graph evolves during the execution of the actions. If there are deadlocks, pick a transaction to abort, and show how the sequence of actions continues.

* a) $r_1(A)$; $r_2(B)$; $w_1(C)$; $r_3(D)$; $r_4(E)$; $w_3(B)$; $w_2(C)$; $w_4(A)$; $w_1(D)$;

  b) $r_1(A)$; $r_2(B)$; $r_3(C)$; $w_1(B)$; $w_2(C)$; $w_3(D)$;

  c) $r_1(A)$; $r_2(B)$; $r_3(C)$; $w_1(B)$; $w_2(C)$; $w_3(A)$;

  d) $r_1(A)$; $r_2(B)$; $w_1(C)$; $w_2(D)$; $r_3(C)$; $w_1(B)$; $w_4(D)$; $w_2(A)$;

Exercise 10.3.2: For each of the action sequences in Exercise 10.3.1, tell what happens under the wound-wait deadlock avoidance system. Assume the order of deadlock-timestamps is the same as the order of subscripts for the transactions, that is, T_1, T_2, T_3, T_4. Also assume that transactions that need to restart do so in the order that they were rolled back.

Exercise 10.3.3: For each of the action sequences in Exercise 10.3.1, tell what happens under the wait-die deadlock avoidance system. Make the same assumptions as in Exercise 10.3.2.

! **Exercise 10.3.4:** Can one have a waits-for graph with a cycle of length n, but no smaller cycle, for any integer $n > 1$? What about $n = 1$, i.e., a loop on a node?

!! **Exercise 10.3.5:** One approach to avoiding deadlocks is to require each transaction to announce all the locks it wants at the beginning, and to either grant all those locks or deny them all and make the transaction wait. Does this approach avoid deadlocks due to locking? Either explain why, or give an example of a deadlock that can arise.

! **Exercise 10.3.6:** Consider the intention-locking system of Section 9.6. Describe how to construct the waits-for graph for this system of lock modes. Especially, consider the possibility that a database element A is locked by different transactions in modes S and IX. If a request for a lock on A has to wait, what arcs do we draw?

*! **Exercise 10.3.7:** In Section 10.3.5 we pointed out that deadlock-detection methods other than wound-wait and wait-die do not necessarily prevent starvation, where a transaction is repeatedly rolled back and never gets to finish. Give an example of how using the policy of rolling back any transaction that would cause a cycle can lead to starvation. Does requiring that transactions request locks on elements in a fixed order necessarily prevent starvation? What about timeouts as a deadlock-resolution mechanism?

10.4   Distributed Databases

We shall now consider the elements of distributed database systems. In a distributed system, there are many, relatively autonomous processors that may participate in database operations. Distributed databases offer several opportunities:

1. Since many machines can be brought to bear on a problem, the opportunities for parallelism and speedy response to queries are increased.

2. Since data may be replicated at several sites, the system may not have to stop processing just because one site or component has failed.

On the other hand, distributed processing increases the complexity of every aspect of a database system, so we need to rethink how even the most basic components of a DBMS are designed. In many distributed environments, the cost of communicating may dominate the cost of processing, so a critical issue becomes how many messages are sent. In this section we shall introduce the principal issues, while the next sections concentrate on solutions to two important problems that come up in distributed databases: distributed commit and distributed locking.

10.4.1   Distribution of Data

One important reason to distribute data is that the organization is itself distributed among many sites, and the sites each have data that is germane primarily to that site. Some examples are:

1. A bank may have many branches. Each branch (or the group of branches in a given city) will keep a database of accounts maintained at that branch (or city). Customers can choose to bank at any branch, but will normally bank at "their" branch, where their account data is stored. The bank may also have data that is kept in the central office, such as employee records and policies such as current interest rates. Of course, a backup of the records at each branch is also stored, probably in a site that is neither a branch office nor the central office.

2. A chain of department stores may have many individual stores. Each store (or a group of stores in one city) has a database of sales at that store and inventory at that store. There may also be a central office with data about employees, chain-wide inventory, credit-card customers, and information about suppliers such as unfilled orders, and what each is owed. In addition, there may be a copy of all the stores' sales data in a "data warehouse," which is used to analyze and predict sales through ad-hoc queries issued by analysts; see Section 11.3.

Factors in Communication Cost

As bandwidth cost drops rapidly, one might wonder whether communication cost needs to be considered when designing a distributed database system. Now certain kinds of data are among the largest objects managed electronically, so even with very cheap communication the cost of sending a terabyte-sized piece of data cannot be ignored. However, communication cost generally involves not only the shipping of the bits, but several layers of protocol that prepare the data for shipping, reconstitute them at the receiving end, and manage the communication. These protocols each require substantial computation. While computation is also getting cheaper, the computation needed to perform the communication is likely to remain significant, compared to the needs for conventional, single-processor execution of key database operations.

---

3. A digital library may consist of a consortium of universities that each hold on-line books and other documents. Search at any site will examine the catalog of documents available at all sites and deliver an electronic copy of the document to the user if any site holds it.

In some cases, what we might think of logically as a single relation has been partitioned among many sites. For example, the chain of stores might be imagined to have a single sales relation, such as

```
Sales(item, date, price, purchaser)
```

However, this relation does not exist physically. Rather, it is the union of a number of relations with the same schema, one at each of the stores in the chain. These local relations are called *fragments*, and the partitioning of a logical relation into physical fragments is called *horizontal decomposition* of the relation Sales. We regard the partition as "horizontal" because we may visualize a single Sales relation with its tuples separated, by horizontal lines, into the sets of tuples at each store.

In other situations, a distributed database appears to have partitioned a relation "vertically," by decomposing what might be one logical relation into two or more, each with a subset of the attributes, and with each relation at a different site. For instance, if we want to find out which sales at the Boston store were made to customers who are more than 90 days in arrears on their credit-card payments, it would be useful to have a relation (or view) that included the item, date, and purchaser information from Sales, along with the date of the last credit-card payment by that purchaser. However, in the scenario we are describing, this relation is decomposed vertically, and we would have to join the credit-card-customer relation at the central headquarters with the fragment of Sales at the Boston store.

10.4.2   Distributed Transactions

A consequence of the distribution of data is that a transaction may involve processes at several sites. Thus, our model of what a transaction is must change. No longer is a transaction a piece of code executed by a single processor communicating with a single scheduler and a single log manager at a single site. Rather, a transaction consists of communicating *transaction components*, each at a different site and communicating with the local scheduler and logger. Two important issues that must thus be looked at anew are:

1. How do we manage the commit/abort decision when a transaction is distributed? What happens if one component of the transaction wants to abort the whole transaction, while others encountered no problem and want to commit? We discuss a technique called "two-phase commit" in Section 10.5; it allows the decision to be made properly and also frequently allows sites that are up to operate even if some other site(s) have failed.

2. How do we assure serializability of transactions that involve components at several sites? We look at locking in particular, in Section 10.6 and see how local lock tables can be used to support global locks on database elements and thus support serializability of transactions in a distributed environment.

10.4.3   Data Replication

One important advantage of a distributed system is the ability to *replicate* data, that is, to make copies of the data at different sites. One motivation is that if a site fails, there may be other sites that can provide the same data that was at the failed site. A second use is in improving the speed of query answering by making a copy of needed data available at the sites where queries are initiated. For example:

1. A bank may make copies of current interest-rate policy available at each branch, so a query about rates does not have to be sent to the central office.

2. A chain store may keep copies of information about suppliers at each store, so local requests for information about suppliers (e.g., the manager needs the phone number of a supplier to check on a shipment) can be handled without sending messages to the central office.

3. A digital library may temporarily cache a copy of a popular document at a school where students have been assigned to read the document.

However, there are several problems that must be faced when data is replicated.

a) How do we keep copies identical? In essence, an update to a replicated data element becomes a distributed transaction that updates all copies.

b) How do we decide where and how many copies to keep? The more copies, the more effort is required to update, but the easier queries become. For example, a relation that is rarely updated might have copies everywhere for maximum efficiency, while a frequently updated relation might have only one or two copies.

c) What happens when there is a communication failure in the network, and different copies of the same data have the opportunity to evolve separately and must then be reconciled when the network reconnects?

10.4.4 Distributed Query Optimization

The existence of distributed data also affects the complexity and options available in the design of a physical query plan (see Section 7.7). Among the issues that must be decided as we choose a physical plan are:

1. If there are several copies of a needed relation R, from which do we get the value of R?

2. If we apply an operator, say join, to two relations R and S, we have several options and must choose one. Some of the possibilities are:

   (a) We can copy S to the site of R and do the computation there.

   (b) We can copy R to the site of S and do the computation there.

   (c) We can copy both R and S to a third site and do the computation at that site.

   Which is best depends on several factors, including which site has available processing cycles, and whether the result of the operation will be combined with data at a third site. For example, if we are computing $(R \bowtie S) \bowtie T$, we may choose to ship both R and S to the site of T and take both joins there.

If a relation R is in fragments $R_1, R_2, \ldots, R_n$ distributed among several sites, we should also replace a use of R in the query by a use of

$$R_1 \cup R_2 \cup \cdots \cup R_n$$

as we select a logical query plan. The query may then allow us to simplify the expression significantly. For instance, if the R_i's each represent fragments of the `Sales` relation discussed in Section 10.4.1, and each fragment is associated with a single store, then a query about sales at the Boston store might allow us to remove all R_i's except the fragment for Boston from the union.

10.4.5 Exercises for Section 10.4

*!! **Exercise 10.4.1 :** The following exercise will allow you to address some of the problems that come up when deciding on a replication strategy for data. Suppose there is a relation R that is accessed from n sites. The ith site issues q_i queries about R and u_i updates to R per second, for $i = 1, 2, \ldots, n$. The cost of executing a query if there is a copy of R at the site issuing the query is c, while if there is no copy there, and the query must be sent to some remote site, then the cost is $10c$. The cost of executing an update is d for the copy of R at the issuing site and $10d$ for every copy of R that is not at the issuing site. As a function of these parameters, how would you choose, for large n, a set of sites at which to replicate R.

10.5 Distributed Commit

In this section, we shall address the problem of how a distributed transaction that has components at several sites can execute atomically. The next section discusses another important property of distributed transactions: executing them serializably. We shall begin with an example that illustrates the problems that might arise.

Example 10.15 : Consider our example of a chain of stores mentioned in Section 10.4. Suppose a manager of the chain wants to query all the stores, find the inventory of toothbrushes at each, and issue instructions to move toothbrushes from store to store in order to balance the inventory. The operation is done by a single global transaction T that has component T_i at the ith store and a component T_0 at the office where the manager is located. The sequence of activities performed by T are summarized below:

1. Component T_0 is created at the site of the manager.

2. T_0 sends messages to all the stores instructing them to create components T_i.

3. Each T_i executes a query at store i to discover the number of toothbrushes in inventory and reports this number to T_0.

4. T_0 takes these numbers and determines, by some algorithm we shall not discuss, what shipments of toothbrushes are desired. T_0 then sends messages such as "store 10 should ship 500 toothbrushes to store 7" to the appropriate stores (stores 7 and 10 in this instance).

5. Stores receiving instructions update their inventory and perform the shipments.

□

10.5.1 Supporting Distributed Atomicity

There are a number of things that could go wrong in Example 10.15, and many of these result in violations of the atomicity of T. That is, some of the actions comprising T get executed, but others do not. Mechanisms such as logging and recovery, which we assume are present at each site, will assure that each T_i is executed atomically, but do not assure that T itself is atomic.

Example 10.16: Suppose a bug in the algorithm to redistribute toothbrushes might cause store 10 to be instructed to ship more toothbrushes than it has. T_{10} will therefore abort, and no toothbrushes will be shipped from store 10; neither will the inventory at store 10 be changed. However, T_7 detects no problems and commits at store 7, updating its inventory to reflect the supposedly shipped toothbrushes. Now, not only has T failed to execute atomically (since T_{10} never completes), but it has left the distributed database in an inconsistent state: the toothbrush inventory does not equal the number of toothbrushes on hand. □

Another source of problems is the possibility that a site will fail or be disconnected from the network while the distributed transaction is running.

Example 10.17: Suppose T_{10} replies to T_0's first message by telling its inventory of toothbrushes. However, the machine at store 10 then crashes, and the instructions from T_0 are never received by T_{10}. Can distributed transaction T ever commit? What should T_{10} do when its site recovers? □

10.5.2 Two-Phase Commit

In order to avoid the problems suggested in Section 10.5.1, distributed DBMS's use a complex protocol for deciding whether or not to commit a distributed transaction. In this section, we shall describe the basic idea behind these protocols, called *two-phase commit*.[3] By making a global decision about committing, each component of the transaction will commit, or none will. As usual, we assume that the atomicity mechanisms at each site assure that either the local component commits or it has no effect on the database state at that site; i.e., components of the transaction are atomic. Thus, by enforcing the rule that either all components of a distributed transaction commit or none does, we make the distributed transaction itself atomic.

Several salient points about the two-phase commit protocol follow:

- In a two-phase commit, we assume that each site logs actions at that site, but there is no global log.

- We also assume that one site, called the *coordinator*, plays a special role in deciding whether or not the distributed transaction can commit. For example, the coordinator might be the site at which the transaction originates, such as the site of T_0 in the examples of Section 10.5.1.

---

[3]Do not confuse two-phase commit with two-phase locking. They are independent ideas, designed to solve different problems.

- The two-phase commit protocol involves sending certain messages between the coordinator and the other sites. As each message is sent, it is logged at the sending site, to aid in recovery should it be necessary.

With these points in mind, we can describe the two phases in terms of the messages sent between sites.

Phase I

In phase 1 of the two-phase commit, the coordinator for a distributed transaction T decides when to attempt to commit T. Presumably the attempt to commit occurs after the component of T at the coordinator site is ready to commit, but in principle the steps must be carried out even if the coordinator's component wants to abort (but with obvious simplifications as we shall see). The coordinator polls all the sites with components of the transaction T to determine their wishes regarding the commit/abort decision.

1. The coordinator places a log record <Prepare T> on the log at its site.

2. The coordinator sends to each component's site (in principle including itself) the message prepare T.

3. Each site receiving the message prepare T decides whether to commit or abort its component of T. The site can delay if the component has not yet completed its activity, but must eventually send a response.

4. If a site wants to commit its component, it must enter a state called *precommitted*. Once in the precommitted state, the site cannot abort its component of T without a directive to do so from the coordinator. The following steps are done to become precommitted:

   (a) Perform whatever steps are necessary to be sure the local component of T will not have to abort, even if there is a system failure followed by recovery at the site. Thus, not only must all actions associated with the local T be performed, but the appropriate actions regarding the log must be taken so that T will be redone rather than undone in a recovery. The actions depend on the logging method, but surely the log records associated with actions of the local T must be flushed to disk.

   (b) Place the record <Ready T> on the local log and flush the log to disk.

   (c) Send to the coordinator the message ready T.

   However, the site does not commit its component of T at this time; it must wait for phase 2.

5. If, instead, the site wants to abort its component of T, then it logs the record <Don't commit T> and sends the message don't commit T to the coordinator. It is safe to abort the component at this time, since T will surely abort if even one component wants to abort.

The messages of phase 1 are summarized in Fig. 10.15.

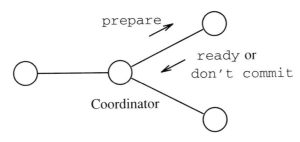

Figure 10.15: Messages in phase 1 of two-phase commit

Phase II

The second phase begins when responses ready or don't commit are received from each site by the coordinator. However, it is possible that some site fails to respond; it may be down, or it has been disconnected by the network. In that case, after a suitable timeout period, the coordinator will treat the site as if it had sent don't commit.

1. If the coordinator has received ready T from all components of T, then it decides to commit T. The coordinator

    (a) Logs <Commit T> at its site, and

    (b) Sends message commit T to all sites involved in T.

2. If the coordinator has received don't commit T from one or more sites, it:

    (a) Logs <Abort T> at its site, and

    (b) Sends abort T messages to all sites involved in T.

3. If a site receives a commit T message, it commits the component of T at that site, logging <Commit T> as it does.

4. If a site receives the message abort T, it aborts T and writes the log record <Abort T>.

The messages of phase 2 are summarized in Fig. 10.16.

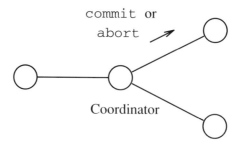

Figure 10.16: Messages in phase 2 of two-phase commit

10.5.3   Recovery of Distributed Transactions

At any time during the two-phase commit process, a site may fail. We need to make sure that what happens when the site recovers is consistent with the global decision that was made about a distributed transaction T. There are several cases to consider, depending on the last log entry for T.

1. If the last log record for T was <Commit T>, then T must have been committed by the coordinator. Depending on the log method used, it may be necessary to redo the component of T at the recovering site.

2. If the last log record is <Abort T>, then similarly we know that the global decision was to abort T. If the log method requires it, we undo the component of T at the recovering site.

3. If the last log record is <Don't commit T>, then the site knows that the global decision must have been to abort T. If necessary, effects of T on the local database are undone.

4. The hard case is when the last log record for T is <Ready T>. Now, the recovering site does not know whether the global decision was to commit or abort T. This site must communicate with at least one other site to find out the global decision for T. If the coordinator is up, the site can ask the coordinator. If the coordinator is not up at this time, some other site may be asked to consult its log to find out what happened to T. In the worst case, no other site can be contacted, and the local component of T must be kept active until the commit/abort decision is determined.

5. It may also be the case that the local log has no records about T that come from the actions of the two-phase commit protocol. If so, then the recovering site may unilaterally decide to abort its component of T, which is consistent with all logging methods. It is possible that the coordinator already detected a timeout from the failed site and decided to abort T. If the failure was brief, T may still be active at other sites, but it will never be inconsistent if the recovering site decides to abort its component of T and responds with don't commit T if later polled in phase 1.

The above analysis assumes that the failed site is not the coordinator. When the coordinator fails during a two-phase commit, new problems arise. First, the surviving participant sites must either wait for the coordinator to recover or elect a new coordinator. Since the coordinator could be down for an indefinite period, there is good motivation to elect a new leader, at least after a brief waiting period to see if the coordinator comes back up.

The matter of *leader election* is in its own right a complex problem of distributed systems, beyond the scope of this book. However, a simple method will work in most situations. For instance, we may assume that all participant sites have unique identifying numbers; IP addresses will work in many situations. Each participant sends messages announcing its availability as leader to all the other sites, giving its identifying number. After a suitable length of time, each participant acknowledges as the new coordinator the lowest-numbered site from which it has heard, and sends messages to that effect to all the other sites. If all sites receive consistent messages, then there is a unique choice for new coordinator, and everyone knows about it. If there is inconsistency, or a surviving site has failed to respond, that too will be universally known, and the election starts over.

Now, the new leader polls the sites for information about each distributed transaction T. Each site reports the last record on its log concerning T, if there is one. The possible cases are:

1. Some site has <Commit T> on its log. Then the original coordinator must have wanted to send `commit` T messages everywhere, and it is safe to commit T.

2. Similarly, if some site has <Abort T> on its log, then the original coordinator must have decided to abort T, and it is safe for the new coordinator to order that action.

3. Suppose now that no site has <Commit T> or <Abort T> on its log, but at least one site does *not* have <Ready T> on its log. Then since actions are logged before the corresponding messages are sent, we know that the old coordinator never received `ready` T from this site and therefore could not have decided to commit. It is safe for the new coordinator to decide to abort T.

4. The hard case is when there is no <Commit T> or <Abort T> to be found, but every surviving site has <Ready T>. Now, we cannot be sure whether the old coordinator found some reason to abort T or not; it could have decided to do so because of actions at its own site, or because of a `don't commit` T message from another failed site, for example. Or the old coordinator may have decided to commit T and already committed its local component of T. Thus, the new coordinator is not able to decide whether to commit or abort T and must wait until the original coordinator recovers. In real systems, the database administrator has the ability

to intervene and manually force the waiting transaction components to finish. The result is a possible loss of atomicity, but the person executing the blocked transaction will be notified to take some appropriate compensating action.

10.5.4   Exercises for Section 10.5

! Exercise 10.5.1 : Consider a transaction T initiated at a home computer that asks bank B to transfer $10,000 from an account at B to an account at another bank C.

* a) What are the components of distributed transaction T? What should the components at B and C do?

  b) What can go wrong if there is not $10,000 in the account at B?

  c) What can go wrong if one or both banks' computers crash, or if the network is disconnected?

  d) If one of the problems suggested in (c) occurs, how could the transaction resume correctly when the computers and network resume operation?

Exercise 10.5.2 : In this exercise, we need a notation for describing sequences of messages that can take place during a two-phase commit. Let (i, j, M) mean that site i sends the message M to site j, where the value of M and its meaning can be P (prepare), R (ready), D (don't commit), C (commit), or A (abort). We shall discuss a simple situation in which site 0 is the coordinator, but not otherwise part of the transaction, and sites 1 and 2 are the components. For instance, the following is one possible sequence of messages that could take place during a successful commit of the transaction:

$$(0, 1, P),\ (0, 2, P),\ (2, 0, R),\ (1, 0, R),\ (0, 2, C),\ (0, 1, C)$$

* a) Give an example of a sequence of messages that could occur if site 1 wants to commit and site 2 wants to abort.

*! b) How many possible sequences of messages such as the above are there, if the transaction successfully commits?

! c) If site 1 wants to commit, but site 2 does not, how many sequences of messages are there, assuming no failures occur?

! d) If site 1 wants to commit, but site 2 is down and does not respond to messages, how many sequences are there?

!! Exercise 10.5.3 : Using the notation of Exercise 10.5.2, suppose the sites are a coordinator and n other sites that are the transaction components. As a function of n, how many sequences of messages are there if the transaction successfully commits?

10.6 Distributed Locking

In this section we shall see how to extend a locking scheduler to an environment where transactions are distributed and consist of components at several sites. We assume that lock tables are managed by individual sites, and that the component of a transaction at a site can only request a lock on the data elements at that site.

When data is replicated, we must arrange that the copies of a single element X are changed in the same way by each transaction. This requirement introduces a distinction between locking the *logical* database element X and locking one or more of the copies of X. In this section, we shall offer a cost model for distributed locking algorithms that applies to both replicated and nonreplicated data. However, before introducing the model, let us consider an obvious (and sometimes adequate) solution to the problem of maintaining locks in a distributed database — centralized locking.

10.6.1 Centralized Lock Systems

Perhaps the simplest approach is to designate one site, the *lock site*, to maintain a lock table for logical elements, whether or not they have copies at that site. When a transaction wants a lock on logical element X, it sends a request to the lock site, which grants or denies the lock, as appropriate. Since obtaining a global lock on X is the same as obtaining a local lock on X at the lock site, we can be sure that global locks behave correctly as long as the lock site administers locks conventionally. The usual cost is three messages per lock (request, grant, and release), unless the transaction happens to be running at the lock site.

The use of a single lock site can be adequate in some situations, but if there are many sites and many simultaneous transactions, the lock site could become a bottleneck. Further, if the lock site crashes, no transaction at any site can obtain locks. Because of these problems with centralized locking, there are a number of other approaches to maintaining distributed locks, which we shall introduce after discussing how to estimate the cost of locking.

10.6.2 A Cost Model for Distributed Locking Algorithms

Suppose that each data element exists at exactly one site (i.e., there is no data replication) and that the lock manager at each site stores locks and lock requests for the elements at its site. Transactions may be distributed, and each transaction consists of components at one or more sites.

While there are several costs associated with managing locks, many of them are fixed, independent of the way transactions request locks over a network. The one cost factor over which we have control is the number of messages sent between sites when a transaction obtains and releases its locks. We shall thus count the number of messages required for various locking schemes on the assumption that all locks are granted when requested. Of course, a lock request may be denied, resulting in an additional message to deny the request and a later message when the lock is granted. However, since we cannot predict the rate of lock denials, and this rate is not something we can control anyway, we shall ignore this additional requirement for messages in our comparisons.

Example 10.18 : As we mentioned in Section 10.6.1, in the central locking method, the typical lock request uses three messages, one to request the lock, one from the central site to grant the lock, and a third to release the lock. The exceptions are:

1. The messages are unnecessary when the requesting site is the central lock site, and

2. Additional messages must be sent when the initial request cannot be granted.

However, we assume that both these situations are relatively rare; i.e., most lock requests are from sites other than the central lock site, and most lock requests can be granted. Thus, three messages per lock is a good estimate of the cost of the centralized lock method.   □

Now, consider a situation more flexible than central locking, where each database element X can maintain its locks at its own site. It might seem that, since a transaction wanting to lock X will have a component at the site of X, there are no messages between sites needed. The local component simply negotiates with the lock manager at that site for the lock on X. However, if the distributed transaction needs locks on several elements, say X, Y, and Z, then the transaction cannot complete its computation until it has locks on all three elements. If X, Y, and Z are at different sites, then the components of the transactions at that site must at least exchange synchronization messages to prevent the transaction from "getting ahead of itself."

Rather than deal with all the possible variations, we shall take a simple model of how transactions gather locks. We assume that one component of each transaction, the *lock coordinator*, has the responsibility to gather all the locks that all components of the transaction require. The lock coordinator locks elements at its own site without messages, but locking an element X at any other site requires three messages:

1. A message to the site of X requesting the lock.

2. A reply message granting the lock (recall we assume all locks are granted immediately; if not, a denial message followed by a granting message later will be sent).

3. A message to the site of X releasing the lock.

Since we only wish to compare distributed locking protocols, rather than give absolute values for their average number of messages, this simplification will serve our purposes.

If we pick as the lock coordinator the site where the most locks are needed by the transaction, then we minimize the requirement for messages. The number of messages required is three times the number of database elements at the other sites.

10.6.3 Locking Replicated Elements

When an element X has replicas at several sites, we must be careful how we interpret the locking of X.

Example 10.19: Suppose there are two copies, X_1 and X_2, of a database element X. Suppose also that a transaction T gets a shared lock on the copy X_1 at the site of that copy, while transaction U gets an exclusive lock on the copy X_2 at its site. Now, U can change X_2 but cannot change X_1, resulting in the two copies of the element X becoming different. Moreover, since T and U may lock other elements as well, and the order in which they read and write X is not forced by the locks they hold on the copies of X, there is also an opportunity for T and U to engage in unserializable behavior. $\square$

The problem illustrated by Example 10.19 is that when data is replicated, we must distinguish between getting a shared or exclusive lock on the logical element X and getting a local lock on a copy of X at the site of that copy. That is, in order to assure serializability, we need for transactions to take global locks on the logical elements. But the logical elements don't exist physically — only their copies do — and there is no global lock table. Thus, the only way that a transaction can obtain a global lock on X is to obtain local locks on one or more copies of X at the site(s) of those copies. We shall now consider methods for turning local locks into global locks that have the required properties:

- No two transactions can have a global exclusive lock on a logical element X at the same time.

- If a transaction has a global exclusive lock on logical element X, then no transaction can have a global shared lock on X.

- Any number of transactions can have global shared locks on X, as long as no transaction has a global exclusive lock.

10.6.4 Primary-Copy Locking

An improvement on the centralized locking approach is to distribute the function of the lock site, but still maintain the principle that each logical element has a single site responsible for its global lock. This distributed-lock method is called the *primary copy* method. This change avoids the possibility that the central lock site will become a bottleneck, while still maintaining the simplicity of the centralized method.

In the primary copy lock method, each logical element X has one of its copies designated the "primary copy." In order to get a lock on logical element X, a transaction sends a request to the site of the primary copy of X. The site of the primary copy maintains an entry for X in its lock table and grants or denies the request as appropriate. Again, global (logical) locks will be administered correctly as long as each site administers the locks for the primary copies correctly.

Also as with a centralized lock site, most lock requests generate three messages, except for those where the transaction and the primary copy are at the same site. However, if we choose primary copies wisely, then we expect that these sites will frequently be the same.

Example 10.20 : In the chain-of-stores example, we should make each store's sales data have its primary copy at the store. Other copies of this data, such as at the central office or at a data warehouse used by sales analysts, are not primary copies. Probably, the typical transaction is executed at a store and updates only sales data for that store. No messages are needed when this type of transaction takes its locks. Only if the transaction examined or modified data at another store would lock-related messages be sent.   □

10.6.5   Global Locks From Local Locks

Another approach is to synthesize global locks from collections of local locks. In these schemes, no copy of a database element X is "primary"; rather they are symmetric, and local shared or exclusive locks can be requested on any of these copies. The key to a successful global locking scheme is to require transactions to obtain a certain number of local locks on copies of X before the transaction can assume it has a global lock on X.

Suppose database element A has n copies. We pick two numbers:

1. s is the number of copies of A that must be locked in shared mode in order for a transaction to have a global shared lock on A.

2. x is the number of copies of A that must be locked in exclusive mode in order for a transaction to have an exclusive lock on A.

As long as $2x > n$ and $s + x > n$, we have the desired properties: there can be only one global exclusive lock on A, and there cannot be both a global shared and global exclusive lock on A. The explanation is as follows. Since $2x > n$, if two transactions had global exclusive locks on A, there would be at least one copy that had granted local exclusive locks to both (because there are more local exclusive locks granted than there are copies of A). However, then the local locking method would be incorrect. Similarly, since $s + x > n$, if one transaction had a global shared lock on A and another had a global exclusive

---

Distributed Deadlocks

There are many opportunities for transactions to get deadlocked as they try to acquire global locks on replicated data. There are also many ways to construct a global waits-for graph and thus detect deadlocks. However, in a distributed environment, it is often simplest and also most effective to use a timeout. Any transaction that has not completed after an appropriate amount of time is assumed to have gotten deadlocked and is rolled back.

---

lock on A, then some copy granted both local shared and exclusive locks at the same time.

In general, the number of messages needed to obtain a global shared lock is $3s$, and the number to obtain a global exclusive lock is $3x$. That number seems excessive, compared with centralized methods that require 3 or fewer messages per lock on the average. However, there are compensating arguments, as the following two examples of specific (s, x) choices shows.

- *Read-Locks-One; Write-Locks-All.* Here, $s = 1$ and $x = n$. Obtaining a global exclusive lock is very expensive, but a global shared lock requires three messages at the most. Moreover, this scheme has an advantage over the primary-copy method: while the latter allows us to avoid messages when we read the primary copy, the read-locks-one scheme allows us to avoid messages whenever the transaction is at the site of *any copy* of the database element we desire to read. Thus, this scheme can be superior when most transactions are read-only, but transactions to read an element X initiate at different sites. An example would be a distributed digital library that caches copies of documents where they are most frequently read.

- *Majority Locking.* Here, $s = x = \lceil (n + 1)/2 \rceil$. It seems that this system requires many messages no matter where the transaction is. However, there are several other factors that may make this scheme acceptable. First, many network systems support *broadcast*, where it is possible for a transaction to send out one general request for local locks on an element X, which will be received by all sites. Similarly, the release of locks may be achieved by a single message. However, this selection of s and x provides an advantage others do not: it allows partial operation even when the network is disconnected. As long as there is one component of the network that contains a majority of the sites with copies of X, then it is possible for a transaction to obtain a lock on X. Even if other sites are active while disconnected, we know that they cannot even get a shared lock on X, and thus there is no risk that transactions running in different components of the network will engage in behavior that is not serializable.

10.6.6   Exercises for Section 10.6

! Exercise 10.6.1 : We showed how to create global shared and exclusive locks from local locks of that type. How would you create:

* ***** a) Global shared, exclusive, and increment locks.

    b) Global shared, exclusive, and update locks.

!! c) Global shared, exclusive, and intention locks for each type.

from local locks of the same types?

Exercise 10.6.2 : Suppose there are five sites, each with a copy of a database element X. One of these sites P is the dominant site for X and will be used as X's primary site in a primary-copy distributed-lock system. The statistics regarding accesses to X are:

    i. 50% of all accesses are read-only accesses originating at P.

    ii. Each of the other four sites originates 10% of the accesses, and these are read-only.

    iii. The remaining 10% of accesses require exclusive access and may originate at any of the five sites with equal probability (i.e., 2% originate at each).

For each of the lock methods below, give the average number of messages needed to obtain a lock. Assume that all requests are granted, so no denial messages are needed.

* ***** a) Read-locks-one; write-locks-all.

    b) Majority locking.

    c) Primary-copy locking, with the primary copy at P.

10.7   Long-Duration Transactions

There is a family of applications for which a database system is suitable for maintaining data, but the model of many short transactions on which database concurrency-control mechanisms are predicated, is inappropriate. In this section we shall examine some examples of these applications and the problems that arise. We then discuss a solution based on "compensating transactions" that negate the effects of transactions that were committed, but shouldn't have been.

10.7.1 Problems of Long Transactions

Roughly, a *long transaction* is one that takes too long to be allowed to hold locks that another transaction needs. Depending on the environment, "too long" could mean seconds, minutes, or hours; we shall assume that at least several minutes, and probably hours, are involved in "long" transactions. Three broad classes of applications that involve long transactions are:

1. *Conventional DBMS Applications.* While common database applications run mostly short transactions, many applications require occasional long transactions. For example, one transaction might examine all of a bank's accounts to verify that the total balance is correct. Another application may require that an index be reconstructed occasionally to keep performance at its peak.

2. *Design Systems.* Whether the thing being designed is mechanical like an automobile, electronic like a microprocessor, or a software system, the common element of design systems is that the design is broken into a set of components (e.g., files of a software project), and different designers work on different components simultaneously. We do not want two designers taking a copy of a file, editing it to make design changes, and then writing the new file versions back, because then one set of changes would overwrite the other. Thus, a *check-out-check-in* system allows a designer to "check out" a file and check it in when the changes are finished, perhaps hours or days later. Even if the first designer is changing the file, another designer might want to look at the file to learn something about its contents. If the check-out operation were tantamount to an exclusive lock, then some reasonable and sensible actions would be delayed, possibly for days.

3. *Workflow Systems.* These systems involve collections of processes, some executed by software alone, some involving human interaction, and perhaps some involving human action alone. We shall give shortly an example of office paperwork involving the payment of a bill. Such applications may take days to perform, and during that entire time, some database elements may be subject to change. Were the system to grant an exclusive lock on data involved in a transaction, other transactions could be locked out for days.

Example 10.21: Consider the problem of an employee vouchering travel expenses. The intent of the traveler is to be reimbursed from account A123, and the process whereby the payment is made is shown in Fig. 10.17. The process begins with action A_1, where the traveler's secretary fills out an on-line form describing the travel, the account to be charged, and the amount. We assume in this example that the account is A123, and the amount is $1000.

The traveler's receipts are sent physically to the departmental authorization office, while the form is sent on-line to an automated action A_2. This process checks that there is enough money in the charged account (A123) and reserves

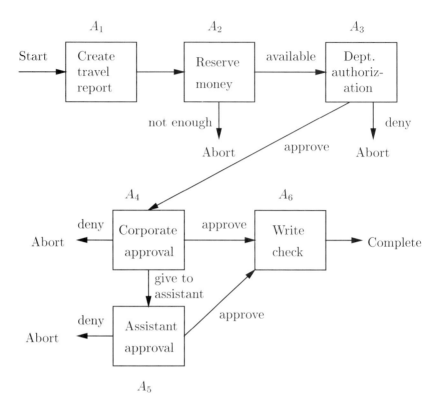

Figure 10.17: Workflow diagram for a traveler requesting expense reimbursement

the money for expenditure; i.e., it tentatively deducts $1000 from the account but does not issue a check for that amount. If there is not enough money in the account, the transaction aborts, and presumably it will restart when either enough money is in the account or after changing the account to be charged.[4]

Action A_3 is performed by the departmental administrator, who examines the receipts and the on-line form. This action might take place the next day. If everything is in order, the form is approved and sent to the corporate administrator, along with the physical receipts. If not, the transaction is aborted. Presumably the traveler will be required to modify the request in some way and resubmit the form.

In action A_4, which may take place several days later, the corporate administrator either approves or denies the request, or passes the form to an assistant,

---

[4]Of course the traveler (who does not work for Stanford anyway) would *never* charge the travel inappropriately to another government contract, but would use an appropriate source of funds. We have to say this because government auditors, who have no clue about how a university should operate, are still swarming all over Stanford.

who will then make the decision in action A_5. If the form is denied, the transaction again aborts and the form must be resubmitted. If the form is approved, then at action A_6 the check is written, and the deduction of $1000 from account A123 is finalized.

However, suppose that the only way we could implement this workflow is by conventional locking. In particular, since the balance of account A123 may be changed by the complete transaction, it has to be locked exclusively at action A_2 and not unlocked until either the transaction aborts or action A_6 completes. This lock may have to be held for days, while the people charged with authorizing the payment get a chance to look at the matter. If so, then there can be no other charges made to account A123, even tentatively. On the other hand, if there are no controls at all over how account A123 can be accessed, then it is possible that several transactions will reserve or deduct money from the account simultaneously, leading to an overdraft. Thus, some compromise between rigid, long-term locks on one hand, and anarchy on the other, must be used. □

10.7.2 Sagas

A *saga* is a collection of actions, such as those of Example 10.21, that together form a long-duration "transaction." That is, a saga consists of:

1. A collection of actions.

2. A graph whose nodes are either actions or the special *Abort* and *Complete* nodes, and whose arcs link pairs of nodes. No arcs leave the two special nodes, which we call *terminal* nodes.

3. An indication of the node at which the action starts, called the *start node*.

The paths through the graph, from the start node to either of the terminal nodes, represent possible sequences of actions. Those paths that lead to the *Abort* node represent sequences of actions that cause the overall transaction to be rolled back, and these sequences of actions should leave the database unchanged. Paths to the *Complete* node represent successful sequences of actions, and all the changes to the database system that these actions perform will remain in the database.

Example 10.22: The paths in the graph of Fig. 10.17 that lead to the *Abort* node are: A_1A_2, $A_1A_2A_3$, $A_1A_2A_3A_4$, and $A_1A_2A_3A_4A_5$. The paths that lead to the *Complete* node are $A_1A_2A_3A_4A_6$, and $A_1A_2A_3A_4A_5A_6$. Notice that in this case the graph has no cycles, so there are a finite number of paths leading to a terminal node. However, in general, a graph can have cycles, in which case there may be an infinite number of paths. □

Concurrency control for sagas is managed by two facilities:

When are Database States "The Same"?

When discussing compensating transactions, we should be careful about what it means to return the database to "the same" state that it had before. We had a taste of the problem when we discussed logical logging for B-trees in Example 10.6. There we saw that if we "undid" an operation, the state of the B-tree might not be identical to the state before the operation, but would be equivalent to it as far as access operations on the B-tree were concerned. More generally, executing an action and its compensating transaction might to restore the database to a state literally identical to what existed before, but the differences must not be detectable by whatever application programs the database supports.

---

1. Each action may be considered itself a (short) transaction, that when executed uses a conventional concurrency-control mechanism, such as locking. For instance, A_2 may be implemented to (briefly) obtain a lock on account A123, decrement the amount indicated on the travel voucher, and release the lock. This locking prevents two transactions from trying to write new values of the account balance at the same time, thereby losing the effect of the first to write and making money "appear by magic."

2. The overall transaction, which can be any of the paths to a terminal node, is managed through the mechanism of "compensating transactions," which are inverses to the transactions at the nodes of the saga. Their job is to roll back the effect of a committed action in a way that does not depend on what has happened to the database between the time the action was executed and the time the compensating transaction is executed. We discuss compensating transactions in the next section.

10.7.3 Compensating Transactions

In a saga, each action A has a *compensating transaction*, which we denote A^{-1}. Intuitively, if we execute A, and later execute A^{-1}, then the resulting database state is the same as if neither A nor A^{-1} had executed. More formally:

- If D is any database state, and $B_1 B_2 \cdots B_n$ is any sequence of actions and compensating transactions (whether from the saga in question or any other saga or transaction that may legally execute on the database) then the same database states result from running the sequences $B_1 B_2 \cdots B_n$ and $A B_1 B_2 \cdots B_n A^{-1}$ on the database state D.

If a saga execution leads to the *Abort* node, then we roll back the saga by executing the compensating transactions for each executed action, in the reverse order of those actions. By the property of compensating transactions stated above, the effect of the saga is negated, and the database state is the same as if it had never happened. An explanation why the effect is guaranteed to be negated is given in Section 10.7.4

Example 10.23: Let us consider the actions in Fig. 10.17 and see what the compensating transactions for A_1 through A_6 might be. First, A_1 creates an online document. If the document is stored in the database, then A_1^{-1} must remove it from the database. Notice that this compensation obeys the fundamental property for compensating transactions: If we create the document, do any sequence of actions α (including deletion of the document if we wish), then the effect of $A_1 \alpha A_1^{-1}$ is the same as the effect of α.

A_2 must be implemented carefully. We "reserve" the money by deducting it from the account. The money will stay removed unless restored by the compensating transaction A_2^{-1}. We claim that this A_2^{-1} is a correct compensating transaction if the usual rules for how accounts may be managed are followed. To appreciate the point, it is useful to consider a similar transaction where the obvious compensation will not work; we consider such a case in Example 10.24, next.

The actions A_3, A_4, and A_5 each involve adding an approval to a form. Thus, their compensating transactions can remove that approval.[5]

Finally, A_6, which writes the check, does not have an obvious compensating transaction. In practice none is needed, because once A_6 is executed, this saga cannot be rolled back. However, technically A_6 does not affect the database anyway, since the money for the check was deducted by A_2. Should we need to consider the "database" as the larger world, where effects such as cashing a check affected the database, then we would have to design A_6 to first try to cancel the check, next write a letter to the payee demanding the money back, and if all remedies failed, restoring the money to the account by declaring a loss due to a bad debt.   □

Next, let us take up the example, alluded to in Example 10.23, where a change to an account cannot be compensated by an inverse change. The problem is that accounts normally are not allowed to go negative.

Example 10.24: Suppose B is a transaction that adds $1000 to an account that has $2000 in it initially, and B^{-1} is the compensating transaction that removes the same amount of money. Also, it is reasonable to assume that transactions may fail if they try to delete money from an account and the balance would thereby become negative. Let C be a transaction that deletes $2500 from the same account. Then $BCB^{-1} \not\equiv C$. The reason is that C by itself fails, and leaves the account with $2000, while if we execute B then C, the account is left with $500, whereupon B^{-1} fails.

---

[5]In the saga of Fig. 10.17, the only time these actions are compensated is when we are going to delete the form anyway, but the definition of compensating transactions require that they work in isolation, regardless of whether some other compensating transaction was going to make their changes irrelevant.

Our conclusion that that a saga with arbitrary transfers among accounts and a rule about accounts never being allowed to go negative cannot be supported simply by compensating transactions. Some modification to the system must be done, e.g., allowing negative balances in accounts. □

10.7.4 Why Compensating Transactions Work

Let us say that two sequences of actions are *equivalent* ($\equiv$) if they take any database state D to the same state. The fundamental assumption about compensating transactions can be stated:

- If A is any action and α is any sequence of legal actions and compensating transactions, then $A\alpha A^{-1} \equiv \alpha$.

Now, we need to show that if a saga execution $A_1 A_2 \cdots A_n$ is followed by its compensating transactions in reverse order, $A_n^{-1} \cdots A_2^{-1} A_1^{-1}$, with any intervening actions whatsoever, then the effect is as if neither the actions nor the compensating transactions executed. The proof is an induction on n.

BASIS: If $n = 1$, then the sequence of all actions between A_1 and its compensating transaction A_1^{-1} looks like $A_1 \alpha A_1^{-1}$. By the fundamental assumption about compensating transactions, $A_1 \alpha A_1^{-1} \equiv \alpha$; i.e., there is no effect on the database state by the saga.

INDUCTION: Assume the statement for paths of up to $n - 1$ actions, and consider a path of n actions, followed by its compensating transactions in reverse order, with any other transactions intervening. The sequence looks like

$$A_1 \alpha_1 A_2 \alpha_2 \cdots \alpha_{n-1} A_n \beta A_n^{-1} \gamma_{n-1} \cdots \gamma_2 A_2^{-1} \gamma_1 A_1^{-1} \qquad (10.1)$$

where all Greek letters represent sequences of zero or more actions. By the definition of compensating transaction, $A_n \beta A_n^{-1} \equiv \beta$. Thus, (10.1) is equivalent to

$$A_1 \alpha_1 A_2 \alpha_2 \cdots A_{n-1} \alpha_{n-1} \beta \gamma_{n-1} A_{n-1}^{-1} \gamma_{n-1} \cdots \gamma_2 A_2^{-1} \gamma_1 A_1^{-1} \qquad (10.2)$$

By the inductive hypothesis, expression (10.2) is equivalent to

$$\alpha_1 \alpha_2 \cdots \alpha_{n-1} \beta \gamma_{n-1} \cdots \gamma_2 \gamma_1$$

since there are only $n - 1$ actions in (10.2). That is, the saga and its compensation leave the database state the same as if the saga had never occurred.

10.7.5 Exercises for Section 10.7

*! Exercise 10.7.1 : The process of "uninstalling" software can be thought of as a compensating transaction for the action of installing the same software. In a simple model of installing and uninstalling, suppose that an action consists of *loading* one or more files from the source (e.g., a CD-ROM) onto the hard disk of the machine. To load a file f, we copy f from CD-ROM, replacing the file with the same path name f, if there was one. To distinguish files with the same path name, we may assume each file has a timestamp.

a) What is the compensating transaction for the action that loads file f? Consider both the case where no file with that path name existed, and where there was a file f' with the same path name.

b) Explain why your answer to (a) is guaranteed to compensate. *Hint*: Consider carefully the case where after replacing f' by f, a later action replaces f by another file with the same path name.

! **Exercise 10.7.2:** Describe the process of booking an airline seat as a saga. Consider the possibility that the customer will query about a seat but not book it. The customer may book the seat, but cancel it, or not pay for the seat within the required time limit. The customer may or may not show up for the flight. For each action, describe the corresponding compensating transaction.

10.8 Summary of Chapter 10

✦ *Dirty Data*: Data that has been written, either into main-memory buffers or on disk, by a transaction that has not yet committed is called "dirty."

✦ *Cascading Rollback*: A combination of logging and concurrency control that allows a transaction to read dirty data may have to roll back transactions that read such data from a transaction that later aborts.

✦ *Strict Locking*: The strict locking policy requires transactions to hold their locks (except for shared-locks) until not only have they committed, but the commit record on the log has been flushed to disk. Strict locking guarantees that no transaction can read dirty data, even retrospectively after a crash and recovery.

✦ *Group Commit*: We can relax the strict-locking condition that requires commit records to reach disk if we assure that log records are written to disk in the order that they are written. There is still then a guarantee of no dirty reads, even if a crash and recovery occurs.

✦ *Restoring Database State After an Abort*: If a transaction aborts but has written values to buffers, then we can restore old values either from the log or from the disk copy of the database. If the new values have reached disk, then the log may still be used to restore the old value.

✦ *Logical Logging*: For large database elements such as disk blocks, it saves much space if we record old and new values on the log incrementally, that is, by indicating only the changes. In some cases, recording changes logically, that is, in terms of an abstraction of what blocks contain, allows us to restore state logically after a transaction abort, even if it is impossible to restore the state literally.

✦ *View Serializability*: When transactions may write values that are overwritten without being read, conflict serializability is too strong a condition on schedules. A weaker condition, called view serializability requires only that in the equivalent serial schedule, each transaction reads the value from the same source as in the original schedule.

✦ *Polygraphs*: The test for view serializability involves constructing a polygraph, with arcs representing writer-to-reader passing of values, and arc pairs that represent requirements that a certain write not intervene between a writer-reader connection. The schedule is view serializable if and only if selection of one arc from each pair results in an acyclic graph.

✦ *Deadlocks*: These may occur whenever transactions have to wait for a resource, such as a lock, held by another transaction. The risk is that, without proper planning, a cycle of waits may occur, and no transaction in the cycle is able to make progress.

✦ *Waits-For Graphs*: Create a node for each waiting transaction, with an arc to the transaction it is waiting for. The existence of a deadlock is the same as the existence of one or more cycles in the waits-for graph. We can avoid deadlocks if we maintain the waits-for graph and abort any transaction whose waiting would cause a cycle.

✦ *Deadlock Avoidance by Ordering Resources*: Requiring transactions to acquire resources according to some lexicographic order of the resources will prevent a deadlock from arising.

✦ *Timestamp-Based Deadlock Avoidance*: Other schemes maintain a timestamp and base their abort/wait decision on whether the requesting transaction is newer or older than the one with the resource it wants. In the wait-die scheme, an older requesting transaction waits, and a newer one is rolled back with the same timestamp. In the wound-wait scheme, a newer transaction waits and and an older one forces the transaction with the resource to roll back and give up the resource.

✦ *Distributed Data*: In a distributed database, data may be partitioned horizontally (one relation has its tuples spread over several sites) or vertically (a relation's schema is decomposed into several schemas whose relations are at different sites). It is also possible to replicate data, so presumably identical copies of a relation exist at several sites.

✦ *Distributed Transactions*: In a distributed database, one logical transaction may consist of components, each executing at a different site. To preserve consistency, these components must all agree on whether to commit or abort the logical transaction.

✦ *Two-Phase Commit*: This approach supports an agreement among transaction components whether to commit or abort, often allowing a resolution even in the face of a system crash. In the first phase, a coordinator component polls the components whether they want to commit or abort. In the second phase, the coordinator tells the components to commit if and only if all have expressed a willingness to commit.

✦ *Distributed Locks*: If transactions must lock database elements found at several sites, a method must be found to coordinate these locks. In the centralized-site method, one site maintains locks on all elements. In the primary-copy method, the home site for an element maintains its locks.

✦ *Locking Replicated Data*: When database elements are replicated at several sites, global locks on an element must be obtained through locks on one or more replicas. The majority locking method requires a read- or write-lock on a majority of the replicas to obtain a global lock. Alternatively, we may allow a global read lock by obtaining a read lock on any copy, while allowing a global write lock only through write locks on every copy.

✦ *Sagas*: When transactions involve long-duration steps that may take hours or days, conventional locking mechanisms may limit concurrency too much. A saga consists of a network of actions, each of which may lead to one or more other actions, to the completion of the entire saga, or to a requirement that the saga abort.

✦ *Compensating Transactions*: For a saga to make sense, each action must have a compensating action that will undo the effects of the first action on the database state, while leaving intact any other actions that have been made by other sagas that have completed or are currently in operation. If a saga aborts, the appropriate sequence of compensating actions is executed.

10.9 References for Chapter 10

Some useful general sources for topics covered here are [2], [1], and [9]. View serializability and the polygraph test is from [10]. Deadlock-prevention was surveyed in [7]; the waits-for graph is from there. The wait-die and wound-wait schemes are from [11].

The two-phase commit protocol was proposed in [8]. A more powerful scheme (not covered here) called three-phase commit is from [12]. The leader-election aspect of recovery was examined in [4].

Distributed locking methods have been proposed by [3] (the centralized locking method) [13] (primary-copy) and [14] (global locks from locks on copies). Long transactions were introduced by [6]. Sagas were described in [5].

1. N. S. Barghouti and G. E. Kaiser, "Concurrency control in advanced database applications," *Computing Surveys* **23**:3 (Sept., 1991), pp. 269–318.

2. S. Ceri and G. Pelagatti, *Distributed Databases: Principles and Systems*, McGraw-Hill, New York, 1984.

3. H. Garcia-Molina, "Performance comparison of update algorithms for distributed databases," TR Nos. 143 and 146, Computer Systems Laboratory, Stanford Univ., 1979.

4. H. Garcia-Molina, "Elections in a distributed computer system," *IEEE Trans. on Computers* **C-31**:1 (1982), pp. 48–59.

5. H. Garcia-Molina and K. Salem, "Sagas," *Proc. ACM SIGMOD Intl. Conf. on Management of Data* (1987), pp. 249–259.

6. J. N. Gray, "The transaction concept: virtues and limitations," *Proc. Intl. Conf. on Very Large Databases* (1981), pp. 144–154.

7. R. C. Holt, "Some deadlock properties of computer systems," *Computing Surveys* **4**:3 (1972), pp. 179–196.

8. B. Lampson and H. Sturgis, "Crash recovery in a distributed data storage system," Technical report, Xerox Palo Alto Research Center, 1976.

9. M. T. Ozsu and P. Valduriez, *Principles of Distributed Database Systems*, Prentice-Hall, Englewood Cliffs NJ, 1999.

10. C. H. Papadimitriou, "The serializability of concurrent updates," *J. ACM* **26**:4 (1979), pp. 631–653.

11. D. J. Rosenkrantz, R. E. Stearns, and P. M. Lewis II, "System-level concurrency control for distributed database systems," *ACM Trans. on Database Systems* **3**:2 (1978), pp. 178–198.

12. D. Skeen, "Nonblocking commit protocols," *Proc. ACM SIGMOD Intl. Conf. on Management of Data* (1981), pp. 133–142.

13. M. Stonebraker, "Retrospection on a database system," *ACM Trans. on Database Systems* **5**:2 (1980), pp. 225–240.

14. R. H. Thomas, "A majority consensus approach to concurrency control," *ACM Trans. on Database Systems* **4**:2 (1979), pp. 180–219.

Chapter 11

Information Integration

While there are many directions in which modern database systems are evolving, a large family of new applications fall under the general heading of *information integration*. Such applications take data that is stored in two or more databases (*information sources*) and build from them one large database, possibly virtual, containing information from all the sources, so the data can be queried as a unit. The sources may be conventional databases or other types of information, such as collections of Web pages.

In this chapter, we shall introduce important aspects of information integration. We begin with an outline of the principal approaches to integration: federation, warehousing, and mediation. A specialized database architecture, called the "data cube," is introduced as a way to organize the integrated data in some applications. Our study also covers specialized applications that have grown around our ability to integrate information: "OLAP" (on-line analytic processing) and "data mining."

11.1 Modes of Information Integration

There are several ways that databases or other, possibly distributed, information sources can be made to work together. In this section, we consider the three most common approaches:

1. *Federated databases.* The sources are independent, but one source can call on others to supply information.

2. *Warehousing.* Copies of data from several sources are stored in a single database, called a (*data*) *warehouse.* Possibly, the data stored at the warehouse is first processed in some way before storage; e.g., data may be filtered, and relations may be joined or aggregated. The warehouse is updated periodically, perhaps overnight. As the data is copied from the sources, it may need to be transformed in certain ways to make all data conform to the schema at the warehouse.

3. *Mediation.* A mediator is a software component that supports a *virtual database*, which the user may query as if it were *materialized* (physically constructed, like a warehouse). The mediator stores no data of its own. Rather, it translates the user's query into one or more queries to its sources. The mediator then synthesizes the answer to the user's query from the responses of those sources, and returns the answer to the user.

We shall introduce each of these approaches in turn. One of the key issues for all approaches is the way that data is transformed when it is extracted from an information source. We discuss the architecture of such transformers, called *wrappers* or *extractors*, in Section 11.2. Section 11.1.1 first introduces some of the problems that wrappers are designed to solve.

11.1.1 Problems of Information Integration

Whatever integration architecture we choose, there are subtle problems that come up when trying to attach meaning to the raw data in the various sources. We refer to (collections of) sources that deal with the same kind of data, yet differ in various subtle ways, as *heterogeneous* sources. An extended example will help expose the issues.

Example 11.1 : The Aardvark Automobile Co. has 1000 dealers, each of which maintains a database of their cars in stock. Aardvark wants to create an integrated database containing the information of all 1000 sources.[1] The integrated database will help dealers locate a particular model if they don't have one in stock. It also can be used by corporate analysts to predict the market and adjust production to provide the models most likely to sell.

However, the 1000 dealers do not all use the same database schema. For example, one dealer might store cars in a single relation that looks like:

        Cars(serialNo, model, color, autoTrans, cdPlayer,...)

with one boolean-valued attribute for every possible option. Another dealer might use a schema in which options are separated out into a second relation, such as:

        Autos(serial, model, color)
        Options(serial, option)

Notice that not only is the schema different, but apparently equivalent names have changed: `Cars` becomes `Autos`, and `serialNo` becomes `serial`.

To make matters worse, the data in the various databases, while having the same meaning, can be represented in many different ways.

---

[1] Most real automobile companies have similar facilities in place, and the history of their development may be different from our example; e.g., the centralized database may have come first, with dealers later able to download relevant portions to their own database. However, this scenario serves as an example of what companies in many industries are attempting today.

1. *Data type differences.* Serial numbers might be represented by character strings of varying length at one source and fixed length at another. The fixed lengths could differ, and some sources might use integers rather than character strings.

2. *Value differences.* The same concept might be represented by different constants at different sources. The color black might be represented by an integer code at one source, the string BLACK at another, and the code BL at a third. Worse, the code BL might stand for "blue" at yet another source.

3. *Semantic differences.* Many important terms can be given different interpretations at different sources. One dealer might include trucks in the Cars relation, while another puts only automobile data in the Cars relation. One dealer might distinguish station wagons from minivans, while another doesn't.

4. *Missing values.* A source might not record information of a type that all or most of the other sources provide. For instance, one dealer might not record colors at all. To deal with missing values, we can sometimes use NULL's or default values. However, a modern trend is to use a "semistructured" data model to represent integrated data that may not conform entirely. Some references to semistructured approaches appear in the bibliographic notes for this chapter.

Each of these kinds of inconsistencies among sources require a form of translation that must be implemented before the integrated database can be built. □

11.1.2 Federated Database Systems

Perhaps the simplest architecture for integrating several databases is to implement one-to-one connections between all pairs of databases that need to talk to one another. These connections allow one database system D_1 to query another D_2 in terms that D_2 can understand. The problem with this architecture is that if n databases each need to talk to the $n - 1$ other databases, then we must write $n(n - 1)$ pieces of code to support queries between systems. The situation is suggested in Fig. 11.1. There, we see four databases in a federation. Each of the four needs three components, one to access each of the other three databases.

Nevertheless, a federated system may be the easiest to build in some circumstances, especially when the communications between databases are limited in nature. An example will show how the translation components might work.

Example 11.2: Suppose the Aardvark Automobile dealers want to share inventory, but each dealer only needs to query the database of a few local dealers

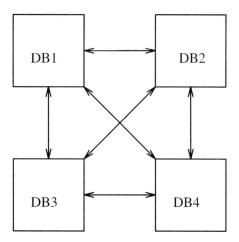

Figure 11.1: A federated collection of four databases needs 12 components to translate queries from one to another

to see if they have a needed car. To be specific, consider Dealer 1, who has a relation

```
NeededCars(model, color, autoTrans)
```

whose tuples represent cars that customers have requested, by model, color, and whether or not they want an automatic transmission. Dealer 2 stores inventory in the two-relation schema discussed in Example 11.1:

```
Autos(serial, model, color)
Options(serial, option)
```

Dealer 1 writes an application program that queries Dealer 2 remotely for cars that match each of the cars described in NeededCars. Figure 11.2 is a sketch of a program with embedded SQL that would find the desired cars. The intent is that the embedded SQL represents remote queries to the Dealer 2 database, with results returned to Dealer 1. We use the convention from standard SQL of prefixing a colon to variables that represent constants retrieved from a database.

These queries address the schema of Dealer 2. If Dealer 1 also wants to ask the same question of Dealer 3, who uses the first schema discussed in Example 11.1, with a single relation

```
Cars(serialNo, model, color, autoTrans,...)
```

the query would look quite different. But each query works properly for the database to which it is addressed.   □

```
for(each tuple (:m, :c, :a) in NeededCars) {
    if(:a= TRUE) { /* automatic transmission wanted */
        SELECT serial
        FROM Autos, Options
        WHERE Autos.serial = Options.serial AND
              Options.option = 'autoTrans' AND
              Autos.model = :m AND
              Autos.color = :c;
    }
    else { /* automatic transmission not wanted */
        SELECT serial
        FROM Autos
        WHERE Autos.model = :m AND
              Autos.color = :c AND
              NOT EXISTS (
                  SELECT *
                  FROM Options
                  WHERE serial = Autos.serial AND
                        option = 'autoTrans'
              );
    }
}
```

Figure 11.2: Dealer 1 queries Dealer 2 for needed cars

11.1.3 Data Warehouses

In a *data warehouse* integration architecture, the data from several sources is extracted and combined into a *global* schema. The data is then stored at the warehouse, which looks to the user like an ordinary database. The arrangement is suggested by Fig. 11.3, although there may be many more than the two sources shown.

Once the data is in the warehouse, queries may be issued by the user exactly as they would be issued to any database. On the other hand, user updates to the warehouse generally are forbidden, since they are not reflected in the underlying sources, and can make the warehouse inconsistent with the sources.

There are at least three approaches to constructing the data in the warehouse:

1. The warehouse is periodically reconstructed from the current data in the sources. This approach is the most common, with reconstruction occurring once a night (when the system can be shut down so queries aren't issued while the warehouse is being constructed), or at even longer intervals. The main disadvantages are the requirement of shutting down

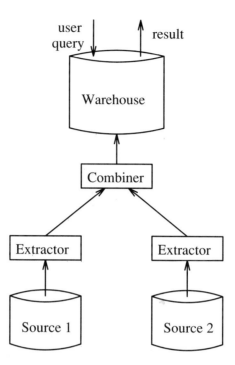

Figure 11.3: A data warehouse stores integrated information in a separate database

the warehouse, and the fact that sometimes reconstructing the warehouse can take longer than a typical "night." For some applications, another disadvantage is that the data in the warehouse can become seriously out of date.

2. The warehouse is updated periodically (e.g., each night), based on the changes that have been made to the sources since the last time the warehouse was modified. This approach can involve smaller amounts of data, which is very important if the warehouse needs to be modified in a short period of time, and the warehouse is large (multigigabyte and terabyte warehouses are in use). The disadvantage is that calculating changes to the warehouse, a process called *incremental update*, is complex, compared with algorithms that simply construct the warehouse from scratch.

3. The warehouse is changed immediately, in response to each change or a small set of changes at one or more of the sources. This approach requires too much communication and processing to be practical for all but small warehouses whose underlying sources change slowly. However, it is a subject of research and a successful warehouse implementation of this type would have a number of important applications, such as automated stock trading at the warehouse.

Example 11.3: Suppose for simplicity that there are only two dealers in the Aardvark system, and they respectively use the schemas

    Cars(serialNo, model, color, autoTrans, cdPlayer,...)

and

    Autos(serial, model, color)
    Options(serial, option)

We wish to create a warehouse with the schema

    AutosWhse(serialNo, model, color, autoTrans, dealer)

That is, the global schema is like that of the first dealer, but we record only the option of having an automatic transmission, and we include an attribute that tells which dealer has the car.

The software that extracts data from the two dealers' databases and populates the global schema can be written as SQL queries. The query for the first dealer is simple:

    INSERT INTO AutosWhse(serialNo, model, color,
            autoTrans, dealer)
        SELECT serialNo, model, color, autoTrans, 'dealer1'
        FROM Cars;

The extractor for the second dealer is more complex, since we have to decide whether or not a given car has an automatic transmission. We use the strings 'yes' and 'no' as values of the attribute autoTrans, with the obvious meanings. The SQL code for this extractor is shown in Fig. 11.4.

In this simple example, the combiner for the data extracted from the sources is null. Since the warehouse is the union of the relations extracted from each source, we showed the data as being loaded directly into the warehouse. However, many warehouses perform operations on the relations that they extract from each source. For instance relations extracted from two sources might be joined, and the result put at the warehouse. Or we might take the union of relations extracted from several sources and then aggregate the data of this union. More generally, several relations may be extracted from each source, and different relations combined in different ways. □

11.1.4 Mediators

A mediator supports a virtual view, or collection of views, that integrates several sources in much the same way that the materialized relation(s) in a warehouse integrate sources. However, since the mediator doesn't store any data, the mechanics of mediators and warehouses are rather different. Figure 11.5 shows a mediator integrating two sources; as with the warehouse architecture, there

```
INSERT INTO AutosWhse(serialNo, model, color,
        autoTrans, dealer)
    SELECT serial, model, color, 'yes', 'dealer2'
    FROM Autos, Options
    WHERE Autos.serial = Options.serial AND
        option = 'autoTrans';

INSERT INTO AutosWhse(serialNo, model, color,
        autoTrans, dealer)
    SELECT serial, model, color, 'no', 'dealer2'
    FROM Autos
    WHERE NOT EXISTS (
        SELECT *
        FROM Options
        WHERE serial = Autos.serial AND
            option = 'autoTrans'
    );
```

Figure 11.4: Extractor for translating Dealer-2 data to the warehouse

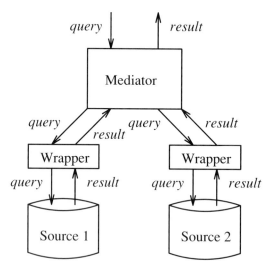

Figure 11.5: A mediator and wrappers translate queries into the terms of the sources and combine the answers

would typically be more than two sources. To begin, the user issues a query to the mediator. Since the mediator has no data of its own, it must get the relevant data from its sources and use that data to form the answer to the user's query.

Thus, we see in Fig. 11.5 the mediator sending a query to each of its wrappers, which in turn send queries to their corresponding sources. In fact, the mediator may send several queries to a wrapper, and may not query all wrappers. The results come back and are combined at the mediator; we do not show an explicit combiner component as we did in the warehouse diagram, Fig. 11.3, because in the case of the mediator, the combining of results from the sources is one of the tasks performed by the mediator.

Example 11.4: Let us consider a scenario similar to that of Example 11.3, but use a mediator. That is, the mediator integrates the same two automobile sources into a view that is a single relation with schema:

        AutosMed(serialNo, model, color, autoTrans, dealer)

Suppose the user asks the mediator about red cars, with the query:

        SELECT serialNo, model
        FROM AutosMed
        WHERE color = 'red';

The mediator, in response to this user query, can forward the same query to each of the two wrappers. The way that wrappers can be designed and implemented to handle queries like this one is the subject of Section 11.2, and for more complex scenarios, translation and distribution of query components could be necessary. However, in this case, the translation work can be done by the wrappers alone.

The wrapper for Dealer 1 translates the query into the terms of that dealer's schema, which recall is

        Cars(serialNo, model, color, autoTrans, cdPlayer,...)

A suitable translation is:

        SELECT serialNo, model
        FROM Cars
        WHERE color = 'red';

An answer, which is a set of `serialNo`-`model` pairs, will be returned to the mediator by the first wrapper.

At the same time, the wrapper for Dealer 2 translates the same query into the schema of that dealer, which is:

        Autos(serial, model, color)
        Options(serial, option)

Thus, a suitable translated query is

```
SELECT serial, model
FROM Autos
WHERE color = 'red';
```

The second wrapper returns to the mediator a set of `serial-model` pairs, perhaps performing the minor task of changing `serial` to `serialNo` in the schema for the returned pairs.

The mediator can take the union of these sets and return the result to the user. Since we expect the serial number to be a "global key," with no two cars, even in different databases, having the same serial number, we may take the bag union, assuming that there will not be duplicates anyway.   □

There are several options, not illustrated by Example 11.4, that a mediator may use to answer queries. For instance, the mediator may issue one query to one source, look at the result, and based on what is returned, decide on the next query or queries to issue. This method would be appropriate, for instance, if the user query asked whether there were any Aardvark "Gobi" model sport-utility vehicles available in blue. The first query could ask Dealer 1, and only if the result was an empty set of tuples would a query be sent to Dealer 2.

11.1.5 Exercises for Section 11.1

Exercise 11.1.1: Go to the Web pages of several on-line booksellers, and see what information about this book you can find. How would you combine this information into a global schema suitable for a warehouse or mediator?

! **Exercise 11.1.2:** Computer company A keeps data about the PC models it sells in the schema:

```
Computers(number, proc, speed, memory, hd)
Monitors(number, screen, maxResX, maxResY)
```

For instance, the tuple $(123, \text{PIII}, 500, 128, 18.7)$ in `Computers` means that model 123 has a Pentium-III processor running at 500 megahertz, with 128M of memory and an 18.7G hard disk. The tuple $(456, 19, 1600, 200)$ in `Monitors` means that model 456 has a 19-inch screen with a maximum resolution of 1600×1200.

Computer company B only sells complete systems, consisting of a computer and monitor. Its schema is

```
Systems(id, processor, mem, disk, screenSize)
```

The attribute `processor` is an integer speed; the type of processor (e.g., Pentium-III) is not recorded. Neither is the maximum resolution of the monitor recorded. Attributes `id`, `mem`, and `disk` are analogous to `number`, `memory`, and `hd` from company A, but the disk size is measured in megabytes instead of gigabytes.

a) If company A wants to insert into its relations information about the corresponding items from B, what SQL insert statements should it use?

* b) If Company B wants to insert into `Systems` as much information about the systems that can be built from computers and monitors made by A, what SQL statements best allow this information to be obtained?

*! **Exercise 11.1.3:** Suggest a global schema that would allow us to maintain as much information as we could about the products sold by companies A and B of Exercise 11.1.2.

Exercise 11.1.4: Write SQL queries to gather the information from the data at companies A and B and put it in a warehouse with your global schema of Exercise 11.1.3. You may consult the solutions for the global schema if you wish.

Exercise 11.1.5: Suppose your global schema from Exercise 11.1.3 (or the schema in the solutions if you don't like your own answer) is used at a mediator. How would the mediator process the query that asks for the maximum amount of hard-disk available with any computer with a 500 megahertz processor speed?

! **Exercise 11.1.6:** Suggest two other schemas that computer companies might use to hold data like that of Exercise 11.1.2. How would you integrate your schemas into your global schema from Exercise 11.1.3?

! **Exercise 11.1.7:** In Example 11.3 we talked about a relation `Cars` at Dealer 1 that conveniently had an attribute `autoTrans` with only the values "yes" and "no." Since these were the same values used for that attribute in the global schema, the construction of relation `Autos1` was especially easy. Suppose instead that the attribute `Cars.autoTrans` has values that are integers, with 0 meaning no automatic transmission, and $i > 0$ meaning that the car has an i-speed automatic transmission. Show how the translation from `Cars` to `Autos1` could be done by an SQL query.

Exercise 11.1.8: How would the mediator of Example 11.4 translate the following queries?

* a) Find the serial numbers of cars with automatic transmission.

b) Find the serial numbers of cars without automatic transmission.

! c) Find the serial numbers of the blue cars from Dealer 1.

11.2 Wrappers in Mediator-Based Systems

In a data warehouse system like that of Fig. 11.3, the source extractors consist of:

1. One or more queries built-in that are executed at the source to produce data for the warehouse.

2. Suitable communication mechanisms, so the wrapper can:

   (a) Pass ad-hoc queries to the source,

   (b) Receive responses from the source, and

   (c) Pass information to the warehouse.

The built-in queries to the source could be SQL queries if the source is an SQL database as in our examples of Section 11.1. Queries could also be operations in whatever language was appropriate for a source that was not a database system; e.g., the wrapper could fill out an on-line form at a Web page, issue a query to an on-line bibliography service in that system's own, specialized language, or use myriad other notations to pose the queries.

However, mediator systems require more complex wrappers than do most warehouse systems. The wrapper must be able to accept a variety of queries from the mediator and translate any of them to the terms of the source. Of course, the wrapper must then communicate the result to the mediator, just like a wrapper in a warehouse system communicates with the warehouse. In the balance of this section, we study the construction of flexible wrappers that are suitable for use with a mediator.

11.2.1   Templates for Query Patterns

A systematic way to design a wrapper that connects a mediator to a source is to classify the possible queries that the mediator can ask into *templates*, which are queries with parameters that represent constants. The mediator can provide the constants, and the wrapper executes the query with the given constants. An example should illustrate the idea; it uses the notation $T \Rightarrow S$ to express the idea that the template T is turned by the wrapper into the source query S.

Example 11.5 : Suppose we want to build a wrapper for the source of Dealer 1, which has the schema

        Cars(serialNo, model, color, autoTrans, cdPlayer,...)

for use by a mediator with schema

        AutosMed(serialNo, model, color, autoTrans, dealer)

Consider how the mediator could ask the wrapper for cars of a given color. Whatever the color was, if we denote the code representing that color by the parameter $c, then we can use the template shown in Fig. 11.6.

Similarly, the wrapper could have another template that specified only the parameter $m representing a model, yet another template in which it was only specified whether an automatic transmission was wanted, and so on. In this

```
SELECT *
FROM AutosMed
WHERE color = '$c';
    =>
SELECT serialNo, model, color, autoTrans, 'dealer1'
FROM Cars
WHERE color = '$c';
```

Figure 11.6: A wrapper template describing queries for cars of a fixed color

case, there are eight choices, if queries are allowed to specify any of three attributes: model, color, and autoTrans. In general, there would be 2^n templates if we have the option of specifying n attributes.[2] Other templates would be needed to deal with queries that asked for the total number of cars of certain types, or whether there exists a car of a certain type. The number of templates could grow unreasonably large, but some simplifications are possible by adding more sophistication to the wrapper, as we shall discuss starting in Section 11.2.3. □

11.2.2 Wrapper Generators

The templates defining a wrapper must be turned into code for the wrapper itself. The software that creates the wrapper is called a *wrapper generator*; it is similar in spirit to the parser generators (e.g., YACC) that produce components of a compiler from high-level specifications. The process, suggested in Fig. 11.7, begins when a specification, that is, a collection of templates, is given to the wrapper generator.

The wrapper generator creates a table that holds the various query patterns contained in the templates, and the source queries that are associated with each. A *driver* is used in each wrapper; in general the driver can be the same for each generated wrapper. The task of the driver is to:

1. Accept a query from the mediator. The communication mechanism may be mediator-specific and is given to the driver as a "plug-in," so the same driver can be used in systems that communicate differently.

2. Search the table for a template that matches the query. If one is found, then the parameter values from the query are used to instantiate a source

---

[2]If the source is a database that can be queried in SQL, as in our example, you would rightly expect that one template could handle any number of attributes equated to constants, simply by making the WHERE clause a parameter. While that approach will work for SQL sources and queries that only bind attributes to constants, we could not necessarily use the same idea with an arbitrary source, such as a Web site that allowed only certain forms as an interface. In the general case, we cannot assume that the way we translate one query resembles at all the way similar queries are translated.

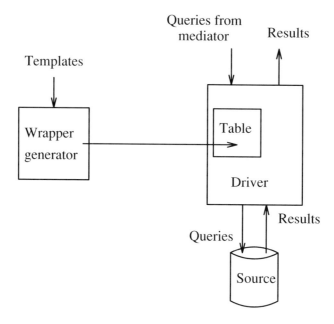

Figure 11.7: A wrapper generator produces tables for a driver; the driver and tables constitute the wrapper

query. If there is no matching template, the wrapper responds negatively to the mediator.

3. The source query is sent to the source, again using a "plug-in" communication mechanism. The response is collected by the wrapper.

4. The response is processed by the wrapper, if necessary, and then returned to the mediator. The next sections discuss how wrappers can support a larger class of queries by processing results.

11.2.3 Filters

Suppose that a wrapper on a car dealer's database has the template shown in Fig. 11.6 for finding cars by color. However, the mediator is asked to find cars of a particular model *and* color. Perhaps the wrapper has been designed with a more complex template such as that of Fig. 11.8, which handles queries that specify both model and color. Yet, as we discussed at the end of Example 11.5, it is not always realistic to write a template for every possible form of query.

Another approach to supporting more queries is to have the wrapper *filter* the results of queries that it poses to the source. As long as the wrapper has a template that (after proper substitution for the parameters) returns a superset of what the query wants, then it is possible to filter the returned tuples at the wrapper and pass only the desired tuples to the mediator. The decision

```
SELECT *
FROM AutosMed
WHERE model = '$m' AND color = '$c';
    =>
SELECT serialNo, model, color, autoTrans, 'dealer1'
FROM Cars
WHERE model = '$m' AND color = '$c';
```

Figure 11.8: A wrapper template that gets cars of a given model and color

whether a mediator query asks for a subset of what the pattern of some wrapper template returns is a hard problem in general, although in simple cases such as the examples we have seen, the theory is well-developed. The references contain some pointers for further study.

Example 11.6 : Suppose the only template we have is the one in Fig. 11.6 that finds cars given a color. However, the mediator needs to find blue 'Gobi' model cars, as with the query:

```
SELECT *
FROM AutosMed
WHERE color = 'blue' and model = 'Gobi';
```

A possible way to answer the query is to:

1. Use the template of Fig. 11.6 with $c = 'blue' to find all the blue cars.

2. Store the result in a temporary relation

```
TempAutos(serialNo, model, color, autoTrans, dealer)
```

3. Select from TempAutos the Gobi's and return the result, as with the query

```
SELECT *
FROM TempAutos
WHERE model = 'Gobi';
```

The result is the desired set of automobiles. In practice, the tuples of TempAutos would be produced one-at-a-time and filtered one-at-a-time, in a pipelined fashion, rather than having the entire relation TempAutos materialized at the wrapper and then filtered. □

Position of the Filter Component

We have, in our examples, supposed that the filtering operations take place at the wrapper. It is also possible that the wrapper passes raw data to the mediator, and the mediator filters the data. However, if most of the data returned by the template does not match the mediator's query, then it is best to filter at the wrapper and avoid the expense of shipping unneeded tuples.

11.2.4 Other Operations at the Wrapper

It is possible to transform data in other ways at the wrapper, as long as we are sure that the source-query part of the template returns to the wrapper all the data needed in the transformation. For instance, columns may be projected out of the tuples before transmission to the mediator. It is even possible to take aggregations or joins at the wrapper and transmit the result to the mediator.

Example 11.7: Suppose the mediator wants to know about blue Gobis at the various dealers, but only asks for the serial number, dealer, and whether or not there is an automatic transmission, since the value of the model and color fields are obvious from the query. The wrapper could proceed as in Example 11.6, but at the last step, when the result is to be returned to the mediator, the wrapper performs a projection in the SELECT clause as well as the filtering for the Gobi model in the WHERE clause. The query

```
SELECT serialNo, autoTrans, dealer
FROM TempAutos
WHERE model = 'Gobi';
```

does this additional filtering, although as in Example 11.6 relation TempAutos would probably be pipelined into the projection operator, rather than materialized at the wrapper. □

Example 11.8: For a more complex example, suppose the mediator is asked to find dealers and models such that the dealer has two red cars, of the same model, one with and one without an automatic transmission. Suppose also that the only useful template for Dealer 1 is the one about colors from Fig. 11.6. That is, the mediator asks the wrapper for the answer to the query of Fig. 11.9. Note that we do not have to specify a dealer for either A1 or A2, because this wrapper can only access data belonging to Dealer 1. The wrappers for all the other dealers will be asked the same query by the mediator.

A cleverly designed wrapper could discover that it is possible to answer the mediator's query by first obtaining from the Dealer-1 source a relation with all the red cars at that dealer:

```
SELECT A1.model A1.dealer
FROM AutosMed A1, AutosMed A2
WHERE A1.model = A2.model AND
      A1.color = 'red' AND
      A2.color = 'red' AND
      A1.autoTrans = 'no' AND
      A2.autoTrans = 'yes';
```

Figure 11.9: Query from mediator to wrapper

```
RedAutos(serialNo, model, color, autoTrans, dealer)
```

To get this relation, the wrapper uses its template from Fig. 11.6, which handles queries that specify a color only. In effect, the wrapper acts as if it were given the query:

```
SELECT *
FROM AutosMed
WHERE color = 'red';
```

The wrapper can then create the relation RedAutos from Dealer 1's database by using the template of Fig. 11.6 with $c = 'red'. Next, the wrapper joins RedAutos with itself, and performs the necessary selection, to get the relation asked for by the query of Fig. 11.9. The work performed by the wrapper[3] for this step is shown in Fig. 11.10. □

```
SELECT DISTINCT A1.model, A1.dealer
FROM RedAutos A1, RedAutos A2
WHERE A1.model = A2.model AND
      A1.autoTrans = 'no' AND
      A2.autoTrans = 'yes';
```

Figure 11.10: Query performed at the wrapper (or mediator) to complete the answer to the query of Fig. 11.9

11.2.5 Exercises for Section 11.2

* **Exercise 11.2.1:** In Fig. 11.6 we saw a simple wrapper template that translated queries from the mediator for cars of a given color into queries at the dealer

---

[3]In some information-integration architectures, this task might actually be performed by the mediator instead.

with relation `Cars`. Suppose that the color codes used by the mediator in its schema were different from the color codes used at this dealer, and there was a relation `GtoL(globalColor, localColor)` that translated between the two sets of codes. Rewrite the template so the correct query would be generated.

Exercise 11.2.2: In Exercise 11.1.2 we spoke of two computer companies, A and B, that used different schemas for information about their products. Suppose we have a mediator with schema

```
PCMed(manf, speed, mem, disk, screen)
```

with the intuitive meaning that a tuple gives the manufacturer (A or B), processor speed, main-memory size, hard-disk size, and screen size for one of the systems you could buy from that company. Write wrapper templates for the following types of queries. Note that you need to write two templates for each query, one for each of the manufacturers.

* a) Given a speed, find the tuples with that speed.

  b) Given a screen size, find the tuples with that size.

  c) Given memory and disk sizes, find the matching tuples.

Exercise 11.2.3: Suppose you had the wrapper templates described in Exercise 11.2.2 available in the wrappers at each of the two sources (computer manufacturers). How could the mediator use these capabilities of the wrappers to answer the following queries?

* a) Find the manufacturer, memory size, and screen size of all systems with a 400 megahertz speed and a 12 gigabyte disk.

! b) Find the maximum amount of hard disk available on a system with a 500 megahertz processor.

  c) Find all the systems with 128M memory and a screen size (in inches) that exceeds the disk size (in gigabytes).

11.3   On-Line Analytic Processing

We shall now take up an important class of applications for integrated information systems, especially data warehouses. Companies and organizations create a warehouse with a copy of large amounts of their available data and assign analysts to query this warehouse for patterns or trends of importance to the organization. This activity, called *OLAP* (standing for *On-Line Analytic Processing* and pronounced "oh-lap"), generally involves highly complex queries that use one or more aggregations. These queries are often termed *OLAP queries* or *decision-support queries*. Some examples will be given in Section 11.3.1; a

Warehouses and OLAP

There are several reasons why data warehouses play an important role in OLAP applications. First, the warehouse may be necessary to organize and centralize corporate data in a way that supports OLAP queries; the data may initially be scattered across many different databases. But often more important is the fact that OLAP queries, being complex and touching much of the data, take too much time to be executed in a transaction-processing system with high throughput requirements. OLAP queries often can be considered "long transactions" in the sense of Section 10.7.

Long transactions locking the entire database would shut down the ordinary OLTP operations (e.g., recording new sales as they occur could not be permitted if there were a concurrent OLAP query computing average sales). A common solution is to make a copy of the raw data in a warehouse, run OLAP queries only at the warehouse, and run the OLTP queries and data modifications at the data sources. In a common scenario, the warehouse is only updated overnight, while the analysts work on a frozen copy during the day. The warehouse data thus gets out of date by as much as 24 hours, which limits the timeliness of its answers to OLAP queries, but the delay is tolerable in many decision-support applications.

---

typical example is to search for products with increasing or decreasing overall sales.

Decision-support queries used in OLAP applications typically examine very large amounts of data, even if the query results are small. In contrast, common database operations, such as bank deposits or airline reservations, each touch only a tiny portion of the database; the latter type of operation is often referred to as *OLTP* (*On-Line Transaction Processing*, spoken "oh-ell-tee-pee").

Recently, new query-processing techniques have been developed that are especially good at executing OLAP queries effectively. Furthermore, because of the distinct nature of a certain class of OLAP queries, special forms of database management systems, called *data cube* systems, have been developed and marketed to support OLAP applications. We shall discuss these systems in Section 11.4.

11.3.1 OLAP Applications

A common OLAP application uses a warehouse of sales data. Major store chains will accumulate terabytes of information representing every sale of every item at every store. Queries that aggregate sales into groups and identify significant groups can be of great use to the company in predicting future problems or opportunities.

Example 11.9: Suppose the Aardvark Automobile Co. builds a data warehouse to analyze sales of its cars. The schema for the warehouse might be:

```
Sales(serialNo, date, dealer, price)
Autos(serialNo, model, color)
Dealers(name, city, state, phone)
```

A typical decision-support query might examine sales on or after April 1, 1999 to see how the recent average price per vehicle varies by state. Such a query is shown in Fig. 11.11.

```
SELECT state, AVG(price)
FROM Sales, Dealers
WHERE Sales.dealer = Dealers.name AND
      date >= '1999-01-04'
GROUP BY state;
```

Figure 11.11: Find average sales price by state

Notice how the query of Fig. 11.11 touches much of the data of the database, as it classifies every recent Sales fact by the state of the dealer that sold it. In contrast, common OLTP queries, such as "find the price at which the auto with serial number 123 was sold," would touch only a single tuple of the data. □

For another OLAP example, consider a credit-card company trying to decide whether applicants for a card are likely to be credit-worthy. The company creates a warehouse of all its current customers and their payment history. OLAP queries search for factors, such as age, income, home-ownership, and zip-code, that might help predict whether customers will pay their bills on time. Similarly, hospitals may use a warehouse of patients — their admissions, tests administered, outcomes, diagnoses, treatments, and so on — to analyze for risks and select the best modes of treatment.

11.3.2   A Multidimensional View of OLAP Data

In typical OLAP applications there is a central relation or collection of data, called the *fact table*. A fact table represents events or objects of interest, such as sales in Example 11.9. Often, it helps to think of the objects in the fact table as arranged in a multidimensional space, or "cube." Figure 11.12 suggests three-dimensional data, represented by points within the cube; we have called the dimensions car, dealer, and date, to correspond to our earlier example of automobile sales. Thus, in Fig. 11.12 we could think of each point as a sale of a single automobile, while the dimensions represent properties of that sale.

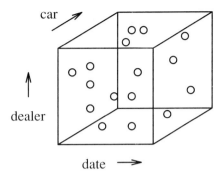

Figure 11.12: Data organized as a multidimensional cube

We shall, in Section 11.4, introduce "data cubes," a specific architecture for management of OLAP data, that takes a somewhat different point of view of multidimensional data. In the data cube, points may represent aggregated data. For instance, instead of the "car" dimension representing each individual car, that dimension might be aggregated by model only, and a point of a cube such as Fig. 11.12 would represent the total sales of all cars of a given model by a given dealer on a given day. The distinction between these two interpretations of multidimensional data are reflected in the two broad directions that have been taken by specialized systems that support cube-structured data for OLAP:

1. *ROLAP*, or *Relational OLAP*. In this approach, data may be stored in relations with a specialized structure called a "star schema." One of these relations is the fact table, which contains the *raw*, or unaggregated, data. The query language and other capabilities of the system may be tailored to the assumption that data is organized this way. We shall discuss star schemas in Section 11.3.3.

2. *MOLAP*, or *Multidimensional OLAP*. Here, a specialized structure, the "data cube" mentioned above, is used to hold the data. Often, this data is partially aggregated, as mentioned above. Nonrelational operators may be implemented by the system to support OLAP queries on data in this structure.

11.3.3 Star Schemas

A *star schema* consists of the schema for the fact table, which links to several other relations, described below, called "dimension tables." The fact table is at the center of the "star," whose points are the dimension tables. A fact table normally has several attributes that represent *dimensions*, and one or more *dependent* attributes that represent properties of interest for the point as a whole. For instance, dimensions for sales data might include the date of the sale, the place (store) of the sale, the type of item sold, the method of payment (e.g., cash or a credit card), and so on. The dependent attribute(s) might be the sales price, the cost of the item, or the tax, for instance.

Example 11.10: The Sales relation from Example 11.9

```
Sales(serialNo, date, dealer, price)
```

is a fact table. The dimensions are:

1. serialNo, representing the automobile sold, i.e., the position of the point in the space of possible automobiles.

2. date, representing the day of the sale, i.e., the position of the event in the time dimension.

3. dealer, representing the position of the event in the space of possible dealers.

The one dependent attribute is price, which is what OLAP queries to this database will typically request in an aggregation. However, queries asking for a count, rather than sum or average price would also make sense, e.g., "list the total number of sales for each dealer in the month of May, 1999." □

Supplementing the fact table are *dimension tables* describing the values along each dimension. Typically, each dimension attribute of the fact table is a foreign key, referencing the key of the corresponding dimension table, as suggested by Fig. 11.13. The attributes of the dimension tables also describe the possible groupings that would make sense in an SQL GROUP BY query. An example should make the ideas clearer.

Example 11.11: For the automobile data of Example 11.9, two of the dimension tables are obvious:

```
Autos(serialNo, model, color)
Dealers(name, city, state, phone)
```

Attribute serialNo in the fact table

```
Sales(serialNo, date, dealer, price)
```

is a foreign key, referencing serialNo of dimension table Autos.[4] The attributes Autos.model and Autos.color give properties of a given auto. We could have added many more attributes in this relation, such as boolean attributes indicating whether the auto has an automatic transmission or one of many other possible options. If we join the fact table Sales with the dimension table Autos,

---

[4]It happens that serialNo is also a key for the Sales relation, but there need not be an attribute that is both a key for the fact table and a foreign key for some dimension table.

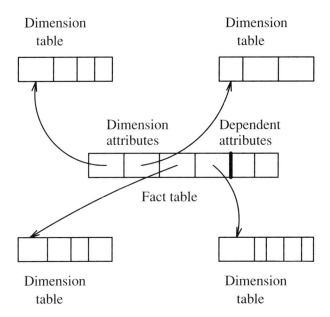

Figure 11.13: The dimension attributes in the fact table reference the keys of the dimension tables

then the attributes `model` and `color` may be used for grouping sales in interesting ways. For instance, we can ask for a breakdown of sales by color, or a breakdown of sales of the Gobi model by month and dealer.

Similarly, attribute `dealer` of `Sales` is a foreign key, referencing `name` of the dimension table `Dealers`. If `Sales` and `Dealers` are joined, then we have additional options for grouping our data; e.g., we can ask for a breakdown of sales by state or by city, as well as by dealer.

One might wonder where the dimension table for time (the `date` attribute of `Sales`) is. Since time is a physical property, it does not make sense to store facts about time in a database, since we cannot change the answer to questions such as "in what year does the day July 5, 2000 appear?" However, since grouping by various time units, such as weeks, months, quarters, and years, is frequently desired by analysts, it helps to build into the database a notion of time, as if there were a time dimension table such as

> `Days(day, week, month, year)`

A typical tuple of this "relation" would be

> `(5, 27, 7, 2000)`

representing July 5, 2000. The interpretation is that this day is the third day of the seventh month of the year 2000; it also happens to fall in the 27th full week of the year 2000. There is a certain amount of redundancy, since the week is calculable from the other three attributes. However, weeks are not exactly commensurate with months, so we cannot obtain a grouping by months from a grouping by weeks, or vice versa. Thus, it makes sense to imagine that both weeks and months are represented in this "dimension table."   □

11.3.4 Slicing and Dicing

We can think of the points of the data cube as partitioned along each dimension at some level of granularity. For example, in the time dimension, we might partition ("group by" in SQL terms) according to days, weeks, months, years, or not partition at all. For the cars dimension, we might partition by model, by color, by both model and color, or not partition. For dealers, we can partition by dealer, by city, by state, or not partition.

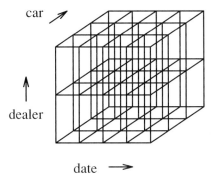

Figure 11.14: Dicing the cube by partitioning along each dimension

A choice of partition for each dimension "dices" the cube, as suggested by Fig. 11.14. The result is that the cube is divided into smaller cubes that represent groups of points whose statistics are aggregated by a query that performs the partitioning in its GROUP BY clause. Through the WHERE clause, a query also has the option of focusing on particular partitions along one or more dimensions (i.e., on a particular "slice" of the cube). The effect is that the query will ask for aggregation of values only in some subspace of the entire cube.

Example 11.12 : Figure 11.15 suggests a query in which we ask for a slice in one dimension (the date), and dice in two other dimensions (car and dealer). The date is divided into four groups, perhaps the four years over which data has been accumulated. The shading in the diagram suggests that we are only interested in one of these years.

The cars are partitioned into three groups, perhaps sedans, SUV's, and convertibles, while the dealers are partitioned into two groups, perhaps the eastern and western regions. The result of the query is a table giving the total sales in six categories for the one year of interest.   □

The general form of a so-called "slicing and dicing" query is thus:

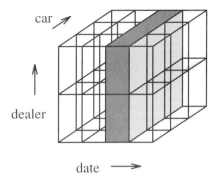

Figure 11.15: Selecting a slice of a diced cube

```
SELECT grouping attributes and aggregations
FROM fact table joined with zero or more dimension tables
WHERE certain attributes are compared with constants
GROUP BY grouping attributes;
```

Example 11.13 : Let us continue with our automobile example, but include the conceptual Days dimension table for time discussed in Example 11.11. If the Gobi isn't selling as well as we thought it would, we might try to find out which colors are not doing well. This query uses only the Autos dimension table and can be written in SQL as:

```
SELECT color, SUM(price)
FROM Sales NATURAL JOIN Autos
WHERE model = 'Gobi'
GROUP BY color;
```

This query dices by color and then slices by model, focusing on a particular model, the Gobi, and ignoring other data.

Suppose the query doesn't tell us much; each color produces about the same revenue. Since the query does not partition on time, we only see the total over all time for each color. We might suppose that the recent trend is for one or more colors to have weak sales. We may thus issue a revised query that also partitions time by month. This query is:

```
SELECT color, month, SUM(price)
FROM (Sales NATURAL JOIN Autos) JOIN Days ON date = day
WHERE model = 'Gobi'
GROUP BY color, month;
```

It is important to remember that the Days relation is not a conventional stored relation, although we may treat it as if it had the schema

```
Days(day, week, month, year)
```

The ability to use such a "relation" is one way that a data-cube system is a specialization of a DBMS.

We might discover that red Gobis have not sold well recently. The next question we might ask is whether this problem exists at all dealers, or whether only some dealers have had low sales of red Gobis. Thus, we further focus the query by looking at only red Gobis, and we partition along the dealer dimension as well. This query is:

```
SELECT dealer, month, SUM(price)
FROM (Sales NATURAL JOIN Autos) JOIN Days ON date = day
WHERE model = 'Gobi' AND color = 'red'
GROUP BY month, dealer;
```

At this point, we find that the sales per month for red Gobis are so small that we cannot observe any trends easily. Thus, we decide that it was a mistake to partition by month. A better idea would be to partition only by years, and look at only the last two years (1999 and 2000, in this hypothetical example). The final query is shown in Fig. 11.16. □

```
SELECT dealer, year, SUM(price)
FROM (Sales NATURAL JOIN Autos) JOIN Days ON date = day
WHERE model = 'Gobi' AND
      color = 'red' AND
      (year = 1999 OR year = 2000)
GROUP BY year, dealer;
```

Figure 11.16: Final slicing-and-dicing query about red Gobi sales

11.3.5 Exercises for Section 11.3

* **Exercise 11.3.1:** An on-line seller of computers wishes to maintain data about orders. Customers can order their PC with any of several processors, a selected amount of main memory, any of several disk units, and any of several CD or DVD readers. The fact table for such a database might be:

```
Orders(cust, date, proc, memory, disk, cd, quant, price)
```

We should understand attribute `cust` to be an ID that is the foreign key for a dimension table about customers, and understand attributes `proc`, `disk`, and `cd` similarly. For example, a disk ID might be elaborated in a dimension table giving the manufacturer of the disk and several disk characteristics. The `memory` attribute is simply an integer: the number of megabytes of memory ordered. The `quant` attribute is the number of machines of this type ordered by this customer, and the `price` attribute is the total cost of each machine ordered.

Drill-Down and Roll-Up

Example 11.13 illustrates two common patterns in sequences of queries that slice-and-dice the data cube.

1. *Drill-down* is the process of partitioning more finely and/or focusing on specific values in certain dimensions. Each of the steps except the last in Example 11.13 is an instance of drill-down.

2. *Roll-up* is the process of partitioning more coarsely. The last step, where we grouped by years instead of months to eliminate the effect of randomness in the data, is an example of roll-up.

---

a) Which are dimension attributes, and which are dependent attributes?

b) For some of the dimension attributes, a dimension table is likely to be needed. Suggest appropriate schemas for these dimension tables.

! **Exercise 11.3.2:** Suppose that we want to examine the data of Exercise 11.3.1 to find trends and thus predict which components the company should order more of. Describe a series of drill-down and roll-up queries that could lead to the conclusion that customers are beginning to prefer a DVD drive to a CD drive.

11.4 Data Cubes

An alternative to executing decision-support queries as ad-hoc queries is to pre-compute all possible aggregates in a systematic way. Surprisingly, the amount of extra storage needed is often tolerable, and as long as the warehoused data does not change, there is no penalty incurred trying to keep all the aggregates up-to-date. In this section we consider the family of DBMS's called *data-cube* systems, or MOLAP (Multidimensional OLAP) systems, which support directly the cube model of data that we suggested by Fig. 11.12, and support the most important OLAP operations.

In data-cube systems, it is normal for there to be some aggregation of the raw data of the fact table before it is entered into the data-cube storage system. For instance, in our cars example, the dimension we thought of as a serial number in the star schema might be replaced by the model of the car. Then, each entry of the data cube becomes a description of a model, a dealer and a date, together with the sum of the sales for that model, on that date, by that dealer. We shall continue to call the points of the data cube the "fact table," even though the interpretation of the points may be slightly different from fact tables in a star schema.

11.4.1 The Cube Operator

Given a fact table F, we can define an augmented table CUBE(F) that adds an additional value, denoted $*$, to each dimension. The $*$ has the intuitive meaning "any," and it represents aggregation along the dimension in which it appears. Figure 11.17 suggests the process of adding a border to the cube in each dimension, to represent the $*$ value and the aggregated values that it implies. In this figure we see three dimensions, with the lightest shading representing aggregates in one dimension, darker shading for aggregates over two dimensions, and the darkest cube in the corner for aggregation over all three dimensions. Notice that if the number of values along each dimension is reasonably large, but not so large that most points in the cube are unoccupied, then the "border" represents only a small addition to the volume of the cube (i.e., the number of tuples in the fact table). In that case, the size of the stored data CUBE(F) is not much greater than the size of F itself.

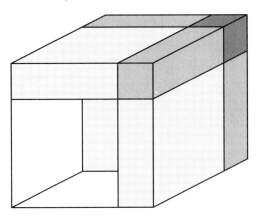

Figure 11.17: The cube operator augments a data cube with a border of aggregations in all combinations of dimensions

A tuple of the table CUBE(F) that has $*$ in one or more dimensions will have for each dependent attribute the sum (or another aggregate function) of the values of that attribute in all the tuples that we can obtain by replacing the $*$'s by real values. In effect, we build into the data the result of aggregating along any set of dimensions. Notice, however, that the CUBE operator does not support aggregation at intermediate levels of granularity based on values in the dimension tables. For instance, we may either leave data broken down by day (or whatever the finest granularity for time is), or we may aggregate time completely, but we cannot, with the CUBE operator alone, aggregate by weeks, months, or years.

Example 11.14: Let us reconsider the Aardvark database from Example 11.9 in the light of what the CUBE operator can give us. Recall the fact table from that example is

```
Sales(serialNo, date, dealer, price)
```

However, the dimension represented by `serialNo` is not well suited for the cube, since the serial number uniquely identifies an automobile, and thus `serialNo` is a key for `Sales`. Thus, summing the price over all dates, or over all dealers, but keeping the serial number fixed has no effect; we would still get the "sum" for the one auto with that serial number. A more useful data cube would replace the serial number by the two attributes — model and color — to which the serial number connects `Sales` via the dimension table `Autos`. Notice that if we replace `serialNo` by `model` and `color`, then the cube no longer has a key among its dimensions. Thus, an entry of the cube would have the total sales price for all automobiles of a given model, with a given color, by a given dealer, on a given date.

There is another change that is useful for the data-cube implementation of the `Sales` fact table. Since the CUBE operator normally sums dependent variables, and we might want to get average prices for sales in some category, we need both the sum of the prices for each category of automobiles (a given model of a given color sold on a given day by a given dealer) and the total number of sales in that category. Thus, the relation `Sales` to which we apply the CUBE operator is

```
Sales(model, color, date, dealer, val, cnt)
```

The attribute `val` is intended to be the total price of all automobiles for the given model, color, date, and dealer, while `cnt` is the total number of automobiles in that category. Notice that in this data cube, individual cars are not identified; they only affect the value and count for their category.

Now, let us consider the relation CUBE(`Sales`). A possible tuple, which is in both `Sales` and CUBE(`Sales`), is

```
('Gobi', 'red', '1999-05-21', 'Friendly Fred', 45000, 2)
```

The interpretation is that on May 21, 1999, dealer Friendly Fred sold two red Gobis for a total of $45,000. The tuple

```
('Gobi', *, '1999-05-21', 'Friendly Fred', 152000, 7)
```

says that on May 21, 1999, Friendly Fred sold seven Gobis of all colors, for a total price of $152,000. Note that this tuple is in CUBE(`Sales`) but not in `Sales`.

Relation CUBE(`Sales`) also contains tuples that represent the aggregation over more than one attribute. For instance,

```
('Gobi', *, '1999-05-21', *, 2348000, 100)
```

says that on May 21, 1999, there were 100 Gobis sold by all the dealers, and the total price of those Gobis was $2,348,000.

```
('Gobi', *, *, *, 1339800000, 58000)
```

Says that over all time, dealers, and colors, 58,000 Gobis have been sold for a total price of $1,339,800,000. Lastly, the tuple

```
(*, *, *, *, 3521727000, 198000)
```

tells us that total sales of all Aardvark models in all colors, over all time at all dealers is 198,000 cars for a total price of $3,521,727,000. □

Consider how to answer a query in which we specify conditions on certain attributes of the Sales relation and group by some other attributes, while asking for the sum, count, or average price. In the relation CUBE(Sales), we look for those tuples t with the following properties:

1. If the query specifies a value v for attribute a, then tuple t has v in its component for a.

2. If the query groups by an attribute a, then t has any non-* value in its component for a.

3. If the query neither groups by attribute a nor specifies a value for a, then t has * in its component for a.

Each tuple t has the sum and count for one of the desired groups. If we want the average price, a division is performed on the sum and count components of each tuple t.

Example 11.15: The query

```
SELECT color, AVG(price)
FROM Sales
WHERE model = 'Gobi'
GROUP BY color;
```

is answered by looking for all tuples of CUBE(Sales) with the form

$$('Gobi', c, *, *, v, n)$$

where c is any specific color. In this tuple, v will be the sum of sales of Gobis in that color, while n will be the number of sales of Gobis in that color. The tuple asked for by the query is $(c, v/n)$. That is, the average price, although not an attribute of Sales or CUBE(Sales) directly, is obtained by dividing the total sales by the number of cars. The answer to the query is the set of $(c, v/n)$ pairs obtained from all $('Gobi', c, *, *, v, n)$ tuples. □

> ## The Different Notions of "Cube"
>
> We started thinking of "cubes" in Section 11.3, but the notion there was more philosophical: it is useful to think of certain kinds of relational data as comprising a fact table and dimension tables. The "cube" in that case is our perception of the fact table.
>
> In Section 11.4, we introduced a formal cube operator, that computes certain aggregates along a dimension or dimensions. This operator works for the fact tables of Section 11.3, as long as the only aggregations that make sense along a dimension are all-or-nothing. We also saw in Example 11.14 how we could take one dimension, say "the car," and break it into several dimensions representing aspects of cars (model and color, in this example) that we obtained from a dimension table. That change gave the CUBE operator more power, since it could aggregate along any of several new dimensions — i.e., model, or color, or both — instead of only having the option to aggregate all cars or not aggregate cars.
>
> Then in Section 11.4.2 we introduced the possibility that subdividing a dimension into several independent dimensions (as with cars into model and color) was not enough. Dimensions could have a more complex aggregation structure, where individuals fall into a hierarchy of granularities, like dealer, or into an even more complex structure, as time units do. Dimensions that cannot be subdivided make the CUBE operator less useful, but the techniques of pre-aggregating certain views is a generalization of the CUBE operator that can be effective, and is actually used in several commercial systems.

11.4.2 Cube Implementation by Materialized Views

We suggested in Fig. 11.17 that adding aggregations to the cube doesn't cost much in terms of space, and saves a lot in time when the common kinds of decision-support queries are asked. However, our analysis is based on the assumption that queries choose either to aggregate completely in a dimension or not to aggregate at all. For some dimensions, there are many degrees of granularity that could be chosen for a grouping on that dimension.

We have already mentioned the case of time, where numerous options such as aggregation by weeks, months, quarters, or years exist, in addition to the all-or-nothing choices of grouping by day or aggregating over all time. For another example based on our running automobile database, we could choose to aggregate dealers completely or not aggregate them at all. However, we could also choose to aggregate by city, by state, or perhaps by other regions, larger or smaller. Thus, there are at least six choices of grouping for time and at least four for dealers.

When the number of choices for grouping along each dimension grows, it becomes increasingly expensive to store the results of aggregating by every possible combination of groupings. Not only are there too many of them, but they are not as easily organized as the structure of Fig. 11.17 suggests for the all-or-nothing case. Thus, commercial data-cube systems may help the user to choose some *materialized views* of the data cube. A materialized view is the result of some query, which we choose to store in the database, rather than reconstructing (parts of) it as needed in response to queries. For the data cube, the views we would choose to materialize will typically be aggregations of the full data cube.

The coarser the partition implied by the grouping, the less space the materialized view takes. On the other hand, if we want to use a view to answer a certain query, then the view must not partition any dimension more coarsely than the query does. Thus, to maximize the utility of materialized views, we generally want some large views that group dimensions into a fairly fine partition. In addition, the choice of views to materialize is heavily influenced by the kinds of queries that the analysts are likely to ask. An example will suggest the tradeoffs involved.

```
INSERT INTO SalesV1
    SELECT model, color, month, city,
        SUM(val) AS val, SUM(cnt) AS cnt
    FROM Sales JOIN Dealers ON dealer = name
    GROUP BY model, color, month, city;
```

Figure 11.18: The materialized view `SalesV1`

Example 11.16 : Let us return to the data cube

```
Sales(model, color, date, dealer, val, cnt)
```

that we developed in Example 11.14. One possible materialized view groups dates by month and dealers by city. This view, which we call `SalesV1`, is constructed by the query in Fig. 11.18. This query is not strict SQL, since we imagine that dates and their grouping units such as months are understood by the data-cube system without being told to join `Sales` with the imaginary relation representing days that we discussed in Example 11.11.

Another possible materialized view aggregates colors completely, aggregates time into weeks, and dealers by states. This view, `SalesV2`, is defined by the query in Fig. 11.19. Either view `SalesV1` or `SalesV2` can be used to answer a query that partitions no more finely than either in any dimension. Thus, the query

```
Q1: SELECT model, SUM(val)
    FROM Sales
    GROUP BY model;
```

```
INSERT INTO SalesV2
    SELECT model, week, state,
        SUM(val) AS val, SUM(cnt) AS cnt
    FROM Sales JOIN Dealers ON dealer = name
    GROUP BY model, week, state;
```

Figure 11.19: Another materialized view, SalesV2

can be answered either by

```
SELECT model, SUM(val)
FROM SalesV1
GROUP BY model;
```

or by

```
SELECT model, SUM(val)
FROM SalesV2
GROUP BY model;
```

On the other hand, the query

```
Q2: SELECT model, year, state, SUM(val)
    FROM Sales JOIN Dealers ON dealer = name
    GROUP BY model, year, state;
```

can only be answered from SalesV1, as

```
SELECT model, year, state, SUM(val)
FROM SalesV1
GROUP BY model, year, state;
```

Incidentally, the query immediately above, like the queries that aggregate time units, is not strict SQL. That is, state is not an attribute of SalesV1; only city is. We must assume that the data-cube system knows how to perform the aggregation of cities into states, probably by accessing the dimension table for dealers.

We cannot answer $Q2$ from SalesV2. Although we could roll-up cities into states (i.e., aggregate the cities into their states) to use SalesV1, we cannot roll-up weeks into years, since years are not evenly divided into weeks, and data from a week beginning, say, Dec. 29, 1999, contributes to years 1999 and 2000 in a way we cannot tell from the data aggregated by weeks.

Finally, a query like

```
Q3: SELECT model, color, date, SUM(val)
    FROM Sales
    GROUP BY model, color, date;
```

can be answered from neither SalesV1 nor SalesV2. It cannot be answered
from SalesV1 because its partition of days by months is too coarse to recover
sales by day, and it cannot be answered from SalesV2 because that view does
not group by color. We would have to answer this query directly from the full
data cube.   □

11.4.3   The Lattice of Views

To formalize the observations of Example 11.16, it helps to think of a lattice of
possible groupings for each dimension of the cube. The points of the lattice are
the ways that we can partition the values of a dimension by grouping according
to one or more attributes of its dimension table. We say that partition P_1 is
below partition P_2, written $P_1 \leq P_2$ if and only if each group of P_1 is contained
within some group of P_2.

Figure 11.20: A lattice of partitions for time intervals

Example 11.17: For the lattice of time partitions we might choose the diagram of Fig. 11.20. A path from some node P_2 down to P_1 means that $P_1 \leq P_2$.
These are not the only possible units of time, but they will serve as an example
of what units a system might support. Notice that days lie below both weeks
and months, but weeks do not lie below months. The reason is that while a
group of events that took place in one day surely took place within one week
and within one month, it is not true that a group of events taking place in one
week necessarily took place in any one month. Similarly, a week's group need
not be contained within the group corresponding to one quarter or to one year.
At the top is a partition we call "all," meaning that events are grouped into a
single group; i.e., we make no distinctions among different times.
   Figure 11.21 shows another lattice, this time for the dealer dimension of our
automobiles example. This lattice is simpler; it shows that partitioning sales by
dealer gives a finer partition than partitioning by the city of the dealer, which is

All
|
State
|
City
|
Dealer

Figure 11.21: A lattice of partitions for automobile dealers

in turn finer than partitioning by the state of the dealer. The top of the lattice is the partition that places all dealers in one group. □

Having a lattice for each dimension, we can now define a lattice for all the possible materialized views of a data cube that can be formed by grouping according to some partition in each dimension. If V_1 and V_2 are two views formed by choosing a partition (grouping) for each dimension, then $V_1 \leq V_2$ means that in each dimension, the partition P_1 that we use in V_1 is at least as fine as the partition P_2 that we use for that dimension in V_2; that is, $P_1 \leq P_2$.

Many OLAP queries can also be placed in the lattice of views. In fact, frequently an OLAP query has the same form as the views we have described: the query specifies some partitioning (possibly none or all) for each of the dimensions. Other OLAP queries involve this same sort of grouping, and then "slice" the cube to focus on a subset of the data, as was suggested by the diagram in Fig. 11.15. The general rule is:

- We can answer a query Q using view V if and only if $V \leq Q$.

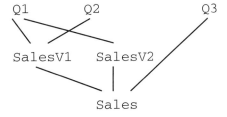

Figure 11.22: The lattice of views and queries from Example 11.16

Example 11.18: Figure 11.22 takes the views and queries of Example 11.16 and places them in a lattice. Notice that the `Sales` data cube itself is technically a view, corresponding to the finest possible partition along each dimension. As we observed in the original example, Q_1 can be answered from either SalesV1 or SalesV2; of course it could also be answered from the full data cube Sales, but there is no reason to want to do so if one of the other views is materialized. Q_2 can be answered from either SalesV1 or Sales, while Q_3 can only be answered from Sales. Each of these relationships is expressed in Fig. 11.22 by the paths downward from the queries to their supporting views.   □

Placing queries in the lattice of views helps design data-cube databases. Some recently developed design tools for data-cube systems start with a set of queries that they regard as "typical" of the application at hand. They then select a set of views to materialize so that each of these queries is above at least one of the views, preferably identical to it or very close (i.e., the query and the view use the same grouping in most of the dimensions).

11.4.4 Exercises for Section 11.4

Exercise 11.4.1 : What is the ratio of the size of CUBE(F) to the size of F if fact table F has the following characteristics?

* a) F has ten dimension attributes, each with ten different values.

  b) F has ten dimension attributes, each with two different values.

Exercise 11.4.2 : Let us use the cube CUBE(Sales) from Example 11.14, which was built from the relation

    Sales(model, color, date, dealer, val, cnt)

Tell what tuples of the cube we would use to answer the following queries:

* a) Find the total sales of blue cars for each dealer.

  b) Find the total number of green Gobi's sold by dealer "Smilin' Sally."

  c) Find the average number of Gobi's sold on each day of March, 2000 by each dealer.

*! **Exercise 11.4.3 :** In Exercise 11.3.1 we spoke of PC-order data organized as a cube. If we are to apply the CUBE operator, we might find it convenient to break several dimensions more finely. For example, instead of one processor dimension, we might have one dimension for the type (e.g., AMD K-6 or Pentium-III), and another dimension for the speed. Suggest a set of dimensions and dependent attributes that will allow us to obtain answers to a variety of useful aggregation queries. In particular, what role does the customer play? Also, the price in Exercise 11.3.1 referred to the price of one machine, while several identical machines could be ordered in a single tuple. What should the dependent attribute(s) be?

Exercise 11.4.4: What tuples of the cube from Exercise 11.4.3 would you use to answer the following queries?

a) Find, for each processor speed, the total number of computers ordered in each month of the year 2000.

b) List for each type of hard disk (e.g., SCSI or IDE) and each processor type the number of computers ordered.

c) Find the average price of computers with 400 megahertz processors for each month from Jan., 1999.

! **Exercise 11.4.5:** The computers described in the cube of Exercise 11.4.3 do not include monitors. What dimensions would you suggest to represent monitors? You may assume that the price of the monitor is included in the price of the computer.

Exercise 11.4.6: Suppose that a cube has 10 dimensions, and each dimension has 5 options for granularity of aggregation, including "no aggregation" and "aggregate fully." How many different views can we construct by choosing a granularity in each dimension?

Exercise 11.4.7: Show how to add the following time units to the lattice of Fig. 11.20: hours, minutes, seconds, fortnights (two-week periods), decades, and centuries.

Exercise 11.4.8: How would you change the dealer lattice of Fig. 11.21 to include "regions," if:

a) A region is a set of states.

* b) Regions are not commensurate with states, but each city is in only one region.

c) Regions are like area codes; each region is contained within a state, some cities are in two or more regions, and some regions have several cities.

! **Exercise 11.4.9:** In Exercise 11.4.3 we designed a cube suitable for use with the CUBE operator. However, some of the dimensions could also be given a nontrivial lattice structure. In particular, the processor type could be organized by manufacturer (e.g., SUN, Intel, AMD, Motorola), series (e.g., SUN UltraSparc, Intel Pentium or Celeron, AMD K-series, or Motorola G-series), and model (e.g., Pentium-III or AMD K-6).

a) Design the lattice of processor types following the examples described above.

b) Define a view that groups processors by series, hard disks by type, and CD's by speed, aggregating everything else.

c) Define a view that groups processors by manufacturer, hard disks by speed, and aggregates everything else except memory size.

d) Give examples of queries that can be answered from the view of (b) only, the view of (c) only, both, and neither.

*!! Exercise 11.4.10: If the fact table F to which we apply the CUBE operator is sparse (i.e., there are many fewer tuples in F than the product of the number of possible values along each dimension, then the ratio of the sizes of CUBE(F) and F can be very large. How large can it be?

11.5 Data Mining

A family of database applications called *data mining* or *knowledge discovery in databases* has captured considerable interest because of opportunities to learn surprising facts from existing databases. Data-mining queries can be thought of as an extended form of decision-support query, although the distinction is informal (see the box on "Data-Mining Queries and Decision-Support Queries"). Data mining stresses both the query-optimization and data-management components of a traditional database system, as well as suggesting some important extensions to database languages, such as language primitives that support efficient sampling of data. In this section, we shall examine the principal directions data-mining applications have taken. We then focus on the problem called "association rules," that has received the most attention from the database point of view.

11.5.1 Data-Mining Applications

Broadly, data-mining queries ask for a useful summary of data, often without suggesting the values of parameters that would best yield such a summary. This family of problems thus requires rethinking the way database systems are to be used to provide such insights about the data. Below are some of the applications and problems that are being addressed using very large amounts of data. Since the best use of a DBMS in many of these problems is open, we shall not discuss the solutions to these problems, merely suggesting why they are hard. In Section 11.5.2 we shall discuss a problem where measurable progress has been made, and there we shall see a nontrivial, database-oriented solution.

Decision Tree Construction

Users of data want to find in that data a way to decide an important question. For instance, Example 5.7 introduced us to what could be the basis for an interesting data-mining problem: "who buys gold jewelry?" In that example, we were only concerned with two properties of customers: their age and income.

Data-Mining Queries and Decision-Support Queries

While decision-support queries may need to examine and aggregate large portions of the data in a database, the analyst posing the query usually tells the system exactly what query to execute; i.e., on which portion of the data to focus. A data-mining query goes a step beyond, inviting the system to decide where the focus should be. For example, a decision-support query might ask to "aggregate the sales of Aardvark automobiles by color and year," while a data-mining query might ask "what are the factors that have had the most influence over Aardvark sales?" Naive implementations of data-mining queries will result in execution of large numbers of decision-support queries, and may therefore take so much time to complete that the naive approach is completely infeasible.

However, customer databases today can record much more about the customer or obtain the information from legitimate sources that are then integrated with the customer data into a warehouse. Examples of such properties could include the customer's zip code, marital status, own-or-rent-home, and information about any number of other items that he or she purchased recently.

Unlike the data in Example 5.7, which includes only data about people known to buy gold jewelry, a *decision tree* is a tree designed to guide the separation of data into two sets, which we might think of as "accept" and "reject." In the case of gold jewelry, the data would be information about people. The accept-set would be those we think would be likely to buy gold jewelry and the reject-set those we think are not likely to buy gold jewelry. If our predictions are reliable, then we have a good target population for direct-mail advertising of gold jewelry, for instance.

The decision tree itself would look something like Fig. 5.13, but without the actual data at the leaves. That is, the interior nodes each have an attribute and a value that serves as a threshold. The children of a node are either other interior nodes, or a decision: accept or reject. A given tuple, representing data to be classified, is passed down the tree, going left or right at each step according to the value the tuple has in the attribute mentioned at the node, until a decision node is reached.

The tree is constructed by a *training set* of tuples whose outcome is known. In the case of gold jewelry, we take the database of customers, including information about which customers bought gold jewelry and which did not. The data-mining problem is to design from this data the decision tree that most reliably decides for a new customer, whose characteristics (age, salary, etc.) we know, whether or not they are likely to buy gold jewelry. That is, we must decide the best attribute A to put at the root and the best threshold value v for that attribute. Then, for the cases that the decision is to go left, we find the best attribute and threshold for those customers who have $A < v$, and we do the same for those customers that have $A \geq v$. The same problem is faced at each level, until we can no longer profitably add nodes to the tree (because too few instances of the training data reach a given node for us to make a useful decision). The query asked as we design each node involves aggregating much of the data, so we can decide which attribute-threshold pair divides the data so the greatest fraction of "accepts" go to one side and "rejects" to the other side.

Clustering

Another class of data-mining problems involves "clustering," where we try to group our data items into some small number of groups such that the groups each have something substantial in common. Figure 11.23 suggests a clustering of two-dimensional data, although in practice the number of dimensions may be very large. In this figure we have shown the approximate outlines of the best three clusters, while some points are far from the center of any cluster; they would be considered "outliers" or grouped with the nearest cluster.

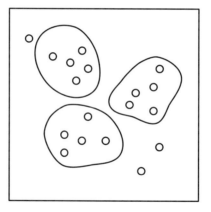

Figure 11.23: Three clusters in two-dimensional data

As an example application, Web search engines often find hundreds of thousands of documents that match a given query. To help organize these documents, the search engine may cluster them according to the words they use. For example, the search engine could place documents in a space that has one dimension for each possible word, perhaps excluding the most common words (*stop words*) such as "and" or "the," which tend to be present in all documents and tell us nothing about the content. A document is placed in this space according to the fraction of its word occurrences that are any particular word. For instance, if the document has 1000 word occurrences, two of which are "database," then the document would be placed at the .002 coordinate in the dimension corresponding to "database." By clustering documents in this space, we tend to get groups of documents that talk about the same thing.

For instance, documents that talk about databases might have occurrences of words like "data," "query," "lock," and so on, while documents about baseball are unlikely to have occurrences of these words.

The data-mining problem here is to take the data and select the "means" or centers of the clusters. Often the number of clusters is given in advance, although that number may be selectable by the data-mining process as well. Either way, a naive algorithm for choosing the centers so that the average distance from a point to its nearest center is minimized involves many queries, each of which does a complex aggregation.

11.5.2 Association-Rule Mining

Now, we shall see a data-mining problem for which algorithms using secondary storage effectively have been developed. The problem, finding so-called "association rules," is most easily described in terms of its principal application: the analysis of *market-basket* data. Stores today often hold in a data warehouse a record of what customers have bought together. That is, a customer approaches the checkout with a "market basket" full of the items he or she has selected. The cash register records all of these items as part of a single transaction. Thus, even if we don't know anything about the customer, and we can't tell if the customer returns and buys additional items, we *do* know certain items that a single customer buys together.

If items appear together in market baskets more often than would be expected, then the store has an opportunity to learn something about how customers are likely to traverse the store. The items can be placed in the store so that customers will tend to take certain paths through the store, and attractive items can be placed along these paths.

Example 11.19: A famous example, which has been claimed by several people, is the discovery that people who buy diapers are unusually likely also to buy beer. Theories have been advanced for why that relationship is true, including the possibility that people who buy diapers, having a baby at home, are less likely to go out to a bar in the evening and therefore tend to drink beer at home. Stores may use the fact that many customers will walk through the store from where the diapers are to where the beer is, or vice versa. Clever marketers place beer and diapers near each other, with potato chips in the middle. The claim is that sales of all three items then increase. □

We can represent market-basket data by a relation

```
Baskets(basket, item)
```

where the first attribute is a "basket ID," or unique identifier for a market basket, and the second attribute is the ID of some item found in that basket. Note that it is not essential for the relation to come from true market-basket data; it could be any relation from which we want to find associated items. For instance, the "baskets" could be documents and the "items" could be words, in which case we are really looking for words that appear in many documents together.

The simplest form of *association rule* in market-basket data is a set of items. The significance of a set of items $\{i_1, i_2, \ldots, i_n\}$ can vary. The most elementary property we might search for is that the number of baskets in which *all* these items appear is large. The *support* for a set of items is the number of baskets in which all those items appear. The problem of finding *high-support sets of items* is to find, given a support threshold s, all those sets of items that have support at least s.

If the number of items in the database is large, then even if we restrict our attention to small sets, say pairs of items only, the time needed to count the support for all pairs of items is enormous. Thus, the straightforward way to solve even the high-support pairs problem — compute the support for each pair of items i and j, as suggested by the SQL query in Fig. 11.24 — will not work. This query involves joining Baskets with itself, grouping the resulting tuples by the two items found in that tuple, and throwing away groups where the number of baskets is below the support threshold s. Note that the condition I.item < J.item in the WHERE-clause is there to prevent the same pair from being considered in both orders, or for a "pair" consisting of the same item twice from being considered at all.

```
SELECT I.item, J.item, COUNT(I.basket)
FROM Baskets I, Baskets J
WHERE I.basket = J.basket AND
      I.item < J.item
GROUP BY I.item, J.item
HAVING COUNT(I.basket) >= s;
```

Figure 11.24: Naive way to find all high-support pairs of items

11.5.3 The A-Priori Algorithm

There is an optimization that greatly reduces the running time of a query like Fig. 11.24 when the support threshold is sufficiently large that few pairs meet it. It is reasonable to set the threshold high, because a list of thousands or millions of pairs would not be very useful anyway; we want the data-mining query to focus our attention on a small number of the best candidates. The *a-priori* algorithm is based on the following observation:

- If a set of items X has support s, then each subset of X must also have support at least s.

Other Forms of Association Rules

A more general form of association rule relates a set of items to another item; the rule has the form $\{i_1, i_2, \ldots, i_n\} \Rightarrow j$. Two possible properties that we might want in useful rules of this form are:

1. *Confidence*: the probability of finding item j in a basket that has all of $\{i_1, i_2, \ldots, i_n\}$ is above a certain threshold, e.g., 50%, e.g., "at least 50% of the people who buy diapers buy beer."

2. *Interest*: the probability of finding item j in a basket that has all of $\{i_1, i_2, \ldots, i_n\}$ is significantly higher or lower than the probability of finding j in a random basket. In statistical terms, j correlates with $\{i_1, i_2, \ldots, i_n\}$, either positively or negatively. The discovery in Example 11.19 was really that the rule $\{diapers\} \Rightarrow$ beer has high interest.

Note that even if a rule has high confidence or interest, it will tend not to be useful unless the set of items involved also has high support. The reason is that if the support is low, then the number of instances of the rule is not large, which limits the benefit of a strategy that exploits the rule.

In particular, if a pair of items, say $\{i, j\}$ appears in, say, 1000 baskets, then we know there are at least 1000 baskets with item i and we know there are at least 1000 baskets with item j.

The converse of the above rule is that if we are looking for pairs of items with support at least s, we may first eliminate from consideration any item that does not by itself appear in at least s baskets. The *a-priori algorithm* answers the same query as Fig. 11.24 by:

1. First finding the set of "OK" items — those that appear in a sufficient number of baskets by themselves — and then

2. Running the query of Fig. 11.24 on only the items in the OK set.

The a-priori algorithm is thus summarized by the sequence of two SQL queries in Fig. 11.25. It first computes OkBaskets, the subset of the Baskets relation whose items have high support by themselves, then joins OKBaskets with itself, as in the naive algorithm of Fig. 11.24.

Example 11.20: To get a feel for how the a-priori algorithm helps, consider a supermarket that sells 10,000 different items. Suppose that the average market-basket has 20 items in it. Also assume that the database keeps 1,000,000 baskets as data (a small number compared with what would be stored in practice).

```
INSERT INTO OkBaskets
    SELECT *
    FROM Baskets
    WHERE item IN (
        SELECT item
        FROM Baskets
        GROUP BY item
        HAVING COUNT(*) >= s
);

SELECT I.item, J.item, COUNT(I.basket)
FROM OkBaskets I, OkBaskets J
WHERE I.basket = J.basket AND
      I.item < J.item
GROUP BY I.item, J.item
HAVING COUNT(*) >= s;
```

Figure 11.25: The a-priori algorithm first finds high-support items before high-support pairs

Then the Baskets relation has 20,000,000 tuples, and the join in Fig. 11.24 (the naive algorithm) has 195,000,000 pairs. This figure represents one million baskets times $\binom{20}{2}$, which is 195, pairs of items. These 195,000,000 tuples must all be grouped and counted.

However, suppose that s is 10,000, i.e., 1% of the baskets. It is impossible that more than $20,000,000/10,000 = 2000$ items appear in at least 10,000 baskets, because there are only 20,000,000 tuples in Baskets, and any item appearing in 10,000 baskets appears in at least 10,000 of those tuples. Thus, if we use the a-priori algorithm of Fig. 11.25, the subquery that finds the high-support items cannot produce more than 2000 items, and will probably produce many fewer than 2000.

We cannot be sure how large OkBaskets is, since in the worst case *all* the items that appear in baskets will appear in at least 1% of them. However, in practice OkBaskets will be considerably smaller than Baskets, if the threshold s is high. For sake of argument, suppose OkBaskets has on the average 10 items per basket; i.e., it is half the size of Baskets. Then the join of OkBaskets with itself in step (2) has 1,000,000 times $\binom{10}{2} = 45,000,000$ tuples, less than 1/4 of the number of tuples in the join of Baskets with itself. We would thus expect the a-priori algorithm to run in about 1/4 the time of the naive algorithm. In common situations, where OkBaskets has much less than half the tuples of Baskets, the improvement is even greater, growing quadratically with the reduction in the number of tuples involved in the join.   □

11.6 Summary of Chapter 11

✦ *Integration of Information*: Frequently, there exist a variety of databases or other information sources that contain related information. We have the opportunity to combine these sources into one. However, heterogeneities in the schemas often exist; these incompatibilities include differing types, codes or conventions for values, interpretations of concepts, and different sets of concepts represented in different schemas.

✦ *Approaches to Information Integration*: Early approaches involved "federation," where each database would query the others in the terms understood by the second. More recent approaches involve warehousing, where data is translated to a global schema and copied to the warehouse. An alternative is mediation, where a virtual warehouse is created to allow queries to a global schema; the queries are then translated to the terms of the data sources.

✦ *Extractors and Wrappers*: Warehousing and mediation require components at each source, called extractors and wrappers, respectively. A major function is to translate queries and results between the global schema and the local schema at the source.

✦ *Wrapper Generators*: One approach to designing wrappers is to use templates, which describe how a query of a specific form is translated from the global schema to the local schema. These templates are tabulated and interpreted by a driver that tries to match queries to templates. The driver may also have the ability to combine templates in various ways, and/or perform additional work such as filtering, to answer more complex queries.

✦ *OLAP*: An important application of data warehouses is the ability to ask complex queries that touch all or much of the data, at the same time that transaction processing is conducted at the data sources. These queries, which usually involve aggregation of data, are termed on-line analytic processing, or OLAP, queries.

✦ *ROLAP and MOLAP*: It is frequently useful when building a warehouse for OLAP, to think of the data as forming a cube, with dimensions corresponding to independent aspects of the data represented. Systems that support such a view of data take either a relational point of view (ROLAP, or relational OLAP systems), or specialize to the data cube (MOLAP, or multidimensional OLAP systems).

✦ *Star Schemas*: If the ROLAP approach is used, each data element (e.g., a sale of an item) is represented in one relation, called the fact table, while information helping to interpret the values along each dimension (e.g., what kind of product is item 1234?) is stored in a dimension table for each dimension. This type of database schema is called a star schema;

the fact table is the center of the star, and the dimension tables are the points.

✦ *The Cube Operator*: When the MOLAP approach is chosen, a specific operator that pre-aggregates the fact table along all subsets of dimensions, is quite useful. It may add little to the space needed by the fact table, and greatly increases the speed with which many OLAP queries can be answered.

✦ *Dimension Lattices and Materialized Views*: A more powerful approach than the CUBE operator, used by some data-cube implementations, is to establish a lattice of granularities for aggregation along each dimension (e.g., different time units like days, months, and years). The warehouse is then designed by materializing certain views that aggregate in different ways along the different dimensions, and the view with the closest fit is used to answer a given query.

✦ *Data Mining*: Warehouses are also used to ask broad questions that involve not only aggregating on command, as in OLAP queries, but searching for the "right" aggregation. Common types of data mining include clustering data into similar groups, designing decision trees to predict one attribute based on the value of others, and finding association rules regarding commonly occurring pairs or larger combinations of values.

✦ *The A-Priori Algorithm*: An efficient way to find association rules is to use the a-priori algorithm. This technique exploits the fact that if a set occurs frequently, then so do all of its subsets.

11.7 References for Chapter 11

Recent surveys of warehousing and related technologies are in [10], [4], and [8]. Federated systems are surveyed in [12]. The concept of the mediator comes from [14]. Implementation of mediators and wrappers, especially the wrapper-generator approach, is covered in [6].

Much of recent information-integration is based on a "semistructured" model of data that copes with missing values and other differences among schemas. The idea originates in [11]; recent surveys include [1] and [13].

The cube operator was proposed in [7]. The implementation of cubes by materialized views appeared in [9].

[5] is a survey of data-mining techniques. The a-priori algorithm is from [2] and [3].

1. S. Abiteboul, "Querying semi-structured data," *Proc. Intl. Conf. on Database Theory* (1997), Lecture Notes in Computer Science 1187 (F. Afrati and P. Kolaitis, eds.), Springer-Verlag, Berlin, pp. 1–18.

2. R. Agrawal, T. Imielinski, and A. Swami, "Mining association rules between sets of items in large databases," *Proc. ACM SIGMOD Intl. Conf. on Management of Data* (1993), pp. 207–216.

3. R. Agrawal, and R. Srikant, "Fast algorithms for mining association rules," *Proc. Intl. Conf. on Very Large Databases* (1994), pp. 487–499.

4. S. Chaudhuri and U. Dayal, "An overview of data warehousing and OLAP technology," *SIGMOD Record* **26**:1 (1997), pp. 65–74.

5. U. M. Fayyad, G. Piatetsky-Shapiro, P. Smyth, and R. Uthurusamy, *Advances in Knowledge Discovery and Data Mining*, AAAI Press, Menlo Park CA, 1996.

6. H. Garcia-Molina, Y. Papakonstantinou, D. Quass, A. Rajaraman, Y. Sagiv, V. Vassalos, J. D. Ullman, and J. Widom) The TSIMMIS approach to mediation: data models and languages, *J. Intelligent Information Systems* **8**:2 (1997), pp. 117–132.

7. J. N. Gray, A. Bosworth, A. Layman, and H. Pirahesh, "Data cube: a relational aggregation operator generalizing group-by, cross-tab, and subtotals," *Proc. Intl. Conf. on Data Engineering* (1996), pp. 152–159.

8. A. Gupta and I. S. Mumick, *Materialized Views: Techniques, Implementations, and Applications*, MIT Press, Cambridge MA.

9. V. Harinarayan, A. Rajaraman, and J. D. Ullman, "Implementing data cubes efficiently," *Proc. ACM SIGMOD Intl. Conf. on Management of Data* (1996), pp. 205–216.

10. D. Lomet and J. Widom (eds.), Special issue on materialized views and data warehouses, *IEEE Data Engineering Bulletin* **18**:2 (1995).

11. Y. Papakonstantinou, H. Garcia-Molina, and J. Widom, "Object exchange across heterogeneous information sources, *Proc. Intl. Conf. on Data Engineering* (1995), pp. 251–260.

12. A. P. Sheth and J. A. Larson, "Federated databases for managing distributed, heterogeneous, and autonomous databases," *Computing Surveys* **22**:3 (1990), pp. 183–236.

13. D. Suciu (ed.) Special issue on management of semistructured data, *SIGMOD Record* **26**:4 (1997).

14. G. Wiederhold, "Mediators in the architecture of future information systems," *IEEE Computer* **C-25**:1 (1992), pp. 38–49.

Index